YACHTING MONTHLY
THE CHANNEL
CRUISING COMPANION

A yachtsman's guide to the
Channel coasts of England & France

NEVILLE FEATHERSTONE & DEREK ASLETT
EDITED BY
LUCINDA ROCH

© Nautical Data Limited 2003

Cruising Companion series editor: Lucinda Roch

Published by Nautical Data Ltd, The Book Barn,
Westbourne, Hampshire, PO10 8RS

ISBN I-904358-12-8

NAUTICAL DATA LIMITED

OTHER CRUISING COMPANIONS

This Cruising Companion is one of a series. Other titles include:

Solent Cruising Companion by Derek Aslett
West Country Cruising Companion by Mark Fishwick
East Coast Rivers Cruising Companion by Janet Harber
North France & Belgium Cruising Companion by Neville Featherstone
North Brittany & The Channel Islands Cruising Companion by Peter Cumberlidge
West France Cruising Companion by Neville Featherstone
North West Spain Cruising Companion by Detlef Jens
South West Spain & Portugal Cruising Companion by Detlef Jens

Also published by Nautical Data: *Reeds Nautical Almanac, Reeds Channel Almanac,*
Racing Charts including: Solent, Mid Solent, West Solent, East Solent and Chichester Harbour

IMPORTANT NOTE

This Companion is intended as an aid to navigation only. The information contained within should not solely be relied on for navigational use, rather it should be used in conjunction with official hydrographic data. Whilst every care has been taken in compiling the information contained in this Companion, the publishers, authors, editor and their agents accept no responsibility for any errors, omissions or alterations, or for any accidents or mishaps which may arise from its use. They will be grateful for any information from readers to assist in the update and accuracy of the publication. Readers are advised at all times to refer to official charts, publications and notices. The charts and chartlets in this book are sketch plans and are not to be used for navigation. Some details are omitted for the sake of clarity and the scales have been chosen to allow best coverage in relation to page size.

THE AUTHORS & EDITOR

Neville Featherstone

Derek Aslett

Lucinda Roch

Design & production by Chris Stevens and Scott Stacey
Printed in Italy

PREFACE

The English Channel, or La Manche to those on the other side, conjures up two words: Contrast and Challenge. Contrast because on either shore of its 330 mile length can be found coastal scenery ranging from the legendary white cliffs of Dover and the even more magnificent alabaster cliffs of eastern Normandy to the granite rocks of Brittany, the sand dunes of the Somme and the wooded charm of such rivers as the Helford, Yealm and Rance.

The best in natural beauty, wildlife and geology is to be found along the East Devon and Dorset coast. Fittingly it has been granted the status of England's first natural World Heritage Site.

And the Challenge? Crossing the Channel in a small boat, whether for the first or five hundredth time, is still a heady achievement worthy of quiet satisfaction. You overcame the elements; your DR navigation (remember that?) tallied closely with GPS; you polished up your radar skills – and you postponed taking up golf for another decade. If you have learned your trade in the Channel, you are probably good enough to sail the whole world.

If the weather has not always been kind, do not forget that the sun does shine, gentle zephyrs blow and we all enjoy those halcyon days of which memories are made. There are countless harbours to be investigated. They will usually charm, and only occasionally tantalise you.

The merit of this book is that it covers everything you might reasonably wish to know about cruising the Channel. Its unique aims are:

a) To describe the lands off which you are cruising and go ashore with you to locate the needs of the modern world (the best restaurants, the nearest supermarket, the launderette, the beaches, places to visit, transport etc).

b) To give well-illustrated and comprehensive guidance into each port or anchorage, answering the questions which you did not like to ask as well as anticipating any potential pitfalls. There are waypoints aplenty and the aerial photographs show you what lies behind the harbour wall.

To achieve this has meant a careful economy with words, which does not imply loss of quality. Indeed, it suits the yachtsman threading the eye of a narrow channel, grasping the bull points of a complex tidal regime or simply looking for the nearest supermarket not to be swamped by turgid prose. This Companion is written as if the authors were with you in the cockpit as you enter a strange port for the first time. This is a privilege for us and, hopefully, of value to you.... and so *Bon Voyage* and to business.

Neville Featherstone and Derek Aslett. May 2003

The National Maritime Museum and Pendennis Marina at Falmouth

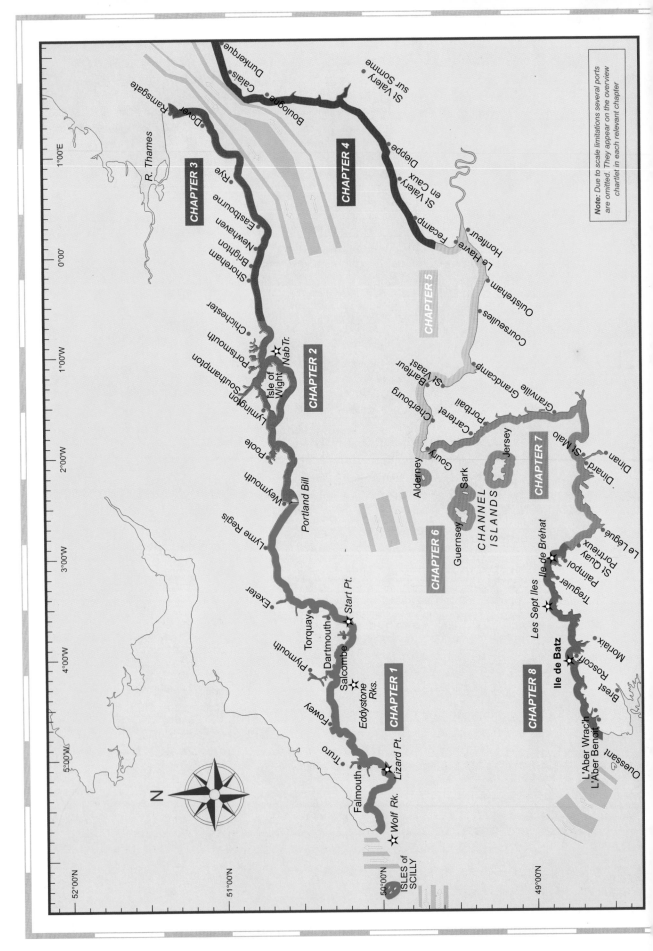

Note: Due to scale limitations several ports are omitted. They appear on the overview chartlet in each relevant chapter

ISLES of SCILLY

Wolf Rk.
Lizard Pt.
Falmouth
Truro
Fowey
Eddystone Rks.
Salcombe
Plymouth
Dartmouth
Start Pt.
Torquay
Exeter
Lyme Regis
Portland Bill
Weymouth
Poole
Southampton
Lymington
Isle of Wight
Nab Tr.
Portsmouth
Chichester
Shoreham
Brighton
Newhaven
Eastbourne
Rye
Dover
Ramsgate
R. Thames

Calais
Dunkerque
Boulogne
St Valéry sur Somme
Dieppe
St Valéry en Caux
Fécamp
Le Havre
Honfleur
Ouistreham
Courseulles
Grandcamp
St Vaast
Barfleur
Cherbourg
Carteret
Portbail
Granville
Alderney
Goury
Guernsey
Sark
Jersey
CHANNEL ISLANDS
St Malo
Dinard
Dinan
Le Légué
St Quay
Portrieux
Paimpol
Tréguier
Ile de Bréhat
Les Sept Iles
Ile de Batz
Roscoff
Morlaix
Brest
L'Aber Wrac'h
L'Aber Benoît
Ouessant

CHAPTER 1
CHAPTER 2
CHAPTER 3
CHAPTER 4
CHAPTER 5
CHAPTER 6
CHAPTER 7
CHAPTER 8

N

52°00'N
51°00'N
50°00'N
49°00'N

5°00'W
4°00'W
3°00'W
2°00'W
1°00'W
0°00'
1°00'E

CONTENTS

INTRODUCTION

St Malo: Le Château and yacht pontoons seen from Bassin Vauban

Sequence and contents Chapters one to three cover Scilly to Ramsgate. 'Crossing the Channel', possibly the most demanding part of the cruise, is dealt with in the Main Introduction. Chapters four to eight incorporate Dunkerque to L'Aber Benoit, with the Channel Islands in chapter six.

Each chapter has introductory words which aim to paint a picture of the region as a whole. Next the Passage Notes provide a thread of continuity. Each harbour, marina, anchorage and town is fully and accurately portrayed. Shoreside facilities and local attractions are described in as much detail as the navigation and pilotage.

Chapters two and three were written by Derek Aslett. Neville Featherstone wrote the rest.

Acknowledgements The authors and publisher gratefully acknowledge the material contributions of the UK and French Hydrographic Offices. We thank countless English and French Harbour Masters for imparting their specialised knowledge and reference materials.

And, most importantly, we thank the following yachtsmen who have helped in various ways: Hans and Mary Bye-Jorgensen, John Frankland, Rear Admiral Terry Loughran, Grenville Hancock, Ian Buxton, Bill Stevens, Chris Springell, David Brockhurst, Souter Harris, Michael Hayes and Annie Aslett.

Photo credits The authors took the sea-level shots in their respective chapters. Aerial photographs from Anvil Point to Ramsgate are by Derek Aslett; and those from Scilly to Portland Bill and from Dunkerque to L'Aber Benoit are by Patrick Roach.

We thank: David Featherstone for the pictures of Charlestown and Sarah Featherstone for those of Alderney; The National Maritime Museum (Cornwall) for the picture of the NMMC by Bob Berry; Roger Graffy of Mylor Yacht Harbour for the aerial picture of MYH by John Such; Ocean Images for the photograph of racing off Cowes; Penwith District Council for the photograph of Penzance harbour entrance; Chris Stevens for his photograph of the Spinnaker Tower in Portsmouth.

England The south coast needs little introduction and is fully described in chapters one to three. It is in parts sublimely beautiful, but also over-crowded. Along the foreshore developers encroach, local authorities legislate and marinas are well aware that the demand for berths exceeds supply.

Despite all this it remains a supreme pleasure to

cruise our historic shores or depart foreign-bound on a misty dawn. Weeks later, sated by the European experience, a landfall on the English coast is a moment of sadness as the cruise ends, coupled with joy at a home-coming.

IN FRANCE

French Customs and/or Marine Police are active both at sea and in harbour. If boarded, business will be quickly and pleasantly transacted if you remain polite and friendly throughout (no harm in offering a cup of coffee, although it is usually declined). Above all it creates a good impression and speeds up proceedings if your personal and yacht papers are easily visible in a folder, with clear plastic envelopes.

Public holidays Public holidays (*jours fériés*) are: 1 Jan/New Year's Day (*Nouvelle Année*); Easter Day and Easter Monday (*Pâques*); 1 May/Labour Day; 8 May/Liberation Day; Ascension Day (40 days after Easter); Whit Sunday and Monday (Pentecost, 7th Sunday after Easter); 14 July/Bastille Day; 15 Aug/Assumption Day; 1 Nov/All Saints Day (*Toussaint*); 11 Nov Remembrance Day (*L'Armistice*); 25 Dec Christmas Day (*Noël*).

Crew-changing
Ferries A table in the *RNA* (p 15) lists ferries from UK and Irish ports to France and the Channel Islands.
The Channel Tunnel, by car or Eurostar, may be a quicker way of getting to northern France.
Low cost flights As of Spring 2003, Brest (Ryanair), Dinard (Ryanair), Guernsey (Flybe) and Jersey (BMI Baby, Flybe) could be reached by low cost carriers from various UK/Irish airports; and in some cases by scheduled airlines.
BMI Baby, ☎ 0870 2642229; www.bmibaby.com
Flybe, ☎ 01392 366669; www.flybe.com
Ryanair, ☎ 0871 2460000; www.ryanair.com

The French National Tourist Office, 178 Piccadilly, London W1J 9AL is worth a visit before leaving the UK. ☎ 0906 824 4123; 🖷 0207 493 6594; info@mdlf.co.uk; www.franceguide.com
Tourist Offices in France A close second to your first glass of wine or plate of moules is a visit to the Tourist Office; details are listed under each harbour. Even quite small communities have one, sometimes known as the *Syndicat d'Initiative* and possibly incorporated in the *Mairie* (Town Hall); they are a mine of useful information, and at the very least will usually provide a *Plan de Ville* and transport timetables.

Restaurants Eating in France is usually a huge pleasure. A pleasant greeting and good service is the norm. Do not feel disadvantaged if you barely speak the lingo. As a foreigner you are deemed of unsound mind and therefore to be indulged, whereas the Frenchman has to argue and cajole. Sadly it was not possible to visit every restaurant as neither time, wallet nor waistband permitted. Those listed are where a good meal was enjoyed, plus many others where only the prices of set menus and general ambience could be recorded.

The *ouvrier* or workman's café, often found in fishing ports, adds greatly to the fun with a friendly welcome and good value food in unpretentious surroundings.

NAVIGATION

Nautical data is correct to 24 April 2003, Notices to Mariners Weekly Edition 17/2003.
Annual corrections will be included on the publisher's website: www.nauticaldata.com

Conventions 'Yachtsmen' embraces both women and men who sail and/or motor their boat. Times are local unless specified as Universal Time. Bearings and courses are True. Magnetic variation in 2003 is 4°–5°W in the western Channel, 3°–4°W in the central Channel and $2\frac{1}{2}$°W in the Dover Strait; these values decrease by approx 7′ to 10′ per annum.

Distances are in nautical miles (M) or, if less than 1M, in cables (ie one tenth of 1M, or 185 metres).

Short distances may be stated in metres (m) and, when ashore, in kilometres.

Charted depths and drying heights are in metres respectively below and above Chart Datum.

Other reference books Current editions include: *The Solent Cruising Companion* (Nautical Data Ltd/Derek Aslett, 2003); *The West Country Cruising Companion* (Nautical Data Ltd/Mark Fishwick, 2001), Portland Bill to Scilly; *The North France & Belgium Cruising Companion* (Nautical Data Ltd/Neville Featherstone, 2001) Goury to Antwerp, including the Seine to Paris; *North Brittany and Channel Islands Cruising Companion* (Nautical Data Ltd/Peter Cumberlidge, 2001) Diélette to Le Conquet and the Channel Islands.

The Admiralty *Channel Pilot* (NP 27, 5th edition 2002) covers England from Scilly to the Owers (just E of Selsey Bill); and France from Pointe de Penmarc'h (S of Brest) to Cap d'Antifer (N of Le Havre). The *Dover Strait Pilot* (NP 28, 6th edition 2003) continues east from the Owers to Southwold and Cap d'Antifer to Scheveningen, Netherlands.

The *Reeds Nautical Almanac* and *Channel Almanac* (both Nautical Data Ltd) provide tidal predictions and other annually changing information for the English Channel. *Votre Livre de Bord* (Almanac) covers France (with translations) and the Channel Islands, plus some English ports.

Charts & maps Admiralty and/or SHOM charts are listed for each harbour, largest scale last. Admiralty paper charts cost £16.70 (Nov 2002). Leisure Charts, formerly Small Craft charts, are better value at £12.95. Leisure folios are the best value at £37 for up to 12 charts reduced to A2 size for yacht chart tables. Folios SC 5600–5603 and 5605 cover the English coast. SC 5604 covers the Channel Islands. Admiralty charts & publications can be obtained from Admiralty chart agents or Kelvin Hughes Ltd, Mail Order Dept, Kilgraston House, Southampton St, Southampton SO15 2ED. ☎ 023 8063 4911; ✆ 023 8033 0014; southampton@kelvinhughes.co.uk; www.bookharbour.com

SHOM charts & publications can most easily be obtained in advance by mail order from: Nautic Service, ZA de Rogerville-Oudalle, BP 60, 76700 Harfleur; ☎ 02 35 51 75 30, ✆ 02 35 45 70 85.

Librairie Maritime Outremer, 17 rue Jacob, 75006 Paris; ☎ 01 46 33 47 48; ✆ 01 43 29 96 77. Both these suppliers specialise in mail order and are also Admiralty chart agents.

Waypoints Usually two waypoints are given for each harbour in this book. The first waypoint normally appears under the sub-headings of 'Approach' or 'Pilotage', and is an approach waypoint. This is a position in safe water, ie adequate depth and clear of nasties, from which you may either start an approach or can see your destination harbour. It might be a few miles away, for example in a buoyed channel requiring further pilotage and/or buoy-hopping, or just a few cables from the harbour entrance.

The second waypoint is the harbour entrance (or an equivalent, specified feature) as given after the title name. This serves as the final waypoint in your route plan – it also enables you to find the place on a chart in the first instance.

Three things are worth stressing:
a) Plot any waypoint before using it, so that you can appreciate the overall navigational scene and anticipate any potential problems. This may also help to eliminate finger trouble, ie inserting the wrong digits (forgive the pun).
b) The first waypoint is advisory only, but bear in mind that it is based on first-hand experience and a detailed study of charts and other relevant information. You can of course discard or modify it to take account of prevailing conditions or other factors.
c) With the removal of Selective Availability, GPS is very good indeed – as even traditionalists might concede. But despite its excellence, and any additional cross-checking which you might rightly employ, it is vital not to lose the Big Picture by a slavish, over-reliance on 'the numbers'.

By that is meant, keep your head out of the office, be alert to everything around you, take nothing for granted and if you sense that all is not well – do something positive at once: eg stop the boat, turn back, plot a fix, re-assess the situation and decide on a safe course of action.

Horizontal Datums Planet Earth is by no means a perfect sphere. Charts are based on many different models of Earth (called Horizontal Datums as distinct from the vertical Chart Datum used in tide heights). Until recently UK charts were based on OSGB 36 (the 1936 Ordnance Survey of Great Britain). European and French charts are/were based on ED 50 (the 1950 European Datum). The Datum used is given in the title block of paper and electronic charts.

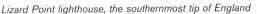
Lizard Point lighthouse, the southernmost tip of England

But GPS (and DGPS), based on WGS 84 (the 1984 World Geodetic System), is changing all this. The unprecedented accuracy of GPS shows up differences between Local Datums and WGS 84. These are commonly about 100m around the UK. In the Dover Strait, for example, an uncorrected WGS 84 read-out will be about 136m in error if plotted on an OSGB 36 chart; or 161m on an ED 50 chart – critical errors if trying to find a buoy or navigate an unmarked, narrow channel in 100m visibility.

This is not an abstruse hydrographic problem. You should pay close attention to these discrepancies, so as to extract the maximum accuracy out of GPS in relation to your charts. Or to put it slightly differently, charts and GPS have to be reconciled with one another. Therefore all charts are steadily being changed to the WGS 84 Datum.

Throughout this book, Latitude and Longitude values and harbour chartlets for England and the Channel Islands are referenced to WGS 84. Thus a GPS readout can be plotted onto a WGS 84 chart without further ado – provided you have set your GPS receiver to WGS 84.

But along the French coast, all values and harbour chartlets are referenced to ED 50 for two reasons:
a) It is not known when all SHOM & UKHO charts of the French coast (also Spain and Portugal) will have been converted to WGS 84; and b) Many yachtsmen will probably retain and use their existing ED 50 charts until the conversion is complete and/or their wallet can stand the cost of replacement WGS 84 charts.

It is pertinent therefore to consider how best to convert your GPS receiver's WGS 84 read-out to ED 50 prior to plotting. There are three options:
1) Do nothing. Plotting raw WGS 84 read-outs onto an ED 50 chart simply means that you will suffer all the inaccuracies described above.
2) Select your GPS receiver to ED 50 Datum, so that the receiver's software automatically converts the WGS 84 read-out to ED 50 for plotting directly onto the chart. This labour-saving option is what most people do, but it is only as good as your GPS' software, which may not be adequate for coping with the inconsistencies in 3.
3) Apply the small Lat/Long corrections printed in the chart's title block under satellite-derived positions to every WGS 84 read-out; plot the result on your ED 50 chart. This is a chore, but it takes account of the fact that differences between WGS 84 and a local Datum (eg ED 50) are not constant; even the corrections themselves are irregular. A typical example with instructions might read as follows:

Your choice depends on the accuracy to which you navigate using GPS; and the margin of error which you accept in very narrow waters and poor visibility. Plot your position in various marinas on large scale charts so as to assess your receiver's accuracy. Think carefully.

Pilotage We do not waste space by telling you that a red can buoy should be left to port as you approach a harbour; nor that you keep south of a SCM. We assume a level of competence befitting a Coastal Skipper who borders on Yachtmaster Offshore. Such a person is a sound navigator, but values the local knowledge that others have gleaned over the years.

Pilotage has been defined as 'What you do when there's no time to plot', ie you direct the yacht along a pre-planned track, usually by eye and often in narrow waters. Pre-planning, as with so many human activities, is the key. So study the chart, select the turning points (which may be used as GPS waypoints, often abeam buoys or beacons), mark in tracks and distances, write down the plan and memorise as much as you can.

If you have a navigator, ie are not solo, his/her job is to give you courses to steer, identify at least the next mark or two ahead, talk your eyes onto them and feed you other relevant information (which may/may not include the latest Test match score). In other words it is a well-coordinated team effort. If you are solo, the workload is higher and there's no one else to blame.

Tidal streams for the English Channel are covered on pages 16 to 19, based on the Admiralty atlas, NP 250. Similarly localised chartlets provide large scale cover of the Portland Race, the Solent and Isle of Wight and the Channel Islands.

French tidal stream atlases are good value, if you sail regularly in these waters or enjoy intricate pilotage. They cover the following more demanding areas at large scale:
i. 561-UJA (Baie de Seine) for the Barfleur Race.

ii. 562-UJA (like NP 264) for Cap de la Hague.
iii. 563-UJA (Bréhat to Pontusval) for N Brittany.
iv. 560-UJA (Pontusval to Penmarc'h) for Chenal du Four and Raz de Sein – almost essential.

Tidal coefficients are used in France in lieu of tidal range to quantify the size of a tide. A spring tide, for example, has a coefficient of about 95, an average tide 70 and neaps around 40. Hence the window of access to a tidally-restricted harbour is often specified by reference to coefficients. When you are used to them they are quicker and easier to use than Range. See the *RNA* under Brest for further details and daily values.

Lights These are always subject to change and are therefore omitted, unless their characteristics help to identify a buoy/beacon or resolve a possible ambiguity.

Coastguard The English South Coast is covered for SAR purposes by the Maritime Rescue Coordination Centres (MRCC) at Falmouth and Dover, plus Maritime Rescue Sub-Centres (MRSC) at Brixham, Portland and the Solent.

The Channel coast of France is covered by three *Centres Régionaux Opérationnels de Surveillance et de Sauvetage* (CROSS) which equate to MRCCs. They operate via a network of radio relay stations:

CROSS Gris-Nez covers from the Belgian border to Cap d'Antifer (N of Le Havre).

CROSS Jobourg, near Cap de la Hague, covers from Cap d'Antifer to a line joining Mont St Michel to Roches Douvres.

CROSS Corsen, 3M N of Le Conquet, covers from the above line to Pte de Penmarc'h (S of Brest). See the *RNA* for details of English & French Centres.

Weather information There is no shortage of weather information, sometimes contradictory as a result of different sources. On the whole more weight may be attached to French forecasts when dealing with their own backyard, whilst the UK Met Office forecasts are possibly more accurate in the northern half of the Channel sea areas.
a. BBC Radio 4 Shipping forecasts on 198kHz LW and FM remain the mainstay for many yachts and are easily received throughout the English Channel. Broadcast times are 0048, 0535, 1201 and 1754, all UK Local Times. The UK CG repeats the forecasts as in the previous section.
b. Navtex routinely broadcasts weather information twice daily in English and other tongues. For the English Channel, Niton (Isle of Wight) transmits on both 518 and 490kHz as follows:

i. Niton (E) on 518kHz transmits in English at 0840 and 2040UT for Thames, Dover, Wight, Portland, Plymouth, Biscay, Fitzroy, Sole, Lundy

and Fastnet (see the *RNA* for any revised transmission times). It also transmits gale warnings on receipt and every 4 hrs from 0040UT whilst the gale warning remains in force.

ii. Niton (K) on 518kHz transmits no weather; only Nav warnings from Cap Gris Nez to Île de Bréhat every 4 hrs from 0140UT in English;.

iii. Niton (I) on 490kHz transmits forecasts for inshore waters (The Wash to Colwyn Bay) at 0520 & 1720UT, plus a UK three-day outlook.

iv. Niton (T) on 490kHz transmits in French Gale warnings and a 24 hrs forecast for sea areas Humber to Ouessant, every 4 hrs from 0310UT.

CROSS Corsen, at Le Stiff on Ouessant, is on the boundary between MetArea I to the north, controlled by the UK, and MetArea II to the south controlled by France. (This explains why Niton (K) transmits nav warnings as in (ii) above, whilst Niton (T) transmits weather as in (iv) above). CROSS Corsen 'looks' south into MetArea II and transmits weather as follows:

v. Corsen (A) on 518kHz in English at 0000 & 1200 UT for coastal areas Iroise, Yeu, Rochebonne and Cantabrico; and for offshore sea areas Pazenn and Finisterre.

vi. Corsen (E) on 490kHz in French at 0840 & 2040 UT for areas in (v.), plus Casquets, Ouessant, Sole, Lundy, Irish Sea, Fastnet and Shannon.
c. Weather broadcasts by the Coastguard
In the UK MRCCs and MRSCs repeat on VHF the Shipping forecast and Inshore waters forecasts for their associated areas, as follows:
i) Shipping forecasts, all times UT.

Falmouth	0940, 2140. Sole, Fastnet, Lundy and Plymouth.	
Brixham	0850, 2050. Plymouth, Portland.	
Portland	1020, 2220. As Brixham, plus Wight.	
Solent	0840, 2040. Portland, Wight.	
Dover	0905, 2105. Wight, Dover, Thames.	

ii) Inshore waters forecasts, 4 hourly UT from:

Falmouth	0140. St David's Head to Lyme Regis.
Brixham	0050. Scilly to Lyme Regis.
Portland	0220. Scilly to Selsey Bill.
Solent	0040. Lyme Regis to N Foreland.
Dover	0105. Lyme Regis to The Wash.

In France, CROSS Gris Nez and CROSS Corsen on VHF Ch 79 and CROSS Jobourg on Ch 80 broadcast weather messages and gale warnings thrice daily in French (at dictation speed), through remote stations at the times listed in the *RNA*. On request, the forecast can be passed in English.
d. Forecasts and synoptic charts are posted daily at HM/Marina offices and at Capitaineries; they usually include a three-day outlook.

Language Useful French words are listed in the *RNA*. The French ABC, as you might suppose, sounds different from the English version. Below is roughly how the French pronounce the letters of their alphabet.

A	=	ah	N	=	en
B	=	bay	O	=	auh
C	=	say	P	=	pay
D	=	day	Q	=	koo
E	=	ayre	R	=	air
F	=	eff	S	=	ess
G	=	shay	T	=	tay
H	=	ash	U	=	ooh
I	=	ee	V	=	vay
J	=	jee	W	=	doobler vay
K	=	kah	X	=	iks
L	=	el	Y	=	eegrek
M	=	em	Z	=	zee

Note for example how easy it is to go to pontoon 'G' when the Frenchman clearly told you to berth on 'J'; or 'E' instead of 'I'. And your ill-tuned ear may not readily distinguish between E and R, which is why Echo and Romeo and their ilk were introduced into the phonetic alphabet.

HARBOURS AND MARINAS

Marina VHF Channels In England Ch 80 or M (ex-37) are the usual channels; Ch 09 in France, but with a few inevitable exceptions. More and more yachtsmen use mobile phones to pre-book a berth or talk to the HM/marina.

Berthing Three types of berth are mentioned in this book:
a) Alongside/rafting. This implies a long pontoon with no fingers, on which you lie alongside the pontoon itself or raft up; the French are good at rafting *ad infinitum*.
b) Finger berth (*catway* in French). Self evident, and the word *catway* is the key to requesting one.
c) Hammerhead. An alongside berth on the T-pontoon across the end of a long pontoon. They are fair game for a visitor; multihulls like them.

The *Accueil* (welcome) pontoon is a helpful feature but by no means universal. It gives you an obvious check-in point where the paperwork can be sorted out before moving to the assigned berth.

Fuel Many marinas have self-service diesel and petrol pumps which are automatically operated continuously by a € credit card. British cards may not be electronically able to operate these pumps.

Usually the solution is to advise the HM of the problem (it is well known); the pumps will then be switched on for your use and your credit card debited in the normal way.

INTERNATIONAL PORT TRAFFIC SIGNALS

No	Lights		Main message
1		Flashing	Serious emergency – all vessels to stop or divert according to instructions
2			Vessels shall not proceed (*Note:* Some ports may use an exemption signal).
3		Fixed or Slow Occulting	Vessels may proceed. One-way traffic
4			Vessels may proceed. Two-way traffic
5			A vessel may proceed only when she has received specific orders to do so. (*Note:* Some ports may use an exemption signal).
Exemption signals and messages			
6		Fixed or Slow Occulting	Vessels shall not proceed, except that vessels which navigate outside the main channel need not comply with the main message
7			A vessel may proceed when she has received specific orders to do so, except that vessels which navigate outside the main channel need not comply with the main message
Auxiliary signals and messages			
White and/or yellow lights, displayed to the right of the main lights			Local meanings, as promulgated in local port orders

CROSSING THE ENGLISH CHANNEL

The further off from England,
the nearer is to France –
Then turn not pale, beloved snail,
but come and join the dance.
Lewis Carroll: *Alice in Wonderland*

This leg may be the hardest part of a holiday cruise, particularly if the boat is lightly crewed and/or the weather fickle. The return leg may suffer from get-home-itis (or the need to be back at work on Monday morning) to the prejudice of the skipper's better judgement.

The following discussion of considerations and techniques uses as an example the classic crossing from the Needles or Nab Tower to Cherbourg. The lessons apply elsewhere of course, so the busy waters and TSS of the Eastern Channel are next discussed; and finally the longer passages across the Western Channel.

Weather All yachts must carefully consider the developing weather pattern, since in effect they need a safe window of 12–24 hrs in which the winds are forecast to be within their capabilities and fog is not expected. A safe diversion harbour must also be selected because there may be few if any ports of refuge, ie accessible in all conditions.

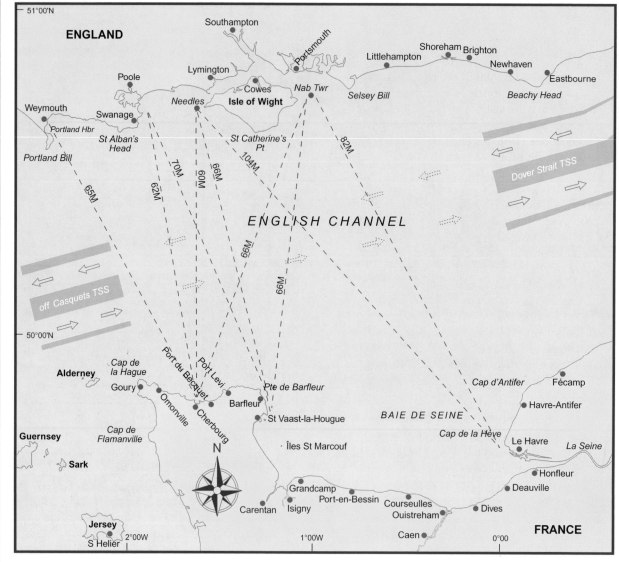

For example many North Brittany harbours can be difficult or even unsafe to enter in onshore winds of F5/6 or more.

The Central Channel broadly covers UK ports from Weymouth to Selsey and on the other side, from the Channel Islands to Le Havre: Alderney, Guernsey, Cherbourg, St Vaast and Le Havre are the most likely destinations. The Casquets TSS may need to be crossed, but shipping between the Casquets and Dover TSS is as much to be avoided as if a TSS did exist; see the diagram above.

Planning is the key to a trouble-free passage. It involves a painstaking process of gathering and analysing facts, then deciding how to play them to best advantage. Ask yourself the following: Is it neaps or springs? When do the tidal streams turn? What does the weather forecast hold in store? Which TSS, if any, have to be negotiated? What other hazards may affect the route? Do departure or arrival procedures influence the choice of route?

Where to go if the destination looks untenable or you have suffered gear failure?

When all these and other questions have been answered, select the route and begin to flesh out the details. In this example leave your home port to reach the Needles/Nab efficiently and at an ETD which thereafter will best utilise tide and wind.

Based on that ETD, carefully extract the hourly tidal vectors which will affect you during the likely time on passage. Sum them together, ie subtract the total vectors in one direction from the larger value in the other. Apply the resultant tidal vector in the correct sense at your departure point and lay off the course to the approach waypoint. This is the course to steer and with good fortune, a fair wind and accurate helming it should get you to that waypoint without altering course again.

Navigation But things rarely work out like that: You started an hour after your ETD. The wind is on the nose; visibility is moderate to poor – not at all as the forecast suggested. Decide whether to continue or turn back to await an improvement.

Assuming all is well, however, log/plot your departure time and position and settle into the routine of passage-making. Write up the log at regular intervals, hourly at first, but maybe half-hourly in say the last dozen miles and perhaps even more frequently if you are battling with the notorious spring tides across the Cotentin peninsula. Plot the fixes which you have logged; these are vital to checking/correcting progress – and, if you lose GPS (unlikely), will allow you to carry on almost routinely with DR navigation.

Keep reviewing your decisions: If hard on the wind, have you adopted the time-honoured and efficient technique of lee-bowing*? Are you aware of when the tidal streams change, and of what VMG (your rate of progress toward the destination) is telling you? Would it pay to tack now or an hour later?

*Lee-bowing is arranging your tacks so that the tidal stream impinges on the yacht's lee bow, thus counteracting leeway and in effect allowing you to sail closer to the wind. It works.

Tidal streams off the French coast are invariably stronger than those off the English coast, as a quick study of the Tidal Stream Atlas makes clear. It is a common misconception that 6 hrs of tide one way will cancel out 6 hrs worth the other way. The streams set east/west across the top of the Cotentin peninsula, $3\frac{1}{2}$ to 4kn at springs and about 2kn at neaps – enough to make tracking difficult. For example, a 5kn boat some 15M north of Cherbourg's west entrance, with a 4kn E-going tide, is likely to be pointing roughly at the Jobourg nuclear plant in order to keep on track or a little up-tide of destination; in other words the drift angle may be up to 35°–40°. This will reduce VMG, which in turn will mean longer exposure to the strong tide.

Thus it becomes painfully clear why it was so important to have pre-calculated tidal vectors, the resultant drift angle and course to steer. Apply these and the boat will track along a classic sine curve, adjusted to keep up-tide of destination.

The Eastern Channel, say Selsey Bill to Rye and Le Havre to Le Tréport, poses few real problems. Distances range from 60 to 80M – a day's sail, or perhaps an overnight passage for a typical family crew. Be aware that

Le Havre and Dieppe are the only sure-fire ports of refuge between Cherbourg and Boulogne.

Crossing TSS The problem, such as it is, concerns crossing the western part of the Dover Strait TSS; see the diagram below. The best solution is to avoid crossing it at all (Rule 10c). For example a track from Newhaven direct to Le Havre crosses the west-bound lane only 5M inside its western end; but a smallish detour will avoid it altogether. When crossing a TSS, the IRPCS require vessels to **head** as nearly as practicable at 90° to the TSS axis. Do **not** steer a heading(s) to make good a track at 90° to the axis of the TSS.

If a TSS cannot be avoided, analyse the tidal streams expected whilst crossing it. Use them so that, whilst heading at 90° to the TSS, the yacht nevertheless tracks as nearly as possible towards the destination. To achieve this, construct a vector triangle based on the total tidal stream vector, boat speed and the 90° cross-TSS heading. 'Juggle' this vector triangle around (tracing paper helps) until its end-point lies on the far side of the TSS and the heading vector is at 90° to the TSS. The start-point is on the near side of the TSS and up-tide of the baseline. From this start-point, head at 90° across the TSS, and monitor progress carefully.

On the day the wind must also be considered:

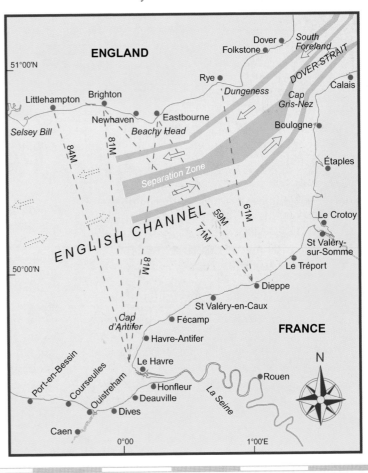

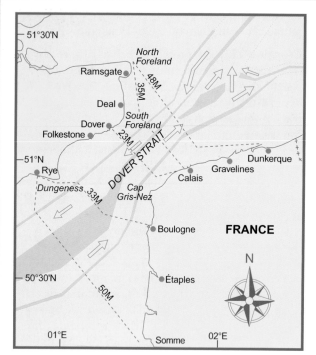

The map shows the Dover Strait area with locations including Ramsgate, North Foreland, Deal, South Foreland, Dover, Folkestone, Rye, Dungeness, Cap Gris-Nez, Calais, Gravelines, Dunkerque, Boulogne, Étaples, Somme, and FRANCE. Distances shown: 35M, 48M, 23M, 33M, 50M. Coordinates: 51°30'N, 51°N, 50°30'N, 01°E, 02°E.

the ATSO buoy should be reached near local HW – to proceed up the Baie de la Somme to St Valéry – a rewarding passage.

b. Dover to Calais (23M). First draw two lines from Dover's Eastern entrance to CA3 and CA4 buoys. Within that narrow cone most of the cross-Channel ferries will track for most of the time; if you can avoid it, do so. Leaving via Dover's Western entrance at once gives almost 1M's lateral separation from ferries, but not Seacats.

Next consider the tidal streams very carefully and also the time of HW Calais (so as to enter the marina without delay). Juggle these factors so that by heading at 90° across the TSS, you will in fact clear the TSS to the NW of CA3 buoy. Hopefully the last six miles to Calais will be with the flood, so as to enter when the bridge into the marina opens, ie at HW Calais –2, HW or HW+1.

The Western Channel embraces passages from UK ports between Scilly and Weymouth to French harbours between Ouessant and the Bay of St Malo, including the Channel Islands (see opposite).

The main problem, if problem it is, concerns the greater distances than those further up-Channel. From Scilly to Ouessant is 108M, whilst from ports between Falmouth and Plymouth to many of the North Brittany ports is typically around 100M. A passage from Dartmouth to Alderney is only 70M. Many yachts may be limited by crew strength and watchkeeping abilities, especially if short-handed. Setting off from the southernmost UK ports can greatly shorten the open-sea passage. For example a yacht out of Exmouth bound for Trébeurden (120M) might do well to coast round to Salcombe (33M) whence the Channel crossing is only 94M or roughly five hours less.

The TSS off Ouessant and off Casquets are not likely to be a hindrance since they can usually be avoided rather than crossed. However the many commercial ships on course between these two TSS pose just as great a hazard as if they were actually in a TSS. Their track (055°/235°) is at an oblique angle to yachts heading generally south or north – thus increasing the time exposed to risk.

Tidal streams set more or less ENE/WSW, ie up and down the Channel axis, and some gain can be extracted. For example, if the likely passage time is 18 hrs, then arrange your southbound departure to benefit from two fair ebb tides, and only one foul flood tide; conversely northbound. This may however be impossible if either the departure or arrival ports are tidally limited. Check tide times at both ETD and ETA. After a long trip it is frustrating to have to await sufficient rise of tide before being able to enter your destination.

Tacking across a lane is out of the question as it blatantly contravenes the 90° heading stipulation. Slow progress under sail, say less than 3kn boat speed, requires motor-sailing so as to spend the least possible time in a lane.

The Dover Strait In these narrow waters the TSS crossing is shorter, but more demanding as traffic intensifies and ferries add a further ingredient. It is no place to be in fog. Yachts departing from the E Sussex/Kent ports or Thames Estuary are likely to be bound for Boulogne, Calais or Dunkerque. See the diagram above.

The Channel Navigation Information Service (CNIS) is a safety service (H24) for all vessels in the Dover Strait. When crossing the TSS or coasting through the ITZ, you should monitor VHF Ch 11 (back-up 16, 67, 80). Dover CG broadcasts at H+40 (and additionally at H+55 if visibility is less than 2M) on Ch 11 reports of adverse weather, exceptional tides, defective navigational aids, hampered vessels (eg oil rigs, deep-draught tankers, cross-Channel swimmers and escorts).

Crossing routes Given the endless permutations, two examples must suffice:
a. Rye to the Somme. The 50M passage to the destination WPT (ATSO buoy) is easily tailored to head across the TSS at 90°. Leaving Rye near HW, the SW-going ebb sets the yacht almost south to the edge of the TSS. Head 145° across it, passing the Bassurelle WCM buoy, and avoiding the bank itself. When clear of the TSS, the growing flood stream will set the yacht up toward the rhumb line track. With careful timing

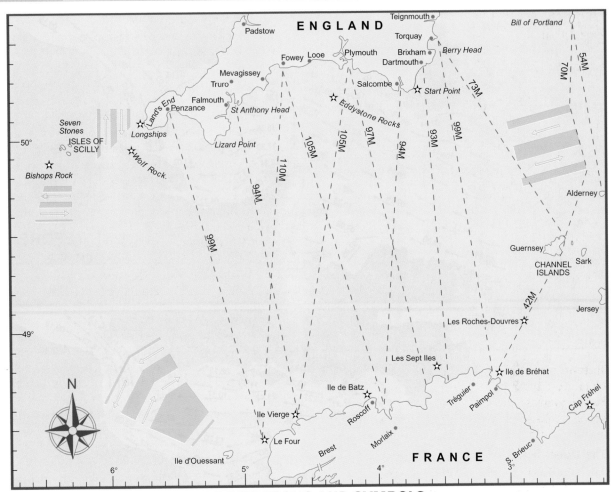

ABBREVIATIONS AND SYMBOLS

The following abbreviations and symbols may be encountered in this book; others may be found which are self-explanatory or are listed in the *Reeds Nautical Almanac*.

AB	Alongside berth	IDM	Isolated Danger Mark	✉	Post Office
AC	Admiralty Chart	🛈	Tourist Office	Q	Quick flashing light
amsl	Above mean sea level	IPTS	Intl Port Traffic Signals	RNA	Reeds Nautical Almanac
⚒, BY	Boatyard	IRPCS	International Rules for	SCM	South Cardinal Mark
⚓, BH	Boathoist		Preventing Collisions at Sea	SHM	Starboard-hand Mark
CH	Chandler	Iso	Isophase light	SHOM	French Hydrographer/chart
⛪	Church	ITZ	Inshore Traffic Zone	SM	Sailmaker
🏴	Direction of buoyage	📷	Launderette	◤	Slip for launching, scrubbing
Ⓔ	Electronic repairs	◆, LB	Lifeboat	SNSM	Société Nationale de
ECM	East Cardinal Mark	Ldg	Leading (light)		Sauvetage en Mer (Lifeboats)
EI	Electrical repairs	≠	Leading line	SPM	Special Mark
F	Fixed Light	L.Fl	Long-flashing light	🛒	Stores/Supermarket
Fl	Flashing light	M	Sea mile(s)	SWM	Safe Water Mark
⛽	Fuel berth	ME	Marine engineering repairs	TSS	Traffic Separation Scheme
FV(s)	Fishing vessel(s)	MHWN	Mean High Water Neaps	Ⓥ	Visitors berth
⊖	Fish Harbour/Quay	MHWS	Mean High Water Springs	Ⓥ	Visitors buoy
FW	Fresh water supply	MLWN	Mean Low Water Neaps	VQ	Very quick flashing light
H+, H–	Minutes after/	MLWS	Mean Low Water Springs	WCM	West Cardinal Mark
	before each hour	➕	Hospital	WPT,⊕	Waypoint
H24	Continuous	NCM	North Cardinal Mark	⚓	Yacht harbour, Marina
🔩	Holding tank pumpout	Oc	Occulting light	⚓	Yacht berths without facilities
⚓, HM	Harbour Master	PHM	Port-hand Mark	◀	Yacht Club

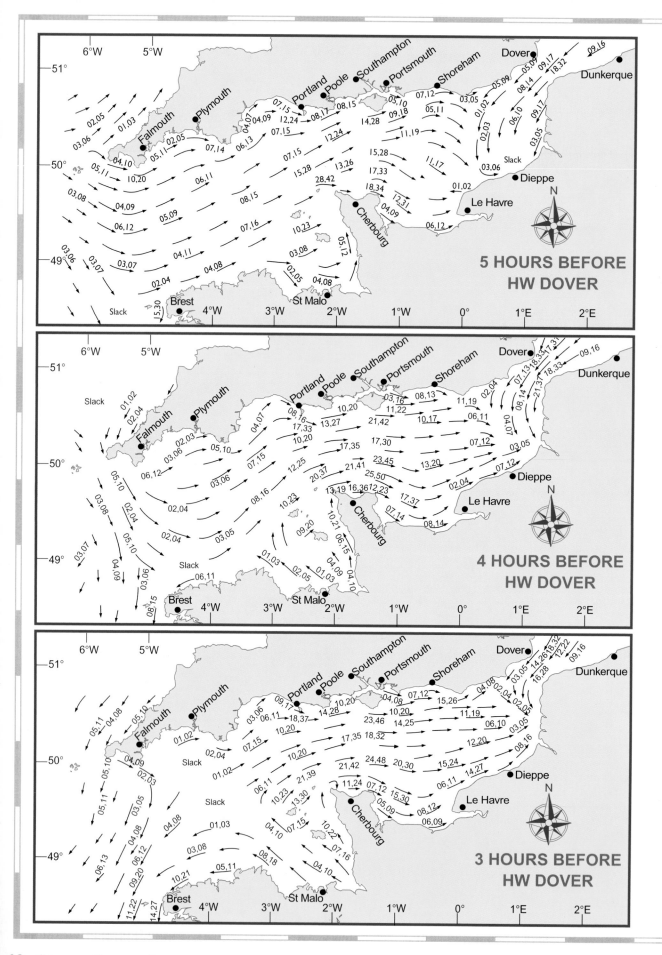

5 HOURS BEFORE HW DOVER

4 HOURS BEFORE HW DOVER

3 HOURS BEFORE HW DOVER

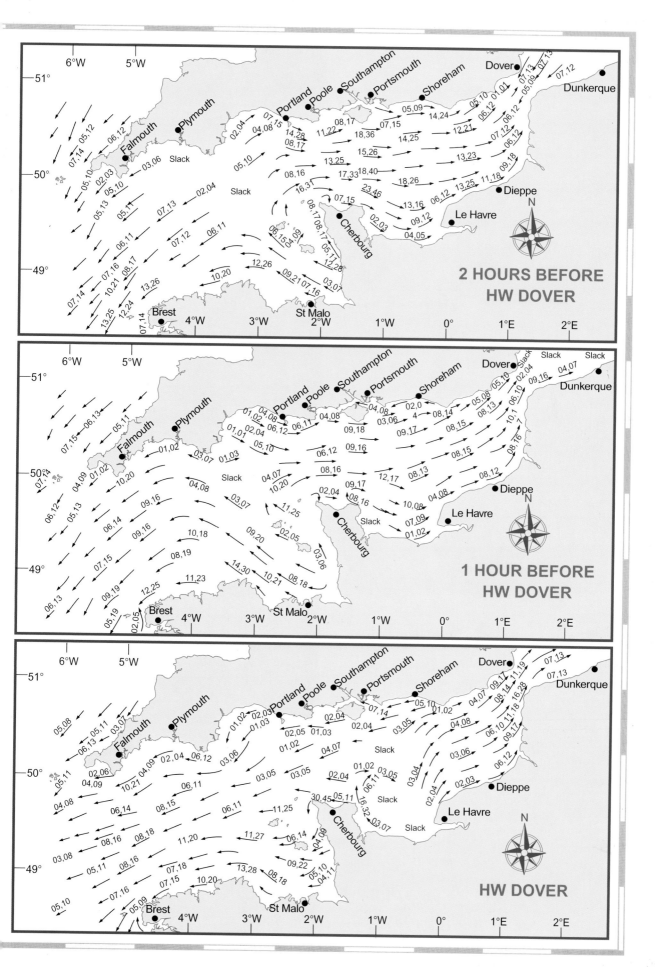

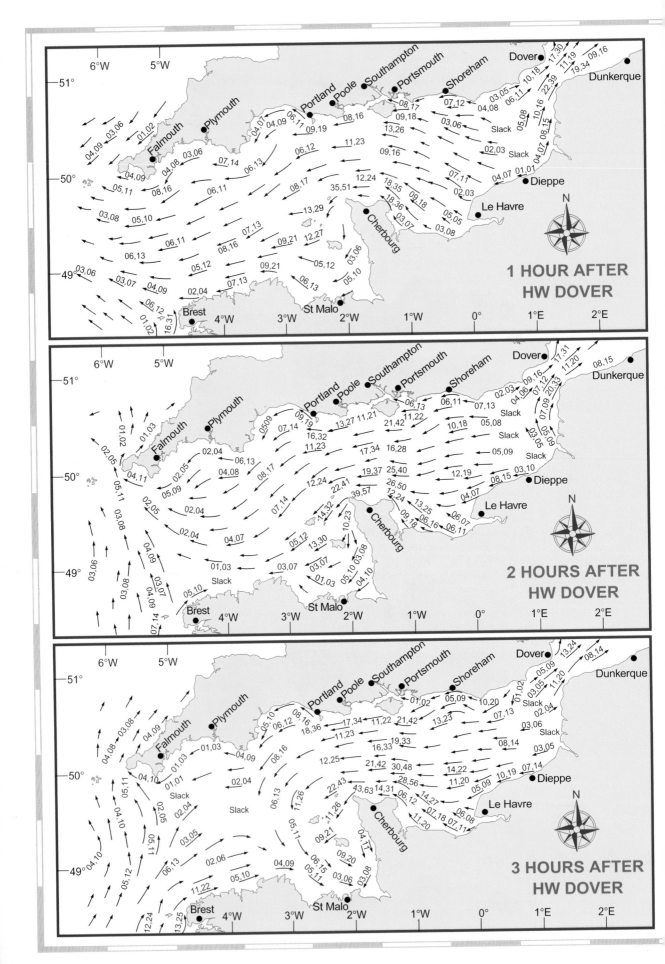

1 HOUR AFTER
HW DOVER

2 HOURS AFTER
HW DOVER

3 HOURS AFTER
HW DOVER

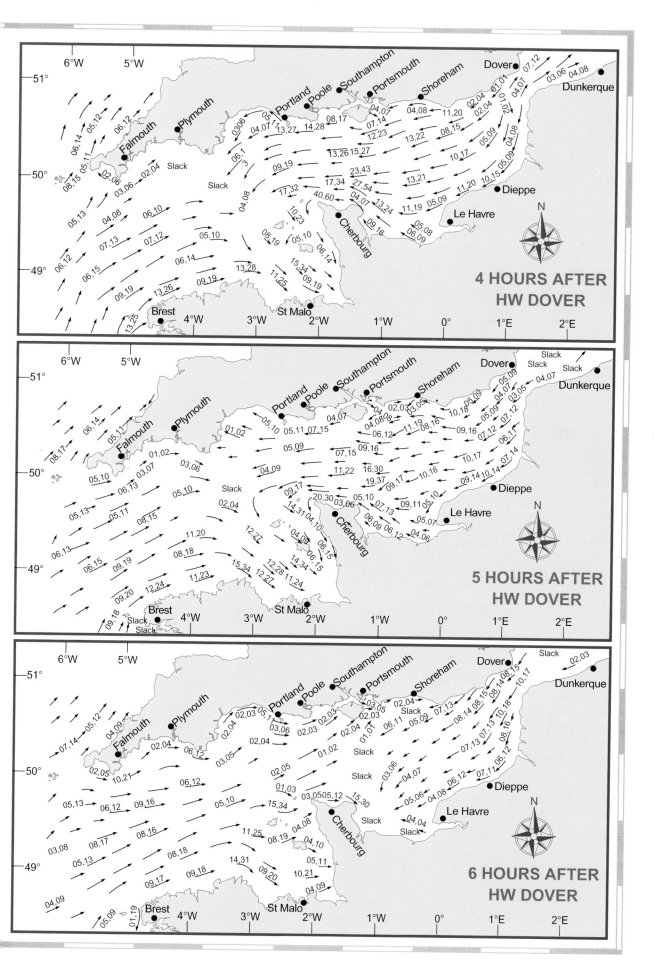

4 HOURS AFTER HW DOVER

5 HOURS AFTER HW DOVER

6 HOURS AFTER HW DOVER

THE WEST COUNTRY AND DORSETSHIRE

ISLES OF SCILLY TO STUDLAND BAY

CONTENTS

INTRODUCTION

The West Country is undoubtedly England's finest cruising ground. The Isles of Scilly, some 20M off Land's End, form a miniature archipelago offering endless scope for cruising in its purest form. Here a yacht may meander for days, never anchoring in the same place. Scilly's relaxed charm and the renowned individuality of the islanders continue to draw 'foreigners' back year after year.

Land's End is a rugged peninsula, fringed by lethal rocks and forbidding cliffs. Mount's Bay has a somewhat gentler face, graced by the fairytale silhouette of St Michael's Mount and minute Cornish fishing villages such as Mousehole or Mullion Cove. And if at times it rains more often than you might wish, remember that the Cornish euphemism for it is Liquid Sunshine.

The Lizard, southernmost point of the UK, is guarded by offlying rocks and swept by strong tides and the attendant race – never a push-over for the cruising yacht. Once east of it and north of the Manacles, Cornwall is at its very best. The Helford River, thanks to Daphne du Maurier, has a multitude of romantic literary associations. To the north the great seaport of Falmouth has served seamen well for centuries and today the River Fal remains a happy haven for yachtsmen to explore.

Beyond the rounded shoulder of the Dodman lie Mevagissey, Charlestown, Fowey and Polruan, Polperro and Looe – all places to savour before passing Rame Head into Plymouth. Nearing the breakwater, history crowds in upon you. Drake, Raleigh, the Pilgrim Fathers, Cook and Darwin all sailed from here and have left their mark upon the city or harbour. On leaving, meander up the River Yealm, surely the most beautiful of Devon's rivers.

Crossing Bigbury Bay find time to loiter at the drying Rivers Erme and Avon or tuck in behind Burgh Island and sound into Hope Cove. Then skirt the high bulk of Bolt Tail and Head, which shield Salcombe from the prevailing westerlies.

After Prawle, the cock's-combed Start Point is a milestone in your voyage up-Channel, usually demanding perseverance if west-bound. Slapton's silver sands give way to high ground cleft by the Dart and the delights of Dartmouth, Kingswear, Dittisham and Totnes. If you have crossed Lyme Bay from Poole or the Solent and time is slipping away, make sure the Dart is your goal.

Northward round flat-topped Berry Head into sub-tropical Tor Bay where Brixham is fun and Torquay pleasant in a different style. Thence past Hope's Nose and across Babbacombe Bay to the wooded bluff of The Ness where Devon's red soil was never more in evidence. Below The Ness slip carefully into Teignmouth if conditions are right or stand on to the largely unspoiled Exe estuary.

Further east the proudly acclaimed East Devon and Dorset World Heritage site stretches around Lyme Bay – and continues east from Portland Bill. Beer Roads and Axmouth's tiny harbour shelter in the lee of Beer Head where quite abruptly the cliffs change from red to white.

In a few more miles The Cobb juts seaward of Lyme Regis and Golden Cap climbs more than 600ft above the sea. At West Bay (Bridport) the narrow entrance is being widened by building a new west pier in lieu of the old. The sweep of Chesil Beach continues to wedge-shaped Isle of Portland and the Bill – off which Portland Race concentrates the mind. Skirt Portland harbour to break your passage in Weymouth.

The matchless scenery, sculptured cliffs and fossil-rich rocks of the Heritage, or Jurassic (as media people insist on calling it), Coast continue east past St Alban's Head and Anvil Point to Old Harry (Handfast Pt) – surely the most inspiring stretch of coast in all England.

PASSAGE NOTES
SCILLY FROM/TO THE MAINLAND

Three TSS (West of Scilly, South of Scilly and Off Land's End; plus ITZ) separate traffic converging here from N, S, E & W. The 'Off Land's End' lanes, orientated N–S, lie about 5M west of Land's End and 7M east of Scilly (see AC 1148). A track from Runnel Stone to Scilly (Peninnis Hd), 254°/26M, crosses the S end of these lanes; but they are just cleared from the Lizard, 267°/46M. Wolf Rock lt ho will be passed fairly close on this leg.

Tidal streams between Scilly and Land's End are rotatory clockwise, ie set W from HW Dover; N from HWD +2; NE from +4; E from −6; SSE from −4; and SW from −2. Spring rates are about 1kn. Optimum use of these streams will decide the ETD from either Scilly or Newlyn/Penzance.

But from/to Falmouth or the Helford R, timings will usually be dictated by the need to carry a fair tide round the Lizard, ie W-bound HWD −2 to +3; E-bound HWD +4 to next HWD −3.

W-bound timing: At HWD −2 leave Newlyn or Penzance (from a ⚓ or ⚓ as the Wet Dock will not be open). Or leave Falmouth/Helford at HWD −4 or −3 to carry the fair tide round the Lizard.

E-bound timing: To Newlyn/Penzance (35M), leave Scilly at HWD +3.
To the Helford R (60M) or Falmouth (65M), leave Scilly at HWD −3 so as to round the Lizard at HWD +5 on the early fair tide. The Lizard tidal window effectively closes at next HWD −5, if the remaining fair tide is to be carried to Falmouth.

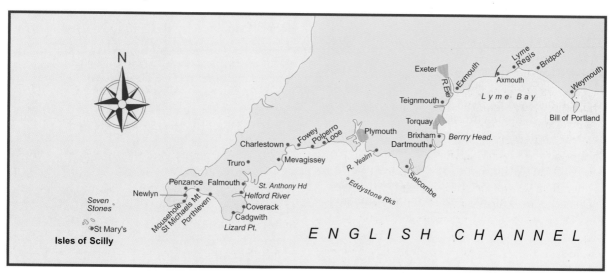

Naval exercise areas extend east from Scilly to beyond the Isle of Wight; and S to approx 49°30'N. In these areas keep a sharp lookout for warships and submarines, especially in the Plymouth areas. The CG and Niton Navtex broadcast information in Gunfacts and Subfacts.

LAND'S END TO LIZARD POINT

Only Gwennap Head to Tater Du, is described here but, 3.3M NW of Gwennap, Longships light remains an important mark by day and night.

The Runnel Stone (drying 0.5m) is 0.7M south of Gwennap. There is no safe passage inshore of it, even in calm weather and at HW, due to rocks and uncharted wrecks. The SCM buoy, 2 cables south of the Runnel Stone, is the mark from which to set course for Scilly, or turn NW for Longships. Irregular depths to seaward cause a bad sea in strong W'lies against a W-going tide. At springs streams exceed 4kn and are unpredictable.

Mousehole's small drying harbour is more easily approached from the SW, inshore of St Clement's Isle. From the NE access is narrower and limited by drying rocks and depths of 1.3m.

SE of Newlyn, Low Lee (1.1m) and Carn Base (1.8m) are dangerous rocks, the former marked by an ECM light buoy. Newlyn is the only harbour in Mount's Bay which is safe to approach in strong onshore winds, but only near HW. From here to Penzance beware Dog Rock and The Gear (1.9m).

From Penzance to St Michael's Mount the head of the Bay is shoal; Cressar, Ryeman, Outer Penzeath and the Hogus are drying rocks up to 4 cables offshore. Mountamopus shoal is marked by a SCM buoy which should be passed to seaward. Porthleven is a small drying harbour exposed to the SW. In offshore weather enter between Great & Little Trigg Rocks and a pier on the south side.

Mullion Cove makes a fair weather, short-stay anchorage between Mullion Island and the tiny drying harbour of Porth Mellin.

The Lizard is a bold, wide headland fronted by drying reefs which extend S for almost 5 cables. Beyond these a dangerous race, which may spread SW and SE of the Lizard, should be skirted at least 3M offshore. Or, if conditions allow, take the far shorter inshore passage; this is never entirely free of rough water nor advised at night. Either side of local LW (= HW Dover) the drying rocks will be seen. Latitude 49°57'·00N clears the southernmost rocks by a bare cable; AC 2345 is essential.

Slack water is at about HW Dover −2½ and +3½. 5M S of the Lizard, the NE-going stream starts at HW Devonport −3½, and SW-going at HW+2½, up to 2.3kn at springs.

To await slack water, anchor in Kynance Cove (1M NW of the Lizard), Housel Bay (close NE of the lighthouse and below a conspicuous hotel) or off Cadgwith or Coverack. 1M E of Lizard lighthouse, which celebrated its 250th anniversary in 2002, avoid Vrogue, a dangerous rock (1.8m), and Craggan Rocks (1.5m) 1M further N.

Manacle buoy, Q (3) 10s

THE LIZARD TO GRIBBIN HEAD

Coverack, 1M N of Black Hd, is a good anchorage in westerlies. The dangerous Manacles reefs, 2½M NE, extend 1M seaward, marked by an ECM lt buoy and the red sector of St Anthony Head light. Here the stream sets NNE from HW Devonport −4½, and SSW from HW+1½, up to 1.7kn springs. North of the Manacles there are no offshore dangers en route to the Helford River or River Fal.

Avoid The Bizzies, 2.5M NE of St Anthony Head, where the sea breaks in rough weather. Off Nare Head the drying Whelps and Gull Rock (38m) can be passed by an inshore route. In the centre of Veryan Bay keep clear of Lath Rock (2.1m).

At the E end of Veryan Bay, Dodman Point is a 112m high, rounded headland, with a stone cross on top. In calm conditions it can be passed close inshore, but in strong winds against tide it is best to pass 2M off to clear heavy overfalls.

Dodman Point from the South

SSE of the Dodman by 2.3 to 4.8M are three yellow target buoys which warships fire at from east of Fowey. Listen out on VHF Ch 74 for firing details.

Gorran Haven, 1M NNE of Dodman Pt, is a tiny drying harbour with an L-shaped pier. Gwineas Rock (8m high), 1M ENE, is marked by an ECM buoy. Further north, anchor off Portmellon or berth in Mevagissey. Charlestown can be entered by prior arrangement or anchor off. St Austell Bay is clear of dangers. Four chimneys at the china-clay port of Par are conspicuous.

GRIBBIN HEAD TO START POINT

On Gribbin Head a 26m high square tower with red and white bands is a highly conspicuous unlit daymark, 104m amsl. It heralds Fowey entrance (1.3M NE) which is not obvious from the east. Off Gribbin keep SE of Cannis Rock SCM buoy. When 3M east of Fowey pass S of Udder Rock (dries 0.6m) and its SCM light buoy.

Tiny Polperro is a safe and delightful anchorage in offshore winds. Looe (or St George's) Island is

Gribbin Head daymark and Cannis Rock buoy

ringed by drying ledges, especially The Ranneys to the E and SE, off which there are overfalls in bad weather. The drying rocky channel inshore of the island should not be attempted. Looe harbour dries utterly, but supports an active fishing fleet.

Eddystone Rocks and offliers are 8M south of Rame Head. Hand Deeps, 3.5M NW of Eddystone, are rocks marked by a WCM light buoy.

Rame Head is a conspicuous conical headland, with a small chapel on top, marking the W side of the entrance to Plymouth Sound. Rocks extend about 200m off it and in wind-over-tide conditions overfalls may be met 1.5M to seaward. Round Draystone PHM buoy and enter The Sound west

Rame Head at the western entrance to Plymouth

of the breakwater. From the E keep clear of Great Mewstone, a conspicuous rocky islet (59m), and the drying Mewstone Ledge SW of it. Then enter The Sound via the Eastern Channel between Tinker shoal and the Shag Stone.

The R Yealm is approached via Wembury Bay which is flanked by the drying Slimers, 2 cables E of Great Mewstone, and by East and West Ebb Rocks awash 2.5 cables off Gara Point. From here to Stoke Pt, dangers extend about 0.3M seaward.

Bigbury Bay is worth a visit in offshore winds to explore the drying Rivers Erme and Avon. Off the latter Burgh Island is an interesting anchorage, as is Hope Cove behind Bolt Tail.

From here to Bolt Head keep 0.5M offshore to clear a series of drying rocks. Below dramatic Bolt

Bolt Head and Salcombe entrance

Head round Little Mew Stone and Mew Stone a safe distance off, before turning north into Salcombe. Prawle Point, 2.5M east of Bolt Head, is rarely difficult to round despite overfalls off it.

START POINT TO STRAIGHT POINT
Start Point is a long spur with a distinctive cockscomb silhouette, conspicuous radio masts and a white lighthouse. Three cables S and E lie Black Stone (6m high) and several drying rocks.

Start Point from close inshore

Overfalls and a race extend 1.5M east and 1M south. In calm weather the slight overfalls can be avoided by passing close to seaward of the rocks; there is no clear-cut inshore passage as such. In bad weather keep at least 2M off Start.

The SSW-going stream begins 1M E of Start at HW Devonport +3½, and the NNE-going at HW−2½. Inshore the stream turns 30 mins earlier. The max rate at springs is 3.1kn. AC 1634 has hourly tidal stream chartlets for Salcombe to Berry Head.

Skerries Bank, least depth 2.1m, is best avoided by passing W or E of it. From Dartmouth to Berry Hd rocks lie up to 5 cables offshore. Nimble Rock, 1.25M NE of the Mew Stone, has only 1m over it.

Berry Head is a sheer, flat-topped cliff (55m); it paints well on radar. East of Torquay avoid Morris Rogue (0.8m), 5½ cables W of Thatcher Rock, and The Sunker, awash 100m SW of Ore Stone.

Teignmouth entrance is dangerous in onshore winds >F4. The River Exe approach is flanked by drying Pole Sand (liable to shift) to the SW, and to the NE by drying rocks and shoals close to the buoyed channel. The safety arc of a firing range extends E of Straight Point, marked by two yellow DZ buoys; when the range is active red flags are flown and a safety vessel is on patrol.

Berry Head and Cod Rock

STRAIGHT POINT TO PORTLAND BILL
The 35M wide segment of coast from Straight Pt to Portland Bill is little visited. Most yachtsmen cross Lyme Bay in a dreary groove between the Bill and Torbay, Dartmouth or Start. In so doing they miss one of England's most glorious coastal stretches, recently elevated to the status of a World Heritage Site. It is true there is no refuge accessible in onshore winds (although this may soon change at West Bay), but with a fair forecast a yacht can make the stunning coastal passage to Torquay in 11 hrs from leaving the Bill.

Streams are weak, rarely more than ¾kn. Further up-Channel, the tidal regime gradually becomes more distorted, especially on the rising tide. The rise is relatively fast for the first hour after LW; then slackens noticeably for the next 1½ hrs before resuming the rapid rate of rise. There is often a stand at HW, not very evident at Straight Point but lasting about

$1\frac{1}{2}$ hrs at Lyme Regis. The Portland tidal curve illustrates the pattern.

In offshore winds there is a good anchorage NE of Beer Head, the most westerly chalk cliff in England. The conspic Golden Cap (186m) is 3.5M E of Lyme Regis. High Ground and Pollock are inshore shoals close to West Bay (Bridport).

Chesil Beach runs SE for about 8M to the north end of the Portland peninsula. From afar The Isle of Portland truly resembles an island, with its distinctive wedge-shaped profile sloping down from N to S. It is mostly steep-to, but rocks extend about 50m off the Bill at its southern tip.

PORTLAND BILL AND THE RACE

Portland lighthouse is conspicuously white with a broad red band. (NE and N of it, Old Low and

Above: Golden Cap, 186m high
Below: Portland Race in good conditions on the E-going flood

Old High are disused lighthouses). It flashes (4) 20s over an arc of 233° (244°–117°); but outside this arc, to the NNE and NNW, the number of flashes progressively reduces from four to one. A lower light shows FR in a 20° arc over The Shambles.

The Race usually extends 2–3M south of the Bill, but further in bad weather. It lies SE of the Bill on the flood and SW on the ebb. Irregular pyramidal seas break dangerously in the race. Conditions deteriorate badly with wind-over-tide, especially at springs. In an E'ly gale against the spring flood, the race may extend eastward to The Shambles. Studiously avoid it even in calm weather although at neaps it may be barely perceptible. National Coastwatch (NCI), ☎ 01305 860178, will advise on conditions 0700–1900 daily.

Plan to pass Portland Bill on a fair neap tide or at slack water springs. If bound up-Channel, time your departure accordingly. Leaving Weymouth W-bound, precise timing is much easier.

Yachts must either pass some 3–5M S of the Bill; or, if conditions suit, via the much shorter inshore passage. This is relatively smooth water 1–3 cables off the Bill, depending on wind; it should not be used at springs nor at night. Keep a sharp lookout for semi-submerged pot floats. From W or E, get close in to Portland and start to ride the S-going stream from at least 2M north of the Bill.

The Tidal Stream chartlets (see page 28) show the approx hourly positions of the Race. They are referenced to HW Portland, for the convenience of those leaving or making for Portland or Weymouth; and to HW Dover for those passing S of the Race.

It is vital to catch 'slackish' water off the Bill, ie:

Westbound: from HW Dover –1 to HW+2 (HW Portland +4 to HW–6).

Eastbound: from HW Dover +5 to HW–4 (HW Portland –3 to HW+1).

Frank Cowper entered the race in some disarray:

Suddenly I saw a great white wall ahead. I went about, but in another minute I was pitched into it, neck and crop. In spite of having tackle on both sides of the tiller, I could not possibly hold it. I was hurled about the deck, holding on to the tiller all the time. The seas came on board fore and aft. I had no steerage way, and could get no command over the boat.

Sailing Tours, Pt II, 1893

Hence the norm: Wear oilskins, lifejacket & safety harness (clipped on), close all hatches, engine at instant readiness – even if the sea looks moderate.

A 7m high, white obelisk on the tip of the Bill warns of a rocky ledge extending about 30m from the Bill. If the lighthouse's top window is visible above the top of the obelisk, you are clear of the outermost rock – but only just, very close inshore.

Clear of the rocks, but it felt close

PORTLAND TO HANDFAST POINT

The Shambles Bank, marked by buoys at each end, should be avoided at all times. In bad weather the sea breaks heavily on it. Its west end is 2M E of the Bill; passage through this 'gap' is inadvisable, especially with a W-going stream which might easily set you into the Race.

From Weymouth to Lulworth rocks lie up to 3 cables offshore. Lulworth Cove, Worbarrow Bay and Chapman's Pool are enchanting anchorages in fair weather and offshore winds. Kimmeridge Ledges extend about 3 cables to seaward and are a trap for the unwary if coasting close inshore.

An Army firing range between Lulworth and St Aldhelm's Hd extends 6M seaward. When active, as shown by red flags and Iso R 2s lts on Bindon Hill and St Aldhelm's Head, yachts should avoid it (and St Aldhelm's Race) by routeing via 50°30′N 02°10′W or transit the range quickly. Some red flags fly permanently to mark the inland range boundaries, whether or not it is in use.

Yachts crossing the active range may be rather firmly 'invited' by *Lulworth Range Safety Boat* (Ch 16, **08**) to leave, but legally they have a right of passage. Morally the Army remains on the low ground, since requisitioning Tyneham village in Dec 1943; see Worbarrow Bay.

The range is inactive at most weekends, at Bank Holidays, for a week at Easter and in early June, and for the whole of August.

It is usually **active** Mon–Thur 0930–1700, Fri 0930–1230 and Tues & Thur nights 3–4 hrs after dark. It is also active for TA training on six weekends (Fri–Sun, 0930–1700) in the year; dates are given in the *RNA*. Further info from Range Control (☎ 01929 404819; 462721 ext 4859/4819), Portland CG, St Aldhelm's Head NCI (☎ 01929 439220), Poole & Weymouth HMs, major YCs, Radio Solent and local papers.

The three Danger Zone buoys on St Aldhelm's Ledge are fired at infrequently by the Navy.

St Aldhelm's Head is 107m high and conspic. A dangerous race extends up to 4.5M SW, along the axis of St Aldhelm's Ledge, least depth 8.5m. The race shifts E on the flood and W on the ebb; the latter is more dangerous. Pass clear to seaward in rough conditions; or in calmer weather avoid the worst of the overfalls by using an inshore passage, which lies between 50m and 2 cables off the steep-to headland, depending on conditions.

One nautical mile south of St Aldhelm's Hd the ESE-going stream starts at HW Dover +5¾, and

Anvil Point lighthouse. Note the two measured mile beacons at the right

the W-going at HWD–¼; max 4¾kn at springs. Along the W side of St Aldhelm's Hd the stream runs almost continuously SE due to a back eddy.

From St Aldhelm's Hd to Anvil Pt the rugged cliffs rise sheer from deep water. Quarrying was a feature of this coast, notably at Seacombe and Dancing Ledge. There are measured mile beacons either side of Anvil Pt lighthouse which squats low on the clifftop, Fl 10s H24.

One nautical mile ESE of Durlston Head the NE-going flood starts at HW Dover +5½ and the SW-going ebb at HWD–½; max rate 3kn at springs.

Off Durlston Head there is often rough water which on the SW-going ebb deteriorates into race conditions. Avoid it by keeping 1M off Durlston. If heading for Handfast Pt (Old Harry), maintain this offing to clear a localised but vicious race which extends almost a mile E of Peveril Point. Peveril Ledge PHM buoy is engulfed in this race which is at its worst on the ebb against strong SE to SW winds.

Looking south from Handfast Point past The Pinnacles to Swanage Bay

Swanage Bay lies between Peveril Pt and Ballard Pt, 1.5M NNE where white cliffs rise impressively to almost 400ft amsl. From here to Handfast Point the Pinnacle rocks lie a cable seaward. Five cables offshore race conditions may apply on the ebb.

DISTANCE TABLE

Approximate distances in nautical miles are by the most direct route, whilst avoiding dangers

		1	2	3	4	5	6	7	8	9	10	11	12	13	14	15	16	17	18	19	20
1.	Longships	1																			
2.	Scilly (Crow Sound)	22	2																		
3.	Penzance	15	35	3																	
4.	Lizard Point	23	42	16	4																
5.	Falmouth	39	60	32	16	5															
6.	Mevagissey	52	69	46	28	17	6														
7.	Fowey	57	76	49	34	22	7	7													
8.	Looe	63	80	57	39	29	16	11	8												
9.	Plymouth (bkwtr)	70	92	64	49	39	25	22	11	9											
10.	R. Yealm (ent)	72	89	66	49	39	28	23	16	4	10										
11.	Salcombe	81	102	74	59	50	40	36	29	22	17	11									
12.	Start Point	86	103	80	63	55	45	40	33	24	22	7	12								
13.	Dartmouth	95	116	88	72	63	54	48	42	35	31	14	9	13							
14.	Torbay	101	118	96	78	70	62	55	50	39	38	24	15	11	14						
15.	Exmouth	113	131	107	90	82	73	67	61	51	49	33	27	24	12	15					
16.	Lyme Regis	126	144	120	104	96	86	81	74	63	62	48	41	35	30	21	16				
17.	Portland Bill	135	151	128	112	104	93	89	81	73	70	55	49	45	42	36	22	17			
18.	Weymouth	143	159	136	120	112	101	97	89	81	78	63	57	53	50	44	30	8	18		
19.	Swanage	165	181	158	142	134	123	119	111	103	100	85	79	75	72	66	52	22	22	19	
20.	Poole	171	187	164	148	140	129	125	117	109	106	91	85	81	78	72	58	28	28	6	20

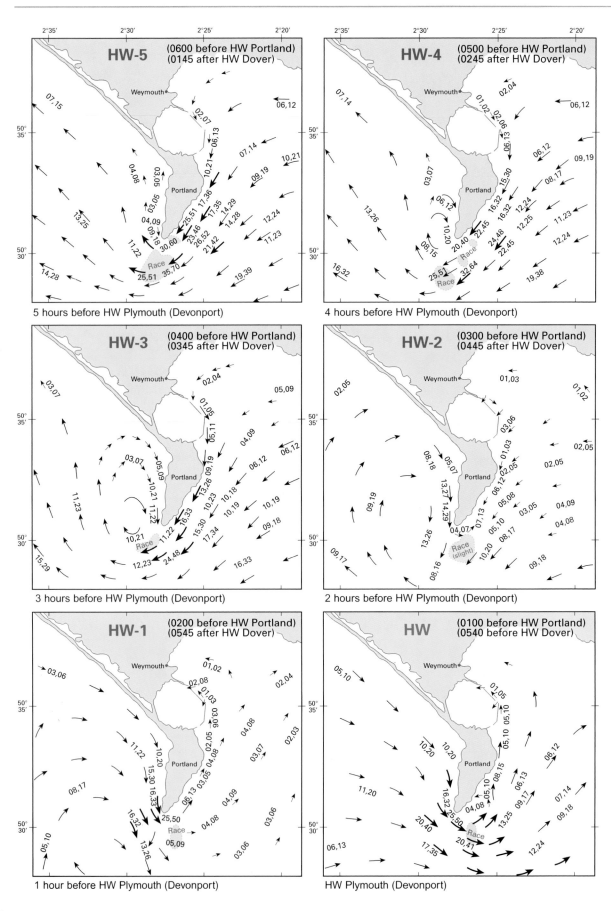

Chapter 1

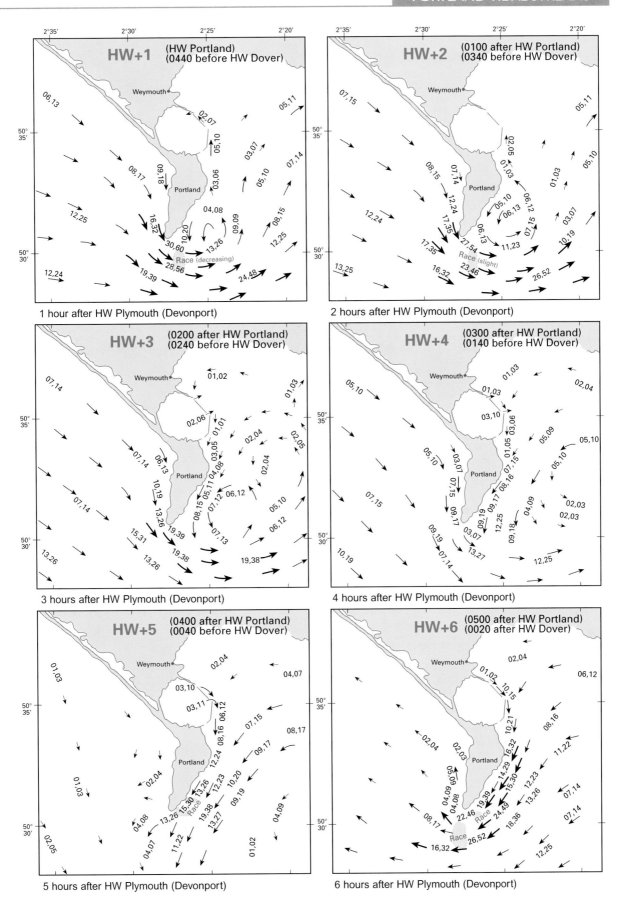

1 hour after HW Plymouth (Devonport)

2 hours after HW Plymouth (Devonport)

3 hours after HW Plymouth (Devonport)

4 hours after HW Plymouth (Devonport)

5 hours after HW Plymouth (Devonport)

6 hours after HW Plymouth (Devonport)

St Mary's. The Pool, visitors' moorings and Scillonian III *in the foreground. Hugh Town and Porth Cressa beyond*

THE ISLES OF SCILLY

St Mary's Pool ⚓s – 49°55´·10N 06°18´·75W

Solitude, freedom from pollution, and a sense of being in a place apart are some of the indelible impressions that linger long after you have left these beautiful, rock-strewn islands (known by locals as the Isles of Scilly or just Scilly; never as the Scilly Isles or The Scillies) – all this, plus the friendliness of the Scillonians – not to mention inquisitive seals and an abundance of bird life.

Visiting Scilly in your own yacht is a rewarding challenge due to the volatile weather and the lack of a 100% safe haven. This concentrates the mind and adds a frisson of excitement, but if the sun shines and the breeze remains F3 or less, you will soon succumb to the charm and indolent lifestyle. Bring walking boots, long johns and bikinis – they could be needed, not necessarily simultaneously.

SHORESIDE (Telephone code 01720)

ST MARY'S
Tourist Office is behind the PO, in Garrison Lane, Hugh Town, TR21 0JD; 422536. Mon–Sat 0830–1730. tic@scilly.gov.uk; www.simplyscilly.co.uk

What to see/do Hugh Town is a bit of a time warp, almost a Toy Town with its neatly ordered shops along Hugh St. On The Quay, things bustle whilst *Scillonian III* disgorges passengers and supplies; when she leaves, peace resumes. Flower growing is a quiet and satisfying business. Pilot gig-racing is strenuous and often noisy: Watch the World Championships in early May, or Ladies' races Wed and Men's Fri evenings. Visit the Isles of Scilly Museum, Church St, ☎ 422337; Easter to Oct, Mon–Sat 1000–1200, 1330–1630, 1930–2100.

Taxi ☎ 422901.

Car hire Call Sibley's ☎ 422431, if you feel the need.

Bike hire Buccabu ☎ 422289 at Porth Cressa, with **launderette** in the same filling station.

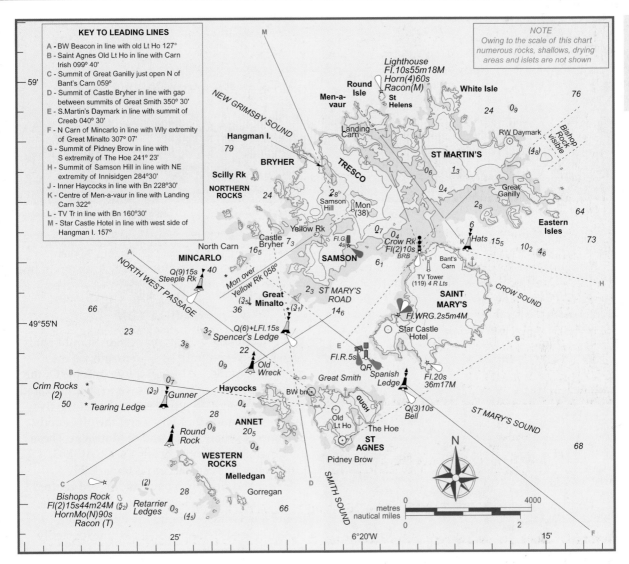

KEY TO LEADING LINES

A - BW Beacon in line with old Lt Ho 127°
B - Saint Agnes Old Lt Ho in line with Carn Irish 099° 40'
C - Summit of Great Ganilly just open N of Bant's Carn 059°
D - Summit of Castle Bryher in line with gap between summits of Great Smith 350° 30'
E - S.Martin's Daymark in line with summit of Creeb 040° 30'
F - N Carn of Mincarlo in line with Wly extremity of Great Minalto 307° 07'
G - Summit of Pidney Brow in line with S extremity of The Hoe 241° 23'
H - Summit of Samson Hill in line with NE extremity of Innisidgen 284°30'
J - Inner Haycocks in line with Bn 228°30'
K - Centre of Men-a-vaur in line with Landing Carn 322°
L - TV Tr in line with Bn 160°30'
M - Star Castle Hotel in line with west side of Hangman I. 157°

NOTE
Owing to the scale of this chart numerous rocks, shallows, drying areas and islets are not shown

Ferries From mid-Apr to end Sep, Mon–Sat, the *Scillonian* leaves Penzance 0915 for Hugh Town (2 hrs 45 mins), departing 1630 or 1700. Pre-book ☎ 0845 710 5555. Inter-island launches, ☎ 422541, run to/from the off-islands after the ferry's arrival and at other times. It's easy to board the wrong one!

Flights From the airfield, ¾ mile E of Hugh Town, helicopters fly (20 mins) about 10 times a day to Penzance, ☎ 01736 363871. Aeroplanes fly (15 mins) to St Just near Land's End, Mon–Sat; or to Bristol, Exeter and Newquay.

Beaches At Hugh Town: Porthmellon, Town and Porth Cressa beaches. Many others ring the island.

Banks Lloyds with cashpoint, Barclays without. Co-op does cashback.

Restaurants Physically atop Garrison Hill and well up the financial stakes, The Star Castle

Hotel, ☎ 422317, has three eateries: The Castle dining room; the Conservatory restaurant (seafood) and the snacky Dungeon Bar. Tregarthen's Hotel, ☎ 422540, is in similar vein. The Pilot's Gig, ☎ 422654, is more fun with the emphasis on seafood. Pubs such as the Atlantic Inn, ☎ 422323, do enjoyable and affordable food. St Mary's is not a pinnacle of *haute cuisine*.

ST AGNES & GUGH

St Agnes is a patchwork of tiny fields given over to flower growing, in contrast to its wild, rocky S and W coasts. PO, general store, wines and books; ☎ 422364. Turk's Head, ☎ 422434, overlooks Porth Conger and the quay; real ales & good pub food. Covean Garden café for cream teas. Gugh, however, is rather featureless with rocky outcrops.

BRYHER

The island is parallel to, but smaller than Tresco. It subsists on flowers and tourists, never having

Looking eastwards over Bryher towards Tresco

St Martins' foreground: Round Island is middle distance to the right

been developed in the same way as Tresco. (Buy large crabs for £4 from a friendly fisherman). Good walking, spectacular bays on the W coast, almost encircled by sandy beaches. PO, general stores, a café and Hell Bay Hotel, with bar food and excellent dining, ☎ 422947, complete the scene.

Tresco abbey in the foreground; Bryher beyond

TRESCO

The island flourishes under the benevolent over-lordship of the Dorrien Smith family. There is an air of well-being and tourists flock to Abbey Gardens (1000–1600) & Shipwreck Museum. Fine sandy beaches around all sides except the N tip. At the S end of New Grimsby Hbr, the Estate Office, ☎ 422849, contains: PO; laundry 0830–1800, same day service if in before 1200; bike hire.

Tresco Stores, ☎ 422806; Mon–Sat 0830–1800, Sun 1000–1300. New Inn, ☎ 422844, is a sociable hostelry; dinner £11.50–15.50, 1800–2100; showers. Island Hotel overlooks Old Grimsby Sound and is impressively up-market, ☎ 422883; dinner £36.50.

ST MARTIN'S

The remotest of the inhabited islands, St Martin's has good heath walks to the N and more pastoral scenery to the S. Lower, Middle and Higher Towns are the three communities. PO, off-licence and stores, ☎ 422801; Mon–Sat 0830–1730, Sun 0900–1000. Vineyard, ☎ 295330, tour & taste. St Martin's on the Isle Hotel, ☎ 422090, offers fine cuisine and all amenities inc ♿s.

NAVIGATION

The Big Picture A first time visitor should study AC 34 & 883 carefully so as to memorise the major landmarks and general topography. Of the 50 or so islands (St Mary's down to small isolated rocks) you might in a week or two visit the five inhabited islands (St Mary's and the off-islands: St Agnes, Bryher, Tresco and St Martin's). These are all on the deceptively large scale AC 883.

In reality this central core is remarkably compact and fits into a circle radius 3M centred on the TV mast (see Landmarks). For example, from New Grimsby Sound the old lt ho on St Agnes is easily seen and looks unexpectedly close. Think small.

Charts AC 777 (1:75,000), 1148 (1:75,000), 34 (1:25,000), 883 (1:12,500), SC 5603.8 – .12 (1:12,500). To emphasise the need for up-to-date charts, the following corrections featured in early 2002: Spanish Ledge buoy lit, Q (3) 10s. Bartholomew Ledge buoy moved/re-named N Bartholomew, Fl R 5s. New beacon installed, Bartholomew Ledge, QR. Crow Rock IDM bcn, lit Fl (2) 10s. Spencer's Ledge marked by a SCM buoy, Q (6) + L Fl 15s. Steeple Rock marked by a WCM buoy, Q (9) 15s. Hulman SHM beacon, lit Fl G 4s.

Approaches Scilly has TSS on its E, S & W sides. The 'Off Land's End TSS' may impinge on your track from the mainland. See Passage Notes in this chapter's introduction.

When planning, do not feel that St Mary's is the sole point of arrival, although it is the likely choice if coming from France or the mainland. A good

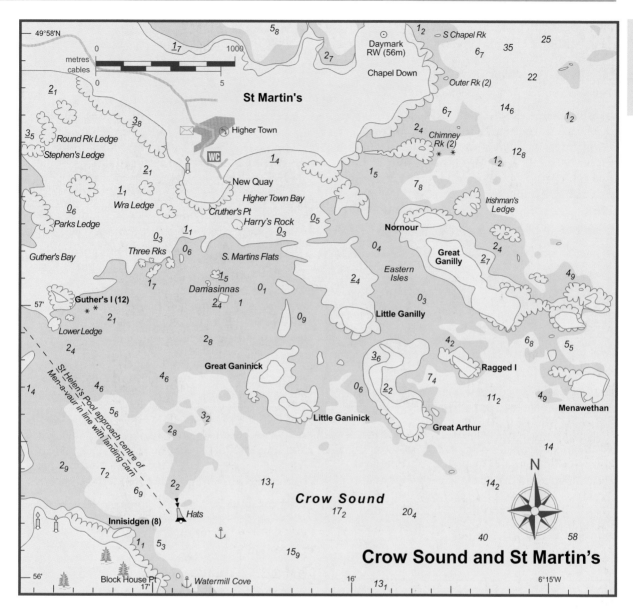

Crow Sound and St Martin's

DEGREE OF SHELTER IN RECOGNISED ANCHORAGES FOR GIVEN WIND DIRECTIONS

Wind direction: Anchorage &/or ⚓s:	N	NE	E	SE	S	SW	W	NW
St Mary's Pool ⚓s	G	VG	VG	VG	VG	–	–	–
Porth Cressa	VG	VG	VG	–	–	–	G	VG
Watermill Cove	–	–	–	–	VG	VG	VG	–
The Cove (St Agnes)	VG	G	G	–	–	G	VG	VG
Porth Conger (St Agnes)	–	G	VG	VG	VG	VG	G	–
New Grimsby ⚓s	G	VG	–	G	G	G	VG	–
Old Grimsby ⚓s	G	G	–	–	G	VG	VG	G
St Helen's Pool	G	G	–	–	G	G	G	G
Tean Sound ⚓s	–	G	–	G	–	–	G	–

Key G = Good; VG = Very good; – means that the degree of shelter is indifferent or worse.

Note The degree of shelter may be modified by: The presence/absence of swell; wind over tide, especially near HW; and by anchoring close-in to obtain a good lee. Official ⚓s are safe for most normal sized boats in gale force winds, although the degree of comfort may be minimal.

Recommendation The *West Country Cruising Companion* by Mark Fishwick, published 2001 by Nautical Data Ltd, provides more detailed information than space permits in a book covering the entire English Channel. It is highly recommended for exploring the Isles of Scilly in depth.

alternative is to make for Round Island, thence to Tean Sound, St Helen's Pool, Old or New Grimsby Sounds. This is an obvious option from Eire and the N. Wind & weather may have a bearing. Later you can visit St Mary's and St Agnes.

Landmarks clockwise from TV mast at N end of St Mary's (119m high, R lights, like an emaciated Eiffel Tower), visible from most parts of Scilly; on St Martin's a R/W banded beacon (like a child's moon rocket); Peninnis Head lt ho (St Mary's, S tip); St Agnes' squat white disused lt ho; Bishop Rock lt ho; white lt ho on conical Round Island.

Round Island lighthouse from the east

In good visibility some of these marks can be seen simultaneously as Scilly is low-lying, max elevation around 40m.

Pilotage Amongst visible, drying or submerged rocks – all potentially dangerous – pilotage is much helped by the crystal clear water and a good bow lookout. Take great care, especially in poor visibility; utilise the top half of the tide. The following three waypoints cater for the S, E and N approaches:
S – 49°53′·59N 06°18′·06W, 307°/0.63M to Spanish Ledge ECM light buoy. St Mary's Sound is well marked/lit, usable day/night and at all tides. After N Bartholomew PHM buoy curve round Garrison Hill to 49°55′·22N 06°19′·71W, which is on the 097° ldg line, 0.6M to ⚓s in St Mary's Pool.
E – 49°55′·79N 06°15′·06W, 287°/1.4M via Crow Sound to Hats SCM buoy; thence Crow Rk IDM lt beacon to St Mary's Pool. Only usable HW±3.
N – 49°59′·34N 06°15′·06W, 266°/2.8M to position 0.4M N of Round Is lt ho. All tide access to Tean Sound & St Helen's Pool from E of Round Is; and to Old and New Grimsby Sounds from further W.

St Mary's Road the epicentre, can also be entered via three little-used, but deep channels, as on AC 34:
a. Smith Sound is a narrow 350.5° transit between unmarked drying rocks off St Agnes and Annet.
b. Broad Sound, on a distant 059° transit, lies north of the Bishop and is situated between

two NCM & two SCM buoys.
c. NW Passage (N Channel on older charts) is the 127° transit of St Agnes Old lt ho ≠ Tins Walbert beacon, clearing buoyed/lit dangers off Samson.

Lights clockwise from St Mary's: Seven Stones light vessel, NE/9.5M; Wolf Rock lt ho, E/18M; Peninnis Hd lt ho (S tip); Bishop Rock lt ho, WSW/5M; and Round Is lt ho, N x W/3M.

Tides HW St Mary's at sp is 1 hr and at nps 35 mins before HW Devonport. LW at nps is 25 mins and at sp 40 mins before LW Devonport. MHWS is 5·7m, MLWS 0·7m; MHWN is 4·3m, MLWN 2·0m. Always keep the height of tide in mind.

Tidal streams around Scilly are rotatory clockwise as shown in hourly chartlets on AC 34. But among the islands they are deflected and hard to predict with much accuracy. They run faster off headlands and over rocks, where overfalls may occur.

Access All anchorages/moorings are accessible above mid-tide; even earlier or H24 in deep water.

Shelter No one anchorage is sheltered from all winds and swell, so anticipate forecast changes and move sooner rather than later. The Table on page 33 shows the degree of shelter afforded in recognised anchorages for given wind directions.

Anchorages/⚓s See individual island entries.

FACILITIES

ST MARY'S

HM (Mr Jeff Penhaligon), The Quay, Hugh Town. ☎/🖷 422768; mobile 07789 273610. 0800–1700.

VHF *St Mary's Harbour* Ch 14, 0800–1700.
⚓s: 38 yellows at St Mary's Pool in 1.5–2m. Land on the beach or inner end of the Quay.

Berthing Short stay (only to uplift fuel, water or

Visitors' moorings in St Mary's Pool

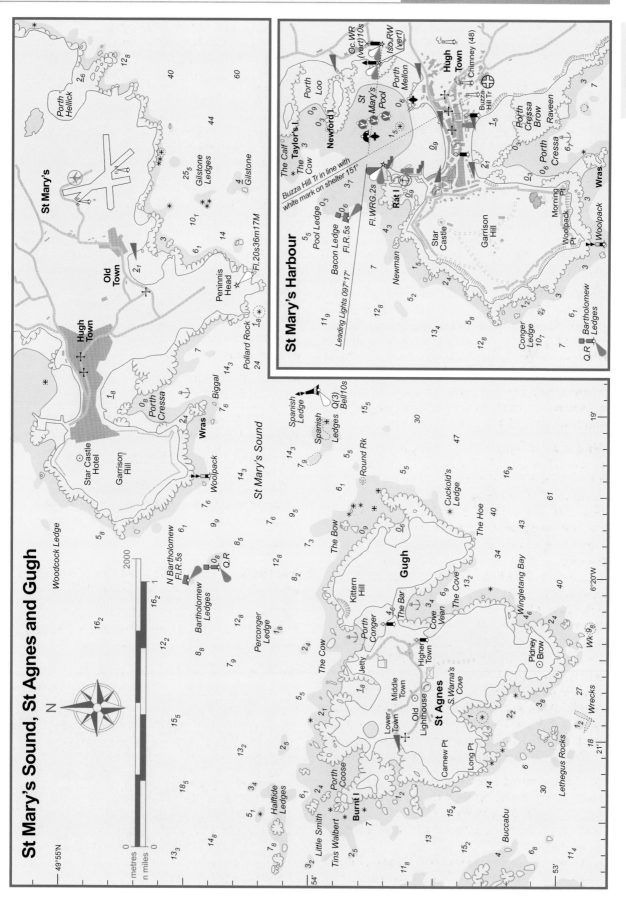

St Mary's Sound, St Agnes and Gugh

St Mary's Harbour

49°55'N

metres

n miles

2000

1

Porth Cressa and Garrison Hill, looking NW

Gugh with St Agnes beyond

stores) alongside the Quay with HM's consent and when *Scillonian* is absent.

Anchorages In St Mary's Pool there is just room to anchor inshore of the ⚓s, but this can become a very adjacent lee shore in NW'lies. In such winds Porth Cressa is a safe bolt hole. Here the entrance is narrowed by Biggal and Wras rocks to port and Raveen and drying ledges to stbd. It is a No-No in S'lies. Watermill Cove at the NE tip of the island is sheltered from SW'lies, if you edge close inshore.

Tariff ⚓ £10/night, fourth night free. ⚓ £5/night.

Showers below HM's Office, 0830–1900.

Fuel Diesel by hose & petrol by cans from Sibleys on the Quay 0830–1130 Mon–Fri and 0930–1200 Sat; ie when *Scillonian* is not alongside. Fresh water also by hose at 5p/gallon (a precious commodity).

Chandlery & repairs Steamship Chandlers, ME, Mon–Fri 0800–1200 & 1300–1700. Southard Engineering, ☎ 422539; CH, outboards. Home Hardware, ☎ 422388, Gas, Camping Gaz. Several boat builders – see HM. Sail repairs, ☎ 422037.

ST AGNES/GUGH

Anchorages St Agnes and Gugh are like Siamese twins: Joined by a sand bar drying 4.6m but covering at HW. To the N, Porth Conger is well sheltered in S'lies; and to the S The Cove is safe in N'lies. Moderate holding on sand/weed at both.

Chandlery & repairs Nil, nor fuel, nor water.

BRYHER

Anchorage See Tresco for New Grimsby Sound, where remote anchorage may also be found north of Hangman Is (complete with gibbet). Green Bay is a good drying anchorage.

A French privateer at anchor north of Hangman Island

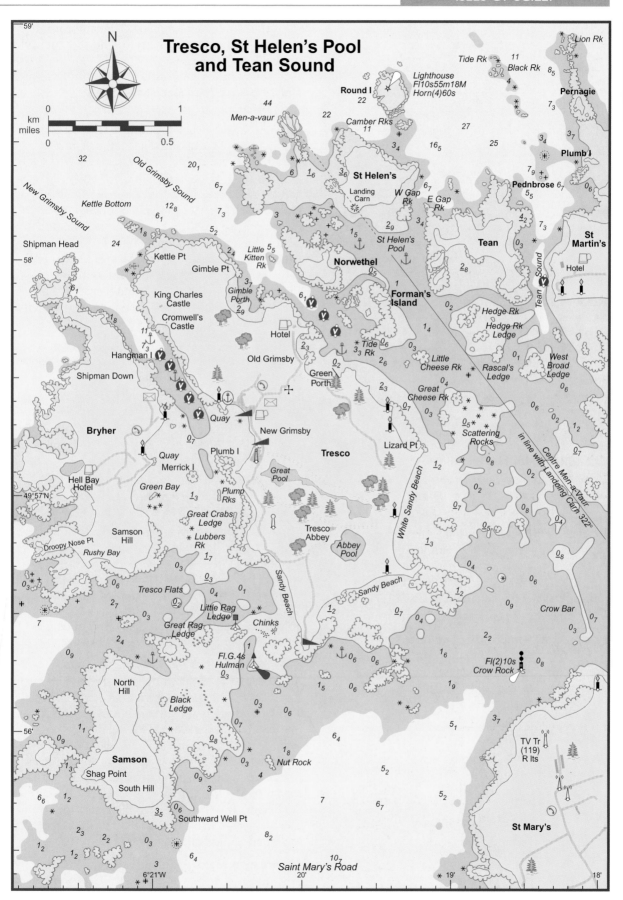

Tresco, St Helen's Pool and Tean Sound

N

km
miles

0   1
0   0.5

Round I

Lighthouse
Fl10s55m18M
Horn(4)60s

Tide Rk

Black Rk

Lion Rk

Pernagie

Men-a-vaur

Camber Rks

Plumb I

St Helen's

Landing
Carn

W Gap
Rk

E Gap
Rk

Pednbrose

Old Grimsby Sound

Tean

St Martin's

Hotel

Kettle Bottom

St Helen's
Pool

New Grimsby Sound

Shipman Head

Kettle Pt

Norwethel

Little
Kitten
Rk

Gimble Pt

Gimble
Porth

Hedge Rk

Hedge Rk
Ledge

King Charles
Castle

**Forman's
Island**

West
Broad
Ledge

Cromwell's
Castle

Hotel

Tide
Rk

Little
Cheese Rk

Rascal's
Ledge

Hangman I

Old Grimsby

Shipman Down

Great
Cheese Rk

Quay

Green
Porth

Bryher

New Grimsby

Tresco

Lizard Pt

Scattering
Rocks

Quay

Plumb I

Merrick I

Great
Pool

In line with Landing Carn 322°

Centre Men-a-Vaur

Hell Bay
Hotel

Green Bay

Plump
Rks

Great Crabs
Ledge

**Samson
Hill**

Lubbers
Rk

Tresco
Abbey

Crow Bar

Droopy Nose Pt

Rushy Bay

Abbey
Pool

White Sandy Beach

Tresco Flats

Little Rag
Ledge

Sandy Beach

Great Rag
Ledge

Chinks

Crow Rock

Fl(2)10s

Fl.G.4s
Hulman

**North
Hill**

Black
Ledge

Sandy Beach

TV Tr
(119)
R lts

Samson

Shag Point

Nut Rock

South Hill

Southward Well Pt

St Mary's

Saint Mary's Road

Above: New Grimsby Sound looking SSE
Below: Moorings in New Grimsby Sound. St Mary's beyond

Chandlery & repairs Blue Boats, ☎ 423095:
Limited CH and repairs. No water or fuel.

TRESCO

HM Mr Henry Birch (The Ever-Helpful) ☎ 422792;
mobile 07778 601237. The busy quay must not be
obstructed by tenders; haul 'em up the beach.

Ⓐs red/yellow, provided by Tresco Estate, £10
per night (fourth night free): 22 in 2–4m at New
Grimsby Sound which is akin to a small Scottish sea
loch. Six Ⓐs at Old Grimsby Sound in about 3m.

Anchorages Same areas as moorings, £5/night.
A day anchorage in 0.9m off Carn Near (landing
at S tip of Tresco) is convenient for the beaches.

Old Grimsby Sound from the Island Hotel

Pilotage When entering New Grimsby Sound
from the ENE, give drying Kettle Bottom rocks
off the N tip of Tresco a wide berth. Entering Old
Grimsby Sound avoid Little Kittern drying 1.9m
and Tide Rock 1.4m just beyond the Ⓐs.

Tresco Flats, drying 1.7m, can be crossed HW±3 to
get from St Mary's to New Grimsby Sound and vice
versa. At nps a yacht drawing 1.6m will have at
least 0.3m under its keel and 0.8m at sps.

From St Mary's go to Nut Rk, 0.9M NW of Bacon
Ledge PHM buoy; then NNW to pass 70m W of
Hulman SHM bcn and 140m E of Little Rag Ledge
PHM bcn. Here pick up the 338° transit of Merrick
Is and Hangman Is. Maintain until 1 cable short of
the former, when jink starboard to pass midway
between it and Plumb Is. A track of 339° toward
Cromwell's Castle then leads into New Grimsby
Sound. Be wary of following shoal-draught tourist
launches which may take short cuts.

Chandlery & repairs Nil. Diesel & petrol in cans
from Estate Office. Water tap on the quay.

New Grimsby Sound and Cromwell's Castle

ST MARTIN'S

Ⓐs Seven at Tean Sound in 7m, provided by
St Martin's on the Isle Hotel, £10/night or free
if you dine in the hotel; showers available.
VHF Ch 12.

Anchorages are limited by large drying areas to
the S and by the rocky approaches to the N coast.
Tean Sound offers moderate holding on rock in
mid-channel to the N and S of the Ⓐs. To the W,
isolated St Helen's Pool is almost landlocked by
St Helen's, Tean and Norwethel. It can be entered
from Old Grimsby Sound; from the SE on the 322°
transit of Men-a-vaur Rk and Landing Carn on
St Helen's; and from the N via St Helen's Gap.
The anchorage in 3–7m is sheltered except from
the E and SE; good holding on sand.

Chandlery & repairs Nothing significant; no fuel
or water.

MOUSEHOLE

Harbour entrance – 50°04´·97N 05°32´·27W

Mousehole (pronounced 'Mouz'l') is a mile south of Newlyn. It may not accommodate a 60ft ocean greyhound, but it has great character, was burned by dastardly Spaniards in 1595 and in the 21st century would be pleased to welcome your modest bilge keeler – fin keelers can lean against piles on the south pier. Ashore pedestrians vie with skilfully driven buses for the right to move and stay alive.

SHORESIDE (Telephone code 01736)

See Penzance and/or Newlyn which meet most mundane needs.

What to see/do Soak up the sun and atmosphere. Stroll the back alleys to find C14 Keigwin House (a private residence) which was spared in 1595, although Squire Keigwin died. Climb up to Paul, where the church of St Pol de Leon was founded by the same man who built the cathedral at St Pol, Brittany (see Roscoff). S of Mousehole, clamber up Raginnis Hill to the Wild Bird Hospital – it does a great job, especially for victims of oil spills, and relies greatly on donations to keep going.

Buses 6A/C & 5A/B to Newlyn/Penzance (15 mins). 6C to Lamorna Cove (12 mins).

Beaches At LW sandy beaches uncover at either end of the harbour.

Restaurants The Ship Inn overlooks the harbour; good bar food and restaurant. On the Newlyn road, the Old Coastguard Hotel, ☎ 731222, does good food, has fine seaviews and friendly staff.

NAVIGATION

Charts As for Newlyn.

Approaches From the N, avoid Carn Base and Low Lee (buoyed). From the S keep at least 0.4M offshore. The passage inshore of St Clement's Isle is usable at most tides, noting a least depth of 1m in the northern part; hence only a S waypoint is quoted.

Landmark The village climbing up the hillside.

Pilotage The waypoint is 50°04´·73N 05°32´·08W; thence 355°/2.5 cables before altering about 260°

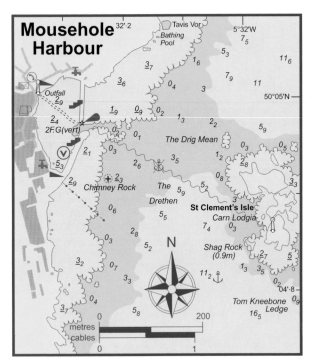

Mousehole Harbour

through the 11m wide entrance (see Anchorage). N pier is lit 2FG (vert), but 2FR if the hbr is closed.

Tides Use differences for Newlyn.

Tidal streams are generally weak and irregular.

Access HW±3, but not in strong onshore winds nor with a heavy ground swell.

Shelter The harbour is well sheltered except in NE, E and S winds; in S'ly gales it may be closed. St Clement's Isle gives some shelter from SE'lies.

FACILITIES

The HM Mr Frank Wallis, whose peaked cap is conspic on his walkabouts. Office by the clock tower, ☎ 731511. Hours include tide times. No VHF.

Berthing The semi-circular harbour is protected by two substantial piers and dries completely up to about 5m. It has many local moorings.

Best to pre-call the HM for a vacant mooring. On the S pier there are two sets of piles for fin-keelers to dry out against on firm, level sand. Bilge keelers may find space against the N pier.

Tariff Daily rate on a mooring or against the piers is £7 for all LOAs.

Anchoring No room in the hbr, but outside ⚓ as marked on AC 2345; good holding on sand in 5–8m. Not ideal as FVs take this inshore passage at speed. If overnighting show an ⚓ light.

Avoid an underwater power cable (to light the Celtic Cross on St Clement's Isle) marked by five small R buoys. The cable is/was to be permanently buried, when the buoys will be removed.

Fuel Diesel/petrol by cans only. **FW** tap on quay.

Chandlery & repairs At Newlyn/Penzance.

NEWLYN

Harbour entrance – 50°06´·19N 05°32´·59W

Newlyn has the great advantage of being accessible at all tides and most weathers, and is therefore a useful passage port. But it is also a large, busy fishing harbour where yachts are accepted only on the fishermen's terms. Yachts raft overnight on FVs; if the fleet is remaining in port, it may be difficult to get out of a long trot when desired.

The town is now planning to 'regenerate' itself and the harbour; a pontoon for up to 60 yachts has been mooted. Early days...

Penzance is a better option, even if it means a restless night at ⚓ or on a waiting buoy. This will not be a problem if all-tide berthing is provided.

Newlyn was once an artist colony, but the easels and palettes have long since migrated to St Ives. Although very different in character, Newlyn and Penzance are almost merged geographically – a pleasant 20 mins walk along the seafront.

SHORESIDE (Telephone code 01736)

Tourist Office None; nearest is in Penzance.

What to see/do Probably just stop the night prior to leaving on the tide for Scilly, Falmouth, Eire or France. Newlyn Art Gallery, Mon–Sat 1000–1700, may catch your eye. The Pilchard Works still functions and also has an interesting museum. Newlyn Fish Festival, late Aug Bank Holiday, is a colourful extravaganza.

Rail See Penzance.

Buses 1, 5, 6 to Penzance, thence Land's End, St Ives, Helston, Truro – the world is your oyster!

Taxi, car & bike hire See Penzance.

Beaches Good sand/shingle beach N of Tolcarne Inn, Newlyn and Penzance.

Supermarkets Co-op by the harbour; open daily.

Market day Fish market, Mon–Sat from 0700.

Banks Barclays, no cashpoints; Mon–Fri 1000–1230.

Restaurants The Smugglers, ☎ 331501, overlooking the harbour, does excellent fish dishes £10–13 from 1800. Tolcarne Inn, Red Lion and Fisherman's Arms all do good pub food. For lunch do not miss Aunty May's Pasty Co (by the tfc lts) for the best range of oggies in Cornwall, if not the world.

NAVIGATION

Charts AC 777 (1:75,000), 2345 (Penzance Bay 1:12,500; hbr plans 1:5,000), SC 5603.7 (1:5,000).

Approaches From the SE, after clearing The Lizard go direct to the WPT, leaving Mountamopus SCM buoy 1.3M to stbd. From Scilly/Land's End, round Lamorna, leave St Clement's Isle (off Mousehole) to port and set course for Low Lee ECM lt buoy; thence to the waypoint.

Landmarks The white lighthouse on the end of S Pier is conspic. Next to it an inconspicuous shed is the Newlyn Tidal Observatory from which Ordnance Datum (Newlyn) originated in 1915.

Pilotage The waypoint is 50°06′·31N 05°32′·06W, 250°/0.35M to the hbr entrance. This track is in an unlit corridor between the N Pier light's G sector and the N edge of the S Pier's arc of visibility. Beware The Gear (IDM lt bcn) to the NE and rocks to the SE: Low Lee (SCM lt buoy) and Carn Base, unmarked.

Tides HW Newlyn at sp is 1 hr 10 mins and at nps 40 mins before HW Devonport. LW at nps is 25 mins and at sp 35 mins before LW Devonport. MHWS is 5·6m, MLWS 0·8m; MHWN is 4·4m, MLWN 2·0m.

Tidal streams within Mounts Bay are weak and irregular.

Newlyn Harbour from the ESE

Access H24, at all tides and most weathers.

Shelter is good, but in SE'lies a heavy swell works in; access should then be limited to HW±2.

VHF *Newlyn Harbour* Ch 12, 16 in office hours.

FACILITIES

HM Mr Andrew Munson. Office at the NW corner of the hbr, beyond the Fishmarket. ☎ 362523, 🖷 332709. Hours 0800–1700, Mon–Fri.

Berthing Berth/raft on a FV at the inner end/SW side of Mary Williams Pier, then check with HM.

Anchorage In W'lies, 3 cables SE of the South Pier head in 5–6m on gravel/weed; show anchor light. No ⚓ in harbour.

Tariff The daily rate for LOA bands remains at the 1994 figures: <8m = £4; <12m = £6; >12m = £9. These are expected to rise substantially as part of the regeneration project.

Showers 50p, next to Fishmarket (security guard has key to blue door); or at Deep Sea Fishermen's base at N Pier, 0700–1600. **Launderette** Penzance.

Electricity Supplies are unsuitable for yachts.

Fuel Bulk diesel by hose from tanker; see HM. Petrol by cans from local garage.

Chandlery & repairs SW Nets, ☎ 360254, CH. Cosalt, ☎ 363094, CH (FV orientated).

Looking ENE from Newlyn to St Michael's Mount

Lodey Sails, ☎ 331557. Mount's Bay Engineering, ☎ 363014, ME. Sea-Com Electronics, ☎ 369695. Marconi Marine, ☎ 361320.

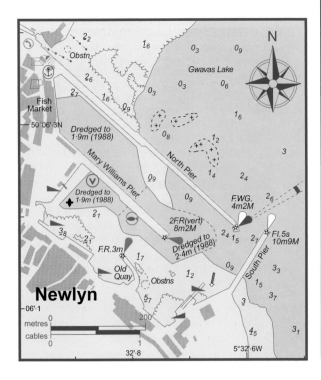

Newlyn

COMMERCIAL FISHING FOR THE UN-HOOKED

Or how the fisherman you are trying to avoid is trying to catch your favourite fish.

Beam trawlers Largest vessels. Long vertical beams are lowered to the horizontal when trawling. From the outer ends heavy metal frames are dragged along the seabed, trailing a mat of chains and an open bag net. Dover sole, lemon sole, monkfish and megrim (flounders) all fall for it.

Side trawlers Heavy metal panels ('doors' or 'otterboards') are dragged astern and plane out to either side, just off the seabed. They keep open the mouth of a net which scoops up whiting, cod, ling, John Dory and red mullet.

Gill netters Usually smaller than trawlers, with enclosed foredeck. Large winches with rubber-coated drums. They lay several miles of panel nets which float vertically from the seabed. Hake, dogfish, ling and cod are caught.

Long liners A traditional method. Tubs are filled with coiled ropes to which hooks are attached by short cords. Hooks are baited with mackerel and the line is stretched across the seabed. Ray, skate, turbot, cod, ling and conger-eel take the bait.

Crabbers Baited 'ink-well' pots are used to catch lobsters, spider crabs, brown crabs and crawfish.

Hand liners Small boats use this method to catch top-quality mackerel. Lines carry about 25 hooks, each with coloured feather lures. See the *Reeds Yachtsman's Handbook* for further information about fishing methods.

PENZANCE

Harbour entrance – 50°07´·07N 05°31´·69W

Penzance doubles as an elegant market town and bustling seaport. Sir Humphrey Davy of miner's lamp fame was its most distinguished son and scientist. Chapel Street is perhaps the most interesting thoroughfare, lined with fine Georgian buildings, notably the Union Hotel, Regent Hotel, the unique Egyptian House with its exotic facade, the Grade II listed Old Custom House and at the bottom the landmark St Mary's Church.

The harbour has a long association with the Royal Navy (press gangs and the first news of Nelson's death). Smuggling, fishing, trading, Trinity House, the RNLI have all played a role – and now yachts, classic craft, tall ships and cruise liners visit.

SHORESIDE (Telephone code 01736)

Tourist Office TR18 2NF, faces the rail and bus stations. ☎ 362207; 📠 363600. Open May–Sep, Mon–Sat 0900–1800; Sun 1000–1300. pztic@penwith.gov.uk; www.west-cornwall-tourism.co.uk

What to see/do Trinity House National Lighthouse Centre, 1030–1630 daily, £3 – illuminating. The Maritime Museum, 19 Chapel St, has a colourful collection of nauticalia housed in a full-sized cross-section of a man o' war; Mon–Sat 1100–1400. At the head of the bay St Michael's Mount (see the end of this entry) is visible from miles around.

Further west towards Gwennap Head, the Minack Theatre has a spectacular setting on the cliffs at Porthcurno; ☎ 810181 and www.minack.com £7 & £5.50; access by 1/1A bus (40 mins). Don't miss!

Rail The station is 550m N of the Wet Dock. Main line trains to London (5–7 hrs) and Birmingham. St Ives (20 mins), Truro (40 mins). Info ☎ 08457 484950.

Bus Land's End (50 mins); Mousehole (20 mins); Helston (45 mins); St Ives (40 mins).

Taxi Stones ☎ 364772; Alberts ☎ 0800 074 6778; ☎ 366366.

Car hire Europcar, ☎ 360536; Economy Hire, ☎ 366636.

Bike hire Pedals Bike hire, ☎ 360600; The Cycle Centre, Chapel St, ☎ 351671; RC Pender, ☎ 365366.

Ferry *Scillonian* to/from St Mary's, Scilly. ☎ 0845 710 5555; www.ios-travel.co.uk Departs Penzance Mon–Fri 0915, arrives St Mary's 1200; dep 1630, arr 1915. Sat: Times vary with the month. Sun, nil.

Helicopters to Scilly www.scillyhelicopter.co.uk; ☎ 363871. Apr–Sep, Mon–Sat approx 11 daily flights to St Mary's; also five to Tresco.

Beaches Walk no further than the sandy beach SW of the harbour, or dive into the Jubilee Pool.

Supermarkets Tesco, Market Jew St. Safeway at Long Rock (E of the heliport) by bus/taxi. Deli Coco's, 27 Market Place, for brilliant delicatessen.

Market day Tues, Flea market. Fri, Farmers' market.

Banks All main banks in/near Market Jew Street.

Restaurants The Abbey, ☎ 330680, is a modern, upmarket restaurant with views across the bay. Bar Coco's at 12/13 Chapel St is a rather stylish continental-type bar/café; ☎ 350222 for tapas etc. Captain's Fish Bar, ☎ 330333, 62 Daniel Place, for top quality fish and chips. The Turk's Head, oldest pub in town, does good meals in a characterful ambience. Harris's, ☎ 364408 in narrow, cobbled New St, serves excellent seafood from £18.50.

NAVIGATION

Charts AC 777 (1:75,000), 2345 (Penzance Bay 1:12,500; hbr plans 1:5,000), SC 5603.7 (1:5,000).

Approaches From the SE, after clearing The Lizard track direct to the WPT, leaving Mountamopus SCM buoy 1M to stbd. From Scilly/Land's End, round Lamorna and set course to seaward of St Clement's Isle for Low Lee ECM buoy, Q (3) 10s; thence to the WPT.

Landmarks St Mary's church tower is conspic, aligned 250° with the Wet Dock gate and S Pier, whose white light tower is prominent by day, but hard to pick out at night. A silver dome on Market House (now a bank) is conspic in certain lights.

Pilotage The waypoint is 50°07′·07N 05°31′·38W, bearing 268°/0.2M to the S Pier head, Fl WR 5s; it is in 3m on the N edge of the light's white sector. Avoid The Gear (IDM lt bcn) to the S and Western Cressar (SCM bcn) to the NE.

Tides HW Penzance at sp is 1 hr 10 mins and at nps 40 mins before HW Devonport. LW at nps is 25 mins and at sp 35 mins before LW Devonport. MHWS is 5·6m, MLWS 0·8m; MHWN is 4·4m, MLWN 2·0m.

Tidal streams within Mounts Bay are weak and irregular.

Access The approach can be difficult in fresh SE/S winds, and dangerous in strong winds. Access to the Wet Dock HW–2 to +1, day/night via an entry gate.

VHF *Penzance Harbour Radio* Ch 12, 16.

IPTS, sigs 2 & 3, shown from mast on NW side of the entry gate, only indicate whether the gate is shut or open; it usually stays open for the whole 3 hrs window. Get clearance to enter/leave on VHF 12. Departures take priority. R/G tfc lts were fitted in 2001 below the mast, but were inop in 2002.

Berthing In the Wet Dock (4.3m) yachts usually raft in four trots on the NE wall (hard stbd after the gate), or as directed. Pick up a waiting buoy or berth temporarily on the S Pier if *Scillonian* is at sea, approx 0915 to 1900, Mon–Fri; Sat variable. The drying basin to the NW is full of local moorings.

Shelter Excellent in the Wet Dock. Yachts can be left unattended in complete safety.

Waiting buoys 12 orange 🛆s are about 100m S of the S Pier head in 2m; often affected by swell.

Anchorages 200m ENE of Albert Pier, clear of the fairway and inshore rocks; or 250m S of the S Pier.

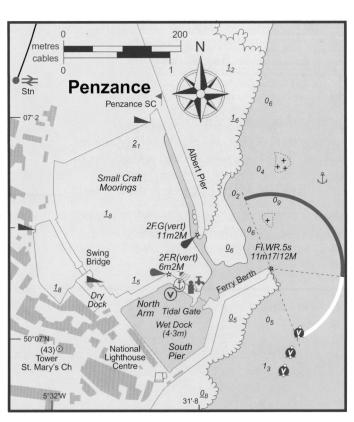

Wet Dock. Yachts rafted to starboard of entry gate

FACILITIES

HM's office is to stbd of the Wet Dock entrance.
☎ 366113, 07779 264335, 🖷 366114. Hours: Mon–
Fri 0900–1300 & 1400–1800 and HW–2 to +1
day/night. www.go cornwall.com/Penzanceharbour

Tariff Daily rates £ berthed/rafted (showers free)
for LOAs: <8m = 9.17; <9m = 10.23; <10m = 11.29;
<11m = 12.72; <12m = 13.76; <13m = 14.82; <14m
= 15.87; <15m = 17.28; <16 = 18.34. Every third
night is free. A week left unattended = half the
above rates; £10 surveillance fee may be added.

Shower basic, below HM's Office; access code.

Electricity free; four sockets on NE wall.

Launderette Superwash, 1 Tolver Rd. Polyclean,
4 East Terrace, near the rail station; daily
0900–1930.

Fuel Diesel by hose/cans from tank by HM's
Office; petrol from garage near rail station.

YCs Penzance SC, Albert Pier, ☎ 364989; bar, food.

Chandlery & repairs Penzance Marine Services,
Wharf Rd, ☎ 361081, most repairs, CH, Gas.
Ocean Blue, CH, sails, rigger, ☎ 364004. Sea-Com,
☎ 369695.

Future developments Existing showers and toilets
for yachtsmen are to be upgraded. In the longer
term an extension to Penzance harbour is planned
which would give H24 access to yacht pontoons
and improved facilities to the Isles of Scilly.

Entering Penzance harbour with the ferry berth and lt twr to port

St Michael's Mount

Harbour entrance – 50°07´·18N 05°28´·66W

Two miles east of Penzance by sea this imposing granite pile is as much a place of pilgrimage for today's tourists as it was 800 years ago when its then Benedictine monastery featured on the long pilgrim trail to Santiago de Compostela. Later the monastery was fortified before becoming, in 1660, the residence of the St Aubyn family. In 1954 it was given to the National Trust. Quite apart from the stunning views, it is well worth a visit.

SHORESIDE (Telephone code 01736)

The Castle can be reached on foot, by bike, 2/2A bus, taxi and of course by sea. At LW walk across a drying 500m long causeway to the little harbour on the N side of the Castle. When the causeway has covered, take a ferry at £1 single.

The Castle is open in season Mon–Fri 1030–1730, ditto most w/ends; £4.60, family £13. The gardens are open by arrangement Apr/May £2.50. Bookings ☎ 710507; 🖷 711544; Tidal/ferry info ☎ 710265. www.stmichaelsmount.co.uk Enjoy The Sail Loft, ☎ 710748, for fresh fishy lunches at sea level.

NAVIGATION

Charts, Tides, Tidal streams As for Penzance.

Approach From Penzance direct to the waypoint. This is basically a fun trip in fair weather. A good tender & reliable outboard is a feasible option if not night stopping. From the E, keep seaward of Mountamopus SCM buoy, thence to the waypoint.

Landmark The castle towers 80m (260ft) above sea level. *Si monumentum requiris, circumspice.*

Pilotage The waypoint is 50°07´·04N 05°29´·26W, 067°/0.4M to the W Pier head. From Penzance, avoid Western Cressar (SCM bcn), Ryeman Rocks

(SCM bcn) and Outer Penzeath Rk, 0.4m. The Mount is ringed by drying rocks and the only safe approach is on its NW side between the W Pier and Great Hogus; dries 5.5m.

Access HW±3, in settled weather. Harbour dries 2.1m; approx 3m at HWS and 2m at HWN.

Anchorage As charted, 140m W of the W pier head in 2.7m; good holding on sand.

Berthing With adequate rise dry out on firm, flat sand against the W Pier by the ladders; fender board advised for fin-keelers as the stone wall is uneven. Keep clear of stone steps used by ferries.

Tariff See **HM** Mr Keith Murch. Office is by the E Pier; ☎ 710265 or 07780 930875. No VHF, facilities.

Marazion PO/general stores. Godolphin Arms Hotel, ☎ 710202, has a good restaurant and possible shower if eating. Mount's Bay SC is dinghies only.

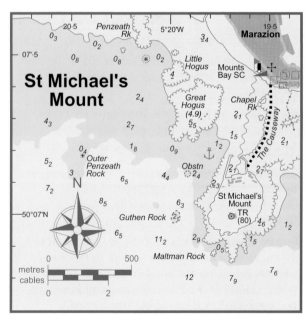

LIZARD PENINSULA

Porthleven Inner Basin 50°05'·04N 05°18'·98W; Cadgwith anchorage 49°59'·10N 05°10'·60W; Coverack harbour entrance 50°01'·38N 05°05'·67W

Around this rocky peninsula, which includes the southernmost point of the UK, are several small harbours and anchorages – separate entities, here described in sequence from W to E. They are: Porthleven, Cadgwith & Coverack – places which an inquiring yachtsman might plan to explore in the right conditions. But all too often the demands of tide and time ('must round the Lizard by so and so') preclude a visit. For St Michael's Mount see under Penzance.

SHORESIDE (Telephone code 01326)

Facilities ashore, such as they are, feature under individual entries. All four harbours share a degree of remoteness, thanks to geography and the vagaries of public transport.

Buses The network is comprehensive, if a little infrequent. Timetables from Penzance, Helston (☎ 565431) or Falmouth Tourist Offices.

Porthleven's outer harbour

Taxis, bike and car hire The HM is most likely to know what, if anything, is available.

PORTHLEVEN

Inner Basin – 50°05'·04N 05°18'·98W

A narrow drying harbour whose long outer arm turns N, via a small middle basin, into a sheltered inner basin. Unfortunately its economic survival has always been held to ransom by the SW-facing entrance which takes the brunt of Atlantic storms. Today a small fishing presence and a few local yachts are all that remain. Yet in settled offshore weather Porthleven is worth a visit and presents no problems to yachts which can dry out.

What to see/do Pleasant cliffy walks to the WNW, or a wooded circuit of Loe Pool. Helston is 2M inland with most facilities; 2, 2A bus (9 mins).

Beaches Porthleven Sands stretch 2M SE, past Loe Bar to Gunwalloe. Choose your spot.

Supermarket Costcutter, Mon–Sat 08–22 (Sun 2100).

Banks in Helston. Cashback at Costcutter.

Launderette Fore St, ☎ 562208; near PO.

Restaurants Critchards Seafood Restaurant at head of hbr; Mon–Sat from 1830, ☎ 562407, £12. Next door: Lugger bistro. Good pub food at the Ship Inn on NW side of hbr and Harbour Inn opposite.

NAVIGATION

Charts AC 777 (1:75,000), 2345 (Penzance Bay 1:12,500; hbr plan 1:5,000), SC 5603.2 (1:7,000).

Approaches From the W, via Mountamopus SCM buoy; beware Welloe Rk $\underline{0}$.8m. From the SE, direct when clear of the Lizard.

Landmarks The clock tower at the root of the pier is conspic; ditto the long shingle beach to the SE.

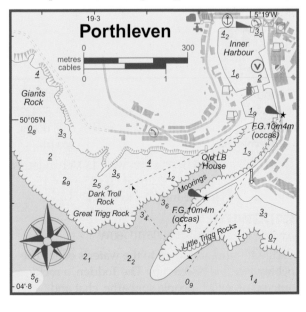

Inner harbour. Visitors berth on the far wall

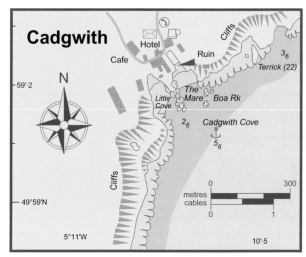

Pilotage The waypoint is 50°04´·61N 05°19´·58W, 053°/800m to abeam the pierhead, and within the visibility arc (033°–067°) of the FG light by the middle basin. This and the pierhead FG light are only shown when the hbr is open to shipping, ie rarely. Great and Little Trigg Rocks, drying about 1·3m, lie close to port and stbd of the channel and extend SW of the pierhead.

Tides HW Porthleven at sp is 1 hr 5 mins and at nps 45 mins before HW Devonport. LW at nps is 25 mins and at sp 30 mins before LW Devonport. MHWS is 5·5m, MLWS 0·8m; MHWN is 4·3m, MLWN 2·0m.

Tidal streams in Mount's Bay are weak.

Access HW±3, but dangerous in fresh S/SWlies.

Shelter The harbour is exposed to S/SW winds, and the inner basin is closed by timber beams if bad weather makes the approach dangerous. A red ball is hoisted on a mast at the pierhead when the harbour is closed, usually for weather!

Anchorage None. Some red waiting buoys in about 2m are abeam the pierhead.

Berthing Yachts dry out on firm sand/mud in the inner basin, to starboard immediately beyond the narrow entrance.

HM Mr Phillip Ward; office near NW corner of the inner basin; **not** in the blue shed labelled 'HM Office' (this is Cornwall); ☎ 574270, 🖷 574225. Hours flexible and at tide times. VHF Ch 08 occas. kathy@porthlevenharbouranddock.fsnet.co.uk

Tariff Daily rates £ berthed on wall, LOA bands: <6m = 8; <9.3m = 10; <12.2m = 12; <15.4m = 15. Showers at Harbour Inn, £1± to RNLI.

CADGWITH
Anchorage – 49°59´·10N 05°10´·60W

Cadgwith tumbles down to the water's edge. The pebbly beach is bisected by The Todden, a rocky outcrop on which people sunbathe, chat and

admire the view. The northern beach is small and much-photographed; here fishermen have hauled up their boats from the year dot. They still do so, with a diesel-powered winch and wire hawsers – careful where you walk.

What to see/do Not a lot, although cliff walking and bike rides down to the Lizard are possible. A little fishing and barbeque, plus watching the pilot gig boats racing, would make the day.

Supermarkets and **banks** Nil; nearest at Helston. PO, general store, café, ice creams.

Restaurant Cadgwith Cove Inn is a friendly pub, full of locals and visitors; main courses about £11.

NAVIGATION

Charts AC 154 (1:35,000), 2345 (1:12,500; hbr plan 1:15,000), SC 5603.6 (1:15,000).

Approaches Cadgwith is most likely to be a day trip from Falmouth or the Helford River. It can also be used to await a fair tide round the Lizard. From the NE, route via The Manacles ECM buoy and Black Head. From the S, having rounded the Lizard avoid The Vrogue and Craggan Rocks.

Landmarks Nothing uniquely obvious.

Pilotage The waypoint is 49°59´·00N 05°10´·00W, 285°/0.4M to the anchorage. Plan to go no further inshore than the 5m line. Take special care to avoid the drying Boa Rock off the N beach and The Mare, drying rocks extending seaward from The Todden.

Access Unlit; day only. Shelter. None in E'lies.

Tides Use differences for the Lizard: HW Lizard Pt at sp is 1 hr and at nps 45 mins before HW Devonport. LW at nps and at sp is 30 mins before LW Devonport. MHWS is 5·3m, MLWS 0·6m; MHWN is 4·2m, MLWN 1·9m.

Fishing boats hauled up on the beach

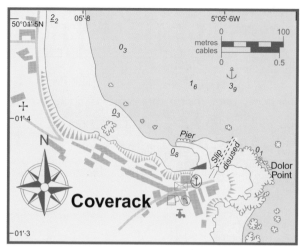

Tidal streams inshore are weak.

Anchorage ⚓ in about 5m on rock/shingle, near the Lat/Long given under the title on page 47, and clear of the approach to the N beach. Beach the dinghy clear of winch wires.

COVERACK

Harbour entrance – 50°01´·38N 05°05´·67W

Whilst there are similarities, Coverack is on a grander scale than Cadgwith. The village straggles round Dolor Pt at the S end of a bay stretching over a mile from Chynhalls Pt to Lowland Pt.

The harbour itself is dinky and chock-a-block with small FVs, so you are unlikely to get in unless you drive a canoe. But out in the bay there is elbow room for all to anchor. When the sun shines, the setting is almost Mediterranean.

What to see/do Much the same as Cadgwith, plus learn to windsurf at the active local centre, ☎ 280687.

Beaches Good sand around the bay, except HW.

Supermarket Only a general store by the harbour.

Restaurants The Paris Hotel down by the harbour is named after a liner which grounded here in 1899; it does good bar food, steaks and seafood at around £10. The Fodder Barn, next to the PO, does main courses around £9.

NAVIGATION

Charts AC 154 (1:35,000), 147 (hbr plan 1:15,000), SC 5603.6 (1:15,000).

Approaches From the NE, round Manacle ECM buoy and avoid the drying ledges off Lowland Pt.

From the S, keep a safe offing from Black Head and drying rocks off Chynhalls Pt.

Landmarks The old LB house (now a café) has a conspic white roof. On Chynhalls Pt a large white hotel is conspic.

Pilotage The waypoint is 50°01´·47N 05°05´·00W, 277°/350m to the anchorage.

Tides HW Coverack at sp is 50 mins and at nps 30 mins before HW Devonport. LW at nps is 15 mins and at sp is 20 mins before LW Devonport. MHWS is 5·3m, MLWS 0·6m; MHWN is 4·2m, MLWN 1·9m.

Tidal streams are weak in the bay.

Access H24, but not in onshore winds.

Shelter The anchorage is exposed to E'lies.

Anchorage Anchor about 300m N of the harbour in 3–5m; good holding on sand. There are no ⚓s, but many lobster pots. Perprean Cove, just S of the Paris Hotel, is a sheltered shoal draught anchorage between rocky drying ledges.

HM Mr Harold Martin, ☎ 280545, next to the shop; open mornings. Anchoring is free.

Looking north to the anchorage

THE HELFORD RIVER

The Pool – 50°05´·83N 05°07´·60W

Helford is the village on the S bank of the river. Helford Passage, mostly holiday apartments, is on the opposite bank. Both boast famous old inns: The Shipwright's Arms at Helford and the Ferryboat at Helford Passage – which add significantly to the attractions of the place. The river is navigable on the tide to Gweek and Trelowarren.

So much for the geography, but it is the ambience which counts for everything: The wooded banks, sunlit waters and shaded creeks of this enchanting river – some would say enchanted if Frenchman's Creek, immortalised by Daphne du Maurier, rates that almost mythical status. If you haven't sailed into the Helford River, do so before you die.

SHORESIDE (Telephone code 01326)

What to see/do Revel in the beautiful surroundings. Glendurgan, ☎ 250906, and Trebah, ☎ 250448, Gardens, both 1030–1730, are an easy walk from Helford Passage. Go by dinghy to Frenchman's Creek; kill the outboard and drift in on your oars – '*Still and soundless, surrounded by the trees, hidden from the eyes of men*'.

Visit the Seal Sanctuary (0900–1700), 3M up-river at Gweek; the kids will love it. Goonhilly Earth station (1000–1700, £5) can be reached by bike or T3 bus (twice daily) from Helford carpark.

Rail Falmouth for Truro and mainline trains.

Buses T8 from Helford Passage to Falmouth (20 mins, every 2 hrs). T2 from Helford village to Helston; change for Falmouth and elsewhere.

Taxi Falmouth Taxis ☎ 312181.

Ferry 0900–1710 dep Helford Passage on the hour to Helford Pt, returning at H+10; £1.60 single.

Beaches Nearest is the small sandy beach at Helford Passage. Also on the N bank: Polgwidden Cove, Robin's Cove, Durgan and Porth Saxon.

Supermarkets Spar at Constantine, Sun–Fri, 0800–2100; Sat 0830–2100. Helford PO/store meets most needs; Mon–Fri 0830–1730 (1700 Sat), Sun 0900–1700.

Banks Falmouth.

Restaurants The Shipwright's Arms, ☎ 231235, BBQ steaks/seafood. The Ferryboat Inn, ☎ 250625, BBQ & seafood. Budock Vean Hotel/restaurant, ☎ 252100, at Porth Navas Creek; dinners daily. See also YCs.

NAVIGATION

Charts AC 154 (1:35,000), 147 (hbr plan 1:12,500), SC 5603.2 (1:75,000), 5603.6 (1:12,500).

Approaches From the NE, set course direct to the waypoint. From the S, round Manacle ECM buoy, thence direct to the waypoint. Expect to see large vessels anchored in Falmouth Bay.

Landmarks None, other than boats & masts; in season August Rock SHM buoy when closer.

Pilotage The waypoint is 50°05′·97N 05°04′·53W, 266°/2M to the seaward end of the fairway which runs W–E through the moorings, alias The Pool. ⚓s are laid either side of the fairway which is easily identified by FV moorings on the S side. Do not anchor in, or obstruct, the fairway. Speed limit 6kn. The SHM Bar buoy lies inconspicuously on its side amid a host of ⚓s; it marks an extensive shoal drying 3.5m off Helford Passage.

Tides HW Helford entrance at sp is 35 mins and at nps 30 mins before HW Devonport. LW at nps is 10 mins and at sp 15 mins before LW Devonport. MHWS 5·3m, MLWS 0·6m; MHWN 4·2m, MLWN 1·9m.

August Rock

Tidal streams in the river reach 2kn at springs.

Access By day (no lights) and at all tides.

Shelter is excellent, except in E'lies which raise a heavy sea in the lower reaches.

Anchorages Off Porth Navas Creek, E of two beige oyster buoys in about 2–3m; off Polgwidden Cove; or ESE of Voose NCM buoy, off Bosahan Cove. No anchoring: Inshore between Toll Pt and Durgan, due to eel grass beds; in Porth Navas Creek and in the upper Helford River, due to oyster beds.

VHF *Moorings Officer* Ch M. HRSC Ch 80, M.

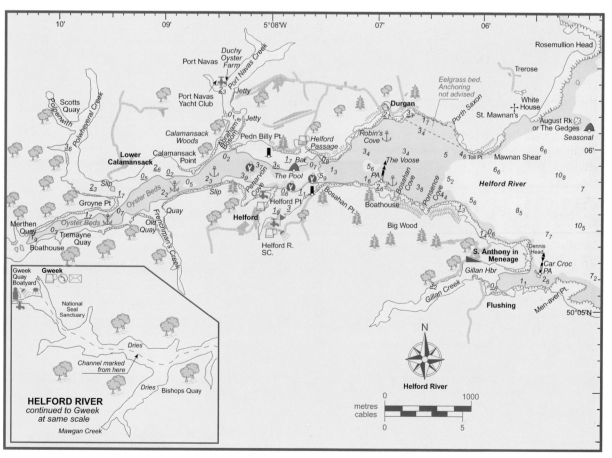

Helford Passage lower right; Helford on the opposite bank

FACILITIES

The Moorings Officer (Mr Simon Walker) has a kiosk on the beach in front of the Ferryboat Inn; ☎ 250770/250749. *Moorings Officer* VHF Ch M. Hours 0900–1700 (–2100 Jul/Aug). moorings@helford-river.com

Moorings 35 green, white or orange ⚓s all have a common and obvious identifying feature: a green pick-up buoy – a shining example to other harbour authorities of how best to indicate a ⚓.

Tariff Daily rate for LOA bands on ⚓s/rafted: <10m = £8; <11m = £10; <12m = £12; >12m = £15. Rafting may be necessary in high season. No fee for anchoring – another shining example!

Water taxi The Moorings launch doubles as a water taxi on request Ch M, approx £1 per head.

Dinghy landings Helford Passage on the beach.

Right: The creek above Helford
Below: Sparkling water and deeply shaded banks

At Helford Pt on a private pontoon (£1 donations welcomed); or at the ferry landing, but dinghies may not be left there; or at HRSC's pontoon, dries.

Showers at HRSC (from 0900) and PNYC.

Fuel None available, except in emergency.

YCs Helford River SC (HRSC on S bank), ☎ 231460: Showers, launderette, bar, restaurant (pre-book). Porth Navas YC (N bank), ☎ 340065: restaurant (pre-book), bar, showers, drying moorings/pontoons.

Chandlery & repairs Sailaway (St Anthony), CH, Sh, repairs, ☎ 231357. Cellar Marine (Porthallow), ☎ 280214, ME. M Wright (Marine Engineering), at Manaccan, ☎ 231502. Gweek Quay Boatyard, ☎ 221657, access HW±2; drying AB, CH, ME, AC, Diesel.

Mylor Yacht Harbour – a haven of tranquillity; Restronguet Creek beyond

FALMOUTH, TRURO
AND ADJACENT RIVERS & CREEKS

Harbour entrance – 50°08´·00N 05°02´·00W

Falmouth is but a part of this vast natural harbour, treasured by every yachtsman. Here is a thumbnail sketch for the newcomer: Enter between St Anthony Head and Pendennis Point. St Mawes and the Percuil River lie to starboard. To port the Penryn River flows seaward past Flushing, three Falmouth marinas and the commercial docks.

From the entrance Carrick Road extends north for almost 4M to Turnaware Pt. Mylor's excellent marina and Restronguet Creek with the popular Pandora Inn are to port. Opposite, St Just Creek is one of the gems of the Roseland peninsula.

Above Turnaware Pt the River Fal leaves Ruan Creek to curve past the sweeping parkland of elegant Trelissick House. King Harry ferry, laid-up merchantmen, Smuggler's Cottage and yacht pontoons punctuate its thickly wooded banks.

In the upper reaches Malpas lies at the junction of the Tresillian River and what has now become the Truro River. Turn port and thread a course to Truro's cathedral and city centre. Some harbour!

SHORESIDE IN FALMOUTH
(Telephone code 01326)

Tourist Office The Moor, near the Prince of Wales Pier. ☎ 312300, 🖷 313457. falmouthtic@yahoo.co.uk www.falmouth-cornwall.org Mon–Sat 0930–1730.

What to see/do The National Maritime Museum (Cornwall) opened, belatedly, in 2003 as a major attraction. Pendennis Castle, 1000–1800, for military history and superb views. Falmouth Art Gallery and Arts Centre for more cultured tastes.

Rail The Town station (aka the Dell) is 5–10 mins walk from VYH and Port Pendennis, but taxi from Falmouth marina. Change at Truro (25 mins) for mainline trains to London, Bristol and the NW.

Buses To all nearby towns and attractions.

Taxi Abacus ☎ 212141; Falmouth Taxis ☎ 312181.

Car hire Central Car Hire, ☎ 315918, near station. Eurodrive ☎ 373575. Falmouth Garage, ☎ 313029.

Bike hire Cycle Solutions, 18 High St; ☎ 317679.

Ferries From Prince of Wales Pier to Flushing, St Mawes, Mylor and up the Fal to Truro.

Beaches Gyllyngvase and Swanpool Beaches are W of Pendennis Castle and S of the town.

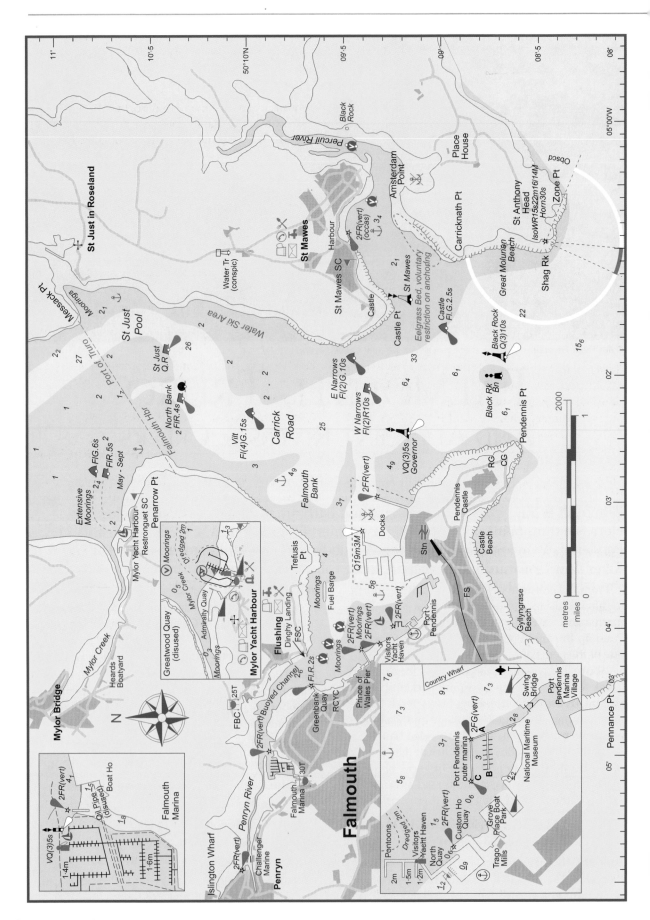

Mylor Bridge

Heards
Boatyard

Mylor Creek

St Just in Roseland

Messack Pt

Moorings

St Just
Pool

2 4

2 1

27

Port of Truro

2 2

2

Falmouth Hbr

1 7

1

Extensive
Moorings

2 4

Fl.G.6s

Fl.R.5s 2

May - Sept

2

Mylor Yacht Harbour

Restronguet SC

Penarrow Pt

North Bank
2 Fl.R.4s

St Just
Q.R

26

2

2 2

2

Vilt
Fl(4)G.15s

Carrick
Road

3

4 9

Falmouth
Bank

3 7

Water Tr
(conspic)

St Mawes SC

St Mawes

Harbour

2FR(vert)
(occas)

3 4

Castle

St Mawes
Castle Pt

2 1

Castle
Fl.G.2.5s

2 1

Eelgrass Bed, voluntary
restriction on anchoring

E Narrows
Fl(2)G.10s

33

W Narrows
Fl(2)R10s

25

2 2

VQ(3)5s
Governor

4 9

2FR(vert)

3 7

5 8

2FR(vert)

Percuil River

Black
Rock

Amsterdam
Point

Place
House

Carricknath Pt

6 1

6 4

Black Rk
Bn

Black Rock
Q(3)10s

22

Great Molunan
Beach

15 6

Carricknath Pt

St Anthony
Head

IsoWR15s22m16/14M
Horn30s

Zone Pt

Obscd

Shag Rk

Pendennis Pt

Black Rk

6 1

Q19m3M

Docks

Stn

Pendennis
Castle

RG
CG

FS

Castle
Beach

Gyllyngrase
Beach

Pennance Pt

Falmouth

Heards
Boatyard

Mylor Creek

N

Greatwood Quay
(disused)

Admiralty Quay

0 5

Dredged 2m

Mylor Creek

Moorings

0 5

Moorings

Mylor Yacht Harbour

Flushing

Dinghy Landing

FSC

Trefusis
Pt

Moorings

Fuel Barge

4

Moorings

5 8

Greenbank
Quay

RCYC

Prince of Wales Pier

FBC 25T

Fl.R.2s

2 6

Fl.R.2s

2FR(vert) Buoyed Channel

Moorings

2FR(vert)
Moorings

Visitors
Yacht Haven

Port
Pendennis

Country Wharf

9 1

7 3

Swing
Bridge

Port
Pendennis
Marina
Village

7 6

2FG(vert)

3 7

Port Pendennis
outer marina

A

2FG(vert)

C B

2 8

National Maritime
Museum

2 2

7 3

Islington Wharf

Pennryn River

Falmouth
Marina

30T

Falmouth
Marina

Penryn

2FR(vert)

Challenger
Marine

VQ(3)5s

Boat Ho

2FR(vert)

4 1

1 5

Oil Pipe
(disused)

1 8

1 4m

1 5m

1 6m

Falmouth
Marina

Pontoons

Dredged 2m

2m

1 5m

1 2m

North
Quay

Visitors
Yacht Haven

1 5

2FR(vert)

Custom Ho
Quay

0 6

0 6

1 2

0 9

Trago
Mills

Place Boat
Park

Grove

5 8

3 7

3

metres

miles

0

2000

1

0

St Anthony Head lighthouse at the harbour entrance

Supermarkets Tesco, Killigrew St, is 600m from VYH and Port Pendennis; Mon–Sat 0700–2000, Sun 1000–1600. See other marinas for nearest option.

Market day Local produce Tues in the Moor.

Banks All in/near town centre, with cashpoints.

Restaurants The Seafood Bar, Quay St, ☎ 315129, £13.50, is off Arwennack St (the S end of the main drag) where the following are near to VYH and Port Pendennis: Seafarers, ☎ 319851, £10.95–14.50. Bistro de la Mer, ☎ 316509, £12.95. Cassis, ☎ 210759, £7–11.50, shut Mon. Hunkydory, ☎ 212977, £11.25–15.95. Further N, Mings Garden, ☎ 314413, £14.50–20. High St, No 33, ☎ 211944, £11.85. Powell's Cellars, No 29, ☎ 311212, £15.50 set menu.

NAVIGATION

Charts AC 1267 (1:75,000), 154 (1:35,000), 32 (1:12,500), 18 (1:5,000); SC 5602.2 (1:75,000), 5602.6 (1:16,000) & 5603.2 (1:75,000).

Harbour/port limits
Falmouth Harbour extends south nearly to the Manacles, up the Penryn River to just short of Falmouth Marina and up Carrick Road to a line from Penarrow Pt to St Just.

The Port of Truro is all north of this line; also the upper Penryn River including Falmouth Marina.

Approaches From the S, round the Lizard, clear Black Hd and the Manacles; thence direct to WPT.

From the E (Prawle Pt), direct to the WPT, passing close S of Eddystone lt ho.

From the ENE (Rame Head) direct to Zone Pt and the WPT. From the NE (Fowey), clear Dodman Pt thence as above; but see Passage Notes for naval targets SSE of Dodman.

Landmarks St Anthony Hd lt ho, but from the E it is obscured by Zone Pt until bearing 295° or more. Pendennis Castle and Falmouth Coastguard bldg are at the W side of the harbour entrance.

Pilotage The waypoint is 50°08´·00N 05°02´·00W, 7 cables S of Black Rock unlit IDM bcn, to stbd of which is the buoyed, lit channel; but yachts can pass to port of it. The Inner Harbour is easily navigated, clear of moorings. The Penryn River is buoyed above Flushing. In Carrick Road, outside the deep, buoyed channel it quickly shoals and near LW care is needed.

Access H24 at all tides and even in a S'ly gale.

Shelter Very good in the Inner Harbour and up the Fal – truly a port of refuge.

Tides Falmouth is a Standard Port; see *RNA* for predictions. MHWS is 5·4m, MLWS 0·8m; MHWN 4·3m, MLWN 2·1m.

Tidal streams do not exceed 1kn at springs.

VHF *Falmouth Harbour Radio* and *Killigrew* (Hbr launch) Ch 12. Fuel barge *Falmouth Industry* Ch 16.

FACILITIES

HM Capt Mark Sansom, Falmouth Hbr Commissioners' (FHC) Office, 44 Arwennack St. ☎ 312285, 🖷 211352.

Moorings FHC offer 18 ⚓s SW of the fairway between VYH and Greenbank Quay; call VHF Ch 12 for exact locations. Daily rates £: <7m = 7;

Channal's Creek and Trelissick House

<12m = 10.60; <15m = 15; >15m = 17.20.

For **❶** pontoons up the River Fal see under Truro.

Fuel Barge *Falmouth Industry* Ch 16, or just berth Mon–Fri 0800–1630 (Sat 1200); 300m SW of Trefusis Pt.

YCs Royal Cornwall YC, ☎ 311105/312126; Bar, moorings. Flushing SC, ☎ 374043. St Mawes SC, ☎ 270686; bar, showers, moorings. Mylor YC, ☎ 374391. Restronguet SC, ☎ 374536, at Mylor.

Water taxi Ocean Aqua Cab, ☎ 07970 242258, rapid transit, daily 1000–0100, to almost all local haunts.

MARINAS

In Falmouth (see also St Mawes, Mylor and Truro) options include from seaward:

Visitors' Yacht Haven at lower left. Pendennis outer marina on the lower right

235° ldg marks and old observatory clear the moorings off the Visitors' Yacht Haven

1. Visitors' Yacht Haven (VYH), run by FHC. Two orange △ ldg marks and Old Observatory tower on the skyline lead 235° clear of moorings. It is handy for the shops and fleshpots of Falmouth.

Tariff Daily rates £ on pontoons (showers free) for LOA bands: <8m = 12.80; <10m = 14.90; <12m = 16.90; <14m = 19; <16m = 26.30. 2 hrs stay, £2.50.

Anchor between VYH and the commercial docks in about 3m on mud/sand/shingle. Anchor rates are approx half those for **❶**s. Land at VYH.

Showers & **launderette** beyond Berthing Office; access by swipe card. **Electricity** By £1 & £5 cards.

Fuel Diesel & petrol pontoon promised by 2003.

Chandlery & repairs Bosun's Locker, ☎ 312212, CH. Penrose, ☎ 312705 & 07977 421970, sailmaker.

2. Port Pendennis Marina Manager Mark Webster. www.portpendennis.com VHF Ch 80, M. ☎ 311113, 🖷 311116. marina@portpendennis.com

Entrance From the commercial docks head S for the tower of the National Maritime Museum. The outer marina (all tide access) is to stbd in 3m.

The inner marina is dead ahead, accessed HW±3 via a flapgate and swing footbridge & traffic lights. Total shelter in 3m; a secure place to leave a boat.

Tariff Daily rate £2/m LOA. **Electricity** £2.50.

Showers & **launderette** plus other facilities on the Museum site. PO/general store/café close SE. 5 mins walk to railway station.

View north across Falmouth Marina

Services, ☎ 313713, all repairs. Spokeshave Yacht Services, ☎ 07890 517711, shipwright. Challenger Marine, ☎ 377222, engines. SKB Sails, ☎ 372107, sail repairs. Europcar, ☎ 315204, at the marina.

ST MAWES (Telephone code 01326)

This peaceful resort, E of its well-preserved castle, overlooks the mouth of the Percuil River.

Above: St Anthony Head lighthouse lower right. St Mawes and Percuil River in the middle ground
Below: St Mawes Castle (right); Pendennis Castle far left

3. Falmouth Marina Manager John Osmond. ☎ 316620, 🖷 313939. www.premiermarinas.com falmouth@premiermarinas.com VHF Ch 80, M.

Entrance Nearing the marina, **keep south of** the rather confusing ECM* beacon, VQ (3) 5s, so as to avoid the drying bank west of it. Disregard the nearby pair of PHM/SHM buoys which solely mark the Penryn River. *This may change.

Berthing Berth initially on 'A' hammerhead (also the fuel berth), then as directed.

Tariff Daily rate Jul/Aug: £2.18/m LOA (£18.50 min); other months £2/m LOA (£17.50 min).

Electricity £3 per day.

Showers are very good and free.

Fuel Diesel only, at the end of 'A' pontoon.

Supermarket Co-op Pioneer. 5 mins walk, from marina turn right to roundabout, then left. Mon–Fri 0800–2200 (Sat 2100), Sun 1000–1600.

Chandlery & repairs The Boat Store, ☎ 318314, CH. Marine Electrical Services, ☎ 378497/07831 482152. Seacom Electronics, ☎/🖷 210031. Seafit Marine

Navigation Lugo Rock, 0.6m and marked by St Mawes unlit SCM buoy, is 240m S of the Castle. There is no marina, just a small drying harbour; ferries/launches berth inside the pier so keep dinghies clear on the beach or slip. Upstream the river bends round to the NNE in beautiful scenery and is crowded with moorings and oyster beds.

Facilities HM, Capt Roy Maddern, whose office is on the quay, ☎ 270553, offers six green ⚓s SE of the pier in 2–3m. Call *St Mawes Harbour Radio* Ch 12.

Tariff LOA <10m =£15; <12m =£20; <15m =£30.

St Mawes SC has five green ⚓s beyond Polvarth Pt @ £6/night via Mr Osborne, ☎ 270528; land at the SC quay. The clubhouse (friendly welcome, bar, food and showers), ☎ 270686, overlooks the harbour.

St Just Creek and church

Banks Barclays & Lloyds, but no cashpoints.

Supermarket Spar, Mon–Sat 0830–1930 (Sun 1900).

Restaurants Idle Rocks Hotel, ☎ 270771, £28.75: three-course dinner. Hotel Tresanton, ☎ 270055, £33: three-course dinner. St Mawes Hotel, £11 main course. The Rising Sun, ☎ 270233, bar food.

St Just Creek inside Messack Pt and 1.6M N of St Mawes Castle, is well sheltered in E'lies. A pink house and the moorings mark the entrance which soon dries. Pick up a vacant mooring or anchor to the south. Then dinghy up the creek and hairpin stbd into a beautiful backwater. Here, surrounded by glorious sub-tropical gardens, the church teeters on the water's edge – a sublime setting.

MYLOR (Telephone code 01326)

Mylor Yacht Harbour has been much improved and expanded in recent years with two substantial breakwaters/outer pontoons, three inner pontoons and 250 moorings. Its idyllic setting, H24 access, good shelter, excellent support facilities and very friendly staff now rank it as one of the best UK south coast marinas. ☎ 372121, ▨ 372120. VHF Ch 80, M. enquiries@mylor.com; www.mylor.com

Make time to visit the historic church (founded 450AD) and its serene churchyard.

Approach Enter the E–W fairway between a pair of PHM/SHM buoys at 50°10´·75N 05°02´·65W; to the NE and SE of this position beware shoal water.

Berthing Call VHF Ch 80, M for a berth/mooring or berth inside/outside the E breakwater, then check in at the Moorings Office. Tenders berth outside the root of the W breakwater.

Tariff Daily rate on pontoons £2/m LOA. £1/m LOA on moorings.

Electricity £1.50 by swipe card, inc fresh water.

Showers are hot, but very brief for 2 x 50p coins.

Launderette Same location.

Fuel Diesel & petrol near root of E bkwtr. LPG at root of 'B' pontoon.

YCs Mylor YC, ☎ 374391; bar and friendly welcome.

Shops Store & café, 0730–1800.

Restaurant Ganges, ☎ 374320, dinner £14.50. Lemon Tree Inn, 15 mins walk up the creek.

Chandlery & repairs Chandlery/rigging, ☎ 375482. Marine Trak Engineering, ☎ 376588. Mylor Shipwrights, ☎ 372121. Seacom Electronics, 377677. Seaweld Fabrications, ☎ 373155.

Restronguet Creek 1M N of Mylor at the creek entrance, the Pandora Inn is a popular watering hole. Around HW±3, anchor or pick up a buoy in the 12.4m pool; or dry out at the Inn's pontoon. The rest of the creek need not distract you.

TRURO (Telephone code 01872)

The river from Turnaware Pt to Truro, or perhaps only up to Malpas (pronounced Mope'us), is for many yachtsmen a favourite sortie. Sheltered by the high wooded banks and away from crowded marinas, the river has good anchorages, moorings and pontoons in peace and seclusion. Enjoy the handsome city of Truro, see below.

NAVIGATION

The river is not difficult, but note the following: SHM lt buoy 'Turnaware Bar' must be obeyed – or run aground S of it. Speed limit 8kn. *King Harry* Ferry gives way to all but sail, but if Rule 27b is applied this will change. Maggoty Bank (0.1m), 8 cables below Malpas, extends well across the river; respect the eponymous SHM lt buoy.

Malpas–Truro Leave Malpas at HW Truro –2 for the 2M trip. HW Truro is approx 8 mins later and 1.8m lower than HW Falmouth. The channel is buoyed from Malpas to a Lighterage Quay (0.7M below Truro); here anti-flood gates normally stay open. The final 0.5M long channel is very exactly marked by perches. At Tesco's carpark it narrows and lies within 2m of the buildings to starboard. At the Y-junction, enter the port arm: Shoal draught boats berth on a pontoon to port (hard bottom); opposite, fin keelers sink into soft mud against the stone quay. A LW recce on foot/bike from Malpas reveals all. Electricity, FW, basic shower/toilet; £6/night. A marina is envisaged, with a bund/sill built across the river's narrowest point abeam Tesco's carpark.

FACILITIES

HM Capt Andy Brigden, ☎ 272130, 🖷 225346; 07790 050554. harbouroffice@carrick.gov.uk www.portoftruro.com VHF Ch 12 *Carrick One* is HM's office; *Carrick Three* is the Harbour launch.

Four Ⓥ pontoons are located: NE of Turnaware Point at 50°12´·58N 05°01´·64W; off Ruan Creek at 50°13´·73N 05°00´·96W; off Woodbury Point at 50°14´·36N 05°00´·91W; and off Malpas Marine at 50°14´·71N 05°01´·39W; this pontoon has only 1m at LWS. Note: The pontoons along Victoria Quay, Malpas are private.

Tariff Pontoons & 🛥: <2 hrs = £2; 2–24 hrs = £6. £3 per day or part thereof for anchoring.

Moorings HM Truro's only 🛥 is off Malpas. 4 cables N of King Harry Ferry are 10 buoys, £6/

Truro at Low Water

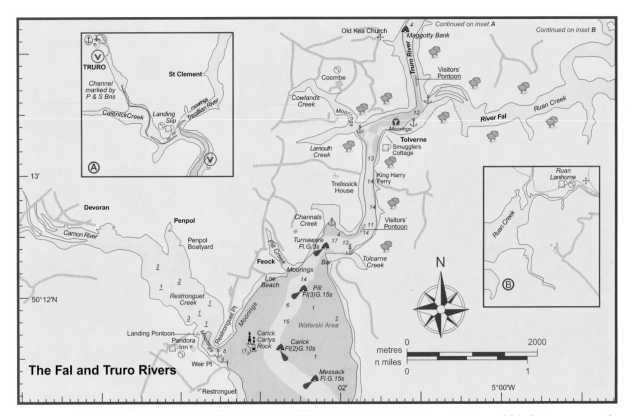

The Fal and Truro Rivers

The drying upper reaches of the Truro River

night or free if eating at the excellent Smuggler's Cottage, ☎ 580309 (much D-Day memorabilia).

Call Malpas Marine, ☎ 271260 (CH, diesel, shower, FW) for a vacant mooring £6. Dinghy landing £2 at jetty accesses village PO, store and Heron Inn.

Anchoring is possible at the mouth of many of the drying creeks. Show an anchor ball/light.

Truro exudes an air of elegance and distinction,

with its cobbled streets, grand Georgian buildings and magnificent cathedral.

Tourist Office Boscawen St, ☎ 274555, 🖷 263031; Mon–Fri 0900–1800 (Sat 1000–1700). tic@truro.gov.uk; www.info@truro.gov.uk Royal Cornwall Museum, ☎ 272205; Mon–Sat 1000–1700.

Supermarket Tesco alongside your berth; open H24 Mon 0800 to 2200 Sat, Sun 1000–1600. Pannier Market, Mon–Sat. All **banks** plus cashpoints.

Transport Car hire: Avis ☎ 262226; Hertz ☎ 223638. Bike hire: Truro Cycles, ☎ 271703. Good bus service and mainline trains to London, 4 hrs 30 mins. Taxi ☎ 0800 318708. Tourist boats to Falmouth on the tide.

Restaurants No 10 Kenwyn St, ☎ 272363. Saffron, ☎ 263771, 5 Quay St. Stars, ☎ 262389, light meals £8.50 on the mezzanine level of Hall for Cornwall, Truro's modernised theatre and concert hall. Wig & Pen, good pub food at Frances St/Castle St.

MEVAGISSEY

Harbour entrance – 50°16´·16N 04°46´·94W

Mevva (useful local shorthand) derives its name from St Meva and St Issey – as if it matters. It is often referred to as the archetypal Cornish fishing village, which today means a declining fishing fleet, Cornish cream teas (yum), tacky tourist gift shops and benches on which visitors nod off in the sun. But all that may change by 2006/7.

Regeneration and European funding are the buzz words. Ambitious and imaginative plans include a 70 berth marina in the N part of the outer harbour, FVs on the S side, (inner harbour unchanged) and a massive detached breakwater lying N/S about 60m E of the existing S Pier – to give year round protection. Book your berth now.

SHORESIDE (Telephone code 01726)

Tourist Office St George's Sq, PL26 6UB; ☎ 844857. www.mevagissey.net Mon–Fri 1000 (Sat 1030)–1700; Sun 1100–1600.

What to see/do Er, nod off in the sun. Or if you're a gardener (not usually compatible with yachting) the Lost Gardens of Heligan (25 mins by footpath) will beckon; daily 1000–1800, £6; allow half a day. The Eden Project may detain you rather longer. Get tickets in advance £9.80 to save queuing; open 1000–1800. 26/26A Bus to St Austell; local bus on.

Rail St Austell is the nearest station.

Buses 26/26A to Heligan, St Austell and beyond; timetables from the Tourist Office.

Taxi ☎ 843001.

Car hire See the Tourist Office.

Bike hire Pentewan Valley Cycle Hire, ☎ 844242.

Ferry To/from Fowey, 35 mins, £7.50 return.

Beaches A small patch of sand at the root of the W Quay – if a multihull has not got there first. At Pentewan, 1M north, there is a much larger beach.

Supermarkets None, but several general stores.

Launderette Behind the King's Arms.

Banks Lloyds, no cashpoint; Mon, Wed, Fri 0930–1230.

Restaurants Alvorada, Portuguese restaurant, 2 Polkirt Hill (one block behind W Wharf), £13.50, ☎ 842055. Opposite is The Oyster Shell, ☎ 842174, £13. Sharksfin Waterside, ☎ 843241, £14, W side of Inner Hbr. The Haven, ☎ 844888, £12.50, shut Mon. The Sundeck, with terrace and

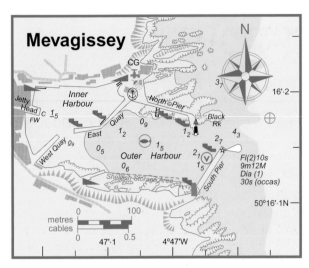

Mevagissey

Fishing boats in the outer harbour

brilliant views seaward, ☎ 843051, is just N of the HM's office; light meals.

NAVIGATION

Charts AC 1267 (1:75,000), 148 (1:30,000), 147 (1:2,500), plus SC 5602.2 (1:75,000 & plan 1:3,500).

Approaches From the S, round the Dodman, pass seaward of Gwineas (rks) and a safe distance off Chapel Pt. From the E/NE direct to the entrance.

Landmarks The S Pier's white lt ho is conspic.

Pilotage An approach waypoint is unnecessary since there are no hazards in Mevagissey Bay. Set course direct to the hbr entrance, but if conditions are poor or foggy, pause 0.5M off to have a think.

South Pier lighthouse is conspicuous

Tides HW Mevagissey at sp is 20 mins and nps 15 mins before HW Devonport. LW at nps is 5 mins and at sp 10 mins before LW Devonport. MHWS is 5·4m, MLWS 0·7m; MHWN is 4·3m, MLWN 2·0m.

Tidal streams in Mevva Bay are insignificant.

Access H24, but not advised in strong E'lies.

Shelter The Outer Harbour is totally exposed to E'lies (unless/until the new outer breakwater is built) and can be uncomfortable in strong N'lies.

VHF Call *Mevagissey Harbour* Ch 16, work 14.

FACILITIES

The HM (Capt Hugh Bowles) has a conspic white office at the root of the N Pier. ☎ 843305, 🖷 842535. Hrs 0900–2100 Apr–Oct. meva.harbour@talk21.com; www.mevagisseyharbour.co.uk

Berthing Berth against the outer harbour's S Pier in 2m, between the stone steps; there are three metal ladders. Keep clear of the inner end where tourist boats/ferries berth and there is a fuel point. It is also possible in very calm settled weather to berth on the seaward side (smooth concrete) of the S Pier. This was widened, slightly lengthened and strengthened in 1998. NB Piling juts out 0.71m at the level of MLWS; use large fenders. Visitors may not berth in the crowded Inner Harbour.

Anchoring in the harbour is prohibited; no room. There are no ⚓ moorings.

Tariff Daily rate £ per m LOA: <6m 4; <9m 6; <12m 7; >12m 9. Pay the HM or the car park attendant.

Showers None.

Fuel Diesel at the root of the S Pier; see HM.

Chandlery & repairs John Moor & Son, ☎ 842964, runs a traditional boatyard & chandlery near the HM's office.

CHARLESTOWN

Harbour entrance – 50°19´·84N 04°45´·35W

This former china clay port, in the NW corner of St Austell Bay, is in sight of the 'Cornish Alps', the slightly eerie whitish-green, conical spoil tips piled up over years of mining. But Charlestown changed its spots in 1993 when the harbour was bought by Square Sail Shipyard Ltd. It is now home to three square riggers which feature in film & TV work, and corporate events (as does the unique harbour).

Subject to prior notice (see below), Square Sail Ltd welcomes visiting yachtsmen, who with luck may find in port the three-masted barques *Kaskelot* (153ft) and *Earl of Pembroke* (145ft) or the two-masted brig *Phoenix* (112ft). If unlucky, the Eden Project is only 4M away. A Shipwreck & Heritage Centre at the port is open 1000–1700; with restaurant above.

SHORESIDE (Telephone code 01726)

Shopping Most of life's mundane needs can be met in Charlestown, PO/stores, or St Austell.

Bike hire Cycle Nucleus, at St Austell, ☎ 68569.

Restaurants Rashleigh Arms, ☎ 73635, pub food & real ale. Pier House Hotel/restaurant, ☎ 67955.

NAVIGATION

Charts AC 1267 (1:75,000), 148 (1:30,000), 31 (plan 1:5,000), plus SC 5602.2 (1:75,000).

Approaches From the S & W, round Black Head and set course for the waypoint. From the E, skirt round Cannis Rock SCM buoy (off Gribbin Head), thence to the waypoint.

Landmarks The 'Cornish Alps' and a hotel 0.7M east of the port are conspicuous.

Pilotage The waypoint is 50°19´·73N 04°44´·98W, 293°/500m to the narrow harbour entrance, with a ruined, sunken wall to stbd. Pierheads are lit, two FR/FG (vert), but a night approach is not advised.

Tides Use differences for Par (see Fowey, *RNA*).

Tidal streams in St Austell Bay are weak.

Access The approach can be dangerously rough in strong winds from E to SSW. Enter the inner basin via an entry gate (10.7m wide), open HW±1.

Shelter The outer basin is exposed to SE'lies, but the inner basin offers total shelter in 4.6m.

Charlestown Harbour

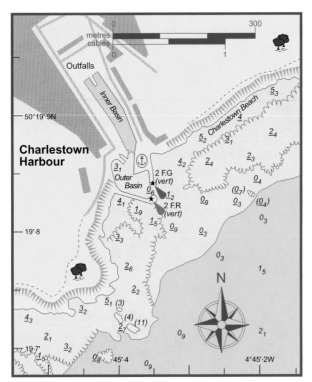

Charlestown Harbour

Anchorage Anchor in 4m near the waypoint in good holding on sand. A mooring buoy is 2 cables SSE of the harbour. Near HW yachts can wait in the outer basin for the gate to open.

VHF When nearing the harbour call *Charlestown* Ch 14 for entry/berthing instructions.

FACILITIES

Clearance to visit must be obtained ideally three days in advance, but at least 24 hrs, by calling HM ☎ 70241, Mon–Fri 0830–1700. He will advise whether a Square Sail vessel is scheduled to enter/leave at about your ETA (see Tariff). 🖷 61839. info@square-sail.com; www.square-sail.com

Berthing As directed. Max LOA 57m; beam 9.8m; draught 4.3m.

The outer basin and entry gate

Tariff (2003) inc VAT. Daily rate/LOA: <6.1m = £18.80; >6.1m = £3.08/m. These rates include gate opening fees, if arriving/leaving at the same time as a Square Sail vessel. If not, each opening = £29.37.

Electricity £4.70 per day. **Showers** None.

Fuel Diesel on request.

Chandlery & repairs Skywave Marine, CH and electronics. Square Sail Shipyard undertake all types of ship repairs, rigging and sailmaking etc for traditional/classic yachts and boats.

Above: The north end of the inner basin
Below: Square riggers – a fine sight

FOWEY

Harbour entrance – 50°19´·63N 04°38´·56W

Fowey is at the heart of Daphne du Maurier's Cornwall, whose mystery and charm is so lucidly evoked in her books. If you have not already done so, may I suggest that you immerse yourself in her writings. Or, if time does not permit, at least read *Daphne du Maurier's Cornwall*, a pictorial memoir which covers her life and has excerpts from her books (ISBN 1-900064-00-6, £4.99 from the D du M Literary Centre next to the church).

Fowey to port, Polruan to starboard

Up-river by Bodinnick car ferry, to starboard you can see Ferryside, the house where D du M spent her earlier years. Sir Arthur Quiller-Couch and Kenneth Grahame (*Wind in the Willows*) also found literary inspiration at Fowey.

The harbour entrance is an impressive, rocky portal into the river. To port Fowey clambers up the hill-side, whilst to starboard Polruan barely maintains a toehold on the even steeper slopes.

SHORESIDE (Telephone code 01726)

Tourist Office in the PO (right from Albert Quay), Tues/Fri ☎ 833616. Mon–Fri 0900–1730 (Sat 1700); Sun 1000–1700. foweytic@visit.org.uk; www.fowey.co.uk

What to see/do Brilliant walking includes the SW Coastal Path. A local section from Readymoney Cove, via Polridmouth (pronounced '*Pridmouth*') beach and Gribbin Hd, to Polkerris Cove and the Rashleigh Arms is not to be missed. D du M Festival is held mid-May. The Eden Project is about 7M WNW, 1000–1800; £9.80. At Lostwithiel, Restormel Castle, an imposing mound-top ruin, and Lanhydrock House make a great day out.

Rail Par (16 mins by No 24 bus) is nearest station.

Bus No 24/24A to St Austell. No 293 to Plymouth.

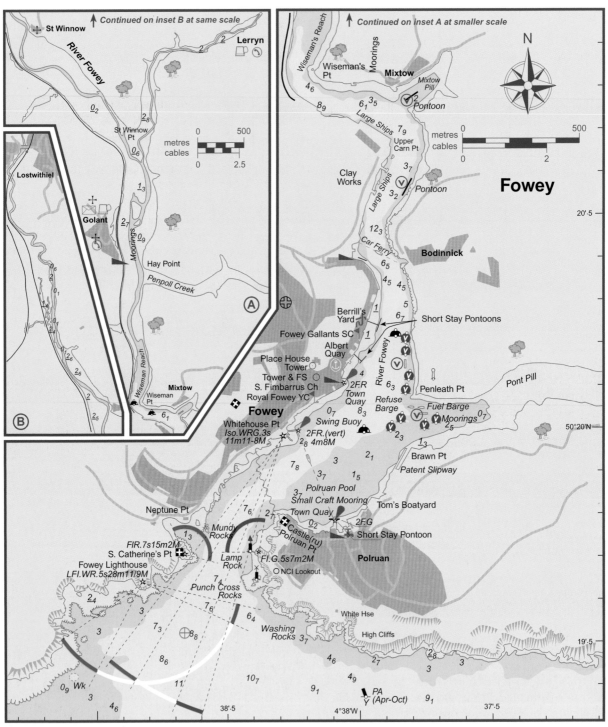

Taxis ☎ 832429; 832676; 814095.

Car hire St Austell ☎ 74743, 75700.

Ferries Frequent passenger ferries to Polruan and car ferry to Bodinnick. In season to Mevagissey, 35 mins/£7.50 return.

Beaches The sandy Readymoney Cove, at the entrance by the ruined castle, is the place to be.

Launderette Nil, surprisingly.

Supermarkets None, but Mini-Mart, Fore St has most essentials.

Banks Three, of which two have cashpoints.

Restaurants Food for Thought, ☎ 832221, Town Quay, £15. The Other Place, ☎ 833636, Fore St, £11. Sam's bistro, £9, Fore St. Ellis', ☎ 832359, The Esplanade, £16. Ibid: Waterside (Marina Hotel), ☎ 833315, set menu £32.50.

Whitehouse Point light on the left

NAVIGATION

Charts AC 1267 (1:75,000), 148 (1:30,000), 31 (1:6,250), plus SC 5602.7 (1: 6,250 and 1:15,000).

Approaches From the SW, give the Dodman and Gwineas a safe berth. From the E keep seaward of Udder Rk SCM buoy and at least 3 cables off the Polruan headland until the harbour opens. The approach is well lit by Whitehouse Pt directional Iso WRG 3s and by Fowey lt ho (keep out of its R sector). The entrance is lit by a Fl R 7s and Fl G 5s.

Albert Quay, the HM's office and tower of St Fimbarras Church

Landmarks A daymark column 104m (red/white bands) on Gribbin Head is conspic, as is a white house 3 cables E of the harbour entrance.

Pilotage The waypoint, 50°18´·10N 04°39´·70W, S of Cannis Rock SCM buoy, bears 027°/1.7M to the harbour entrance. Give way to Bodinnick car ferry.

Golant, Lostwithiel and Lerryn can be explored on the tide by shoal draught boats. Between Golant and Lostwithiel the height of CD rises in steps below/above OD (Newlyn); see diagram on AC 31.

Tides HW Fowey at sp is 15 mins and at nps 10 mins before HW Devonport. LW at nps is 5 mins and at sp 10 mins before LW Devonport. MHWS is 5·4m, MLWS 0·6m; MHWN is 4·3m, MLWN 2·0m.

Tidal streams In the entrance the flood starts at HW Devonport +0610 and the ebb at –0015.

Access H24, but strong SSW'lies against the ebb can make the entrance boisterous or even difficult.

Fowey Gallants Sailing Club, a hospitable watering hole

Shelter Good, but the lower reaches, including Pont Pill, become uncomfortable in SSW'lies >F5.

Moorings Øs are yellow or white, marked 'FHC Visitors' and lie mainly in Pont Pill (creek); most are swinging, some fore-&-aft. There are more on the E bank just N of Pont Pill; two fore-&-aft Øs at Mixtow Pill; and two just N of Wiseman's Pt.

Visitors' pontoons Two are in Pont Pill east of the refuse skip; one faces Albert Quay; one is 850m further N, off the E bank; and one is at Mixtow Pill (inner pontoon is for locals). NB At Mixtow Pill new Ⓥ pontoons are joined to the shore; showers & FW.

Dinghy landing and short stay (<2 hrs) pontoons are at Albert Quay, Berrill's Yard and Polruan Town Quay.

Anchorage Yachts may only anchor, with the HM's permission, in the swinging ground close W of Pont Pill. Cruise liners sometimes moor here.

VHF *Fowey Harbour Radio* Ch 12. *Fowey Refueller* Ch 10. *Fowey Water Taxi* Ch 06.

FACILITIES

The **HM**'s office (Capt Mike Sutherland) is at Albert Quay, PL23 1AJ. Hrs 0830–2100. ☎ 832471/832472; ▨ 833738; fhc@foweyharbour.co.uk

Tariff Daily rates £/m LOA on Øs & Ⓥ pontoons:<8m 9; <9m 10; <10m 12; <11m 13; <12m 14.50; <13m 15.50; <14m 16.50; <15m 17.50; <16m 18.50; <17m 19.50; <18m 21. Reductions (or vouchers in Jul/Aug) are available for three or seven night payments.

Showers at the RFYC and the FGSC, see below.

Fuel Diesel 0900–1800 from Fowey Refueller (Pont Pill), ☎ 833055 and Ch 10. Petrol only by cans.

YCs The Royal Fowey YC, ☎ 832245, is 250m S of the HM's office. The Fowey Gallant SC, ☎ 832335, is 100m N. Both offer a friendly welcome, showers, bar and food – roughly in that order! Fowey Royal Regatta and Carnival, third week in August, takes over both town and harbour.

Chandlery & repairs Upper Deck Marine, ☎ 832287, CH; and Outriggers, ☎ 833233, both by Albert Quay. Fowey Hbr Marine Engineers, ☎ 832806. Marine Electronics SW, ☎ 833101. Mitchell Sails, ☎ 833731, North St. Fowey BY, ☎ 832194, Passage St N of Fowey Gallants SC. Fowey Marine Services, ☎ 833236, Station Rd by car ferry to Bodinnick. **Polruan**: C Toms & Sons, ☎ 870232, BY, ME.

POLPERRO

⚓ mooring buoys – 50°19´·83N 04°30´·88W

Polperro is a tiny (and I mean tiny) fishing port about 3M west of Looe. Think small and you will not be surprised when you poke your bows into the narrow cleft in the high cliffy surrounds. In peak season legions of tourists throng the narrow alleys, cheek by jowl. For all that it is a place not to be missed, either for a lunch stop or overnight in suitable conditions.

SHORESIDE (Telephone code 01503)

Visitor Information from a small office near the PO. www.polperro.org

What to see/do Museum of Smuggling & Fishing, ☎ 272423; 1000–1800 daily, £1.50. Land of Legend and Model Village (whatever next?), ☎ 272378.

Rail Liskeard is the nearest mainline station.

Buses No 290 to Polruan & Looe; No 77 to Liskeard. See the Tourist Office for timetables.

Taxi, car and bike hire See the Tourist Office.

Beaches Sand has given way to gravel/boulders.

Supermarkets None, just general stores.

Banks None, but the PO has a cash dispenser.

Restaurants Neville's (no relation), ☎ 272459, £12, near the hbr. Some 400m up the hill: The Kitchen, ☎ 272780, £12; and The Cottage, ☎ 272217, £12. Various pubs with bar food.

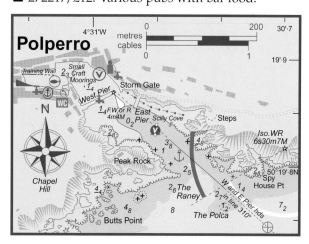

NAVIGATION

Charts AC 1267 (1:75,000), 148 (1:30,000 and plan 1:3,500), plus SC 5602.3 (1:75,000 and plan 1:3,500).

Approaches From the W keep seaward of Udder Rock (SCM lt buoy). The harbour does not open up until you are S/SE of it. From the E give Looe Island and The Ranneys a safe berth.

Landmarks A spindly TV mast, 3 cables W of the hbr, is fairly conspic from W and E. The village straggling up the valley orientates you on WNW, as does the jagged Peak Rock to port.

As seen from the waypoint with the tide well down

Pilotage The waypoint is 50°19'·60N 04°30'·46W, bearing 310°/3 cables to the ⚓s, with the E and W Pier heads in transit; binos may be needed.

Caution: Polca Rock, with 1m over it, is only 20m to port of the transit. The Raney, 2.5m, extends 40m E from Peak Rock. Drying rock ledges on both sides narrow the outer harbour to about 50m.

The only lights are the Iso WR 6s on Spy Glass Pt whose W sector (288°–060°) shows to seaward; and a FW light on the W Pierhead, which shows FR (or a black ball by day) when the storm gate is closed. A night approach is not advised for a first visit.

Access H24 to the outer harbour, but HW±3 to the inner harbour, drying approx 1.3m @ ⓥ berth.

Shelter is good except in onshore winds, when stay well away. When the wind has any S in it, the inner hbr may be closed by a steel storm gate, which stops swell but still allows the tide to flow.

Tides Use differences for Looe.

VHF *Polperro Harbour Master* Ch 10.

FACILITIES

The HM (Mr Chris Curtis) may be found at/near the Fish Quay or on his FV *Girl Jane* (SD 80). Office ☎ 272809, Mob 07968 374118. Hours flexible.

Berthing The three options from seaward are:
1. Anchor to seaward of the ⚓s in about 3m, as space permits. Holding on sand/rock is poor.
2. Moor fore & aft (NW/SE) to a pair of the four red ⚓s in the outer harbour; these lie in about 1.8m and may be occupied by FVs waiting to enter the drying inner harbour. Raft up in calm conditions.
3. Dry out on firm mud/sand with fender board against piled quay*, stbd side of the inner hbr, just beyond a sign for the Museum of Smuggling & Fishing. *A pontoon may be laid here in 2003. Keep clear of the FV fuel berth, first to stbd.

Tariff Daily rate for LOAs <10m £5; >10m £6.

Showers None. **FW** tap on quayside. No electricity.

Fuel In extremis, diesel by cans from a fisherman.

Chandlery & repairs None, but check with HM.

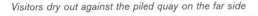

Visitors dry out against the piled quay on the far side

LOOE

Harbour entrance – 50°21´·05N 04°27´·07W

Looe attracts tourists mainly by dint of being an active fishing port, complete with lobster pots on the quayside and gnarled old salts mending their nets. Throw in the Shark Angling Club of Great Britain (no less) and a maze of narrow alleyways – and there you have it.

E Looe (EL) has most of the action; W Looe (WL) is a tad more refined, but only a tad! Unsurprisingly yachts barely make the agenda, given that the harbour dries to the head of the Banjo Pier, apart from a trickle along the E quays. Upstream a seven arched bridge with a mere 2m clearance effectively bars exploration of the upper reaches to all but kayaks.

SHORESIDE (Telephone code 01503)

Tourist Office is an annex to EL's Guildhall, with conspic clock tower. ☎ 262072; 🖷 265426. Open 1000–1700 daily. www.southeastcornwall.co.uk

What to see/do Looe Island (aka St George's) is a bird sanctuary and still inhabited by the surviving Atkins sister ('We bought an island'); visit by pleasure boat from EL. The SE Cornwall Discovery Centre (WL), ☎ 262777 and the Old Guildhall Museum (EL), ☎ 263709, will keep for a rainy day.

Rail The Looe Valley Line from the station, 400m N of the bridge, winds scenically beside the river to Liskeard (30 mins, £2.60 return); thence mainline.

Buses No 290 to Polruan; No 77 to Liskeard. See the Tourist Office for timetables.

Taxi ☎ 262405; 264193.

Car hire See the Tourist Office.

Bike hire Looe Mountain Bike hire, ☎ 262877.

Ferry Cross the river between WL & EL for 30p.

Beaches E Looe beach, E of the Banjo Pier, is large and sandy; further E is Plaidy beach. WL's Hannafore beach looks across to Looe Island.

Supermarkets WL: Spar is one block behind the ❖ berth; Mon–Sat 0730–2200, Sun 0800–2200. EL: Somerfield is by the Guildhall, Mon–Sat 0830–2000, Sun 1000–1800.

Market day 0500 at the daily fish-market.

Banks EL has three, with cashpoint; None in WL.

Launderette The oddly named 'Press-on-Linen', ☎ 263810, has branches in both WL and EL.

Restaurants WL: Tom Sawyer, ☎ 262782, is an inn/restaurant on Marine Drive, views across to Looe Island; does good seafood. EL: The Water

Rail, Lower Market St, ☎ 262314, £14. Café Rue, 3 Lower Chapel St, is much more than a café, ☎ 264285, £11. The Grapevine, Fore St, ☎ 263913, £13.

NAVIGATION

Charts AC 1267 (1:75,000), 148 (1:30,000), 147 (1:5,000), plus SC 5602.3 (1:75,000 & 1:6,000 plan).

Approaches From the W give Looe Island and The Ranneys (drying rocks) a wide berth; there may be overfalls to the SE. Do not attempt the drying rocky channel inshore of the island. From the E, there are no hazards across Whitsand Bay.

Landmarks Wooded Looe Island is an obvious feature (although mistaken by the Luftwaffe for a warship - and bombed accordingly). Banjo Pier, with a white band, is less obvious until near.

Pilotage The waypoint is 50°20′·83N 04°26′·37W, 295°/0.5M to the harbour entrance. At night stay in the white sector of the Banjo light. There are no other navigational lights, but many shore lights.

Tides HW Looe at sp & nps is 10 mins before HW Devonport. LW at sp & nps is 5 mins before LW Devonport. MHWS is 5·4m, MLWS 0·6m; MHWN is 4·2m, MLWN 2·0m.

Tidal streams in the harbour can reach 5kn at springs on both flood and ebb.

Access HW±3, but the entrance is dangerous in strong SE'lies, when seas break on the bar.

Shelter Good.

Anchorage 2 cables ENE of the Banjo Pier in 3m on sand. Stay N of the white sector (267°–313°) of the Banjo's light, Oc WR 8s; show an anchor light.

VHF *Looe Harbour* Ch 16, occas.

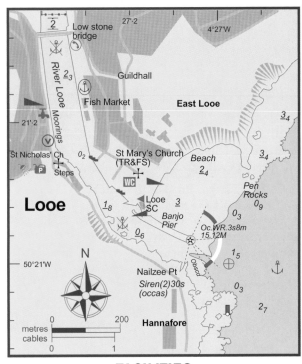

FACILITIES

The HM (Mr Webb) has an office in part of the Fishmarket. ☎ 262839. Hrs 0900–1700.

Berthing The ⓥ berth is on the W bank, just past the clock tower of St Nicolas church and next to the foot ferry. The adjacent white shower building is clearly marked 'Visitor's Berth', but may be occupied by the usual small FV. Dry out on firm level sand against the piled quay (use a fender board). Rafting is permitted, max three deep.

Local yachts dry out up-river in mid-stream. The E bank is very obviously FV country; keep clear.

Tariff Daily rate for LOA bands (shower inc): <6m £5.18; <9m £7.77; >9m £10.35.

Showers free in adjacent block. The key can be obtained from the ferryman.

Fuel Diesel (from Looe Fish) in small amounts.

YCs Looe SC, Buller St (EL), ☎ 262559: Bar, showers.

Chandlery & repairs MarineCo, ☎ 265444, 🖷 264760, behind the Fishmarket. Looe Chandlery, ☎ 264355, also organises sea fishing trips.

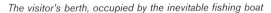
The visitor's berth, occupied by the inevitable fishing boat

PLYMOUTH

South Winter SCM buoy – 50°21′·40N 04°08′·55W

The Sound from just north of the breakwater. Drake's Island and silo are conspicuous in the centre

Plymouth is one of England's greatest harbours, set amidst dramatic scenery with Cornwall to port and Devon to starboard. At centre stage The Hoe commands the Sound and it requires little imagination to visualise Drake biding his time before seeing off the Spanish Armada. A plaque in Sutton Harbour commemorates *Mayflower* in which the Pilgrim Fathers set sail for the New World. Raleigh, Grenville, Hawkins, Captain Cook and Darwin all sailed from Plymouth – a noble roll-call of history. Frank Cowper, in his *Sailing Tours* of the 1890s, called Plymouth another Portsmouth, but apart from the presence of the Royal Navy the comparison does little justice to Plymouth.

Today you may see aircraft carriers, Trident submarines and gas-turbine powered destroyers at close quarters (not too close), together with all manner of commercial ships, ferries, fishing boats and flotillas of yachts. The latter are catered for by several marinas and some of the best anchorages in the West Country. The R Tamar and its creeks offer a mini-cruising ground in all weathers.

Ashore the city centre has been rebuilt since the ravages of WWII and the modern Royal Parade is in sharp contrast to the historic areas around the Barbican. Truly there is something for all tastes.

SHORESIDE (Telephone code 01752)

Tourist Office (small), SW corner of Sutton Hbr. ☎ 304849/227865; 🖷 257955. Apr–Oct, Mon–Sat 0900–1700; Sun 1000–1600. barbicantic@ plymouth.gov.uk; www.plymouth.gov.uk

What to see/do The Barbican is full of interest: The Glassworks, Elizabethan House (sea captain's house), Mayflower Visitor Centre, Plymouth Gin Distillery, National Marine Aquarium (E of Sutton Hbr). The Hoe, Smeaton's Tower, The Citadel, Plymouth Dome (successful), history of Plymouth.

Further afield: Mount Edgcumbe, restored Tudor House in glorious parkland; walk to Cawsand and Whitsand Bay. Morwhellam Quay, former copper port near Tavistock. National Trust: Buckland Abbey (Drake's house), Cotehele, Saltram House. Finally, as a break from the sea, wander Dartmoor, 'the high untrespassed sanctity of space'; www.dartmoor-npa.gov.uk For the western moor take a No 86 bus to Tavistock/Lydford, walking to Brent Tor and Gibbet Hill.

Rail The station is N of the City centre. Mainline trains to London (3–3hrs 30 mins), Penzance and Bristol.

Buses The bus station is on Bretonside, close NW

of Sutton Hbr. No 25 bus to railway station, Royal Parade, the Hoe and the Citadel. Regional buses to Exeter, Okehampton, Yelverton, Tavistock. Coach to London (Heathrow & Victoria), ☎ 0990 808080.

Taxis ☎ 666222; 252525; 606060; 363638; 222222.

Car hire Avis ☎ 221550; Hertz ☎ 207207.

Bike hire Plymouth Cycle Hire ☎ 258944.

Ferries Brittany Ferries (☎ 0990 360360) to Roscoff and Santander. Torpoint chain ferry to Cornwall. Local ferries: Sutton Hbr to Cawsand;

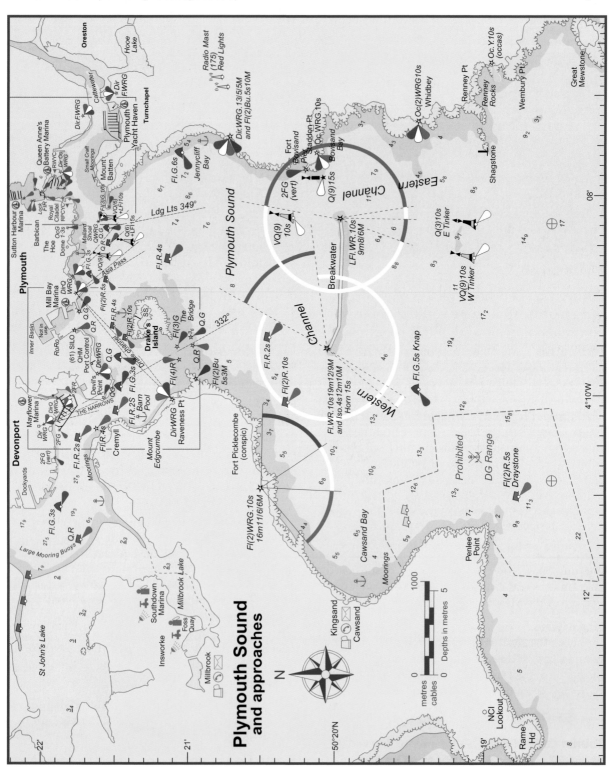

Plymouth Sound and approaches

Admiral's Hard (Stonehouse) to Cremyll, via Mayflower Marina if requested; VHF Ch 14 *Northern Belle* or ☎ 07816 603561.

Flights Airport, ☎ 705151, (N outskirts) to Gatwick, Bristol, Jersey, Guernsey and Cork.

Beaches Whitsand Bay, 1M W of Cawsand by coastal path, has vast sandy beaches and rollers.

Supermarkets Sainsbury, M & S and Tesco in the city centre. See also under Marinas.

Banks Plenty in the centre, all with cashpoints.

Restaurants The Barbican has an amazing variety of eateries, pubs. See also under Marinas.

NAVIGATION

Charts AC 1900 (1:25,000), 30 (1:12,500), 1967 (1:7,500), 1901 (1:5,000), 1902 (1:5,000) and 871 (1:12,500 with 1:20,000 insets) progress up-harbour at ever larger scale; plus SC 5602.8 and 5602.9 (1:25,000).

The Dockyard Port of Plymouth is controlled by a QHM who has wide powers. See VHF and IPTS. QHM ☎ 836952; DQHM ☎ 836485; Port Control ☎ 663225.

Approaches The Western and Eastern Channels lie either side of Plymouth Breakwater. The former is the main deep-water (DW) channel; the latter carries a least depth of 3.2m and normally is no problem, but in strong W'lies breaking seas and the lee shore make it dangerous for yachts.

From the W round Rame Hd to the **W waypoint**, 50°18′·85N 04°11′·07W (Draystone PHM buoy off Penlee Pt). Thence 032°/3M crosses the Western Channel, toward S Winter buoy; see under Title.

From the E, the **E waypoint**, 50°18′·00N 04°07′·70W, is 7 cables WSW of Mewstone Ledge and Great Mew Stone. Thence track 355°/3.5M via the East Channel toward S Mallard buoy, leaving the unlit Shag Stone beacon 2 cables to starboard and Tinker shoal 2 cables to port. Never venture inshore of the Mew Stone or Shag Stone.

Pilotage For a first visit, and especially at night, the many marks and lights may appear confusing. But The Sound is deep enough, except at the rocky fringes, for yachts to sail freely where big ships cannot go. Stay clear of the DW Channel. If caught out in fog, anchor close inshore.

Pilotage may be a direct track (see Approaches) if the wind serves, or buoy hopping outside the DW channel. Identify each mark in sequence and

Looking E past the breakwater to Staddon Heights

do not get distracted by extraneous features. If you lose the thread, pause to fix and re-orientate.

S Winter and S Mallard buoys (see Approaches) are 'aiming points' where you will either fork east for QAB, Sutton Hbr or Plymouth Yacht Haven; or west for Mayflower Marina and the R Tamar.

The Bridge, between Drake's Island and Mount Edgcumbe, is a useful short cut to the NW, with the left-hand, blue-painted of three conspic high-rise blocks bearing 327°. It is well marked by two SHM and two PHM light beacons and carries 1.7m least depth. Do your tidal sums and check the depth gauges on Nos 1 and 4 bns. Near LW take it through the middle to avoid possible foul patches. Note that the stream sets mainly NNW/SSE, max 2.4kn.

Access H24 at all tides, but fresh/strong onshore winds against the ebb can make conditions lively.

Landmarks From the W, the conical-shaped Rame Head is easily seen; the Eddystone lighthouse lies 8M SSW of it. From the E, Great Mew Stone (57m) is conspicuous; ditto the white lighthouse on the W end of the Breakwater, from all directions. When closer, Drake's Island and an ugly grey silo (61m) at Millbay are obvious.

Tides Plymouth is a Standard Port. Predictions & local secondary port differences are in the *RNA*. MHWS is 5·5m, MLWS 0·8m; MHWN is 4·4m, MLWN 2·2m.

South Winter buoy, Smeaton's Tower and the war memorial almost in transit

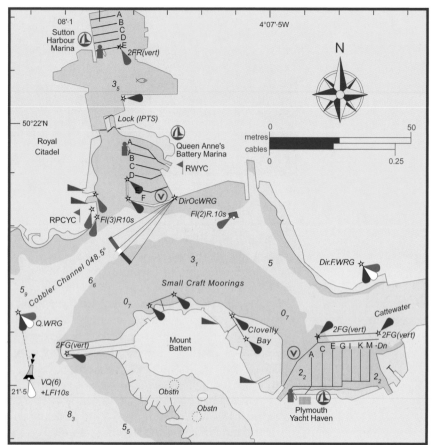

Tidal streams generally follow the channels, but see tidal diamonds on large scale charts for detail.

VHF *Longroom Port Control* Ch 14 controls the movements of vessels >25m LOA; yachts should monitor Ch 14 only for traffic, tidal, wind & fog info.

Marinas See individual entries.

IPTS Nos 1 and 4 (modified to stipulate a wide berth from warships) are shown from a mast atop Drake's Island and from Longroom Port Control. If unlit, there are no restrictions. The *RNA* lists two other signals not affecting craft <20m LOA. Wind strength warning lts may be shown: 1 Oc white = F5–7; 2 Oc white = F7+.

Day sailing In the Hamoaze the Torpoint chain ferry has right of way. For a free commentary on the warships off the Naval Dockyard, fall in beside a tourist launch.

The Lynher River is entered some 7 cables below the Tamar/Albert road/rail bridges. With AC 871 to hand, St Germans village, quay and Elliot Arms can be reached on the tide. Most of this quiet creek dries, but stay afloat at anchor off the north bank (Forder Lake and Ince Pt) or in Dandy Hole (3m).

From the bridges, the Tamar proper is navigable on the flood with care to Calstock (12M) even by deep draught boats. Off Cargreen pick up a ⚓ and repair to the Crooked Spaniard. Or, if your mast is shorter than 16m (overhead cables), make for Weir Quay BY which offers ⚓s and showers. Upstream, depths shoal gradually to 0.6m (4.1m at HWN), but pre-arrange to dry out at Calstock BY (☎ 01822 833331; showers and diesel) alongside their quay. The River Yealm, 4M ESE of The Breakwater, is quite delightful, hence (too) popular.

Anchorages From seaward, there are ⚓s: Off Cawsand in about 4m on sand, well protected from W'lies. In Jennycliff Bay in 4–7m on mud, well sheltered from E'lies. In the bay close SW of the Hoe in 3–7m on mud. A cable N of Drake's Is in 3–6m on gravel/shells (where there are also ⚓s), but exposed to wash from passing traffic. Barn Pool (5 cables S of Mayflower Marina) in 5–7m on mud/gravel, sheltered from W'lies in peaceful surroundings, but the bottom is foul in places.

FACILITIES

Marinas

The four major marinas, from E to W are:

1. Plymouth Yacht Harbour (PYH) in Cattewater, 50°21′·59N 04°07′·15W, access H24 all tides. Manager Bobbie Blackler. ☎ 404231, 🖷 484177, Mob 07721 498422. plymouth@yachthavens.com; www.yachthavens.com Internet café in reception. From humble origins PYH has become a well-run marina with excellent support facilities on site.

Berthing Ⓥ berths on P6 pontoon outside the wavebreak can be uncomfortable in fresh W'lies; if so, call Ch 80, M (H24) for an inside berth. Beware, quite large tankers berth at Cattedown Wharves on the N bank.

Tariff Daily rate on pontoons (showers and electricity included), Apr–Sep = £2/metre LOA.

Plymouth Yacht Harbour seen looking across the Cattewater

The lock into Sutton Harbour

Launderette by token.

Fuel Diesel only at berth near boat hoist, H24.

Chandlery & repairs Mt Batten Boathouse
☎ 482666; Rock Run Yachts ☎ 482445; Dex Tamar
☎ 491454; Osen Sails, ☎ 563666; Rigger ☎ 0800
9158609; Webber Marine ☎ 405403; FSCD
☎ 837890; Mt Batten Boathouse ☎ 482666.

Facilities Water taxi, ☎ 07930 838614, to Barbican.

Eating Stroll to Turnchapel where the Boringdon
Arms, ☎ 402053, and the New Inn, ☎ 402765,
both serve good pub food; or try Shaw's
Restaurant at Mount Batten.

Food shop Basic groceries on site. Hooe (5 mins
walk): Mini-market, butcher, PO. Plymstock
Broadway (12 mins by bus): Safeway (Mon–Sat
0800–2300; Sun 1100–1700); Lidl, banks, PO.

2. Queen Anne's Battery (QAB) 50°21´·90N
04°07´·93W. Manager Nicola Walsh ☎ 671142;
🖷 266297; Mobile 07967 939017. VHF Ch 80, M,
H24. qab@mdlmarinas.co.uk; www.marinas.co.uk
Ⓥ berth/raft alongside red pontoon (no fingers),
next to the outer breakwater. In season it is often
crowded with racers and akin to a mini-Cowes.

Tariff Daily rate on pontoons: £2.35/m LOA.

Electricity = £2.50 per day.

Showers free, coded access. **Launderette** by token.

Fuel Diesel and petrol from fuel barge on white
pontoon, 7/7 0830–1830 in season.

Chandlery & repairs Yacht Parts, ☎ 252489.
Sea Chest, ☎ 222012, books/charts. Ocean
Marine, ☎ 222550. Danvic BY, ☎ 268677.
Allspars (rigger), ☎ 266766.

Facilities Chandler's Bistro/bar. Water taxi to
Barbican. Royal Western YC, ☎ 66007, visitors
welcome. Food shops: As Sutton Hbr.

3. Sutton Harbour Marina Lock at 50°21´·98N
04°07´·96W. Manager Susan Tansy. ☎ 204737;
🖷 205403. VHF 12, H24. admin@sutton-
harbour.co.uk; www.sutton-harbour.co.uk

VHF Call *Sutton Hbr Radio* Ch 12 for lock entry
and a berth (pre-book in season).

Access H24 via a lock, ☎ 204186, marked by
R/G chevrons. (Ignore the emergency gate close
W of the lock). One-way entry/exit, via swinging
footbridge, is controlled by IPTS sigs 1, 2 & 3.
In the lock (floodlit) secure to narrow pontoons.
Freeflow is in force when height of tide is >3.7m
(approx HW±3).

Shelter is very good in 3.5m. FVs berth to the SE.

Tariff Daily rates £ on pontoons (showers free)
for LOA bands: <8m = 15.50; <9m = 18.10; <10m =
20.30; <11m = 22.40; <12m = 24.60; <13m = 26.75;
<14m = 28.90; <15m = 31; <16 = 33.10.

Electricity £3.50/24 hrs.

Fuel Diesel and petrol at fuel berth, 0800–1830.

Chandlery & repairs Plymouth Chandlers
☎ 268826; Marine Bazaar ☎ 201023; Harbour
Marine ☎ 204694. Sutton Rigging ☎ 269756;
Sutton Marine ☎ 662129.

Launderette Coin-operated.

Food shop Southside (Barbican) 0800–2000.

4. Mayflower Marina 50°21´·79N 04°10´·00W,
SE entrance. Office 0800–1800; Manager
Charles Bush. ☎ 556633, 🖷 606896;
mayflower@ mayflowermarina.co.uk;
www.mayflowermarina.co.uk VHF Ch 80, M.
Pontoons are being renewed/extended and many
other improvements made 2002–2012.

Berthing Tidal streams set diagonally through
the pontoons. A S'ly swell may be uncomfortable.

Tariff Daily rate £/m LOA (showers and electricity included), April–Sep: 2.20.

Fuel Diesel, petrol & LPG at fuel berth, 0800–1800.

Chandlery & repairs Chandlery ☎ 500121; M & G Marine services ☎ 563345, engineering/general; Androdian Yacht service, repair/maintain, ☎ 606707; Rigger ☎ 226609; Osen Sails ☎ 563666; A Blagdon's BY, ☎/▨ 561830, Mobile 07468 914556.

Showers or bath. Free, access by key (£10 deposit).

Launderette By tokens: wash £2, dry 50p/10 mins.

Mayflower Marina and The Narrows

Facilities Brasserie restaurant £16.50, daily 1100–1500 & 1900–2300, bar, café, ☎ 500008. Courtesy bus, Mon–Sat Jun/Aug, to City centre (Sainsbury's): Out 1030 & 1530; back 1330 & 1700.

Food shop Plymco, daily 0800–2200, 15 mins walk. Limited groceries at Chandlery, daily 0900–1730.

Other marinas Millbay Village Marina has no ❶ berths. Southdown Marina/BY, ☎ 823084, in Millbrook Lake, dries. Torpoint Yacht Harbour (Ballast Pound on older charts) may have a spare berth in 2m within its four walls; ☎ 813658. At Saltash a pontoon (walk ashore) is 150m N of Tamar bridge: 12 hrs free, no return within 24 hrs.

Yacht Clubs Royal Western YC, ☎ 660077, at QAB. Royal Plymouth Corinthian YC, ☎ 664327, below the Citadel. Mayflower SC, ☎ 662526, E of the Citadel. Mosquito SC at Torpoint, ☎ 812508. Quay SC (St German's), ☎ 01503 250370. Saltash SC, ☎ 845988.

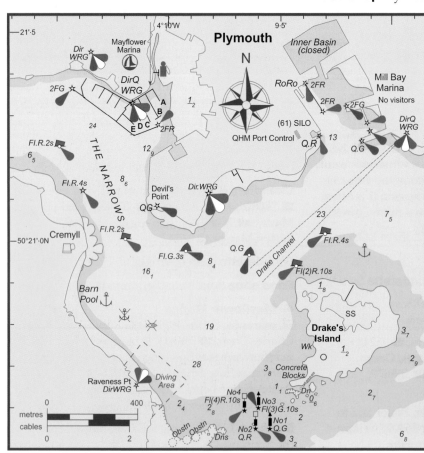

RIVER YEALM

First **V** pontoon – 50°18´·68N 04°03´·14W

Arguably the Yealm ranks with the Dart as South Devon's most attractive navigable river (strictly there is no river at Salcombe; it is a drowned ria). Its steeply wooded banks form a handy hideaway for weekend yachtsmen out of Plymouth – hence it is so popular in season that the HM may sometimes have to limit the number of visitors.

An unusual view, looking south down river

Newton Ferrers on the N bank of Newton Creek is full of character(s) with shops on Newton Hill, the steep main street. Opposite is little Noss Mayo and the Ship Inn, reached at LW by a drying causeway, or by ferry to Baring Pt at other times.

SHORESIDE

(Telephone code 01752. NB Mobiles here only work on Orange; no service from Vodafone)

Tourist Office None.

What to see/do Walk the South Devon Coastal Path, or parts of it; also glorious riverside walks detailed in the Yealm Hbr booklet. Lazing in the sun (?) may be an option. Or fishing, although not for Bass, 1/5–31/12, as the Yealm is a Bass Nursery area.

Rail Via Plymouth.

Bus The 94 bus leaves Yealm Steps, Mon–Sat @ 0757, 0957, 1157 & 1627 to Plymouth (45 mins).

Taxi Bridge Cabs ☎ 696969.

Car & bike hire In Plymouth.

Ferry Local ferry from Yealm Steps to Warren Pt and Baring Pt.

Beaches None, but you can still enjoy a quick dip.

Supermarkets Plymco, at the top of Newton Hill, Mon–Sat 0800–2000, Sun 0900–1900. The PO/general store has groceries, Mon–Fri 0830–1730 (Sat 1300), Sun 0900–1200.

Banks None, but Plymco do cashback and the PO cashes cheques.

Restaurants Bistro Ferrers, ☎ 873146, £16. Village Fayre, ☎ 872491. Excellent pub food/meals at The Dolphin, £10.

The north face of Great Mewstone looking east. The 089° leading marks are just visible

NAVIGATION

Charts AC 1613 (1:75,000), 1900 (1:25,000), 30 (1:12,500); SC 5602.8 (1:25,000 & 1:12,500 plan).

Approaches From Plymouth and the W, keep S of Great Mewstone with its Ledge to the SW and the Slimers to the E; thence to the approach waypoint.

From the E, skirt Bolt Head and pass 7 cables off Hillsea Pt and Yealm Head. As soon as St Werburgh's conspic church tower bears 002° (to clear the W and E Ebb Rks) turn N to the approach waypoint.

Landmarks Great Mewstone and St Werburgh's church tower.

Pilotage The waypoint, 50°18′·59N 04°04′·97W, is 5.5 cables from the river entrance, in transit 089° with two B/W beacons above Cellar Bay; this transit clears Mouthstone Ledge. To clear the sandbar, drying 0.6m, which extends S from Season Pt across the river entrance, jink S of two PHM buoys (the first Fl R 5s). Then alter NE toward a R/W beacon on the N bank; this leg carries least depth of 0.9m past Misery Pt. Here the river and moorings open to the SE, trending

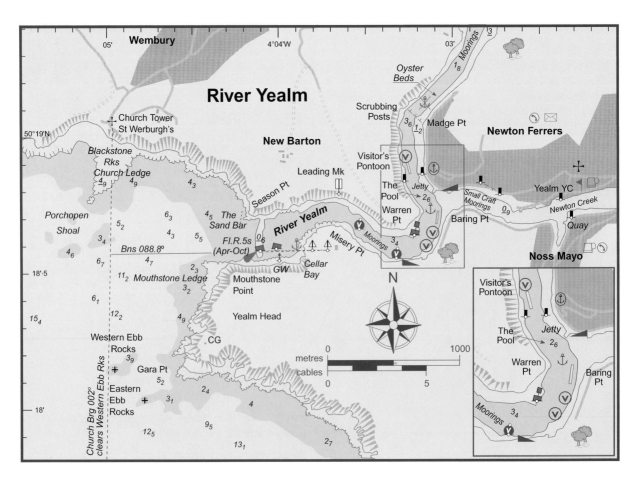

089° leading marks, buoyage and Cellar Bay

A quiet corner up Newton Creek

NE into Yealm Pool past Spit PHM buoy. This marks the drying spit and can be obscured by moored yachts; take the bend wide.

Tides HW at the entrance to the R Yealm at sp & nps is 6 mins after HW Devonport. LW at nps & at sp is 2 mins after LW Devonport. MHWS is 5·4m, MLWS 0·7m; MHWN is 4·3m, MLWN 2·1m.

Tidal streams in the river reach $2\frac{1}{2}$kn. The flood starts at HW Devonport $-5\frac{3}{4}$ hrs and the ebb at $+\frac{1}{4}$.

Access By day; unlit. Near LW check rise of tide.

Shelter is good in The Pool and up-river.

VHF None, except water taxi Ch 08, 1000–2300.

FACILITIES

The **HM**'s office (Julian Stapley, ☎ 872533) is above Yealm Steps in the drive of the Yealm Hotel. Open 0930–1200 and evenings in season.

Yealm Steps pontoon, least depth 1.5m at LW, for FW (max stay 30 mins) and dinghy landing; also the ferry.

Berthing The first ❶ pontoon is in The Pool (Lat/Long under the title); the second is about 3 cables N. Rafting is the norm. There is one ⚓ E of Misery Pt for boats < 23m/25 ton and two ⚓s in The Pool, each for three rafted yachts; a local mooring may only be used if the HM

approves. Newton Creek, drying to 1.5m, has local moorings only.

Anchoring Cellar Bay is a popular anchorage, but exposed to strong W'lies. Within the river space is limited by the many moorings; before anchoring get the HM's consent – the fee is the same as for ❶ pontoons and ⚓s. No anchoring above Madge Pt.

Tariff Daily rates £/m LOA on pontoons, ⚓s and at anchor are: <7m 7; <8m 8; <9m 9.50; <10m 10.50; <11m 11.50; <12m 12.50; <13m 13.50; <14m 15; <15m 16; <16m 17; <17m 18.

Water taxi VHF Ch 08, ☎ 880079; 1000–2300.

Showers at Yealm YC, £1 coins, by the slipway. If YC shut, The Dolphin or chemist Tubb has a key.

Fuel None by hose; cans from Yealmpton 4M.

YCs Yealm YC, ☎ 872291, on the N bank of Newton Creek; bar, food Mon–Sat pm. Showers as above.

Chandlery & repairs None.

SALCOMBE

Southernmost 🛥s – 50°14´·04N 03°46´·09W

Looking NNE from Bolt Head. Kingsbridge is visible in the background

Salcombe lies on the west bank of what is a sea inlet, since no river flows seaward from any of the creeks. This inlet, or ria, hosts a myriad of marine life, which in turn attracts a variety of birds – seeking a ready supply of food. Bottle-nosed dolphins and seals may be seen in the harbour approaches.

Respect the area as a Site of Special Scientific Interest and a Local Nature Reserve. 'Take nothing but photographs, leave nothing but footprints'.

Meanwhile the inlet is a relatively peaceful haven for pleasure craft, although plagued by the ceaseless drone of outboards. Common-sense, courtesy and a dash of good seamanship are essential with so many and varied craft at close quarters.

SHORESIDE (Telephone code 01548)

Tourist Office Market St, ☎ 843927, 🖷 842736. Open Mar–Sep Mon–Sat 1000–1700 (Sun 1600). info@salcombeinformation.co.uk; www.salcombeinformation.co.uk

What to see/do The interesting old town is invaded by vast numbers of holiday-makers. If you feel the need to break out, take the coastal path via Bolt Head to Bolt Tail and Hope Cove, a 15 mile round-robin in inspiring scenery – or perhaps a shorter version.

Rail Nearest station at Totnes (☎ 01752 221300); to Plymouth (30 mins) and Exeter (40 mins).

Buses Via Kingsbridge (25 mins), to Plymouth (1 hr), Totnes (45 mins). Western National ☎ 01752 660411.

Taxi ☎ 561577; 842914, 07976 551532.

Car hire See under Kingsbridge.

Bike hire Diventure, Island St, ☎ 843663.

Ferries Ferry Steps to East Portlemouth, 90p one way; to Kingsbridge on the tide, £6 return; and from Whitestrand to South Sands.

Beaches S of the town are super sandy beaches at S and N Sands Bays. East Portlemouth, Small's Cove, Mill Bay & Sunny Cove are on the E bank.

Supermarkets Spar on the outskirts, but in Fore St the Food Hall, daily 0830–2200, is adequate; whilst at the other end The Delicatessen, ☎ 842332, sells the tastier things in life.

000° ldg marks: Front, Pound Stone; rear, Sandhill Pt Dir WRG 2s. The gabled house is conspicuous

Banks Three in Fore St, each with cashpoints.

Restaurants From S–N in Fore St: Clare's, ☎ 842646, £13; shut Sun, except in Aug; pre-book and be punctual. Spinnakers, ☎ 843408, £14, superb views. Dusters Bistro, ☎ 842634, £12. Boatswain's Brasserie in Russell Court (alley off Fore St), ☎ 842189, £14.50. The Galley, ☎ 842828, £13.50. Regan's, ☎ 844534, £14, at 50°14´·30N 03°45´·96W (so they say!).

NAVIGATION

Charts AC 1613 (1:75,000), 1634 (1:25,000), 28 (1:12,500), SC 5602.10 (1:15,000 & 1:6,000 plan).

Approaches From the W, keep 0.5M offshore from Bolt Tail to Bolt Head. The entrance is dominated by the towering bulk of Bolt Head (128m), below which shape a course around the Mewstone rocks.

From the E, round Prawle Pt and set course direct for the Bar (see Access).

Landmarks Bolt Head's craggy massif, and 1M NW a radio mast, mark the W side of the entrance. Prawle Pt is 2.2M E of the waypoint.

Pilotage The waypoint is 50°12´·29N 03°46´·67W, on the 000° ldg line/1.35M to the front mark on Poundstone Rk and rear at Sandhill Pt. The latter is lit Dir Fl WRG 2s, W357.5°–002.5°. Maintain 000° until just past Wolf Rk SHM buoy, QG; then alter stbd 042.5° into the Fairway. At night this track is defined by ldg lts, both Q, on Scoble Pt.

Speed limit 8kn (offenders may be prosecuted), but go slower near jetties, pontoons, slipways, moorings and beaches.

Tides HW at Salcombe at sp is 10 mins after, and at nps the same as, HW Devonport. LW at nps is 5 mins before and at sp 5 mins after LW Devonport. MHWS is 5·3m, MLWS 0·7m; MHWN is 4·1m, MLWN 2·1m.

Tidal streams off the town reach 3kn on the spring ebb, although diamond 'A' indicates 1.9kn max.

Access H24 in calm weather with no swell, but the bar (greatly over-publicised since Tennyson wrote his piece) demands thought. In SE–S winds and/or swell the seas break dangerously on it, especially on the ebb below half-tide. If in doubt await HW and/or an improvement, ask the HM's advice, or divert. NB There is 2.5m depth 150m W of the 1.3m shown on the bar at the leading line.

Shelter is good on moorings and at anchorages.

VHF *Salcombe Harbour* Ch 14. *Harbour Taxi* Ch 12. *Fuel barge* Ch 06.

FACILITIES

HM's (Capt Stephen Tooke) office at Whitestrand, TQ8 8BU; ☎ 843791; 🖷 842033; VHF Ch 14. salcombe.harbour@south-hams-dc.gov.uk Open Mon–Thur 0900–1300 & 1400–1645 (Fri 1615); plus, mid-May to mid-Sep, Sat/Sun hours as for Fri.

Moorings Request a ⚓ on VHF 14 to which a hbr launch will direct you – or to a vacant local buoy. Expect to have to raft in season.

The 21 ⚓s are hard to find and identify amongst local moorings. They are not uniformly coloured, nor uniquely marked (not all have a 'V' & max

A view of the town from the north east

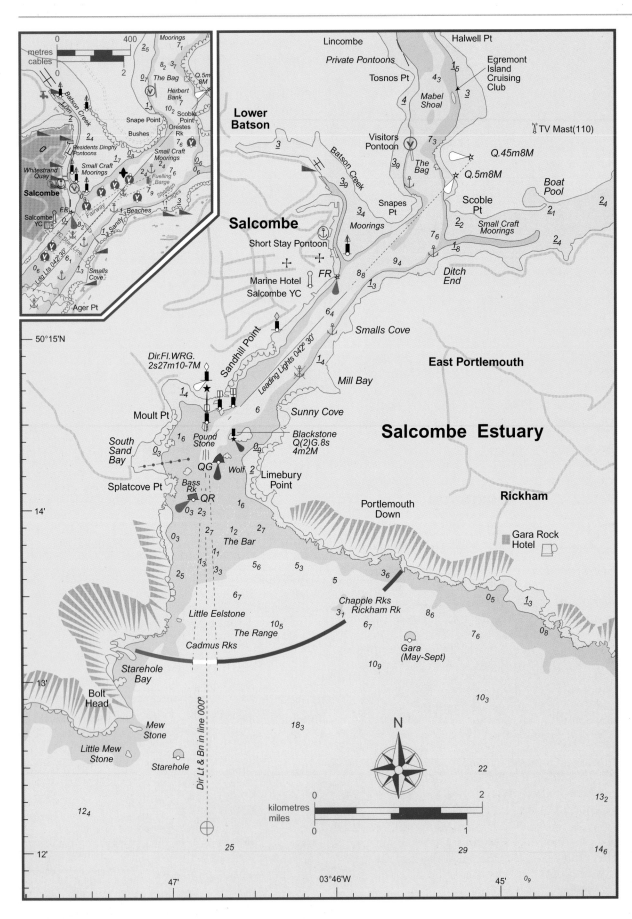

Moorings
7₁

2₅

8₂ 3₇

The Bag
0₇

Q.5m
8M

Herbert Bank
7

1₃

10₂

Scoble Point
Orestes
Rk

Snape Point

Bushes

Residents Dinghy Pontoons

2₄

Small Craft Moorings

1₇

Whitestrand Quay

Small Craft Moorings

2₄ 7₆

0₆

0₈

Fuelling Barge

2₄ 7₉

Shellfish Cages

Salcombe

Salcombe YC

FR

WC

0₉

8₂

6₁

Beaches

1₃

0₆

Ldg Lts 042°30'

1₃ Smalls Cove

Sandy

Ager Pt

Lower Batson

Lincombe

Private Pontoons

Tosnos Pt

Halwell Pt

Egremont Island Cruising Club

1₅

4₃

3

Mabel Shoal

4

Visitors Pontoon

7₃

TV Mast (110)

Q.45m8M

3₉

The Bag

Q.5m8M

Boat Pool

Salcombe

3

Batson Creek

Scoble Pt

Small Craft Moorings

2₄

3₉

Snapes Pt

3₄

2₂

2₁

Short Stay Pontoon

Moorings

7₆

2₄

1₈

Marine Hotel
Salcombe YC

FR

8₈

1₃

9₄

Ditch End

50°15'N

6₄

Smalls Cove

Short Stay Pontoon

Sandhill Point

East Portlemouth

Dir.Fl.WRG.
2s27m10-7M

1₄

Leading Lights 042°30'

1₄

Mill Bay

Moult Pt

6

Sunny Cove

Salcombe Estuary

1₆

Pound Stone

Blackstone
Q(2)G.8s
4m2M

0₉

South Sand Bay

0₃

QG

Wolf

2

Limebury Point

Rickham

Bass Rk

QR

1₆

Splatcove Pt

0₃ 2₃

2₇

1₂

Gara Rock Hotel

14'

0₃

2₇

The Bar

2₇

Portlemouth Down

1₃

1₁

5₆

5₃

0₅

1₃

2₅

3₃

5

3₆

Little Eelstone

6₇

Chapple Rks
Rickham Rk

8₆

7₆

0₈

10₅

The Range

3₁

6₇

Cadmus Rks

Gara
(May-Sept)

Starehole Bay

10₉

Bolt Head

18₃

10₃

Mew Stone

N

22

Little Mew Stone

Starehole

13₂

12₄

kilometres
miles

2

0

1

Dir Lt & Bn in line 000°

12'

25

29

14₆

47'

03°46'W

45'

0₉

LOA). This confuses visitors and makes needless work for hbr staff; it may in part explain why the latter are 'constantly harassed over many issues', to quote the Hbr Guide. See also Helford River.

Berthing A ♥ pontoon, rafted capacity 50 boats, is in The Bag, 300m N of Snapes Pt.

Off Whitestrand Quay the Normandy ♥ pontoon (first to port; min depth 1m) is for max stay of 30 mins to take on stores, fresh water; no rafting; no berthing 1900–0700. Tenders (marked T/T) can berth on the inboard side. Other pontoons/jetties in Batson Creek, which dries extensively, are for ferries and locals.

Anchorages a) Sunny Cove (ENE of Blackstone). b) W and N of Small's Cove (on the E bank facing the Marine Hotel), clear of underwater cables and the SYC start line. c) Close N of the fuel barge. d) Off the entrance to Frogmore Creek. e) West of Salt Stone. No anchoring from Sunny to Small's Coves (due to cables); nor in the fairway from abeam Marine Hotel to Salt Stone.

Tariff Daily rate/m LOA for ⚓s and ♥ pontoon: Apr–Sep £1.30; Oct–Mar £0.65. Anchoring £0.65/m.

Water taxi Call *Harbour Taxi* Ch 12, 843791; £1. May–Sep 0800–2300; other months, see HM. Water taxi also runs to/from E Portlemouth on the hour up to 2300, after the ferry stops; pre-book.

YCs Salcombe YC (SYC), ☎ 842872/842593, in its rather grand, if sepulchral, building in Cliff Road, 250m S of HM's office, offers a warm welcome, showers, bar and food – presumably in that order. Island Cruising Club (ICC), ☎ 531775, in The Bag aboard *Egremont*; showers, bar, bistro (pre-book).

Showers at SYC, 0900–2200, £1; and on *Egremont*. **Launderette** in Fore St behind Cranch's Sweet Shop; Mon–Sat 0900–1700, Sun 1000–1700.

Fuel Diesel & petrol from *Fuel barge* VHF Ch 06; ☎ 07801 798862. End Jun–mid-Sep, 0900–1700, daily. (2.5 cables E of Whitestrand).

Refuse skip is off the Normandy pontoon.

Chandlery & repairs are mostly in Island St near the top end of Batson Creek: Salcombe Boatstore, CH, Rigger ☎ 843708. Winters Marine ☎ 843580, BY, CH. Quayside Marine ☎ 844300. Starey Marine ☎ 843655; also H24 emergency repairs, ☎ 843053 and VHF Ch 13. J Alsop,

☎ 843702, SM. A Jedynak, ☎ 843321, electronic repairs. Reddish Marine, ☎ 844094, ME.

KINGSBRIDGE – 50°16´·86N 03°46´·52W
Kingsbridge is a pleasant market town, 'capital' of the South Hams area of S Devon. The bias is more towards agriculture than seafaring, since its creek dries completely. But on the tide it is an attractive river jaunt for shoal draught boats or more adventurous fin keelers.

SHORESIDE (Telephone code 01548)
Tourist Office ☎ 853195, 🖷 854185. Mon–Sat 0900–1730, Sun 1000–1600. advice@ kingsbridgeinfo.co.uk; www.kingsbridgeinfo.co.uk
Mace Foodstore, turn left 100m past Tourist Office; also Somerfield in town. A fair selection of eateries and pubs. Banks & cashpoints. Wills Marine, ☎ 852424, is the chandlery. Car hire, SMG Motors, ☎ 843600.

Navigation HW is 5 mins after HW Salcombe. From The Bag the 2.5M channel is navigable HW±2½ to the basin drying up to 3.4m. Above Salt Stone SHM beacon it is marked by R/W perches (ignore the red PHM buoys which slowly diverge starboard into Balcombe Creek), and by small PHM buoys in the final reach. See AC 28. A prior recce by dinghy/ferry may be instructive.

Berthing HM Salcombe may be able to advise on berth availability. Shoal draught boats, max LOA 11m, berth off the E bank on a ♥ pontoon (outboard at its S end) which is often cluttered by small craft. Deep draught (up to 1.5m) boats sink into soft mud against the West wall, between two pairs of iron ladders which stand proud of the wall; fender board advised; no bollards. There is a broad slipway at the S end of the W wall.

Kingsbridge. The west quay where fin-keelers could 'park' next to the car park

DARTMOUTH

Harbour entrance – 50°20´·50N 03°33´·75W

Dartmouth is always an impressive, but totally straightforward, entrance through a chink in the Devon hills. Frank Cowper thought otherwise: 'Dartmouth is the most baffling, anxious place I know to enter' – having had a snarl-up with a tug.

As you pass the Castle, the town first opens to port and then ahead. Next the Britannia Royal Naval College (BRNC) heaves into view, majestically commanding the estuary. Turning further to starboard, the little village of Kingswear is seen clinging to the steep slopes of the E bank. All is now revealed.

The Dart, rising high on Dartmoor, is a charming and interesting river and its lower reaches can readily be explored on the tide to Totnes; an ideal inland mini-cruising ground, when it's foul at sea.

SHORESIDE (Telephone code 01803)

Tourist Office The Engine House, Mayor's Ave. ☎ 834224; 🖾 835631. Mon–Sat 0900–1730;

Sun 1000–1600. enquiries@dartmouth-information.fsnet.co.uk; www.dartmouth-information.co.uk

What to see/do Guided tour of BRNC, via Tourist Office. Dartmouth Museum, on the half-timbered Butterwalk, ☎ 832923, is full of nautical memorabilia. Reach Dartmouth Castle by walking 1M past cobbled Bayard's Cove or by ferry; 1000–1800. The steam train from Kingswear to Paignton is a fun trip and a useful connection to mainline trains.

Rail From Paignton a branch line to Newton Abbot connects with trains for Plymouth or Exeter and London (Waterloo or Paddington).

Buses No 91 Dartmouth–Totnes (45 mins). Kingswear-Brixham, No 22, No 24 (17 mins).

Entrance to the River Dart, looking west

RN college

Dartmouth Castle

Kingswear Castle

No 120, to Torquay (55 mins). Timetables from buses or the Tourist Office.

Taxi ☎ 833522; 833778; 832526; 07968 760613; 834407.

Car hire AMMB ☎ 834255/833277.

Bike hire Hot Pursuit, 44 Fore St, Totnes; ☎ 865174.

Ferries from seaward: Lower car ferry, near DYC to Kingswear. Passenger ferry, Town jetty to Kingswear. Shuttle ferry, Town jetty to Dittisham via Dart and Noss Marinas. Higher car ferry (on cables, avoid) from near Dart Marina to east bank. Dittisham to Greenway, VHF Ch 10, ☎ 844010.

Beaches Blackpool Sands, near Stoke Fleming 2M SW, is the nearest beach; 25 mins by No 93 bus.

Supermarket Plymco, Mon–Sat 0800–2100, Sun 1000–1600. Somerfield, Fairfax Place; Mon–Sat 0800–2000, Sun 1000–1600.

Market day Fri in Market Sq; Tues, lesser market.

Banks NatWest, Lloyds & HSBC, with cashpoints. Nil in Kingswear.

Restaurants Sails, ☎ 839281, S Embankment above DYC; brilliant food £12, friendly service, modern surroundings, with splendid river and sea views. Anzac St Bistro, ☎ 835515, £11.50; by the church. Hooked, ☎ 831022, three-course dinner £19.50; shut Mon. Hauleys (Dart Marina Hotel), ☎ 832580; set £18.95. Carved Angel, ☎ 832465; three-course dinner £42. Carved Angel Café, 11 Foss St; ☎ 834842. Everyday, but imaginative eating, dinner Thur–Sat. Spice Bazaar (Indian) £9, ☎ 832285, St Saviour's Square.

NAVIGATION

Charts AC 1613 (1:75,000), 1634 (1:25,000), 2253 (1:6,250), SC 5602.11 (1:8,000 plan) & .12 to Totnes.

Approaches From the S/SW, after passing Start Point make for the waypoint, keeping E or W of Skerries Bank. From the N/NE, keep seaward of rocks between Berry Head and the Mew Stone; see Passage Notes.

Dartmouth Castle to port and the town beyond

Landmarks 8.5 cables E of the harbour entrance, a Day Beacon (grey obelisk, 24m high, 167m amsl) is conspic, unless lost in the cloudbase. Dartmouth Castle is on the port side of the harbour entrance.

Pilotage The waypoint is 50°19′·53N 03°32′·88W, 328°/1.2M to the harbour entrance, 150m wide. Pass between Homestone PHM and Castle Ledge SHM buoys. Western Blackstone (2m) is visible to port; Checkstone is marked by a PHM buoy. In fog the entrance is readily navigated on radar.

At night stay in the W sector, 325°–331°, of the Iso WRG 3s, Kingswear directional light. A second directional light at Bayard's Cove, Fl WRG 2s, will bring you in on 293°, if need be. (When leaving, stay in the W sector, 102°–107°, of a FW light opposite Dartmouth Castle). In the harbour are many two FG/FR (vert); up-river, only Anchor Stone, Fl (2) R 5s, and Stoke Gabriel beacon QG.

Speed limit in the harbour and up-river is 6kn, but 'Dead Slow' in the last mile to Totnes.

Homestone buoy and the Day Beacon

Tides Dartmouth is a Standard Port. Predictions for the entrance and differences for Dittisham and Totnes are given in the *RNA*. MHWS is 4·9m, MLWS 0·6m; MHWN is 3·8m, MLWN 2·0m.

Tidal streams outside the harbour set weakly NE/SW. Within the harbour they follow the fairway, max rate abeam the Castle is 1.5kn springs.

Access H24, but care is needed in strong SE'lies.

Shelter The harbour is virtually land-locked and provides excellent shelter, as does the Dart itself.

Fuel barge, N of No 6 buoy: Diesel/petrol, 0800–1800 in season. VHF Ch 06 *Dart Crusader*; ☎ 07801 798861. Dart marina is the only other diesel source.

VHF *Dartnav* Ch 11. Marinas Ch 80. Fuel Ch 06.

Water taxi *The Maid* VHF Ch 69, ☎ 07970 346571.

FACILITIES

The Dart Harbour and Navigation Authority (DHNA), Oxford St, the S Embankment, is where the **HM** (Capt Simon Dowden) reigns supreme. ☎ 832337, 🖷 833631. Out of hrs emergency ☎ 835220. Mon–Wed 0900–1700 (Thur 1800, Fri 1600, Sat 1200; Sun shut). *Dartnav* Ch 11. dhna@dartharbour.org.uk; www.dartharbour.org.uk

Berths The three marinas are listed separately below. DHNA provides ✪ jetties, ✪ pontoons (identified by blue flags) & approx 200 ✪s, plus anchorages, as follows from seaward, W bank then E bank (NB 'a' to 'g' are annotated on the chartlet):
a) ✪ **pontoon**, linked to S Embankment. Max LOA 9.1m. Raft four deep outboard; tenders inboard.
b) **Town Jetty**, S Embankment. Raft on inboard side during the day; plus outboard 1700–0900. Electricity, FW.
c) ✪ **pontoon**, detached, just N of Town Jetty.
d) **Pontoon/jetty**, just S of Higher ferry. ✪ berths at N tip inboard side, linked to shore.
e) **Pontoon**, detached and parallel to (d). ✪ berths at N tip outboard side.
f) **Quayside** berthing against the wall is possible at S & N Embankments, but not advised for small yachts/cruisers; fender board essential.
g) **East bank** Two ✪ pontoons, opposite (e) on E side of fairway. Max LOA 24m in 6–7m depths.
h) ✪s, light blue with black 'V', are well dispersed and include those off Dittisham and Stoke Gabriel. Call *Dartnav* **VHF** 11 for directions to a vacant ✪.

Anchorages Mainly off Dartmouth, between the yellow big-ship buoys (avoid their ground tackle, as on AC 2253) and Darthaven Marina and trots further N. Also up-river clear of the main channel. Anchoring is prohibited off Sandquay and Noss Point where big ships turn, and off Dittisham. If in doubt, ask a hbr launch VHF Ch 11.

DHNA Tariff Four daily rates £/m LOA, including Harbour dues and VAT, apply as follows: £1.50 at (b) see adjoining column. £1.25 at (a) and (d). £1 at (c) and (e) to (g); and £1 on a ✪ and at anchor.

YCs Dartmouth YC, ☎ 832305, at S Embankment. Bar, showers and a warm welcome. Royal Dart YC, ☎ 752272, at Kingswear. Short-stay ✪ pontoon, welcoming bar, restaurant & showers.

Chandlery & repairs Shipmates, ☎ 839292, CH. Calibra, ☎ 833094, Foss St; CH, Rigging, Electronics. Dartmouth Dock Services, ☎ 832776, CH.

MARINAS

1. Darthaven Marina (Kingswear). ☎ 752545; 🖷 752722. Manager John Holman. 0830–1800 7/7. darthaven@darthaven.co.uk; www.darthaven.co.uk Berth as directed or on twin ✪ pontoons S of the marina. The outer pontoon is part of Darthaven, the inner is shared with DHNA for short-stay berthing <2 hrs on the inboard side; landing only (no berthing) on the outboard side.

Tariff Daily rate £2.35/m, inc hbr dues and VAT.

Electricity Normally included in the berthing fee.

Showers (free) & **launderette,** access by code.

Fuel None. Refuel at Dart Marina or Fuel barge.

Chandlery & repairs Chandlery, ☎ 752733; 🖷 752790. On-site boatyard: repairs, ME. Chris Hoyle Marine, ☎ 752221; outboards.

Facilities Kingswear village stores; Mon–Sat 0700–1800, Sun 0830–1300. Ship Inn (C15), good bar food. Zanne's Bistro and takeaway.

2. Dart Marina (W bank, just above Higher car ferry). ☎ 833351, 🖷 835150. Manager Tony Tucker. marinas@dartmarina.com; www.dartmarina.com VHF Ch 80.

Tariff Daily rate £3.44/m, inc Hbr dues & VAT; the highest fees between Poole and Isles of Scilly.

Electricity £2.35 per night.

Showers, baths and **launderette.**

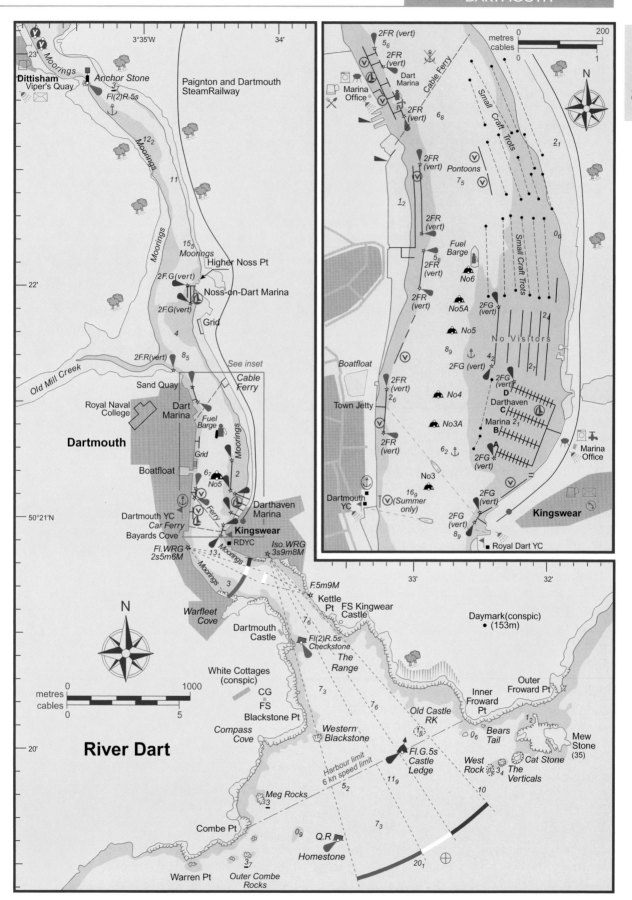

3°35'W
34'
23'

Dittisham
Viper's Quay
Moorings
Anchor Stone
Fl(2)R.5s

Paignton and Dartmouth
SteamRailway

2FR (vert)
5₆
2FR (vert)
Dart Marina
Cable Ferry

metres 0 200
cables 0 1

Marina Office

Moorings
12₂

2FR (vert)
6₈

Small Craft Trots

N

11

2FR (vert)

2₁

Moorings

Pontoons
7₅

15₅
Moorings
Higher Noss Pt
2F.G (vert)
Noss-on-Dart Marina
2F.G(vert)
Grid
4

2FR (vert)
1₂

2FR (vert)
5₈
Fuel Barge
No6

Small Craft Trots

0₆

22'

2F.R (vert)
8₅
See inset
Cable Ferry

2FR (vert)
No5A
2FG (vert)

2FR (vert)
No5
2₄

Old Mill Creek

Sand Quay
Royal Naval College
Dartmouth
Dart Marina
Fuel Barge
Grid
Boatfloat
6₇₀
No5
2

Boatfloat
Town Jetty

2FR (vert)
2₆
No4

8₉
4₂
2FG (vert)

No Visitors
7₁
2₇

2FG (vert)
D
Darthaven
C
Marina 2₁
B

50°21'N
Dartmouth YC
Car Ferry
Bayards Cove
Fl.WRG 2s5m6M
Moorings
Ferry
Darthaven Marina
Kingswear
RDYC
Iso.WRG 3s9m8M
13₁

2FR (vert)
No3A

2FR (vert)
6₂
2FG (vert)
A

Marina Office

Moorings
3

No3
16₉
(Summer only)

2FG (vert)

Kingswear

Dartmouth YC
2FG (vert)
8₉
Royal Dart YC

Warfleet Cove

F.5m9M
Kettle Pt
FS Kingwear Castle
33'
32'

N

Dartmouth Castle
Fl(2)R.5s
Checkstone
The Range
7₆

Daymark(conspic)
• (153m)

metres 0 1000
cables 0 5

White Cottages (conspic)
CG
FS
Blackstone Pt

7₃

Compass Cove

Western Blackstone

Inner Froward Pt
Old Castle RK
0₈

Outer Froward Pt

1₂
Bears Tail

Mew Stone (35)

River Dart

20'

Fl.G.5s
Castle Ledge

West Rock
3₄
Cat Stone
The Verticals

Harbour limit
6 kn speed limit
5₂
11₉

10

Meg Rocks
3

Combe Pt

0₉
Q.R
Homestone

7₃

20₁
⊕

Warren Pt
Outer Combe Rocks
3₇

The Royal Naval College commands the river. The Royal Dart YC is to starboard

Fuel Diesel at fuel berth, second pontoon from the S.

Chandlery & repairs See Noss-on-Dart.

Services Bike hire £11.75 per day.

3. Noss-on-Dart Marina (E bank, 0.5M N of Dart Marina); both are run by the same company, with the same ☎/✉ Nos. *Noss Marina* VHF Ch 80. Noss is rather more workaday than the sybaritic luxury downstream. Rafting is the norm.

Tariff Daily rate £2.55/m on pontoons, inc VAT & hbr dues.

Electricity £2.35 per night.

Showers and **launderette.**

Fuel Diesel from Dart marina.

Chandlery & repairs Dart Chandlers ☎ 833772. Marine Services, ☎/✉ 833343; Mob 07768 815872.

UP THE DART

Navigation *The DHNA Handbook*, £2, contains detailed, illustrated directions to be used with AC 2253. Dartmouth (BRNC) to Totnes bridge is ±10M so start about HW−3; leave Anchor Stone to port.

Dittisham (*Ditchem*) is a peaceful spot for a night or two on a ✿, light blue with black 'V'. The Ferry Boat Inn, ☎ 722368, on the water's edge, or the

Red Lion, ☎ 722235, up the hill will wine/dine you. Across the river visit Greenway, Agatha Christie's house and garden; Wed–Sat, 1030–1700, £2.75. Off Stoke Gabriel Creek are ✿s. Keep to the outside of the two buoyed S-bends up-river to Berry Rock. Home Reach is about 50m wide, enough to pass tourist boats; there are no commercial ships.

Totnes On the W bank dry out in soft mud at Baltic Wharf BY at a 30m pontoon; pre-call ☎ 867922. Daily rate £/m LOA, inc showers, FW & electricity: <9.1m = 14.69; >9.1m = 17.62. The Steam Packet Inn, ☎ 863880, close upstream, has four free ❶ berths alongside, drying to soft mud; electricity, restaurant, bar food, real ales.

Beyond the Steam Packet the river is divided by Vire Island. In the left arm drying berths belong to Baltic Wharf BY; the bottom is glutinous mud, sloping in places, but just usable by bilge keelers. On the E bank dry out against Steamer Quay, run by South Hams DC and DHNA (no showers, FW or electricity; harbour dues may not be collected). Keep clear of tourist boats which berth at the N end of Steamer Quay.

Lack of space precludes a description of this old and interesting town. Tourist Office, Coronation Rd; ☎ 863168; ✉ 865771; enquire@totnesinfo.org.uk; www.totnesinfo.org.uk

BRIXHAM

Harbour entrance – 50°24´·31N 03°30´·86W

The harbour is well laid out. Fishing boats and yachts co-exist peacefully

Brixham is an honest working port onto which a marina was successfully grafted in 1989. Stir in the seasonal ingredient of tourists and you have an appealing hotchpotch of character with the rough edges for all to see. 'Roll up, roll up all the fun of the fair ...' could well be Brixham's motto.

Brixham trawlers long epitomised fishing. One of the last gaff-rigged trawlers, *Vigilance*, built in 1926, still sails out of Brixham; call ☎ 07764 845353 to book a trip or visit her on the Town pontoon.

Halfway up Tor Bay Paignton is notable only for its zoo and traffic jams, whilst Torquay at the northern end offers shelter beneath a veneer of glossy tourism.

SHORESIDE (Telephone code 01803)

The Tourist Office is in front of the inner harbour. ☎ 0906 680 1268; ✉ 852939. Open in season Mon–Sat 0930–1800; Sun 1000–1800.

What to see/do Walk out to Berry Head Nature Reserve (seabirds), Napoleonic forts and terrific views. Replica of Drake's tiny, round-the-world

Golden Hind in the inner harbour. And on a wet day, the Heritage Museum, New Rd, ☎ 856267 with an interesting Maritime Gallery.

Rail The nearest station is Paignton.

The inner harbour and Golden Hind

Bus 12/A to Paignton/Torquay. 22 to Kingswear.

Taxi ☎ 883883; 853000; 856367.

Car hire Chief Vehicle Rentals ☎ 663838.

Beaches Breakwater Beach at the root of Victoria Breakwater is the nearest to the marina; pebble/shingle & good facilities. Shoalstone Beach, 300m E, is shingle/rock with a seawater swimming pool & good facilities. Fishcombe Cove and Churston Cove both have quiet sand/shingle beaches.

Supermarkets Somerfield and Co-Op in Fore St; both Mon–Sat 8–8, Sun 0900–1800.

Market Indoor Pannier Market Tues & Fri in Market St. Fish market 0600–0900, Mon–Fri, Fish Quay.

Banks All the usual, with cashpoints, in Fore St.

Restaurants Quayside Hotel, King St (pink hotel overlooking the inner hbr), ☎ 855751; £14. Pilgrims, ☎ 853983, 64b Fore St (above Lloyds bank); £12.50, shut Mon. Armada, 14 The Quay, ☎ 853418; £13. Poop Deck, 15 The Quay, ☎ 858681; £12.50. Beamers, 19–20 The Quay, ☎ 854777; £11. See also Brixham YC.

NAVIGATION

Charts AC 1613 (1:75,000), 3315 (1:75,000), 1634 (1:25,000), 26 (1:12,500 with 1:7,500 inset), plus SC 5602.5 (1:75,000 with 1:7,500 inset).

Approaches From the S, keep a safe offing from Skerries Bank (NNE of Start Pt) and rocks between Dartmouth and Berry Head. From the E, Tor Bay is not easy to identify, except on radar, until quite close; two tall radio masts behind Paignton give general guidance. From the N, keep seaward of Ore Stone, off Hope's Nose. In the near approach expect to encounter large ships at anchor. The shores of the Bay are mostly marked by small SPM buoys, indicating Controlled Areas (swimming, water ski etc); speed limit 5kn.

Landmarks Berry Head's vertical cliff, 1.3M E of the hbr, is a good radar return and conspic from S & N. Victoria breakwater's white lt ho is conspic. The MOD vessel, *Longbow*, for so long moored by the lt ho, is due to go elsewhere in 2004.

Pilotage Most yachts track direct to the head of Victoria breakwater; but at night/in poor visibility go via 50°24′·58N 03°31′·00W, in the white sector of the Dir Iso WRG 5s 6M; thence 159°/0.3M to the hbr entrance, plus 0.4M through the buoyed/lit fairway to the marina entrance.

Tides Use differences for Torquay.

Tidal streams in Tor Bay are very weak.

Access H24, at all tides.

Shelter Tor Bay is well sheltered from W'lies and large vessels often anchor there. The harbour is exposed only to strong NNW'lies, when a short sea makes the Town and Events pontoons very uncomfortable. The marina however is well protected by a wavebreak. Long term plans for a breakwater (North Arm) across the entrance from Battery Pt toward Victoria breakwater would be a huge benefit for all.

Brixham

The Town pontoon and Events pontoon lie close SW of the marina

VHF *Brixham Marina* Ch 80; *Brixham Hbr* Ch 12; *Brixham YC* Ch M.

Anchorages Fishcombe Cove is delightful, close W of Battery Pt; ⚓ inside the Y buoy in about 3m on sand/shingle. It is also possible to anchor free of charge in the outer harbour, if space can be found clear of the fairway and local moorings.

FACILITIES

The **HM**'s (Capt Paul Labistour) office overlooks the FV Basin. ☎ 853321, 🖷 852434; brixham.harbour@ torbay.gov.uk; www.tor-bay-harbour.co.uk Mon–Fri 0900–1700; Sat/Sun 1000–1300.

Berthing Three options: a) The marina; b) The town pontoon; and c) the YC's two ❶ pontoons. The inner harbour dries and has no ❶ berths. Note that the two long, N/S parallel pontoons lie close W of the marina's 'A' & 'B' pontoons: The E'ly is the marina's Events pontoon; the W'ly is the HM's town pontoon. Both are lit 2FR (vert).

Marina, Victoria Breakwater and Torquay in the distance

a) **Marina**, Manager Neil Salter, plus his friendly team. ☎ 882929, 🖷 882737. Open 0900–1730, Mon–Fri; Dock Office open H24; mobile 07740 806034. brixham@mdlmarinas.co.uk; www.marinas.co.uk

Tariff Daily rate £/m LOA on fingers: 1.95 <10m; 2.20 >10m. 20p less berthed/rafted on the Events pontoon (no FW/electricity). Short stay, <4 hrs = £5.

Electricity £2.50/day.

Showers free; **launderette** is coin operated.

Fuel Diesel from barge at end of 'C' pontoon, 0900–1800 Apr–Sep; also water, if berthed on the marina's Events pontoon. Petrol from garages only.

b) **Town pontoon** Call *Brixham Harbour* asap Ch 12 for a berth. Daily rate £1.10/m LOA, inc FW. Short stay <3 hrs free. **Electricity**: £2 (10kW card).

c) **Brixham YC** Two 10m long ❶ pontoons in front of the YC; no electricity/FW; daily rate £0.82/m LOA. Welcoming bar & restaurant. Showers 50p.

Brixham CG overlooks the inner harbour and, if not too busy, welcomes interested yachtsmen.

CHANDLERY & REPAIR FACILITIES

The Boat Shop, CH, ☎ 850582 (near the Events pontoon). Brixham Yacht Supplies, Middle St, CH; Mon–Sat 0900–1730, Sun 1000–1600. There is a grid in the inner harbour. CCS Marine, King St, ☎ 883444; electronics.

TORQUAY

SHM buoy off Harbour entrance – 50°27´·42N 03°31´·80W

The potential for a close encounter at the harbour entrance is obvious

Torquay markets itself as 'The English Riviera' – which slightly taxes the imagination. True, palm trees and white buildings do sprout in this popular seaside resort, but they also proliferate elsewhere in Devon and Cornwall.

Torquay paradoxically suffers an unusually high crime rate, evidently fuelled by drugs and alcohol. Some locals even fear to be in the pedestrianised Fleet Walk shopping precinct after dark.

To improve this Jekyll and Hyde image, Torquay is undergoing a major, if largely cosmetic, facelift. The centrepiece inner harbour no longer bares its muddy bottom; water is retained H24 by a sill at the entrance which is crossed by a lifting foot-bridge. Small boats now bob at their moorings, more tourist attractions have been installed, streets cleaned up – for £21 million by the end of 2004. Does this get to the root of the problem?

SHORESIDE (Telephone code 01803)

Tourist Office is on Vaughan Parade. ☎ 0906 680 1268; 🖷 214885; torquaytic@torbay.gov.uk;

www.torbay.gov.uk Summer hours: Mon–Sat 0930 (Sun 1000)–1800.

What to see/do Agatha Christie is the local lady made good, and a gallery in Torquay Museum is devoted to her life and detective novels. Kents Cavern, ENE of the marina, is a palaeolithic site where half a million years ago cavemen and dinosaurs walked. Paignton Zoo is just that, and a good one too. Its managers will also run *Living Coasts*, a quasi-educational display of marine life along the tide-line – part of Torquay's facelift. Babbacombe Model Village intrigues all ages. The ruined Torre Abbey is set in parkland NW of the marina, great for a picnic or to visit Abbey Mansion which among other things houses Agatha Christie's reconstructed study.

Rail The station is on a branch line from Paignton

to Newton Abbot for mainline trains to Penzance, London and the North West.

Buses Timetables from the Tourist Office. Heavy summer traffic greatly delays some services.

Taxi ☎ 213521; 211611.

Car hire Hertz, ☎ 294786, at the railway station. A J Blacker, ☎ 400808. Laburnham, ☎ 292300.

Bike hire Simply The Bike, 101/2 Belgrave Rd, ☎ 200024.

Pleasure boats to Paignton, Brixham and the Dart.

Beaches W of the marina: Torre Abbey Sands, the nearest and largest except at HW. Easy access from a busy road; cafés, ice cream vans, WCs, shops to hand. Livermead Sands (also shingle), good access but popular with water skiers etc. E of the marina: Meadfoot Beach, pebble/sand, rock pools at LW, easy access, bus X80; WCs, café. N of Hope's Nose: Anstey's Cove, shingle/rock, steep access, good anchorage in offshore winds; WCs, café. Babbacombe Beach, sand/shingle, moderate access by bus; WCs, café; good anchorage in offshore winds. Oddicombe Beach, sand/shingle, easy access by bus & cliff lift; WCs, café.

Supermarkets Iceland in the Union Square Mall is the only one within walking distance; plus a number of small Spar branches. Basic needs in the Marina Dockmaster's office.

Banks Plenty with cashpoints in Fleet Walk/Union St.

Restaurants No 7 Fish Bistro, ☎ 295055 (just below the RTYC), super fresh fish £12. Café Sol, 1 Palk St, behind the marina; relaxed, but more than a Café, £14, ☎ 296090. Marina Restaurant, ☎ 292255, is convenient, £11.75. Imperial Hotel,

The Old Harbour before its facelift

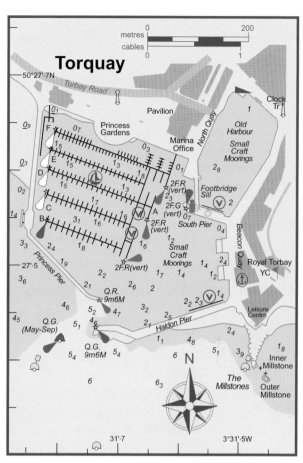

☎ 294301, £16–23. Howlers, ☎ 296421, 248 Union St (top of hill), £13.50. The London Inn, by the clock tower, does good food most evenings at reasonable prices.

NAVIGATION

Charts AC 3315 (1:75,000), 1613 (1:75,000), 26 (1:12,500 with 1:4,000 inset), plus SC 5602.5 (1:75,000 with 1:4,000 inset).

Approaches From the S, keep a safe distance off Berry Head, thence direct. From the E, Tor Bay is not easy to identify, except on radar, until fairly close; two tall radio masts W of Paignton provide some guidance. From the N, keep seaward of Ore Stone and inshore rocks to the W of it.

Off Tor Bay expect to find large ships at anchor. The shores of the Bay are mostly marked by small SPM buoys, indicating Controlled Areas (swimming, water ski etc); speed limit 5kn.

Landmarks Large white hotels and other bldgs, inc Princess Theatre at the harbour's NW corner.

Pilotage The waypoint is 50°27′·02N 03°31′·80W, 000°/0.4M to a seasonal SHM buoy, QG, (Lat/Long under title) off the hbr entrance.

To reduce the collision risk in the 40m wide, semi-blind entrance: Slow down, 5kn max. On arrival turn close round the SHM buoy onto E; then hug Haldon Pierhead (white paint) until the harbour opens up. Departing vessels keep close to Princess Pierhead and turn wide around the SHM buoy.

Tides HW Torquay at sp is 45 mins and at nps 25 mins after HW Devonport. LW at nps is the same as, and at sp 10 mins after, LW Devonport. MHWS 4·9m, MLWS 0·7m; MHWN is 3·7m, MLWN 2·0m.

Tidal streams in Tor Bay are very weak.

Access H24 at all tides, but in strong SE'lies seas rebound off the piers – Brixham would be easier.

Shelter Good in the Harbour.

Anchorage 3–4 cables outside the harbour in an arc from SE to SW, but only in offshore winds. No anchoring in the harbour.

VHF *Torquay Harbour* Ch 14. *Torquay Marina* Ch 80. *Riviera Fuels* Ch M (see under Facilities).

IPTS At Haldon Pierhead: Three R balls by day or three R lts (vert) at night = No entry, navigational hazard.

FACILITIES

The HM (Capt Kevin Mowat) is at Beacon Quay; ☎ 292429, 🖷 299257, Emergency ☎ 550405. Mon–Fri, 0900–1700, Sat/Sun 1000–1300.

Berthing There are three options:

1. **Torquay Marina** Manager Neil Salter. ☎ 200210; 🖷 200225; Mobile 07779 556651. VHF Ch 80. Hrs Mon–Fri 0900–1730. Dockmasters office H24. A well equipped and friendly marina. ❶ berth on 'A' pontoon, or as directed. torquaymarina@mdlmarinas.co.uk; www.marinas.co.uk

    Tariff Daily rate £2.20/m LOA. Short stay <4 hrs, £10. **Electricity** £2.50/night.

    Showers very good and free; plus **launderette.**

2. **Outer Harbour** ❶ pontoon at the inner end of Haldon Pier; run by HM. £1.10/m LOA.

    Showers Near the HM's office. Limited electricity, one FW tap.

3. **Old (inner) Harbour** which no longer dries. ❶ pontoon in 2m on the N side of the S Pier. Across the entrance a wall with flapgate retains depths of 1m to 2.8m. Above it a footbridge with lifting centre section opens on request Ch 14 when the flapgate is in use, approx HW–3½ to +3, 0700 to 2300, Apr–Sept. It is illegal to pass under the bridge when it is not open.

Fuel Diesel, petrol & LPG 0830–1800 from *Torquay Fuel*, VHF Ch M; S side of South Pier, ☎ 294509.

YC The Royal Torbay YC, ☎ 292006, has an elegant Georgian clubhouse, 12 Beacon Terrace, SE corner of the outer hbr. admin@ royaltorbayyc.org.uk; www.royaltorbayyc.org.uk The restaurant, ☎ 295009 opens Wed & Fri, 1900–2230; and daily for lunch. Showers, free or donate. Torbay Royal Regatta is in late August.

Chandlery & repairs Torquay Chandlers (in the Pavilion), ☎ 211854; open 7/7. Coastal Chandlery, 7 Palk St (near Tourist Office), ☎ 211190. Brixham and Dartmouth offer a range of repair facilities.

The Royal Torbay extends a friendly welcome

TEIGNMOUTH

Harbour entrance (130m NE of The Ness) – 50°32´.34N 03°29´.72W

Teignmouth (pronounced *'Tinmuth'*) is a pleasing mixture of Victorian seaside gentility, handsome Regency townhouses, fishing boats hauled up on the Back Beach and a workaday commercial port. Shaldon on the south side of the harbour is a picturesque village with some worthy pubs.

The slightly intimidating approach channel lies between shifting sand banks – but take heart: 1,500 ton coasters of 5m max draught routinely wend their way up to the commercial quays. The Salty, a large bank drying 3.3m, and the low bridge to Shaldon limit the waterspace inside the harbour.

If ever that elusive commodity 'local knowledge' was needed, it is here. To acquire it, a land recce at LW is revealing. Then call the ever-helpful HM for an update, or better still visit him to study aerial photographs of the entrance taken over the years: A certain pattern emerges in the movement of the banks. History doth repeat itself...

SHORESIDE (Telephone code 01626)

Tourist Office is inshore of the pier. ☎ 215666; 🖷 778333. In season Mon–Sat 0900–1700; Sun 1030–1630.

What to see/do The Templar Way is an 18M walk from Teignmouth to Haytor (Dartmoor); it can be reduced by bus links. Experience the ferry to Shaldon and take the Smugglers Tunnel to Ness

beach to fish, swim and sunbathe. On a wet day the Museum, by the station, regales visitors with local stories; Mon–Sat 1000–1630, Sun 1400–1630. The 1690 attack by the French is commemorated in Shaldon every Wed (May–Sep) when residents in C18 costumes run stalls and entertainments.

Rail The station is on the Penzance–London line.

Buses Nos 85, 85A & 85C to Exeter (55 mins) and Torquay (30 mins).

Take your pick. Shaldon beyond

Taxi ☎ 779079; 776396; 777922; 776011.

Car & bike hire See the Tourist Office.

Ferry Since the 13th century a passenger ferry has plied between Teignmouth and Shaldon beaches. The black & white gunwales emulate Elizabethan galleons. £1 single, Mon–Sat 0800 (Sun 0900)–2200. ☎ 873060; 07880 713420.

Beaches Red sandy beaches are N & S of the pier.

Supermarkets Co-op, Higher Brook St East; Mon–Sat 0800–2200, Sun 0900–1500. A smaller Co-op is in Bank St, further south.

Banks The usual, with cashpoints, around the centre.

Launderette George St, 0700–1930. Supawash, 100 Bitton Park Rd; 7/7 0700–1900.

Restaurants Bay Hotel, ☎ 774123, £12. Goodfillas, 1st floor, ☎ 776999, £9.50. Dukes, ☎ 774652, £10. Shaldon: La Provence, ☎ 872384.

NAVIGATION

Charts AC 3315 (1:75,000), 26 (1:7,500); and SC 5602.5 (1:75,000 & 1:7,500 plan).

Approaches From the S, E and NE make for a big yellow outfall buoy, 104°/1.3M from The Ness.

Close the waypoint 50°32´·34N 03°29´·07W in about 5m depth with caution, as it may not relate to the latest situation. Inshore features can be identified with binos.

Landmarks The Ness, a high red sandstone cliff is conspic S of the entrance. To the N, the town and St Michael's church tower are easily seen.

Pilotage In July 2002 the entry channel (dredged to approx 0.5 to 1.0m) lay 270°/090° between Pole Sand and East Pole Sand, whose S edge was marked by a yellow conical SPM buoy (treated as a starboard-hand buoy). The N edge of Pole Sand was identified by three tiny, nondescript buoys laid by the pilots. These unofficial buoys could at

The Ness glows in early morning sunlight

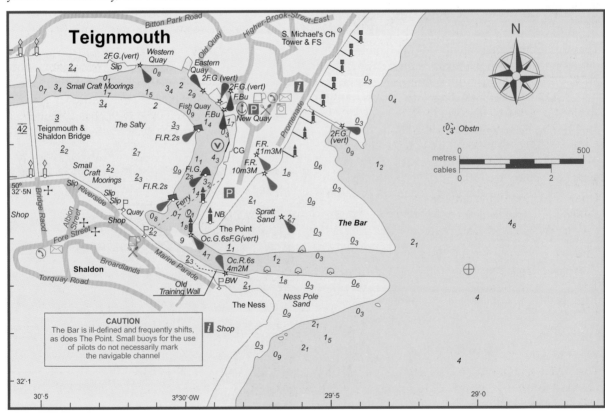

Tiny, nondescript buoys are laid by the pilots

Looking seaward past The Point bn, training wall bn & The Ness

that time be treated as port-hand buoys. NB The past tense indicates that all or any of this data may have changed; pre-check with HM. Disregard: Various yellow spherical buoys marking inshore bathing areas; the FR lts SW of the pier; and the F Bu lts by New Quay – neither pair are leading lts.

From the waypoint the pilot buoys, if in place, should be visible. Ditto the white beacon, Oc R 6s, on the training wall to port and a tall green lattice beacon, Oc G 6s, beyond and to starboard on the end of The Point. Keep mid-channel and once abeam the Oc G 6s beacon alter smartly onto 030° for the ❶ pontoon. It is by no means as difficult as you might imagine. Speed limit 10kn.

Tides HW Teignmouth at sp is 40 mins and at nps 25 mins after HW Devonport. LW at nps and sp is the same as LW Devonport. MHWS is 4·8m, MLWS 0·6m; MHWN is 3·6m, MLWN 1·9m.

Tidal streams outside the bar set NNE from HW Devonport $-1\frac{1}{2}$, and SSW from $+5\frac{1}{4}$. Inside the Bar the in-going stream begins at $-5\frac{1}{2}$ and out-going at $+\frac{3}{4}$. Off The Point streams reach 4–5kn with eddies/overfalls forming when >3kn. Hence it is safest to arrive near slack water.

Access Avoid springs, enter at HW–1. Don't try it at night (there are better things to do) nor in E'lies > F3 when the entrance breaks dangerously.

Shelter is good inside, but in a fresh W'ly it may be choppy near HW when The Salty is covered.

VHF *Teignmouth Port Radio* Ch 12; not H24.

FACILITIES

The **HM**'s (Ian Hayward) office is next to the New Quay Inn. Hours 0800–2000. ☎ 773165, 07810 615009,

07796 178456 in emergency, ✉ 770317. VHF 12. teignmouthharbourmaster@eclipse.co.uk

Berthing A 20m ❶ pontoon in 2–3m has replaced the two charted ⚓s. Two 9m boats can berth either side, plus rafting if calm. Land on the beach.

Tariff Daily rate £/m LOA on ❶ pontoon/rafted: £0.90; weekly rate £5.40.

Anchorage No room in the harbour to anchor afloat; but a bilge keeler could dry out on The Salty if a vacant mooring is available.

Showers in the TCYC.

Fuel Only by cans from garage.

YC The Teign Corinthian YC, ☎ 772734, is on the seafront, just N of St Michael's church; not as shown on AC 26. Bar (Wed & Fri) and showers.

Chandlery & repairs Bosun's Locker, CH, ☎ 779721. Addicott Electrics Ltd, ☎ 774087. Chris Humphrey, BY, ME, ☎ 772324. At Shaldon: The Brigantine, CH, ☎ 872400. Sleeman & Hawken Ltd, Diesel centre, ☎ 872750. Mariners Weigh, Outboards, ☎ 873698.

The new visitors' pontoon

RIVER EXE

Exmouth Dock entrance – 50°37´·00N 03°25´·47W

The Exe is little visited by cruising yachts, quite why is unclear. Perhaps Mark Fishwick, local boy and author of the laudable *West Country Cruising Companion*, over-publicised his confessional to a minor grounding off Topsham Quay and off-put lesser mortals? Your present Companion, a raw tyro fresh out of Teignmouth, sailed to Exmouth, decided against grounding up-river and retired unscathed, quite fun – in hindsight.

The estuary is greatly loved by those who moor there, enjoying its wide horizons and cyclic mud and water. Wildlife abounds and human haunts in Exmouth, Topsham and Exeter are pleasing. The estuary, river and canal may best be treated in three geographic sections:
a. From sea to Exmouth, the first port of call;
b. Thence up-river to Topsham; and
c. The Exeter Ship Canal above Turf Lock.
These sections include Shoreside, Navigation and Facilities. But clearly to reach Turf or Topsham you must have studied the entrance from sea, whether or not you pause en route at Exmouth.

SHORESIDE

EXMOUTH (Telephone code 01395)

Tourist Office Alexandra Terrace. ☎ 222299; 🖷 269911; exmouth@btinternet.com; www.exmouthguide.co.uk Mon–Sat 0930–1700; Sun 1000–1500 Jul/Aug.

What to see/do Exmouth is a small seaside resort whose former commercial dock is now a marina. Fishing and tourism flourish. Walk the banks of the estuary or enjoy the Devon countryside. Visit À la Ronde (National Trust), an extraordinary 16-sided house N of Exmouth built for two C18 spinster cousins.

Rail A branch line runs from Exmouth, via Topsham, to Exeter (25 mins; mainline trains).

Bus X57 Exeter-Topsham-Exmouth; every 20 mins.

Taxi ☎ 222268; 227588; 223033. **Car hire** See Exeter.

Bike hire Knobblies, ☎ 270182, Exeter Road.

Ferries To Starcross and Turf Lock. Water taxi to The Warren £2.35 return.

Beaches 2M of sandy beach is a great attraction, plus more sand at Dawlish Warren, by ferry.

Supermarket Somerfield, Magnolia Walk centre.

Market day Covered market, 12 The Strand; daily 9–5, selling everything under the sun.

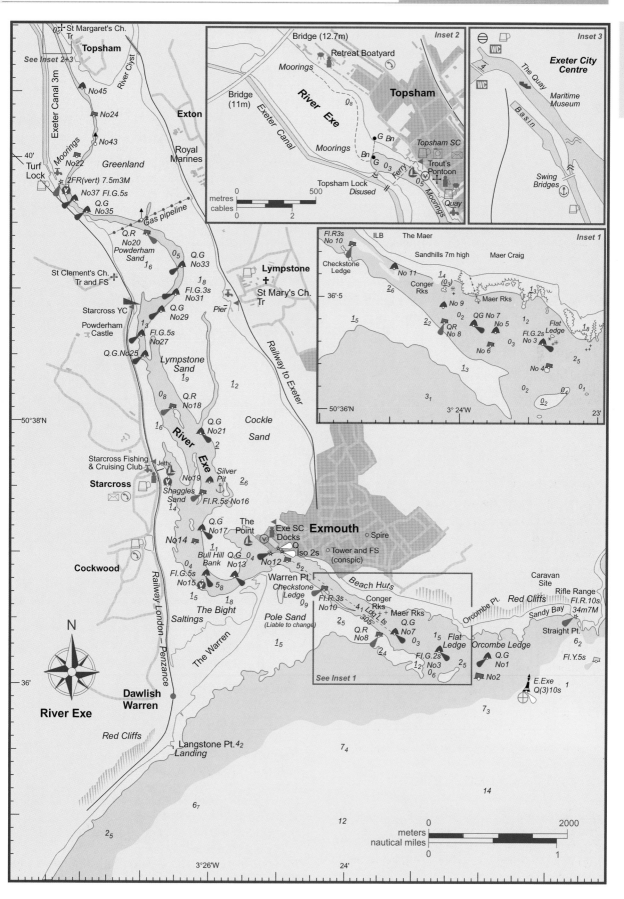

Bridge (12.7m)

Retreat Boatyard

Moorings

River Exe

Topsham

Bridge (11m)

Exeter Canal

Moorings

0.8

G Bn

Bn

Topsham SC

G

Ferry

Trout's Pontoon

Moorings

0.3

0.5

Topsham Lock
Disused

Quay

metres
cables

0   500

0   2

WC

WC

The Quay

Exeter City Centre

Maritime Museum

Basin

Swing Bridges

Fl.R3s
No 10

ILB   The Maer

Checkstone Ledge

No 11

Sandhills 7m high   Maer Craig

2.6

Conger Rks

1.4
(0.3)

No 9

Maer Rks

1.3

1.5

2.2

QR
No 8

0.2

QG No 7
No 5

1.2

Flat Ledge

1.8

0.3

Fl.G.2s
No 3

36'.5

No 6

1.3

50°36'N

3.1

No 4

0.2

0.2

0.4

2.5

0.1

3° 24'W   23'

St Margaret's Ch. Tr

0.5

Topsham

See Inset 2+3

Exeter Canal 3m

River Clyst

No45

No24

Exton

No43

40'

Moorings

No22

Royal Marines

Turf Lock

Greenland

2FR(vert) 7.5m3M

No37 Fl.G.5s

Q.G
No35

Q.R
No20

Powderham Sand

0.5

Q.G
No33

Gas pipeline

1.6

St Clement's Ch. Tr and FS

1.8

Fl.G.3s
No31

Lympstone

St Mary's Ch. Tr

Starcross YC

Q.G
No29

Pier

Powderham Castle

1.3

Fl.G.5s
No27

Q.G.No25

Lympstone Sand

1.9

Railway to Exeter

1.2

50°38'N

0.8

Q.R
No18

1.6

River Exe

Q.G
No21

Cockle Sand

2

Starcross Fishing & Cruising Club

Jetty

Silver Pit

Starcross

No19

2.6

Shaggles Sand

1.4

Fl.R.5s No16

Q.G
No17

The Point

Exe SC
Docks

Exmouth   Spire

Q

No14

1.1

Bull Hill Bank

0.4

Q.G
No13

0.4

Iso 2s

No12

Tower and FS (conspic)

Cockwood

0.4

Fl.G.5s
No15

5.8

5.2

Warren Pt.

Checkstone Ledge

Beach Huts

Caravan Site

Rifle Range

Red Cliffs

Fl.R.10s

1.5

1.8

Fl.R.3s
No10

Conger Rks

4.1

Ldg 1 ts

Maer Rks

Orcombe Pt.

Sandy Bay

34m7M

0.9

305°

1.5

Q.G
No7

0.3

1.5

Flat Ledge

Straight Pt.

The Bight

Saltings

Pole Sand
(Liable to change)

2.5

Q.R
No8

2.4

Fl.G.2s
No3

2.5

Orcombe Ledge

Q.G
No1

6.2

The Warren

1.5

1.2

0.6

No2

Fl.Y.5s

N

E.Exe
Q(3)10s

1

Red Cliffs

7.3

36'

River Exe

Dawlish Warren

Langstone Pt.

Landing

4.2

7.4

14

6.7

12

meters

0   2000

nautical miles

0   1

2.5

3°26'W   24'

Launderette in the High St.

Banks The main ones, with cashpoints, in the centre.

Restaurants Seafood restaurant, 9 Tower St, ☎ 269459; £13.50; Tues–Sat. The Beach Hotel by the marina and The Deer Leap, The Esplanade, do bar food.

TOPSHAM (Telephone code 01392)

Tourist Office None, but visit www.topsham.org

What to see/do Topsham Museum, 150m S of the Quay (Sat, Sun, Mon, Wed 1400–1700; ☎ 873244) is good on local colour. Beyond are attractive gabled-houses of Dutch origin. The ambience is *très chaleureux*.

Rail A branch line runs to Exeter (14 mins; main-line trains) and Exmouth, 11 mins.

Buses X57 to Exeter, 19 mins; Exmouth, 25 mins.

Car & bike hire See Exeter.

Ferries From Trout's BY to Turf lock; £3.50 return, ☎ 07778 370582. Cross R Exe to canal swing bridge.

Market day Sat morning in Town Hall.

Banks Plenty around the centre.

Restaurants The Galley, 41 Fore St, ☎ 876078, mains £15–25; strong on seafood and tapas. The Lighter Inn at the Quay has a restaurant and does good bar food. Georgian Tearoom: lunch, £4.50, Tues, Thur, Sun, and cream teas.

EXETER (Telephone code 01392)

This fair city is a delight to visit, especially the area around Rougemont Castle, the cathedral and down to the rejuvenated Quay. By 2005, when the City Basin on the SW bank has been refurbished, motor cruisers and shorter-masted yachts will be able to stay in central Exeter via the Ship Canal.

Tourist Office Paris St. ☎ 265700; 🖷 265260. Jun–Aug, Mon–Sat 0900–1700; Sun 1000–1600. A smaller Visitor Centre, ☎ 265213, is on the Quay, Easter–Oct. tic@exeter.gov.uk; www.exeter.gov.uk

Facilities All that might be expected in Devon's county town, plus good road, rail, bus & air links.

Taxi ☎ 218888; 433433; 422888. **Airport** ☎ 367433.

Car hire Avis, 259713; Budget, ☎ 496555.

Bike hire Saddles & Paddles, ☎ 424241; Mud Docks Cycleworks, ☎ 279999 – both on The Quay.

Restaurants A wide variety around Fore St, South and North Streets and The Quay.

NAVIGATION AND FACILITIES

FROM SEA TO EXMOUTH

River & Canal Manager's (Mr Jack Nott) office is by the City Basin in Haven Rd, Exeter EX3 0AZ; ☎ 274306, 07801 203334, 🖷 250234. VHF Ch 12 *Port of Exeter*. His bailiwick extends up-river to Exeter from a line joining Straight Pt, the East Exe ECM buoy and Langstone Pt (Dawlish Warren). river_canal@exeter.gov.uk; www.exeter.gov.uk

Charts AC 3315 (1:75,000), 2290 (1:12,500 with Exmouth plan 1:2,500); SC 5601.2 (1:75,000) and .6 (1:16,000).

Approaches From the SSW, go direct to the WPT. If coasting close inshore from Teignmouth, do not go N of Langstone Pt – unless clear of Pole Sand. From the E/SE, go direct to the waypoint. From the ENE avoid Straight Point firing range where the Royal Marines grapple with their recalcitrant SA80 rifles. The range safety sector extends 1.5M east to two large Y DZ buoys (not to be confused with a small Y SPM outfall buoy 2 cables SSE of Straight Pt). When active, red flags fly and a safety boat patrols; monitor VHF Ch 08.

East Exe buoy with tiny topmark

Landmarks W of Straight Point, the 200ft high red cliffs, topped by a caravan site, are conspicuous. These mark the start of the natural World Heritage Site which runs 95M E to Studland Bay. Exmouth church tower gives general orientation, if needed.

Pilotage The WPT is East Exe ECM lt buoy, 50°36′·00N 03°22′·37W, 304°/0.4M to No 1 buoy; or 2.25M to Exmouth Marina. For best water hug SHM buoys 1–9. (Unlit buoys 2, 4, 5, 6 & 9 appear to be 'capsized', but are OK). Least water, 0.3m, is between Nos 3 and 7 buoys; thereafter depths increase. Stay within the buoyed channel throughout. Shoal depths/positions are liable to change, esp Pole Sand to port, drying up to 3.5m. It is vital to use a corrected and in-date AC 2290.

The 305° ldg line (Iso 2s 6m/Q 12m) is only valid from No 9 buoy to 300m short of the front leading lt. The marks/lights are hard to see by day/night.

Many grains of sand; add salt and water − stir and you have the Exe estuary

Tides HW East Exe buoy at sp is 50 mins and at nps 30 mins after HW Devonport. LW at nps is 5 mins and at sp 15 mins after LW Devonport. MHWS is 4·6m, MLWS 0·5m; MHWN is 3·4m, MLWN 1·7m. Exmouth differences: in the *RNA*.

Tidal streams Slack water at No 10 buoy is at HW Devonport +1; a good ETA for a first visit. In the channel the ebb exceeds 4.5kn when the banks uncover. In the narrows off Warren Point the flood reaches 3–4kn; it sets across the marina entrance.

Access In fresh/strong S/SE'lies do not attempt to enter. If Exmouth is your destination, start the approach at HW−1. But if going further up-river, start at HW−2 so as to carry the flood all the way.

Anchorage No space and strong tidal streams.

Water Taxi Call *Conveyance* Ch M, 16 or ☎ 07970 918418; 0800–1915.

VHF *Port of Exeter* Ch 12. *Exmouth Dock* Ch 14.

EXMOUTH FACILITIES

Dockmaster's (Mr Keith Graham) office is to stbd of the footbridge (a Portakabin, due to be bricks & mortar). ☎ 269314. VHF Ch 14 *Exmouth Dock*. By the time you read this, the marina could be totally corralled by apartments in assorted pastel tints.

Access A long pontoon to stbd of the entrance is host to ferries, workboats and yachts (waiting to enter the marina). A lifting footbridge opens on request and stays open at night.

Shelter Very good in the tidal marina, but near HW some surge may enter in strong SW'lies.

Berthing A vacant berth can usually be found in approx 2m; pre-booking is advised. If full, stay on the entrance pontoon with HM's consent.

Tariff Daily rate on finger pontoon (showers inc) £11.75, regardless of size. ⚓s by No 15 buoy £6.

Showers, to be built, next to Dockmaster's office.

Fuel Diesel only from short pontoon first to stbd of entrance; petrol by cans from filling station.

YC Exe SC, ☎ 264607, is 80m N of the marina. Visitors are welcome: Clubhouse, bar, showers.

Chandlery & repairs Dixons, CH, ☎ 273248. Victoria Marine, ☎ 265044; outboard maintenance.

EXMOUTH TO TOPSHAM, passing Turf Lock

Landmarks Concentrate on the buoys, which are numbered 12 to 24 PHM and 13 to 45 SHM from Warren Pt; No 23 buoy does not exist. Above Turf Lock the buoys are unlit. In some stretches the channel is defined by mooring trots. After No 45 buoy, the channel to Topsham Quay is almost aligned with St Margaret's church tower.

Pilotage The estuary is in parts over a mile wide, the channel in places as narrow as 40m, charted depths as little as 0.1m. Waypoints play no further part; 21 lateral buoys, mostly lit, guide you 5.5M to Topsham – well almost. For best water shape a seamanlike curved track between buoys, rather than a dead straight line. The narrowest part of the channel is at No 31 buoy.

Tides HW Topsham at sp is 65 mins and at nps 45 mins after HW Devonport. LW times and heights: no data. MHWS is 4·0m; MHWN 2·8m. Starcross differences: See the *RNA*.

Access To carry the flood up to Topsham, leave E Exe buoy at HW–2 or –3.

Moorings Four 🛥s, and one big-ship buoy, lie 2 cables W of No 13 buoy; £6 per day.

Anchorage Yachts can anchor in a 2.1m hole 240m east of No 16 buoy. Also off Turf Lock.

VHF *Port of Exeter* Ch 12.

TOPSHAM FACILITIES

The River & Canal Manager (Mr Jack Nott) or his ferryman are responsible for Topsham Quay.

Berthing Topsham Quay, 50°40′·85N 03°27′·91W: berth/raft at pontoon below a conspic redbrick building to stbd. Fin keelers sink into soft mud; or use a long fender board if berthing against piles. 100m beyond, at Trouts BY (pre-book ☎ 873044) shoal draught boats can berth in 1m on the three hammerheads; hard gravel unsuitable for fin keels.

Tariff Daily rate on Topsham Quay £5.50. Trouts BY: <8.5m = £10; >8.5m = £12.50, inc electricity.

Showers at Trouts BY £1.

Electricity At Topsham Quay on request to ferryman ☎ 01780 1203338. At Trouts BY, free of charge.

Fuel Diesel at Trouts BY and Retreat BY; petrol by cans only.

YCs Starcross Fishing & Cruising Club, ☎ 01626 891996. Starcross YC, ☎ 890470. Topsham SC, ☎ 877524.

Entering Exmouth Dock at HW

Chandlery & repairs Trouts, ☎ 873044, a traditional family BY, CH, M, over 100 years old. Retreat BY, ☎ 874720, CH, D (below the M5 bridge). Ash Marine, ☎ 876654, CH (N end of Topsham). Exe Leisure, CH, ☎ 879055, at the Quay.

THE EXETER SHIP CANAL

The canal offers peaceful charm, rural scenery and good walking/cycling on the towpath. By 2005, when the City Basin will have been fitted with pontoons, electricity, FW etc, yachts will be able to stay overnight or longer in Exeter; they are at present limited to up & back in a day (5.5M each way) with an overnight stop at Turf Basin.

Turf Lock, abeam No 39 buoy, is the Canal entry. Lock times: Out @ HW Exmouth –5; In @ HW Exmouth. One locking per day, 7/7; on request.

The Canal is 3m deep. The M5 bridge, 1.6M above Turf, has an overhead clearance of 10m, restricting passage to motor cruisers, shorter-masted yachts and tenders. Swing/lift bridges are as AC 2990.

CANALSIDE FACILITIES

Tariff One yellow 🛥 off the lock: £6 per day; £4 short stay awaiting lock. Alongside/rafted in Turf Basin: £9 per night, including lock & showers.

Inns Turf Hotel, ☎ 893128, is isolated and tranquil, with fine views over the river. Good bar food, BBQs. There is a small crane for de-masting. The Double Locks Pub, ☎ 256947, is 3M up-stream. Exeter: see under Shoreside.

Ferries Day trips to Turf Lock from Topsham or Exmouth are popular. A small ferry from Topsham canal bridge crosses the R Exe to Topsham, 60p.

Chandlery & repairs John Bridger Marine, ☎ 250970, by City Basin.

AXMOUTH

Harbour entrance – 50°42´·13N 03°03´·27W

Where the River Axe meets the English Channel stout hearts quail

Salute the seafarers of Axmouth whom St Matthew clearly had in mind when he wrote: *Strait is the gate and narrow is the way which leadeth unto life, and few there be that find it.* Amend 'Strait' to read 'Tortuous' and the description is apt.

It is a pity that few yachts visit Axmouth since the setting is spectacular, the achievement rewarding and the welcome warm. But you do need bilge keels or shoal draught, max 1.2m, and LOA preferably <8.5m; plus of course local knowledge and a nerveless helms(wo)man – surely not a lot to ask?

SHORESIDE (Telephone code 01297)

Tourist Office The Underfleet, Harbour Road, Seaton; ☎ 21660; 🖳 21689. Mon–Sat 1000–1700 (Sun 1000–1700 in Jun–Aug). inf@seatontic.freeserve.co.uk www.eastdevon.net/tourism/seaton www.axmouth-uk.com (run by the Ship Inn)

What to see/do The 'chocolate box' (and most people like chocolate) village of Axmouth is 0.75M inland, a pleasant riverside stroll past the nature reserve. Or walk west, if needs be, to the semi-Victorian seaside resort of Seaton. Great walking country on the SW Coast Path, so at least climb up Haven Cliff for an aerial view of

the harbour. If you have nothing better to do, ride the touristy Seaton to Colyford Tramway, £5.15 return.

Rail Nearest station is Axminster (6M) on the Exeter (40 mins) to Waterloo (2 hrs 30 mins) line.

Buses No 885 Axminster (30 mins). No X53 Exeter (1 hr)–Seaton–Weymouth (1 hr 25 mins).

Taxis ☎ 20038/23366; 552719.

Car & bike hire None at Seaton.

Beaches To the west, Seaton beach is a substantial shingle bank; sand is a scarce commodity here.

Supermarket Co-op in The Undercliff, Seaton.

Banks The usual, plus cashpoint, in Seaton.

Launderette In Fore St, Seaton; closed Wed.

Restaurants The Harbour Inn, ☎ 20371, and The Ship, ☎ 21838, both in Church St, Axmouth, spoil you for choice; visit both for good food and ales. Seaton is closer, but unvisited by this Companion.

NAVIGATION

Charts AC 3315 and SC 5601.2 (both 1:75,000). The scale is inadequate, but remember Captain Cook who had no aerial photos – and take heart.

Approaches From the W, Beer Hd is fairly steep-to. From the E, keep 0.5M offshore to clear drying rocky ledges and cliff falls. Beware pot markers.

Landmarks A handsome white house overlooking the harbour is conspic from the SW, but from the E is obscured by Haven Cliff. Beer Head, 2M WSW, with large caravan site is conspic. A SHM beacon, Fl G 4s, is on the entrance jetty.

Access By day only for strangers and never in onshore winds >F4. The 10m narrow entrance is a bottleneck which constrains both river current and the tidal streams. Thus water levels outside and inside may effectively differ; when they are in balance is the optimum time to enter, as follows: at springs HW$-2\frac{1}{2}$ or $-\frac{1}{2}$ (not between these times); and at neaps from HW$-2\frac{1}{2}$ to $+1\frac{1}{2}$. Note: If you enter at HW-1, as per conventional wisdom, the spring flood will still be running strongly.

Pilotage The waypoint is 50°41´·83N 03°03´·27W, 000°/3 cables to the harbour entrance. A shingle bar close offshore shifts E or W, varying the final

The entrance and SHM beacon at LW

approach track between parallel to the coast and at 90° to it. Cross the bar if you know where the 'hole' in it is; or call the HM for an update; or recce the scene by dinghy. At the entrance hug the short concrete jetty to starboard (which deflects river currents and tidal streams through the large shingle bank). The channel then turns sharply 90° to port passing a piled quay on the N bank and into a wider pool just before the low (2m) bridges.

Tides Use differences for Lyme Regis, 5M east. At Axmouth MHWS is 4·4m and MHWN 2·7 to 3·1m.

Tidal streams are weak and parallel to the coast.

Shelter Good – once you're inside the entrance.

Anchorage No room inside. Outside, ⚓ near the waypoint if conditions permit, to await the tide.

FACILITIES

The HM's office is near the far end of the mooring trots. The Ass't HM, Mr Pete Paulson, is usually around; ☎ 22180, mobile 07939 044109. No VHF.

Berthing On a vacant mooring or alongside a moored yacht. Larger craft against the N Quay with fender board, as directed by the Ass't HM. Land at the club pontoon where FW is available. Piles may replace the mooring buoys in the future.

Tariff Daily rate £4.50; no electricity.

YC Axe YC, ☎ 20742, offers a warm welcome, bar & showers, also diesel. Access via the Beachmaster.

Fuel Diesel from AYC; the local garage has closed.

Chandlery & repairs At the harbour: Chandlery, ☎ 24774. HJ Mears, Boat builder, ☎ 23344.

BEER

Anchorage – 50°41´·63N 03°05´·27W
Beer (alas no hops & yeast) sits between imposing Beer Head (BH) and Seaton. Beer Roads is a good passage anchorage, well sheltered from WSW to N winds in the lee of BH, the first chalk cliff as you head up-Channel. Beware many mooring buoys. Anchor in 3–5m on sand in front of the village. Two powerful security lights are aligned with the church and centre of the beach.

Land on the steep shingle beach up which local fishing boats have been hauled for centuries – and repair to the Dolphin Hotel for excellent food. In mid-August Beer SC holds an energetic regatta which includes odd sports such as rolling barrels along the main drag. Jimmy Green Marine, ☎ 20744, The Meadows, CH, ropes, rigging.

View NE in early season. The orange visitors' moorings are clearly visible

LYME REGIS

Harbour entrance – 50°43´·20N 02°56´·20W

On rounding the massive Grade I-listed Cobb, the hooded figure of Meryl Streep, alias *The French Lieutenant's Woman*, might not be there to greet you. But you may see the less beautiful, albeit ever happy face of Harbour Master Mike Poupard ('one of the friendliest on the south coast' to quote his own words).

This counts for a lot, especially if it has been a difficult passage or you are worried about leaning your plastic, fin-keeled shell against Lyme's weather-beaten timbers. It is the sort of welcome you can count on at a traditional, old-fashioned port – the most westerly in Dorset.

SHORESIDE (Telephone code 01297)

Tourist Office, Church St, Lyme Regis. ☎ 442138; 🖷 444668. Monday–Saturday 1000–1700 (Sunday 1600). lymeregis.tic@westdorset-dc.gov.uk www.lymeregistourism.co.uk

What to see/do Lyme's steep main drag, Broad St, is full of interest but mightily congested at the bottom. Most things are to hand and the town is mercifully free of the gaudier excesses of a seaside resort. Walk W below the cliffs looking for fossils, like a latter day Mary Anning who in 1811, aged 12, discovered an icthyosaur – now in the Natural History Museum, London. Be glad if you find an ammonite, a spiral-shaped extinct mollusc. Take a very informative walk – guided by expert fossils. Or visit Dinosaurland Fossil Museum which even has a Fossil Clinic – for analysing your pet fossil.

Rail Nearest station is Axminster (7M) on the Exeter (40 mins) to Waterloo (2 hrs 30 mins) line.

Buses No 31 Axminster (20 mins); No X53 Weymouth (1 hr 25 mins).

Taxis ☎ 444555; 442070; 444747; 445884; 442222.

Car & bike hire See the Tourist Office.

Beaches The harbour has more than its fair share of clean golden sand on which lies beetroot flesh. To W and E the beaches are more shingly.

Supermarket Co-op in Broad St, and good Delis.

Banks The usual, plus cashpoints, around the centre.

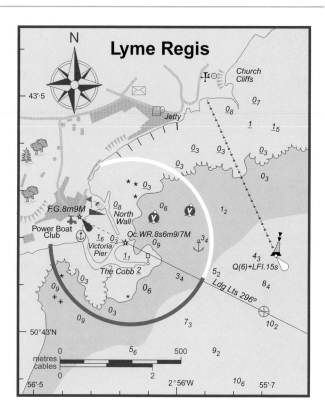

FVs berth on the outer end of Victoria Pier

Restaurants Victoria Hotel, Uplyme Rd, ☎ 444801, £13.50. Mariners Hotel, Silver St, ☎ 442753, £11. Turles, Broad St, ☎ 445792, £13. Good pub food at: The Cobb Arms, Harbour Inn, Royal Standard, Nag's Head and Pilot Boat.

NAVIGATION

Charts AC 3315 (1:75,000 & 1:12,500 plan); ditto SC 5601.3.

Approaches From the W, to clear rocky ledges keep at least 0.5M offshore. From the E, go direct to the waypoint.

Landmarks The town itself sprawling up the hill is more obvious from the E. About 0.5M W of the harbour, distinctive smooth grey 'slabs' lie below the wooded upper cliffs.

Pilotage The waypoint is 50°43´·03N 02°55´·66W, 296°/600m to the front leading lt. At 300m to go, turn 20° stbd to clear the end of The Cobb (PHM bcn), then open up the harbour entrance on about 255°. Do not stray north of the ⚓s, due to drying, rocky shoals. 300m N of the WPT, a SCM (outfall) buoy, Q(6) + L Fl 15s, gives useful orientation.

Tides HW Lyme at sp is 1 hr and at nps 40 mins after HW Devonport. LW at nps is 5 mins before, and at sp 5 mins after, LW Devonport. MHWS is 4·3m, MLWS 0·6m; MHWN is 3·1m, MLWN 1·7m.

Pink flesh on the drying sand north of the harbour

Tidal streams are weak and parallel to the coast.

Access to Victoria Pier, dries 0.3 to 2.1, is approx HW±2, depending on draught.

Shelter Good, except in strong easterly/south easterly winds, when the North Wall provides a more sheltered berth; or it may be advisable to go elsewhere.

VHF Call *Lyme Regis Harbour Radio* Ch 16; then work 14, which is not routinely monitored.

FACILITIES

The **HM**'s office is at the root of The Cobb. ☎/📠 442137; mobile 07770 636728. 0800–2000 Jul/Aug. lrharmar@aol.com; www.lymeharbour.com

Moorings Eight orange ⚓s lie east of the

The hbr entrance, nearing Low Water. Boats inside are already drying

harbour. Those inshore are in about 0.6m, so if drawing more than 1.5m go for the outers in about 1m. In fresh E to SSW winds the ⚓s can be uncomfortable.

Anchorage Deep draught boats should anchor about 50–100m south of the ⚓s in 4–5m, free of charge.

Berthing Dry out against Victoria Pier beyond the knuckle on firm level sand, as directed by the HM who can provide a fender board plus local advice. Multihulls usually dry out on the beach. FW taps.

Tariff Daily rate against Victoria Pier/rafted; no electricity: LOA >8m = £10.50; max LOA 10m+. ⚓s £5.

Showers at the SC, between the Cobb Arms and Harbour Inn, Marine Parade; keys from HM.

Fuel Diesel/petrol by cans from 4M away!

YCs Lyme Regis SC, ☎ 442800, is open Wednesday and Saturday evenings and Sunday: warm welcome, bar & showers.

CHANDLERY & REPAIR FACILITIES

Rob Perry Marine, ☎ 445816, ME, Gas.
Axminster Chandlery, ☎ 33980.
Jimmy Green, ☎ 20744, CH at Beer.

Work in progress (March 2003) on the new West Pier

WEST BAY (BRIDPORT)

Harbour entrance – 50°42´·54N 02°45´·84W

Bridport derives its name from the patriotic R Brit which flows through. Thomas Hardy called it Port Bredy, a name which is still perpetuated. One and a half miles south, prosaic Bridport Harbour was re-branded West Bay in 1884 as an embryonic seaside resort; spin is nothing new – but what of East Bay?

Today West Bay is getting a new lease of life as can be seen from the chartlet, photographs and text below. Under Navigation a dual entry (Old & New/Before & After) describes the harbour as it is now and as it is expected to be during the lifespan of this edition.

SHORESIDE (Telephone code 01308)

Tourist Office is at 47, South St, Bridport.
☎ 424901; ▦ 421060. Open Apr–Oct, Mon–Sat 0900–1700.
West Bay: A Visitors' Centre in the Old Salt House contains a graphic exhibition of the new harbour developments. ☎ 422807; ▦ 421509. Apr–Oct, 7/7 1000–1700. westbay.vc@westdorset-dc.gov.uk

What to see/do Bridport is twinned with St Vaast, France; see Chapter 5, page 329. Palmers Brewery, West Bay Rd does guided tours Tues, Wed, Thur @ 1100 sharp; sample real ales; ☎ 427500. Bridport Museum, Mon–Sat 1000–1700, does the usual things, plus rope-making and the 'Bridport Dagger'. West Bay has a vertiginous golf course on the crumbling E Cliff.

Rail Nearest station is Crewkerne on the Exeter (50 mins) to Waterloo (2 hrs 20 mins) line.

Buses B3: West Bay to Bridport, 10 mins. 47: Bridport to Crewkerne 40 mins.

Taxi Pat's Cabs ☎ 424715.

Car hire See Tourist Office.

Bike hire Wheels 'n Deals, ☎ 420586; 37 St Michael's Trading Estate, Bridport.

Beaches Shingle beaches E and W of West Bay.

Supermarkets Somerfield and Spar in Bridport; large Safeway 15 mins walk from West Bay.

Launderette George St, West Bay, 0800–2000. Also in large caravan site close NW of the harbour.

Market days Wed & Sat, as in the last 1,000 years.

Banks All the usual, with cashpoints, in Bridport.

Restaurants Riverside, N of West Bay basin; pre-book ☎ 422011; brill (literally) seafood, £16; shut Mon. Good food at the George and Bridport Arms.

NAVIGATION

Charts AC 3315 (1:75,000 & 1:3,500 plan); ditto SC 5601.3.

Approaches From the W, avoid High Ground a rocky patch close inshore 1.4M W of the harbour with only 3m over it. From the SE route direct to the waypoint.

Landmarks To W and E, especially the latter, the harbour is sign-posted by the orangey cliffs.

Pilotage The waypoint is 50°41´·99N 02°46´·47W, a yellow SPM (outfall) lt buoy, 032°/6.5 cables to the harbour entrance.

Tides HW Bridport (West Bay) at sp is 40 mins and at nps 25 mins after HW Devonport. LW at nps and sp is the same as LW Devonport. MHWS is 4·1m, MLWS 0·6m; MHWN is 3·0m, MLWN is 1·6m. Differences for Chesil Beach and Chesil Cove are listed in the *RNA* under Bridport.

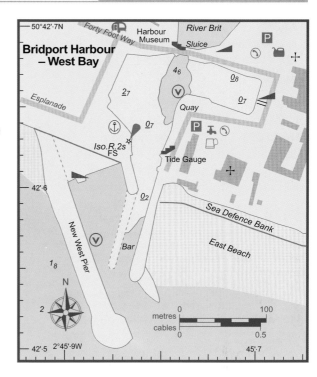

Tidal streams are weak and parallel to the coast.

VHF Pre-call *Bridport Radio* Ch 16, 11 for a berth.

Anchorage About 3 cables SW of the harbour in 3m, but only in settled offshore conditions.

OLD WEST BAY, before...

Entrance HW±2, only in quiet offshore weather. The entrance between two chunky, but vulnerable piers is 180m long, 12m narrow and dries 0.6m. In S'ly gales breaking seas in the entrance make entry dangerous/impossible; it is even difficult in an onshore F4, or less if ground swell is present. *It is easier for a camel to go through the eye of a needle,*

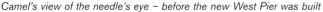

Camel's view of the needle's eye − before the new West Pier was built

than for a visiting yachtsman to enter West Bay's inner sanctum – until the new works are completed.

Shelter The inner basin is safe, but exposed to strong onshore winds and susceptible to swell.

Berthing As directed by the HM. There is little or no room amongst permanent drying moorings. A yacht would stay afloat in 3.5m at The Quay (close NW of the lofty Pier Terrace building) where in the past coasters berthed. Use a fender board.

NEW WEST BAY, after...

In late April 2002 work began on a new West Pier to replace the old. This and related works are due to be finished by April 2004 – a trifle optimistic?

The new West Pier starts from the shoreline where today's AC 3315 shows a small spur and PHM beacon. It extends 230m SE to form a 43m wide entrance, with 5m @ MLWS, due S of the present East Pier. The outer 100m of the existing West Pier (as depicted by a pecked outline) will be demolished, leaving a stub jetty. SW of this will be a 'spending ramp' and 10m wide slipway. At this early stage what follows can only be a statement of intent rather than of hard fact: The new West Pier and entrance are designed to ensure calmish water in the outer harbour in up to storm force winds, with a similar improvement in the inner harbour. In lesser winds the accessibility of the harbour will improve by 50%, ie from 220 to 330 days per annum.

The half-completed new West Pier

The west side of the outer harbour, including the new slipway, is intended for leisure craft. There will be no mooring buoys, but it is hoped to install two pontoons alongside the West Pier for visiting yachts.

The east side of the harbour is intended for commercial vessels/FVs; when berthed on the East Pier they will have continuous access to/from seaward.

Dredging may be possible up to the sluice gates at the head of the inner harbour and ideally to either side, depending on underwater structures.

FACILITIES

The **HM** (Mr Tony Preston) has a temporary office at 3c George St, behind the George Hotel. ☎/🖷 423222, in emergency ☎ 07967 739020. Hrs 0800–2000 Jul/Aug. When building work is complete, HM's office and showers will return to 'The Mound', N of the new slipway.

Tariff Daily rate for yachts LOA >7m = £10.50 in the inner harbour; no electricity.

Showers near to HM's Office.

Fuel Diesel and petrol by cans from Texaco garage at NE corner of the village.

Chandlery & repairs An electronics shop is visible just E of the inner basin. Only basic repairs are possible.

The inner harbour at HW

Looking NW along Chesil Beach and the western part of the harbour

PORTLAND HARBOUR

Harbour, N entrance – 50°35´·72N 02°25´·91W

The Isle of Portland, or the Island as it is known locally, is but a slight misnomer. Only a large bank of pebbles, alias Chesil Beach, connects this wedge of limestone to the mainland and prevents it being truly an island. Not surprisingly Thomas Hardy called it the Gibraltar of Wessex.

Fortuneswell and Easton are the main places on it. The Bill and its offlying Race are perhaps Portland's most dubious claims to fame; see Passage Notes on page 25.

Portland Harbour is now a commercial port – once described as 'so vast for small craft as to be hardly like a harbour at all'. It is of only passing interest to the majority of cruising yachtsmen. But Castle Cove SC is in the NW part of the harbour; and Weymouth & Portland Sailing Academy is at Osprey Quay (the former RN helicopter base).

SHORESIDE (Telephone code 01305)

Tourist Office Visitors' Centres are at Chesil Beach, ☎ 760579; and at Portland Bill lighthouse, ☎ 861233. Or visit the Centre at Weymouth.

What to see/do Lighthouse & Visitor Centre at the Bill: You can climb the lighthouse's 153 steps (£2; 1100–1700, not Sat), but only if you are taller than 1.1m/43in – to avoid falling between the balusters. Portland Castle, ☎ 820539, 1000–1800 £3.50 – look out for the ghosts. Portland Museum, ☎ 821804, above Church Ope Cove, 1030–1700; £2.10.

Rail See Weymouth.

Buses Nos 1, 7 & 10 to Weymouth. No 501 (Jun–Aug) the Bill to Weymouth. Timetables from Tourist Offices.

Taxis ☎ 821600; 822822; 821397; 823456.

Car & bike hire See Weymouth.

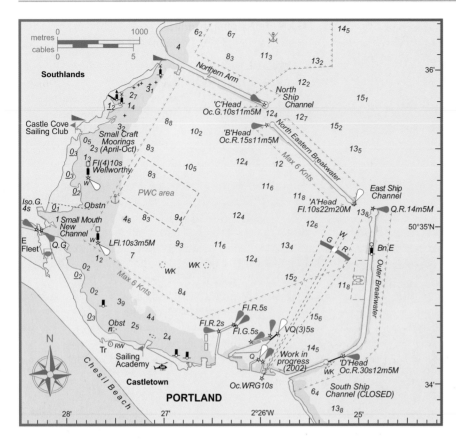

Ferries From Portland Castle jetty to Weymouth in season, ☎ 785000/07778 286892.

Beaches Er... Chesil Beach, all 17 miles of it, if you don't mind the pebbles (said to be largest at the SE end); but swimming is not advised. Castle Cove SC had a pleasant sandy beach at their former site.

Supermarkets A small Co-op in Fortuneswell.

Launderette One in Fortuneswell.

Market day Open-air market, Tues in summer, near the Portland Heights Hotel (great viewpoint).

Banks Lloyds, with cashpoint, at Easton.

Restaurants Some 35 restaurants, cafés and pubs are listed in a 20p booklet from the Tourist Office. Try Slingers, ☎ 822288, at Chesil; Vaughans, ☎ 822226, at Weston; or the Portland Heights Hotel, ☎ 821361.

NAVIGATION

Charts AC 2615 (1:75,000), 2610 (1:40,000), 2255 (1:20,000), 2268 (1:10,000); SC 5601.7 (1:20,000).

Approaches From the W, via the inshore passage, keep close to the E side of Portland and the outer breakwater. From outside the Race, it is safer to route east of The Shambles. An acoustic range at 50°34′N 02°24′W is marked by four SPM light buoys. From the E track direct to the waypoint, avoiding Lulworth firing ranges; see Passage Notes on page 26.

Reporting system Only vessels >50m LOA must comply. Yachts should monitor *Portland Harbour Radio* Ch 74, but need not get clearance to enter.

Landmarks From E and W the steep N face (The Verne) of Portland is conspic, as is the white 'golf-ball' radome. By day/night the lt ho, Fl 10s, on 'A' Head (East Channel) is obvious. Weymouth's shore lights are very bright.

The Race is visible NE of the lighthouse

Pilotage The waypoint is 50°35′·89N 02°25′·17W, 250°/0.5M to the N Channel entrance, which yachts should use for entry/exit, thus avoiding commercial activity in the SE part of the harbour. The commercial port lies within a Controlled Area which may only be entered if so cleared.

Speed limits 6kn applies to all power-driven vessels within a broad band around the harbour's periphery and within 150m of all breakwaters; see chartlet. Elsewhere the limit is 12kn, but this may be exceeded by vessels <10m long. A jet ski area, as shown on the chartlet, is best avoided.

Tides Portland is a Standard Port. Predictions are given in the *RNA*. MHWS is 2·1m, MLWS 0·1m; MHWN is 1·4m, MLWN 0·8m. Note the very small tidal range.

Tidal streams in the harbour are imperceptible.

Access H24, but take extra care in strong E'lies. The S Channel entrance is permanently closed by a scuttled vessel and an overhead power cable.

Shelter Good in fair weather, but the harbour is large and particularly exposed to W and E winds. Chesil Beach and the breakwaters do not give total protection. Strong winds can raise a rough sea, but in summer yacht moorings are usually safe.

Anchorages Yachts can anchor in 4–6m east of the local moorings (see YCs) which line the W side of the harbour. Do not obstruct the 288° leading line into New Channel and The Fleet.

Moorings See under YCs.

FACILITIES

HM (Mr Stan Mault), ☎ 824044, 🖷 824055. a.baker.po@portland-port.co.uk; www.portland-port.co.uk

Tariff Harbour dues £/day for LOA bands: <9.1m = 3.80; <12.2m = 5.20; <15.2m = 6.40; <20m = 7.50. These dues apply to visiting yachts on a mooring or at anchor. If collected, they help to maintain the breakwaters and navigational lights.

Fuel Diesel by hose in Weymouth; petrol only by cans from garages.

Weymouth & Portland Sailing Academy (WPSA) ☎ 860101, 🖷 820099; info@wpsa.org.uk; www.wpsa.org.uk WPSA trains racing crews to Olympic standards and organises international and national championships for keel boats and dinghies within the harbour.

SAR Helicopter, funded by MCA, operates from a site close to WPSA. Long may it continue to do so.

YCs Castle Cove SC, ☎ 783708; moorings, landing. Note: In Dec 2002 CCSC moved 500m SW to the site of the former Weymouth Sailing Centre. The Royal Dorset YC, ☎ 786258, has adjacent moorings – ditto W & PCA, Ferrybridge Marine, RNSA and Portland Boat Club – along the W side of the hbr.

CHANDLERY & REPAIR FACILITIES

Ferrybridge Marine, ☎ 781518, CH, repairs. Bluecastle Chandlers, ☎ 822298, CH. Relling One Design, Osprey Quay, ☎ 826555, SM. Clark's Boatworks, 41 Chiswell, ☎ 860265; all repairs and maintenance. At Weymouth there is a wider range of service and repair facilities.

Portland Bill lighthouse and Pulpit Rock from the inshore passage

WEYMOUTH

Harbour entrance – 50°36´.59N 02°26´.49W

Glorious sands, the outer harbour, lifting bridge and marina are all clearly visible

Weymouth somehow merges its Georgian charm with modern developments and more pubs per square metre than a man can count! George III introduced sea bathing here in the 18th century, but later this popular king succumbed to insanity.

Today the superbly manicured sandy beach – complete with Punch & Judy – is that of a classic seaside resort. A great sweep of hotels embellishes the seafront. The outer harbour retains a lot of its original character with pastel-tinted, bow-fronted Georgian houses on either side. High-speed Cats berth to starboard on entry. Where the harbour broadens into The Cove, yachts are rafted at least fourfold on both sides, followed by fishing boats berthed almost up to the lifting bridge. Beyond the bridge are municipal pontoons and a tightly-packed 250-berth marina which opened in 1996.

SHORESIDE (Telephone code 01305)

Tourist Office is on the Esplanade near KG III's statue. ☎ 785747; 🖷 788092. Mon–Fri 0900–1230 & 1330–1830; Sat 0900–1830; Sun 1000–1200 & 1500–1700. tic@weymouth.gov.uk; www.weymouth.gov.uk

What to see/do Close to hand, stroll into Brewers Quay, a redeveloped site near The Cove. Continue to Nothe Fort for its museum and kids'

assault course. Radipole Lake, just N of the marina, is a nature reserve/minor swannery run by the RSPB. Further afield visit Abbotsbury Swannery, gardens and Children's Farm; daily 1000–1800, £5.50. Or take the 501 bus to Portland Bill (see page 113).

Rail The station is about 500m N of the marina. London (Waterloo) 2 hrs 45 mins.

Buses Timetables/info: First, ☎ 0870 608 2608.

Taxi ☎ 773636/783636.

Car hire Dorset Vehicle Rentals, ☎ 814444.

Bike hire Tilleys, ☎ 785672, St Thomas St (N end). Westham Cycles, ☎ 776977.

Ferries Condor Cats to Guernsey, Jersey, St Malo. A rowing boat ferry, 20p, across the harbour near the ldg lts, has right of way over all other vessels.

Beaches Weymouth sand is known world-wide as being of talc-like fineness which bonds when wet. Good for sculpting sand castles.

Supermarkets Small Tesco in St Thomas St Spar,

St Edmund St, near bridge. Roberts Food Services at NW side of bridge; Mon–Sat 0830–1700, Sun 1000–1300 in summer. Asda at SW corner of the marina.

Market day Thur, open-air in Swannery car park.

Banks Plenty around the centre.

Restaurants Isobar, ☎ 750666, by the bridge £13.50; shut Mon. Mallams, ☎ 776757, two-course dinner £19.95, and Perrys, ☎ 785799, £14, are alongside each other SE of the bridge; essential to pre-book. Along the N Quay, The Ship, ☎ 773879, £8 is mass eating in reasonable comfort. Next door the Sea Cow, ☎ 783524, £13, has changed hands. Floods, ☎ 772270, £12.50 excellent very fresh fish.

NAVIGATION

Charts AC 2615 (1:75,000), 2610 (1:40,000), 2255 (1:20,000), 2172 (1:5,000), plus SC 5601.7 (1:5,000).

Approaches From the W, via the inshore passage, keep close to the E side of Portland and the outer breakwaters. From outside the Race, it is safer to route east of The Shambles. An acoustic range at 50°34′N 02°24′W is marked by four SPM light buoys. A de-gaussing range, 600m S of the waypoint, is marked by three SPM buoys, only one of which is lit. From the E track direct to the waypoint, avoiding Lulworth firing ranges if possible.

Landmarks The church spire is conspic 0.7M NW of the waypoint. At night guidance is given by the lighthouse, Fl 10s, on Portland's 'A' Head breakwater. Weymouth is a blaze of shore lights.

Pilotage The waypoint is 50°36′·66N 02°26′·27W, bearing 240°/300m to the S pierhead. The 240° FR ldg lights lead clear of shallows along the S side of the entrance, but are not primarily for yachts. Speed limit = Dead slow; avoid making wash.

Tides Portland predictions apply. MHWS is 2·1m, MLWS 0·1m; MHWN is 1·4m, MLWN 0·8m. Note: The range is small (2·0m sp, 0·6m nps), and double LWs occur; predictions are for the first LW.

Tidal streams in Weymouth Bay are weak, but nearly always W-going.

Anchorage Yachts can anchor in 3–6m on sand in an arc 015°–060° from the N pierhead, clear of the buoyed swimming/watersport areas and fairway.

Access H24, but demanding in strong E'lies.

Shelter The outer harbour is exposed to E'lies, but the marina is well sheltered.

VHF *Weymouth Harbour* & *Weymouth Town Bridge* Ch 12. *Weymouth Marina* Ch 80. Fuel Ch 60.

Traffic Signals (with slightly different meanings from IPTS) are shown omni-directionally from a mast halfway along the S pier; they are difficult to see against a low morning/evening sun. Given

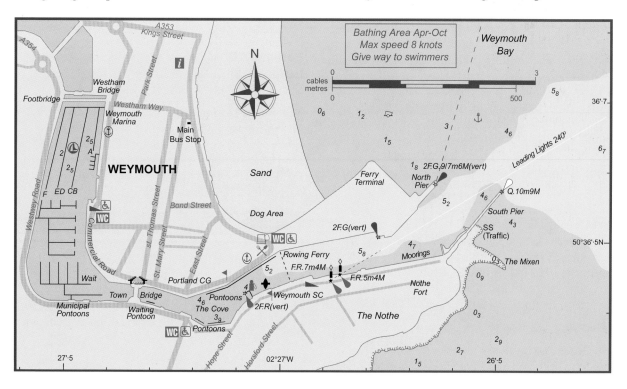

Outward bound from the marina. Note triple reds either side of the bridge

that ferry/commercial traffic is slight, yachtsmen are only likely to be affected by the following:
No signals = Clear to enter/leave.
Signal 2 = A vessel is leaving harbour; no vessel shall approach so as to obstruct the entrance.
Signal 3 = A vessel is approaching the entrance from seaward; no vessel is to leave the harbour.
IPTS and their standard meanings are in the Main Introduction which starts on page 6.

Lifting bridge 10 & 5 mins before lifts, a bridge broadcast on Ch 12 confirms the bridge lift and prioritises in/outbound traffic. Yachts should be visible to the bridge and minimise transmissions. Three R or three G (vert lights) on the bridge control traffic. Waiting pontoons are on or near the S bank, close down and up-stream of the bridge.

Mid-Apr to mid-Sep lifts are @ 0800, 1000, 1200, 1400, 1600, 1800 & 2000LT; and 2100, 1 Jun–31 Aug. Mid-Sep to mid-Apr lifts are @ 0800, 1000, 1200, 1400, 1600 & 1800. In these months give 1 hr's notice of a required lift on VHF Ch 12, HM ☎ 206423.

FACILITIES

HM's (Capt David Stabler) building is conspic at 13 Custom House Quay. ☎ 838423 (+ answer phone), ⚏ 767927. Bridge ☎ 789357. Open, in summer 0730 to last bridge lift; in winter to 1715, if 1800 bridge lift is not booked. corinnegillard@weymouth.gov.uk; www.weymouth.gov.uk

Berthing The two options, from seaward, are:

1. Outer Harbour; see chartlet. Motor cruisers and yachts >10m LOA berth/raft on pontoons N side. Yachts <10m LOA berth/raft on pontoons in The Cove, S side. Or as directed by HM.

Tariff Daily rate £/m LOA: Mar–Sep £1.70; Oct–Feb £1.20.

Showers, free and superb, plus coin **launderette** are below HM's Office; access 0500–2300 by code.
Electricity On both quays, free; ditto **FW** by hose.

2. Weymouth Marina
(Manager Russ Levett).
☎ 767576, ⚏ 767575. Summer 0730 to last bridge lift +30 mins; winter 0830–1700. sales@weymouth-marina.co.uk; www.weymouth-marina.co.uk Pre-call Ch 80 for a berth. After the lifting bridge (times above), keep round to stbd (past municipal pontoons, no Ⓥs). Ⓥ berths at N end of pontoons 'C' & 'D'; motor cruisers on 'F'; or as directed by dory.

Tariff Daily rate Apr–Sep £2.40/m LOA. £1.20/m other months. Showers included. **Electricity** £3.

Fuel Raybar Ch 60, ☎ 787039 or 07860 912401 for diesel at fuel pontoon on S bank of outer harbour. Quayside Fuel, Ch 60, ☎ 772318, or ☎ 07747 182181; a small bowser delivers diesel as convenient in the outer harbour or near marina. Petrol only by cans.

Portland CG (MRSC) is on Customs House Quay; call ☎ 760439 or Ch 16 > 67 for advice/assistance.

YCs Royal Dorset YC, 11 Customs House Quay, ☎ 786258; rdyc@weymouthharbour.fsnet.co.uk; www.rdyc.freeuk.com Visitors welcome; bar & food, 1200–1500 & 1800–2300, daily; moorings in Portland Hbr. Weymouth SC, ☎ 785481, at outer harbour's S bank has a bar.

CHANDLERY & REPAIR FACILITIES
WL Bussell, ☎ 785633, 30 Hope St, just S of The Cove. Kingfisher Marine, ☎ 766595, just W of bridge. Rigger, A D Gordon ☎ 07774 633419. Mobile Yacht Maintenance, ☎ 07900 148806. Mechanical Services ☎ 07831 263524. Marine Electronics, ☎ 07970 855775, 23 Trinity Rd (S bank, W of the bridge).

THE PURBECK COAST

Lulworth Cove – 50°36´·99N 02°14´·82W; Worbarrow Bay W Anchorage – 50°37´·09N 02°13´·29W;
Chapman's Pool – 50°35'·53N 02°03'·91W; Swanage – 50°36'·69N 01°56'·94W

In 2001 UNESCO designated the East Devon and Dorset coast from Exmouth to Studland Bay as England's first natural World Heritage site. Thus it ranks with Scotland's St Kilda, Northern Ireland's Giant's Causeway, America's Grand Canyon and Australia's Great Barrier Reef.

Fame at last – even if the site is already known as the Jurassic Coast. For those too young to recall, the Jurassic age was a mere 150–200 million years ago, ie about mid-life in the geology of planet Earth. The evidence is before your eyes.

The Purbeck Coast from Weymouth to Studland Bay is one section of this site, and arguably may be judged the finest, not only for scientific reasons but mainly for its sheer aesthetic beauty.

Happily it contains at least five anchorages where yachtsmen can enjoy varying measures of tranquillity, solitude, scenic splendour, wildlife – also the inescapable proximity of other humans! Not to mention an army firing range which limits freedom of coastal passage-making; see page 26 for details. But the pros far, far outweigh the cons.

Charts and references

Visit www.jurassiccoast.com for geological savvy. Telephone code for all five places and all Purbeck is ☎ 01929.

Charts comprise AC 2615 (1:75,000), 2610 (1:40,000), 2172 (1:12,500); SC 5601.11 Lulworth Cove (1:5,000), Worbarrow Bay and Chapman's Pool (1:12,500). 5601.8 Swanage & Studland Bays (1:12,500). Peter Bruce's *Inshore along the Dorset Coast* goes closer inshore than most yachtsmen would dare to go.

LULWORTH COVE

Entrance – 50°36´·99N 02°14´·82W

This (too) popular anchorage is in a circular cove below the soaring chalk of Bindon Hill. The primaeval ambience is almost tangible.

Ashore By the carpark a Heritage Centre, ☎ 400587, explains the geology. Then walk to The Stairhole close W or 1M further along to Durdle Door and other rock formations. Just E of the entrance is the Fossil Forest, ie fossilised tree stumps.

Restaurants Lulworth Cove Hotel, ☎ 400333; £11. Lulworth Beach Hotel, ☎ 400404; £12. Lulworth Beach Café cooks seafood at the beach; bring your own bottle. A general store is situated at West Lulworth.

Chandlery Lulworth Marine, Boathouse, ☎ 400560.

Approaches From the W, a simple inshore trip to the waypoint. From the E, see Passage Notes (page 26) for St Aldhelm's Race and Lulworth Range, whose W limit is at 02°14´·38W, ie the Cove is outside it.

Landmarks From seaward the narrow entrance is not easy to discern against the inner background, until you glimpse a forest of masts.

Stairhole's folded strata; the Cove beyond

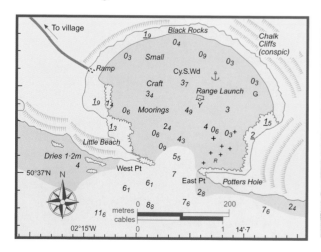

Pilotage The waypoint is 50°36´·69N 02°14´·82W, 000°/3 cables to the entrance, which is biased towards the eastern point. Speed limit 5kn.

Access By day (unlit), but not in fresh onshore winds or swell as the anchorage will be marginal.

Shelter Good in offshore winds, but otherwise exposed; leave at the first sign of onshore winds.

Anchor roughly in the NE quadrant in 2–4m with moderate holding on clay/sand/weed. The SE quadrant is rocky and much of the W half is taken up by local moorings, rocks and shoals. Land on the NW beach. The Range safety boat's yellow mooring buoy is nearly in the centre of the cove.

Tides HW Lulworth Cove at sp is 15 mins and at nps 5 mins after HW Portland. LW at nps is the same as, and at sp 5 mins before, LW Portland. MHWS is 2·2m, MLWS 0·2m; MHWN is 1·5m, MLWN 1·0m. Tidal streams inside are slight.

WORBARROW BAY

W Anchorage – 50°37´·09N 02°13´·29W
E Anchorage – 50°37´·04N 02°11´·13W
The 1.5m wide, crab-shaped bay is wholly within Lulworth range. At the W end Mupe Bay is tucked in behind Mupe Rocks and below the massif of Bindon Hill. In centre stage the skyline plummets down to the gap at Arish Mell, before rising once more to Flowers Barrow; then down to the E end and the appendage of Worbarrow Tout.

Ashore Land on the beaches at either end; not at Arish Mell. From Mupe Bay it is easy to visit the Fossil Forest at Lulworth Cove. From the E end, walk 0.75M E to the abandoned and infinitely sad ruins of Tyneham. In Dec 1943 the villagers were evicted from their homes by the War Office – with a clear assurance that they would be able to return. Sixty years on, the Army is still there.

Landmarks The skyline's cleavage at Arish Mell and chalk falls at Bindon Hill are eye-catching.

Chalk falls at Bindon Hill. Mupe Rock in front

Pilotage A third waypoint is not needed. Simply avoid Mupe Rks and rocky ledges W & E of Arish Mell, and NW of Worbarrow Tout. An outfall from Winfrith Heath nuclear power station runs from Arish Mell to the 'Atomic' buoy 2.4M offshore.

Access By day (unlit), but not in fresh onshore winds or swell as the anchorage will be marginal.

Anchorages At Mupe Bay in W'lies and at the E end in E'lies; leave if onshore winds freshen.

Tides HW & LW times and heights for Mupe Rocks are as for Lulworth Cove, above.

CHAPMAN'S POOL

Anchorage – 50°35´·53N 02°03´·91W 'Far from the madding crowd's ignoble strife...' beneath Houns-tout Cliff and Emmetts Hill.

Ashore Climb the hill to Worth Matravers (1.5M), to feast on pasties and real West Country ales at the Square and Compass, ☎ 439229 – you will not be true to your heritage if you fail in this pleasant task.

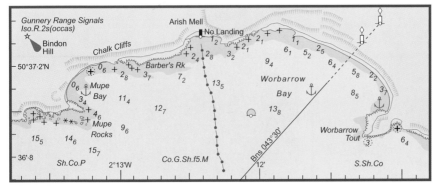

Chapman's Pool from Emmetts Hill

Walk to the C12 eponymous chapel on St Aldhelm's Hd and chat with the NCI lookouts (see page 25).

Pilotage Approaching from the W, stay 4 cables offshore to clear the drying Kimmeridge Ledges. A waypoint of 50°35´·03N 02°04´·43W, 033°/0.6M to the anchorage, clears rocks either side of the Pool.

Anchorage In the centre of the Pool in 2–5m, good holding on mud/sand, well sheltered from N to E winds. Land on the beach or at the slip to the SE. The Range launch's yellow mooring is 300m SW.

Tides Use Mupe Bay (Worbarrow) differences.

Tidal streams run almost constantly SSE down the W side of St Aldhelm's Head, due to a back eddy.

SWANAGE (Thomas Hardy's *Knollsea*)
Anchorage – 50°36´·69N 01°56´·94W
This small seaside resort is a metropolis compared to the other four anchorages. But nautically Swanage has simply a bay and a pier. There is no harbour, therefore no Harbour Authority and no HM. Self-help is the name of the game at Swanage: For example every plank of the beautifully restored pier was paid for by private donations.

SHORESIDE

Tourist Office is at Shore Rd. ☎ 422885; 🖷 423423. mail@swanage.gov.uk; www.swanage.gov.uk Jul/Aug, open 7/7, 1000–1700.

What to see/do Heritage Centre, 1000–1700 7/7 for local colour and history. Say hello to NCI at Peveril Pt. Durlston Country Park, 1M S of town, is good cliff-top walking amid flora & fauna. The whole Isle of Purbeck is prime walking country.

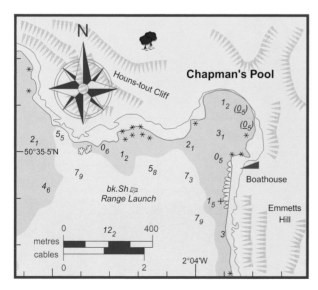

Rail To Corfe Castle by steam train, £6 return, ☎ 425800. Join Weymouth-London line at Wareham.

Bus Traveline, ☎ 0870 608 2608 for timetable info.

Taxi ☎ 422007; 425350; 25800; 427440.

Car hire U-Drive, ☎ 553870; 1 Johns Rd, Wareham.

Bike hire Bike About, ☎ 425050, 71 High St.

Beaches Excellent, E-facing; narrow at HW.

Supermarkets Somerfield and Leo by the station.

Banks Plenty around the centre.

Launderette 59 King's Rd, ☎ 422780.

Restaurants The Cauldron, 5 High St, ☎ 422671; £15, shut Mon. The Galley, Fish & Game Restaurant, 9 High St, ☎ 427299; £16.50. The Trattoria, 12 High St, ☎ 423784; £15. All at the pier end of town.

NAVIGATION

Approaches From the S, be aware of Peveril Pt race; see Passage Notes on page 27. Peveril Pt Ledge is marked by a PHM buoy, QR. From the N/E go direct to the anchorage. Avoid the Phippards and Tanville Ledges, drying to the NNW of the pier.

Shelter is good in SW–N winds, but poor in NE–SE winds, especially if swell works in.

Facilities The pier is run by Piermaster, Mr Russ Johnston ☎ 427058. A No-Anchoring area covers 100m either side and 200m ENE of the pierhead. Outside this area private moorings are laid to no

Looking west past Wellington clock tower and the pier to the seafront

perceptible pattern; be very wary of using one. Pleasure boats berth on the pier and yachts could do so in calm conditions, with the PM's consent.

Anchor clear of moorings to the N/NW of the pier in about 5m on sand & broken shells. Land at a stone jetty 200m W of the pier or near the SC.

Tides LW Swanage at sp is 45 mins, and at nps 55 mins, before LW Poole Harbour. Times of HW are not given due to the ill-defined tidal curve; double HWs occur. MHWS is 2·0m, MLWS 0·5m; MHWN is 1·6m, MLWN is 1·2m.

Tidal streams rotate oddly around the Bay. Avoid Peveril Pt Race, especially on the SW-going ebb.

YC Swanage SC, ☎ 422987. Open Thur & w/ends for dinghy racing; friendly bar and showers.

Chandlery Swanage Chandlery ☎ 424989.

POOLE BAY & THE SOLENT

Racing off Cowes

CONTENTS

INTRODUCTION

Heading east along the Purbeck coast brings you to the safe and popular anchorage of Studland Bay, close to the start of the Swash Channel into Poole Harbour. One of the largest natural harbours in the world, Poole's modern marinas to the north contrast with its peaceful anchorages set among acres of nature reserve to the south.

From here it is just a short hop to the Solent. Stretching roughly 25 to 30 miles from Hurst Point in the W towards Chichester Harbour in the E, it is one of the most popular coastal areas in Britain,

offering a variety of cruising grounds from the lively, bustling marinas of Cowes and Portsmouth to the quiet backwaters of Wootton Creek and Newtown River. As it is a centre of yachting excellence, you are never too far away from a boatyard or chandlery should you need any repairs carried out.

PASSAGE NOTES

CROSSING POOLE BAY

Sheltered from W'ly and N'ly winds, the passage across Poole Bay is straightforward, whether

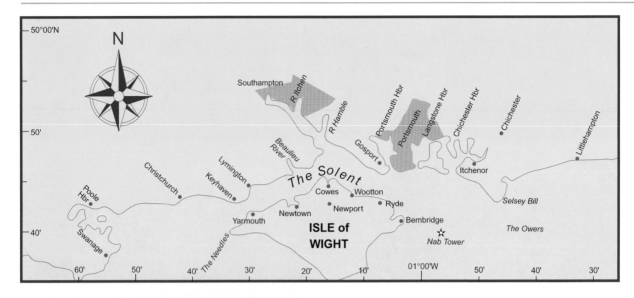

An unusually benign Needles

making for The Needles or towards Hurst Point. Tidal streams are weak N of a line between Handfast Pt and Hengistbury Hd, as well as within Christchurch Bay. Take care around Hengistbury Hd, S of Christchurch Hbr, where a groyne extends a cable south, with Beerpan Rks lying a further 100m SE of it. The tide runs fast and sometimes breaks over Christchurch Ledge, which stretches 2.75M from Hengistbury Hd.

APPROACHING THE SOLENT FROM THE NEEDLES CHANNEL

As the Solent is among the busiest waters in Britain, you need to enter it with the due care that it deserves. If you are approaching the Western Solent, you can't fail to spot the distinctive Needles Rocks at the western end of the Isle of Wight, along with the adjacent chalk cliffs of High Down. By night the lighthouse at the end of the

Needles flashes Oc (2) WRG 20s 24m 17–13M. A couple of good deterrents from getting too close to this area are the Goose Rock, situated about 50m WNW of the lighthouse, and the wreck of the Greek ship *Varvassi* which sank about 150m WSW of the rock. Three miles SW of the Needles Rock the fairway buoy signifies the deep water entrance to the Needles Channel, although most yachts enter the fairway between the SW Shingles Buoy and the Bridge Buoy. To the NW of the channel are the Dolphin Bank and Shingles Bank, the latter being one of the most prominent features in the Solent. Keep away from this bank, as parts of it dry at LW and seas break on it even if there's not much swell. The channel is clearly marked and lit by the standard buoyage, so if you stick to that you can't go wrong. Be aware, however, of the strengths of the tides in this area, particularly on the ebb when the stream sets in a WSW direction across the Shingles at a rate of about 3 to 4kn.

To the SE of the Needles Channel is the Pot Bank, where the minimum depths are around 15m. Pay particular attention in bad weather to the Bridge, a reef that runs eight cables W of the lighthouse, the end of which is marked by a WCM lt buoy. Also bear in mind that dangerous seas can form in the Needles Channel in S to W gales, particularly when the tide is on the ebb. In these circumstances you would be better off approaching the eastern Solent via the Nab Tower or, alternatively, sheltering in Poole Harbour.

Again in strong winds, or if you are coming from St Alban's Head or Poole, it may be preferable to use the clearly marked North Channel which is situated just N of the Shingles Bank. The North and Needles Channels merge S of Hurst Point, where you should to be aware of the Trap, a shoaling spit about 150m SE of Hurst Castle.

THE WESTERN SOLENT – KEYHAVEN TO BEAULIEU RIVER

With considerably less commercial traffic and several tranquil harbours, the western Solent is popular with yachtsmen. The backdrop of the New Forest stretching along the shoaling shores of the mainland and the unspoilt coastline of the Isle of Wight make it a particularly attractive cruising ground.

Apart from the Needles Channel, the western Solent has few serious hazards to watch out for, provided you keep to reasonable soundings. Along the Island's shores, Black Rock, Hamstead Ledge, Salt Mead Ledges and Gurnard Ledge are all clearly marked with buoys. In strong winds and tides, heavy overfalls can occur at these particular spots but if you stay to the correct side of the buoyage you will not encounter any problems.

On the mainland coast, between Hurst Point and Lymington, the chart shows that you should not try to cut inshore where the shallow water off Pennington extends some 0.75M offshore. East of Lymington's entrance, the Pylewell Lake shallows also protrude approximately 1M offshore. To the W of Beaulieu entrance, the Beaulieu spit can easily catch out anyone heading for the harbour. With patches drying to around 0.3m about 100m S of the spit, make sure you do not cut the corner.

It is worth remembering that throughout the Solent, even short hops between harbours need to be carefully planned using a tidal stream atlas, especially on spring tides.

THE CENTRAL SOLENT – SOUTHAMPTON TO COWES

The central Solent is a busy but exciting area to sail. With Cowes as the hub of British yachting and Southampton a magnet for large container vessels and high speed ferries, cruising between these two harbours needs constant vigilance.

An Area of Concern (AOC) dominates this region in order to improve safety for commercial ships. Many pleasure boats cut across the AOC, used by large vessels bound to or from Southampton normally via the eastern Solent. To reduce the risk of collision, vessels over 150m in length, when entering the AOC, are given a Moving Prohibited Zone (MPZ), extending 1,000m ahead of the craft and 100m on either beam. Craft under 20m LOA are prohibited from entering this zone. The Vessel Traffic Service (VTS), operated by Southampton on VHF Ch 12 and Ch 14, controls the shipping throughout the Solent, (with the exception of Portsmouth Harbour and its approaches north of a line from Gilkicker Point to Outer Spit buoy, which is regulated by QHM Portsmouth on VHF Ch 11). If near the AOC, listen out on VHF Ch 12 for the regular broadcasts transmitted by Southampton VTS.

Hazards along the Isle of Wight shoreline are mainly close inshore and are avoided by staying in reasonable soundings. If sailing along the shore from Osborne Bay to Cowes, the rocks off Norris Castle can easily catch you out. The popular anchorage in Osborne Bay is well sheltered from the prevailing wind and out of the main tidal stream, but watch out for the rocks at its eastern end and the drying patches some 150m offshore to the west.

On the mainland side, Horseshoe Spit, E of the entrance to Beaulieu River, runs S of Stansore Point, but is clearly marked by the Lepe Spit SCM. Extending well out from the shore, Calshot Spit can be a trap to newcomers, especially as you may well have to stay quite close to its eastern edge to keep clear of the main fairway with its AOC.

Being one of the few 'mid channel' hazards in the Solent, the Bramble Bank lies roughly halfway between Cowes and Southampton Water. It is very easily misjudged, despite being well marked by Hill Head and East Knoll buoys to the N, East Bramble ECM, West Knoll green conical buoy and the Brambles post to the S. Approximately 1M N of the East Bramble ECM and NW of Lee Point are two buoyed areas for jet skiing and water skiing, both of which you may want to avoid.

DISTANCE TABLE

Approximate distances in nautical miles are by the most direct route, whilst avoiding dangers

		1	2	3	4	5	6	7	8	9	10	11	12	13	14	15
1.	Poole Hbr ent	1														
2.	Needles Lt Ho	14	2													
3.	Lymington	24	6	3												
4.	Yarmouth (IOW)	22	4	2	4											
5.	Beaulieu R. ent	29	11	7	7	5										
6.	Cowes	27	14	10	9	2	6									
7.	Southampton	34	20	16	16	9	9	7								
8.	R. Hamble (ent)	34	18	12	13	6	6	5	8							
9.	Portsmouth	35	23	19	19	12	10	18	13	9						
10.	Langstone Hbr	39	25	21	21	14	12	21	18	5	10					
11.	Chichester Bar	42	28	23	24	17	15	23	18	8	5	11				
12.	Bembridge	39	24	18	19	13	10	18	15	5	6	8	12			
13.	Nab Tower	44	29	23	24	18	15	24	19	10	7	6	6	13		
14.	St Catherine's Pt	25	12	19	21	27	15	36	29	20	20	19	17	15	14	
15.	Littlehampton	61	46	44	45	38	36	45	42	31	28	25	28	22	35	15

No Man's Land Fort

THE EASTERN SOLENT – WOOTTON CREEK TO CHICHESTER

The eastern end is probably the most diverse section of the Solent, with ports ranging from the large modern marinas of Portsmouth through to the rural charm of Chichester and Langstone. With its deep water berthing capacity recently increased, Bembridge is also proving ever more popular with locals and visitors alike. However, less protected from the Isle of Wight, the eastern Solent can be more exposed than the other two areas in rough weather. You should avoid crossing Langstone and Chichester bars in strong onshore winds, particularly against the ebb on spring tides.

Like the rest of the Solent, hazards in this part are all clearly marked on the charts. Among the sand banks to look out for are the East and West Pole sands on either side of Chichester Harbour entrance and the East and West Winner banks flanking the channel to Langstone. Beware of the expansive Ryde Sands, which can easily catch you out, although when coming from the E, staying N of No Man's Land Fort and the SW Mining Ground Y buoy should keep you out of trouble.

Bembridge Ledge is one of the few rocky hazards in the eastern approach. Watch out too for the prominent Wootton Rocks just to the W of Wootton Creek. Although a passage between these rocks and Wootton Point exists at HW, it is best not to use this without local knowledge. Passing N of the conspicuous Royal Victoria Yacht Club starting platform will keep the rocks at arm's length. The man-made barrier between Southsea and Horse Sand Fort could also be considered a potential hazard and can only be safely crossed through the well marked Main Passage with a favourable tide. However, with the right tide and local knowledge, smaller yachts do use the Boat Passage close inshore when sailing between Langstone and Portsmouth. As is the case in the Central Solent, the biggest hazards are the ferries and large commercial ships entering and leaving the Solent between Horse Sand Fort and No Man's Land Fort. Listen out on VHF Ch 12 or VHF Ch 11 for the Portsmouth area for regular updates of shipping movement.

EASTWARD SOUTH OF THE ISLE OF WIGHT

The passage eastward S of the Isle of Wight can be plotted close inshore (approx 1 to 2 cables) from the Needles to Freshwater Bay. Further E, however, look out for Brook and Atherfield Ledges which need at least a 5-cable offing, especially when the E-going stream sets towards them. Off St Catherine's Pt, with its conspic lighthouse (Fl 5 41m 25M & FR 35m 13M), St Catherine's race can be extremely dangerous, particularly at or near springs with wind over tide. It is therefore best to give it a wide berth of around 3M. Approx 1.25M SE of the point, the tide turns E x N at HW Portsmouth +0520 and W x S at HW Portsmouth –0055, with a rate of up to 3.75kn at springs.

Five and a half miles NE of St Catherine's Pt, rocks extend 2.5 cables either side of Dunnose, at times creating a race. Sandown Bay, with its weak tidal streams, offers a temporary anchorage, but from here to Bembridge there are drying rocks extending up to 3 cables offshore, so keep to the E of the Bembridge Ledge ECM (Q (3) 10s). The final approach to the eastern Solent is very straightforward and far safer in SW/W gales than the Needles Channel, although the commercial shipping tends to be pretty heavy. Coming from France, head for the Nab Tower, which is approximately 4.5M east of Foreland. You will see that the main channel into the Solent is well marked and easy to follow. For passage details to or from the Sussex Ports, see the introduction to chapter three.

Due to the heavy shipping that you are likely to encounter when approaching the Solent, particularly towards the eastern end, a radar reflector is essential. Once in the Solent, there are plenty of harbours and marinas to choose from, most of which offer all the necessary facilities, including maintenance and repair services. A useful service for breakdowns in the area is Sea Start. Based in the Hamble, it can be contacted on ☎ 0800 885500.

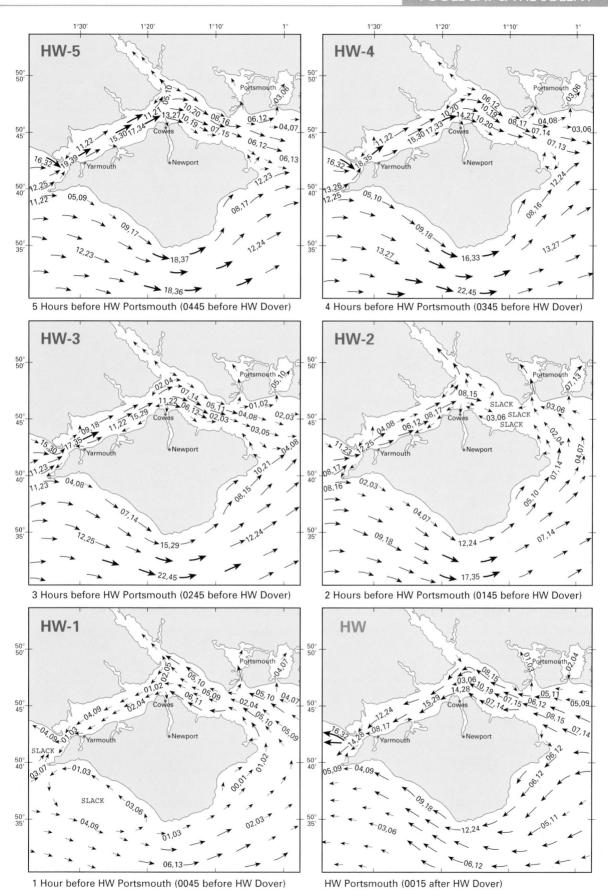

5 Hours before HW Portsmouth (0445 before HW Dover)

4 Hours before HW Portsmouth (0345 before HW Dover)

3 Hours before HW Portsmouth (0245 before HW Dover)

2 Hours before HW Portsmouth (0145 before HW Dover)

1 Hour before HW Portsmouth (0045 before HW Dover)

HW Portsmouth (0015 after HW Dover)

Chapter 2

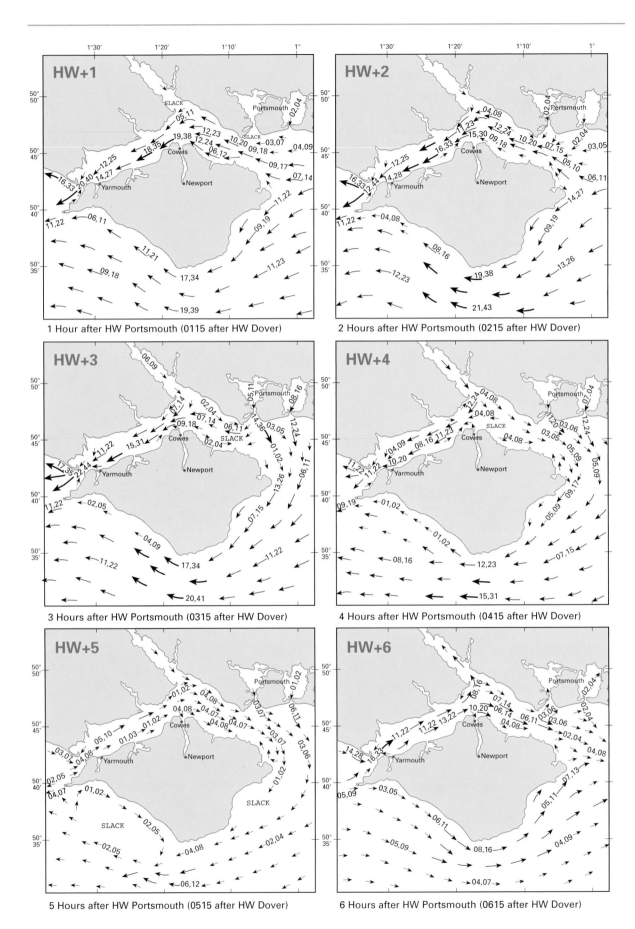

1 Hour after HW Portsmouth (0115 after HW Dover)

2 Hours after HW Portsmouth (0215 after HW Dover)

3 Hours after HW Portsmouth (0315 after HW Dover)

4 Hours after HW Portsmouth (0415 after HW Dover)

5 Hours after HW Portsmouth (0515 after HW Dover)

6 Hours after HW Portsmouth (0615 after HW Dover)

POOLE HARBOUR

Poole Harbour entrance – 50°40'·93N 01°56'·96W

One of the largest natural harbours in the world, Poole is also considered by many to be among the finest. Boasting 10,000 acres of channels, creeks, mudflats and nature reserves, it is accessible at all states of the tide and in all conditions, except in strong E to SE'ly winds. Due care and attention, however, is needed when entering the harbour as the entrance is only 300m wide, with a chain ferry plying to and fro across its narrowest point. Once inside you can have the best of both worlds: To the North are several modern marinas (some of which can be expensive) in close proximity to a multitude of shops and restaurants while to the South are a few tranquil anchorages set within the unspoilt nature reserves that are home to an abundance of wildlife.

SHORESIDE (Telephone code 01202)

Tourist Office Poole Tourism, Waterfront Museum, 4, High St, Poole, Dorset, BH15 2ZX. ☎ 253253; 🖾 633888; tourism@poole.gov.uk; www.pooletourism.com

What to see/do Poole Pottery is one of Dorset's premier attractions. Open Mon–Sat 0900–1700 and Sun 1030–1630; ☎ 668681. Great for children is the Tower Park Leisure Complex in Poole, ☎ 722917, which offers water rides, mega bowls, cinemas and restaurants. A more sedate way to pass the time is to visit the Waterfront Museum in Old High St, ☎ 262600. To try to recoup some of your marina charges go to the greyhound racing at Poole Stadium in Wimborne Rd (☎ 677449), held every Tues, Thur and Sat evening at 1930hrs.

A stopover at Poole should not exclude a landing on Brownsea Island, the largest and only publicly-owned island in the harbour. Managed by the National Trust, its 500 acres are a sanctuary for wildlife and the numerous woodland walks and trails are fun to explore. You could either drop anchor off the W end of the island and row in to Pottery Pier, paying a small landing fee for each person (£3.70 per adult; £1.70 per child (under 5yrs goes free); £9 for a family ticket comprising two adults

Poole Quay, no longer packed with boats

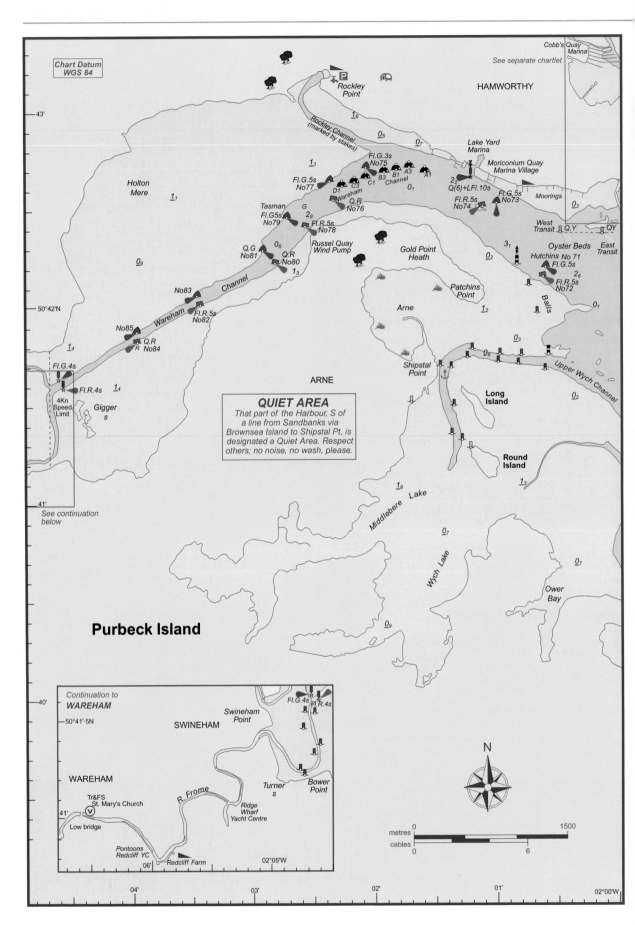

Chart Datum
WGS 84

43'

HAMWORTHY

Cobb's Quay
Marina

See separate chartlet

Rockley
Point

Rockley Channel
(marked by stakes)

1_6

0_5

0_7

Lake Yard
Marina

Moriconium Quay
Marina Village

Holton
Mere

1_3

Fl.G.3s
No75

Fl.G.7s
No77

D1
Nareham
Q.R
No76

B3
C3
C1
B1
A3
A1

Channel

0_1

Q(6)+LFl.10s
2_2

Fl.R.5s
No74

Fl.G.5s
No73

Moorings

0_3

1_1

Tasman
Fl.G.5s
No79

G
2_9
Fl.R.5s
No78

West
Transit
Q.Y
Q.Y
East
Transit

Q.G
No81

0_6
Q.R
No80

Russel Quay
Wind Pump

Gold Point
Heath

0_2

3_1

Oyster Beds
Hutchins No 71
Fl.G.5s

0_9

1_3

Fl.R.5s
No72
2_6

50°42'N

No83

Channel

Wareham

Patchins
Point

Arne

1_2

Balls

0_1

No85

Fl.R.5s
No82

Q.R
R
No84

0_3

Upper Wych Channel

0_6

1_4

Fl.G.4s

1_4

Shipstal
Point

Long
Island

0_2

4Kn
Speed
Limit

Fl.R.4s

Gigger
s

ARNE

QUIET AREA
That part of the Harbour, S of
a line from Sandbanks via
Brownsea Island to Shipstal Pt, is
designated a Quiet Area. Respect
others; no noise, no wash, please.

Round
Island

1_3

41'

See continuation
below

1_8

Middlebere Lake

0_7

40'

Wych Lake

0_7

Ower
Bay

Purbeck Island

0_9

Continuation to
WAREHAM

50°41'·5N

SWINEHAM

Swineham
Point

Fl.G.4s

Fl.R.4s

WAREHAM

R. Frome

Turner
s

Bower
Point

Tr&FS
St. Mary's Church

41'

Low bridge

Ridge
Wharf
Yacht Centre

N

Pontoons
Redcliff YC

06'

Redcliff Farm

02°05'W

metres
cables

0

0

1500

6

04'

03'

02'

01'

02°00'W

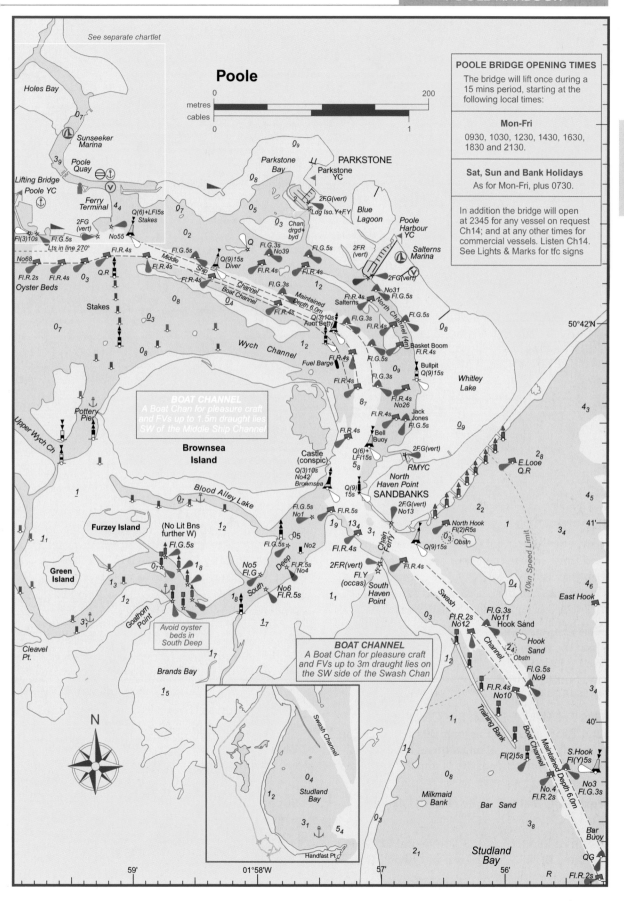

See separate chartlet

Poole

Holes Bay

0₇

Sunseeker Marina

3₉

Poole Quay

Lifting Bridge
Poole YC

Ferry Terminal

4₄

2FG (vert)

Fl(3)10s

Fl.G.5s

Lts in line 270°

No55

Q(6)+LFl5s
Stakes

0₇

No68

Fl.R.2s

Fl.R.4s

0₃

Q.R

Oyster Beds

Stakes

0₇

0₃

0₈

0₈

Upper Wych Ch

Pottery Pier

1

BOAT CHANNEL
*A Boat Chan for pleasure craft
and FVs up to 1.5m draught lies
SW of the Middle Ship Channel*

**Brownsea
Island**

Blood Alley Lake

0₇

Furzey Island

1₂

Green
Island

1₃

1₂

3₁

Goathorn Point

*Avoid oyster
beds in
South Deep*

Cleavel
Pt.

1₇

Brands Bay

1₅

N

PARKSTONE

0₉

Parkstone Bay

Parkstone YC

11

0₈

0₅

2

2FG(vert)

Ldg Iso.Y+F.Y

0₃

Chan
drgd+
byd

Blue
Lagoon

0₂

Middle

Fl.R.4s

Fl.G.5s

Q(9)15s
Diver

Fl.G.3s
No39

Fl.R.4s

Ship

Fl.R.4s

Q

Fl.G.5s

0₈

Channel

Boat Channel

0₄

Fl.R.4s

Fl.R.4s

Fl.R.4s

Fl.G.3s

Wych Channel

Maintained
Depth 6.0m

Aunt Betty
Q(3)10s

1₂

1₂

Fuel Barge

Fl.R.4s

Fl.R.4s

Fl.G.5s

Fl.R.4s

Fl.G.3s

8₇

Fl.R.4s
No26

Fl.R.4s

Bell
Buoy

Castle
(conspic)

Q(3)10s
No42/
Brownsea

Q(6)+
LFl15s

5₈

Fl.G.5s
No1

Fl.R.5s

Fl.G.5s

Fl.G.5s
No2

Fl.G.5s

No5
Fl.G

0₇

1₈

Deep

0₅

Fl.R.5s
No4

South

No6
Fl.R.5s

1₈

1₇

2FR
(vert)

No31
Fl.G.5s

Salterns

Poole
Harbour
YC

Salterns
Marina

2FG(vert)

North Channel (4m)

Basket Boom
Fl.R.4s

0₈

Bullpit
Q(9)15s

Whitley
Lake

4₃

Jack
Jones
Fl.G.5s

0₉

50°42'N

2FG(vert)

RMYC

North
Haven Point

SANDBANKS

2FG(vert)
No13

Q(9)
15s

2₈

E.Looe
Q.R

4₅

North Hook
Fl(2)R5s

0₃ Obstn

2₂

1

Q(9)15s

3₄

41'

4₆

East Hook

10kn Speed Limit

1₉

13₄

3₁

Chain
Ferry

Fl.R.4s

Fl.Y
(occas)

South
Haven
Point

1₁

Fl.R.4s

0₃

0₄

Swash

Fl.G.3s
No11

Hook Sand

Hook
Sand

Fl.R.4s
No10

2₄
Obstn

Channel

Fl.G.5s
No9

3₄

Fl.R.2s
No12

1₂

Training Bank

Boat Channel

Maintained
Depth 6.0m

BOAT CHANNEL
*A Boat Chan for pleasure craft
and FVs up to 3m draught lies on
the SW side of the Swash Chan*

1₁

1₂

0₈

Milkmaid
Bank

Bar Sand

3₈

Fl(2)5s

S.Hook
Fl(Y)5s

No3
Fl.G.3s

No.4
Fl.R.2s

Bar
Buoy

QG

*Studland
Bay*

2₁

Swash Channel

0₄

*Studland
Bay*

3₁

5₄

Handfast Pt

R

Fl.R.2s

59'

01°58'W

57'

56'

POOLE BRIDGE OPENING TIMES

The bridge will lift once during a
15 mins period, starting at the
following local times:

Mon-Fri

0930, 1030, 1230, 1430, 1630,
1830 and 2130.

Sat, Sun and Bank Holidays

As for Mon-Fri, plus 0730.

In addition the bridge will open
at 2345 for any vessel on request
Ch14; and at any other times for
commercial vessels. Listen Ch14.
See Lights & Marks for tfc signs

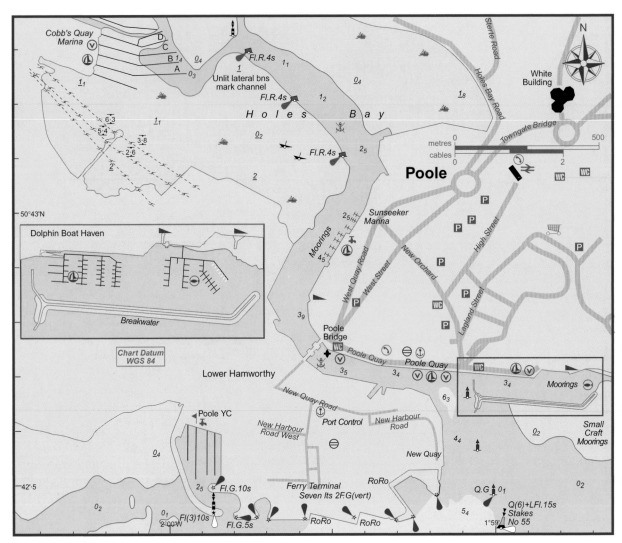

and three children), or take one of the ferries from Sandbanks or Poole Quay. For information on ferry times call Brownsea Island ☎ 707744 or Brownsea Island Ferries ☎ 01929 462383.

Rail The station is about a 10–15mins walk from the High Street. Good rail connections to Weymouth, London Waterloo (approx 2 hrs) and Southampton. National Rail Enquiries ☎ 0845 7484950.

Bus The Wilts & Dorset Bus Company, ☎ 673555, offers an Explorer Bus Ticket giving you unlimited travel on its buses for one day. Also valid on many of the Hampshire Bus and Solent Blue Line buses.

Taxi Poole Radio Cabs ☎ 666333; Dial–A–Cab ☎ 666822.

Car hire Budget Car and Van Rental ☎ 723343; U-Drive ☎ 747275; National Car Rental ☎ 667300.

Bike hire Action Bikes, Dolphin Centre ☎ 680123.

Ferries Brittany Ferries, ☎ 08705 360360, runs services from Poole to Cherbourg. Condor Ferries, ☎ 01305 761551, provides services from Poole to Jersey, Guernsey and St Malo. For the Sandbanks to Studland Ferry, The Floating Bridge, call ☎ 01929 450203. Wight Link operates ferries to and from the Isle of Wight, ☎ 0870 5827744. For Brownsea Island see above.

Flights European flights from Bournemouth International Airport, ☎ 364000.

Beaches Three sandy beaches on the E side of the hbr are Sandbanks Beach, Shore Road Beach and Branksome Chine Beach. Studland Bay to the W.

Supermarkets Sainsbury's in the High St is within easy walking distance from the Town Quay, or else go to Marks & Spencer's food section in the Dolphin Shopping Centre. On the Town Quay is The Cabin newsagents for essential items, with a greengrocer just a bit further along.

Brownsea Island dominates the eastern harbour area

Banks Several major high street banks and building societies, with cashpoints, are in the High St.

Restaurants The Quay incorporates several eateries including The Warehouse Brasserie, ☎ 677238, good for seafood, The Custom House, ☎ 676767, with its continental café bar and *à la carte* menu, and the convivial Mexican restaurant, Las Margaritas, ☎ 670066. Leading off from The Quay in the High St are several other eating places that can be highly recommended, including Storm Fish, ☎ 674970, and John B's French Restaurant, ☎ 672440. For outstanding cuisine, go to the Mansion House in Thames St, again a stone's throw from The Quay, ☎ 685666, while the Guildhall Tavern in Market St, ☎ 671717, offers Mediterranean food in a pub-like atmosphere. Over at Sandbanks try La Roche Brasserie at the Haven Hotel, ☎ 707333, which provides spectacular views of Poole Bay and Studland. On the other side of the bay, not far from the S slipway of the Sandbanks chain ferry, is the popular Shell Bay Seafood Restaurant, ☎ 01929 450363.

NAVIGATION

Charts AC SC 5601.5 (1:75,000); 5601.9 (1:12,500); 5601.10 (1:12,500); 2611 (1:12,500), 2175 (1:20,000).

Approaches From the E make directly for the WPT (see Pilotage). Approaching from the S, give Old Harry Rocks off Handfast Pt a good offing. Note that the tide runs fiercely here and a considerable sea can be expected, particularly when there is a strong wind over tide.

Landmarks The prominent white Old Harry Rocks are approx 1.25M S of the seaward end of the Swash Channel SH Bar Buoy. Another useful landmark is the conspic white Haven Hotel on Sandbanks, on the E side of the hbr entrance.

Pilotage The WPT 50°39'·14N 01°55'·00W lies approx 0.25M SE of the Swash Channel Bar Buoy (QG), from where the Swash Channel, dredged to 6m and well buoyed and lit, runs NW for approx 2M to the mouth of the harbour. The channel is flanked by the Hook Sand shoals, drying in places to 0.8m, to the E and a training wall, which covers at HW, to the W. This training wall is well marked with red PH posts but only the outer one is lit (2FR (vert)). A Small Boat Channel for draughts of up to 3m runs between these posts and the PHMs identifying the Swash Channel. The mouth of the harbour is bordered by Studland to port and Sandbanks to stbd, with the large white Haven Hotel providing a useful landmark.

If coasting from the E and with weather and tide permitting, the East Looe Channel between Sandbanks beach and the Hook Sand shoals is a useful short cut. The E Looe PHM (QR) marks its eastern end and the North Hook PHM (Fl (2) R5s) its western end. From the latter leave the lit green beacons close to stbd and the Swash WCM (Q (9)) buoy to port before joining the main fairway. A chain ferry regularly crosses the mouth of the harbour but at present has no right of way over boats using the entrance; although there are moves afoot to reverse this. A black ball displayed at its forward end indicates that it is

The Small Boat Channel, with the training wall to port

about to move off the slipway while a white flashing strobe is shown at its forward end to identify the direction in which it is going. When stationary at night the chain ferry displays a FW lt and in fog sounds one long and two short blasts every 2 mins. For ferry crossings see under 'Chain Ferry' below. It is important to anticipate the ferry movements in advance, as the tide runs very fast in the entrance, and remember that the chains are taut at the front so try to pass well astern of it. Use your engine, if you have one, when entering the harbour to give greater control.

Once inside the entrance, with the conspic Brownsea Island dead ahead, the fairway divides at the Brownsea Buoy ECM (Q (3) 10s), with the designated Quiet Area to the S and the vibrant town and marinas to the N. The channels in Poole harbour comprise the following:

1) The Middle Ship Channel, leading towards the Town Quay and Dolphin Boat Haven, is primarily used by ferries coming to and from the Hamworthy terminal. Small yachts with draughts of up to 1.5m should use the Boat Channel which runs parallel S of the dredged Middle Ship Channel, leaving the PHMs just to starboard (see chartlet). To get to Dolphin Boat Haven, enter the Little Channel, passing the No 55 Stakes SCM (Q (6) +LFl 5s) to stbd, before turning on to a course of about 349°. Dolphin Boat Haven is behind the bkwtr on your stbd side.

2) The North Channel, providing access to Salterns Marina and Parkstone Haven, is well marked and lit, but keep to the outside of the bends for the best water.

3) The Wych Channel branches to port from the Middle Ship Channel between No 46 PHM (Fl R 4s) and No 48 PHM (Fl R 4s), with the fuel barge situated within this vicinity. Marked by unlit port and stbd hand stakes, the channel runs close to

the N side of Brownsea Island and has approx 2.5m of water around Pottery Pier.

4) The South Deep Channel to the SW of Brownsea ECM buoy takes you into the dedicated Quiet Area with its numerous anchorages (see page 138).

5) The Wareham Channel See under Wareham on page 137.

Access to Poole Hbr H24 in all conditions except very strong E/SE winds. The bar across the entrance is dangerous in strong SE-S winds, especially on the ebb. At springs, try to time your arrival on the flood or during the long high water stand (see under 'Tides' on page 135).

Shelter in the harbour is good.

Keep a good distance behind the ferry

Traffic signals Traffic lts shown from Poole Bridge, above The Quay, are as follows: R = Do not approach the bridge; Fl G = Bridge is lifting, therefore proceed with caution; G = Proceed.

Poole bridge opens each day for small craft at: Mon–Fri 0930, 1030, 1230, 1430, 1630, 1830, 2130; Sat, Sun & Bank Hols = as Mon-Fri, plus 0730. In May to Sept the bridge also opens 1930. An additional lift is at 2345 each day, but only if specifically asked for. Yachts may also pass when the bridge lifts on request by a commercial vessel. For bridge movements, monitor VHF Ch 14 or call ☎ 674115.

Chain Ferry Ferry crossing times are generally on the hour from the Haven Hotel (N side of the hbr) and every 20 mins from thereon from 0700 to 2300 all year, except for Christmas Day. From Studland (S side of the hbr), crossing times are from 0710 and every 20mins until 2310. Note that during peak periods in the summer season this timetable may be subject to change and a continuous shuttle service may be provided.

Speed restrictions A 6kn speed limit is enforced from Stakes SCM buoy, past Poole quay and Poole Bridge up to Cobbs Quay in Holes Bay. It also applies within the southern half of the hbr, the designated Quiet Area. A 4kn speed limit should be adhered to in the Dolphin Boat Haven and in the River Frome, leading to Wareham. A 10kn speed limit applies to the rest of the hbr, from the seaward approach channels westward to the junction of the River Frome with the River Trent. Speeding fines of up to £1,000 can be imposed.

Tides Poole is a Standard Port. HW times are not indicated as they cannot be predicted with accuracy. Approx times can be found by using LW times and the tidal curves (refer to the *RNA*). LW sp at the hbr entrance are 25 mins before and LW nps 10 mins before LW Poole Hbr (near the Ro-Ro terminal). MHWS is 2·2m, MLWS 0·6m; MHWN is 1·7m, MLWN 1·2m. Double HWs occur except at nps. The second HW is always about 1.8m; only the height of the first HW varies from sp to nps. The tide is above Mean Level (1.6m) from about LW+2 to the next LW−2. Strong and continuous winds from the E to SW may raise sea levels by as much as 0.2m; W to NE winds may lower levels by 0.1m.

Tidal streams Due to the narrow entrance, tidal streams are fast, with the spring ebb reaching between 4.5 to 5kn.

VHF *Poole Hbr Control* Ch 14, 16 (H24); *Dolphin Boat Haven* Ch 80; *Salterns Marina* Ch 80, M; *Parkstone Haven* Ch 80, M; Poole YC Haven, callsign *Pike* Ch M, 80; *Pool Bridge* Ch 14; *Cobb's Quay* Ch 80; *Lake Yard* Ch M, M1.

FACILITIES

HM The Harbour Office, 20, New Quay Rd, Hamworthy, Poole, Dorset, BH15 4AF. ☎ 440233; 🖷 440231; harbourmaster@phc.co.uk; www.harbours.co.uk

Harbour dues £2.23 per metre per week; £0.55 per metre per day.

MARINAS

1) Poole Quay – Dolphin Boat Haven, 50°42'·70N 01°59'·11W. Access H24 from the Little Channel. VHF Ch 80; ☎/🖷 649488; harbourmaster@phc.co.uk Despite the fact that there are 100 berths designated entirely to visitors, due to its central location it gets busy in season so

Steering 349° past the SCM takes you to the Town Quay and Dolphin Boat Haven

reserve a berth ahead of time. The berthing office is immediately to port on the holding jetty. Note that the Town Quay is only used for berthing yachts of less than 15m if the Dolphin Boat Haven is full. Most of the time larger vessels of over 15m LOA will be moored alongside the quay.

Tariff £2.56 per metre per day. A short stay of up to 4 hrs is £5 for up 10m, £10 for 10–20m, £15 for over 20m. All prices are inclusive of harbour dues.

Launderette None on site, but a laundry service is available; ☎ 07788 767840.

Showers and toilets within the marina complex.

Electricity (£2.50 per hook up) and **FW** on the pontoons.

Fuel from Corralls, ☎ 674551, opposite the Town Quay just before the bridge, or from the fuel barge S of Aunt Betty buoy in the entrance to Wych Channel which is manned during the day.

Chandlery & repairs Piplers Chandler on The Quay, ☎ 673056, sells gas. For information on boatyards and repairs see page 138. Other marinas from seaward are:

The entrance to Dolphin Boat Haven, with the office and waiting pontoon to port

2) Salterns Marina, 50°42'·25N 01°57'·11W. Access H24 at any state of the tide. VHF Ch M, 80; ☎ 709971; 📠 700398; www.salterns.co.uk Situated off the North Channel, it is approached from the No 31 STM. With few **❶** berths, call ahead to find out about berthing availability.

Tariff £31.70 per day or £133.50 per wk for a 10m yacht; £37.60 per day or £205.60 per wk for a 12m yacht.This does not include the hbr dues.

Launderette (coin-operated) and **showers** are located in the Marina Office block and are accessed by a security code.

Electricity (£4.50 per day or £24 per wk) and **FW** on the pontoons.

Fuel Diesel and petrol available 24 hrs per day from the on site chandlery; located at the end of 'A' pontoon.

Food shop A convenience store is within easy walking distance of the marina, as is a Barclays Bank.

Eating On site is the Salterns Harbourside Restaurant,☎ 707321, offering alfresco dining and an *à la carte* menu. The chandlery, open seven days a week, incorporates a coffee shop.

Chandlery & repairs Salterns Chandlery, ☎ 701556, sells gas. Other facilities include a BH (45 ton), storage and electrical, engine and sail repairs.

3) Parkstone Yacht Haven, 50°42'·58N 01°57'·60W. Access H24 at any state of the tide. VHF Ch 80, M; ☎ (Parkstone YC) 743610; 📠 716394; haven@parkstoneyc.co.uk

Approach from the North Channel near No 35 SHM (Fl G 5s). Its channel has been dredged to 2.5m and is clearly marked by buoys. Leading daymarks are Y ◇s on a bearing of 006°; the ldg lts are: front Iso Y 4s; rear FY. The Haven has

eight **❶** berths, but will accommodate more visitors if resident berth holders are away.

Tariff 8–9m £14.80; 9–10m £18; 10–11m £20.10. NB All prices do not include the Poole Harbour daily dues of £0.55 per metre per day.

Showers and toilets in the clubhouse.

Launderette None on site, the nearest one being Strides Launderette in Church Rd, Parkstone ☎ 748751.

Electricity (£2.50 per day) and **FW** available on the pontoons.

Gas available on site.

Fuel No pump on site. For the nearest fuel go to Salterns Marina.

Food shop A Courts convenience store is in Sandbanks Rd, within walking distance of the marina.

Eating Visitors are welcome to use the club's bar and restaurant.

Chandlery & repairs No chandlery on site, the nearest one being a short distance away at Mitchell's Boatyard in Turks Lane. The yard on site offers boat maintenance and repair services, marine engineering, pressure washing and boat storage.

4) Poole YC Marina, 50°42'·46N 01°59'.81W; just W of the ferry terminal. Access H24, but only to visitors from affiliated yacht clubs. VHF Ch M, 80 (callsign Pike); ☎ 672687; 📠 661174. As there are no designated berths for visitors, you must contact the club before entering the marina. If space is available you will be allocated a vacant berth or asked to go alongside the waiting pontoon. After berthing, all visitors must report to the haven office or main office situated inside the front entrance to the clubhouse.

The tightly-packed Salterns Marina

The approach into Parkstone Yacht Haven

Tariff £28 per night for a 10m yacht, inclusive of hbr dues.

Facilities include showers, bar and restaurant. As it is a private club, there are no repair/fuel services on site.

5) Lake Yard, 50°42'·69N 02°01'·21W; situated towards the NW end of the harbour, just beyond SHM No 73. The entrance is marked by 2FR (vert) and 2FG (vert). Access H24 at all stages of the tide. VHF Ch M, M1; ☎ 674531; 🖷 677518. No designated ♥ berths, but Lake Yard will accommodate you if one of the resident berth holders is away.

Tariff Between £26–£42 per night for craft of between 6–15m. Does not include hbr dues.

Showers and toilets on site; no security code or swipe card needed. No **launderette** on site.

Electricity (£6 per day) and **FW** on the pontoons.

Fuel None on site, so go to Corralls or the fuel barge (see page 138).

Food shop A convenience store is a 5 mins walk from marina.

Restaurant The Waterfront Club on site serves lunchtime and evening meals seven days a week.

Water Taxi operates on weekends during the summer; VHF Ch 37, M1.

Chandlery & repairs The nearest chandlery is at Cobb's Quay, which is a 10 mins walk from Lake Yard. Full maintenance and repair services are on site, as well as hard standing, a 5 ton crane and 50 ton BH.

6) Cobbs Quay Marina 50°43'·25N 01°59'·94W. Access HW±5. ☎ 674299; 🖷 665217. Lies on the W side of Holes Bay, further upstream of Sunseeker International. Three port hand buoys (Fl R 4s) lead to the entrance. With fully serviced pontoons for yachts up to 25m LOA, the marina can normally accommodate visiting yachts, although has no designated berths for visitors.

Tariff price on application; would not include the hbr dues.

Showers North Block is next to 'D' pontoon; South Block next to 'A' pontoon. Access is by a security code.

Launderette (coin operated) is behind the north shower block and can be accessed 24 hrs a day.

Electricity (metred or daily rate, depending on length of stay) and **FW** on the pontoons.

Fuel/gas A fuel pump on site, with diesel and petrol available H24 by prior arrangement with the Dock Office. Calor, camping and LPG Gas are also sold here.

Food shop Within 5 mins of the marina is a supermarket on the corner of Woodlands Ave and Blandford Rd. Poole's town centre is about a 20–30 mins walk away.

Eating Cobb's Quay Yacht Club, ☎ 673690, is on site and welcomes visitors to its bar and restaurant; open lunchtimes and evenings.

Chandlery & repairs An on site chandlery, ☎ 682095, is situated next to the main slipway and opens seven days a week. Services include boat lifting and hard standing as well as full maintenance and repairs.

WAREHAM

For shoal draught yachts, a trip up to the ancient market town of Wareham should not be overlooked. Tucked between the Rivers Frome and Trent, it is packed full of cafés, pubs, restaurants and shops. Yachts drawing more than a metre are not advised to navigate the river right up to the quay and those with about a metre draught should only do so approx HW±1 to be certain of not going aground. However, deeper draught yachts can always moor at Ridge Wharf Yacht Centre or Redclyffe YC and go the rest of the way by dinghy.

Pilotage To enter Wareham Channel, which leads to the River Frome, continue heading W past Stakes SCM, leaving the ferry terminal to stbd. About 0.75 M further on from here you will come to No 73 SHM (Fl G 5s) and No 74 PHM (Fl R 5s) just before the entrance to Lake Pier to stbd, following on from which is a line of big ship moorings veering SW that should be left to port. Beyond this, the channel is clearly marked by buoys and posts lit to N of Giggers Island. For the best water keep to the centre of the channel, veering to the outside of all the bends.

BERTHING

1) Ridge Wharf Yacht Centre, 50°41'·04N 02°05'·38W; on the S bank of the River Frome. ☎ 01929 552650; 🖷 01929 554434; No VHF. Has a few visitors berths for yachts with a draught up to 1.5m. At LW the berths dry out to soft mud. Access for a 1.5m draught is HW±1.

Tariff £14 per night. Does not include harbour dues.

Showers and toilets accessible H24, with no security code or swipe card. No launderette on site.

Electricity (approx £2 per day) and **fresh water** on the pontoons.

Fuel pump is open from 0900–1700 Mon–Fri and 1000–1600 on weekends.

Food shop Nearest convenience store is a Spar, about half a mile away in Stoborough.

Eating The closest restaurants and cafés are in Stoborough, or else go to Wareham.

Chandlery & repairs The on site chandlery sells gas. Full repair and maintenance services are available along with hard standing and a 20-ton BH.

2) Redclyffe Yacht Club, 50°40'·82N 02°05'·99W. ☎ 01929 551227. No dedicated ❷ berths but can accommodate you if one of its members is away. Fore and aft moorings or from Mon–Fri there is space for approx four boats alongside its pontoon. Suitable for yachts drawing about 1.4m, although the moorings sometimes dry out to soft mud at LWS.

Tariff £10 per day. Not inclusive of hbr dues.

Facilities Showers, water. No other facilities on site, but the town of Wareham, full of shops and restaurants, is only about a mile away along the tow path.

3) Wareham Quay, with a depth of 0.2m at MLWS, is only advisable for bilge keelers or yachts that can take the ground. In summer it becomes very crowded with commercial pleasure craft, so mooring can be difficult. ☎ (Purbeck District Council) 01929 557220 from Mon–Fri 0900–1700.

Tariff Permitted to stay 48 hrs free of charge, although you will be expected to pay hbr dues. There are no facilities on the quay.

ANCHORAGES IN POOLE HARBOUR

The most peaceful anchorages are to be found on the S side of the hbr between Patchins Pt and South Haven Pt in the Quiet Area. Here you find a nature reserve full of creeks and shoals set against the picturesque backdrop of the Purbeck Hills. A few suggested areas (see chartlets) are:

1) In the South Deep Channel, where you can anchor off Goathorn Point or further W below Green Island.

2) To the W of Brownsea Island off Pottery Pier.

3) In the Upper Wych Channel off Shipstal Point.

4) Outside of Poole Harbour, an anchorage in Studland Bay proves very popular (see opposite), with good holding ground and plenty of protection in W to SW winds.

YCs Poole Yacht Club ☎ 672687; Parkstone Yacht Club ☎ 743610; Royal Motor Yacht Club, Sandbanks ☎ 707227; Cobb's Quay Yacht Club ☎ 673690.

Fuel in Poole Harbour Corralls ☎ 674551, opposite the Town Quay just before the bridge. Open Mon-Fri 0500–2300; Sat 0900–1600; Sun 0900–1400. Fuel barge S of Aunt Betty buoy in the entrance to Wych Channel which is manned during the day. Salterns Marina ☎ 709971; diesel and petrol available 24 hrs per day. Ridge Wharf Yacht Centre ☎ 01929 552650; although situated up the Wareham Channel, which is only accessible HW±2 for 1.5m draughts.

CHANDLERY & REPAIRS IN POOLE HARBOUR

Chandlers
Piplers, The Quay ☎ 673056; Mitchell's Boatyard, Turks Lane, Parkstone ☎ 747857; Salterns Chandlery, Lilliput ☎ 701556; CQ Chandlers, Cobbs Quay ☎ 682095

Repairs
Lifeline Marine Services ☎ 669676; Lathams Boatyard, Turks Lane, Parkstone ☎ 748029; Davis's Boatyard, Cobbs Quay ☎ 674349; Dorset Yacht Company, Hamworthy ☎ 674531; Sandbanks Yacht Co ☎ 707500

Sailmakers
Quay Sails, Lagland St ☎ 681128; The Rig Shop ☎ 677717; Southern Sails ☎ 677000.

Goathorn Point, one of several anchorages in the Quiet Area

STUDLAND BAY
Anchorage – 50°38´·73N 01°55´·90W

Walks From the village walk 1M E to Old Harry Rocks and circuit round Ballard Down with fine views over Poole Bay to the Isle of Wight. South Beach is the nearest for yachtsmen.

Ashore The Bankes Arms, ☎ 450225, is the place to be; good bar meals £8.50. The Manor House Hotel, ☎ 450288, is friendly and traditional; £25 for four-course dinner. Joe's Café is on the beach. PO, general store/tearoom. Knoll House Hotel, ☎ 450450 is north of the village and Shell Bay Restaurant, ☎ 450363, is close to the Sandbanks ferry (3M+).

Chandlery Shell Bay Marine & Watersports Centre, Ferry Rd; ☎ 450340.

NAVIGATION

Approaches The Bay is easily entered from Poole via the Boat Channel. From the S, avoid rough water on the SW-going ebb by keeping 1M off Ballard and Handfast Points; note the Pinnacles.

Landmarks Old Harry Rocks are conspicuous off Handfast Pt, at the SE end of the bay. The S side of the bay is lined by attractive 20m high chalk cliffs. At the E end these are deeply indented between promontories known as The Yards.

Pilotage Make for the Lat/Long of the anchorage and choose your spot. Depths are modest, 3–4m, and shoal steadily as the SW corner of the bay is entered. Avoid Redend Rocks, awash at CD.

Access By day, or by night with care (unlit).

Shelter Excellent in S to NW winds, but totally exposed in the NE quadrant.

Anchorage Good holding on fine sand in 3–4m, as shown. Shoal draught boats can anchor further WSW where there are also 12 dayglow red ⚓s owned by the Bankes Arms, free of charge. Land on the beach.

CHRISTCHURCH

Christchurch Harbour entrance – 50°43´·59N 01°43´·97W

The historic port of Christchurch lies about 6M E of Bournemouth Pier and 7M W of Hurst Point. Uniquely situated where the Rivers Stour and Avon converge, the picturesque town is dominated by the 11th century Priory Church, renowned for its beautiful architecture.

Although well worth a visit, Christchurch harbour virtually dries out and is difficult to navigate, with entry very much restricted to shoal draught yachts that can take the bottom.

SHORESIDE (Telephone code 01202)

Tourist Office 23, High St, Christchurch, Dorset, BH23 1AZ. ☎ 471780; ▨ 476816; www.christchurchtourism.info Summer opening times 0930–1730 Mon–Fri; 0930–1700 Sat. Closed Sun.

What to see/do The Priory, at approx 95m in length, is allegedly the longest parish church in England. Open 1000–1700 every day except Christmas; ☎ 485804. The Norman Constable's Hall, ☎ 495127, boasts one of the oldest Norman chimneys in Britain. Open all year, admission is free. The Red House Museum & Gardens in Quay Rd vividly depicts Christchurch's history. Open Tues–Sat 1000–1700; Sun 1400–1700; ☎ 482860. Also worth visiting are Place Mill on Quay Rd, ☎ 487626, and Highcliffe Castle, just outside Christchurch, ☎ 01425 278807.

Rail South-West Trains provides regular services from Christchurch to London Waterloo, Southampton, Bournemouth, Poole and Weymouth. National Rail Enquiries ☎ 0845 748 4950.

Bus Yellow Buses and Wilts & Dorset operate services from Christchurch to Bournemouth as well as to other nearby towns and villages. For bus timetables contact the Tourist Office.

Taxi Taxi ranks in the High St, opposite the Tourist Office, and in Bargates. Avon Taxis ☎ 477766; Christchurch Radio Cabs ☎ 484848.

Supermarkets A Co-op in Bargates and Somerfield in Saxon Square. Mudeford has a village store which is open seven days a week.

The Haven House Inn and Café on Mudeford Quay

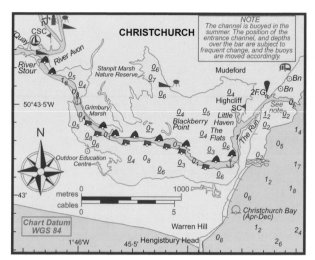

Banks Most of the major banks, with cashpoints, are in the High St.

Restaurants A varied selection ranging from the Italian La Mamma Pizzeria and Trattoria in Bridge St, ☎ 471608, through to the Lychee Chinese Restaurant, ☎ 478378, and the Starlight Bengali and Indian Cuisine, ☎ 484111, both of which are in the Bargates and offer takeaway services. Also try the Boathouse on the Quay at Christchurch, ☎ 480033, the Hut Beach Café & Bistro ☎ 423474 at Hengistbury Hd or the Haven House Inn and Café at Mudeford Quay, ☎ 01425 272609.

NAVIGATION

Charts AC SC 5601.5 (1:75,000), 5601.12 (1:7,500), 2172 (1:7,500), 2035 (1:25,000).

Approaches Coming from the E, the North Channel takes you from the Solent across Christchurch Bay. From the W, beware of the groyne S of Hengistbury Hd as well as Beerpan Rocks just a cable beyond. Approx 0.5M NE of Hengistbury Hd are Clarendon Rocks; a groyne of rocks extending about 1.5 cables from shore which needs to be left well to port before heading for the WPT 50°43'·60N 01°43'·20W. Do not attempt to cut the corner into the hbr entrance as the ground shoals to 0.9m.

Landmarks The hbr is approx 1M NE of the prominent Hengistbury Hd. Christchurch Priory is also a conspic landmark.

Pilotage The WPT 50°43'·60N 01°43'·20W is 0.5M E of the hbr entrance. Note that the unlit buoys in the approach channel are laid from April–Oct and their positions vary to correspond with the changing depths across the bar and in the fairway. On entering the channel, which is

The Run, with Mudeford Quay to starboard and the conspicuous black house to port

narrow and shallow (approx 0.3m over soft mud), keep rigidly to the buoyage which will bring you into The Run. This stretch of water is flanked by Mudeford Quay (lit 2 FG (vert) on its NE end) to the N and a shingle spit to the S. Once through The Run, the channel turns to port and is well marked with unlit port and starboard buoys as far as Grimbury Marsh. Beyond this point, follow the line of moorings to stay in the best water. The harbour speed limit is 4kn.

Access The bar and channel are prone to shifting, therefore the entrance is only really suitable for yachts drawing approx 1m about 1 hr before HW. Without local knowledge, only attempt to navigate the river on a rising tide.

Shelter Hengistbury Head offers some protection, but otherwise the harbour entrance can be exposed in strong winds blowing from the E through to the SW.

Tides (in harbour entrance) Double HWs occur except near nps; predictions are for the higher HW. Near nps there is a stand, in which case predictions refer to the middle of the stand. HW sp are 2 hr 30 mins before and HW nps are 30 mins after HW Portsmouth. LW sp and LW nps are both 35mins before LW Portsmouth. MHWS is 1·8m, MLWS 0·6m; MHWN is 1·4m, MLWN 0·7m.

Tidal streams Strong in the entrance, averaging 3–5kn. The tides are also strong in The Run, reaching an average of 3–5kn. On the ebb it has even been known to gush out at 7kn.

VHF None.

FACILITIES

Harbour Authorities Leisure and Technical Services, Civic Offices, Bridge St, Christchurch,

Dorset, BH23 1AZ. ☎ 495061; ⎙ 482200. Bournemouth & West Hampshire Water Co, Knapp Mill, Mill Rd, Christchurch, Dorset, BH23 2JY. ☎ 444646; ⎙ 444617.

Berthing Two options for berthing:

1) **Rossiter Yachts** ☎ 483250; situated in the E arm of the River Avon, about a cable S of Waterloo Bridge. Offers a couple of ❶ pontoon berths suitable for yachts up to 8m LOA. The depth at LW is just over 1m.

   Tariff £13.50 per night

   Facilities Electricity (metred) and FW on the pontoons. Diesel (no petrol) from fuel pump. A chandlery and full boat repair and maintenance services are on site. For a launderette go to Bargates.

2) **Christchurch SC** (CSC) ☎ 483150; situated to the W of Priory Quay. Offers two ⚓s which can take two boats each as well as pontoon berths for three yachts of less than 7.6m or for two yachts of over 7.6m LOA. Berths are only suitable for bilge keelers with less than a metre draught.

   Tariff (NB May be subject to a slight increase in Summer 2003) £8.50 per night on a pontoon and £6 per night in the river.

   Facilities Visitors are entitled to use the club's facilities including the bar (open Tues–Sun during lunchtime and in the evenings) and shower amenities (open 0800–2300; Sun to 2230). FW from the pontoon and in front of the club. Diesel can be obtained in cans with the purchase of a five litre ticket at the YC bar. On production of this ticket, fuel will be issued between 0900–1000 (except Tues) from Mr Peter Gillard, the club handyman.

Anchorage ⚓ is free of charge. Two designated areas are S of the main channel to the W of the ferry jetty and at the SE end of Steepbank below the moorings on the left hand side.

CHANDLERY & REPAIR FACILITIES

The Christchurch Boatshop, Bridge St ☎ 482751, CH; Rossiter Yachts, Bridge St ☎ 483250, CH, BY; South Coast Marine, Bridge St ☎ 482695, CH, ME; Power Afloat, Elkins Boatyard ☎ 489555, ME.

Chapter 2

KEYHAVEN

Keyhaven harbour entrance – 50°42'·85N 01°33'·22W

A view of Keyhaven's entrance showing the anchorage tucked inside North Point

Keyhaven is situated at the western tip of the Solent and forms part of a nature reserve extending over 2,000 acres of saltings and mudflats. Tucked away behind the historical Hurst Castle, it is really only accessible to small craft that can take the ground, although there is a small deep water anchorage just inside the entrance.

SHORESIDE (Telephone code 01590)

Tourist Office Lymington and New Forest Visitor Information Centre, New Street, Lymington ☎ 689000; ☎/📠 689090; information@nfdc.gov.uk; www.thenewforest.co.uk Open 1000–1700 Mon–Sat.

What to see/do Keyhaven is a conservation area and bird sanctuary, offering plenty of interesting shore side walks. Hurst Castle, completed in 1544, was one of a string of coastal defences constructed by Henry VIII. Today owned by the English Heritage, it is open 1000–1730 in season and 1000–1600 out of season; ☎ 642344. A ferry runs regularly from Keyhaven to Hurst Castle, ☎ 642500, or else you can walk out across the spit, which takes a good 30 mins. If you opt for the latter, be sure to wear a strong pair of shoes to cope with the shingle.

Rail The nearest train station is at Lymington, a taxi ride from Keyhaven or a bus ride from Milford on Sea.

Buses None between Keyhaven and Milford on Sea. Wilts and Dorset runs regular bus services between Milford and Lymington as well as to Christchurch ☎ 672382.

Taxi J Hall, Milford on Sea ☎ 644896; Galleon Taxi Service, New Milton ☎ 01425 611907.

Beaches The nearest beaches are from Milford on Sea through to Christchurch.

Shops None in Keyhaven, but the village of Milford, about half an hour away by foot, fulfills most shopping needs. A Spar convenience store is in the High Street, Mon–Fri 0700–2000, Sat–Sun 0700–2100, along with a Post Office and chemist.

Banks An HSBC with cash machine on Church Hill in Milford.

Restaurants The attractive Gun Inn at Keyhaven, ☎ 642391, serving local fish and shellfish, is famous for its real ales and extensive malt whisky selection. Among several good pubs in Milford are the Red Lion, ☎ 642236, on the High Street and the White Horse, ☎ 642360, on Keyhaven Road, with a reputation for great homemade food.

NAVIGATION

Charts AC 2021 (1:7,500), plus SC 5600.1 (1:150,000), 5600.2 (1:75,000), 5600.4 (1:25,000), 2021 (1:7,500), 2035 (1:25,000).

Approaches The entrance to Keyhaven, lying approx 5 cables NW of Hurst Point, is flanked by a low shingle bank to the S and mud flats beyond. From the E, there are no real dangers, although watch out for the regular Lymington–Yarmouth ferries. From the W, beware of the Shingles Bank and the Trap, just inside Hurst Point, which should be given a wide berth.

Landmarks The old pier, N of the Hurst Tower lt (Fl (4) WR 15s/Iso WRG 4s), is 5 cables SE of the harbour entrance.

Pilotage The waypoint 50°42′·73N 01°32′·58W brings you to within 0.5M of the entrance. From here two leading red and white-striped beacons, positioned on mudflats just inside the entrance, bear 283°. These are hard to spot until fairly close in, so you may find that you pick up the port and starboard hand entrance buoys more easily. At times there are strong tides across the entrance, particularly on the ebb, making the approach difficult.

   Depth is only 0.3m LAT just inside the North Point entrance where the channel, marked by green starboard buoys, heads S. Once in the channel, stay close to the line of moorings for the deepest water. Do not follow the shallow-draught ferry as you could end up going aground. The fairway soon turns to the NW where the moorings still need to be closely followed until you reach the green buoy indicating the beginning of the drying stretch of the channel to the quay. When closing the quay, the best water is to port by the ferry jetty. At the top of sp tides there is about 2.5m of water at the quay but, with changing depths, drying out is not recommended. Speed limit of 4kn in the channel. With an unlit entrance and fairway, a night approach is unwise.

Access is at HW±2 for yachts with a 1.5m draught. Try to avoid entering Keyhaven in strong easterly winds, especially as the bar is constantly shifting.

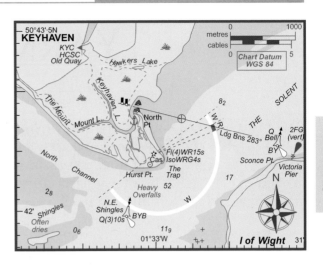

Shelter All moorings and anchorages are exposed to winds across the marshland, particularly from the E.

Tides HW sp at Hurst Point are 1 hr 15 mins before and HW nps 5 mins before HW Portsmouth. LW sp are 30 mins and LW nps 25 mins before LW Portsmouth. MHWS is 2·7m, MLWS 0·7m; MHWN is 2·3m, MLWN 1·4m.

Tidal streams On the approach to Keyhaven off Hurst Point, tidal streams can exceed 4kn at sp.

VHF *Keyhaven River Warden* Ch M.

FACILITIES

Keyhaven River Warden Anthony Wilkinson ☎ /📠 645695; anthony.wilkinson@nfdcgov.uk

Berthing Tie up alongside the quay for a short stay at HW unless you are happy to dry out.

Tariff An overnight stay against the quay is £8, including **FW** from a tap next to the Warden's office.

Anchorage Space to ⚓ in approx 3m of water just inside the entrance at North Point. Anchor rates are £7 per night. A popular ⚓ in favourable conditions is outside the harbour, close to the old pier, which is mainly used for a short lunchtime stopover or for waiting for the tide.

Fuel No fuel pump, but fuel can be had in cans from the garage at Milford on Sea, a 30 mins walk away.

YCs Keyhaven YC, ☎ 642165, adjacent to the quay, welcomes visitors and offers showers, bar and lounge.

Chandlery & repairs West Solent Boatbuilders, ☎ 642080, CH, 9.5 ton crane, 25 ton slip.

YARMOUTH

Yarmouth harbour entrance – 50°42'·42N 01°30'·05W

The most western port on the Isle of Wight, Yarmouth is not only a convenient passage stopover but has become a very desirable destination in its own right, with virtually all weather and tidal access, although strong N to NE winds can produce a considerable swell. The pretty harbour and town offer plenty of fine restaurants and amenities and are within easy reach of many of the Isle of Wight tourist attractions.

SHORESIDE (Telephone code 01983)

Tourist Office The Square, Yarmouth. ☎ 642344 813818; ☏ 823033; post@islandbreaks.co.uk; www.islandbreaks.co.uk

What to see/do Yarmouth Castle, constructed in 1547 by order of Henry VIII after the sinking of the *Mary Rose* in 1545, is worth a visit. Open 1000–1800 from 29 March–30 Sept and 1000–1700 from 1–31 Oct. A 15 mins walk from the harbour brings you to Fort Victoria Country Park, ☎ 760283, incorporating an aquarium, planetarium, Britain's largest model railway and the Sea-bed Heritage Exhibition; open 1000–1800 from Easter–Oct. The Needles Park at Alum Bay, ☎ 0870 458 0022, provides a great day out for children. Open 1000–1700 from Easter to early Nov. Alternatively, explore the Island on horse-back; Come Riding, ☎ 752502.

Buses Southern Vectis, Tel 292082 – Services 7/7A/42/43/47 from Bridge Road to all Island Destinations. (NB Several routes operate during summer only).

Taxi The Quay rank ☎ 760024; Yarmouth Harbour Taxis ☎ 761758/9.

The entrance to Yarmouth Harbour can be easily identified by the Wightlink ferries plying to and from Lymington

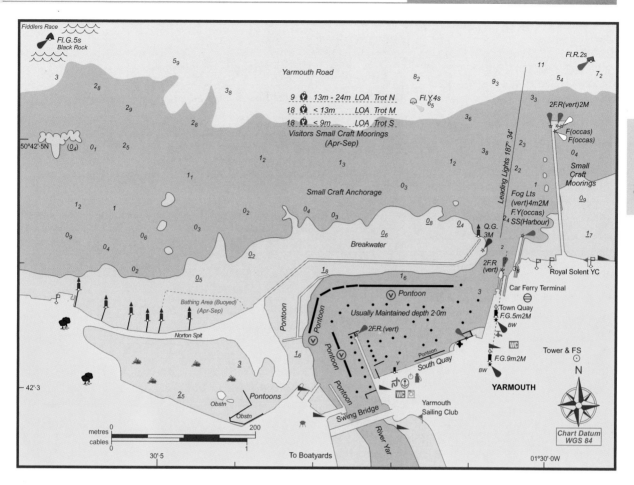

Car Hire See under Cowes/Newport on page 159.

Cycle Hire Isle Cycle Hire ☎ 760219/760738.

Ferries Wightlink ferries run every half hour between Yarmouth and Lymington on the mainland from where there are train services to Poole and London, ☎ 0870 5827744.

Beaches Easy access to safe, sandy beaches from Yarmouth, the nearest ones being Colwell Bay and Totland Bay. Alum Bay, just N of The Needles, is renowned for its multi-coloured sand cliffs. All these beaches have beach shops and cafés.

Shops An adequate range of shops in the town centre, from small delicatessens to mini supermarkets. A chemist and Post Office, with cashpoint, are in Quay Street.

Banks Lloyds Bank is in the Square and offers a cash machine.

Restaurants in Yarmouth get very busy during the summer so book ahead of time. Highly recommended but not cheap is the George Hotel in Quay St, ☎ 760331. Otherwise, the Bugle, ☎ 760272, provides two restaurants and three bars; offering a wide variety of beers, it proves popular with yachtsmen. Salty's is good for seafood and has a lively atmosphere, ☎ 761550, while the Wheatsheaf in Bridge Road, ☎ 760456, is reputed for its bar meals. Close to the steps above the ferry terminal is Baywatch on the Harbour, ☎ 760054. Only open in the high season, it serves bistro-type food.

The George in Quay Street, renowned for its quality cuisine

NAVIGATION

Charts AC 2021 (1:12,500), plus SC 5600.1 (1:150,000), 5600.2 (1:75,000), 5600.5 (1:25,000; inset of 1:6,000), 2021 (1:3,000), 2037 (1:25,000).

Approaches From the W Black Rock, marked by a green conical buoy (Fl G 5s), and shoal water N of the outer E–W pier are the only dangers. From the E, apart from the unlit historic wreck buoy (Y SPM) and the conspic yacht club moorings E of the pier, there are no hazards. Perhaps the biggest concern is the regular Lymington ferry. NB The tide runs strongly E/W at half flood and ebb, so in your final approach make sure you do not get swept either side of the narrow entrance.

It is possible to moor at the Town Quay with the HM's permission

Landmarks Yarmouth is easily located by its conspic pier, church tower (and constant stream of ferries). At night the pier-head lights (2FR) and the flood-lit ferry can be clearly identified.

Pilotage The E Fairway buoy (Fl R 2s) and W Fairway buoy (Fl G 2s) will bring you to the WPT 50°42'·58N 01°30'·01W, two cables N of the entrance WPT. The leading beacons are 2 W ◊ on B/W masts and leading lights FG 9m 2M on the quay bearing 188°. The W breakwater is QG 3M and the E short ferry pier 2FR vert lights.

Once past the breakwater, most of the ❶ berths lie to starboard. The speed limit is 6kn in the approaches and 4kn in the harbour. Do not enter under sail.

Access H24 at all tides.

Lights When the harbour is closed (eg when full on a summer weekend) a R flag is flown on the pierhead and a 'Harbour Full' sign is displayed at the entrance; illuminated at night. In fog a high intensity W Lt is shown from the pierhead and from the inner E pier.

Shelter Good from all directions, although a swell forms in strong N/NE winds.

Tides HW sp are 1 hr 5 mins before and nps 5 mins after HW Portsmouth. LW sp are 25 mins before and nps 30 mins before LW Portsmouth. MHWS is 3·0m, MLWS 0·8m; MHWN is 2·6m, MLWN 1·6m.

Tidal streams Outside the harbour, a NE stream runs from HW Portsmouth +5 to HW–2. A SW going stream runs from HW–1 to HW+4.

VHF *Yarmouth HM launch* Ch 68; *Yarmouth Water Taxi* Ch 15.

FACILITIES

HM Bryn Bird, South Quay ☎ 760321; 📠 761192; info@yar-iow-harbour.demon.co.uk; www.harbours.co.uk

Berthing The HM launch patrols the harbour entrance and will direct you to pontoon berths or piles. With the exception of the Town Quay, access ashore is by dinghy or water taxi. Also 38 ⚓s outside the harbour in Yarmouth Roads.

Tariff Rates per night for a 10m yacht, in or outside the harbour, are £11 Tues–Thur; £13.50 Fri–Mon. A short stay of up to 4 hrs for a 10m yacht is £5.50 Tues–Thur; £6.50 on all other days.

FW from a tap beside the harbour office on the S Quay as well as on the Town Quay.

Fuel (including LPG) is next to the HM office.

Gas, ice, showers (£1/token) and **launderette** available at HM office.

YCs Royal Solent Yacht Club ☎ 760256; Yarmouth Sailing Club ☎ 760270.

Scrubbing piles to the N of the inner harbour, but book ahead of time with the HM.

CHANDLERY & REPAIR FACILITIES

Harwoods, ☎ 760258, CH; Harold Hayles, ☎ 760373, CH, ME; Buzzard Marine, ☎ 760707, CH, ME; Isle of Wight Outboards, ☎ 760436; Saltern Sail Company, ☎ 760120.

LYMINGTON

Lymington harbour entrance – 50°44′·37N 01°30′·54W

Lymington is an attractive old market town situated at the western end of the Solent, just three miles from the Needles Channel. Despite the fact that the river is monopolised by the regular ferries plying to and from the Isle of Wight, it is sheltered and accessible at all states of the tide, proving a popular destination with visiting yachtsmen.

The moorings give a good indication of the channel

SHORESIDE (Telephone code 01590)

Tourist Office Lymington and New Forest Visitor Information Centre, New Street, Lymington ☎ 689000; ☎/🖷 689090; information@nfdc.gov.uk; www.thenewforest.co.uk Open 1000–1700 Mon–Sat.

What to see/do Begin with the St Barbe Museum and Art Gallery on New Street, ☎ 676969, which depicts the history of the New Forest as well as exhibiting works from local artists and sculptors. Open 1000–1600 from Mon–Sat. For recreational pursuits, the local open-air sea baths are adjacent to the Yacht Haven, ☎ 674865, or the Lymington Recreation Centre in North Street, Pennington, ☎ 670333, has a 25m indoor swimming pool. Horticulturists may enjoy a trip to Spinners Garden at Boldre, ☎ 673347; open during summer Tues–Sat 1000–1700. With the New Forest on the doorstep, small villages and towns such as Brockenhurst and Lyndhurst are only a bus, train or taxi ride away.

The Bluebird Seafood restaurant in the cobbled Quay Street

Rail Train station in Station St, just off Gosport St. Direct services to Poole and London. For National Rail Enquiries call ☎ 0845 7484950.

Buses Direct bus services to Brockenhurst, Lyndhurst, Beaulieu, Southampton and Bournemouth. Wilts and Dorset Bus Company ☎ 672382.

Flights Lymington is conveniently situated between Bournemouth, ☎ 01202 364234, and Southampton, ☎ 023 8062 0021, airports.

Taxi Allports Taxi ☎ 679792; Lymington Taxis ☎ 672842; Grosvenor Taxis ☎ 688888.

Car hire None in Lymington; nearest one is 2–3 miles away in Sway, ☎ 683684.

Cycle hire None in Lymington, but several in nearby Brockenhurst ☎ 623133; 622627.

Ferries Wightlink runs a car and passenger ferry service every half hour between Lymington and Yarmouth, ☎ 0870 582 7744/673301.

Beaches The nearest beaches are between Milford on Sea and Christchurch.

Supermarkets Several in the town centre, including a Tesco Metro in the High St, open 24 hrs from 20 May–14 Sept, and a Waitrose in St Thomas' St. Opposite Tesco is the delicatessen Lymington Larder. For the Post Office and chemists, also go to the High St and St Thomas St.

Market day Held in the High St every Saturday.

Banks Most of the mainstream banks, with cash points, are in the High St.

Restaurants The Haven Bar and Bistro is convenient if moored at the Yacht Haven, ☎ 679971. In Lymington itself, Limpets is a privately run, 40-seater restaurant in Gosport St, ☎ 675595. Closed on Tuesdays, it gets crowded during summer so you need to book ahead of time.

Recommended for its seafood is Bluebird Seafood Restaurant in Quay St, ☎ 676908, while Fat Cats, ☎ 675370, tucked away down Ashley Lane, offers a convivial atmosphere, especially on weekends when they play live jazz. Other restaurants include the Indian, Lal Quilla, ☎ 671681, and the Italian Caffe Uno, ☎ 688689. For pub food go to the Ship Inn, ☎ 676903, right on the quay, or Chequers in Woodside Lane, ☎ 673415.

NAVIGATION

Charts AC 2021 (1:5,000), plus SC 5600.1 (1:150,000), 5600.2 (1:75,000), 5600.5 (1:25,000), 2021 (1:5,000), 2035 (1:25,000).

Approaches Besides the shoals to the east and west of the harbour entrance and the regular Lymington to Yarmouth car ferry, there are no real hazards to watch out for. The ferry has right of way at all times, so it is advisable to use your engines when entering or leaving Lymington Harbour.

If approaching from the west, try to time your arrival on the flood due to the strength of the tides through Hurst Roads.

The ferry leaves little room for manoeuvring in the channel

Conspic marks The starting platform (Fl G2s) to the E and the Jack-in-the-Basket port hand channel marker (Fl R 2s) to the W make the entrance easily identifiable by day and night.

Pilotage The waypoint 50°44'·20N 01°30'·30W brings you to a position approx 2 cables SE of the platform. From this WPT the FR leading lts bear 319° and the channel is clearly marked by stbd (Fl G 2s) and port hand (Fl R 2s) beacons. After about five cables on a course of 319° you come to Tar Barrel Beacon (Fl G 2s), at which point turn to stbd, coming on to a course of 007°. This brings you to the inbound ferry transit, identified by black and white leading marks.

The channel turns to port at the No 9 Cage Boon beacon (Fl G 2s), from where the Lymington Yacht Haven entrance bears approx 280°. Harper's Post ECM and two FY leading lts bearing 244° from WPT 50°45'·12N 01°31'·42W mark the entrance to the Yacht Haven.

Continuing further up river, you pass the Royal Lymington YC to port and car ferry terminal to stbd before reaching Lymington Marina to port. Beyond this point, the river bends sharply to the left, after which the Town Quay comes into view. Observe the 6kn speed limit.

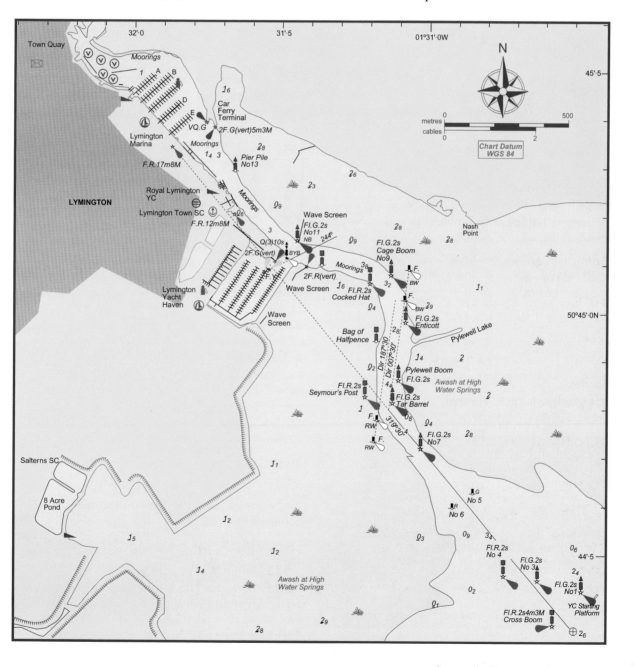

Access River is accessible at all states of the tide.

Shelter Good in both marinas as well as at the Town Quay.

Tides HW sp are 1 hr 10 mins before and HW nps 5 mins after HW Portsmouth. LW sp and LW nps are 20 mins before LW Portsmouth. MHWS is 3·0m, MLWS 0·7m; MHWN is 2·6m, MLWN 1·4m.

Tidal streams See Solent tidal streams on page 127.

VHF *Lymington Yacht Haven* Ch 80; *Lymington Marina* Ch 80. NB Lymington HM cannot be contacted on VHF.

FACILITIES

HM Bath Road, Lymington ☎ 672014; ⌨ 671823; www.harbours.co.uk

Berthing The Town Quay has space for more than 150 visiting yachts (with a max LOA of 12m) on the pontoon and fore and aft moorings. Anchoring is strictly forbidden anywhere in the river.

Tariff For a 10m yacht rates are £11.50 per night or £5 for a short stay of up to 4 hrs.

Showers, launderette No ablution facilities, but this is reflected in the cheaper berthing prices.

Fuel Go to Lymington Marina or Lymington Yacht Haven.

YCs The Royal Lymington YC, ☎ 672677, and the Lymington Town SC, ☎ 674514, welcome visiting yachtsmen from affiliated clubs.

MARINAS

Options include from seaward:

1. Lymington Yacht Haven 50° 45'·10N 01°31'·50W. Full tidal access. VHF Ch 80;

The pontoon at the Town Quay can get crowded in summer

☎ 677071; ⌨ 678186; www.yachthavens.com Approx a 15 mins walk from Lymington town centre. Although no allocated **V** berths, visiting yachts can usually be accommodated in summer when resident berthholders are away.

Tariff Peak rate is £2.59 per metre per day; short stay of up to 4 hr is half the daily rate.

Showers and **launderette** (coin operated) open 24 hrs a day.

Electricity (metred) and **FW** available on the pontoons.

Fuel Diesel, LPG and 2 stroke oil from the fuel station on the sea wall in front of marina office.

CHANDLERY & REPAIR FACILITIES

Nick Cox Chandlery ☎ 673489; Force 4 Chandlery ☎ 673698; Greenham Regis, for electronic repairs, ☎ 671144; Tinley Electronics ☎ 610071; Ocean Rigging ☎ 676292; Hood Sailmakers ☎ 675011; Yacht Care Ltd, ranging from electronics to sail repairs and valeting, ☎ 688856.

Chandlery on site; sells gas. Other services on site include riggers, electronic engineers, bar-cum-bistro serving coffees, teas, snacks and breakfast from 0800–1015 daily. Waterford Stores, selling basic provisions, is within easy walking distance.

2. Lymington Marina 50°45'·48N 01°31'·87W. Accessible at all states of the tide. VHF Ch 80; ☎ 673312; ⌨ 676353; marina@berthon.co.uk; www.berthongroup.co.uk Half a mile up river of the Yacht Haven on the port hand side, it offers between 60 to 70 **V** berths.

Tariff £2.76 per metre per day (£0.84 per foot per day); a short stay is half the daily rate.

Showers and **launderette** (token operated) are accessed by code.

Electricity, £3.52 per day (incl VAT), and **FW** on the pontoons.

Fuel Floating fuel dock selling diesel, petrol and oil. Other facilities include a hard standing area and a 45-ton hoist. Marina office sells gas, ice, milk and orange juice.

A clear view of the narrow, but steep-to entrance into Newtown River

NEWTOWN RIVER

Newtown River Entrance – 50°43'·69N / 01°24'·90W

During the Middle Ages Newtown was a thriving and busy commercial harbour. However, it was attacked in 1377 by the French who, by burning it to the ground (after which the town's prosperity never recovered), turned it into probably the most unspoiled anchorage in the Solent today. Newtown River estuary is now a nature reserve owned by the National Trust. Its only downside is its popularity, so try to time your visits on weekdays or, better still, out of season.

SHORESIDE (Telephone code 01983)

Tourist Office The Square, Yarmouth.
☎ 813818; 🖷 823033; post@islandbreaks.co.uk; www.islandbreaks.co.uk. The National Trust ☎ 741020.

What to see/do A quiet haven for wildlife, Newtown Estuary offers several lovely walks, including the Hamstead Trail that starts from the banks of Newtown River and crosses via the small hamlet of Wellow to the S shore at Brook Bay. Barbecues are popular on the W entrance spit, although should be held below the HW mark to preserve the rare plants. To protect the important nesting area for birds, landing on the E spit is strictly forbidden.

Buses run from Shalfleet to Yarmouth and Newport; Southern Vectis ☎ 292082.

Taxi Shalfleet ☎ 524081.

Beaches To the west are the sandy beaches of Colwell, Totland and Alum bays. To the east is Gurnard Bay, a gently shelving sand and shingle beach.

Shops Past the Shalfleet Church and left at

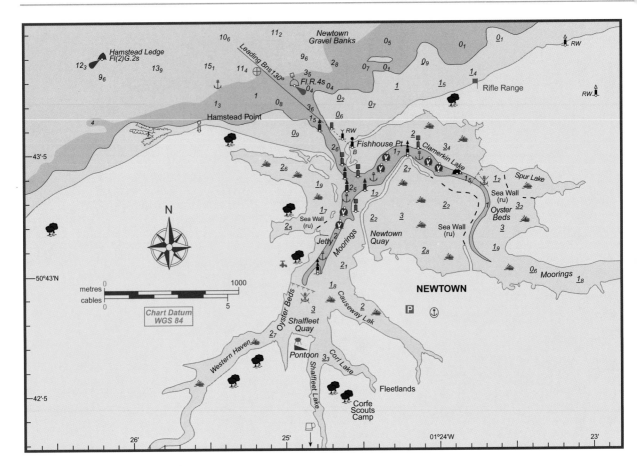

Warlands Lane is the Shalfleet Post Office and shop. For supermarkets and banks go to Yarmouth or Cowes.

Restaurants A trip in the dinghy to Shalfleet Quay (not accessible at LW sp), followed by a pleasant 15 mins riverside walk brings you to the New Inn pub, ☎ 531314. Dating back to the 17th century, it specialises in seafood and serves various real ales. In the height of summer, it is best to book in advance.

NAVIGATION

Charts AC 2021 (1:12,500), plus SC 5600.1 (1:150,000), 5600.2 (1:75,000), 5600.5 (1:25,000), 2021 (1:12,500), 2035 (1:25,000), 2036 (1:25,000).

Approaches From the E keep north of Salt Mead buoy (Fl (3)G 10s) and at least 0.5M from the Island's shore to clear the Newtown Gravel Banks. Hamstead Ledge (Fl (2)G 5s) provides a good approach from the W.

Landmarks The conspic TV mast (152m) helps to identify the entrance, which is narrow and difficult to spot from seaward.

Pilotage From WPT 50°43'·85N 01°25'·20W the TV mast bears approx 150°, providing the initial approach to Newtown River entrance. Also from this WPT, the leading beacons on the NE side of the entrance, bearing approx 130°, show a front RW banded beacon with a 'Y' shaped top mark and a rear BW beacon with a 'W' disc in a 'B' circle. Both sides of the channel shoal, but by keeping the BW circle in the 'V' of the 'Y' top mark on a course of 130° and with a minimum depth of 1.5m, you should have no problems. The transit takes you close to a port hand R beacon. When abeam, turn a few degrees to stbd and steer towards the middle of the two shingle spits that mark the entrance. The gap is narrow but the spits are steep-to. Apart from the port hand buoy at the mouth of the harbour (Fl R4s), the channel is unlit, making a first time night entry unwise.

Once inside, the channel is marked by R and G withies. Where it divides into the Clamerkin Lake to the E and Newtown R to the W, marks can appear confusing, so tread carefully and study the charts. If taking the W branch to Shalfleet, do not cut into stbd as there is a hard drying bank. Keep a close eye on the echo sounder when manoeuvring in hbr, although most of the bottom

Chapter 2

is soft mud and is easy to back off. Speed limit is restricted to 5kn.

Access For newcomers, the best time to enter is HW–4, on the flood but while the mud flats are still visible.

Shelter Good other than in N'ly winds.

Tides HW sp are 1 hr before and nps the same as HW Portsmouth. LW sp are 25 mins before and nps 20 mins before LW Portsmouth. MHWS is 3·4m, MLWS 0·7m; MHWN is 2·8m, MLWN 1·6m.

Tidal streams See Solent tidal streams on page 127.

VHF HM can only be contacted by telephone.

FACILITIES

HM David Flannagan ☎ 531424; 🖾 531914; sisnew@smtp.ntrust.org.uk

Moorings and anchorage A row of 18 ⚓ in the main arm of the river leading to Shalfleet Quay and six in Clamerkin Lake. White buoys are for visitors, red for local boats. Anchor just inside the entrance or in Clamerkin Lake; be careful to avoid the oyster beds on either side and do not ⚓ beyond boards showing 'Anchorage Limit'. Holding ground is excellent, but on a crowded summer weekend strong winds and unpredictable eddies make for close quarter sparring.

The leading beacons bear 130°. Turn to starboard for the entrance abeam the beacon

Tariffs Short stay on a mooring costs £3–£5; overnight ranges from £8–£10. Anchoring from £1 (if a member of the National Trust) to £5.

Fuel and **gas** available from garage at Shalfleet, ☎ 531315.

Water from the end of the footbridge at Newtown Quay (accessible HW±3). For all other marine supplies, go to Yarmouth or Cowes.

Looking across the visitors' moorings towards Newtown Quay

BEAULIEU RIVER

Beaulieu River entrance – 50°46'·90N 01°21'·72W

Looking down the Beaulieu River. The marina at Buckler's Hard welcomes visiting yachtsmen

Meandering through the New Forest, the Beaulieu River is by far the most romantic harbour on the mainland side of the Solent. A few miles upstream from the mouth of the river lies Buckler's Hard, an historic 18th century village where shipwrights skilfully constructed warships for Nelson's fleet.

SHORESIDE (Telephone code 01590)

Tourist Office Lymington and New Forest Visitor Information Centre, New Street, Lymington ☎ 689000; ☎/🖷 689090; information@nfdc.gov.uk; www.thenewforest.co.uk Open 1000–1700 Mon –Sat. Lyndhurst and New Forest Visitor Information Centre, Main Car Park, Lyndhurst ☎ 023 8028 2269; 🖷 023 8028 4236.

What to see/do As Buckler's Hard is renowned for its shipbuilding history, the Maritime Museum, ☎ 616203, is worth a visit. Among the displays are models of ships built by Henry Adams for Lord Nelson, the most notable of which was the *Agamemnon*. Rich in birdlife, the Riverside Walk between Buckler's Hard and Beaulieu should not be overlooked. If you do get as far as Beaulieu, go to the National Motor Museum or see the ruins of Beaulieu's ancient monastery, established by French monks over 800 years ago. Alternatively visit Palace House where 'Victorian' staff will give you an insight into what life was like then. For any of the Beaulieu attractions call ☎ 612345.

Rail Train stations at Beaulieu Rd or Brockenhurst station; both a taxi ride away. National Rail Enquiries ☎ 0845 748 4950.

Bus No 112 runs via Beaulieu (bus stop in front of garage) between Lymington and Hythe. Wilts and Dorset Bus Company ☎ 672382.

Buckler's Hard village

The seasonal yellow racing buoy is slightly west of the transit waypoint, making the entrance easily identifiable

Taxi Marchwood Motorways, Hythe ☎ 023 8084 4210.

Bike hire Forest Leisure Cycling, National Motor Museum, Beaulieu ☎ 611029.

Beaches The closest beaches are Lepe and Calshot, to the E of Beaulieu River.

Supermarkets None, but at Buckler's Hard the village store, behind the Maritime Museum, provides essential items and incorporates an off-licence. Otherwise shops at Beaulieu include a general store, bakery and Post Office. For larger supermarkets and banks go to Lymington, Brockenhurst or Lyndhurst.

Restaurants The Master Builder's House Hotel, ☎ 616253, where the Yachtsman's Bar and Gallery is a popular choice with visiting sailors. For something a little smarter, try the Hotel's Riverview Restaurant and Terrace. A bit further afield in Beaulieu is the Montagu Arms Hotel, ☎ 612324, providing restaurant and bar meals as well as incorporating Monty's, a bistro which is highly recommended. The Captain's Cabin, ☎ 616293, amalgamated with Buckler's Hard village store, serves hot and cold snacks.

NAVIGATION

Charts AC 2021 (1:10,000), plus SC 5600, 2021 (1:10,000), 2035 (1:25,000), 2036 (1:25,000).

Approaches From the E, keeping the Lepe Spit SCM (Q(6)+LFl 15s YB) to stbd, steer towards the Y spherical racing buoy (Fl 4s; March–Oct; position 50°46'·59N 01°21'·46W) in order to stay well clear of the shallows off Stone Point until you get to the transit WPT 50°46'·57N 01°21'·37W. From the W, to avoid the shallows leave the Y spherical racing buoy (March–Dec; position 50°46'·15N 01°22'·20W) to port, steering a course towards the transit WPT above.

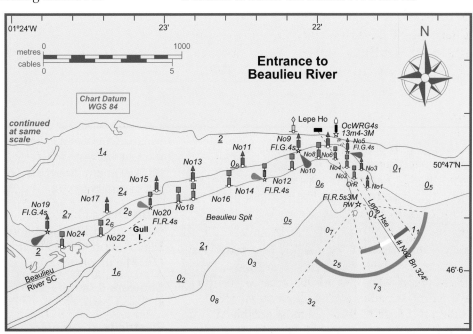

Landmarks With its prominent new Millennium Beacon and sector lt as well as the old CG cottages and white boathouse, the mouth of Beaulieu River is easily identified day and night.

Pilotage From the transit WPT (see under Approaches), the ldg marks, bearing 324°, must be aligned carefully to avoid the shoal water either side. The front mark is No 2 port beacon with orange dayglow topmark; the rear is Lepe House. Keep the Beaulieu Spit dolphin Fl R 5s 3M (Vis 277°–037°) 40m to port.

In the river, the channel is marked with numbered R and G beacons, of which nos 12 and 20 are lit with Fl R 4s and 5, 9 and 19 with Fl G 4s. Once past No 19 stbd beacon, the channel turns NW and is marked by withies. Follow the line of mooring buoys for the best water. The 5kn speed limit must be observed.

The moorings make it easier to stay in the deep water

Access Due to the bar and shifting sands, entering can be dangerous and should not be attempted until LW±2.

Shelter Good, although anchoring in the first reach can be exposed in strong E winds.

Tides HW sp are 40 mins and nps 10 mins before HW Portsmouth. LW nps are 10 mins before and sp 5 mins after LW Portsmouth. MHWS is 3·7m, MLWS 0·5m; MHWN is 3·0m, MLWN 1·7m.

Tidal streams Outside the river entrance, the E-going tide runs from HW–6 to HW–2, reaching 3.2kn in the second hour on springs. Slack water is at HW–1 before the W-going tide runs from HW to HW+4, reaching 2.6kn in the second hour.

VHF The HM at Buckler's Hard cannot be contacted on VHF.

FACILITIES

HM John Edward, ☎ 616200/616234; 🖷 616211; beaulieu@tcp.co.uk; www.beaulieu.co.uk

Berthing No ⚓s, although vacant ones may be used with HM's permission. Visitors are welcome to enter the marina (dredged to 1.8m below MLWS) at any time or moor fore and aft to piles above and below the marina.

Tariff Overnight fees in the marina are £26 for yachts up to 12m LOA and £38 for those up to 18m. A short stay, only applicable up to 1530hr, is £10. Pile moorings are £8 per day.

Showers & launderette (coin-operated) can be accessed 24 hr.

Leave the Beaulieu Spit Dolphin 40m to Port on the approach

Electricity £2 per night.

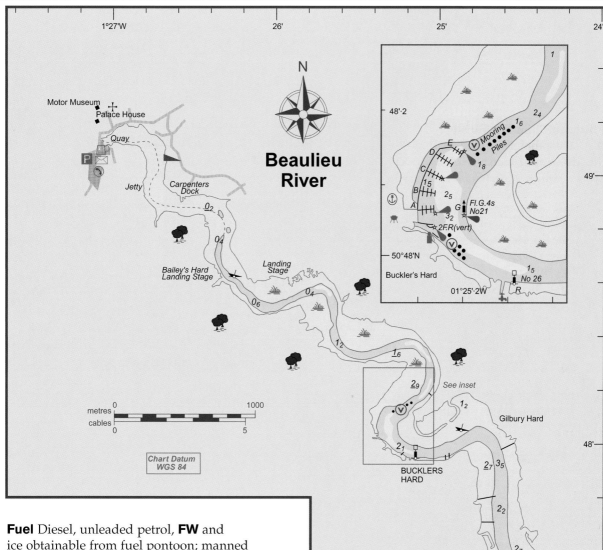

Beaulieu
River

Fuel Diesel, unleaded petrol, **FW** and ice obtainable from fuel pontoon; manned until sunset.

Gas from Buckler's Hard Garage (BHG Marine/☎ 616249); open seven days a week in summer.

Scrubbing grid £22, & valet service (midweek only) must be booked in advance at HM.

YCs Members of affiliated YCs are welcome at the Royal Southampton Yacht Club, which has a small offshoot at Gins Farm, ☎ 616213.

Chandlery & repairs The Agamemnon CH is next door to the shower block. Ask at the HM office for ME, El, SM etc. Other facilities include a hard standing area and mobile BH.

Anchorage The only recognised ⚓ is in the first reach on the S side of the channel opposite Gull Island. Good holding ground on mud, but can be uncomfortable in strong E winds. Anchoring in the river costs £5.

COWES/NEWPORT

Cowes harbour entrance – 50°46'·08N 01°17'·93W

Situated virtually at the centre of the Solent, Cowes is best known as Britain's premier yacht racing centre and offers all types of facilities to yachtsmen. Although not all the yacht clubs welcome visitors, the town boasts an array of pubs and restaurants as well as many places of interest.

For the non-racing cruiser it is probably best to avoid the mayhem of Skandia Life Cowes Week at the beginning of August, unless you want to experience the vibrant atmosphere and don't mind burning a large hole in your pocket. At the top of the Medina River lies the town of Newport, the capital of the Isle of Wight, which can only be reached by deep-draught yachts on favourable tides.

SHORESIDE (Telephone code 01983)

Tourist Office Cowes Tourist Office, The Arcade, Fountain Quay W, ☎ 813818.

What to see/do Cowes Maritime Museum on Beckford Rd, ☎ 293394; open Mon–Wed and Fri 0930–1800; Sat 0930–1630, admission free. On the Parade, the IoW Model Railways Exhibition & Museum, ☎ 280111, conveys 100 years' development of toy or model trains; open daily (except for Sun in winter) 1100–1700. In the High St is the Sir Max Aitken Museum, ☎ 292191, dedicated to Sir Max's collection of nautical instruments, paintings and maritime artefacts. Opens May to end Sept, Tues–Sat 1000–1600.

Situated on a high ridge two miles SW of Newport is Carisbrooke Castle; dates back to Norman times, although the original site was

Looking straight down the Medina on what would be considered a quiet day

The popular Folly Inn two miles up river from Cowes

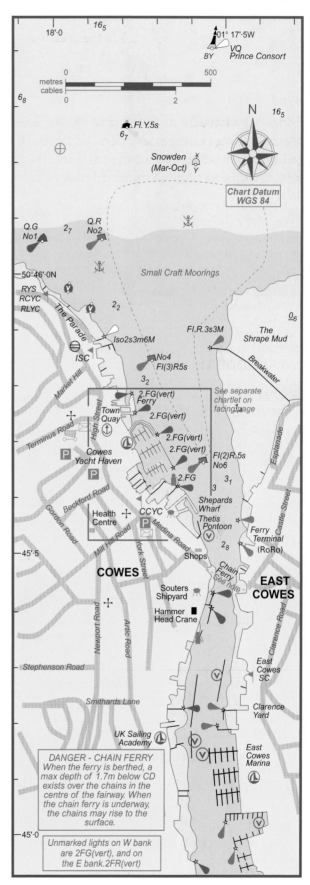

Saxon. It was here that Charles I was imprisoned before being taken to London for his trial and subsequent execution in 1649. Open daily from 1000–1800 in summer and from 1000–1600 in winter. To the E of Cowes is Osborne House, the country retreat that Queen Victoria and Prince Albert built between 1845 and 1850. Now belonging to English Heritage, it opens 29 March–30 Sept 1000–1800. Both house and grounds are open daily throughout Oct 1000–1700; ☎ 200022.

Buses run between Newport and Cowes as well as to other towns and villages on the Isle of Wight. Southern Vectis ☎ 292082.

Taxi Alpha Cars ☎ 280280; Gange Taxis ☎ 281818; Taxi Rank ☎ 297134.

Car hire Solent Self Drive, Cowes ☎ 282050.

Bicycle hire Offshore Sports, Cowes ☎ 290514; Mobile Cycle Hire ☎ 294910.

Ferries Red Funnel provides a daily car ferry service every 50 mins to an hour and a high speed foot passenger service every 30 mins between Cowes and Southampton ☎ 0870 444 8898. The chain ferry operates between East Cowes and Cowes, ☎ 293041.

Beaches To the W of Cowes is Gurnard Bay, suitable for swimming and surfing, or else a sand and shingle beach runs along the Princes Esplanade at West Cowes. East Cowes has a shingle beach; a good spot for watching the yacht racing during Skandia Life Cowes Week.

Supermarkets *Cowes*: Somerfield in the High St or Co-op in Terminus Road. *East Cowes*: Somerfield in York Avenue; Alldays on Well Road includes the Post Office.

Watch House Lane, off the High St

Banks *Cowes*: Major banks can be found in the High St, most of which have cash machines. *East Cowes*: None, but Alldays incorporates an Abbeylink cash machine.

Restaurants *Cowes*: As a centre for yachting, Cowes has a plethora of pubs and restaurants. Opposite Cowes Yacht Haven is the Anchor Inn, ☎ 292823. Claiming to be the oldest and most traditional pub in Cowes, it offers a broad selection of fine ales and bar meals. Also the Globe Inn on the Parade, ☎ 293005, and the Union Inn in Watch House Lane, ☎ 293163. Situated about 2M up river and with its own pontoon for berthing is the famous Folly Inn, ☎ 297171, specialising in local fish as well as home-made casseroles and grills.

For breakfast go to Tiffins, ☎ 292310, or Eegon's Café, ☎ 291815, in the High St; otherwise the 'Wicked' Espresso Bar on Shooters Hill, ☎ 289758.

The Red Duster on the High St, ☎ 290311, is good for high quality, reasonably-priced food. Also on the High St is Murrays Seafoods, ☎ 296233. For fish and chips try Chip Ahoy on Victoria Rd, ☎ 269763. *East Cowes*: Besides the Lifeboat on Britannia Way in East Cowes Marina, ☎ 292711, the majority of restaurants are in Cowes. The Pizza Oven, opposite the Floating Bridge, ☎ 200433, offers a takeaway and delivery service. Pubs include the Ship & Castle in Castle St and the White Hart Inn in Dover Rd.

NAVIGATION

Charts AC SC 5600.1 (1:150,000), 5600.11(1:25,000), 5600.12 (1:3,500), 2793 (1:3,500), 2035 (1:25,000), 2036 (1:25,000).

Approaches From the east, Old Castle Pt needs to be kept at least 2 cables off, staying outside the Y racing spherical buoy (Fl Y 4s; March–Dec; position 50°46'·15N 01°16'·64W). From here aim for the Cowes Roads Trinity House buoy (Fl Y 5s) to avoid the Shrape mud shallows to port.

From the west, the inshore Grantham Rks between Egypt Pt and the SHM QG entrance buoy should be given a good offing. If coming from the north, beware of the Restricted Entry Area NE of the line between Gurnard NCM in the W and the Prince Consort NCM in the east, enabling large vessels to turn easily. A mile further north of Prince Consort buoy is the Bramble Bank; part dries to 1.2m and catches out deep-keeled yachts. Keep west of the G conical W Knoll buoy to avoid it.

Conspic marks The channel is marked by a No 1 SHM buoy (QG) and the No 2 PHM buoy (QR).

Pilotage From the WPT 50°46'·23N / 01°17'·99W, a course of 167° puts you in mid-channel between the No 1 stbd hand and the No 2 port hand fairway buoys. Use the main channel but keep close to the W shore as the ferries take up a lot of room. On the E side of the fairway are two further PHMs, No 4 (Fl (3) R5s) and No 6 (Fl (2) R5s). To stbd, the Jubilee Pontoon, the outer limits of Cowes Yacht Haven and the fuel jetty between the marina and Shepards Wharf are clearly lit at night (2FG (vert)). Likewise all port and stbd jetties and pontoons between the chain ferry and the National Power Jetty are marked with 2FR (vert) and 2FG (vert) lights respectively, making the channel easy to identify at night. Beyond the National Power Jetty the channel starts to narrow and shoals rapidly. For the best water stay as close as possible to the stbd moorings.

There is a 6kn speed limit in the river, and the HM advises all yachts to use their engines, especially when approaching the chain ferry, although this is meant to give way to yachts.

Swinging moorings for visitors lie just off the Parade

Access The lower reaches of the River Medina are accessible at all states of the tide.

Shelter Good at Cowes Yacht Haven and in the upper reaches, but the outer harbour is exposed in N to NE winds.

Tides HW sp are 15 mins before and nps 15 mins after HW Portsmouth. LW nps are 20 mins before and sp the same as LW Portsmouth. MHWS is 4·2m, MLWS 0·8m; MHWN is 3·5m, MLWN 1·8m.

Tidal streams run strongly in the outer parts of Cowes Roads, but less so inshore. In the River Medina, the flood starts at HW Portsmouth +0530 and the ebb at HW Portsmouth +0015. Both are strong, particularly the ebb.

VHF *Cowes Harbour Control* Ch 69; *Cowes Yacht Haven* Ch 80; *East Cowes Marina* Ch 80; *Marine Support & Towage* (fuel) Ch 69; I*sland Harbour Marina* Ch 80; *Cowes Water Taxi* Ch 77; *Chain Ferry* Ch 69; *Folly Waterbus* Ch 77.

FACILITIES

Marinas The three major marinas in Cowes from seaward are:

1. Cowes Yacht Haven (CYH) 50°45'·72N 01°17'·69W; access H24 at all tides. ☎ 299975; 📠 200332; info@cowesyachthaven.demon.co.uk; www.cowesyachthaven.com

Berthing With few permanent moorings, CYH is dedicated to catering for visitors and events. Expect multiple rafting at peak times. For events such as Skandia Life Cowes Week and Hoya Round the Island Race, book in advance. Offers good protection, although there can be a swell in N to NE winds.

Tariff During peak season, £2.55 per metre per day Fri–Sat; £2 per metre per day Sun–Thur. A short stay of 4 hrs is £0.90 per metre. During Cowes Week prices are geared to the serious racers.

Showers, launderette (coin-operated).

Electricity (£3 per day) and **FW** on the pontoons.

Fuel Diesel and LPG can be obtained on site or at Lallows Boatyard, ☎ 292111, approx 50m S of marina.

Shops/restaurants Within very easy walking distance of Cowes' High St.

Chandlery & repairs Aquatogs ☎ 295072, CH; Hunter & Combes ☎ 299599, CH; Marine Bazaar

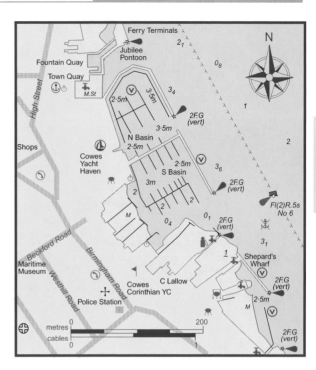

☎ 298869, CH; Pascall Atkey & Sons ☎ 292381, CH; Adrian Stone Yacht Services ☎ 297898; Lallows Boatyard ☎ 292111; Victory Marine Services ☎ 200226; Greenham Regis Electronics ☎ 293996; DG Wroath ☎ 281467, EI; Ratsey & Lapthorn ☎ 294051, SM; McWilliams ☎ 281100, SM; Saltern Sail ☎ 280014, SM.

2. East Cowes Marina 50°45'·17N 01°17'·53W. Access H24 at all states of the tide. ☎ 293983; 📠 299276; sales@eastcowesmarina.co.uk; www.eastcowesmarina.co.uk Situated in a relaxed semi-rural setting about 0.5M above the chain ferry.

Berthing Can accommodate approx 120 visiting yachts. Takes advance bookings.

Entrance to the North Basin in Cowes Yacht Haven

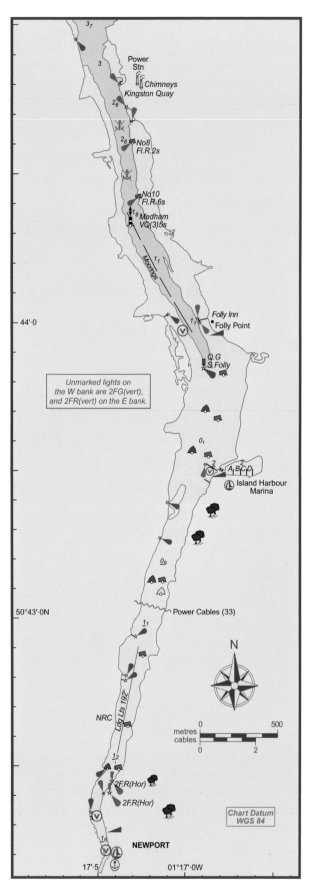

Tariff In summer £2.40 per metre per night; in winter £1.20 per metre per night. A short stay of up to 4 hrs is £6 in summer, £3 in winter.

Showers and **toilets** by marina office. Existing facilities are good, but plans are underway for a new block to be completed by the start of the 2004 season.

Launderette None at present, but one will be included in the new building (see above).

Electricity (£3 per day) and **FW** on the pontoons.

Gas available from the on site chandlery, Island Chandlers.

Fuel No pump on site; go to the Marine Support & Towage barge, VHF Ch 69/☎ 293041, 200m S of the Chain Ferry on the stbd side. Also sells gas.

Chandlery & repairs Island Chandlers, ☎ 293983. Also on site are a drying out dock, rigger's workshop, cranage and repair facilities.

Water Taxi VHF Ch 77/☎ 07050 344818; provides a service to Cowes and back; £3 return.

Eating The Lifeboat, in Britannia Way, East Cowes Marina, ☎ 292711. Barbecue and marquee during season. For other suggestions see page 160.

Food shops The on site chandlery sells essential provisions. Otherwise nearest shops are in East Cowes, about 15 mins away on foot.

3. Island Harbour Marina 50°43'·51N 01°16'·80W; accessible HW±4 with 1.5m draught. The deep water channel is marked by port hand withies. ☎ 822999; 🖷 526020; info@island-harbour.co.uk; www.island-harbour.co.uk The lock is operated daily from 0700–2100 in summer and from 0800–1730 in winter; holding pontoon outside the lock to stbd. Entrance to the lock is controlled by R and G traffic lts; mooring ropes are provided once inside.

Tariff £2.55 per metre per night; commit to six nights and you get the seventh one free. Short stay rates; £3.50<9m; £4.50>9m.

Launderette (coin-operated) in the shower block, behind the large car park, next to the workshop. Access code needed.

Electricity (metred) on 'A' and 'B' pontoons.

Fuel Go to the Marine Support & Towage barge, VHF Ch 69/☎ 293041, 200m S of the Chain Ferry on the stbd side.

Looking up the River Medina, with the Folly Inn moorings in the foreground and the Island Harbour Marina further upstream to port

Chandlery & repairs On site chandlery. Richardsons, a family run business within marina complex, ☎ 821095, provides engineering, boatbuilding and repairs. Slipway, boat hoist and crane available.

Eating A licensed on site restaurant, Harbour View ☎ 07866 701546; also sells essential provisions and newspapers. For the nearest shops, go to Newport, see page 164.

OTHER BERTHING FACILITIES

Cowes Harbour Commission has four swinging moorings inside the harbour entrance alongside the Parade to stbd. During special events extra moorings are laid to the E and W of the river mouth. Cowes Water Taxi provides a regular service, VHF Ch 77/☎ 07050 344818. Also under the Harbour Commission's control are Shepards Wharf, a cable upstream of the Yacht Haven on the stbd side; Thetis Pontoon, a

cable further up river of Shepards Wharf; and Ⓥ pontoons on the W bank of the River Medina, just N of Folly Point (NB Due to the latters' close proximity to the Folly Inn, they can be very crowded in summer). Contact Cowes Harbour Control on VHF Ch 69 or ☎ 293952.

Tariff In season prices for swinging moorings are £0.83 per metre per day; pontoon berths are £1.40 per metre per day. If committed to six nights, get seventh one free. For a short stay, rates are: £2.80 >9m; £3.90 9–12m; £5 12–15m; £6 for 15m and over.

UK Sailing Academy, upstream of the chain ferry on stbd side, has an outside Ⓥ pontoon; 15 mins walk from centre of Cowes. ☎ 294941.

Tariff £1.50 per metre per night; £5.50 for a short stay of up to 4 hrs.

Anchoring prohibited in harbour.

YCs The Royal Yacht Squadron ☎ 292191;

The Royal London YC ☎ 299727; The Royal Corinthian YC ☎ 293581; The Island Sailing Club ☎ 296621; The Cowes Corinthian YC ☎ 296333. The Island SC and Cowes Corinthian YC are particularly welcoming to visitors.

NEWPORT

If you sail about 4M up the River Medina from Cowes you come to the ancient port of Newport Harbour, which is well protected in all conditions and acts as an ideal base for exploring the Isle of Wight.

Tourist Office Newport Tourist Office, The Guildhall, High St, ☎ 813818.

What to see/do Newport also has its fair share of museums, in particular the Museum of Island History, ☎ 823366. Housed in the old clock-tower Town Hall, it illustrates the Island's history from the time of the dinosaurs. Open Mon–Sat 1000–1700 and Sun 1100–1500. The Island's only arts centre, Quay Arts, ☎ 822490, is also worth a visit. Open Mon–Sat 1000–1600.

Buses run between Newport and Cowes as well as to other towns and villages on the Isle of Wight. Southern Vectis ☎ 292082.

Taxi Amar Cabs ☎ 522968; Prices Taxi Rank ☎ 522084.

Car hire Ford Rental, Newport ☎ 523441.

Supermarkets Sainsbury's in Foxes Road; Safeway in South St; Somerfield in Pyle St; Marks & Spencer in Church Litten.

Market day A stall market every Tues; Farmer's market on Fri.

Banks All the major banks, most of which have cashpoints, are in the High St, St James' St or St James' Sq.

Restaurants Bargeman's Rest, ☎ 525828, situated on Little London Quay overlooking Newport Harbour, serves real ales and good home-cooked food. Equally popular is the Wheatsheaf Inn, ☎ 523865, in St Thomas' Sq. Restaurants include Joe Daflo's on the High St, ☎ 532220, and Moulin Rouge café-bar in St Thomas' Sq, ☎ 530001. For a light lunch go to the Sunflower Tea & Coffee House in Holyrood St, ☎ 528989; open Mon–Sat, although shuts early on a Sat.

NAVIGATION

Approach/pilotage Located 1.5M S of the Folly, Newport is reached by a well buoyed and partially lit drying channel (about HW Portsmouth ±2 you find a depth of approx 2m), which favours the W bank. Moving S of the Folly Point, two pairs of FG lts are positioned on the W bank at the Cement Mills site, while at Dodnor, a further pair of FG lts signify the end of a small jetty protruding from the W bank. Power lines have a 33m clearance. Upstream, shallow patches are marked with seven port and three stbd hand buoys. The approach to Newport is easily identified by large W bcns on the E bank showing pairs of hor R lts at night. When these bcns are lined up they should bear 192°, leading you to the hbr entrance. A first time entry is not recommended at night. Speed limit is restricted to 6kn.

FACILITIES

HM VHF Ch 69, ☎ 525994.

Berthing ⊕ pontoons, suitable for bilge keelers or multihulls, are on the E side of the hbr. Single-keeled boats should lie S of the pontoons against the quay. The hbr dries HW±5 to reveal a firm, level, mud bottom.

Tariff 1 April–31 Oct, rates are £1 per metre per day; a minimum charge of £5. Winter rates are 50% off the summer rates. Short stay of up to 4 hrs: £2.50<7m; £3>7m; no discounts out of season.

Shower and **launderette** on quayside.

Electricity and **FW** on the pontoons. Other facilities include rubbing boards for the wall berths, available from HM office, four slipways, a hand-operated crane and winter storage.

Berthed in front of Bargeman's Rest at Newport

SOUTHAMPTON

A cable W of West Bramble buoy – 50°47′·20N 01°18′·82W
A cable E of East Bramble buoy – 50°47′·23N 01°13′·48W

At the head of the six-mile stretch of Southampton Water lies the city of Southampton. Founded in around 70AD, when the Romans first built a town on the banks of the River Itchen, the city has always held an important place in maritime history and today hosts what is considered to be one of Europe's finest on-water annual boat shows.

Boasting several major marinas with comprehensive facilities, Southampton Water over recent years has become increasingly accommodating to visitors and is well protected in all but strong E winds.

SHORESIDE (Telephone code 023 80)

Tourist Office 9, Civic Centre Rd, Southampton. ☎ 023 8083 3333; ✉ 023 8083 3381; city.information@southampton.gov.uk; www.southampton.gov.uk/cityinfo Open Mon–Sat 0830–1730, except Wed, 1000–1730.

What to see/do An exhibition at the Maritime Museum at Town Quay, ☎ 635904, gives a fascinating account of the sinking of the *Titanic* in 1912. Also conveys the history of Southampton since 1838. Open Tues–Fri 1000–1700; Sat 1000–1600; Sun 1400–1700; admission free. The Hall of Aviation on Albert Rd, ☎ 635830, commemorates the work of RJ Mitchell who pioneered the legendary WWII Spitfire fighter aircraft. Open Tues–Sat

1000–1700; Sun 1200–1700. For more cultured tastes, go to the Southampton City Art Gallery in the Civic Centre, Commercial Rd, ☎ 832277. Further afield: Lyndhurst, the 'capital of the New Forest' is only a 20 mins bus ride away; full of cafés/restaurants and surrounded by beautiful forest walks.

Three cinemas provide evening entertainment: UGC in Ocean Village, ☎ 0870 1555132; Harbour Lights Picture House, Ocean Village, ☎ 335533; Odeon in Leisure World on West Quay Rd, ☎ 0870 5050007. Leisure World, ☎ 237988, also includes a bowling alley, casino, bars and restaurants.

If in the Solent during the second to third week in Sept, don't miss the annual Southampton International Boat Show at the Mayflower Park.

Rail Southampton train station is a 15-20 mins walk from Town Quay and Ocean Village; direct links to London Waterloo, Poole, Weymouth, Portsmouth and Brighton. National Rail Enquiries ☎ 08457 484950.

Town Quay, with the entrance between the breakwaters

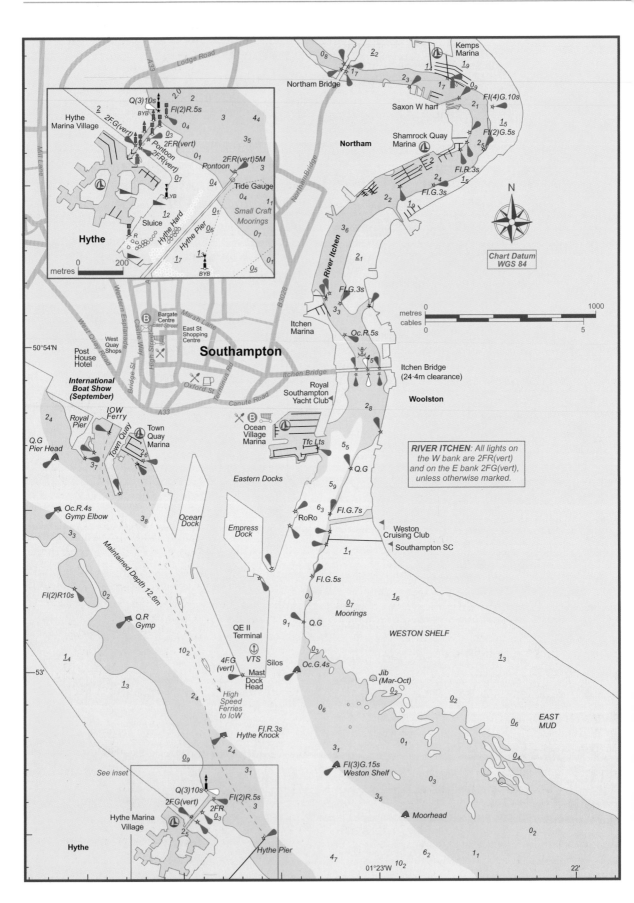

Hythe (inset)

Q(3)10s
BYB
Fl(2)R.5s
Hythe Marina Village
2·F·G(vert)
2F.R(vert)
Pontoon
2F.R(vert)
2F.R(vert)
Pontoon
2F.R(vert)5M
Tide Gauge
Small Craft Moorings
Sluice
Hythe Hard
Hythe Pier
R
YB
BYB

Hythe

metres 0 200

Main chart

Lodge Road
A33
Kemps Marina
Northam Bridge
Fl(4)G.10s
Saxon Wharf
Fl(2)G.5s
Northam
Shamrock Quay Marina
Fl.R.3s
Fl.G.3s
Northam Bridge
B3028
River Itchen

N

Chart Datum WGS 84

Fl.G.3s
Itchen Marina
Oc.R.5s

metres
cables
0   1000
0   5

50°54'N
Post House Hotel
West Quay Road
Western Esplanade
Marsh Lane
Bargate Centre East Street
East St Shopping Centre
Castle Way
High Street
Bridge St
Terminus Rd
Oxford St
Southampton
Canute Road
A33

Itchen Bridge
Itchen Bridge (24·4m clearance)
Woolston

Royal Southampton Yacht Club

RIVER ITCHEN: *All lights on the W bank are 2FR(vert) and on the E bank 2FG(vert), unless otherwise marked.*

International Boat Show (September)
IOW Ferry
Royal Pier
Town Quay
Town Quay Marina
Ocean Village Marina
Tfc Lts
Eastern Docks

Q.G
Pier Head
Oc.R.4s
Gymp Elbow
Ocean Dock
RoRo
Fl.G.7s
Weston Cruising Club
Southampton SC

Maintained Depth 12·6m
Fl(2)R10s
Q.R Gymp
Empress Dock
Fl.G.5s

Moorings
Q.G
WESTON SHELF

QE II Terminal
VTS
4F.G (vert)
Silos
Mast Dock Head
High Speed Ferries to IoW
Oc.G.4s
Jib (Mar-Oct)

EAST MUD

Fl.R.3s
Hythe Knock

See inset
Q(3)10s
2FG(vert)
Fl(2)R.5s
2FR
Hythe Marina Village
Hythe
Hythe Pier

Fl(3)G.15s
Weston Shelf
Moorhead

01°23'W
22'

The conspicuous Fawley Power Station chimney

Buses Various bus companies offer frequent services throughout the city as well as to the surrounding areas. Solent Blue Line ☎ 618233; First Southampton ☎ 224854; First Provincial ☎ 01329 232208.

Flights Southampton International Airport provides flights to and from several key UK and European destinations, ☎ 620021; its terminal is less than 50m from Southampton Airport (Parkway) railway station.

Taxi Radio Taxis ☎ 666666; Shirley Cabs ☎ 393939; West Quay Cars ☎ 223450.

Car hire Avis Rent-a-car ☎ 226767; National Car Rental ☎ 227373; Europcar ☎ 332973.

Cycle hire AA Bike Hire, Gosport Lane, Lyndhurst ☎ 283349.

Ferries Red Funnel runs a high-speed ferry service between Southampton and the Isle of Wight every half hour throughout the day as well as a car ferry service each hour, ☎ 0870 444 8898. White Horse Ferries operates a half hourly service between Southampton and Hythe, providing links with the New Forest, ☎ 840722.

Beaches Lepe Beach to the E and Lee-On-Solent to the W, although both are shingle beaches.

Supermarkets Waitrose and Marks & Spencer in West Quay; alternatively go to Asda in the Marlands Shopping Centre.

Banks A Nat West Bank close to Ocean Village Marina, with a cashpoint. You will find all other major high street banks in the city centre, most of which have cash machines.

Restaurants Numerous bars and restaurants at Ocean, Town and Shamrock Quays. Other recommended eating places in Southampton are the Olive Tree in Oxford St, ☎ 343333; the adjacent Oxford Bar Restaurant, ☎ 224444; the cheap and cheerful Italian, La Lupa, in the High St, ☎ 331849; Bouzy Rouge in East Bargate, ☎ 220545. For excellent fish and chips go to Harry Ramsden's in West Quay Shopping Centre, ☎ 230678.

NAVIGATION

Charts AC SC 5600.1 (1:150,000), 5600.8 (1:25,000, with insets of R Itchen 1:10,000 and entrance to River Hamble 1:10,000), 2041 (1: 10,000), 2036 (1: 25,000).

Approaches are controlled by the port of Southampton and all craft should heed the priority given to commercial traffic by the Vessel Traffic Services (VTS) VHF Ch 12. No right of way for sail, and specific care should be taken around the area of concern which covers the main channel from the Cowes Prince Consort NCM to the Reach buoy in Southampton Water. Any vessel over 150m LOA in this channel must be given a 'moving prohibited zone' of 1,000m ahead and 100m on either beam. The turning point in the area of the West Bramble WCM and the Calshot Spit lt is particularly restricted.

Southampton Water is fairly expansive, so there is plenty of room for sailing without encroaching too much on the main shipping channel – yachts are advised to keep just outside the buoyed lit fairway and, if possible, cross the channel at right angles (a) abeam Fawley chimney, (b) at Cadland/Greenland buoys, (c) abeam Hythe and (d) abeam Town Quay.

Landmarks The entrance to Southampton Water is clearly marked by Calshot Radar Tower on its W bank, along with the Fawley Power Station and chimney. Southampton Water divides at Dock Head, which is easily identified by conspic silos and a high lattice mast showing traffic signals that are mandatory for commercial vessels but may be disregarded by yachts outside the main channels.

Pilotage Waypoint 50°52'·71N/01°23'·26W brings you to the SHM Weston Shelf Buoy. Approx 3 cables NE of the WPT Southampton Water divides at Dock Head into two rivers –

Chapter 2

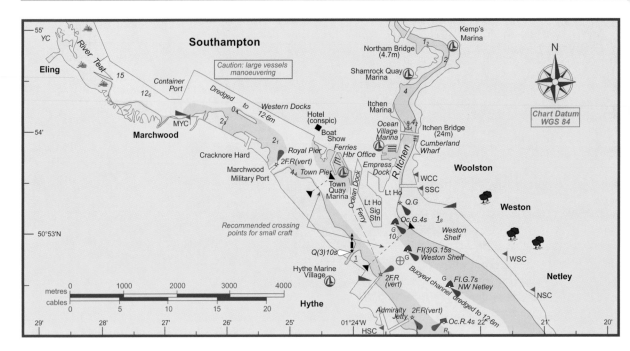

The entrance to the River Itchen with the grain silos to port

the River Test to port and the Itchen to stbd. Due care needs to be taken here to avoid large vessels manoeuvring.

Leaving the Signal Station to port and the G conical buoy (Oc G4s) to stbd, you come to the entrance of the R Itchen. Ocean Village Marina appears shortly after the Empress Dock to port, opposite No 4 bcn. Between the marina and the Itchen Bridge (height clearance of 24m) the best water is to stbd. Above the bridge, marked by 2FR (vert), 2FG (vert) and a FW (indicating the main channel), the channel swings slightly to port and then to stbd, favouring the W bank. Keep the midstream unlit moorings to stbd, sticking to the steep-to docks to port. Opposite No 5 bcn lies Shamrock Quay Marina, above

which the river shallows, although still has just over 2m until Northam Bridge.

To enter the R Test leave the Signal Station to stbd, keeping the dock walls to stbd and the R buoys to port. Town Quay Marina soon appears on your stbd side. There is plenty of water to continue up the R Test as far as the Container port, although beware of foul ground at Marchwood and the Royal Pier. Beyond is Eling Channel, but this is very narrow and dries out; advisable to go up by dinghy unless your boat can take the bottom.

Access Five out of six marinas in Southampton Water are accessible H24 at all tides. Kemp's Marina, at the top of the R Itchen, can be reached HW±3½.

Shelter in Southampton Water is mostly good, although a heavy chop develops in strong SE winds.

Tides Southampton is a standard port. Double HWs occur at sp, about 2 hrs apart; at nps there is a long stand. When there are two, HW predictions are for the first, otherwise they refer to the middle of the stand. MHWS is 4·5m, MLWS 0·5m; MHWN is 3·7m, MLWN 1·8m.

Tidal streams The flood stream, running at a maximum of 1kn at sp, and HW period lasts for about 8 hrs; the ebb, reaching 1¾kn at sp, lasts for 4 hrs.

VHF *Southampton Harbour Patrol* VHF Ch 12, 16;

Hythe Marina Village

Southampton VTS Ch 12, 14, 16 (H24); *Hythe Marina* Ch 80; *Ocean Village Marina* Ch 80; *Shamrock Quay Marina*, Ch 80.

FACILITIES

HM ABP, Ocean Gate, Atlantic Way, ☎ 336402, ✉ 488800.

Fuel Itchen Marine on the River Itchen, just upstream of the Itchen bridge on the port hand side, ☎ 631500. NB cannot be contacted on VHF.

YCs Royal Southampton Yacht Club, ☎ 223352, overlooks Ocean Village Marina and welcomes visitors from affiliated YCs. Open every lunchtime and evening; facilities include bar, buffet and dining room, although it serves evening meals only from Wed–Sat.

MARINAS

In Southampton Water, the options include from seaward:

1. Hythe Marina Village 50°52′·54N 01°23′·98W; Access H24 at all tides. VHF Ch 80; ☎ 207073; ✉ 842424; hythe@mdlmarinas.co.uk; www.marinas.co.uk Situated on the W shores of Southampton Water, the marina is approached by a dredged channel leading to a lock basin. Lock gates are controlled H24, with a waiting pontoon to the S of the approach basin. Call ahead of time for berthing availability and access through the lock gates.

Tariff £2.50 per metre per night; short stay of up to 4 hrs is £5.50 <10m; £6.50 >10m.

Launderette at 'C' basin.

Showers & toilets at each basin.

Fuel pump selling petrol, diesel and gas; opens from 0800–1700. You can also fill up with **FW** here.

Electricity is metred.

Chandlery & repairs On site chandlery; BH (30-ton); hard standing area; Kiss Marine (offers full repair service) ☎ 840100.

Food shop Essential items can be bought in the Marina Village Centre. Hythe is in close walking distance; incorporates a Waitrose in the High St.

Banks An HSBC and Lloyds Bank, with cashpoints, in The Marsh, Hythe.

Restaurants Two in the Marina Village: The Italian La Vista, ☎ 207730; the Boat House pub, ☎ 845594. Pubs in Hythe include two on the High St: The Seagull, ☎ 847188; The Lord Nelson ☎ 842169. Or try the Indian Restaurant, Forest Spice, on Pylewell Rd, ☎ 842315; also offers a takeaway service.

2. Town Quay, the River Test 50°53′·66N 01°24′·22W. Access H24 all tides. ☎ 234397; ✉ 235302. Leaving the silos and Signal Station to stbd brings you to the R Test. Beyond the cruise liner dock, on the stbd side, lies Town Quay Marina. ❶ berths are scarce so contact the marina ahead of time to check availability. Watch out for the fast ferries shuttling between Southampton and the Isle of Wight. The marina entrance is between two floating wavebreaks (2FR (vert) and 2FG (vert)) that can appear continuous from seaward.

Tariff Overnight: £2.50 per metre <15m; £2.75 per metre 15–18m. A short stay of up to 6 hrs is £10.

Showers, launderette (coin-operated) are accessed by code.

Electricity, £2 per day, and **FW** on the pontoons.

Fuel Go to Hythe Marina or Itchen Marine, upstream of the Itchen bridge to port.

Shops and restaurants See page 167.

3. Ocean Village on the River Itchen, 50°53'·72N 01°23'·39W. Access H24 all tides. VHF Ch 80; ☎ 229385; ▨ 233515; oceanvillage@mdlmarinas.co.uk; www.marinas.co.uk The entrance to Ocean Village is to port just before the Itchen bridge. On entering, tie up against the dock office pontoon to enquire about berthing availability. No dedicated ❶ berths, but the marina will accommodate you if there is space.

Tariff £2.60 per metre per night <15m; £3.25 per metre per night 15–18m; £3.60 per metre per night 18.1m and over.

Launderette (coin-operated) and **showers** can be accessed by code.

Electricity (metred) and **FW** on the pontoons.

Fuel Go to Itchen Marine.

Chandlery & repairs Go to nearby Shamrock Quay; see opposite.

The entrance to Ocean Village. The visitors' pontoon is directly ahead

Food shops The on site One Stop is good for general provisions. Also see page 167.

Restaurants Several on site, or else see page 167.

4. Shamrock Quay, the River Itchen 50°54'·55N 01°22'·80W. Access H24, but note that some of the inside berths can get quite shallow at LWS. It is best to arrive at slack water as the cross tide can be tricky when close quarter manoeuvring. VHF Ch 80; ☎ 229461; ▨ 213808; shamrockquay@mdlmarinas.co.uk; www.marinas.co.uk Upstream of the Itchen bridge on the port hand side, it used to be part of the Camper & Nicholsons' yard, taking its name from the J Class yacht *Shamrock V*, which was constructed on the site in 1931 as a challenger for the America's Cup. Contact the marina ahead of time for berthing availability.

Tariff £2.65 per metre per night; £5 for a short stay of up to 4 hrs.

Showers and **launderette** (coin-operated) are accessed by card.

Electricity (metred) and **FW** on the pontoons.

Gas and ice available on site. Make enquiries at the marina office.

Fuel Go to Itchen Marine, about 300m before the Itchen Bridge, on the stbd side, if heading back down the river.

Chandlery & repairs Well stocked chandlery on site. Besides a BH and hard standing area, there are plenty of marine engineers, riggers, sailmakers, electronic and electrical experts on site. Also Rampart Yachts ☎ 234777.

Food shop The closest for basic provisions is the One Stop in Ocean Village.

Eating The Waterfront pub on site, ☎ 632209; offers good meals at reasonable prices. Otherwise try the neighbouring Taps, ☎ 228621. The coffee shop is being refurbished in time for 2003 season and will sell sandwiches, baguettes and cakes, as well as essential items.

5. Saxon Wharf, the River Itchen 50°54'·77N 01°22'·72W. Access H24. VHF Ch 80, ☎ 339490; ▨ 213808; saxonwharf@mdlmarinas.co.uk; www.marinas.co.uk This relatively new development, situated next to Shamrock Quay, is intended to accommodate superyachts and larger vessels. It is equipped with 50-metre marina berths and heavy duty pontoons.

Tariff £2.65 per metre per night; short stay is a flat rate of £5.

Facilities As part of the Shamrock Quay complex, it shares its ablution facilities and launderette with Shamrock Quay Marina.

Repairs BH (200 ton); slipway (500 ton); marine specialists on site include Southampton Yacht Services, ☎ 335266.

6. Kemp's Marina, the River Itchen 50°54'·86N 01°22'·70W. Access HW±3½, with a draught of 1.5m. ☎ 632323. At the head of the R Itchen on the stbd side is Kemp's Marina. A family-run business, it is friendly and has a pleasant, old-fashioned feel. However, its semi-industrial environs mean that it is not located in the most attractive of areas and is quite far from the city centre. It has a limited number of deep water berths, the rest being half-tide, drying out to soft mud. There are no dedicated ❼ berths, so contact the marina ahead of time to check availability.

Tariff £2 per ft per wk or £6.60 per metre per week.

Showers and **toilets** are accessed by code. No launderette.

Electricity (£2.20 per day) and **FW** available on the pontoons.

Fuel Go to Itchen Marine.

Chandlery & repairs A CH on site, along with a BH (10 ton), hard standing, repair and maintenance service.

Food shop The nearby BP garage sells bread and milk while a 5 mins bus ride takes you to Bitterne Centre where you will find a Safeway and Sainsburys.

Chapter 2

The River Itchen

THE HAMBLE

The River Hamble entrance – 50°50'·15N 01°18'·64W

The River Hamble is renowned internationally as a centre for yachting and boatbuilding. With five marinas and several boatyards, it accommodates over 3,000 boats and is a constant hive of activity during the summer. Due to its popularity and the lack of designated berths for visitors, berthing may be difficult so contact the marinas or harbour master slightly ahead of time. Once in the river, you will be spoilt for choice by the number of charming pubs and restaurants lining the water's edge.

SHORESIDE (Telephone code 023 80)

Tourist Office 9, Civic Centre Rd, Southampton. ☎ 023 8083 3333; ▨ 023 8083 3381; city.information@southampton.gov.uk; www.southampton.gov.uk/cityinfo Open Mon–Sat 0830–1730, except Wed, 1000–1730. Fareham Tourist Information Centre, Westbury Manor Museum, 84 West St, Fareham, PO16 0JJ. ☎ 01329 221342; information@ touristboard.freeserve.co.uk Open Mon–Fri 0930–1700, Sat 1000–1600.

What to see/do A walk along the River Hamble is well worth while, if only to reflect on its past maritime history which began as far back as the ninth century when King Alfred's men sank as many as 20 Viking long ships at Bursledon during the Battle of Brixdone. Or on a favourable tide, go by dinghy as far as Botley Village. The Royal Victoria Country Park, two miles from the Hamble on the edge of Southampton Water, proves a popular attraction, especially with children. Open all year round, it has large open spaces, a children's play area and a miniature railway; ☎ 455157. Other places of interest in the area include Manor Farm Country Park in Bursledon, ☎ 01489 787055, a working farm from the Victorian era, and the Bursledon Windmill, reputed for being Hampshire's only working mill. Built between 1813 and 1814, it opens on weekends during the summer from 1000–1600 and on Sun only in the winter; ☎ 023 8040 4999.

Hamble Week, packed full of watersports, takes place towards the end of June/ beginning of July and is combined with the Hamble Valley Food and Drink Festival ☎ 0906 6822 001. The Moody Used Boat Show is also worth going to if you are in the Hamble around the second to third week of

Looking up river, with Swanwick Marina to starboard and the Elephant and Deacon's boatyards to port

The Bugle pub in the Hamble Village

September. At the same time as the Southampton Boat Show, it is held at Moodys Boatyard in Swanwick Marina, ☎ 01489 885000.

Rail Stations at Bursledon, Hamble, Netley, Hedge End and Botley, providing links with Southampton and Portsmouth from where train services run regularly to London. For train enquiries call ☎ 08457 484950.

Buses Many of the marinas are within easy reach of bus stops, with buses running between Warsash, Hamble, Swanwick, Bursledon and Southampton. Contact Solent Blue Line, ☎ 618233, or First Bus network, ☎ 224854.

Flights Good UK and European connections from Southampton International Airport, ☎ 620021, which is only a 5 mins walk from Southampton Parkway railway station.

Taxi Phipps Taxis ☎ 0700 234 5678; Radio Taxis ☎ 666666.

Car hire Performance Hire, Locksheath, ☎ 01489 572722; Peter Cooper Volkswagen, Hedge End, ☎ 01489 783434.

Ferries Red Funnel runs services from Southampton, a 15 mins car ride away, to the Isle of Wight, ☎ 334010. P&O offers cross–Channel services from Portsmouth, 30 mins by car from the Hamble, ☎ 0870 242 4999.

Beaches The nearest is a shingle beach, Lee-on-Solent, to the E of Southampton Water.

Supermarkets The main supermarket is Tesco, with cash machine, at Bursledon on Hamble Lane. Otherwise Hamble Village has several little shops including a PO, Alldays and a delicatessen. On the opposite side of the river, Warsash boasts an Alldays and a One Stop, both of which have cash machines, with the latter incorporating a PO.

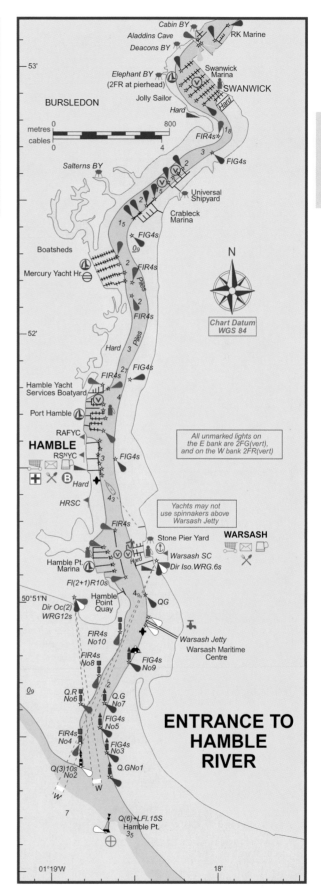

Hamble Point south cardinal mark

Banks Hamble village has two banks, a Nat West and Barclays, although only the latter, which is a 10 mins walk from the village, has a cashpoint.

Restaurants Three pubs highly recommended in Hamble village are the Bugle, ☎ 453104, the Victory Inn, ☎ 453105, and the King & Queen, ☎ 454247. Another well known pub in the area is The Jolly Sailor at Bursledon on the W bank of the river, ☎ 405557. For something special, try either Compass Point Riverside Restaurant in the High St, ☎ 452388, or The Key in Rope Walk, ☎ 454314. During summer, book in advance with both these restaurants. For a good Italian menu go to La Dolce Vita in the Square, ☎ 454567. Also in the Hamble are a fish and chip shop, ☎ 456711, and an Indian restaurant just outside the village, next to Barclays Bank on Hamble Lane.

Among the three pubs in Warsash is the Rising Sun, ☎ 01489 576898, on the quay. Although offering superb views and serving good food, it is more expensive than the other two pubs closer to the village centre – the Ferry Man, ☎ 01489 573088, and the Silver Fern, ☎ 01489 572057. Alternatively try the Indian restaurant, The Chon Chona, on Shore Road, ☎ 573110, or Rumours in Brook Lane, ☎ 573720.

NAVIGATION

Charts AC 2022 (1:5,000), plus SC 5600.1 (1:150,000), 5600.8 (1:10,000), 2036 (1:25,000).

Approaches From the E there are no real hazards except for the extensive but gentle shoaling from Lee Pt to the entrance on your stbd hand side. There is, however, plenty of room to sail outside the North Channel shipping lane. From the W, after rounding Lepe Spit SCM to port and keeping clear of Calshot Spit (Fl 5s 12m), stay to the outside edge of the main channel. Cross over to the E side, heading for the Hamble Point SCM and retaining a distance from commercial vessels. If approaching from Southampton, do not cut inside No 2 ECM for fear of getting caught on the Hamble Spit.

Landmarks The mouth of the River Hamble is virtually opposite Fawley Power Station, a few cables further NW of Calshot Radar Tower which marks the entrance to Southampton Water.

Pilotage From the waypoint 50°50'·15N 01°18'·64W, leaving Hamble Point SCM just to port, steering due N brings you to the No 1 QG pile from whereon the channel is clearly marked with port and stbd piles that are all lit. Once through the entrance stick to the centre of the river between the moorings. At night, from the Hamble Pt SCM, a Dir lt on the shore W of Hamble Pt (Oc (2) WRG12s W351°–353°) at 352° leads you into the entrance. Between the No 5 bn (Fl G 4s) and the No 7 bn (QG) alter course to 028° to bring you into the W sector of the Dir lt (Iso WRG 6s 5m 4M) on the Warsash shore. Beware of the unlit mooring piles at night. During the summer, finding a berth can be difficult and as traffic is heavy, it is recommended that you use your engine. Spinnakers must not be flown N of the Warsash Jetty and anchoring is forbidden in the river.

Access All the marinas on the River Hamble can be accessed H24 at all tides. Note that if moored at Hamble Quay the depth can drop to about 1.5m at LWS.

Shelter is excellent in all weather.

Tides At Warsash, near the entrance to the River Hamble, HW sp are 10 mins after and HW nps 20 mins after HW Southampton. LW nps are 10 mins after and LW sp the same as LW Southampton. MHWS is 4·5m, MLWS 0·8m; MHWN is 3·8m, MLWN 1·9m.

Tidal streams Try to avoid berthing in the Hamble when the tide is ebbing strongly.

VHF *Hamble Harbour Radio* Ch 68 (April–Sep: Daily 0600–2200. Oct–March: Daily 0700–1830); *Water Taxi* Ch 77; *Hamble Point Marina* Ch 80; *Port Hamble Marina* Ch 80; *Mercury Yacht Harbour* Ch 80; *Universal & Crableck Marinas* Ch 80; *Swanwick Marina* Ch 80.

FACILITIES

HM Harbour Office, (conspic black and white striped building), Shore Road, Warsash, SO31 9FR. ☎ 01489 576387; Mobile 07718 146380/146381; ⏚ 01489 580718; www.harbours.co.uk

Berthing The HM offers several midstream **ⓥ** piles and pontoons as well as a couple of jetties. Places cannot be reserved ahead of time and are on a 'first come first served' basis. Hamble Quay is also under the control of the HM.

Tariff Short stay for a 10m yacht on a pontoon berth is £5; for overnight £10; for 24 hrs £15. Piles are charged on a 24 hr or weekly rate; 10m is £5 for 24 hr or £30 per week. Jetties are the most expensive option; a 10m yacht is charged £7.50 for a short stay; £22.50 for 24 hr period. Lying alongside Hamble Quay is free up to 1 hr.

Fuel and **gas** from Stone Pier, ☎ 01489 885400, not far from the HM's office.

YCs Warsash Sailing Club, ☎ 01489 583575; Hamble River Sailing Club ☎ 452070; The Royal Southern YC ☎ 450300; The RAF YC ☎ 452208. All YCs welcome visiting yachtsmen and serve food and drinks.

Water Taxi A river taxi runs between Hamble and Warsash. Contact the Water Taxi on VHF Ch 77; ☎ 454512/Mobile 07720 438402.

Hamble Point Marina

CHANDLERY & REPAIR FACILITIES

Aladdin's Cave, Swanwick Marina ☎ 01489 575828, CH; Aladdin's Cave, Deacon's Boat Yard ☎ 402182, CH; Aladdin's Cave, Mercury Marina, ☎ 454849, CH; Shore Sailmakers ☎ 01489 589450; Bruce Bank Sails ☎ 582444; Elephant Boat Yard ☎ 403268; Deacon's Boat Yard ☎ 402253; Salterns Boatyard ☎ 403911; Moody Service & Construction ☎ 01489 885000; Hamble Yacht Services ☎ 454111; RK Marine (engine stockist) ☎ 01489 583585.

MARINAS

In Hamble, options include from seaward:

1. Hamble Point Marina 50°51'·16N 01°18'·65W. Access H24 at all tides. VHF Ch 80; ☎ 452464; ⏚ 456440; hamblepoint@mdlmarinas.co.uk; www.marinas.co.uk Situated practically opposite Warsash, this is the first marina on the W bank of the River Hamble. There are no dedicated **ⓥ** berths, with availability subject to resident berthholders being away. The marina can accommodate yachts up to 20m LOA.

Tariff £2.30 per metre per night; £7.50 for a short stay of up to 4 hrs for yachts <10m; £10 for a short stay for >10m.

Launderette and **showers** are behind the Ketch Rigger restaurant; accessed by code.

Electricity (metred) and **FW** on the pontoons.

Gas available from the on site chandlery; ice from the dock office.

Fuel Diesel and LPG can be obtained at the fuel pontoon, but contact the Dock Office first.

Repairs Plenty of marine services on hand (ask at the Dock Office) as well as boat lifting facilities, hard standing and undercover storage.

Food shop The nearest convenience store is Alldays in the Hamble Village, a 15 mins walk away; open daily 0700–2200.

Eating The on site bar-cum-restaurant, the Ketch Rigger, ☎ 455601, serves lunchtime and evening meals.

2. Port Hamble Marina 50°51'·65N 01°18'·69W. Access 24 hrs per day at any state of the tide. VHF Ch 80; ☎ 4527421; ✉ 455206; porthamble@mdlmarinas.co.uk; www.marinas.co.uk The second marina on the W bank, it is also the closest one to Hamble village (correctly known as Hamble-le-Rice). Again there are no dedicated places for visitors so berthing availability is often scarce in summer.

Tariff £2.65 per metre per night; £6 for a short stay of up to 4 hrs.

Launderette (coin-operated) directly beneath the Dock Office.

Showers, also below the Dock Office, are open 23 hrs per day, closing for 1 hr for cleaning Accessed by code.

Electricity (metred) and **FW** can be obtained on the pontoons.

Fuel Unleaded petrol and diesel from the fuel barge on the outside of 'B' pontoon

from 0800–1800 in summer and from 0900–1700 in winter.

Chandlery & repairs On site chandlery behind the marina office. No shortage of marine expertise to hand; ask at the office for a full list of contractors. Other facilities include hard standing and craning out.

Food shop The chandlery stocks a small range of provisions; otherwise the closest grocery store is Alldays in Hamble village, open daily 0700–2200.

Eating The on site restaurant, the Square Rigger, ☎ 453446, serves good pub food.

3. Mercury Yacht Harbour 50°52'·27N 01°18'·69W. Access H24. VHF Ch 80; ☎ 455994; ✉ 457369; mercury@mdlmarinas.co.uk; www.marinas.co.uk The marina can accommodate yachts up to 24m LOA. No allocated ❶ berths, although usually space can be found in summer when resident berthholders are away.

Tariff Overnight £2.30 < 15m; £2.90 >15m. Short stay of up to 4 hrs is £6 <10m; £7 >10m.

Launderette (coin-operated) and **showers** are situated in the main marina building.

Electricity (metred) and **FW** on the pontoons.

Gas available from the on site chandlery; ice from the dock office.

Fuel No fuel station on site so go to Swanwick, Port Hamble or Hamble Point Marinas, although contact the marina staff ahead of time.

Repairs BH, hard standing area, SM plus other marine experts (ask at the dock office for more information).

Food shop The on site chandlery stocks a few essential provisions, otherwise the nearest convenience store is Alldays in the Hamble village; open seven days a week 0700–2200.

Eating The Gaff Rigger Bar and Restaurant on the premises serves good food and offers great views of the water, ☎ 457220.

The Jolly Sailor at Bursledon

4. Universal & Crableck Marinas 50°52'·56N 01°18'·59W. Access H24. VHF Ch 80; ☎/🖷 01489 574272; www.universalmarina.co.uk Situated a little further up river from Mercury Yacht Harbour, but on the E shore, are Universal and Crableck Marinas, offering deep water, semi tidal and river berths to yachts between 6–20m LOA. No designated **❶** berths but space may be had on one of the pontoons if residents are away.

Tariff £2 per metre per night or a short stay of up to 4 hrs is a flat rate of £5.

Launderette (coin-operated) as well as a local laundry & dry cleaning collection and delivery service; ☎ 406366.

Showers Various shower and toilet blocks on site, all of which are accessed by code.

Electricity (£2 per day) and **FW** available on some pontoons.

Fuel No facility on site so go a little further upstream to Swanwick Marina or back to Port Hamble.

Chandlery & repairs No chandlery on site, but there is an Aladdin's Cave at Swanwick Marina. A BH (50 ton), hard standing area and an array of marine specialists make it easy to have repairs carried out.

Food shop One of the nearest convenience stores is the One Stop, with cash machine, at Sarisbury Green, about a 15 mins walk away.

Eating See under Swanwick Marina below.

5. Swanwick Marina 50°52'·92N 01°18'·06W. Accessible at any state of the tide. VHF Ch 80; ☎ 01489 885000 during office hrs; ☎ 01489 885262 out of office hrs; 🖷 01489 885509; www.moody.co.uk Situated on the E bank of the River Hamble, just before the Bursledon Bridge, the marina has a few **❶** berths, otherwise availability is dependent on resident berthholders being away. Yachts up to 20m LOA can be accommodated, although any yacht of this size should contact the marina in advance.

Tariff £28 per night for 10m LOA; £17.50 for 8m LOA. A short stay of up to 4 hrs is £6 for 5–10m.

Launderette located below the dock office; open 0800–2000. A key is available for use outside of these hours.

Showers and toilets are also situated below the dock office and are accessed by code.

Warsash pontoons and HM office

Electricity (included in berthing fees) and **FW** on the pontoons.

Gas and **ice** available from the on site chandlery, Aladdin's Cave.

Fuel A fuel berth opens on request at the dock office between 0800 and 1730.

Repairs The Moody (Service and Construction) boatyard on site offers a full range of services from BH (65 tons) to repairs and maintenance. Open-air and under cover storage are available.

Food shop Nearest store is Swanwick Post Office in Swanwick Lane, open to 1730 Mon–Fri and until 1300 on weekends. Or go to the One Stop, with cash machine, at Sarisbury Green, about half a mile from the marina.

Eating The marina's fully-licensed bar and bistro, the Doghouse, ☎ 01489 571602, is open seven days a week. Also within walking distance of the marina are two pubs, the Spinnaker, ☎ 01489 572123, and the Old Ship, ☎ 01489 575646. The Riverside Restaurant, next to the Spinnaker on Bridge Rd, comes highly recommended, ☎ 404100.

Other berthing places Opposite Swanwick Marina is the Elephant Boat Yard; although it has no allocated **❶** berths, it may have space on one of its pontoons, with the added of advantage of being far cheaper than the marinas (£1.28 per metre per night); ☎ 403268.

North of the Elephant Boat Yard is Deacon's, also offering pontoon berths and several swinging moorings. No specific **❶** berths, ☎ 023 8040 2253. Rates are again cheaper at £12 per night.

The channel into Wootton Creek is well marked by port and starboard hand beacons, all of which are lit

WOOTTON CREEK

Wootton Creek entrance – 50°44·32N 01°12'·42W

Despite being the Isle of Wight's main ferry terminal from Portsmouth, Wootton Creek is in fact a charming little harbour. Unfortunately it has few deep-water moorings but offers excellent shelter for shoal draught yachts in all but strong N to NE winds.

SHORESIDE (Telephone code 01983)

Tourist Office 81-83 Union Street, Ryde.
☎ 813818; 🖷 823033; post@islandbreaks.co.uk; www.islandbreaks.co.uk

What to see/do As an area of outstanding natural beauty, a walk along Wootton Creek from Fishbourne to Wootton Bridge is well worth while, especially as you can be rewarded for your efforts in the Sloop Inn.

Buses go from Wootton Bridge to Ryde and Newport; Southern Vectis ☎ 292082.

Taxi Amber Cars ☎ 812222; Ralph Taxis ☎ 811666.

Ferries Wightlink ferries, ☎ 0870 582 7744, runs a car ferry service for Portsmouth every 30 mins on the hour and half hour, depending on the time of year. The crossing takes approx 35 mins.

Beaches The closest are Ryde's extensive sandy beaches, starting with West Beach on the W side of the pier.

The Wootton Creek approach with little room for passing ferries

Shops Wootton Bridge, accessible either by dinghy, depending on the state of the tide, or on foot (about half a mile from the Royal Victoria Yacht Club), has two supermarkets and a PO.

Banks For the nearest bank go to Ryde.

Restaurants Two pubs in the area are the Fishbourne Inn, ☎ 882823, reached by turning left after the ferry car park, and the Sloop Inn at Wootton Bridge, ☎ 882544.

NAVIGATION

Charts: AC 2022 (1:10,000), plus SC 5600.1 (1:150,000), 5600.3 (1:75,000), 2022 (1:10,000).

Approaches From the W, staying N of the Royal Victoria Yacht Club (RVYC) starting platform will keep you clear of the Wootton Rocks. From the E, with a good offing, there are no hazards to look out for apart from the regular Portsmouth to Fishbourne ferries which often heave to just outside the entrance.

Landmarks Situated approx 2M W of Ryde pier, the entrance to Wootton Creek, with the regular Wightlink ferries and the RVYC starting platform just W of it, is not that difficult to make out against the wooded shoreline.

Pilotage From the waypoint 50°44'·53N 01°12'·13W, (ie the Wootton NCM bn (Q 1M)), steering 224° will take you into the straight channel which is well marked by four SHM and two PHM, all of which are lit.The ferry pier is also lit (2FR (vert)) and has a fog light (FY) and bell. Beyond the pier is a ldg sectored Dir lt which at night shows the narrow white sector if you are on course. Manoeuvring in the channel can be restricting so try to time your arrival to avoid the ferries which run every 30 mins on the hour and half hour. Once past the No 7 bn and abeam of the outer ferry terminal, turn to stbd leaving the RVYC pontoon to port; this should bring the two triangular ldg marks on the W bank into line. If continuing further into the creek stick to the row of mooring buoys for the deepest water and look out for a small green buoy, which needs to be kept just to stbd to avoid the gravel spit protruding from the port side. Following on from this, a small red buoy and a line of old piles, both of which must be left to port, bring you to Fishbourne Quay.

Access The initial stretch of channel is well dredged, but above the ferry terminal the creek dries and is really only accessible to shoal draught yachts at HW. The RVYC pontoon dries out at LW. For an overnight stay, it is better for those boats that can take the bottom.

Shelter Good shelter except in strong N to E'ly winds.

Tides Use Ryde differences; see page 182.

Tidal streams in Wootton Creek are weak. See Solent tidal streams on page 127.

FACILITIES

RVYC ☎ 813818; rvyc@lineone.net; www.rvyc.co.uk

Berthing Visiting yachts may tie up alongside the RVYC's pontoon, but bear in mind that this does dry out.

Tariff £1 per metre per night or £4 for a short stay.

Anchorage ⚓ is forbidden in the fairway, but you may anchor ⚓ free of charge directly opposite the yacht club on the N side of the channel where you will dry out at half-tide on soft mud.

Electricity and **FW** on the yacht club pontoon.

Showers and toilets ashore in the clubhouse are available to members of other yacht clubs.

Fuel No facility, therefore you would need to go to Cowes.

Chandlery & repairs As above.

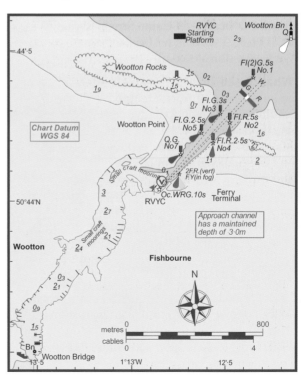

RYDE

Ryde harbour entrance – 50°44'·35N 01°09'·14W

Known as 'the gateway to the Island', Ryde, with its elegant houses and abundant shops, is one of the Isle of Wight's most popular resorts. Its well-protected harbour, although drying to about 2.5m, is conveniently close to the exceptional beaches as well as to the town's restaurants, amusements and 'candy-floss' atmosphere, making it an ideal cruising destination for families.

SHORESIDE (Telephone code 01983)

Tourist Office 81–83 Union Street, Ryde. ☎ 813818; 🖷 823033; post@islandbreaks.co.uk; www.islandbreaks.co.uk

What to see/do The Esplanade offers a host of activities ranging from a tenpin bowling alley and ice rink to a large indoor swimming pool and a small open-air heated junior pool which opens May–Sept. Other options include a canoe lake and the challenging Appley nine-hole pitch and putt golf course. The sea wall promenade provides a popular walk, leading to Puckpool Park where tennis, bowling, crazy golf and refreshments are all on offer. For something less strenuous, visit the Royal Victoria Arcade, incorporating boutiques, antique shops and an intriguing cellar market.

Rail An electric train (comprising refurbished 1930s London Underground carriages) runs from the pierhead to Shanklin with stops at Ryde Esplanade, Ryde St John's, Brading, Sandown and Lake, ☎ 812591.

Buses Services from Ryde to Newport and Cowes as well as to the Island's major tourist attractions. The Rover Ticket is an economical way of travelling by bus or train, ☎ 292082.

Taxi Como Taxis ☎ 563224; Ryde Taxis ☎ 811111.

Ferries Wightlink ferries run from Portsmouth Harbour to Ryde generally twice every hour at 20 mins past and 10 mins to the hour. Crossing takes approx 15 mins. Wightlink ☎ 0870 582 7744.

Hovercraft A half-hourly service between Ryde and Southsea, ☎ 811000.

Beaches Ryde is renowned for its sandy beaches, extending from West Beach on the W side of the pier to Appley, Puckpool and Springvale to the E.

Supermarkets Somerfield in Anglesea St is one of the nearest; to get there go up the High St and turn left at Boots the chemist. Tesco is further out of town on Brading Road; open 24 hrs Mon–Sat and 1000–1600 Sun.

Banks are in Union St, High St or St Thomas Square, most of which have cash machines.

Restaurants For Italian cuisine try Michaelangelo's Restaurant, ☎ 811966, close to the marina, or Dino's on the High St, ☎ 616883, offering eat-in, take away or delivery service. Yelf's Hotel, Bar and Restaurant in Union St, ☎ 564062, provides a variety of dishes including traditional English roast on Sundays. Also incorporates Bar 53, a parisienne-style café-bar serving cocktails, wines, beers, coffees and snacks. Long John Eater in Union St, ☎ 562623, is popular with children. For fish and chips try the Cod Father and Ian's Plaice along the Esplanade.

NAVIGATION

Charts AC SC 5600.1 (1:150,000), 5600.3 (1:75,000), 2037 (1:25,000), 2045 (1:75,000).

Approaches From the E, Ryde Sand is waiting to snare those who take short cuts. First-timers to the Solent should stay N of No Mans Land Fort and the SW Mining Ground Y buoy. From the W, Ryde Pier, with its three sets of 2FR (vert) and FY Fog lights, needs to be kept well to stbd to avoid hindering the high-speed ferry operating from the pier head. E of the pier the Ryde/Portsmouth hovercraft has absolute right of way, with the buoyed channel being your only safe water.

Landmarks The marina is approx 3 cables to the E of the pier and immediately E of a large modern conspic building (incorporating the ice rink). A bearing on the Holy Trinity Church spire can be used as an initial approach.

Pilotage The waypoint is 50°44'·70N 01°09'·00W. From here use the Holy Trinity Church spire, brg 196°, as an initial approach across Ryde Sand until the unlit No 1 SHM puts you in the straight drying channel (1.5m), marked by three stbd and three port unlit buoys. The marina breakwaters,

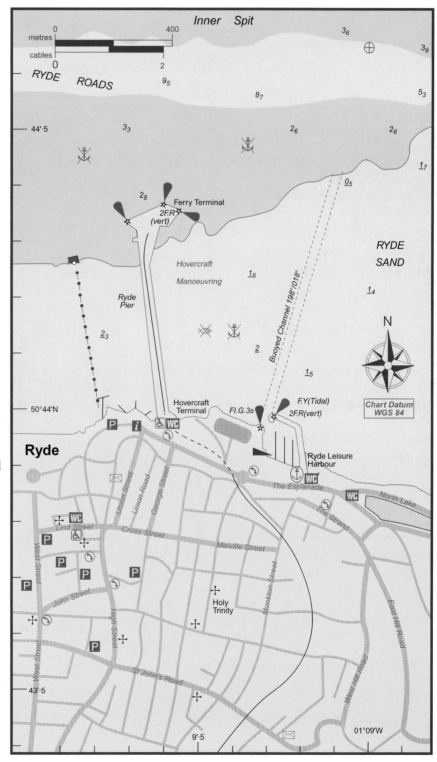

The hovercraft runs between Ryde and Southsea

both of which are lit, are less than 0.5M directly ahead. On entering the marina, turn to port as soon as the port hand breakwater is abeam of you. A tide gauge is situated on the port hand breakwater and at night a FY showing one light indicates that the depth in the harbour is one metre, while two lights signify that there is at least 1.5m of water.

Access The harbour dries to approx 2.5m. Access for shoal draught yachts is HW–2 to +2.

Shelter is good in the harbour.

Tides HW sp are 10 mins before and nps 10 mins after HW Portsmouth. LW nps are 10 mins before and sp 5 mins before LW Portsmouth. MHWS is 4·5m, MLWS 0·9m; MHWN is 3·7m, MLWN 1·9m.

Tidal streams see Solent tidal streams on page 127.

VHF Ryde Harbour Ch 80.

FACILITIES

HM David Brown, The Esplanade, Ryde. ☎ 613879; rydeharbour@amserve.net; www.rydeharbour.com

Berthing The harbour has 75 **Ⓥ** berths, although its popularity with families often makes it crowded in summer. Ideally suited for smaller craft, bilge keelers are berthed on the pontoons, while the E inner breakwater is well equipped with fender boards and mooring cleats to deal with deep-draughted yachts willing to take the sandy bottom.

Tariff £8 per night for an 8m yacht; £4.50 for a short stay.

Showers, toilets and **FW** at the harbour.

Fuel (in cans) and **gas** from the local garage.

Chandlery & repairs None available at Ryde.

Alternative moorings Visitors can also pick up one of the 15 moorings to the W of Ryde Pier, which are currently free of charge. For more information on these call ☎ 811533.

Ryde is a good place for shopping and eating out

The Holy Trinity church spire (centre) can be used as a bearing (196°) to bring you to the channel entrance

Church spire bearing 196°

BEMBRIDGE

Bembridge harbour entrance – 50°42'·34N 01°05'·36W

Bembridge is a compact, pretty harbour whose entrance, although restricted by the tides, is well sheltered in all but N/NE gales. Offering excellent sailing clubs, beautiful beaches and fine restaurants, this Isle of Wight port is a first class haven with plenty of charm.

The channel is well buoyed but unlit, so a night-time entry is not recommended

SHORESIDE (Telephone code 01983)

Tourist Office 81–83 Union Street, Ryde/
8 High St, Sandown. ☎ 813818; 🖷 823033;
post@islandbreaks.co.uk; www.islandbreaks.co.uk

What to see/do The walk over the Culver Down to Sandown provides some of the best views of the Island, while the Bembridge Trail takes you from the harbour along the old sea wall to ancient Brading. Bembridge itself has several attractions ranging from The Shipwreck and Maritime Museum in Sherbourne St, ☎ 872223, open daily 1000–1700 from March–Oct, to an art gallery displaying the work of local artists. A little inland is Bembridge Windmill. Built in 1700, it is today owned by the National Trust and is open to the public. Also open to the public, but only during the summer on three afternoons a week and Bank Holidays, is the Bembridge Lifeboat Station. A bit further afield is the ancient port of Brading, home to the popular Wax Works, ☎ 0870 458 4477, open daily from 1000–1700 from 20 March–2 Nov.

Buses Southern Vectis, ☎ 292082, puts on bus services approx twice an hour in the summer

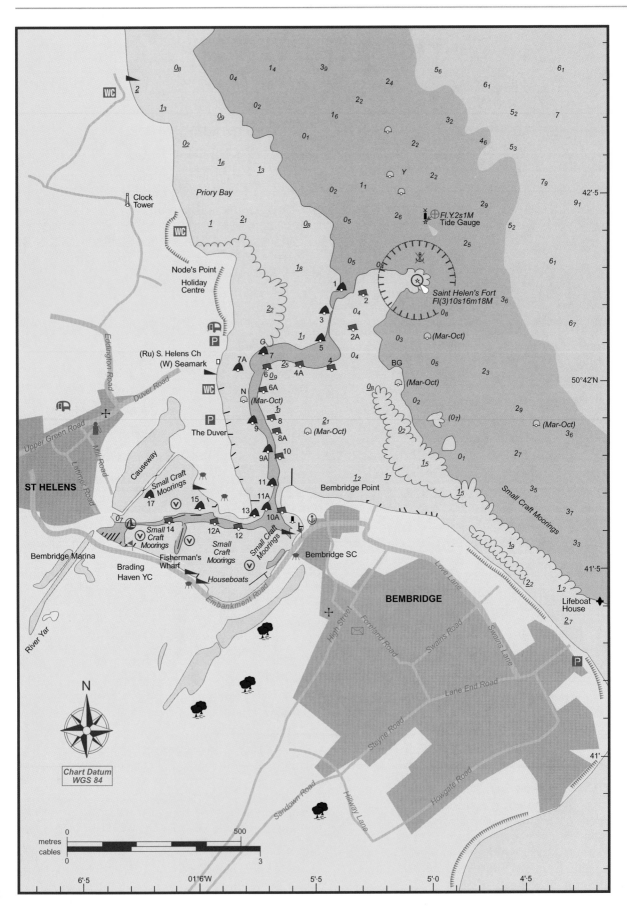

WC

2

0.8

0.4

1.4

3.9

5.6

6.1

13

0.9

0.2

2.2

2.4

6.1

0.2

1.6

2.2

3.2

5.2

7

Clock
Tower

0.2

0.1

2.2

4.6

5.3

Priory Bay

0.2

1.1

Y

2.2

7.9

42'·5

WC

0.2

2.6

⊕ Fl.Y.2s1M
Tide Gauge

2.9

9.1

Node's Point

1

2.1

0.8

0.5

2.5

5.2

Holiday
Centre

1.8

0.5

0.4

6.1

2.2

1

1

2

Saint Helen's Fort
Fl(3)10s16m18M

3.6

6.7

3

0.4

0.8

(Ru) S. Helens Ch
(W) Seamark

1.1

2A

0.3

(Mar-Oct)

G

7

5

4

0.4

BG

0.5

50°42'N

7A

2.5

4A

(Mar-Oct)

2.3

6.1

6

0.9

N

6A

0.8

0.2

2.9

WC

(Mar-Oct)

1.3

(0.7)

(Mar-Oct)

P

8

2.1

3.6

The Duver

9

8A

(Mar-Oct)

0.2

10

0.1

ST HELENS

9A

1.5

2.7

11

1.2

1.7

Bembridge Point

3.5

Small Craft
Small Craft
Moorings

17

15

11A

1.5

3.7

Moorings

13

10A

Small Craft
Moorings

0.7

Small 14
Craft
Moorings

12A

12

Small
Craft
Moorings

1.9

3.3

Bembridge Marina

Brading
Haven YC

Fisherman's
Wharf

Small Craft
Moorings

Bembridge SC

2.2

1.2

Lifeboat
House

Houseboats

2.7

River Yar

Embankment Road

BEMBRIDGE

N

Chart Datum
WGS 84

metres

0

500

cables

0

3

184 Channel Cruising Companion

The Bembridge Shipwreck and Maritime Museum

from Bembridge and the harbour to Ryde and Sandown, from where you will find connections to other parts of the Island.

Taxi Bembridge & Harbour Taxis, ☎ 874132; Ralph's Taxis (Ryde) ☎ 874132.

Beaches Surrounded on three sides by sea, Bembridge is renowned for its quiet, sandy beaches, many of which are covered at HW. North of Bembridge is St Helens, ideal for swimming, with an esplanade, café and slipway. To the south is Whitecliff Bay, accessed by a fairly steep path, but well sheltered by the Culver Cliffs. Also has a café and picnic area.

Supermarkets A good 30 mins walk from the marina, Bembridge village, east of the hbr, has a comprehensive range of shops from supermarkets to a traditional butcher. The closest food shop is Davids supermarket in Sherbourne St. St Helens, on the west side, is closer to the marina and has a local store that stays open from 0800–2000 all year round.

Banks Lloyds TSB, with a cashpoint, is in the High St in Bembridge village. The Post Office at St Helens has a cash machine.

Restaurants On the Bembridge side, The Crab & Lobster Inn, ☎ 872244, has a good reputation for

its bar meals and evening *à la carte* menus; speciality is seafood. Serving bar food of an equally high standard is the Windmill Hotel and Restaurant, ☎ 872875. For a convivial atmosphere, go to Fox's restaurant in the High St, ☎ 973259, serving morning coffees and light lunches as well as evening meals. If you fancy fish and chips, try the Bay Tree on Foreland Rd, ☎ 873334.

On the St Helens' side, the Ganders, ☎ 872014, and St Helens Restaurant and Bar, ☎ 872303, offer high quality, bistro-type food. One restaurant not to be overlooked is Baywatch on the Beach, ☎ 873259. Located in a superb position in St Helens Bay, it offers outstanding seafood as well as steaks, pastas, vegetarian dishes and light snacks. To really spoil your crew go to the Priory Bay Hotel, ☎ 613146. Set in spectacular surroundings, it is quite a walk from the marina so you may prefer to go by taxi. Ingredients are sourced locally and all dishes are cooked and prepared to order.

NAVIGATION

Charts AC 2022 (1:5,000), plus SC 5600.1 (1:150,000), 5600.3 (1:75,000 with an inset of Bembridge Hbr 1:15,000), 2022 (1:5,000), 2037 (1:25,000), 2045 (1:75,000).

Approaches From the NW, the rocks and shoals off Nettlestone and Nodes Pt should be given a good offing. Coming from the SE, Bembridge Ledge (BYB Q (3) 10s) and St Helens Fort (Fl 3 10s 16m) are the port hand marks. During March–Oct there are numerous unlit, yellow racing buoys around Bembridge and Seaview.

Landmarks The conspic St Helens Fort and the Duver shore white seamark make the entrance to Bembridge easy to identify.

Pilotage The waypoint is 50°42'·34N 01°05'·36W, about 2 cables SW of the Bembridge tide gauge. When approaching, make a course for Bembridge tide gauge (Fl Y 2s top mark 'X'), keeping at least

The well buoyed, sinuous approach channel

a cable off St Helens Fort. The tide gauge, marked in metres, indicates the minimum depth of water in the approach channel. When Portsmouth HW is less than 4m, the depth in the channel sometimes does not exceed 1.6m, so on those days in particular do not ignore the tide gauge.

A course of 240° brings you to the above WPT in the start of the channel and the first of the numbered buoys (even nos to port, odd to stbd). Once through the entrance, past 11A, turn W and follow the narrow marked channel towards the marina. Passing the small craft ♥ pontoon to stbd, the tightly-packed marina lies straight ahead. Speed limit is 6kn. A night time entry is not advisable.

Access Recommended entry for a 1.5m draught is HW–2½.

Shelter Entry can be difficult in N to NE gales.

Tides HW sp are 20 mins after and nps the same as HW Portsmouth. LW nps are 20 mins and sp 1 hr after LW Portsmouth. MHWS is 3·2m, MLWS 0·2m; MHWN is 2·4m, MLWN 0·6m.

VHF Bembridge Marina Ch 80; Harbour Launch Ch M; Bembridge Water Taxi Ch 80.

FACILITIES

Bembridge Marina ☎ 872828; ▨ 872922; www.harbours.co.uk

Berthing Bembridge harbour can accommodate approx 100 visiting yachts, but during the summer, esp at weekends, it often gets completely full. The marina and ♥ pontoon area are dredged to about 2m. The marina, at the W end of the hbr, is compact and manoeuvring can be difficult, whereas the mid-harbour ♥ pontoons, just W of no 15 G buoy, are more user friendly, particularly with the new shoreside pontoon access to Finlays yard. There are also some small craft drying ♥s SW of Bembridge SC, while multi hull and bilge keel vessels are permitted (for a flat fee of £6 per night) to run up the beach to port just inside the entrance. Fisherman's Wharf on the S shore has a few ♥ berths but numbers are very restricted.

Tariff £1.60 per metre per day for the marina; £1.50 per metre per day for ♥ pontoons; £90 for seven nights for a 10m yacht in the marina.

Anchorage is forbidden in the harbour.

Showers and a **launderette** at the marina.

Fuel Diesel can be obtained from the H Attril & Sons pontoon, ☎ 872319, or Ken Stratton's Boatyard, ☎ 875961, N of the marina. Petrol in cans is available from Hodge & Childs Peugeot garage in Church Row, Bembridge. None is open on Sun and it is best to call in advance.

Water Taxi ferries people around the harbour and can be contacted on VHF Ch 80 or ☎ 872828/ 07816 558855.

YCs Brading Haven YC, ☎ 872289, E of the marina, and Bembridge SC, ☎ 872686, in the E corner of the hbr, have their own private jetties for tenders. The former is happy to welcome visitors to its bar and restaurant.

Chandlery & repairs A slipway can be used for boats up to 25 tons. Boatyards and marine engineers in the area include Bembridge Boatyard Marine Works, ☎ 872911; Ken Stratton Boatyard, ☎ 875961; H Attrill & Sons, ☎ 872319.

FUTURE DEVELOPMENTS

Plans are underway for new visitors' facilities to be completed by the end of 2003. These will include water and electricity on the pontoons as well as a new complex incorporating showers, toilets, restaurants and shops.

The channel turns west towards the marina, with the mid-harbour pontoons to starboard

PORTSMOUTH HARBOUR

Portsmouth Harbour entrance – 50°47'·38N 01°06'·67W

As one of the world's great naval bases, Portsmouth is inextricably linked with maritime history. Among Britain's premier waterfront destinations, it is a naturally formed and well protected harbour, offering yachtsmen a choice of marinas with comprehensive facilities.

SHORESIDE (Telephone code 023 92)

Tourist Office Portsmouth Information Centre, The Hard, Portsmouth, PO1 3QJ. ☎ 826722; ▦ 827519; tic@portsmouthcc.gov.uk.

What to see/do No visit to Portsmouth is complete without a trip to the Historic Dockyard, ☎ 861512, home to Henry VIII's *Mary Rose*, Nelson's HMS *Victory* and the first iron battleship, HMS *Warrior*, built in 1860. The D-Day Museum in Southsea, ☎ 827261, vividly depicts the Allied landings in Normandy on 6 June 1944. Also in Southsea is the Royal Marines Museum, ☎ 819385, portraying the colourful and exciting history of the Royal Marines and housing one of the most extensive collections of medals in the world. Over on the Gosport side of the

hbr is the Royal Navy Submarine Museum, ☎ 529217, and the Museum of Naval Firepower 'Explosion', ☎ 505600.

Historical attractions include Fort Brockhurst, ☎ 581059, Southsea Castle, ☎ 827261, and Portchester Castle, ☎ 378291, not far from Port Solent Marina.

Rail Portsmouth has two train stations, Portsmouth Harbour and Portsmouth City Centre, with frequent direct services to London (80 mins) and Southampton (45 mins). National Rail Enquiries ☎ 0845 748 4950.

Buses There are good bus connections linking Portsmouth with all the nearby towns and villages. Contact First Provincial ☎ 586921; National Express ☎ 0870 580 8080.

Taxi Bridge Cars ☎ 522333; Ferry Taxis ☎ 551166; Sky Cars ☎ 522522; Streamline ☎522222; Avacar Taxis ☎ 384495.

Car hire National ☎ 870701; Hertz ☎ 753820; Avis ☎ 694851.

Ferries run regularly not just across the harbour and to the Isle of Wight but also to the N coast of France, the Channel Islands and Spain. Contact: P&O ☎ 0870 242 4999; Brittany Ferry ☎ 0870 536 0360; Wightlink ☎ 0870 582 7744; Hovertravel ☎ 811000; Gosport Ferry ☎ 524551.

Beaches In Portsmouth itself, Southsea's shingle beaches are safe for swimming. Alternatively to the W of Portsmouth are the gentle shelving beaches off Hillhead and Lee-on-Solent, while to the E is Hayling Island.

Supermarkets Three supermarkets in Gosport, all of which are no more than a 15 mins walk from either Haslar or Gosport Marinas. In Portsmouth itself, go to Sainsbury's in Commercial Rd or Tesco in Paradise St.

Banks All the major banks in Gosport can be found in the High Street. On the Portsmouth side, Commercial Rd and Palmerston Rd are the two main locations for the high street banks, all of which have cash machines.

Restaurants *In Gosport*: Chinese restaurants include the Great Wall in the High St, ☎ 503388, and the T&J in South St, ☎ 582564. For Indian cuisine try the New Bengal on Stoke Rd, ☎ 583722, or the nearby New Jalalabad Balti House, ☎ 582927. A good view can be had at The Pebble Beach, ☎ 510789, situated on the beach at Stokes Bay. *In Portsmouth*: You will be spoilt for choice at Gunwharf Quays alone. Otherwise try the Chinese restaurant, Yellow River Café, ☎ 837111, Tootsies, ☎ 833787, or Pizza Express, ☎ 832989.

NAVIGATION

Charts AC 2628 (1:5,000), 2629 (1:5,000), plus SC 5600.1 (1:150,000), 5600.9 (1:25,000), 2631 (1:7,500), 2037 (1:25,000), 2045 (1:75,000).

Approaches From the W, craft can use the Swashway channel NW of Spit Sand Fort, which has a depth of about 2m. Ideally you should cross Spit Sand on approx 049°, giving you the transit of the prominent war memorial and the right hand side of an isolated block of flats on the Southsea shore. Resident boats often use the inner Swashway channel, a short cut

HMS Warrior, *moored at the Historic Dockyard*

along the Haslar shore, but with numerous obstructions and the unpredictable Hamilton Bank, it needs local knowledge.

From the E, the submerged barrier running from Horse Sand Fort N to Southsea means passing S of the fort unless you take a short cut through the barrier at the Main Passage (WPT 50°46'·00N 01°04'·10W), which is marked by a S dolphin (QR) and a stbd pile.

Landmarks In the inner approaches to Portsmouth there are three conspic forts: Horse Sand Fort, Iso G 2s; No Man's Land Fort, Iso R 2s, and Spit Sand Fort, Fl R 5s. Southsea Castle, St Judes church spire and the war memorial are on the E side of the entrance. Spinnaker Tower is the centrepiece of the Gunwharf Quays development and is being built with support from the Millennium Commission. When completed the Tower will top an impressive 165 metres and will be visible for many miles across the Solent.

The Spinnaker Tower at Gunwharf Quays under construction

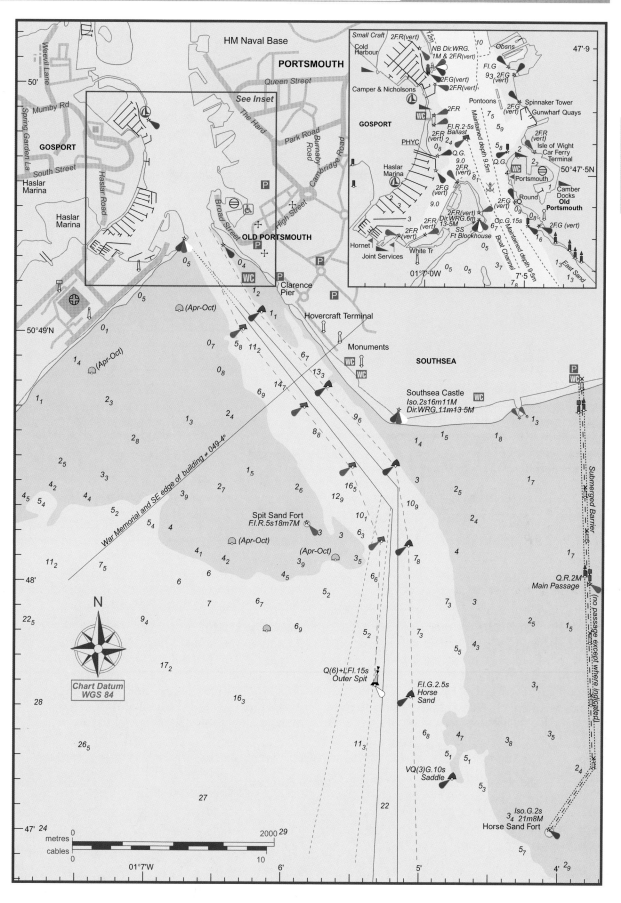

Chapter 2

The Gunwharf Quays Marina entrance

Access H24, but try to avoid entering on the ebb, which in the third and fourth hours can reach 5kn plus.

Local signals displayed at Fort Blockhouse. These do not apply to craft <20m LOA, which may use the Small Boat channel H24 provided they proceed with caution and do not impede shipping in the main channel. For more details on the signals, see the *Reeds Nautical Almanac*.

Pilotage When entering or leaving the harbour, craft up to 20m LOA must use the Small Boat channel on the western edge of the main channel and all yachts with engines are obliged to motor from abeam the war memorial to the inner PHM Ballast buoy. Note that yachts are no longer permitted to use the inshore passage on the eastern side when entering Portsmouth harbour.

The Small Boat channel starts from No 4 Bar Buoy (QR), which is about 0.5M from the entrance bearing 332° to the WPT 50°47·38N 01°06'·67W. It extends approx 50m from the Fort Blockhouse (keep as close to the R bcns as possible) and runs inside the harbour to the Ballast PHM (Fl R 2.5s). At night the Oc R sector (324°–330°) of the Dir WRG lt (6m 13-5M) on Fort Blockhouse covers the Small Boat channel until close to the entrance, after which the Iso R 2s sector 337.5°–345° of the Dir WRG lt (2m 1M) to the E of Gosport Marina takes you through the entrance on 341° to close abeam the PHM Ballast buoy. Yachts using the Small Boat channel wishing to cross from the W to the E side of the main channel should not do so until north of the Ballast Buoy.

The Small Boat channel approach to Portsmouth Harbour

Shelter Excellent. Protection can always be found in some part of the harbour from any wind.

Tides Portsmouth is a Standard Port. MHWS is 4·7m, MLWS 0·8m; MHWN is 3·8m, MLWN 1·9m.

Tidal Streams The flood runs at 3½kn in the last 2 hrs. See above under 'Access' for the ebb, while for tidal directions see Solent tidal streams on page 127.

VHF Yachts should monitor Ch 11 for shipping movement/navigational information. *Haslar Marina*, Ch 80; *Gosport Marina*, Ch 80/M; *Gunwharf Quays Marina*, Ch 80; *Port Solent Marina*, Ch 80.

FACILITIES

Marinas from seaward:

1. Haslar Marina 50°47'·54N 01°06'·94W. Access H24 at all states of the tide. VHF Ch 80; ☎ 601201; ✉ 602201; sales@haslarmarina.co.uk; www.haslarmarina.co.uk This marina lies on the W side of the hbr entrance and is easily recognised by its prominent lightship. **Ⓥ** pontoons are immediately shoreside of the lightship.

Tariff In summer: £2.40 per metre per night; a short stay of up to 4 hrs is a flat fee of £6. In winter: £1.20 per metre per night; a short stay is £3.

Launderette (coin-operated) in the lightship.

Showers in the lightship as well as on 'A' and 'G' pontoons.

Electricity (metered) and **FW** on the pontoons.

Fuel No fuel pump on site, the nearest being at Gosport Marina, approx 4 cables N of Haslar.

BoatScrubber A unique drive through 'boat wash', ☎ 510567.

Chandlery & repairs An on site chandler (sells gas), ☎ 588815, as well as a comprehensive range of independent marine operators from engineering to yacht rigging.

Food shop For basic provisions go to the Ferry Garage and Murco convenience store on Mumby Rd. Otherwise Gosport has several supermarkets.

Eating A bar and restaurant in the lightship, *Mary Mouse II*.

2. Gosport Marina 50°47'·82N 01°06'·96W. Access H24 at all states of the tide. VHF Ch 80/M; ☎ 524811; 📠 589541; www.harbours.co.uk A few cables N of Haslar Marina, just N of the PHM Ballast Buoy, Gosport Marina has 150 **⓿** berths.

Tariff During the summer season, an overnight stay for a 10m yacht is £21.21; a short stay of up to 4 hrs is £5.

Launderette (coin-operated) and **showers** on site; no code or key necessary for access.

Electricity (included in berthing fees) and **FW** on the pontoons.

Fuel a barge on the S entrance breakwater is manned in summer 0900–1745 and in winter 0900–1445.

Chandlery & repairs Solent Marine, Mumby Rd, ☎ 584622. Numerous boatyard and engineering facilities in and around the site, including the legendary Camper & Nicholsons yard, ☎ 580221.

3. Gunwharf Quays Marina

50°47'·66N 01°06'·50W. Access is H24, with plenty of depth. ☎ 836732; 📠 836738; berth.masters@gunwharf-quays.com On the E side of the harbour, close to Portsmouth's waterside attractions, it caters mainly for the

Haslar Marina with its distinctive lightship

likes of the Tall Ships and various other major waterborne events in season, leaving little room for the cruising yacht. Visitors can berth here when no events are in progress. Care should be taken around the marina entrance to keep clear of the car ferries manoeuvring in and around their dock just S of Gunwharf.

Tariff In summer: An overnight stay is £2.75 per metre; a 4 hr short stay is £6. In winter: An overnight stay is £1.75 per metre; a short stay is £3.

Facilities Not comprehensive, although a new shower block is currently under construction and is due to be completed by the 2003 summer season. Meanwhile visitors can use the temporary portakabin® containing showers and toilets.

4. Port Solent Marina 50°50'·63N 01°06'·20W. Access H24 via a channel, dredged to 1.5m, leading to a lock. VHF Ch 80; ☎ 210765; 📠 324241; www.premiermarinas.com Located to the NE of the hbr, not far from Portchester Castle. The approach channel is well marked with port and stbd-numbered piles – PHMs are numbered 57 to 74 (from seaward) and SHMs 95 to 75. Do not linger when crossing Tipner Range, its S limit marked by Nos 63/87 piles and N by Nos 70/78. Contact the marina when passing stbd pile 78 just below Portchester Castle to request a 'lock in'. If the lock is available you will be told to continue up the channel and enter the lock on a green light. Once in the lock, a crew member should contact the lockmaster for berthing instructions.

Tariff £2.17 per metre per night; 88p per metre for a short stay of up to 4 hrs.

Launderette (coin operated) and **showers** are accessed by card.

Electricity (min charge £2.75 per day when metred supply unavailable) and **FW** on the pontoons.

Fuel A 24 hr fuel service provides diesel, unleaded petrol and LPG as well as gas. Contact the marina on VHF Ch 80 ahead of time.

Chandlery & repairs Marine Super Store, ☎ 219843, CH. Goodacre Yacht Services, ☎ 210220, ME, EI; Motortech Marine Engineering ☎ 201171; Yacht Solutions, ☎ 200670, ME, EI; A&V Leisure, ☎ 510204, SM. Facilites include a mobile crane (18 ton) and travel hoist (40 ton).

Food shop An Alldays convenience store on site sells most essential items and incorporates a cashpoint. Or go to the large 24 hr Tesco, also with cashpoints; about a 10 mins walk from the marina.

Eating Several restaurants along the Boardwalk, adjacent to the marina pontoons, include Slackwater Jacques, ☎ 780777, the Italian restaurant Olivo, ☎ 201473, and the Mexican Chiquito, ☎ 201181.

Other berthing Hardway Marine, N of Gosport Marina, on your port hand side, has some deep water ⚓s. A flat rate of £3 per night; ☎ 580420. Facilites include toilets, showers, gas, diesel, FW as well as a full repair service and on site chandlery.

YCs Portsmouth Harbour YC, ☎ 222228; Port Solent YC, ☎ 718196. Gosport Ferry, ☎ 524551. Runs regular services between Portsmouth and Gosport.

The self-contained Port Solent Marina

FAREHAM

Fareham is situated approx 4½M N of Portsmouth Harbour entrance at the head of Fareham Lake.

SHORESIDE (Telephone code 01329)

Tourist Office Westbury Manor, 84, West St, Fareham. ☎ 221342; 🖷 282959.

What to see/do & **transport** See page 187–188.

Supermarkets Somerfield in West St and a Marks & Spencer in the shopping centre.

Banks The major banks, most of which have cash machines, are in West Street.

Restaurants Among the more expensive restaurants are Edwins Brasserie, ☎ 221338, Truffles Restaurant Français, ☎ 231265, and Lauro's Brasserie, ☎ 234179, all of which are in the High St. For Italian cuisine go to L'Ancora, ☎ 829445, or ASK, ☎ 239210, both in West St. Or try the Castle in the Air, ☎ 280320, serving good bar food and ales.

NAVIGATION

Leave the entrance to Portchester Lake to stbd, following the main channel to the NNW. Keep to the line of mooring buoys until you reach a SCM (VQ (6) + LFl 10s) to stbd and a PHM (Fl (2) R), which lead you into the Fareham Lake channel. The channel is clearly marked by piles but is only partially lit up until Bedenham Pier. Note that craft should not come within 12m of this pier without permission. The final mile, although still well marked, is unlit except at Foxbury Point (2FR (hor)). Here the channel starts to shallow, with the final 5 cables to the Town Quay drying to 0.9m. Yachts drawing 1.5m should only attempt to get up this fairway HW–2½ to 3hrs either side of HW.

FACILITIES

Berthing from seaward:

1. Wicor Marine 50°50'·34N 01°08'·99W, ☎ 237112. Situated N of Bedenham Pier, on the E side of the channel, Wicor Marine has several deep water moorings and is happy to accommodate visiting yachtsmen. Cannot be contacted on VHF.

Tariff Price is on application.

Facilities include water, fuel, gas as well as a 10-ton BH, slip, chandlery and repairs. On site specialists range from sailmakers to electronic, electrical and marine engineering experts.

Food shop The village of Wicor is about 10 mins away by foot and includes several grocery shops, a bakery and a Post Office.

Eating For restaurants, go to Fareham town centre, either a short bus ride away (a bus stop is very close to Wicor Marine) or about a 45 mins walk. For suggestions, see page 192.

2. Portsmouth Marine Engineering/Fareham Yacht Harbour
50°50′·77N 01°10′·63W, ☎ 232854; 🖷 822780. Although there are no allocated Ⓥ berths, the Yacht Harbour will accommodate visiting yachts when resident berthholders are away. Berths dry out and are therefore only suitable for yachts that can take the bottom. Cannot be contacted on VHF.

Tariff A flat rate of £10 per night.

Facilities are limited, comprising fresh water, showers and a crane out service. Local independent engineers can be arranged on request. For the nearest fuel station, go to Wicor Marine, Hardway Marine or Gosport Marina.

Food shop The closest convenience store is a One Stop, situated about 400m away; incorporates a cash machine. For restaurants go to Fareham town centre.

3. Trafalgar Yachts/Fareham Marina
50°50′·89N 01°10′·72W. ☎ 822445; 🖷 221565; info@westerly-yachts.co.uk Has no dedicated berths for visitors, but will accommodate visiting yachtsmen if there is space. Again, berths dry out and are only suitable for yachts that can take the bottom. Cannot be contacted on VHF.

Tariff No set rates, so call the marina ahead of time.

Facilities are basic, consisting of FW, electricity, but no fuel or showers. For fuel, go to Wicor Marine, Hardway Marine or Gosport Marina.

Food shop The One Stop is within easy walking distance. Otherwise go to the town centre; also for restaurants.

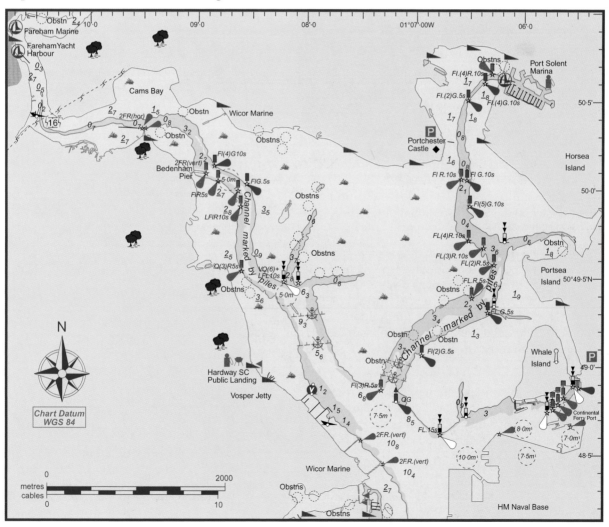

LANGSTONE HARBOUR

Langstone Harbour entrance – 50°47'·21N 01°01'·51W

On entering Langstone Harbour, take the port hand channel for Southsea Marina

As an expansive tidal bay situated between Hayling Island and Portsmouth, Langstone Harbour is a rather muddy, slightly desolate but charming haven. Incorporating a few deep water moorings as well as a modern marina on the W shore, it is regarded as a Special Area of Conservation and is therefore home to a wealth of wildlife.

SHORESIDE (Telephone code 023 92)

Tourist Office *Southsea* (summer only), Clarence Esplanade, Southsea, PO5 3ST. ☎ 826722; tic@portsmouthcc.gov.uk *Hayling Island* (summer only), Beachlands, Southfront, Hayling Island, PO11 OAG. ☎ 467111.

What to see/do If moored in Southsea Marina, go to Southsea Castle on Clarence Esplanade, ☎ 827261. Built in 1545, it opens daily 1000–1730 April to Oct. Also on Clarence Esplanade is the D-Day Museum & Overlord Embroidery, ☎ 827261, while the Royal Marines Museum is on the seafront towards the Eastney end of Southsea, ☎ 819385.

Rail The nearest railway station to the marina is Portsmouth and Southsea, which is actually in Fratton, about 40 mins walk from the marina. Havant is the closest station to Hayling Island.

Buses Bus services run between the marina and Southsea Central, as well as in the Hayling Island area: Provincial, ☎ 862412; Stagecoach Coastline ☎ 0845 121 0170.

Taxi *Southsea*: Aqua ☎ 654321; Streamline Taxis ☎ 811111; *Hayling Island*: C Cars ☎ 468888; Island Cars ☎ 422828; Lady Cars ☎ 465400.

Car hire *Southsea*: Enterprise Rent-A-Car ☎ 475566; *Hayling Island*: Ford Rental ☎ 467612.

Ferry runs between Southsea and Hayling Island; make contact on VHF Ch 10.

Hovercraft A frequent hovercraft service runs between Southsea and Ryde, ☎ 811000.

Beaches Hayling Island is renowned for its long sandy beaches which have been awarded for their cleanliness and outstanding facilities.

The Langstone Fairway Beacon

Supermarkets *Southsea*: A bus ride away from the marina are Tesco and Somerfield in Albert Rd and Waitrose in Marmion Rd. There are smaller convenience stores within walking distance of the marina. *Hayling Island*: the nearest is a One Stop, with cashpoint, in West Town.

Banks *Southsea:* Banks are situated in Albert Rd and Palmerston Rd, all of which have cash machines. *Hayling Island:* A Nat West, Lloyds and Barclays, with cashpoints, in Mengham.

Restaurants *Southsea:* Fatty Arbuckles in Osborne Rd, ☎ 739179, serves generous portions. A little more sophisticated is Sur-La-Mer in Palmerston Rd, ☎ 876678, or Truffles in Castle St, ☎ 730796. Oddballs in Clarendon Rd is good value for money, ☎ 755291, while the Spice Merchants in Osborne Rd, ☎ 828900, is a pleasant Indian restaurant. *Hayling Island:* Close to the shore is the Ferry Boat Inn, ☎ 463459, serving high quality bar food. Further E, on Station Rd, Jaspers, ☎ 463226, and Capers, ☎ 637775, come highly recommended, although you need to book in advance in summer.

NAVIGATION

Charts AC SC 5600.1 (1:150,000), 5600.7 (1:25,000), 5600.9 (1:25,000), 3418 (1:20,000), 2045 (1:75,000).

Approaches From the W, sailing due east from south of the Horse Sand Fort to the WPT 50°45′·00N 01°01′·00W leaves plenty of sea-room from the West Winner bank and its shoals. With the right tide underneath you, especially if you are coming from Portsmouth, using the Main Passage (WPT 50°46′·00N 01°04′·10W), which cuts through the Horse Sand Fort to Southsea barrier (the gap is marked by a S dolphin (QR) and a green pile), saves a good deal of time. From the gap a course of approx 120° and a distance of about 2M brings you to the WPT transit. From the E stay well clear of the E Winner bank, which protrudes about 1¼M offshore. Leave the unlit SCM to stbd, making for the WPT 50°45′·00N 01°01′·00W.

Landmarks The prominent chimney on its W bank identifies the entrance to Langstone Harbour.

Pilotage From the WPT 50°45′·00N 01°01′·00W the chimney should bear 348°. Once abeam of the Langstone Fairway bn (LFl 10s), which must not be confused with the R

and B IDM (Fl (2) 5s), a course of 352° takes you into the entrance, although make allowance for any cross tides. At night there is a transit of 348° from the Fairway bn to the QR dolphin lt on the W side of the entrance.

Access Best attempted from HW–3 to +1. Try to avoid going in on an ebb tide, especially at sp if a strong offshore wind is blowing, and do not negotiate the entrance in S to SE gales.

Shelter is very good in Southsea Marina, to the W of the entrance.

Tides HW sp and nps are the same as HW Portsmouth. LW nps and sp are 10 mins after LW Portsmouth. MHWS is 4·8m, MLWS 0·8m; MHWN is 3·9m, MLWN 1·9m.

Tidal streams The W-going stream starts at HW Portsmouth –2; the E-going starts at HW Portsmouth +4.

VHF Langstone Harbour Master Ch 12 (Summer 0830–1700 daily, Winter Mon–Fri 0830–1700, Sat–Sun 0830–1300; Southsea Marina Ch 80/M; Hayling Island Ferry CH 10.

FACILITIES

HM Ferry Point, Hayling Island, Hants, PO11 ODG. ☎ 463419; 🖷 467144; www.harbours.co.uk

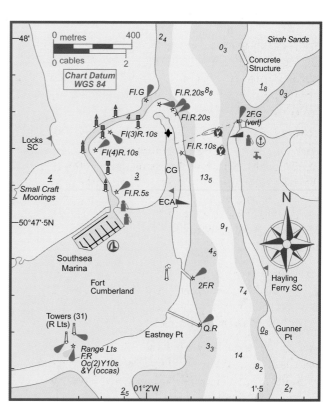

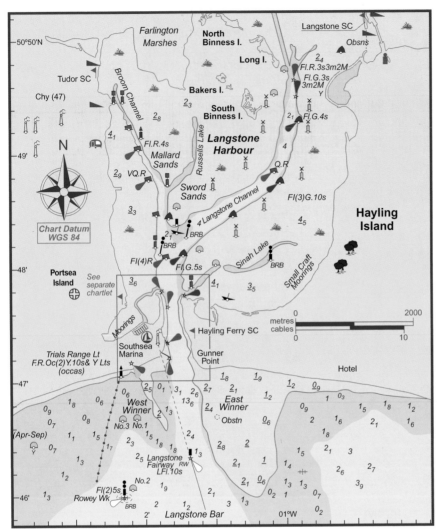

Marina Southsea Marina, Fort Cumberland Rd, Southsea, Hants, PO4 9RJ. ☎ 822719; 🖷 822220; office@premiermarinas.com; www.Southsea–marina.co.uk

Entrance The entrance to Southsea Marina lies to the NW of the Southsea ferry pontoon, with its twisting channel clearly marked by five SHM (only the first of which is lit), and nine PHM. A tidal gate operates the marina entrance which closes at HW+3 and opens at HW–3 when the depth over the sill is about 1.6m. With a tide gauge giving you depths over the sill, a R lt indicates the gate is closed and a G means it is open. A waiting pontoon with shore access is on the port hand side of the entrance. Contact the marina ahead of time for berthing availability.

Tariff £1.50 per metre per day, with a minimum charge of £12. At present there are no short stay fees.

Anchorage ⚓ only with the permission of the HM; favoured spots are in Langstone Fairway or in Russells Lake. Hayling Island Ferry services both shores, VHF Ch 10.

YCs Langstone SC, ☎ 484577; Locks SC ☎ 829833; Tudor SC ☎ 662002; Eastney Cruising Association ☎ 734103.

Mooring Several deep-water ⚓s to port and stbd of the inner entrance; subject to fierce tides, esp on the ebb. The two to stbd come under the HM's authority, while the six to port are owned by the Eastney Cruising Association (ECA) ☎ 734103. NB yachts over 7.6m are not permitted to use them.

Tariff Daily dues for the hbr moorings are £4.30 per boat. Prices on arrival for the ECA buoys.

Fuel and **FW** from the ferry pontoon to stbd.

Showers, toilets and bar are incorporated at Eastney Cruising Association.

Launderette token operated.

Showers and **toilets** are accessed by code.

Electricity (daily provisional service charge of £1.18 incl VAT) and **FW** on the pontoons.

Fuel pump is open 24 hrs a day.

Chandlery & repairs A chandlery on site. Marina staff will organise a range of services from marine electronics through to sail repairs and laundering. Other chandlers in the area include Chris Hornsey, Southsea ☎ 734728; Ship'N Shore, Sparkes Marina, Hayling Island ☎ 637373; Mengham Marine, Hayling Island ☎ 464333.

Food shop A small shop on site for essential items. Otherwise the nearest convenience stores are a 10-15 mins walk away. For more serious provisioning go to the centre of Southsea.

Eating The on site restaurant Top Deck, ☎ 874500, serves traditional English and European cuisine.

Emsworth Channel

Chichester Channel

Sparkes Marina

CHICHESTER HARBOUR

Chichester Harbour entrance – 50°45'·73N 00°56'·45W

Chichester Harbour, although technically not in the Solent, is still considered by most locals to be part of the Solent scene. Set against a backdrop of the Sussex Downs, it boasts 17 miles of wide, deep water channels flanked by picturesque, historic towns and villages. Well served with moorings and anchorages,

it is a must for visiting yachtsmen. On summer weekends you will have to share the channels with the local dinghy and keelboat racing community but by Sunday evening the harbour empties, becoming one of the most beautiful rural ports on the South Coast.

SHORESIDE (Telephone code 01243)

Tourist Office *Chichester*, 29a, South Street, Chichester, PO19 1AH. ☎ 775888; 🖾 539449; chitic@chichester.gov.uk *Hayling Island* (summer only), Beachlands, Southfront, Hayling Island, PO11 OAG. ☎ 467111.

What to see/do Of Norman origin with Gothic additions, Chichester Cathedral, ☎ 782595, is open daily 0715–1900 in summer and 0715–1800 in winter. Pallant House Gallery in North Pallant St houses one of the finest permanent collections of British Modern Art. Open Tues–Sat 1000–1700, ☎ 536038. Also worth a visit is Fishbourne Roman Palace, Tel 785859, built in 75AD. As an area of outstanding natural beauty, there are plenty of walks and cycle paths to choose from along with several pretty harbour villages to visit. For more information contact the Chichester Tourist Office.

Rail Many of the smaller towns and villages have train stations, with frequent connections to Chichester and Portsmouth. National Rail Enquiries ☎ 0845 748 4950.

Buses Good bus services link Chichester to the surrounding villages and towns.

Taxi *Chichester:* Dunnaways Taxis ☎ 782403; Central Cars ☎ 789432; *Hayling Island:* C Cars ☎ 468888; Lady Cars ☎ 565400.

Car hire Hendy Hire, Chichester ☎ 536100; Panther Cars, Chichester ☎ 778109, Enterprise Rentacar, Chichester ☎ 779500.

Cycle hire Barreg (situated just W of Fishbourne – see chart), Portsmouth Rd, Fishbourne ☎ 786104.

Beaches Sandy beaches flank both sides of Chichester Harbour entrance. To the W are those on Hayling Island and to the E is West Wittering, popular with bathers and windsurfers alike.

Supermarkets The easiest well stocked supermarket to get to (by bus or taxi) from most of the marinas/berths in Chichester Harbour is Tesco on the Fishbourne roundabout. Open until 2200 Mon–Sat and until 1600 on Sun. Also in Chichester

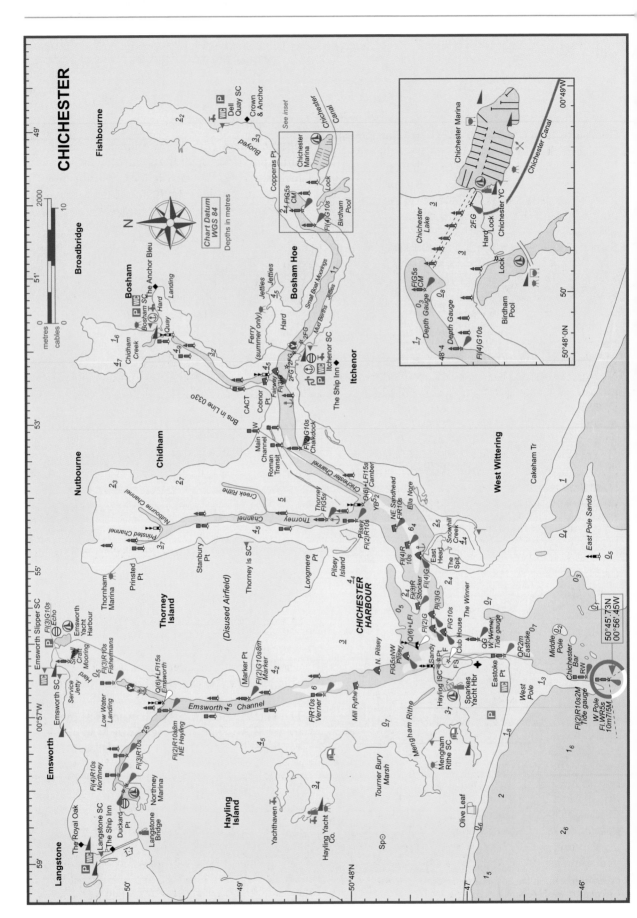

CHICHESTER

Fishbourne

Broadbridge

Bosham

Nutbourne

Chidham

Emsworth

Langstone

Hayling Island

Thorney Island

(Disused Airfield)

West Wittering

Itchenor

Bosham Hoe

CHICHESTER HARBOUR

Chart Datum WGS 84
Depths in metres

N

See inset

Chichester Marina
Chichester Canal

Chichester Lake
Lock
Chichester YC
2FG
Hard
Lock
Birdham Pool
Fl(4)G10s
Depth Gauge
Fl G5s CM
Depth Gauge

50°48'·0N
00°49'·W
00°49'·W

50°45'·73N
00°56'·45W

itself are a Tesco Metro and Marks & Spencer on East St and an Iceland in South St.

Banks Several major high street banks, with cash machines, are in East St, Chichester. Emsworth has a Nat West, Barclays and Lloyds, with cashpoints.

Restaurants In **Chichester**: Woodies Wine Bar in St Pancras St ☎ 779895, on the E side of the city, has a convivial atmosphere. For Italian cuisine go to Pizza Express in South St, ☎ 786648, or ASK on East St, ☎ 775040. The Old Cottage on West St is reputed for good quality Indian food, ☎ 780859, while Confucius in Cooper St, ☎ 783712, is one of the best Chinese restaurants in the area. At **Itchenor** is The Ship Inn, ☎ 512284, a minute's walk from the jetty. At **Dell Quay**, the Crown and Anchor pub, ☎ 791712, is located right on the waterfront, as is the Anchor Bleu, ☎ 573956, at Bosham. Other restaurants/pubs in the **Bosham** area include the Berkeley Arms, ☎ 573167, the Millstream Hotel, ☎ 573234, and the popular Indian restaurant, Memories of India, ☎ 572234. **Emsworth** boasts at least 10 pubs, which include the Blue Bell in South St, ☎ 373394, and the Sussex Brewery, ☎ 371533, renowned for 37 different types of sausages. Among the recommended restaurants in Emsworth are Fat Olives in South St, ☎ 377914, 36 on the Quay, ☎ 375592, (expensive) and Spencers in North St, ☎ 372744. **Langstone** has two popular waterside pubs serving bar meals: The Ship Inn, ☎ 023 9247 1719, and the Royal Oak, ☎ 023 9248 3125.

NAVIGATION

Charts AC SC 2045 (1:75,000), 5600.2 (1: 75,000), 5600.10 (1: 25,000), 3418 (1: 20,000).

Approaches From the W a course of 090° from Horse Sand Fort keeps you clear of the East Winner

West Pole, marking the entrance to Chichester Harbour; the Chichester Bar Beacon is just beyond

and West Pole Sands. From the E or SE, via the Looe Channel, give the Bracklesham shoals and East Pole sands a wide berth, keeping due W for at least 2M before altering course to the NW until the Nab Tower bears 184° astern of WPT 50°44'·80N 00°56'·70W (about 1M S of the West Pole bn).

Conspic marks With its low lying entrance set against the backdrop of the South Downs, Chichester Hbr is not easy to identify until close to the beacons. Chichester Bar bn comprises a white and red lattice tower on top of a four-legged dolphin (Fl (2) R 10s 14m). Two cables S is West Pole PHM (Fl WR 5s 10m).

Pilotage From WPT 50°44'·80N 00°56'·70W steer 013° in order to pass the West Pole bn (Fl WR 5s) close to port. The Chichester Bar bn should also be left about a cable to port. Continue to steer 013° towards the gap between Eastoke bn (Q R 2m) and W Winner bn (QG), leaving Eastoke at least 50m to port. Once past Eastoke, the Winner shoal to stbd is marked by three stbd hand buoys – NW Winner (Fl G 10s), N Winner (Fl (2) G 10s) and Mid Winner (Fl (3) G 10s). These are right on the edge of the shingle bank so do not attempt to cut inside them.

The channel divide is indicated by the Fishery SCM. Leaving this to stbd, the Emsworth Channel continues northwards and is clearly marked by day and partially lit by night. Heading ENE from this cardinal buoy takes you towards Chichester, with Stocker sand to port marked by four PHMs – Stocker (Fl (3) R 10s), the unlit Copyhold, Sandhead (Fl (4) R 10s) and NE Sandhead (Fl R 10s). The East Head SHM (Fl (4) G 10s) signifies the beginning of the East Head anchorage.

A night time entry should only be attempted in favourable conditions and you need to stay in the W sector of the West Pole bn (Fl WR 5s, 10m, 7/5M, vis W 321°–081°, R 081°–321°).

The **Emsworth Channel**, which is well marked and lit, runs for about 2.5M to the Emsworth SCM, where Sweare Deep forks NW to Northney Marina.

The entrance to **Thorney Channel** is at the Camber SCM. From here, head due N to pass between the Pilsey PHM (Fl (2) R 10s) and the Thorney SHM (Fl G 5s). The channel divides above Stanbury Point, with the Prinsted branch, full of moorings and ultimately leading to Thornham Marina, to port and the Nutbourne Channel to starboard. Both channels dry out towards their northern ends.

The **Chichester Channel** runs NE to the Bosham Channel and then to the Itchenor Reach and on to Birdham Pool, Chichester Marina and Dell Quay.

Chapter 2

Itchenor Reach, looking towards the conservancy offices

From the NE Sandhead PHM (Fl R 10s), a transit of 033° on the PH Roman bn and the Main Channel bn, on the shore NW of Cobnor Pt, brings you to Chaldock bn (Fl (2) G 10s). From Chaldock the Itchenor Fairway buoy (Fl (3) G 10s) bears approx 080°. Just beyond the Fairway buoy the Deepend SCM signals the divide into the N-bound Bosham Channel and the ESE-running Itchenor Reach.

The **Bosham Channel** has a depth of about 1.8m at LW on a moderate sp tide until approx 2 cables from the quay. Although the channel is marked with R and G withies, for the best water stay between the port and stbd swinging moorings. The approach to the quay is made when the quay and the old wooden pilings open up. Keep the SCM at the end of the dinghy slip about 4m to port, taking care on a sp flood not to be carried onto the steep-to slip between the end of the quay and the SCM.

In **Itchenor Reach** you should stick between the swinging moorings until the Birdham SHM (Fl (4) G 10s), marking the beginning of the approach to Birdham Pool. About 100m further NE is the CM stbd hand pile (Fl G 5s), identifying the start of the Chichester Marina channel. Beyond this marina, the channel leads to Dell Quay although it shallows quickly and is not advisable for deep-draughted yachts.

Chichester Harbour's speed limit of 8kn must be observed.

Access Best entry is HW–3 to +1, to avoid confused seas on the ebb, especially in onshore winds of >F5.

Shelter Good in all five channels.

Tides HW sp are 5 mins after and nps 10 mins before HW Portsmouth. LW nps are 15 mins after and sp 20 mins after LW Portsmouth. MHWS is 4·9m, MLWS 0·9m; MHWN is 4·0m, MLWN 1·9m.

Tidal streams see under Langstone on page 195.

VHF *Chichester Hbr Radio* Ch 14/16 (Apr–Sept: 0830–1700; Sat 0900–1300) or *Chichester Hbr Patrol* (weekends Apr-Sept); *Northney Marina* Ch 80; *Emsworth Yacht Harbour* Ch 80; Emsworth Ferry (callsign *Emsworth Mobile*) Ch 14; Itchenor Ferry (callsign *Ferry*) Ch 8; *Birdham Pool Marina* Ch 80; *Chichester Marina* Ch 80.

FACILITIES

HM Chichester Harbour Conservancy, The Harbour Office, Itchenor, Chichester, West Sussex, PO20 7AW. ☎ 512301; 🖷 513026; harbourmaster@conservancy.co.uk; www.conservancy.co.uk Office hours: Weekdays 0830–1700; Sat (1 Apr–30 Sept) 0900–1300.

Ferries A ferry operates in Emsworth Hbr on weekends and bank holidays from Easter to end of Sept, HW±2½ from 0800 until 2000 or sunset, whichever is the earlier. Call *Emsworth Mobile* on VHF Ch 14. The Itchenor ferry runs from the

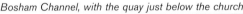
Bosham Channel, with the quay just below the church

Itchenor jetty to Smugglers Lane, Bosham, or to and from moorings from Deep End to Birdham. Call *Ferry* on VHF Ch 8 or ☎ 07970 378350. Operates daily from 0900–1800 May–Sept and on weekends and bank holidays only during March to May and the month of October.

MARINAS

There are six marinas in the harbour, only two of which (Sparkes and Northney) have full tidal access. From seaward:

1. Sparkes Marina 50°47'·16N 00°56'·60W. Access H24 at all states of the tide. VHF Ch 80, ☎ 023 9246 3572; 🖷 023 9246 5741; info@sparkes.co.uk; www.sparkes.co.uk Located just inside the entrance to Chichester Hbr on the E shores of Hayling Island. Its approach channel, dredged to 2m MLW, is identified by an unlit ECM. Sparkes has several ❶ berths.

Tariff £2.30 per metre per day or £13 per metre per week. A short stay is a flat rate of £5.

Launderette token operated.

Showers and toilets have 24 hr access via a code.

Fuel pontoon sells diesel and petrol seven days a week: 0930–1730 in winter (closing 1300–1400 for lunch); 0900–1800 in summer (without closing for lunch).

Electricity (metered) and **FW** on the pontoons.

Chandlery & repairs The on site chandlery, Ship'N Shore, ☎ 023 9263 7373, sells gas. Services offered are craning out and hard standing as well as maintenance and repairs ranging from electronics and engineering to painting and carpentry.

Food shop The on site chandlery sells essential items; otherwise go to the newsagents, with cashpoint, on Creek Rd. For more serious provisioning catch a bus or taxi to the Somerfield in Mengham.

Eating The Mariners Bistro, ☎ 023 9246 9459, is on site, but gets busy in summer. Several takeaways are on Southwood Rd, a 15 mins walk from the marina, or else try the Olive Leaf pub on the seafront, well known for its bar menu.

2. Northney Marina 50°50'·01N 00°57'·95W. Accessible at all states of the tide. VHF Ch 80; ☎ 023 9246 6321; 🖷 023 9246 1467; www.marinas.co.uk Northney Marina is on the N shore of Hayling Island in the well marked Sweare Deep Channel, which branches off to port

almost at the end of the Emsworth Channel. Providing good shelter, it welcomes visitors, although no designated ❶ berths so availability is subject to whether resident berthholders are away.

Tariff £2.20 per metre per night; a flat rate of £5.50 for a short stay of up to 4 hrs.

Launderette coin-operated.

Showers and **toilets** are currently located in the dock office building; accessed by code. A new facilities building has recently been constructed and opened in early 2003.

Electricity and **FW** on the pontoons.

Fuel berth at the end of 'G' pontoon, selling diesel, oil, LPG and gas; open 24 hrs.

Chandlery & repairs On site chandler, Pumpkin Marine Supplies ☎ 023 9246 8794. Hard standing and BH (35 ton). Ask at marina office for yacht repair and maintenance services.

Food shop Basic items are sold at a petrol station at the end of Northney Road, half a mile or less from the marina. The new facilities opening in Spring 2003 will also include a small grocery shop. Otherwise go to Havant Town Centre, about two miles away.

Eating The Langstone Hotel, ☎ 023 9246 5011, within the marina complex, serves lunch and evening meals. Close by are the Ship Inn, ☎ 023 9247 1719, and the Royal Oak, ☎ 023 9248 3125, both situated at the head of Sweare Deep.

3. Emsworth Yacht Harbour 50°50'·59N 00°55'·89W. Access HW±1½ to 2. VHF Ch 80; ☎ 377727; www.emsworth–marina.co.uk Office hours: Mon–Fri 0800–1630; Sat 0930–1700; Sun (summer only) 0930–1500. Above the red Fishermen's bcn in Emsworth Channel, follow the

LW at the head of Sweare Deep.

Chapter 2

line of red piles marking a drying fairway heading NNE. The channel swings to stbd at the green Echo beacon, where further stbd and port piles lead to the sill. The sill, with tide gauge, is pretty narrow, but favour the port side for the deeper water.

Tariff £2/metre per day or £9.50/metre per week.

Showers and toilets are in the main office block between 'C' and 'D' pontoons.

Electricity (included in berthing fee) and **FW** on the pontoons.

Fuel pontoon is open during office hours.

Chandlery & repairs An on site chandlery selling gas. Facilities include a 40 ton crane, hard standing and engineering/repair services.

Food shop Go to either the One Stop or Co-op in Emsworth.

Eating Plenty of restaurants in Emsworth; see page 199.

4. Thornham Marina 50°50'·19N 00°54'·99W. Access for a 1.5m draught is HWS±1. ☎ 375335; 🖳 371522; www.enigma.mcmail.com Situated at the head of Prinsted Bay on the E side of Thorney Island, about 2M along the Thorney Channel. No allocated ❶ berths, although will accommodate them if space permits. Berthing comprises several drying pontoons as well as a small number of pontoon berths within a gated basin for draughts up to 1.75m.

Tariff A flat rate of £7.50 per night.

Showers and toilets are accessed by key. No launderette.

Electricity (metered) and **FW** on the pontoons.

Repairs A BH (12 ton) lifts yachts of up to 35m LOA. On site services include a marine engineer and general repair specialist.

Food shop Convenience stores in either Southbourne or Emsworth, both approx a mile from the marina.

Eating The Boaters Bar and Restaurant on site, ☎ 377465, serves lunchtime and evening meals during summer.

5. Birdham Pool Marina 50°48'·18N 00°49'·83W. Access HW±3 via a lock. VHF Ch 80; ☎ 512310. A charming and rustic marina, Birdham Pool is approached via a channel starting at Birdham SHM bn (Fl (4) G 10s) with tide gauge. The channel to the lock is marked by G piles which

The final approach to Emsworth Yacht Harbour

should be left no more than 3m to stbd.

Tariff £1.80 per metre per night; 20% discount if you stay for seven consecutive nights.

Showers and toilets accessed by code. No launderette.

Electricity (new tariffs were in the process of being set at the time of going to press) and **FW** on the pontoons.

Fuel Diesel and petrol are sold from 0700–1000 weekdays and 0600–1000 weekends during the summer season.

Chandlery & repairs Small on site chandlery is open weekdays and Sat mornings; otherwise go to the one at Chichester Marina, open seven days a week. Comprehensive repair facilities with a 20 ton slip and 10 ton crane.

Food shop For essential items go to the small shop at Chichester Marina, a 5 mins walk away if cutting across the lock at the end of the canal. Also a Spar (Birdham Stores), incorporating a Post Office, on the Birdham Rd.

Eating Go to The Spinnaker restaurant at Chichester Marina, ☎ 511032, or the Black Horse pub, ☎ 784068, on the Birdham Rd (about a 15–20 mins walk away). For more suggestions see page 199.

6. Chichester Marina 50°48'·29N 00°49'·46W. Access LWS±1½ for draughts of 1m; a waiting pontoon outside the lock. VHF Ch 80; ☎ 512731; 🖳 513472; chichester@premiermarinas.com; www.premiermarinas.com The marina has more than 1,000 berths and welcomes visiting yachtsmen. Situated a little further upstream from Birdham Pool, still on the stbd side, its channel is identified by the CM SHM (Fl G 5s). The channel dries to 0.5m, but there are two tide gauges (one on pile No 6 and one in the lock). A flashing R lt on the roof of the lock control signifies that the depth has dropped

Entry to Birdham Pool Lock – keep the approach green piles close to starboard

to less than a metre. The lock is manned H24.

Tariff £1.95 per metre per day, with a minimum charge of £13.65. A short stay of up to 4 hrs is £0.90 per metre, with a minimum charge of £7.20.

Launderette, showers and toilets are accessed by code.

Electricity (first two days are free, after which it is metered) and **FW** on the pontoons. Fuel pontoon sells diesel and petrol; open 24 hrs. For gas ask at the Marina Office. Outboard engine flush tank near 'M' pontoon.

Chandlery & repairs On site Peters chandlery, ☎ 511033, is well stocked and opens seven days a week. Facilities include a BH, full boat repair services and a hard standing area.

Food shop A small shop on the marina complex provides basic provisions. Otherwise go to the Spar on Birdham Rd or catch a bus/taxi into Chichester (10 mins drive away).

Eating The Spinnaker (☎ 511032) on site serves excellent breakfasts each day from 0830–1200 as well as lunch time and evening meals throughout the summer. For more suggestions, see page 199.

OTHER BERTHING

1. Hayling Yacht Company VHF Ch 80; ☎ 023 9246 3592; haylingyacht@cwcom.net; www.haylingyacht.co.uk A family-run boatyard at the end of Mill Rithe Creek, about 1M from the S end of Emsworth Channel. Within its complex is a half tide marina accommodating 116 boats up to 18m.

Tariff £1.05 per metre per day.

Facilities include boat repairs, general maintenance, showers, toilets, fresh water and electricity.

Food shop The nearest shop is the Co-op in Church Rd, about a 15–20 minute walk away.

Eating Two pubs in Havant Rd, The Maypole ☎ 023 9246 3670 and the Yew Tree ☎ 023 9246 5258.

2. Emsworth Ⓥ pontoon VHF Ch 14 (callsign *Chichester Harbour Radio* or *Chichester Harbour Patrol*); ☎ 512301. There is designated space for visitors on the floating pontoon in Emsworth Harbour.

Tariff £5 per night plus £3 per night for harbour dues. Charges for a week are £30 per week for a max of six weeks. Harbour dues for a weekend, Fri–Sun, are £4.50 and £9 per week.

Facilities FW from Emsworth Jetty, which should only be approached HW±2 for draughts of 1.5m. For fuel go to Emsworth Yacht Harbour, see pages 201–2.

3. Bosham Quay ☎ 573336/No VHF. Craft drawing up to 2m can dry out against Bosham Quay (access is HW±2) in soft mud. At the E end there is room for four boats to sit on the purpose built grid. Swinging moorings are occasionally available with the permission of the Quay Master.

Tariff Yachts between 9m–10.6m pay £3.50–£4 for 6 hrs or £8 for 12 hrs. If moored at the scrubbing area, rates are £0.58 per foot per day.

Facilities Fender boards from the quay as well as pressure washers for scrubbing off, FW, limited electricity and a small two ton crane for lifting masts/engines. Bosham SC offers showers and toilets.

Food shop Bosham Farm Shop in Delling Lane, a 15–20 mins walk from the quay. Open seven days a weeks until 2100, it incorporates a Post Office and cashpoint.

Eating The closest eateries are the Anchor Bleu, ☎ 573956, or the Mariners (café) in the High St, ☎ 572960. For more suggestions see page 199.

4. Itchenor moorings VHF Ch 14 (callsign *Chichester Harbour Radio* or *Chichester Harbour Patrol*); ☎ 512301. Visitors can normally pick up

Chapter 2

a swing mooring off the village of Itchenor. All moorings are accessible by dinghy from the hard at any state of the tide.

Tariff £5 per night for a mooring and £3 per night for harbour dues. Charges for a week are £30 per week for a max of six weeks. Harbour dues for a weekend, Fri–Sun, are £4.50 and £9 per week.

Facilities Go alongside Itchenor Jetty at any state of the tide for water and fuel (supplied in cans). Showers are in the Harbour Office building and are token-operated. Tokens cost £1 from the Harbour Office. Scrubbing piles, electrical, electronic and marine engineering repair services are also on site. A ferry operating in summer, ☎ 07970 378350/VHF Ch 8, runs between Itchenor and Smugglers Lane in Bosham; will also drop you off at your mooring.

Food shop None in the immediate vicinity; the nearest is the Spar on Birdham Rd, 15–20 mins away on foot.

Eating The Ship Inn, ☎ 512284, is a stone's throw from the jetty. The Itchenor SC, ☎ 512400, opposite the pub, welcomes visiting yachtsmen and serves lunchtime and evening meals.

Anchorages Three recognised anchorages in Chichester Harbour. East Head, the most popular one, is close to the hbr entrance, just to the E of the East Head Spit Buoy (Fl (4) G) and N of the beach outside the main channel. Further along the channel towards Chichester, inside and to stbd of the Thorney Channel, is the quieter ⚓ off Pilsea Island, although is slightly more exposed than East Head. Also ⚓ 0.5M W of Itchenor, N of Chaldock Pt along the S edge of the channel; convenient if waiting for the tide to get to Bosham or Birdham. All anchored craft must display day or night time anchorage signals.

YACHT CLUBS

Hayling Island SC ☎ 023 9246 3768
Mengham Rithe SC ☎ 023 9246 3337
Langstone SC ☎ 023 9248 4577
Emsworth SC ☎ 373065
Emsworth Slipper SC ☎ 372523
Thorney SC ☎ 371731
Chichester YC ☎ 512918
Itchenor SC ☎ 512400
Dell Quay SC ☎ 780601
West Wittering SC ☎ 514153

Bosham Quay, where the dinghy hard is exposed at LW

EASTERN CHANNEL
LITTLEHAMPTON TO RAMSGATE

Beachy Head lighthouse

CONTENTS

INTRODUCTION

The eastern end of the English Channel sees the greatest volume of commercial shipping in the world. Here yachtsmen have to watch out for large tankers plying up and down the shipping lanes, while fast ferries travel between English and Continental ports. Even for coastal passages you need to have an understanding of the TSS and ITZ, being fully aware that the SW-bound TSS lane from Dover Strait passes only 4M off Dungeness.

Although this low-lying stretch of coastline between Sussex and Kent incorporates several interesting harbours, it offers little protection in S'ly to SW'ly winds and in heavy weather the funnelling effect of the Dover Strait can cause the sea to become very rough.

PASSAGE NOTES

THE SOLENT TO BEACHY HEAD

Heading E from the Solent, approx 6M past Chichester, you come to Selsey Bill, off which there are extensive rocks and shoals. These can be passed either via the Looe Channel, so long as conditions are favourable, or to seaward of the Owers SCM lt buoy. In good visibility and moderate conditions,

the Looe Channel, running in an E/W direction about 1M S of Mixon Beacon and marked at its W end by the Boulder buoy (Fl R 2.5s), is a preferable shortcut. However, a fair tide is generally necessary – an E-going stream begins at HW Portsmouth +0430 and a W-going at HW Portsmouth –0135, with springs running at around 4kn. Also, keep an eye out for the lobster pots in this area. When conditions are bad it is best to keep S of the Owers SCM lt buoy, which is about 6.5M SE of Selsey Bill. The depth is less than 3m over much of the Owers, so strong winds and tidal streams can cause breaking seas in this area.

From Selsey to Brighton the coastline is low, predominantly comprising a shingle beach. Offlying dangers to look out for are Bognor Rks, extending 1.75M E from a point 1M W of the pier, and the Bognor Spit that stretches E and S from the end of these rocks. About 1.5M E of Bognor Pier is Middleton Ledge, a ridge of rocks running 8 cables offshore with depths of less than 1m. Five cables S of this ledge are Shelley Rocks, again with depths of less than 1m. A little further along the coast, Winter Knoll, approx 2M SSW of Littlehampton hbr entrance, has depths of 2.1m, while lying about

3.25M ESE of the entrance are Kingston Rocks with a depth of 2m. When approaching W of Shoreham, watch out for Church Rocks, with depths of 0.3m, which are situated 2.5 cables from shore, while on the E side of the entrance Jenny Ground has a depth of 0.9m.

From Brighton to Beachy Head there are no real dangers more than 3 cables offshore until you come to Birling Gap, marking the start of a rocky ledge on which Beachy Head lt ho is built. Head Ledge extends approx 4 cables south. In rough weather give Beachy Head a berth of 2M to avoid any overfalls. Two miles S of Beachy Hd the E-going stream begins at HW Dover –0520 while the W-going stream starts at HW Dover +0030. At springs it can reach 2¼kn.

BEACHY HEAD TO DUNGENESS

The Royal Sovereign lt tr (Fl 20s 28m) lies 7.5M E of Beachy Head, with the extensive Sovereign Shoals (a minimum depth of 3.5m) stretching 3M NW of it to 1.5M N of it. Note that there are strong eddies over the shoals at springs and the sea breaks on them in bad weather. Along the coast across Pevensey Bay and Rye Bay a 2.5M offing keeps you clear of any dangers except for Boulder Banks and Tower Knoll in the W of Rye Bay. This stretch of coast between Beachy Head and Dungeness, with its conspic power station, is unforgiving in bad weather, offering no real refuge other than the Royal Sovereign Harbour to the NE of Beachy Head. The inauguration of this marina 10 years ago has greatly improved passage making along this coastline, particularly if W bound when the tide and weather conditions prevent you from rounding Beachy Head. To the W of Dungeness the Lydd Firing Ranges sometimes make it necessary to keep S of Stephenson Shoal, although note the closeness of the TSS to Dungeness.

DUNGENESS TO NORTH FORELAND

From Dungeness to Folkestone the coast sweeps round in a bay, with no offlying dangers apart from Roar Bank, E of

New Romney, with a depth of approx 2.7m, and Hythe Firing Range, where a Sea Danger Area extends 2M offshore between Hythe and Dymchurch (to the W). Red flags and lights are displayed when the range is in use. Off Folkestone the tide runs ENE 2 hrs before HW Dover, reaching between 2–3kn at springs, and sets WSW between 3½ to 4 hrs after HW Dover. When passing Dover, keep at least 1M offshore to avoid the ferries and jetfoils leaving the hbr at speed as well as the lumpy seas off the breakwater created by their wash. Between the S and N Foreland the N-going tide starts about HW Dover – 0150 and the S-going at about HW Dover +0415.

Sailing from S Foreland to Ramsgate, you will have to negotiate the Goodwin Sands, extensive drying shoals that are prone to shifting. Most yachts will opt for the well buoyed Gull Stream between Goodwin Sands to the E and the Brake Shoals to the W. The Ramsgate Channel, inshore of the Brake and Cross Ledge Shoals, can also be used, but is quite shallow with unpredictable depths and doesn't save much time. Kellett Gut is an unmarked channel running SW/NE through the middle of the sands, but is not recommended as it is not regularly surveyed and is liable to change.

		DISTANCE TABLE Approximate distances in nautical miles are by the most direct route, whilst avoiding dangers									
1.	Littlehampton	**1**									
2.	Shoreham	13	**2**								
3.	Brighton	17	5	**3**							
4.	Newhaven	24	12	7	**4**						
5.	Beachy Head Lt	30	20	14	8	**5**					
6.	Eastbourne	34	24	19	12	7	**6**				
7.	Rye	56	46	41	34	25	23	**7**			
8.	Dungeness Lt	60	50	44	38	30	26	9	**8**		
9.	Folkestone	76	65	60	53	43	40	23	13	**9**	
10.	Dover	81	70	65	58	48	45	28	18	5	**10**
11.	Ramsgate	96	85	80	73	63	60	43	33	20	15	**11**

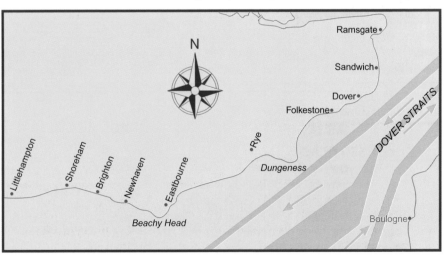

LITTLEHAMPTON

Littlehampton Harbour entrance – 50°47'·88N 00°32'·43W

The narrow entrance with a training wall and shoals to starboard

A typical English seaside town with funfair, promenade and fine sandy beaches, Littlehampton lies roughly midway between Brighton and Chichester at the mouth of the River Arun. It provides a convenient stopover for yachts either east or west bound, providing however that you have the right tidal conditions (the bar across the entrance has a charted depth of 0.7m) and you can find adequate berthing. Beware that the entrance becomes difficult, if not dangerous, in strong SE winds, with a considerable swell running up the river.

SHORESIDE (Telephone code 01903)

Tourist Office Windmill Complex, Coastguard Rd, Littlehampton, BN17 5LH. ☎/📠 721866; tourism@arun.gov.uk; www.sussexbythesea.com

What to see/do The Harbour Park on the seafront is a great day out for children, incorporating funfair rides, amusement arcades, restaurants and burger bars; ☎ 721200. Other more civilised attractions include the new Visitor and Field Study Centre on the redeveloped E bank of the harbour, the Littlehampton Miniature Railway, ☎ 716127, open daily from Easter to Sept, and the Littlehampton Museum, ☎ 738100, in Church St. Open 1030–1630, admission is free. A bus ride away is the picturesque hilltop town of Arundel whose prime attraction is the castle.

Rail Good connections to London (Victoria), Brighton and Portsmouth. National Rail Enquiries ☎ 0845 748 4950.

Bus Stagecoach runs services along the whole of the South Coast, linking all the major ports and cities. Bus No 700; Stagecoach Coastline ☎ 0845 121 0170.

Taxi Arun Taxis ☎ 717200/717832; Drivers Taxis ☎ 713713.

Car hire Ford Rental ☎ 714367; Ace Car Hire ☎ 713208.

Bike hire Splash Mountain Bikes, Worthing, ☎ 872300.

Beaches East Beach has been carefully zoned off to ensure safe swimming and is popular with families. West Beach is a Site of Special Scientific Interest (SSSI), providing a haven for wildlife and rare plants.

Supermarkets A Somerfield in High St and Safeway in Anchor Springs, both of which are in the town centre. A little further away in Bridge Rd is a 24 hr Tesco.

Market day A Farmers' market takes place in the High Street on the last Wed morning of each month.

Banks All the major banks and building societies, with cashpoints, are in the High Street.

Restaurants The Arun View Inn, ☎ 722335, in Wharf Road alongside the footbridge has a dining room overlooking the River Arun. Adjacent to it is The Steam Packet pub, ☎ 715994, popular with the locals. The Silk Road in Arcade Rd, ☎ 722055, is an unusual Turkish and Mediterranean restaurant, complete with belly dancer. In contrast, for fish and chips go to Fred's Fish and Chips on Pier Rd, ☎ 721255, or for a takeaway pizza the Favourite Pizza in the High Street, ☎ 722777, which also offers a free delivery service.

NAVIGATION

Charts AC SC 5605.3 (1:75,000 with Littlehampton inset 1:15,000), 1991 (1:6,250), 1652 (1:75,000).

Approaches From the W, if passing through the Looe Channel via Boulder (Fl G 2.5s), carry on due E for approx 2M, leaving the Mixon with its beacon (Fl R 5s) well to N, before turning on to a course of 060°. Keep on this course until either Littlehampton's leading lts or the West Pier bear 346°. From the E, a prudent offshore offing is all that is needed until you pick up the leading marks. The approach from the SW or W is straightforward assuming you keep the Owers (Q (6) + LFl 15s) well to port.

Landmarks A high-rise building (38m) is conspic 0.4M NNE of the harbour entrance, along with a funfair (Harbour Park) to the E of the entrance. There is also a pile with small platform and lt (Fl (5) Y 20s 5M) 2.5M SE of the harbour entrance.

Leading lts Front: FG on a black column. Rear: lt ho (Oc WY 7.5s 9m 10M)

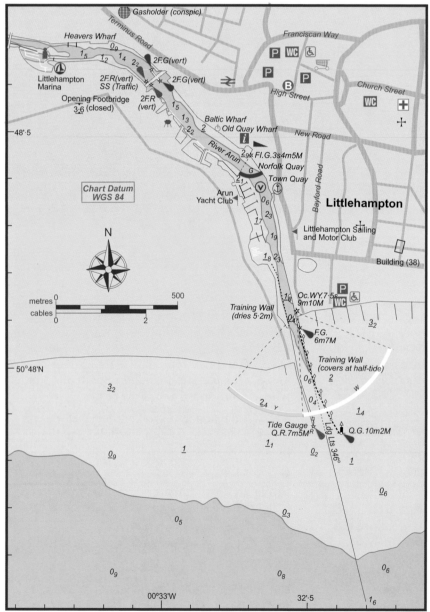

at the root of the E breakwater; W 290°–356°, Y 356°–042°. The Fl G 3s 4m 5M at Fisherman's Quay guides yachts upstream.

Pilotage From the WPT 50°46'·92N 00°32'·02W, 1M SE of the entrance, steer 346° over the bar which, drying to 0.7m, extends 900m S of the West Pier. A training wall that covers at half tide is marked by seven perches and stretches S from the East Pierhead, its seaward end identified by a beacon (QG 10m 2M) with triangular top mark. Once abeam the West Pierhead, with its tide gauge giving heights in metres above chart datum, (to obtain depth on the bar subtract 0.7m from indicated depth) steer towards the East Pierhead both to stay in the deeper water and to avoid the strong W-going tidal stream (see below) that can set you onto the West Pier from HW−1 to HW+4. Once past the East Pier, keep to stbd of the mid channel, heading for Fisherman's Quay (Fl G 3s 4m 5M) ahead. About 3 cables above Town Quay and Fisherman's Quay (both on the stbd side of the River Arun) a retractable footbridge (3.6m clearance MHWS) provides access to Littlehampton Marina, on the port hand side. It is opened on request to the HM, although you need to contact him by 1630 the day before you require entry. Beyond this point, the River Arun, leading to Ford, Arundel and beyond, is best explored by dinghy.

Access HW−3 to HW+2½ for a 1.5m draught.

Shelter Strong SE winds can cause a swell in the harbour. Do not attempt to cross the bar in strong SW'lies.

Signals When a pilot boat with P1 at the bow

Littlehampton Marina looking downstream towards the lifting bridge

displays the Pilot flag 'H' (WR vert halves) or W over R lts, all boats must keep clear of the entrance as a large ship is manoeuvring. Signals on the retractable footbridge providing access to Littlehampton Marina: Fl G lt = open; Fl R = closed.

Tides HW sp at the entrance are the same as HW Shoreham; HW nps are 10 mins after HW Shoreham. LW sp are 10 mins before and LW nps 5 mins before LW Shoreham. MHWS is 5·9m, MLWS 0·4m; MHWN is 4·4m, MLWN 1·7m. NB The tidal height inside the harbour is affected by the River Arun and seldom falls below 0.7m above chart datum.

Tidal streams A strong W stream runs from HW−1 to HW+4 across the entrance, so keep to the E side. Inside the harbour the ebb reaches 4–6kn at sp, making entry difficult for yachts.

VHF *Littlehampton HM* Ch 71, 16 (0900–1700LT); Pilots Ch 71, 16 when a ship is due; Bridge Ch 71; *Littlehampton Marina* Ch 80, M (office hours).

FACILITIES

HM The Harbour Office, Town Quay, Pier Road, Littlehampton, BN17 5LR. ☎ 721215; www.harbours.co.uk

Berthing For berthing availability it is best to

The Arun View Inn with its popular riverside terrace

The Arun Yacht Club on the west bank, with the new Town Quay development opposite

contact the HM/marina ahead of time. The Town Quay has undergone major changes in time for the start of the season 2003 and incorporates 100m of **Ⓥ** pontoons dredged to chart datum. For more information call the HM office.

Tariff Under 8m £13 per night; 8m+ £16 per night. Catamarans are charged 1½ times these charges. A short stay is free of charge.

Showers, toilets and drying room accessed by code. No launderette.

Electricity (card system) and **fresh water** on the pontoons.

Fuel see under Littlehampton Marina.

Chandlery and repairs Facilities include a small storage area and crane, plus a number of repairs specialists within the area, including David Hillyard (shipyard) ☎ 713327; Arun Canvas and Rigging ☎ 732561, Davis's Yacht Chandler ☎ 722778; absolute marine ☎ 734411, CH; Arun Craft ☎ 723667, ME; Hooper Marine ☎ 731195, ME.

Eating Restaurant and bar are included within the recent developments.

Littlehampton Marina lies N of the footbridge on the port hand side. VHF Ch 80, M; ☎ 713553; 🖷 732264. No allocated visitors' berths, so call in advance for availability. Remember also that you have to contact the HM by 1630 on the previous day for access through the bridge.

Tariff £2 per metre per night.

Showers, toilets and **launderette** (token operated) can be accessed without a code or key H24.

Electricity (daily rate of £2) and **fresh water** on the pontoons.

Fuel pump open 0800–1700 daily, except in June–Aug, when it stays open until at least 1800. Diesel and petrol available.

Chandlery & repairs Three chandlers just outside the marina entrance. For marine repair specialists ask at the marina office. Other facilities include boat hoist, slipway and hard standing area.

Food shop Within a 5 mins walk is a Tesco supermarket, with cash machine.

YCs Arun Yacht Club ☎ 714533. On the W side of the river, opposite the Town Quay. Can accommodate visitors in the summer, but must be contacted in advance to check availability. The berths dry out and are only accessible HW±2½.

Tariff £8.50 per night.

Facilities Electricity (included in the tariff) and FW on the pontoons. Showers, bar and restaurant (lunch and evening meals are served every day except Tues).

Other berthing may be available at Hillyards Shipyard, ☎ 713327, although moorings are scarce and facilities are limited.

Anchorage ⚓ is forbidden in the harbour and within 100m of the West Pier.

SHOREHAM

Shoreham Harbour entrance – 50°49'·48N 00°14'·84W

Only five miles west of Brighton Marina lies the commercial port of Shoreham. Established originally during the Roman era, the port's prosperity took off during the Norman times with the importation of wine and exportation of English wool. Despite its chequered history, Shoreham still remains one of the South Coast's major commercial ports handling, among other products, steel, grain, tarmac and timber. On first impressions it may seem that Shoreham has little to offer the visiting yachtsman, but once through the lock into the eastern arm of the River Adur, the quiet Lady Bee Marina, with its Spanish waterside restaurant, and the friendly Sussex Yacht Club can make this harbour an interesting alternative to the urban atmosphere of Brighton Marina.

SHORESIDE (Telephone code 01273)

Tourist Office Adur District Council, Civic Centre, Ham Road, Shoreham-by-Sea, West Sussex. ☎ 263162; ▦ 454847.

What to see/do The Marlipins Museum, ☎ 462994, in Shoreham-by-Sea's town centre depicts the area's local and maritime history. Housed in an historic Norman Secular building, it opens 1030–1630 Tues–Sat from 1 May–30 Sept. Adjacent to the lighthouse on Kingston Beach is the Lifeboat Station containing historical artefacts and memorabilia. Phone prior to any visit on ☎ 593403. The Museum of D-Day Aviation, ☎ 0374 971971, at Shoreham Airport is open Mon–Fri between April–Oct. For recreational pursuits go to Southwick Leisure Centre in Old Barn Way; ☎ 263200.

Rail Trains go direct from Shoreham to London, Portsmouth and Brighton. National Rail Enquiries ☎ 0845 748 4950.

Bus Brighton and Hove Bus and Coach Company runs services between Shoreham and Brighton as well as links to Chichester; ☎ 01273 886200.

Taxi Shoreham Taxis ☎ 441010; Bel-Cabs ☎ 454455.

Car hire United Rental Systems ☎ 454287.

Flights Scheduled flights to France and the Channel Islands go from Shoreham Airport, ☎ 296900. Gatwick airport is only a 35 mins drive away, ☎ 0870 000 2468.

Beaches Shoreham has a shingle beach.

Supermarkets There is a small convenience store just outside the Lady Bee Marina, otherwise go to the Co-op in Southwick Square, about a 5 mins walk away.

Banks All the major high street banks can be found in Southwick Square.

Keep clear of the regular commercial traffic

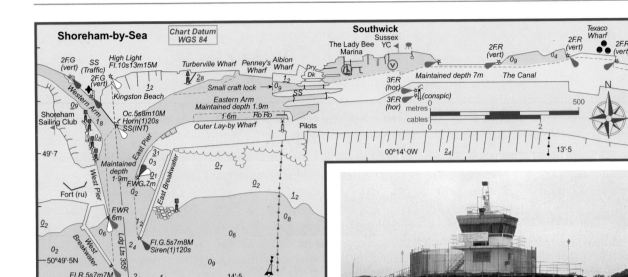

Chart showing Shoreham-by-Sea and Southwick.

Chart Datum WGS 84

Shoreham-by-Sea

2F.G (vert) — SS (Traffic) — High Light Fl.10s13m15M — Turberville Wharf — Penney's Wharf — Albion Wharf — Dry Dk — Southwick Sussex — The Lady Bee Marina YC — Texaco Wharf — 2F.R (vert) — 2F.R (vert)

2F.G (vert) — Kingston Beach — 1.2 — 2.8 — Small craft lock — 0.9 — 1.2 — Maintained depth 7m — The Canal — 0.9 — 0.4 — 2F.R (vert)

Shoreham Sailing Club — Western Arm — 0.9 — Oc.5s8m10M Horn(1)20s SS(INT) — 1.8 — 0.8 — Eastern Arm Maintained depth 1.9m — 1.6m — Ro Ro — Outer Lay-by Wharf — 3F.R (hor) — 3F.R (hor) — (conspic) — metres — cables — 500

49'·7 — East Pier — 3.1 — 0.3 — 0.1 — 0.7 — Pilots — 00°14'·0W — 2.4 — 13'·5

Maintained depth 1·9m — F.WG.7m — 0.2 — East Breakwater — 0.2 — 1.2 — 0.8

Fort (ru) — West Pier — F.WR 6m — 1.2 — 0.6 — 0.2

0.2 — West Breakwater — Ldg Lts 355° — 2.4 — 1.2 — Fl.G.5s7m8M Siren(1)120s — 0.6 — 0.9

50°49'·5N — 0.2 — Fl.R.5s7m7M — 2.4 — 1.1 — 14'·5

15'

Restaurants
La Cala in Lady Bee Marina, ☎ 597422, serves Spanish cuisine and has a terrace overlooking the moorings. Just 100m away in Albion St, overlooking the canal, is The Schooner Inn, ☎ 592252, while in Station Road The Pilot, ☎ 591789, serves traditional pub food at very reasonable prices.

NAVIGATION

Charts AC 2044 (1:5,000), SC 5605.4 (1:75,000 including inset of Shoreham 1:15,000), 1652 (1: 75,000).

Approaches From the E there are no real dangers except for the Brighton piers and the Jenny Rocks (0.9m), approx 1.75M from the entrance. From the W beware of Church Rocks (0.3m), about 0.25M from the shore and just over 1M from the breakwater. Do not attempt to enter in strong onshore winds, especially when the tide is on the ebb.

Landmarks/conspic marks A radio mast is conspic 170m N of the lighthouse. A 100m high silver chimney with a black top to the E of the

Approaching the outer breakwaters

The Middle Pier watch house is left to port

entrance is easily identified. A SCM, marking outfall diffusers, bears 155° and is 1.75M from the hbr entrance.

Pilotage The waypoint is 50°49'·23N 00°14'·81W, around 0.5M due S from the entrance, which is sandwiched between two concrete outer breakwaters lit with Fl R5s 7m 7M to port and Fl G5s 7m 8M (fog siren 120s) to starboard. From this WPT, a course of 355° brings you on to the leading lts, the front one being Oc 5s 8m 10M on the Middle Pier watch house and the rear one being Fl 10s 13m 15M on the lighthouse beyond. From seaward, when entering for the first time, the breakwaters and piers can look confusing, but once past the outer breakwater all becomes clear.

Just inside the breakwaters the W pier lies to port (FWR 6m), while further on the E pier (FWG 7m) indicates the turn into the eastern dredged arm of the harbour, leading to Southwick Canal. The western arm (the River Adur) dries out and is not really recommended to visitors unless their yachts can take the bottom.

Once in the eastern arm, having left the Middle Pier with its watch house to port, the commercial Prince Philip and the small craft Prince George Locks are immediately ahead. The northern Prince George Lock is manned H24, although the sill is 0.26m below CD, therefore preventing access at about LWS±1. The lock entrance is 6m wide and a waiting pontoon is inside on the S wall. Entry times to the canal are H+30 while departure times are on the hour. Yachts waiting

The conspic chimney E of the entrance

for the Prince George Lock are allowed to wait on the outer lead-in and inner lead-in piers, but must be manned at all times. Keep clear of both commercial ships using the southern lock and the Ro-Ro terminal to the S of the locks. The harbour speed limit of 4kn must be observed and yachts are not permitted to proceed E of Lady Bee Marina without the HM's permission.

IPTS From the Middle Pier Oc Y 3s means do not enter the eastern or western arm. From the LB house, Oc R 3s directed at either the E or W arm means no exit.

Lock signals Three R (vert) means do not approach the lock. GWG (vert) means clear to approach the lock.

Access H24, although contact Shoreham Hbr Radio for berthing instructions before entering. Due to the shallow water (dredged to 1.9m) in the inner entrance, it can be very rough in strong onshore winds and dangerous in onshore gales.

Shelter Once through the lock and into the canal, shelter is excellent.

Tides Shoreham is a Standard Port. MHWS is 6·3m, MLWS 0·6m; MHWN is 4·8m, MLWN 1·9m.

Tidal streams The W-going stream starts approx 2 hrs after HW, with the E-going stream occurring about 6 hrs later. Strong tidal streams in the Western arm, but weak in the Eastern arm.

VHF *Shoreham Hbr Radio* VHF Ch 14, 16. The HM will advise Lady Bee Marina of your arrival.

FACILITIES

HM Harbour Office, Southwick, BN42 4ED.
☎ 593801; ✆ 592492/870349;
www.portshoreham.co.uk

Berthing The Lady Bee Marina, on the port side of the eastern arm, has a few ❶ berths but check availability ahead of time. Access as lock times. ☎ 593801; ✆ 870349. If full, the marina may direct you to Aldrington Quay Marina at the E end of the canal which, like the Lady Bee, comes under the HM's jurisdiction.

Tariff For yachts <15m £16.50 for first night (incl of lock fee) and £12 after that. Vessels <7m £12 and £9.50 after that.

Electricity (included in berthing fees) and **FW** on the pontoons. No **launderette** on site, but one can be found in Southwick Square, about a 5 mins walk away.

Showers and toilets are code accessed.

Fuel in cans from the local Southwick garage. Diesel pump at Corral's, Wharf House, Brighton Rd, in the western arm. No VHF, but can be contacted on ☎ 455511. Open 0830–1700 Mon–Fri and 0900–1200 Sat. Access for a 1.5m draught is HW±2½.

Chandlery & repairs On site chandlery GB Barnes, ☎ 596680, sells gas. With a range of marine specialists on site, most repairs can be carried out.

The Sussex Yacht Club, ☎/✆ 464868. Welcomes visitors but only has limited pontoon berths above the Lady Bee Marina in the eastern branch and moorings that dry out at half tide in the western branch. Call in advance for availability. £7 per day applies to both the pontoon and moorings. Electricity is available on the pontoon, provided you have your own cable, as is FW. The clubhouse at Southwick is unmanned but does provide showers. The clubhouse at Shoreham has showers as well as a bar and restaurant. Serves food every day except Mon and Fri/Sat evenings.

Lady Bee Marina from the lock

Chapter 3

BRIGHTON

Brighton Marina entrance – 50°48'·49N 00°06'·34W

Situated halfway between Portsmouth and Dungeness, Brighton Marina, with its extensive range of shops, restaurants and facilities, is a popular and convenient stopover for east and west-going passagemakers. Only half a mile from here is the historic city of Brighton itself, renowned for being a cultural centre with a cosmopolitan atmosphere.

The ideal track is slightly to the left of this military approach

Although the marina gets busy in season, its huge capacity normally enables it to accommodate visitors without any difficulty. However, the approach and entrance to the marina, despite being straightforward, can be surprisingly bumpy, even in moderate conditions and it is not advisable to attempt to enter in strong S to SE winds.

SHORESIDE (Telephone code 01273)

Tourist Office 10 Bartholomew Square, Brighton BN1 1JS. ☎ 0906 711 2255 (calls charged at 50p per minute); 🖷 292594; brighton-tourism@ brighton-hove.gov.uk

What to see/do The marina is practically a small town in its own right, with a bowling alley, eight-screen UGC cinema, ☎ 0870 1555145, a health

centre and a variety of shops. The city of Brighton is only a short bus ride or walk away, where your first port of call should be the exotic Royal Pavilion, ☎ 290900. Built for King George IV in the 1800s, it was subsequently used by William IV and Queen Victoria. Open April–Sept 0930–1745; Oct–March (except 25 & 26 Dec) 1000–1715. Accessed from the Pavilion gardens is the newly refurbished Brighton Museum & Art Gallery, ☎ 290900. Open Tues 1000–1900, Wed–Sat 1000–1700, Sun 1400–1700. Admission is free. A stroll along the beachfront brings you to the Fishing Museum, ☎ 723064, W of Brighton Pier, illustrating Brighton's history as a fishing village. On Marine Parade is the Sea Life Centre, ☎ 604234; open daily from 1000. Don't miss the Lanes, with its multitude of antiques shops. For plenty of other attractions and places of interest, contact the Tourist Office.

Rail Brighton has a mainline station with regular trains to Chichester, Portsmouth, London (approx 1 hr) and Gatwick (30 mins). National rail enquiries ☎ 0845 748 4950. In the summer the Volks Railway, ☎ 292718, runs along the beach from Brighton Pier to a few hundred metres short of the marina. It operates 1100–1700 every 15 mins; adults cost £1; children 50p.

Bus A No 7 bus runs from the Katarina Beefeater pub and restaurant in the centre of the marina village to the centre of Brighton every 15 mins. Brighton & Hove Bus Company ☎ 886200.

Taxi Taxi ranks can be found: Alongside the marina bus shelter; in East Street; in Queens Rd near the Clock Tower; outside Hove Town Hall. You can also hail cabs on the streets. Streamline Taxis ☎ 747474; Car Cabs ☎ 414141; Brighton & Hove Radio Cabs ☎ 204060; Taxi Link ☎ 595959.

Car hire Avis has an office within the marina village, ☎ 673738; Hertz Rent-a-Car ☎ 738227; National Car Rental ☎ 202426.

Bike hire Lifecycle Preston Rd, ☎ 542425.

Flights By road or rail Brighton is only 30 mins from Gatwick, ☎ 0870 000 2468, and approx 90 mins from Heathrow, ☎ 0870 000 0123.

Beaches Brighton's pebble beach stretches several miles from the marina in the E to Hove in the W. Safe for bathing, it is fringed by numerous restaurants and traditional seaside shops.

Supermarkets Asda supermarket, with cashpoints, is in the marina village. Opens 24 hrs from Mon 0800–Sat 2200. Open Sun from 1100–1700.

Banks Most of the major high street banks and building societies, with cashpoints, are in North Street or Western Road.

Restaurants There are more than 10 restaurants and bars on the marina site, ranging from the excellent Italian, the Bella Napoli, ☎ 818577, to the fast food chain, McDonalds, ☎ 819111. The city of Brighton has over 400 restaurants and bars which, in true cosmopolitan style, range from traditional English and French to Mexican, Chinese and Japanese. Several good eating places

Chapter 3

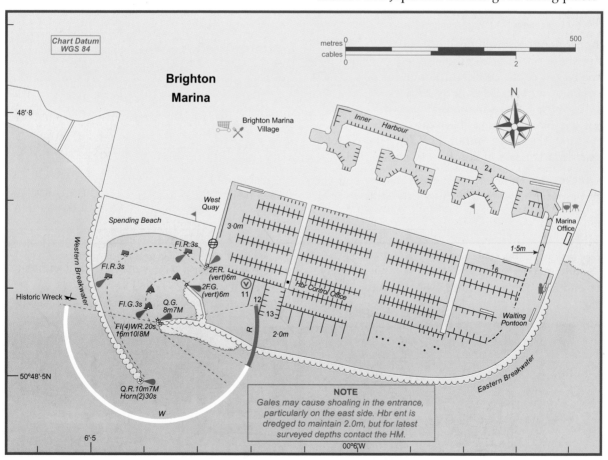

The on-site Bella Napoli Italian restaurant

A conspic high-rise hospital block with a large white vertical stripe, bearing 334°, leads to the entrance.

Lights At night the hbr entrance lights can be confusing with the bright streetlights in the background. However the E bkwtr now has a high intensity sector lt (Fl (4) WR 20s 16m 10M; vis R260°–295°, W295°–100°) with a smaller lt at its head (QG 8m 7M). The W bkwtr is lit with a QR 10m 7M with a foghorn ((2) 30s) that comes into play when the visibility is less than 1,000m in the entrance.

are situated in The Lanes, including Hotel De Vin in Ship St, ☎ 718588, the sophisticated Havana in Duke St, ☎ 773388, and the Santa Fe Restaurant in East St, offering high quality Mexican cuisine, ☎ 823281. For Japanese sushi go to Moshi Moshi in Bartholomew Square, ☎ 719195. A good seafood restaurant is The Regency, ☎ 325014, near the West Pier.

NAVIGATION

Charts AC SC 5605.4 (1:75,000 with an inset of Brighton Marina 1:7,500); 1991 (1:5,000); 1652 (1:75,000).

Approaches Keeping well offshore the W approach presents no problems, except for the Brighton Palace Pier, although this is very conspic and at night is lit by 2 FR lts.

From the E there are no real hazards, except for the lobster grounds N of the can buoy marking the sewer outfall (Fl Y 5s). These can be particularly nasty at night.

Landmarks The marina is at the eastern end of the town where white cliffs extend eastwards.

Pilotage The WPT is 50°48′·08N 00°06′·27W, about a cable E of the Black Rock Ledge Y spar buoy (Fl Y 4s) lying 2 cables S of the entrance. From here the can buoy marking the sewer outfall is 2.95M to the E and the Brighton Pier is 1.5M to the W. Between the W and E breakwaters the entrance is 80m wide and dredged to 2m LAT, but shoaling can occur S of the E bkwtr, especially after gales. Even in moderate conditions it can be extremely choppy S of the entrance, but once inside the W arm you will be well protected. The channel, which is well buoyed and lit, turns to stbd. The inner entrance is marked by two FR (vert) and two FG (vert) lts on the heads of the inner bkwtrs. The speed limit is 5kn.

Access H24, although not advisable in S'ly gales.

Shelter Good in the marina under all conditions, but the approach can be difficult in strong S'ly winds.

Tides HW sp are 5 mins and HW nps 10 mins before HW Shoreham. LW nps and LW sp are 5 mins before LW Shoreham. MHWS is 6·9m, MLWS 0·5m; MHWN is 4·9m, MLWN 1·9m.

The high-rise hospital block bearing 334° leads to the harbour entrance

Tidal streams The W-going stream starts at Brighton HW$-1\frac{1}{2}$ and the E-going at HW$+4\frac{1}{2}$. Inshore the sp rate reaches approx 1.5kn.

VHF Brighton Marina Ch 80, M (37).

FACILITIES

Brighton Marina ☎ 819919; 📠 675082; brighton@premiermarinas.com; www.premiermarinas.com In the marina the reception pontoon (No 10) lies to port. Here you should moor up and report to the Harbour Office on the West Jetty to find out about berthing availability, unless you have already contacted the berthing master ahead of time on VHF or telephone. A 24 hr VHF radio watch is kept on Ch 16, M and 80, although you should contact the marina on Ch 80.

Tariff £1.95 per metre per day; a short stay is £6.

Launderette (token-operated) on the E Jetty (one to also be built on the W Jetty). **Showers** and toilets are accessed by a security card.

Electricity (£2.75 per day) and **fresh water** on the pontoons.

Fuel Diesel, unleaded petrol, LPG, calor and camping gas are available from the fuel pontoon

Brighton Marina is one of the largest on the South Coast

Once inside the marina entrance, moor up alongside the visitors' pontoon to port and report to the harbour office

located at the E end of the marina near the entrance to the inner harbour. Open 24 hrs a day.

Chandlery & repairs Southern Masts & Rigging ☎ 818189, CH (in the Marina Trade Centre). A full range of marine specialists on site as well as a 60-ton travel hoist, a mobile crane and storage.

YCs Brighton Marina YC, ☎ 818711, enjoys a prime position overlooking the hbr entrance. It serves excellent lunch and evening meals as well as breakfasts in its terraced bar and restaurant.

NEWHAVEN

Newhaven Harbour entrance – 50°46'·54N 00°03'·61E

Some seven miles east of Brighton, Newhaven lies at the mouth of the River Ouse. Its fairly straightforward entrance means that it is often used by yachtsmen as a port of refuge when conditions are too bad to get in to Brighton Marina. With its large fishing fleet and regular ferry services to Dieppe, the harbour has over the years become increasingly commercial and therefore care is needed to keep clear of large vessels under manoeuvre. As Newhaven is prone to silting, dredging is virtually a continuous occupation here.

SHORESIDE (Telephone code 01273)

Tourist Office 187, High St, Lewes, East Sussex, BN7 2DE. ☎ 483448; ▨ 484003; lewes.tic@lewes.gov.uk

What to see/do Go to Newhaven Fort, ☎ 517622. Built in the 1860s, it opens daily 23 March–3 Nov 1030–1800. On Avis Road is the Paradise Park, ☎ 616006. Open all year round, (except 25–26 Dec), it incorporates the Sussex History Trail with models of famous buildings, the Local & Maritime Museum and an exhibition depicting the life story of Planet

Earth. A bus or taxi ride away is the English Wine Centre in Alfriston, ☎ 01323 870164, where you can spend an afternoon tasting British wines. Nearby are superb walks over the South Downs with views of the Seven Sisters cliffs.

The inshore end of the West Pier

Bikes can be hired from the Cuckmere Cycle Company, ☎ 01323 870310, within the Seven Sisters Country Park; open March–Nov.

Rail Good rail links between Eastbourne, Brighton and London via Lewes. Contact National Rail Enquiries on ☎ 08457 484950 or the Travel Line on ☎ 0870 6082608.

Buses Stagecoach runs services along the whole of the South Coast, linking all the major ports and cities. Stagecoach Coastline ☎ 0845 121 0170.

Taxi Newhaven Taxis ☎ 611111; Seaford Taxis ☎ 896666; A 2 B Cars ☎ 512151.

Car hire Select Self Drive ☎ 612444.

Beaches The West Quay Beach covers at HW but is sandy at LW.

Supermarkets Somerfield in the town centre, about a 10 mins walk from the marina. Also The Store Supermaket at Newhaven Marina and Sainsbury's in the Drove, a little further from the town but still within walking distance.

Market day Fresh fish from the fishing fleet is

Enter keeping the West breakwater well to port

sold daily in a recently built fish market just a few hundred metres N of the marina.

Banks Several banks, with cash machines, can be found in the High Street.

Restaurants The Villa Adriana, ☎ 513976, serving Italian cuisine, is a short distance S of the marina. Benbows Restaurant on Bridge St, ☎ 526334, does an inexpensive three course lunch for £5.95, although you have to bring your own wine. Two pubs serving good bar meals in the area are The Hope Inn on West Pier, ☎ 515389, and the Ark Inn at West Quay, ☎ 515389. The Coral Cafe on the marina complex provides breakfasts from 0700.

NAVIGATION

Charts AC 2154 (1:5,000); SC 5605.4 (1:75,000 with an inset of Newhaven 1:10,000); 5605.5 (1:75,000); 1652 (1:75,000).

Approaches From the E keep a good distance off Seaford Head and similarly from the W keep well clear of Burrow Head. From either direction make for WPT 50°46'·24N 00°03'·60E, about 0.5M from the W breakwater bearing 348°. The E breakwater is lit with an Iso G 10s 12m 6M.

Landmarks The lighthouse (Oc (2) 10s 17m 12M) on the end of the W breakwater is conspic from seaward.

Pilotage From the above WPT, steer 359° towards the E pier. Once inside the W bkwtr take care not to deviate to port as the outer harbour is silted up. With high speed ferries and commercial craft movements, listen out to the Port Authority on VHF Ch 12 and watch out for the signals from the lt ho on the W bkwtr (see under Signals). The harbour speed limit of 5kn must be observed. Newhaven Marina is about 0.25M from the entrance on the port hand side.

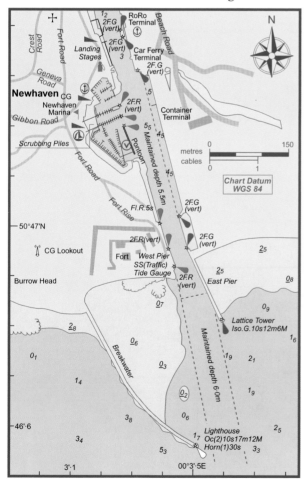

A little further N is a swing bridge, which opens on request through *Newhaven Radio* on Ch 12. Lewes lies 7M upriver and is best navigated by dinghy.

Access H24 at all states of the tide. The channel is dredged to 5.5m. Newhaven Marina, on the W bank of the River Ouse, was dredged 2003 to allow full tidal access except on LWS. Yachts with a 1.5m draught should approach LWS±1, but check with the marina first.

Shelter Generally good in all weathers, although in strong S'ly winds breaking seas on the E side of the dredged channel can make entry difficult.

IPTS

W Pier Signal Station: Three Fl R (vert) = all vessels to stop or divert according to instructions from the Newhaven Port Authority, VHF Ch 12.
Three F R (vert) = vessels may not enter.
Two F G (vert) over W = small craft may proceed; two way traffic.
GWG (vert) = proceed only when instructed by the Port Authority. All other vessels keep clear.
On swing bridge: Fl G = bridge opening or closing.
FG vessels may pass N to S.
FR vessels may pass S to N.
Newhaven Marina: R lts showing on signal mast, at the NE corner of the marina = no vessels may leave any part of Newhaven Marina.
SuperSeaCat berth (North end): R lts showing on signal mast at NW corner of No 2 Ro-Ro pontoon = no vessel may proceed S past these lts.

Tides HW at sp is 10 mins before and nps 15 mins before HW Shoreham. LW at nps and sp is the same as LW Shoreham. MHWS is 6·5m, MLWS 0·4m; MHWN is 4·9m; MLWN 1·8m.

VHF *Newhaven Radio* Ch 12, 16 (H24); Bridge Control (callsign *Newhaven Radio*) Ch 12; *Newhaven Marina* Ch 80 (0800–1700).

FACILITIES

HM Newhaven Harbour, Beach Rd, Newhaven, BN9 0BG, ☎ 612868; 🖷 612878. Harbour Signal Station ☎ 612929.

Newhaven Marina Situated approx 0.25M from the hbr entrance on the W bank, it has recently

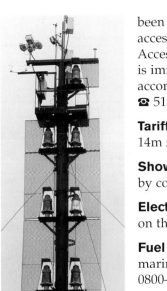

been dredged to allow full tidal access except on LWS (see under Access opposite). The **Ⓥ** pontoon is immediately to port and can accommodate about 12 boats. ☎ 513881; 🖷 510493.

Tariff 8m £13; 10m £16; 12m £19; 14m £22.50.

Showers and toilets are accessed by code. No **launderette** on site.

Electricity (daily rate £2) and **FW** on the pontoons.

Fuel pontoon is 150m N of the marina entrance. Diesel is available 0800–1700 daily.

Chandlery & repairs The on site chandlery, Simpson Marine ☎ 612612, sells gas. Services include a BH (18 ton), crane (10 ton), slipway and marine specialists ranging from engineers to shipwrights. Gary Chabot ☎ 611076, BY; Andy Pace ☎ 516010, ME; Peter Leonard Marine ☎ 515987, BY. Cantells Shipyard, ☎ 514118, offers all forms of boat repairs and has an on site chandlery; situated N of the swing bridge on the port hand side.

Food shop The Store, ☎ 516143, sells a range of provisions or go to Somerfield supermarket in the town centre.

Anchoring No ⚓ in harbour although locals sometimes ⚓ SE of the E Pier for a short stay. This area is also used by waterskiers.

YCs Newhaven YC is based within the marina complex and welcomes visiting yachtsmen to its club nights. Call the Commodore, Graham Jones, on ☎ 589849.

The visitors' pontoon

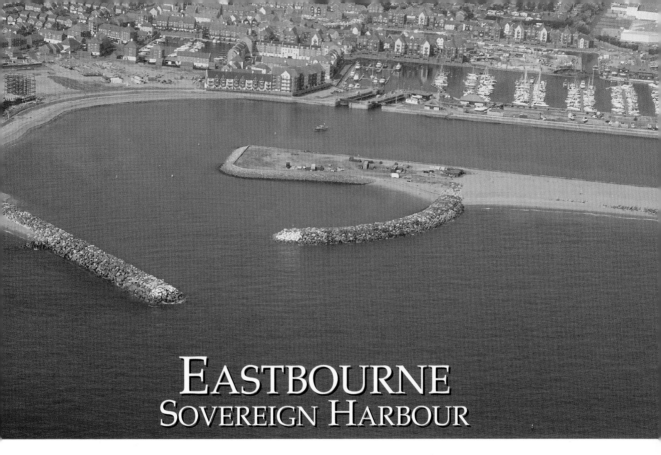

EASTBOURNE
SOVEREIGN HARBOUR

Sovereign Harbour entrance – 50°47'·33N 00°20'·08E

Opened 10 years ago, Sovereign Harbour is situated a few miles NE of Eastbourne and is accessible at all states of the tide and weather except for in strong NE to SE'ly winds. Since its conception it has increasingly become a welcome addition to the ports along the SE coast of England, especially if you miss the tide at Beachy Head when passage making down the Channel. Entered through twin locks which are manned continuously, the marina incorporates five separate harbours covering around 65 acres and boasts a cosmopolitan Waterfront comprising a multitude of shops and restaurants.

SHORESIDE (Telephone code 01323)

Tourist Office Cornfield Rd, PO Box 447, Eastbourne, BN21 4NZ. ☎ 411400; tic@eastbourne.gov.uk Open 0930–1730 Mon–Sat; 1000–1300 Sun in summer only.

What to see/do One of the largest marina complexes in Britain, there is no shortage of things to do at the Sovereign Harbour alone. The Waterfront includes a wide selection of shops and cafés, while behind in the Crumbles Retail Park is a UGC multiplex cinema, ☎ 0870 1555159. A short bus or taxi ride takes you to Eastbourne where places of interest include its famous pier, opened in 1870; ☎ 410466. Visit the 'How We Lived Then' Museum of Shops off Cornfield Terrace to see clothes and items from the Victorian era. To the E of the pier is the Napoleonic Redoubt Fortress, ☎ 410300, while nearby is the Musgrave Collection of Egyptian and Roman artefacts. Among the more vibrant attractions on offer is the Fort Fun Wild West Park, which includes American Adventure Golf and Formula One Go Karts, ☎ 642833.

Rail Regular train services to London Victoria (takes 80 mins) as well as to towns along the coast. National Rail Enquiries ☎ 0845 748 4950.

Buses Frequent buses to Brighton and Newhaven as well as to other surrounding towns and villages. For bus information call ☎ 416416.

Taxi Radio Cars ☎ 735566; Greyhound Taxis ☎ 417555; Sussex Cars ☎ 726726.

Car hire Practical Car and Van Hire ☎ 419944; Vauxhall Car & Van Hire ☎ 720681.

Cycle hire Raggamuffin Action Sports hires out bikes from April–Oct, ☎ 470081.

The safe water mark, with the entrance bearing 258°

The unmarked wreck north of the fairway

Beaches The main shingle beach at Eastbourne is safe for swimming. Includes lifeguards, beach huts and beach cafés. Also beaches to the NE within Pevensey Bay.

Supermarkets An Asda supermarket in The Crumbles retail park just behind the marina is open seven days a week. Has a cashpoint.

Market day Takes place every Tues and Sat and Bank Holiday Mon at Langney Shopping Centre.

Banks None at Sovereign Harbour, although Asda has a cashpoint. For major high street banks and building societies go to Eastbourne's town centre.

Restaurants A wide range of restaurants and bars on The Waterfront within the marina complex. Two to be recommended are the Thai Marina, ☎ 470414, and Simply Italian, ☎ 470911. The Harvester restaurant, ☎ 470074, and Di Lieto's sandwich bar and patisserie, ☎ 470990, are popular choices with families. Go to Seamoor's wine bar for a convivial atmosphere and live music, ☎ 470271. Eastbourne also offers a plethora of eating places to suit all tastes and budgets.

NAVIGATION

Charts AC SC 5605.5 (1:75,000 with inset 1:15,000), 536 (1:75,000)

Approaches From the W once you have rounded Beachy Head, keep approx 1M offshore to clear Holywell Bank and head for the WPT 50°47'·37N 00°21'·40E. From the E be aware of the Royal Sovereign and Horse of Willingdon shoals, while further inshore, to the NE in Pevensey Bay, the Coxheath shoals extend nearly 2M offshore.

Landmarks The marina entrance is 2M NE of Eastbourne Pier (2 FR (vert)). A Martello tower, at the root of the S breakwater, has a high intensity xenon lt, (Fl (3) 15s 12m 7M) which is visible during the day as well as at night.

Another Martello tower is about 0.5M to the N of the entrance.

Pilotage The WPT 50°47'·37N 00°21'·40E is 0.5M due E of the RW safe water buoy (L Fl 10s/ position 50°47'·37N 00°20'·81E). From this buoy the entrance bears 258° and is about 800m away, at which point you should contact Sovereign Harbour to find out navigational information and lock status. At night keep in the W sector of the Dir ldg lt (Fl WRG 5s 4m 1M, W256.5°–259.5°), leading 258° through the approach channel. Do not wander N of the SHM buoys (Fl G 5s and Fl G 3s) which mark a wreck from WWI that is visible at LW. The seaward ends of the breakwaters are both painted white and lit at night – the S bkwtr Fl (4) R 12s 6M; the N bkwtr Fl G 5s 6M. Approx 5 cables S of the S bkwtr off Langney Pt is an unlit PHM. Once through the breakwaters follow the buoyed channel to the two large locks. The locks are manned 24 hrs and close on the hour and half hour. The lock traffic signals are clearly visible as you head up the channel and indicate lock availability (see below under IPTS). You should monitor VHF Ch 17 at all times once in the channel and harbour and observe the speed limit of 5kn.

Access H24, via two locks. Note that the channel

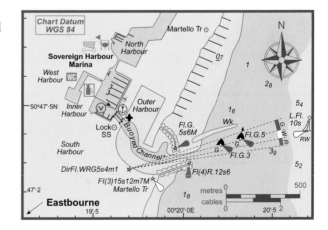

is prone to shoaling after gales and is dredged frequently. If uncertain, contact the HM for the latest information.

Shelter Good in the marina, but the approach is exposed in NE to SE winds above F5. In strong winds, it is best to time your arrival HW±1½.

IPTS Three R lts (vert) mean that vessels must not proceed. Three G lts (vert) mean that vessels may proceed. A GWG (vert) mean that vessels may proceed only after receiving specific instructions from the HM.

Tides HW sp are 5 mins and HW nps 10 mins before HW Shoreham. LW sp are 20 mins and LW nps 15 mins after LW Shoreham.

Tidal streams Slack water outside the hbr entrance is at HW Dover +1 to HW Dover +3. A SW going tide starts at HW+4 to HW–4. An E–NE going stream starts at HW–3 to HW Dover.

VHF *Sovereign Harbour* CH **17**, 15 (H24).

The outer harbour at low tide – the best water is to port

FACILITIES

HM Sovereign Harbour, Pevensey Bay Road, Eastbourne, East Sussex, BN 23 6JH. ☎ 470099; ✉ 470077; sovereignharbour@carillionplc.com; www.sovereignharbour.co.uk

Berthing On entering the lock, with fenders out on both sides, tie up to the pontoon as far to the front as possible. Once secure, wait for the lock-keeper to give you berthing instructions. The ❶ berths are located immediately to port as you enter the marina.

Tariff £2.10 per metre per night; £10.50 per metre per week. A part day is 35% of the daily rate, with a minimum charge of £5.

Electricity (either metered or pre-purchased credit cards) and **FW** on the pontoons.

Launderette (coin-operated) is situated within the Inner Harbour shower building and is accessible 24 hrs per day.

Showers and toilets can be accessed 24 hrs a day in both the Inner and West Harbours. Also temporary facilities in North Harbour.

Fuel A self-service fuel pontoon is open H24. Fuels include Marine Diesel (on two pumps), unleaded petrol, LRP (the old four star leaded) and LPG. Once you have finished filling up, pay at the Harbour Office, which can also supply various grades of engine oil along with calor and camping gas.

Chandlery & repairs Facilities include a BH (50 ton), high pressure wash off and hard standing area. Langney Marine Services, based on site, offers a comprehensive boat and engine repair service, ☎ 470244. Also Felton Marine Engineering (Volvo Penta dealers), ☎ 470211, and Yoldings Marine, ☎ 470882, EI, ME.

YCs The Sovereign Harbour Yacht Club, ☎ 470888, has premises in North Harbour, with views across the marina. It welcomes visitors to its bar and restaurant (closed Mondays; Tuesday–Thursday opens 1800–2300. Opens from 1200 Friday–Sunday).

Once through the lock, the visitors' pontoons are immediately to port

Chapter 3

RYE

Rye Harbour entrance – 50°55'·59N 00°46'·61E

Strand Quay visitors' berths

The mediaeval hilltop town of Rye is one of the most charming and interesting harbours along the SE coast of England. In the 14th century it became a Cinque Port whereby its duty was to supply the King with ships and men in return for being exempt from taxation. During the 18th century much of its prosperity relied on smuggling, with smugglers' caches hidden in old vaulted cellars joined by a network of secret tunnels spreading underneath the entire town. Today its narrow cobbled streets and picturesque historic buildings create an enchanting atmosphere not to be missed. However for first timers the drying entrance can appear rather daunting, especially in heavy onshore winds, and once inside there are no deep water berths, with all the moorings drying out onto soft mud.

NAVIGATION

Charts AC SC 5605.6 (1:75,000 with an insert of Rye 1:25,0000); 1991 (1:25,000); 536 (1:75,000).

Approaches When approaching from either direction keep at least 2M offshore. If coming from the W from Fairlight, look out for Boulder Banks and Tower Knoll. If coming from the E past Dungeness, Lydd Firing Range, to the W of Dungeness, needs to be given a good offing of at least 2M when firing is taking place. A range boat is normally operating in the area to warn you off. Yachts entering Rye Bay should look out for the numerous anchored gill nets, which are normally marked at each end by dan buoys and tend to have a minimum depth of 2m over them.

Landmarks The entrance is difficult to spot, although you should be able to make out a church spire just under 1M to the east. Closer in, the conspic red tripod bcn off the West Groyne allows the entrance to be easily identified.

Pilotage The WPT is 50°53'·70N 00°48'·00E, approx 0.25M S of the Rye Fairway Buoy (Spherical RW Fl 10s). From the Fairway Buoy, which is about 1.85M from the entrance, a course of 329° brings you on to the conspic red-painted tripod bcn (Fl R 5s 7m 6M), about 30m to seaward of the W groyne. Note that the depth over the bar (dries to 1.5m about 2 cables offshore) can be judged during the day by how many horizontal timber frames are showing on this beacon. One, two or three timbers indicate depths of 3.5m, 2m and 0.5m respectively. The E pier, which covers at HW, is another 250m inland and is identified by a square steel structure topped by a green board that is lit at night (Q (9) 15s 7m 5M). The E training wall, which slopes outwards, is easily identified by stbd hand beacons and lights. Beware

329° leads you straight down the river

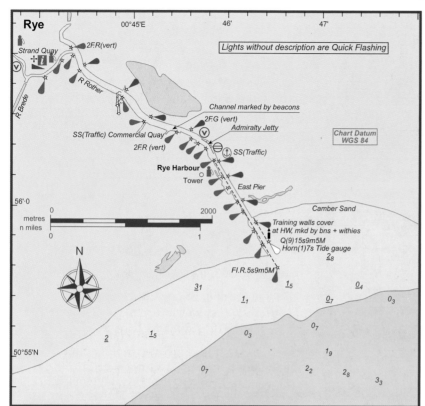

Rye

00°45'E   46'   47'

Strand Quay

2 F.R (vert)

R Rother

R Brede

Lights without description are Quick Flashing

Channel marked by beacons

2 F.G (vert)

Admiralty Jetty

SS (Traffic) Commercial Quay

2 F.R (vert)

SS (Traffic)

Rye Harbour
Tower

East Pier

Chart Datum
WGS 84

56'·0

metres
n miles

0   2000

0   1

N

Camber Sand

Training walls cover
at HW, mkd by bns + withies
Q(9)15s9m5M
Horn(1)7s Tide gauge
2_8

Fl.R.5s9m5M

3_1 1_1 1_5 0_7 0_4 0_3

0_7

50°55'N

2 1_5 0_3 1_9

0_7 2_2 2_8 3_3

The E pier identified by a square steel structure topped by a green board which is lit at night

that the W training wall is submerged at high tide, although remains clearly marked by unlit port hand beacons and withies every 100m. During the flood stream, strong east-going eddies occur inside the W groyne so be prepared to correct your helm. At night, a Dir Oc WG 4s lt on the HM's office identifies the safe approach into the channel, with the W sector (326°–331°) covering the entrance/river.

Inside the piers the channel narrows from 45m to 30m. Keep on a course of 329° from the W groyne for about 0.5M or so. More or less once you reach Rye Harbour village, the W training wall comes to an end. Slightly further upstream of this, on the E bank, is the HM's office and Admiralty Jetty, where visiting yachtsmen must stop to report to the HM

for berthing instructions and navigational advice for the berths at Strand Quay in the centre of Rye. Beyond this point the River Rother is well marked and fairly steep-to right up until the town of Rye. However beware that on each side of the channel mud flats cover at HW so do not deviate from the centre of the channel too much. Look out for the entrance to Rock Channel, on the port hand side, about 1M further on from the Admiralty Jetty. It is marked by two R and G buoys. Do not turn into the channel until these buoys are well open. The N side of Rock Channel is marked by 2 FR (vert) lights. (Note that N of Rock Channel the river leads to the Fishmarket and, due to a road bridge, becomes impassable to masted vessels). Keep to the centre of the Rock Channel until you reach the sluice gate at the top of the River Brede on your port hand side. On this bend, it is best to veer towards the port hand side close to the boat moorings for the deeper water, before heading back to the middle of the channel to continue up to Strand Quay.

Access For yachts with a 1.5m to 2m draught, the best time to enter is about HW–1. Do not approach the entrance more than HW–2 to HW+2 at springs.

Shelter is good in the River Rother, which dries completely to soft mud. Ryde Bay is exposed in strong SW'ly winds, in which case do not attempt entry.

IPTS are located close to stbd of the HM's office and are only switched on when commercial ships are manoeuvring in the channel. It is advisable to contact the HM on VHF Ch 14 before entering the channel to find out about shipping movements in port.

Tides HW sp are 5 mins after and HW nps 10 mins before HW Dover. MHWS is 7·8m; MHWN is 6·0m. No LW data.

Tidal streams The flood runs between 4.5 and 5kn between max HW–3 to HW–1.

VHF *Rye Harbour Radio* Ch 14 0900–1700LT or when a large vessel is due.

Chapter 3

from the HM when tying up against the Admiralty Jetty on the E side of the river. Yachts up to 15m LOA can usually be accommodated at the Strand Quay in the town of Rye. All berths dry out onto soft mud. The Strand Quay berths consist of timber fendering on solid walls, with access ladders every 15m or so.

Tariff An 8–10m yacht pays a flat fee of £10.

Showers and toilet facilities are at the Strand Quay and are accessed by code. Facilities at the HM office are for emergency use only. **Launderette** can be found in The Rope Walk Shopping Centre in Rye.

Electricity and **FW** are supplied with each berth and are included within the berthing fees.

Fuel at Strand Quay in cans from nearby garage.

YCs Rye Harbour Sailing Club welcome visitors to the clubhouse, which is on the opposite side of the river to the Admiralty Jetty, adjacent to the lifeboat station.

Chandlery & repairs Sea Cruisers ☎ 222070, CH; Chippendale Craft ☎ 227707, BY; HJ Phillips ☎ 223234, BY; Rye Harbour Marine ☎ 227667, BY; Versatility Workboats ☎ 224422, BY; Sussex Fishing Services ☎ 223895, Ⓔ.

FACILITIES

HM New Lydd Road, Camber, East Sussex, TN31 7QS. ☎ 225225; ▨ 227429;

Berthing You will be given full berthing instructions

FOLKESTONE

Folkestone Harbour entrance – 51°04'·56N 01°11'·78E

Folkestone is a drying harbour which is full of local craft and fishing boats and is really only accessible to yachts that can take the ground. This, combined with the fact that there are at present no proper facilities for visitors, discourages yachts from staying for any reason other than an emergency and makes it lowdown on the list of desirable stopovers for the cruising yachtsman.

NAVIGATION

Charts AC SC 5605.7 (1:75,000 with an inset of Folkestone 1:6,000); 1991 (1:75,000 with an inset of Folkestone 1:5,000); 1892 (1:75,000).

Approaches If coming from the NE, look out for the Copt Rocks and Mole Head Rks which should be given a good offing, particularly the former due to the extended sewer outfall pipe. Coming from the SW, keep the R can buoy at position 51°04'·16N 01°10'·00E to port to avoid the cluster of rocks to the W of the breakwater. The Hythe Firing Range may be in use, in which case red flags or red lights will be displayed.

Landmarks A hotel block on the W end of the inner harbour is conspic, particularly from the E. The outer bkwtr, with its latticed traffic signal mast and lighthouse (Fl (2) 10s 14m 22M), is easy to spot.

Pilotage From the WPT 51°04'·50N 01°12'·00E a course of 305° keeps you clear of the outer breakwater and old ferry terminal to port as well as the Mole Head Rocks to stbd, bringing you to the entrance between the S Quay and the E pier (its outer end lit with a QG lt). The distance to run from the WPT is about 0.5M. The water shoals towards the entrance of the Inner Hbr

which dries completely at LW. A tide gauge at the head of the E pier indicates how much depth you have beneath you. Plans are being considered to lay a buoy to mark the S edge of the Mole Head Rocks to help navigation into the hbr.

Access is HW±2 for yachts with a 1.5m draught. The northern end of the harbour is the most shallow part, drying to $\underline{3}$.7m in places.

Shelter Does not provide good shelter in rough weather. In strong E to S winds seas break at the hbr entrance.

IPTS Signals on the latticed mast at the seaward end of the outer bkwtr. Ferries no longer operate here, but cargo ships come in about once a week.

Tides HW sp are 20 mins before and HW nps 5 mins before HW Dover. LW sp and nps are 10 mins before LW Dover. MHWS is 7·2m, MLWS 0·7m; MHWN is 5·7m; MLWN 2·1m.

Tidal streams The tide runs ENE 2 hrs before HW Dover, reaching up to 3kn. It sets WSW between $3\frac{1}{2}$ and 4 hrs after HW Dover.

VHF *Folkestone Port Control* Ch 15, 16.

FACILITIES

HM Folkestone Properties Ltd, Folkestone Hbr, Folkestone, Kent, CT21 QH. ☎ (01303) 715354.

Berthing/anchoring The Folkestone Yacht and Motorboat Club, ☎ (01303) 251574, may be able to provide a fore and aft mooring if one of its members is away. Anchoring in the Inner Hbr is frowned upon and should only be done in an emergency.

The harbour dries completely and is therefore only suitable for bilge keelers or motor boats.

Tariff The YC does not charge ⚓s, but you may be asked to pay a small amount by the hbr authorities.

Facilities are extremely limited. Water is available from the slipway, although to access the tap you have to get a key from the fishermen. Diesel can be had from the N edge of the hbr, but you need to call the telephone number displayed there to get assistance. The Yacht Club has showers and a bar that opens on Tues, Wed and Fri evenings, although no bar food is served.

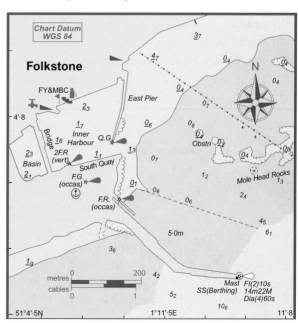

DOVER

Western Harbour entrance – 51°06'·74N 01°19'·73E
Eastern Harbour entrance – 51°07'·25N 01°20'·61E

Nestling under the famous White Cliffs, Dover sits between South Foreland to the NE and Folkestone to the SW. Boasting a maritime history stretching back as far as the Bronze Age, Dover is today one of Britain's busiest commercial ports, with a continuous stream of ferries and cruise liners

plying to and from their European destinations. However, over the past years the harbour has made itself more attractive to the cruising yachtsman, offering well sheltered tidal and non-tidal berths.

SHORESIDE (Telephone code 01304)

Tourist Office The Old Town Gaol, Biggin St, Dover. ☎ 205108; 🖷 245409; tic@doveruk.com; www.whitecliffscountry.org.uk

What to see/do Overlooking the town is Dover Castle, ☎ 211067, which played a significant role in history from the 12th century right up until WWII. Open 29 March–30 Sept 1000–1800 daily; Oct 1000–1700 daily; 1 Nov–31 Mar 1000–1600 daily. Visit the Dover Bronze Age Boat contained within the Dover Museum in Market Square, ☎ 201066. Open daily (except 24, 25 Dec and 1 Jan) 1000–1800 May to 1 Sept; 1000–1730 Sept–Apr. Close to the Wellington Dock in Snargate St is the Grand Shaft, (☎ 201066; open July–Aug 1400–1700, Tues–Sun) a unique spiral stone staircase built

in 1806 for troop movements between the town and the Western Heights above. Here, if not out of breath, you can do one of the walks around the local nature reserve.

Rail Dover Priory Station near the centre of the town, is about a 20 mins walk from the marina, from where there are direct services to London (1 hr 30 mins). National Rail Enquiries ☎ 08457 482950. You can also catch the Eurostar from Ashford to Lille, Paris and Brussels, ☎ 08705 186186, as well as trains from Folkestone to Calais, ☎ 08705 353535, although the latter doesn't cater for foot passengers so is only suitable if you have hired a car.

Buses Stagecoach runs buses between Canterbury, Folkestone, Eastbourne and Dover. ☎ 240024/08702 433711. National Express puts on coaches between Dover and London (£10.50 day return) and runs direct services to Ashford. ☎ 08705 808080.

Taxi Central ☎ 204040/240441; Star Taxis ☎ 201010, 228822; Victory Cars ☎ 227777.

Car hire Avis Rent A Car ☎ 206265; Hertz Rent A Car ☎ 207303; National Car Rental ☎ 201421.

Bike hire None in Dover, but Arc Cycles in Deal, ☎ 360680, will deliver hire bikes to you.

Ferries run regularly between Dover and Calais. Contact P&O ☎ 08705 980980; Seafrance ☎ 08705 711711. Hoverspeed also offers fast services between Dover and Calais on its seacats, ☎ 08705 240241.

Beaches A shingle beach between the Eastern Docks and the Hoverport is safe for swimming.

Supermarkets The closest is Kwik Save in Castle St, open Mon–Sat

Dover's beach and elegant parade overlooked by the castle

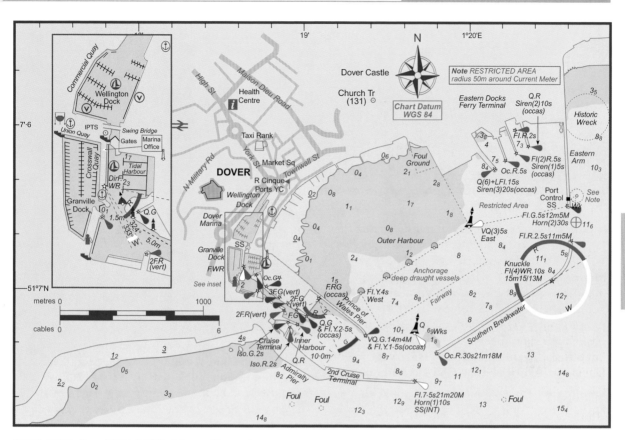

0800–2000, Sun 1000–1600. Also a Co-op in Charlton Green, a little further away, open Mon–Sat 0700–2300, Sun 1000–1600. A free bus runs from the Marine Parade to Tesco in Whitfield (about two miles from the town centre) every Tues & Fri at 0955. For basic provisions, the Shell Garage next to the marina, on Limekiln St, is open 24 hrs a day and has a cash dispenser.

Market day Dover Indoor Market in Pencester Rd. Open Mon–Sat 0900–1700.

Banks All the major high street banks and building societies, with cashpoints, are in the pedestrianised precinct near the Market Square.

Restaurants Dover is well served by restaurants, ranging from Traditional English and European through to Oriental. Most of the local pubs also provide good bar food as well as a wide selection of ales. Cullins Yard Bistro, ☎ 211666, overlooking the Wellington Dock, specialises in local seafood. Prices are around £15, although the excellent weekend brunch costs £8. Also good for seafood is Blakes of Dover in Castle St, ☎ 202194. The closest Indian Restaurants to the marina are Light of India in Townwall St, ☎ 210666, and Curry Garden in High St, ☎ 206357. Three Chinese restaurants are in the High St, one of which is Moonflower, ☎ 212198.

NAVIGATION

Charts AC SC 5605.8 (1:37,500 with an inset of Dover 1:12,500), 1698 (1:6,250), 1828 (1:37,500), 1892 (1:75,000).

Approaches Coming from the E or W observe the traffic separation zones. Dover Port Control supervises all movements in and out of the hbr. Small craft are advised to call the Port Control on VHF Ch 74 about 2M off to receive instructions for entering, although you will not be granted permission to enter the Outer Harbour until you are within 200m of either entrance. You must comply with any directions from the Port Control or the hbr patrol launch. If you have no VHF, you

The eastern entrance

Approaching the western entrance

should stay clear of the entrance and attract the Port Control's attention (from the E entrance) with five short lamp flashes or telephone the marina office on ☎ 241663. If no contact can be made, keep a safe distance off the E arm (do not use the W entrance) and wait for the hbr patrol launch to escort you in. Yachts on passage past Dover should keep at least 1M off the breakwaters. While navigating within the vicinity, keep a listening watch on Ch 74 at all times.

Landmarks The long breakwaters make the harbour easy to identify. Overlooking the hbr is the conspic Dover Castle.

Pilotage The WPT for the western entrance is 51°06'·74N 01°19'·73E. The WPT for the eastern entrance is 51°07'·25N 01°20'·61E. Yachts may use either entrance but should keep a sharp lookout for the entry signals (see under IPTS below). When negotiating either entrance, keep well out of the way of commercial shipping and ferries.

Beware of the lumpy seas/overfalls outside the bkwtrs and note that in strong SW'ly winds, a steep swell can occur off the western entrance. In this situation, you should be extremely cautious, particularly on HWS. Tides run strongly across both entrances, so entering under engine is strongly recommended.

Once through the eastern entrance, identified at night by a port (Fl R 2.5s 11m 5M) and stbd (Fl G 5s 12m 5M) hand light, follow the fairway to the inner hbr, taking care not to venture between the NCM (Q) and the southern bkwtr. Through the western entrance, marked to port by a Fl 7.5s lt and to stbd by an Oc R 30s lt, the dredged channel lies directly ahead. Follow the dredged channel, keeping the green posts to stbd at all times. In the final approach, especially at LW, stay in the deep water until the ldg lt

Granville Dock and the marina approach

Wellington Dock

Granville Dock

Tidal Hbr

The final approach to the marina where contact on VHF Ch 80 should be made

(FW 324°–333°), situated towards the SW end of the reception pontoon, has opened up. The reception pontoon is to port alongside the Lifeboat Station and care must be taken when approaching it at tidal heights below 2m.

Departure from the hbr If leaving the marina, inform the marina office staff who will contact the hbr patrol launch and Port Control to obtain clearance for you.

Shelter Very good in the marina.

Tides Dover is a standard port. MHWS is 6·8m, MLWS 0·8m; MHWN is 5·3m, MLWN 2·1m.

Tidal streams The stream flows N to S except from HW–1 to HW+3. See *RNA* for tidal stream charts.

IPTS Traffic signals operate day and night on light panels near the Port Control at the eastern entrance (on the stbd side) and on the seaward end of the Admiralty Pier at the western entrance. Three R (vert) lts mean do not proceed; GWG (vert) indicate that you may proceed.

VHF *Dover Port Control* Ch **74**, 12, 16; *Hbr launch* Ch 74; *Dover Marina* Ch 80, (NB Should only be contacted once inside the Tidal Hbr/ marina.; *Dover Coastguard* Ch **69**, 16, 80, gives TSS surveillance.

FACILITIES

HM The Port of Dover, Harbour House, Marine Parade, Dover, CT17 9BU. ☎ 240400 Ext 4520; ✉ 225144; pr@doverport.co.uk; www.doverport.co.uk. Dover Port Control ☎ 240400 Ext 5530.

Berthing Inside the entrance to the hbr, continue to keep a listening watch on Ch 74 and inform the Port Control that you are making for the marina. Once past the S pier contact *Dover Marina* on VHF

Ch 80 for berthing instructions or go alongside the reception pontoon and report to the Marine Office. Note that you should only ever contact the marina from within the tidal harbour and marina.

Dover Marina ☎ 241663; ✉ 242549; pr@doverport.co.uk Set well away from the busy ferry terminal, the marina is well sheltered and offers three berthing options:
 a) Tidal Hbr, E of the waiting pontoon (to a depth of 2.5m); access H24. **Tariff** £1.90 per metre per day.
 b) Granville Dock, opposite the tidal harbour; access via a gate approx HW±4. **Tariff** £1.65 per metre per day.
 c) Wellington Dock, via dock gates and swing bridge, access HW±2 at nps and approx HW-1½ to HW+2½ at sp. An ideal option if you want to leave your boat for a period of time. **Tariff** £1.40 per metre per day. N.B all tariffs above include electricity and water. Berths without electricity cost £1.20 per metre per day.

Electricity and **FW** are provided on most pontoons throughout the three areas of the marina.

Showers and toilets are accessible 24 hrs per day. Situated on the E and W side of Wellington Dock as well as the Granville Dock and Tidal Hbr.

Launderette Two on site, one next to the clock tower to the E of the Tidal Hbr, the other next to the shower block on the W side of Wellington Dock.

Fuel Available 24 hrs a day from the fuel berth in the Tidal Hbr.

Chandlery & repairs Sharp & Enright chandlers, ☎ 206295, in Snargate St, (running parallel to Wellington Dock) sells **gas**. The marina has a BH (50 tons) in the Granville Dock area. The Dover Yacht Co, ☎ 201073, offers comprehensive repair facilities including engineering and electronics.

YCs The Royal Cinque Ports YC, ☎ 206262, is on Waterloo Crescent, overlooking the Outer Hbr. Welcomes visitors to its bar and restaurant. Also offers shower facilities and a games room. The White Cliffs Motor Boat and Yacht Club is based at Cullins Yard Bistro, ☎ 211666, where club night is on a Wednesday.

Anchorage Although not encouraged due to the heavy shipping, you can anchor in the Outer Harbour for a few hours free of charge. However this anchorage is exposed to winds from the NE through to the S and SW. Landing on the Prince of Wales Pier is not permitted so you will have to take your dinghy into the beach.

SANDWICH

River Stour entrance waypoint – 51°19'·00N 01°24'·00E

Situated some five miles up the winding River Stour is the ancient town of Sandwich, a Saxon name meaning 'sandy place' or 'a place on sand'. Once a leading Cinque Port, it boasts some of the best preserved mediaeval architecture in Britain and is well worth a visit.

However, despite the fact that the River Stour is Kent's second longest river, it is very shallow, therefore making a trip to Sandwich only suitable for those with shoal draught yachts that can take the ground.

SHORESIDE (Telephone code 01304)

Tourist Office Sandwich Tourist Information Centre, The Guildhall, Sandwich; ☎ 613565; only open April–Oct. Dover Tourist Information Centre, The Old Town Gaol, Biggin St, Dover; ☎ 205108.

What to see/do Guildhall Museum ; ☎ 617197. The River Bus runs daily from the Quay by the Old Toll Bridge to the Richborough Roman Fort. Open 29 March–30 Sept 1000–1800; ☎ 612013.

Rail Connections to Ramsgate and Dover. National Rail Enquiries ☎ 0845 748 4950.

Bus Services are run by Stagecoach ☎ 240024.

Taxi Sandwich Cars ☎ 617424

Supermarkets A Co-op in Moat Sole, behind the Guildhall, is only a 10 mins walk from The Quay.

Banks Several around Cattle Market and Market St.

Restaurants Fisherman's Wharf on the Quay; ☎ 613636. Or try the Quay Side Bar & Brasserie in Bell Lane; ☎ 619899.

NAVIGATION

Charts AC 1827 (1:12,500); SC 1828 (1:37,500).

Approaches The approach waypoint to the River Stour is 51°19'·00N 01°25'·00E, lying just over 0.5M SW of Ramsgate hbr entrance and 0.25M W of the West Quern WCM (Q (9) 15s).

Landmarks The three cooling towers and tall chimney inland of Pegwell Bay are conspic.

Pilotage From the above WPT steer due W until you reach WPT 51°19'·00N 01°24'·00E. From here shape a course of approx 260°, passing close to the RW safe water buoy (April–Sept), until you come to the first unlit port and stbd buoy. From this point on the fairway across Pegwell Bay is marked by port and stbd buoys and beacons which are laid down each season and are moved regularly due to the shifting channel. At the mouth of the River Stour you will come to a scaffold tower (no longer lit), opposite which is a stbd post with a green lattice top mark. From here on in the river is marked by posts and has depths of between 0.5m and 1m LAT (between 2m and 3m at HW). For the best water stay in the centre of the channel as far as Richborough New Wharf, thereafter favouring the W bank. Without local knowledge a visiting yachtsman should only attempt to navigate the River Stour on a rising tide and certainly never at night. It takes approx 30–45 mins to reach the Quay from the river mouth. Just beyond Sandwich's Town Quay is a swing bridge that is manned 24 hrs a day. To open, call ☎ 01304 620644, giving an hour's notice. When closed it has a clearance of 1.7m.

Access Draughts of 1.5m should only attempt to navigate to Sandwich at HW±1 at springs. Visiting yachtsmen should aim to arrive off the entrance at HW Dover +15 mins. With HW at Sandwich 45 mins after HW at the bar, it ensures you come up on a rising tide, while having max depth of water when crossing the bar.

Shelter Entrance exposed in strong E to SE winds.

Tides HW sp and nps at Richborough are 15 mins after HW Dover. LW sp and nps at Richborough are 30 mins after LW Dover. MHWS is 3·4m; MLWS 0·1m; MHWN is 2·7m; MLWN 0·1m.

The tricky entrance to the River Stour

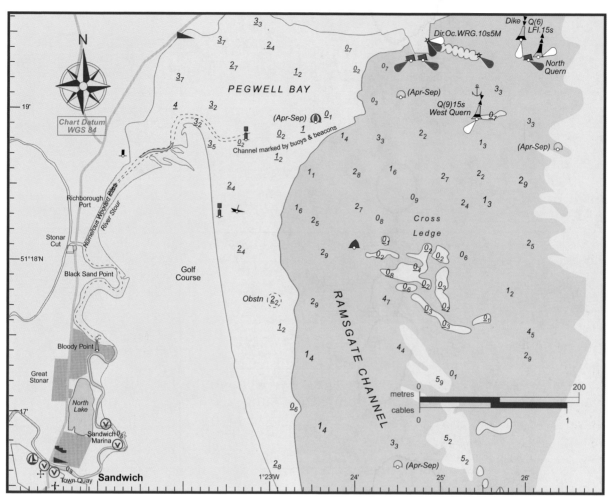

Tidal streams The flood is much stronger than the ebb, rising approx 5.5m in just 1½ hrs.

FACILITIES

HM Sandwich Port & Haven Commissioners, c/o Guildhall, Castle Market, Sandwich, Kent, CT13 9AH; ☎ 617197/612162.

Berthing from seaward:

1) Sandwich Sailing and Motor Club can normally accommodate visitors on one of its pontoon berths for shoal draught yachts. Although the outside berths do not dry out at LW, they are not deep enough to keep a 1.5m draught afloat. Contact the club's treasurer, Alan Humphrey, on ☎ 01843 585711. Tariff on application. No facilities at present except for electricity.

2) Sandwich Marina is undergoing an extensive development programme and will not reopen until the start of the season in 2004. For more details contact the Marina Manager on ☎07974 754558. With deep water berths, the marina's facilities will include water, electricity, fuel and showers.

3) The Town Quay has an area designated to

visitors at its far end towards the swing bridge. The berths do not dry out at LW and can accommodate draughts up to 1.5m. When mooring up, it is best to lie with the bow of the boat down river. However manoeuvring near the swing bridge can cause problems, so it is advisable to slow right down when alongside the quay, swing to stbd putting your bow into the reeds and then stem the tide with your engine until you have picked a mooring place along the quay (90m in length). For berthing availability contact the quaymaster ahead of time, ☎ 614967. Tariff is £6.50 per night. Facilities comprise water and toilets.

4) Highway Marine ☎ 613925. Situated upstream of the Swing Bridge on the port hand side. Has plenty of pontoon and finger berth moorings which dry at LW±2. Tariff is £4 per metre per week. Daily rates on application. Facilities include cranage, hard standing, full repair and maintenance services, electricity and FW on the pontoons, as well as gas from the on site chandlery. There is currently no fuel pump on the River Stour, the nearest being at Ramsgate.

RAMSGATE

Ramsgate Harbour entrance – 51°19'·49N 01°25'·47E

Steeped in maritime history, Ramsgate was originally constructed to provide a safe haven for vessels on passage between the English Channel and the North Sea. The harbour was awarded 'Royal' status in 1821 by George IV in recognition of the warm welcome he received when sailing from Ramsgate to Hanover with the

Royal Squadron. Also one of the main embarkation ports during the Napoleonic Wars, it was to Ramsgate that thousands of soldiers were brought after the rescue of the British Expeditionary and allied forces in Dunkerque in 1940. In recent years the harbour has upgraded its facilities for yachtsmen and is now more than just a convenient stopover between the east and south coast. Offering good shelter, it can be accessed in all conditions except for strong E'ly winds.

SHORESIDE (Telephone code 01843)

Tourist Office 17, Albert Court, York St, Ramsgate, CT11 9DN. ☎ 583333/583334; 585353; tourism@thanet.gov.uk; www.tourism.thanet.gov.uk

What to see/do Ramsgate Maritime Museum, ☎ 570622, is housed in a 19th century Clock House on Pier Yard and depicts the maritime heritage of the East Kent area. Open Easter to end of Sept, Tues–Sun 1000–1700. Closed on Mon; in winter phone for opening times. Ramsgate Motor Museum, ☎ 581948, in the Paragon, exhibits 10 cars from every decade starting from the year 1900. Open daily from Easter to end of Sept 1015–1730. Nearby on West Cliff Promenade is the famous Model Village, ☎ 850043, reproducing some of England's most charming villages. A few

miles W of Ramsgate, the Sandwich & Pegwell Bay National Nature Reserve lies at the mouth of the River Stour. Open all year except 25 Dec from 0830–2000 or dusk, whichever is earlier; admission free. On the cliff top at Pegwell Bay visit a replica of the Viking ship which sailed from Denmark to Thanet in 1949 to celebrate the 1,500th anniversary of the invasion of Britain. For plenty of other places of interest in the area contact the Tourist Office.

Rail Direct train services to London (1 hr 45 mins) and Dover. Via London for trains to

The Ramsgate Maritime Museum

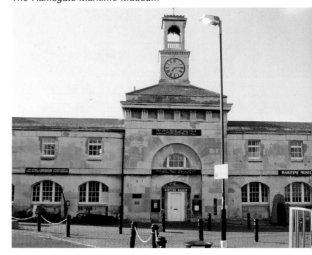

Brighton and Portsmouth. Via Ashford and Hastings for Eastbourne. National Rail Enquiries ☎ 0845 748 4950.

Bus Good bus connections to and from Ramsgate. Operators in the area are: Eastonways ☎ 588033; Stagecoach Kent ☎ 01903 237661.

Taxi Star Cars ☎ 581581; Smiley Radio Cars ☎ 603603.

Car hire Haine Road Car Hire ☎ 570532; Compass Car Hire ☎ 582324.

Bike hire None in Ramsgate; the closest is Ken's Bikeshop in Margate, ☎ 221422.

Beaches Ramsgate Main Sands is a popular beach in summer, with sunloungers for hire, donkey rides and beach cafés. Further NE is the quieter Louisa Bay, although even this has a café and chalets for hire.

Supermarkets Just behind the harbour is Waitrose in Queen St and Iceland in King's St.

Market day Held every Fri and Sat in the High St.

Banks Several major banks and building societies, with cashpoints, are in either High St or Queen St.

Restaurants The Continental Restaurant, ☎ 585795, on the Harbour Parade is good for inexpensive meals ranging from fish and chips to chicken curry; £5. The Royal Temple Yacht Club offers excellent lunch and evening bar meals (see under YCs). Just below the club are a selection of French, Greek, Thai and Indian restaurants, all conveniently close to one another. For breakfast go to the Albion Café in Kent

Place, ☎ 588412. Opening from 0700, it is not far from the Main Sands beach and is well worth the 15 mins walk from the marina.

NAVIGATION

Charts AC 1827 (1:5,000); SC 5605.9 (1:37,500 with an inset of Ramsgate 1:7,500); 5606.3 (1:50,000 with approaches to Ramsgate 1:37,500); 1828 (1:37,500 with an inset of Ramsgate 1:5,000); 323 (1:75,000).

Approaches Small craft must use the recommended Yacht Track which runs directly S of the Main E–W Channel dredged to 7.5m. From the S beware of Quern Bank, close to the channel, and Cross Ledge and Brake shoals further S. From the N look out for Dike Bank. Coming from the S through the well-buoyed Gull

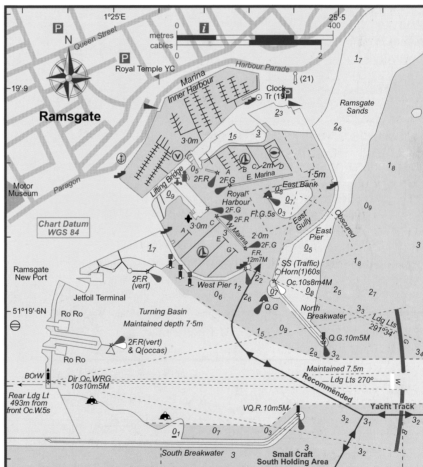

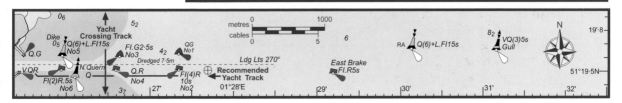

Stream or from the N past North Foreland, the WPT 51°19'·00N 01°28'·00E puts you in the Yacht Track about 1.5M from the harbour entrance. In favourable conditions a short cut can be made from the Gull Stream through the Old Cudd Channel from a WPT 51°19'·00N 01°28'·00E, which is 0.5M S of the Yacht Track on a bearing of 291.5°, leaving N Quern NCM to port. From the N, enter the Yacht Track by crossing the Main Channel at right angles between the No 3 Fl G 2.5s SHM and the No 4 Q R PHM.

Conspic marks The Main Channel is clearly marked with buoys. The breakwaters and Main Channel's leading marks/lights also make the harbour easy to identify. By day the ldg marks are: Front black △ triangle with white stripe; Rear black and white ▽. By night: Front Dir Oc WRG 10s 10m 5M; Rear Oc 5s 17m 5M (about 490m behind front lt).

Pilotage From the WPT 51°19'·45N 01°28'·00E follow the Yacht Track on a course of 270°, keeping the port buoys close to stbd, into the outer harbour. Approx 200m from the S breakwater (VQR 10m 5M) alter course for the entrance, passing the N breakwater (QG 10m 5M) well to stbd to avoid the changing shoal water.

Note that permission to enter or leave the Royal Harbour must be obtained from Ramsgate Port Control on VHF Ch 14. Also look out for the IPTS on the E Pier (see opposite) controlling traffic in and out of the hbr. Small craft should be aware of large vessels manoeuvring and keep well clear. If required to wait for entry, there are holding grounds S of the S breakwater and to the N of the No 3 SHM. All yachts are obliged to enter and leave the harbour under power and the speed limit of 5kn must be observed.

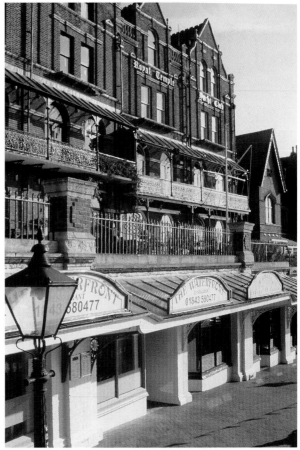

The Royal Temple Yacht Club overlooks the harbour

Once between the breakwaters, sweep round to stbd into the Royal Harbour entrance where the best water is close to the West Pier (FR 12m 7M). Take care to avoid the East Bank once in the Royal Hbr, although it presents no real problem as the channel is well buoyed.

IPTS At E pier, visible from seaward as well as from the Royal Hbr. These signals control the approach in the hbr limits (abeam Nos 1 & 2

When approaching the entrance, keep to the recommended Yacht Track

The sweep round to starboard into the Royal Harbour

buoys) and the entry/exit to or from the Royal Hbr. Three R lts (vert) mean do not enter the approach channel or enter or leave the hbr. Three G lts (vert) mean you are free to enter the approach channel or leave the hbr. In addition a Fl orange lt indicates that a ferry is underway and therefore no vessel may enter the approach channel or leave the Royal Hbr.

Access into the hbr is H24 depending on shipping movement. The Royal Hbr comprises three marinas: The inner marina, with a depth of 3m, can be accessed approx HW±2 via a flap gate and lifting bridge; the W marina in 3m of water has access H24; the E marina, in 2m, has access H24.

Shelter Good, although entry is not advisable in E'ly gales.

Tides HW sp and HW nps are 30 mins after HW Dover. LW nps are 17 mins and LW sp are 7 mins after LW Dover. MHWS is 5·2m, MLWS 0·6m; MHWN is 4·0m, MLWN 1·4m.

Tidal streams The tide sets across the entrance in a NE'ly and SW'ly direction, with the NE'ly going tide running about HW–1$\frac{1}{4}$ to HW+4.

VHF *Ramsgate Port Control* Ch 14; *Ramsgate Marina* Ch 80; Ramsgate Dock Office can be contacted on Ch 14 for information on the Inner marina lock.

FACILITIES

HM, Harbour Office, Military Rd, Ramsgate, Kent, CT11 9LQ. ☎ 572100; 🖷 590941; marina@ramsgatemarina.co.uk; www.ramsgatemarina.co.uk

Berthing Contact the marina staff on VHF Ch 80 or ☎ 572100 (as for HM) once inside the

Royal Hbr for berthing availability. They will probably allocate you a berth in either the E or W marinas, which accommodate visitors staying for a short period of time. The gate to the inner marina is open for approx HW±2. By day a R and Y flag, and by night a single G lt, indicate that the gate is open.

Tariff £1.70 per metre per day in season; £1.45 per metre per day off season. A short stay of up to 4 hrs is 50% of the daily rate.

Showers, toilets and **launderette** (coin-operated) are all accessed by code.

Electricity (included in the tariff) and **FW** on the pontoons.

Fuel barge below the Dockmaster's Office is to the E of the boat hoist. It opens from 0800–2000 on a daily basis, but contact the marina staff on VHF Ch 80 ahead of time.

Chandlery & repairs The Bosun's Locker, ☎ 597158, located in Military Rd next to the inner marina, is well stocked and sells gas. Other services include slipways, 40-ton travel hoist and full boat repairs. Davies Marine Services ☎ 586172, BY (offers comprehensive boat services including rigging and engineering); Marlec Marine ☎ 592176, ME.

Anchorage ⚓ in Ramsgate Roads N of the Quern Bank.

YCs The Royal Temple YC, ☎ 591766, sits at the top of Jacob's Ladder, the long flight of steps linking the West Pier to the top of the cliff. With an impressive bar and terrace, it serves excellent lunchtime and evening meals. Visiting yachtsmen are welcome to use all facilities.

Looking out over the inner marina with flap gate directly ahead

CHAPTER 4

NORD-PAS-DE-CALAIS, PICARDY & NORMANDY
DUNKERQUE TO CAP DE LA HÈVE

CONTENTS

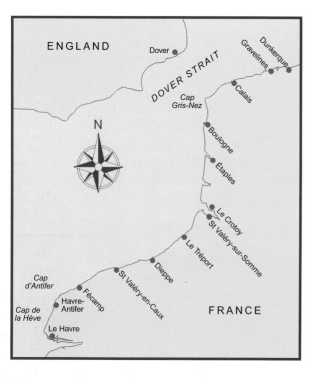

INTRODUCTION

Dunkerque's East Port has character and interest, but the huge industrial sprawl of Dunkerque offers only a dreary progression of iron, steel, coal, gas, cement and petro-chemical works. Happily between here and Calais lies the delightful town of Gravelines fortified by Vauban. This is all part of the Département of Nord-Pas-de-Calais which includes the old provinces of Artois and Flanders. It is also the Opal coast, since this amorphous quartz-like form of hydrated silica abounds.

Just beyond Calais and the Channel Tunnel the land climbs steeply to the impressive Cap Blanc-Nez, rising vertically from the shoals below and crowned by the Dover Patrol monument of WWI. To starboard the narrow waters of the Dover Strait command our attention. Having rounded the well-known but scenically undistinguished Cap Gris-Nez the yacht can at last bear away off the prevailing westerlies.

The coast southwards to Boulogne and Cap

Port d'Antifer (VLCCs only) looking NE

d'Alprech is punctuated by short stretches of low cliffs and the undulating hills of the inland plateau. These gradually give way to the seemingly endless sand dunes which characterise Picardy's short (20M), low-lying coastline. The R Canche meets the sea at Le Touquet and nearby Étaples.

At Berk-Plage the little-known R Authie (do not attempt) flows seaward. The much wider Baie de la Somme, 7M further south, is memorable for the long buoyed channel to St Valéry-sur-Somme. The sand dunes end at Ault and from Le Tréport the limestone cliffs march west almost without interruption to Cap de la Hève, forming the great ramparts of the Seine Maritime and Normandy's Alabaster coast.

Alabaster, lest you ask, is a translucent, usually white form of gypsum, which loosely describes the appearance of the flat-topped cliffs. At Étretat, close NNE of Cap d'Antifer lighthouse, the cliffs have eroded over hundreds of years into spectacular arches. The famous Aiguille, rising a sheer 70m from the water, was originally part of the coastline. The beaches are generally pebbly, where flint has fallen from the cliffs and been rounded and smoothed by the sea's action. The water is supposedly milky white, but only noticeably so at St Valéry-en-Caux.

PASSAGE NOTES

DUNKERQUE TO CAP GRIS-NEZ

Leave Dunkerque's East Port and the Roads via the Intermediate channel (linking East and West Dunkerque) to pass abeam Dunkerque West at DKB. At this point, if Gravelines is your next port of call, steer SW for the breakwaters. Otherwise continue west, paralleling south of the Deep Water channel until nearing DW 5/6 buoys.

DISTANCE TABLE

Approximate distances in nautical miles are by the most direct route, whilst avoiding dangers

1.	Dunkerque	**1**							
2.	Calais	22	**2**						
3	Boulogne	42	20	**3**					
4.	St Valéry-sur-Somme	69	50	30	**4**				
5.	Le Tréport	69	50	30	19	**5**			
6.	Dieppe	96	74	54	35	14	**6**		
7.	St Valéry-en-Caux	103	81	61	45	28	16	**7**	
8.	Fécamp	118	96	76	62	44	29	15	**8**
9.	Le Havre	143	121	101	85	73	54	38	25	**9**

Here decide whether to route seaward of the Ridens de Calais via RCE and CA2 buoys; or, if bound for Calais, whether to take the shallow short cut inshore of the Ridens de la Rade, height of tide permitting. Chances are the west-going ebb may have expired such that it is nearing LW at Calais, in which case go round Ridens de Calais and approach the harbour via CA4, 6 and 8 buoys. Stay outside the buoyed channel.

Fast ferries approach Calais via the 3M wide gap between CA3 and CA4 buoys, thence rounding CA6 buoy and into a narrowing funnel to the port entrance. A gimlet-eyed lookout is essential and a call to Calais Port on Ch 12 with your position and intentions keeps everyone in the picture.

From CA3 buoy set course to Cap Gris-Nez, either direct or via the Abbeville west cardinal if the inshore shoal waters look rough.

CAP GRIS-NEZ TO THE SOMME

Off Cap Gris-Nez ships in the NE-bound lane of the Dover Strait TSS pass only 3M offshore and the ITZ begins. So too does the Bassure de Baas, a long thin bank with least depths of 4.9m, which extends south as far as Berk-Plage, although there

are gaps in it abeam Boulogne and Cap d'Alprech. It lies between 1.5 and 5M offshore. Further to seaward the Vergoyer bank (4.2m) is on the edge of the TSS and inside the ITZ. In the prevailing westerlies the whole coast becomes a hostile lee shore and yachts on passage should stay seaward of the Bassure de Baas.

The R Canche is not difficult to enter near HW, but the marina at Etaples very nearly dries.

Off the Somme estuary find the ATSO NCM buoy which is moved infrequently and to a minor degree; in contrast the buoys marking the volatile channel are often moved. Enjoy the Somme, St Valéry-sur-Somme is very good news and well worth the effort.

THE SOMME TO CAP DE LA HÈVE

Along this coast Le Tréport, Dieppe, St Valéry-en-Caux and Fécamp, each 15M from the next, all have good facilities for yachts, but only Dieppe is an all-weather port of refuge. Le Tréport and St Valéry-en-Caux are both tidally limited to access at HW±3; Fécamp's entrance is exposed to winds from W to N and shallow near LW.

Ault lighthouse will probably be seen 4M NE of Le Tréport. To the west stay at least 1M offshore to clear drying rocks which extend 4 cables seaward and a No Entry area, marked by two SPM light buoys, off St Martin nuclear power station (5M east of Dieppe).

Dieppe is easily seen and approached, but keep an eye out for ferries, Seacats and fishing vessels. Daffodils and Berneval are a pair of WCM wreck buoys, the latter unlit, 6 and 7M north of the port.

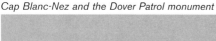
Cap Blanc-Nez and the Dover Patrol monument

L'Aiguille (needle) of Étretat

The DI ECM buoy marks another wreck 2.5M NW of Dieppe. The Roches d'Ailly NCM buoy, 3M further west, identifies a 1.2m wreck; most yachts pass north of it. The 5 cables wide gap south of the wreck and north of the rocks can be negotiated, but little mileage is saved by so doing.

St Valéry-en-Caux is very much a crack in the cliffs, first identified by the light tower on the W breakwater; stand on until aligned with the access channel. Palue NCM buoy, 3M to the west, marks a No Entry area off the nuclear power station at Conteville; keep north of it. Thereafter, en route to Fécamp it is safe to sail at least 5 cables offshore to enjoy the cliff scenery.

Fécamp is readily identified by the vertical cliff face of Pte Fagnet, north of the harbour entrance. When approaching/leaving from/to the east, stay well clear of the offlying Les Charpentiers rocks which dry. To the west resume 5 cables offshore until reaching Étretat with its spectacular cliffs.

Le Havre-Antifer, 1M south of Cap d'Antifer, is a vast oil terminal for 500,000 ton VLCCs which are too large to enter Le Havre. Yachts should cross the access channel at buoys A21/22 which are 1.7M NW of the breakwater and 3M offshore. If bound for Le Havre (page 286), it is then safe to close the coast at Cap de la Hève.

Cap d'Antifer lighthouse

Chapter 4

DUNKERQUE EST

Harbour entrance – 51°03´·70N 02°21´·18E

Dunkerque seems to have a little more style and sense of history than Calais, Boulogne, Le Havre and Cherbourg; its ruins were more interestingly re-constructed; the older parts were more sympathetically preserved; the nautical traditions seem stronger. All this may appear ill-defined, but it should give a flavour of how one man sees Dunkerque, the Church on the Dunes.

SHORESIDE

Tourist Office is in the town centre behind the Belfry Tower of St Eloi church which has recently undergone a face-lift. ☎ 03 28 66 79 21; 📠 03 28 63 38 34. Open Mon–Fri 0900–1230 & 1330–1830; Sat 0900–1830; Sun 1000–1200 & 1500–1700. dunkerque@tourisme.norsys.fr

What to see/do *Duchesse Anne* is a fine three-masted training ship berthed on the N side of the Bassin du Commerce; she is open to visitors. Behind her, on the quai de la Citadelle is the Musée Portuaire. The lighthouse has rather

limited opening hours: Sat 1500–1900 and Sun 1030–1230 & 1500–1900 from mid-Jun to mid-Sept.

Rail The station, ☎ 08 36 35 35 35, is SSW of the Arrière Port. Trains to Calais and Boulogne. TGV via Lens to Paris, Gare du Nord (1 hr 40 mins).

Buses See the Tourist Office for timetables.

Taxi ☎ 03 28 66 73 00.

Car & bike hire See the Tourist Office.

UK access Norfolk Line from Port West to Dover, details in the Introduction; plus the Chunnel.

Beaches The vast sandy beach and children's play areas at Malo-les-Bains are convenient if you happen to be berthed at Port du Grand Large.

Looking ENE to Malo-les-Bains. Port du Grand Large (left) and YCMN Marina (right)

Bassin du Commerce: Marina to starboard; Duchesse Anne beyond

Supermarkets Lidl (slightly downmarket) is at 9 rue du Leughenaer, just off Place du Minck and the nearest to Port du Grand Large. More up-market, but a good 15 mins walk is ATAC by the Marine Gate shopping centre off the Arrière Port.

Market day Large, open-air market in Place du Général de Gaulle, all day Wed and Sat. Fish of every shape and size can be bought straight off the boats or at La Halle at the Bassin de Pêche, off Place du Minck.

Banks Plenty around the city centre.

Restaurants Three restaurants on the quai de la Citadelle abeam *Duchesse Anne* are: L'Estouffade, ☎ 03 21 63 92 78, seafood at €24 & 42; shut Sun afternoon & Mon. Le Corsaire at No 6, ☎ 03 28 59 03 61, €15.75–36.75; shut Sun afternoon & Wed. La Croisette is altogether simpler and cheaper with one menu at €15.75.

From the Port du Grand Large a 15 mins walk to Malo-les-Bains offers numerous downmarket places on the seafront, or go back a block or two for the more traditional Au Rivage, 7 rue de Flandre, ☎ 03 21 63 19 62; very friendly patron and good menus at €14.70, 23 & 27.35. The more modern Entre Ciel et Mer does not have views of sea and sky, but of C19 seaside architecture *à la* red/yellow bricks; menus €9.45 (plat du jour)–25.

NAVIGATION

Charts AC 323 (1:75,000), 1873 (1:60,000), 1350 (1:25,000), plus SC 5605. SHOM 7424 (1:73,900), 7214 (1:60,000) and 7057 (1:20,000).

Approaches From the E, the East channel counts down from E12 (51°07'·90N 02°30'·78E) on the Franco-Belgian border) to E1 buoy, 1.3M ENE of the East Port. The first part, from E12 to E7, is the relatively shallow (3.8m) Passe de Zuydcoote.

From the W, the well-buoyed route starts at Dyck PHM buoy, Fl 3s, (formerly the Dunkerque Lanby), thence to DKA landfall buoy where the DW channel, marked by buoys DW5 to DW30, continues to Dunkerque Est.

For cross-Channel passages from ports between Rye and North Foreland see the Introduction.

Access H24. Fresh to strong onshore winds raise a heavy sea in the entrance.

Landmarks From the west, the sights and smells of Dunkerque's heavy industry warn that you are getting close. The big light-tower on the end of the W jetty is prominent (floodlit at night), but that on the E jetty is certainly not; indeed most of the E jetty covers at HW. It is punctuated by nine small beacons with orange sodium lights. In the centre of town the main lighthouse, white with black top, guides you past Trystram lock to the marinas.

Tides Dunkerque is a Standard Port; see the *RNA* for data. MHWS is 6·0m, MLWS 0·6m; MHWN is 5·0m, MLWN 1·5m.

Tidal streams set ENE across the entrance from HW–2 to +4, peaking at 2½kn at HW. If arriving from the east at local HW, take care not to get set onto the diminutive E Jetty head. Slack water is at HW+4. The WSW-going stream then makes, peaking at 1kn at HW+6.

VHF Dunkerque Port, locks, bridges and Bassin du Commerce: Ch 73 in English. Monitor Ch 73 during the approach to check traffic movements. In poor visibility advise Port Control of your position; they may give navigation assistance or traffic avoidance. Both tidal marinas Ch 09.

IPTS are shown from the light tower on the West jetty and must be heeded. They are visible from without and within the Avant Port. Storm signals may also be shown (*RNA* 9.15.7).

Pilotage The two waypoints, with bearing and distance to the W or E jetty heads, are:

1.   From the east, E2 PHM buoy 51°04′·38N 02°22′·40E, 224°/1.0M to E jetty head.
2.   From the west, DW29 SHM buoy at 51°03′·89N 02°20′·33E, 111°/0.5M to W jetty head.

A very special mark buoy

The nearest basins to the town centre
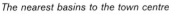

Leughenaer Tower

Fishing basin

Bassin du Commerce

Duchesse Anne

Cruise liner terminal

Bassin Freycinet

The 300m wide harbour entrance opens into the Avant Port, dredged 13.5m, from which big ships lock into the commercial docks via the de Gaulle or Watier locks; but most enter Dunkerque's West Port. Yachts however head SE parallel to the 0.8M long E jetty, with Dunkerque lighthouse fine on the stbd bow and the two marinas just beyond. At night use the 137.5° leading line, both lights Oc (2) 6s 7/10m 12M.

Marinas The Port du Grand Large and YCMN (YC Mer du Nord) are tidal, access H24. A non-tidal marina in the Bassin du Commerce is reached via Trystram lock and four bridges.

1. Port du Grand Large is the first marina to port just beyond the leading lights. Visitors berth/raft on the long E/W pontoon in 3m; local boats on pontoons 'A'–'F'. The **V** pontoon, even at the E

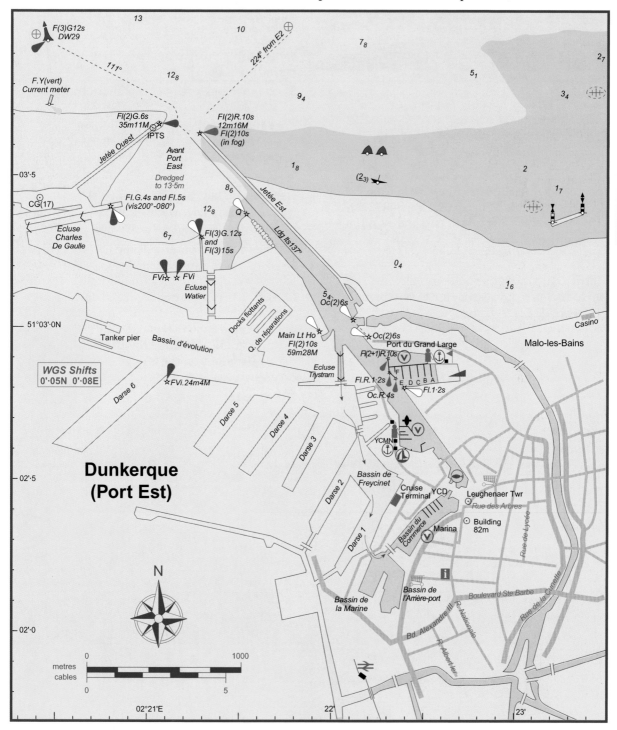

Dunkerque (Port Est)

Yacht Club de la Mer du Nord (YCMN)

end, can be very uncomfortable in a W'ly F6+. Adjacent pilot launches and FVs operate H24. 'Le Grand Large', a café/brasserie by the gangway offers convenient food/bar etc.

The Capitainerie is at the head of the **Ⓥ** pontoon. HM Fabienne Dunes. ☎ 03 28 63 23 00, 🖷 03 28 66 66 62. VHF Ch 09. Open 0800–2000. This marina and the one in Bassin du Commerce are municipally run. www.dunkerque-marina.com

Tariff Daily rates on pontoons (showers included) in €, in season, for LOA bands: 6.5–8m = 11.55; 8–9.5m = 14; 9.5–11m = 17.85; 11–12.5m = 21; 12.5–14m = 23.25; 14–16m = 27.30; 16–18m = 31.50; 18–20m = 35.85; >20m, per extra m LOA = 2. Rates for multihulls are 50% more.

Showers are free, located in the Sailing School building N of the pontoon gangway.

Fuel Diesel and Petrol at fuel pontoon by gangway; open 0800–1000 & 1730–1930.

2. YCMN's marina is to starboard 300m beyond Port du Grand Large. Berth initially on the **Ⓥ** pontoon (3m) and ask HM for a finger berth (2m); good shelter in prevailing W'lies. The atmosphere is noticeably friendly and relaxed.

The Capitainerie is opposite 'E'/'F' pontoon. HM Joël Brats. Open in season 0800–1200 & 1400–2000. ☎ 03 28 66 79 90; 🖷 03 28 66 36 32; VHF Ch 09; info@ycmn.com; www.ycmn.com

Tariff Daily rate on pontoons, 1 Jun–30 Sept = €2 per metre LOA.

Showers in block N of Capitainerie, by jeton €1.20. Launderette ditto; €2 wash, €2.15 dry.

Fuel Diesel and Petrol by 'H' pontoon. Open Mon–Sat, 0800–1200 & 1400–1800; Sun 0900–1200 & 1400–1800. Minor repairs in YCMN workshop.

Restaurant/bar, ☎ 03 28 63 67 33. Menus €12.20–19.95. Bread and sandwiches can be ordered.

3. Bassin du Commerce is the nearest marina to town and the cheapest, but also has the hassle of Écluse Trystram and four bridges to be negotiated (see below). 15 **Ⓥ** berths are listed, but this tends to be a notional figure. Visitors may berth on the pontoon alongside the quai des Hollandais (SE wall), or at the NE end of the Bassin or amongst the six pontoons on the NW side. Shelter is excellent; depths about 5m.

The Capitainerie is at 16 quai de la Citadelle (NW wall). HM Fabienne Dunes.

Port du Grand Large Marina

☎/🖷 03 28 21 13 77. VHF Ch 09. Open 0800–2000. www.dunkerque-marina.com

Tariff Daily rates on pontoons (showers included) in €, in season, for LOA bands: 6.5–8m = 9.45; 8–9.5m = 11.55; 9.5–11m = 13.65; 11–12.5m = 14.70; 12.5–14m = 16.80; 14–16m = 18.90; 16–18m = 21; 18–20m = 23.10; each extra m LOA = 1.20. Rates for multihulls are 50% more.

Showers are free; located at north end of the Bassin.

Fuel None.

Access to Bassin du Commerce The huge de Gaulle lock and the slightly smaller Watier lock are rarely used by yachts which should enter the Trystram lock, daily 1 Jun to 15 Sep, and Sat/Sun/Hols from 2 Apr to 31 May, at the following times:

Entry from sea. 1200–1230, 1530–1600, 1830[3]–1900 & 2100–2130[2,3].

Exit to sea. 0835[2], 1105, 1435 & 1900.

It is best to confirm the above times (and the lock to be used) with the Port Capitainerie Ch 73 or ☎ 03 28 29 72 62, or Watier lock ☎ 03 28 29 72 67. Times may change to accommodate commercial movements. Lock signals are those of the CEVNI code.

Notes
1. The associated bridges open to meet the above locking times.
2. 2 April to 31 May, Mon–Fri: only entry is 2100–2130; only exit 0835.
3. 16 Sep to 1 April: No weekday movements. Sat/Sun/Hols, the 1830 entry is advanced to 1800 and the 2100 entry is cancelled. The 1900 exit is cancelled.

CHANDLERY & REPAIR FACILITIES

Accastillage Diffusion, quai des Monitors (across from YCMN). ☎ 03 28 59 18 19. CH, engineering, sail repairs.

Bleu Marine, terre-plein Guillain (across from YCMN). ☎ 03 28 63 93 33. CH, repairs, electronics, sail repairs.

Technic Boat, 12 route de l'Ecluse Trystram. ☎ 03 28 63 33 90. Diesel specialists.

Debussche, 471 rue des Bancs de Flandres (Port du Grand Large). ☎ 03 28 63 33 90. Diesel specialists, including Volvo and Honda.

GRAVELINES

West pierhead – 51°00′·99N 02°05′·56E

Gravelines is a delightful nautical cul-de-sac which has retained its other-worldly charm and character, despite being sandwiched between two ferry ports, Calais and Dunkerque Ouest. The town is a classic, moated, star-shaped fortress à la Vauban 1706.

The HM was very welcoming and what follows may put Gravelines more on the cruising map. It is known and visited by a few devotees, but is otherwise given a miss by those who don't know what they are missing – if you follow me.

SHORESIDE

Tourist Office 11 rue de la République. ☎ 03 28 51 94 00; 🖷 03 28 65 58 19. Open Jul/Aug, Mon–Sat 0900–1230 & 1400–1900; Sun/Hols 1000–1230 & 1500–1000. gravelines@ tourisme.norsys.fr; www.tourisme.fr/gravelines

What to see/do The Arsenal or castle was the military core of the fortress; there are gunpowder stores, cannon emplacements and a C17 bakery. Part of the castle is now an art museum housing a beautifully restored relief map of C18 Gravelines.

Rail The station is 600m SE of the marina. A local train (Line 9) runs to Dunkerque and Calais.

Buses Line A starts in the Place Valentin and does a round-robin to Petit- and Grand-Fort Philippe.

Taxi ☎ 03 28 23 11 25.

Car & bike hire In Calais and Dunkerque (☎ 03 28 66 30 00); see the Tourist Office.

UK access Calais and Dunkerque ferries and Channel Tunnel.

Beaches A pleasant bike ride gets you to the good sandy beaches at Petit- and Grand-Fort Philippe.

Supermarkets Lidl at NW corner of the marina. Market day: In the place Charles Valentin; check which day(s) with the HM.

Banks In the town centre.

Launderette in town; ask at the Tourist Office.

Restaurants Hostellerie du Beffroi, place C. Valentin, ☎ 03 28 23 24 25. Below its distinctive clock tower this Hôtel/restaurant offers a traditional fare at €15.75, *a menu de Terroir* at €23.10 and a *gastronomique* at €31.50. At 5 rue Léon Blum (behind Hostellerie du Beffroi) is Le Sainte Cecile, an inexpensive brasserie/café; €10.50–13.65. Go north out of town on rue de Dunkerque to: Le Turbot, ☎ 03 28 23 08 54, with interesting dishes at €15.75–31.50. Further north at No 44, La Cheminée is cheaper at €10.50–13.65. Petit-Fort Philippe, due to its size and beach, has more restaurants than Gravelines.

NAVIGATION

Charts AC 323 (1:75,000) & 1350 (1:25,000), plus SC 5605. SHOM 7424 (1:73,900), 6651 (1:43,100) and 7057 (1:20,000).

Approaches From the east, Gravelines is easily reached after crossing Dunkerque Ouest's entry channel, keeping seaward of DKB & DW15 buoys.

From Calais, on the flood, the short-cut outlined on page 252 should be possible. Stay clear of the extensive, steep-to sandbank which dries 1M offshore and is now only partially marked by the unlit Walde beacon on stilts.

From further west, including Dover, approach via CA4 buoy and north of Ridens de la Rade; or via the Dyck buoy (formerly Dunkerque Lanby) and RCE SHM buoy, thence direct to Gravelines. Access. The entrance channel dries between 0.5m and 1.5m, giving access HW±3 for shallow draughts, ±2 for draughts >1.5m; max draught 2.5m. For a first visit an arrival near HW is preferable and straightforward. In fresh onshore winds, stay away.

Landmarks From all directions the industrial structures at and around Dunkerque Port Ouest are conspicuous 2M east of Gravelines. In the near approach the disused lighthouse, with black and white spiral, will be seen at the root of Gravelines' east jetty. There is a church tower and a church spire to W and E respectively of the channel.

Anchorage In moderate winds and to await the

Marina at lower left and star-shaped fortress centre/right foreground looking NW

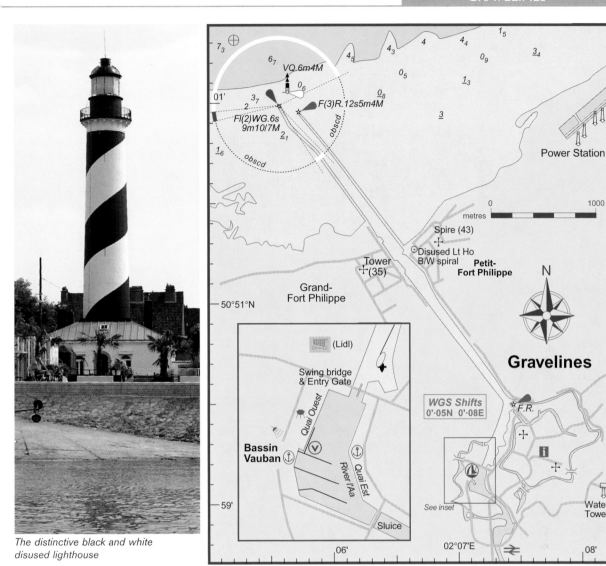

The distinctive black and white disused lighthouse

tide, there is good holding on sand in 5–6m off the jetty heads. The four yellow SPM buoys off the power station to the NE mark outfalls.

Looking seaward near Low Water

Tides HW Gravelines at sp is 5 mins, and at nps 15 mins, before HW Dunkerque; LW at nps is 5 mins before, & at sp 5 mins after, LW Dunkerque. MHWS is 6·3m, MLWS 0·5m; MHWN is 5·1m, MLWN is 1·4m.

Tidal streams 5 cables N of the entrance set ENE from HW Dunkerque $-2\frac{1}{2}$, reaching 2kn at HW Gravelines. At HW Dunkerque +3 there is a brief slack water, followed by the WSW-going ebb.

VHF Marina Ch 09 during office hours.

Pilotage From the approach waypoint 51°01´·29N 02°05´·30E track 143°/4 cables to the jetty heads from which the channel continues straight as an English arrow for 2M to the final bend. A covering extension to the east jetty is marked by a NCM beacon, Q; do not try to cut inside it.

Inside the west jetty head, silting occurs and a

Entry gate and swing bridge into the marina. Note 4.85m digital depth read out

Vauban (marina).

The Marina entry gate, 10m wide, usually stays open HW±3 in season (±1½ out of season), as does the pedestrian swing bridge above it. A very clear digital depth gauge, visible from inside and out, shows depth over the sill which is 0.6m above CD. Night opening requires 24 hrs notice.

Berth on the clearly marked **Ⓥ** pontoon at the NW quay, or as directed to a finger berth on the three pontoons. The depth is maintained at 1.5m, except for short periods when the gate has opened but sluicing from the River Aa has not yet started. The bottom is soft mud in which fin keelers remain upright. Aa is pronounced '*ar-ar*', ie two separate short sounds.

dredger is often at work. Keep to the E side until the channel narrows when hold a middle course. At HW, coefficient 63, a mean depth of 3.5m was found. There is sometimes dinghy sailing near the disused lighthouse. Thereafter the channel is marked by lateral dolphins until the 60° bend stbd to the entry gate into Bassin

CHANDLERY & REPAIR FACILITIES

Flandre Marine, quai Ouest, Bassin Vauban; ☎ 03 28 65 34 01.Good chandlery and workshops.

Marine & Reparation, quai Vauban (E side of marina); ☎ 03 28 23 14 68, Chandlery, sail repairs, engineering.

FACILITIES

The Capitainerie is in the SW corner of the basin. VHF Ch 09, 0800–1200 & 1330–1730. HM Bruno Marcotte; ☎ 03 28 23 19 45; ⊠ 03 28 23 05 36.

Tariff Daily rate (showers included) year round: €1.20 per metre LOA.

Showers, free. In a block across the road.

Fuel By cans from filling station 200m NNE from E end of pedestrian bridge; closed Wed.

CALAIS

Harbour entrance – 50°58´·34N 01°50´·50E

Calais is the definitive frontier town, by sea and tunnel; a magnet for cross-Channel shoppers and an unhappy staging post for those seeking asylum in Britain. Calais was English for over two centuries, until Mary Tudor, who had always regarded it as the jewel in the English crown, lost it to the French in 1558.

Her post-mortem revealed 'Calais' tattooed upon her heart. Today Calais teems with Brits, pubs and English-sounding hotels (George V, Bristol, Windsor) serving *le* English breakfast.

SHORESIDE

Tourist Office 12 quay Gambetta. Open Apr–Aug, Mon–Sat 0900–1900; Sun 1000–1300. ☎ 03 21 96 62 40; ⊠ 03 21 96 01 92; ot@ot-calais.fr; www.ot-calais.fr

Looking NE across the marina, Avant Port and ferry berths

What to see/do Calais is in effect two towns: Calais-Nord, near the marina and almost ringed by canals. The main drag, rue de la Mer and rue Royale, bisects it passing Place d'Armes where much of the action is. The Tourist Office and rail station, Calais-Ville, are as shown on the plan.

Continue south into Calais-Sud, where the ornate Town Hall is fronted by Rodin's famous bronze statue of the Six Burghers of Calais. This recalls Edward III's siege of Calais in 1347. Irked by the town's lengthy resistance he vowed to slaughter the whole population. Six of the town's burghers offered themselves in sacrifice, but were spared by Philippa, Edward's queen, pleading for mercy.

Opposite the Town Hall in the Parc St Pierre is the Museum of War housed in a former German bunker. It tells of the British Expeditionary Force's arrival and later evacuation at Dunkerque; the rearguard evacuation fought at Calais by the Green Jackets; the long years of Occupation; the Resistance; and the Liberation of Calais on 30 Sept 1944. Open 1000–1800, May–Aug, €4.20.

Finally climb the lighthouse, only 271 steps, to enjoy the fantastic views, including on a clear day the white cliffs of Dover. Open Mon–Fri, 1400–1830; Sat/Sun 1000–1200 & 1400–1830; €2.10.

Rail Mainline trains from Calais-Ville via Boulogne, Abbeville and Amiens to Paris (2 hrs). TGV from Calais-Frethun to Paris (1 hr 23 mins).

Buses There is a comprehensive urban network and regional buses to Boulogne and Dunkerque.

Car hire In the Place d'Armes: Avis ☎ 03 21 34 66 50; and Budget ☎ 03 21 96 42 20.

Bike hire Opale Tour, by the lighthouse; ☎ 03 21 34 33 34. €12.60 per day, €8.40 for half a day.

UK access Ferries and Channel Tunnel; see the Introduction for details.

Beaches A good sandy beach and children's play areas are west of the west jetty.

Supermarkets There is a medium-sized Prisunic on bd Jacquard, just before bd Gambetta; a good 30 mins walk from the marina. An Auchan hypermarket is on the outskirts, needing a bus or taxi. A big Carrefour is in the vast new complex which forms part of the Chunnel terminal.

Market day Bustling, colourful market in Place d'Armes on Wed and Sat mornings.

Banks Plenty around the city centre.

Restaurants Cross the marina bridge, and on the corner of the bd Résistance and rue de la Mer is the very good La Sole Meuniere, ☎ 03 21 34

43 01, with seafood at
€15.75–28.35 and a
gastronomique at €36.75.
In Place d'Armes is the
more traditional Coq d'Or,
☎ 03 21 34 79 05, with
menus from €10.50 to
€38.85 for a *gastronomique*.
In the same Place, try
Le St-Charles, ☎ 03 21 96
02 96, at €10.50–29.40
including Filet de boeuf
aux escargots. In rue Royale
eat well in: Le 1900,
☎ 03 21 97 58 41, at
€12.80–45.15, including
a huge choucroute de
poissons. The attractive brasserie, Histoire
Ancienne, cooks over a wood fire in traditional
style; €9.80–25.20 include some Greek dishes;
☎ 03 21 34 11 20. Le George V, ☎ 03 21 97 68 00,
has a fine restaurant with regional menus from
€12.60 and a gastronomique at €45.15. Finally
Le Touquet, ☎ 03 21 97 11 55, is one of Calais'
best known restaurants with bouillabaise, paëlla
and couscous from €11–19.

View from atop the lighthouse, looking WNW to Angleterre

NAVIGATION

Charts AC 1892 (1:75,000), 323 (1:75,000), 1351
(approaches 1:15,000; port 1:7,500), plus SC 5605.
SHOM 7424 (1:73,900), 7323 (1:74,300) and
7258 (1:15,000).

Approaches From the east, (after passing DKB
WCM buoy) route either (a) inshore or (b) to
seaward of Ridens de la Rade, a sandbank with
drying patches, close N of Calais.

Route (a) is via 51°00′·00N 01°53′·41E direct to
the E jetty head and carries a least depth of 1.7m.
It is therefore only viable with sufficient rise of
tide which may not be available if arriving near
LW on the last of the W-going ebb.

In which case take route (b), skirting north of
Ridens de la Rade until clear of the tail of the
bank in about 01°48′·00E, or even further west to
CA6 PHM buoy, before turning back to Calais.

When leaving Calais eastbound on the main
flood, route (a) may be used if the departure is
timed to ensure the necessary rise of tide.

From the WSW, round Cap Gris-Nez at least
6 cables to seaward, then set course direct, or via
Abbeville WCM buoy, to CA3 SHM buoy. The
direct track just clears the shallow waters off Cap
Gris-Nez and Cap Blanc-Nez. From CA3 a direct
track via CA5 to Calais' W jetty head keeps clear
of the unbuoyed southern edge of the ferry access
channel and the drying inshore banks.

Access The entrance and Avant Port can be very
rough in fresh (F5+) onshore winds from WNW to
ENE, when entry may be difficult or impossible.
Calais is accessible at all tides, but outside the
opening hours of the entry gate/bridge into the
marina (see below), yachts should pick up one of
the 23 white conical buoys east of the gate. These
lie in up to 2m of water and can be uncomfortable
in anything other than calm conditions; about half
are occupied by local boats.

Landmarks To the east Dunkerque's industrial
silhouette is evident. Cap Blanc-Nez and the
Dover Patrol monument are prominent 6M west
of Calais. In Calais the following are conspic:
the white/black-top, octagonal lighthouse in
Calais-Nord; the Town Hall tower which from
afar is reminiscent of Big Ben; a large and little
conical-topped silos close east of the entrance;
and a red/white chimney (78m) 1M east of
the lighthouse.

Anchorage There is no recognised yacht
anchorage. Anchorage is prohibited out to 1M
west of the harbour entrance and within the
Avant Port. Do not anchor between CA3 and
CA5 buoys due to underwater cables.

Tides Calais is a Standard Port, but in the *RNA*
is a Secondary Port to Dunkerque. HW Calais
at sp is 20 mins and at nps 30 mins before HW
Dunkerque; LW at nps is 15 mins and at sp 5 mins
before LW Dunkerque. MHWS is 7·2m, MLWS
0·9m; MHWN is 5·9m, MLWN 2·1m.

Tidal streams set NE across the entrance from
HW−2½ to +3½; and SW from HW+3½ to −2½; spring

The main lighthouse is in the background. The IPTS in the foreground is near the root of the West Jetty

rates peak at $2\frac{1}{2}$kn at HW. Slack water is a mere 15 mins at about HW$-3\frac{1}{2}$ and $+2\frac{1}{2}$.

VHF Call Calais Port, or just Ferryport, Ch 12; good English spoken. There is no marina VHF.

Pilotage Three waypoints cater for the three directions of approach:

1. From the E, the position 51°00′·00N 01°53′·41E given under Approaches applies mainly to route (a) above, but is also a decision point for route (b).

2. From the NW, 50°59′·45N 01°45′·19E (CA4 buoy) is on the edge of the ferry channel and west of both Ridens de Calais and Ridens de la Rade. Pass CA6, 8 and 10 buoys keeping outside the ferry channel and holding clear of the entrance until cleared in by IPTS. (NB, *en passant*, that CA 1 and 7 buoys do not exist).

3. From the SW, 50°57′·70N 01°46′·21E (CA5 buoy), as described under Approaches.

IPTS are shown bi-directionally from two places:

(i) Inside the E jetty head, shown to the W for arrivals; and to the S/SE for departures.

(ii) From the W side of the Avant Port (between a FY beacon and a Dir FG; see photo), shown to the NW for vessels entering the Arrière Port; and to the SE for those leaving it.

These signals apply to yachts, as much as to ferries. Thus an arriving yacht must first obey IPTS (i) for clearance into the Avant Port; and then IPTS (ii) for clearance into the Arrière Port for the marina. In the Avant Port hug the western side as you proceed into the Arrière Port, but do not cut the corner off Fort Risban where drying ground is marked by two unlit SHM perches.

Departing yachts follow the reverse procedure; noting that a third IPTS, due east of the marina, solely controls entry to the Arrière Port.

Meticulous compliance with the IPTS cuts out any VHF chatter, but monitor Ch 12 throughout and keep a sharp lookout for fast-moving ferries.

The Marina (Bassin de l'Ouest) is accessed via an entry gate which is open by day/night from HW−2 to +1. If technically possible the gate may open about 15 mins before HW−2. It is 17m wide and has a sill drying 2m.

Entering the marina via gate and swing bridge. Visitors' berths are the first to starboard

The co-located swing bridge opens at HW–2, HW and HW+1. Traffic lights show: Red = no entry; Amber = bridge opening in 10 mins; Green = enter. The operator monitors VHF Ch 12.

Visitors berth/raft on the pontoon in front of the Capitainerie/SRC (where the flags fly). If staying a day or two, a quieter finger berth may be negotiated further to the west.

FACILITIES

The Capitainerie is behind the **Ⓥ** pontoon. Open 0800–1200 & 1400–1800. HM Michel Louf. ☎ 03 21 34 55 23, 🖷 03 21 96 10 78; calais-marina@calais-port.com; www.calais-port.com The Société des Régates de Calais (SRC), ☎ 03 21 97 02 34, is in the same building.

Tariff Daily rates on pontoons (showers included) in €, in season, for LOA bands:
6.5–8m = 7.35; 8–9.5m = 8.40; 9.5–11m = 9.45; 11–13m = 11; 13–14m = 11.75; 14–16m = 12.60; 16–18m = 13. Rates for berthing on the S wall (no pontoons, security nor electricity) are half the above.

Showers Inside the Capitainerie, free.

Fuel Diesel at fuel pontoon 200m west of the Capitainerie. Petrol from the nearest garage.

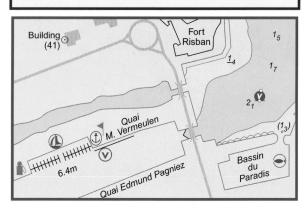

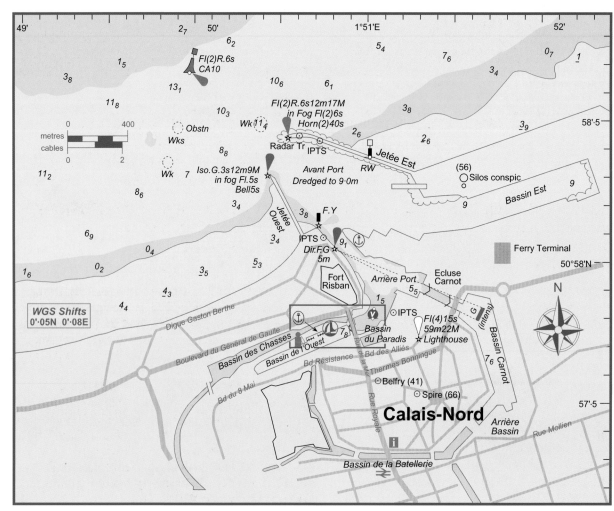

Looking east beyond the industrial sites to Boulogne's fair city

BOULOGNE-SUR-MER

Marina – 50°43´·54N 01°36´·06E

The dome of Notre Dame cathedral rises like a beacon on the skyline. Around it the mediaeval ramparts of the upper town enclose an oasis of peace and calm. Nausicaa, the City of the Sea, turns her glittering face seaward amid trees and grass as you approach the final bend.

However from seaward the industrialised iron, steel, coke and manganese works around the outer basins are visible from afar, black with grime and rust and depositing a brown patina on nearby buildings. Further up harbour, the ferry terminal, devoid of ferries since late 2000, is back in business from May 2003 with ferries to/from Dover.

SHORESIDE

Tourist Office 24 quay Gambetta; see town plan. ☎ 03 21 10 88 10; ℻ 03 21 10 88 11; boulogne@ tourisme.norsys.fr Open in season, Mon–Sat 0845–1230 & 1330–1815; Sun 1000–1230 & 1430–1700.

What to see/do Boulogne is two towns, the lower and the upper or Haute Ville. In the bustle and traffic of the workaday lower town stroll the pedestrianised shopping streets, rues Thiers and Victor Hugo, and the open spaces of place Dalton where the Saturday morning market is an absolute must.

Then climb to the walled Haute Ville and stroll the ramparts, but sadly views over the town and harbour are mostly obscured by trees. Within these ancient walls admire the Town Hall and climb up to its belfry (*beffroi*) for an unobstructed view. Pause to enter the strangely Italianate cathedral. The Château stands attractively in a moat and is entered over an old stone bridge.

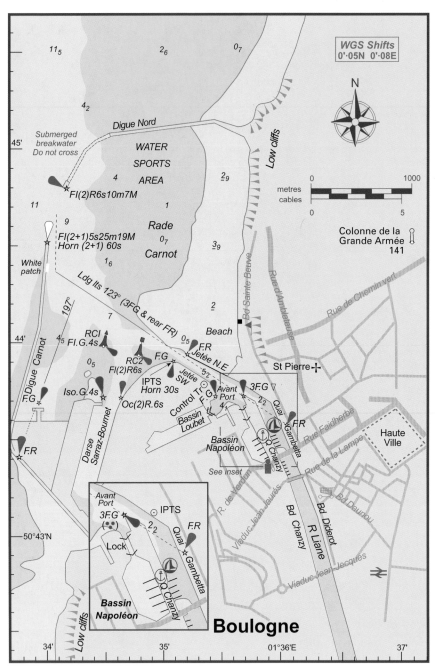

Boulogne

See inset

Rail Mainline trains from Calais to Paris (2 hrs).

Buses There is an urban network and regional services to Calais and Le Touquet.

Taxi ☎ 03 21 91 25 00.

Car hire Autorent, 96 rue Nationale, ☎ 03 21 30 32 23. Ada, 211 rue Nationale, ☎ 03 21 80 80 82.

Bike hire Try Motul, 106 rue Thiers; or make enquiries at the Tourist Office.

UK access Speedferries (www.speedferries.com) operates five daily round trips (50 mins each way) to Dover.

Beaches There is an excellent sandy beach and low cliffs north of Nausicaa.

Supermarkets A large Champion is on the east side of R Liane at corner of bd Liane and bd Daunou, 600m from the marina. The Leclerc and Auchan hypermarkets on the outskirts need a bus or taxi.

Market day Lively and colourful fruit & veg market in place Dalton on Wed and Sat mornings. Or try the fish auction at Bassin Loubet at 0500 on Wednesdays.

Banks In the city centre.

Restaurants proliferate in two main areas:

Nausicaa, the National Sea Centre, is basically a vast aquarium with something for all the family, but in addition there are scientific and educational sections for the dedicated submariner. Open Jul/Aug 0930–2000; €10.50 adult.

From the top of the Colonne de la Grande Armée, 600ft above sea level, you will see Cap Gris-Nez, Calais, possibly Dover and the White cliffs in decent visibility and a panorama across Artois and Flanders. The Colonne was erected somewhat prematurely in 1804 to commemorate Napoleon's invasion of England – a non-event, thanks to Nelson's victory at Trafalgar in 1805.

a. In the lower town in and around Place Dalton. Spread yourself in the vast Chez Jules at No 8, ☎ 03 21 31 54 11; €14.70–35.70. Le Henley, ☎ 03 21 87 51 51; €11.50–24.15. Or off the SW corner of the square in rue Doyen, where in the cosy and unpretentious surroundings of Le Doyen I enjoyed one of the best meals of my cruise; pre-book – it's small.

b. In the Haute Ville along the rue de Lille visit La Poivrière, ☎ 03 21 80 18 18; €13–22. La Pierre Chaude, ☎ 03 21 80 30 32; €13–20. Restaurant de la Haute Ville, ☎ 03 21 80 54 10; €12.50–35.70.

Finally near Nausicaa: La Matelote, 80 bd Ste Beuve, ☎ 03 21 30 17 97. Ideal for pushing out *le bateau* on a grand occasion as the menus suggest, €24–57.75 (*gastronomique*).

NAVIGATION

Charts AC 2451 (1:150,000), 1892 (1:75,000), 438 (1:10,000), plus SC 5605. SHOM 7416 (1:75,000), 7323 (1:74,300) and 7247 (1:10,000).

Approaches The TSS is only 3M off Cap Gris-Nez, 4.4M off Boulogne and 8M offshore abeam Vergoyer N buoy. Vergoyer bank and the Bassure de Baas further restrict the searoom, although the latter has significant gaps, WNW of the harbour and SW of Cap d'Alprech; it peters out 4M south of Gris Nez. Otherwise there are no hazards, but be vigilant in onshore winds when the dunes to the south and

The free-standing structure at the seaward end of the Digue Nord

broken cliffs in the north form a hostile lee shore.

Access H24. Boulogne is a port of refuge, but in bad weather there may be heavy seas in the entrance; here conditions may be less rigorous at slack water, HW+3.

The inner harbour and marinas looking north

Landmarks From the north, the Colonne de la Grande Armée (141m), with Napoleon on top, is 2M east of the port entrance. From the south, Cap d'Alprech lighthouse, with unusual external spiral stairway, is conspic 2.5M S of the port entrance. The conical-roofed cement works in the industrial docks is prominent. The cathedral dome (144m) is on the skyline.

Anchorage There is no recognised yacht anchorage. Anchorage is prohibited in the Avant Port SW of a line from the Digue Nord head to the head of the inner NE jetty.

Tides Boulogne is a Standard Port, but the *RNA* references it to Dunkerque as a secondary port. HW Boulogne at sp is 45 mins and at nps 1 hr before HW Dunkerque; LW at nps is 45 mins and at sp 25 mins before LW Dunkerque. MHWS is 8·8m, MLWS 1·1m; MHWN is 7·2m, MLWN 2·6m.

Tidal streams off the entrance: the N-going flood starts at local HW−0150 and the S-going ebb at HW+0330; spring rates can exceed 4kn.

VHF Boulogne Port Ch 12; marina Ch 09.

IPTS are shown from the SW jetty head, FG; and from the NW side of the bend in the inner channel. The latter are visible from the marina and must be heeded by departing yachts and FVs. If dredging is in progress, a yellow light is shown to the right of the top main light.

Pilotage The waypoint is 50°44′·73N 01°33′·61E, 125°/4 cables to the head of Digue Carnot. The head of the Digue Nord, Fl (2) R 6s, is an isolated structure separated from the visible part of the jetty by an under-water section which must never be crossed.

After rounding Digue Carnot a safe distance off, turn starboard to parallel the jetty until abeam a white-painted mark 1 cable south of the jetty head. This jink keeps clear of shoal waters to the east and intercepts the 122.4° leading line to the inner channel (at night, front three neon FG △; rear FR). By day pass between the conspic green and red light towers on the inner jetties. In the Avant Port give way to vessels locking in/out of the Bassins Loubet and Napoléon.

The 'old' marina and disused ferry terminal beyond, looking NNW

THE INNER HARBOUR AND PORT NAPOLÉON

The east side (Quai Gambetta) of the inner hbr is reserved for medium sized FVs. The marina, in about 2.9m, is to starboard beyond the defunct ferry terminal. The four pontoons with fingers are usually full in season or bad weather, with much rafting on the hammerheads; max LOA 12m. Beyond the pontoons there is shoal water (0.7m) in front of the bridge, sluices and access gate to the inner Bassin F Sauvage where only small local craft berth, with no access to the R Liane. Caution: When sluicing takes place, as indicated by two blue lights (hor) on the E end of the bridge, a significant current and turbulence affects the marina and can make berthing difficult.

Port Napoléon, west of the existing marina, now has 150 + 80 **Ⓥ** finger berths on five pontoons in 3m; max LOA 25m. Enter via a lock which opens at HW±3. Local yachts have been encouraged price-wise to move into Bassin Napoleon. Visitors should therefore plan to berth in the old marina. Large FVs berth on the W and S sides of Bassin Napoléon.

A bustling market in Place Dalton

The Capitainerie on quai Chanzy is new with showers, free, and probably a launderette. HM Christian Allard; ☎ 03 21 31 70 01; 🖷 03 21 99 62 02; boulogne.cci@netinfo.fr; www.portboulogne.com The Yacht Club Boulonnais (YCB; ☎ 03 21 31 80 67) is nearby.

Tariff Daily rates in €, May–Sep, for LOA bands are: 6.5–8m = 12.60; 8–9.5m = 15.75; 9.5–11m = 19.95; 11–13m = 23.10; >13m = 26.25. Short stays of up to 6 hrs may be charged at €4.60–5.25.

Fuel Diesel at root of the third pontoon from a fuel pontoon which is only 7.5m long and sits very low in the water. Petrol by cans from nearest garage.

Chandlery & repairs Opposite the marina four high-rise blocks contain from S to N: Opale Accastillage (first block), chandler. (Second block, Tourist Office). Flagler Accastillage, 44 rue Gambetta (third block) ☎ 03 21 33 90 75; pflagler@magic.fr Good chandlery with reasonable stock of SHOM charts; also a sailmaker.

Chapter 4

ÉTAPLES

Marina – 50°31´·00N 01°38´·00E

Étaples is only feasible for a maximum draught of about 1.2m. The mouth of the Canche estuary dries at least 6.2m and the little marina even more so. The access channel is well marked and short, although by no means a pushover for the first-time visitor.

SHORESIDE

Tourist Office La Corderie, bd Bigot Descelers. ☎ 03 21 09 56 94; 📠 03 21 09 76 96; www.etaples-sur-mer.com In Jul/Aug a small office is open near the bridge roundabout.

What to see/do When you have exhausted the pleasures of Étaples, in the afternoon you could perhaps visit Le Touquet. Or a day trip to the field of the Battle of Agincourt (Azincourt as it is now known) might be more fun. Walk the ground and visit the Centre of Mediaeval History, open 0900–1800 April–Oct. www.azincourt-medieval.com

Rail Mainline from Calais via Boulogne, Abbeville, Amiens to Paris (2 hrs 15 mins). The station is 10 mins walk NE of the marina.

Buses run to Le Touquet and Boulogne.

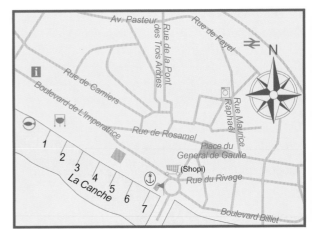

Taxi ☎ 06 07 81 38 66.

Car hire Agence P Gonet (Europcar), 39 bd Daloz. ☎ 03 21 05 21 21.

The marina looking east at sundown

Off Le Touquet looking east across the channel to Étaples

Access to UK Ferry from Calais or Dieppe.

Beaches Excellent beach at Le Touquet.

Supermarkets Champion and ATAC supermarkets are both on the route de Boulogne near the railway station. More convenient is Shopi on rue du Port where it joins the roundabout by the bridge over the Canche.

Market day A large and varied market fills the Place Gen de Gaulle, Tuesday mornings.

Banks Mostly in/near Place Gen de Gaulle.

Launderette Laverie L'Espace, rue Deboffe; close to the railway station.

Restaurants Aux Pêcheurs d'Étaples, ☎ 03 21 94 06 90, is on the upper floor of a pagoda-like building facing the marina, the river and Le Touquet airfield. The morning catch is landed on the ground floor. Elsewhere try Au Vieux Port in the Place Gen de Gaulle; Restaurant des Voyageurs, ☎ 03 21 94 32 70, opposite the railway station; and the Beau Rivage (Hôtel de la Baie), ☎ 03 21 89 99 99, with views downstream to the bay.

NAVIGATION

Charts AC 2451 (1:150,000) is far too small a scale and stops just short of Étaples. SHOM 7416 (1:75,000) at twice the scale is adequate.

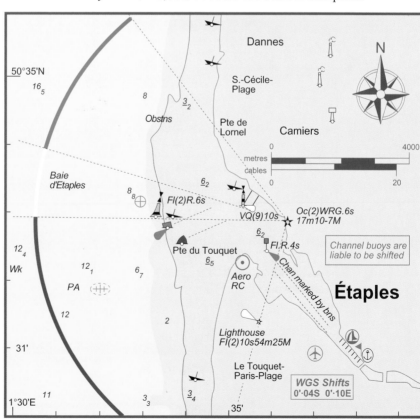

Fishing boats berth down-stream of No 1 pontoon

Approaches Inshore of the Bassure de Baas (least depth 4·9m), there are no hazards, but the Canche estuary mostly dries to about 5 cables offshore, and 1M off Pointe de Lornel. From the first channel buoys (depending on where they are) to the marina is only some 3–4M.

Access Leave the waypoint (see Pilotage) at local HW–1. In onshore winds of F4 or more the approach channel, drying about 6m, is very rough.

Landmarks Le Touquet lighthouse dominates the estuary. N of Pointe de Lornel is a large cement works. The directional light, Oc (2) WRG 6s, at Camiers is on a slender red pylon, initially only visible with binos. Two groynes NW of this light are easily seen, marked by a WCM light beacon and two SPM beacons. The large light beacon, Fl R 4s, at the outer end of the training wall is conspic. Do not approach at night, unless qualified by day.

Anchorage There is no ⚓ in the channel up to Étaples, but see Le Touquet (opposite).

Tides HW Le Touquet at sp is 7 mins and at nps 17 mins after HW Dieppe. LW is 32 mins after LW Dieppe at both nps and sp. MHWS is 9·5m, MLWS 1·2m; MHWN is 7·7m, MLWN 2·9m.

Tidal streams to seaward of the waypoint (below) set N/S at up to $1\frac{3}{4}$kn at springs.

Pilotage The Waypoint at 50°33′·15N 01°32′·80E is in 5m, in the middle of Camiers' white sector; but the first PHM/SHM channel buoys may be to the NE or SE, well outside the white sector. Follow the buoys to the head of the training wall, 50°32′·62N 01°35′·70E, marked by a large red light column. The channel then leads 141°/2M between perched training walls to pass abeam a huge 130 ton yellow boat hoist, thence to the fish quay, marina and road bridge.

The Marina has seven pontoons with fingers. Visitors berth/raft on the hammer-heads of pontoons 1 or 2 and check with the HM; or pre-call Étaples Ch 09 or mobile. Berthing is difficult in the strong current outside HW slack. The river shallows and narrows towards the low road bridge.

FACILITIES

Capitainerie is abeam pontoon 6, in CNE (Club Nautique Étaplois), bar and showers. HM Olivier Imbert; ☎ 03 21 84 54 33. Open at tide times by day.

Tariff Daily rates (showers included) in €, for LOA bands: 5–8m = 12.60; >8m = 14.70.

Fuel By cans from garage on the Le Touquet road.

CHANDLERY & REPAIR FACILITIES
Au Grand Large, bd Descelers, ☎ 03 21 09 53 11; 🖷 03 21 09 08 64.
Co-op Maritime L'Étaploise, quai de la Canche, ☎ 03 21 94 72 77.

Le Touquet is the big name around these parts, but it really only offers a casino and the trappings of a bygone epoch, plus a drying mooring for a draught of about 1m, if you're lucky. Or anchor west of the moorings on sand, with stony patches and allegedly quicksands. Send your man ahead to suss out the bad bits before walking ashore in your DJ. The **Capitainerie** is part of the Cercle Nautique du Touquet (CNT), ☎ 03 21 05 12 77 or VHF Ch 09 or 77.

ST VALÉRY-SUR-SOMME

Marina – 50°10´·91N 01°38´·77E

The marina and canal lock

This place I really like. Wide seascapes, huge expanses of water, sand and glistening mud; overhead the great azure vault of the sky – these are what I visualise when I think of the Somme. St Valéry is the icing on the cake and the last harbour in Picardy.

You have mastered the sluicing tides and slalomed between countless buoys. After passing the town's tree-lined promenades and rounding the final bend, the friendliest of marinas lies in front of you – it is irresistible stuff. St Valéry-sur-Somme is hereinafter abbreviated to St VsS, ignoble treatment for such a place.

SHORESIDE

Tourist Office, quayside at the N end of the marina. ☎ 03 22 60 93 50; 📠 03 22 60 80 34. Open in season 0930–1200 & 1430–1830. http://Perso.wanadoo.fr/St.Valery

What to see/do The town divides into the lower, more workaday part, and the upper or Old Town which rises a dizzy 44m above the flatlands. A pleasant walk along the shaded riverside promenade takes you to the beach by the Iso G 4s light. Here climb the hill to the twin towers of C12 Porte Guillaume with panoramic views of the estuary. Continue out to the Mariners' Chapel set amongst grassy fields, returning via the Old Town's cobbled streets, awash with flowers.

An excursion which will delight all the family is to take the steam train to Le Crotoy, see page 267. This is *Thomas the Tank Engine* in real life, huffing and puffing around the head of the estuary with that evocative smell of coal, steam and hot oil. Three trains daily, an hour each way, €9.45 adult return.

Rail Nearest railway station is Noyelles-sur-Mer;

change for Boulogne or Abbeville/Amiens/Paris.

Buses run infrequently via Noyelles to Abbeville and via Cayeux to Le Tréport.

Taxi ☎ 03 22 26 93 59; 03 22 60 05 05.

Car hire Nothing in St VsS; the nearest firm is at Abbeville, details from the Tourist Office.

Bike hire Le Velocipede, 1 rue du Puits Salé (Old Town); ☎ 03 22 26 96 80.

Beaches There is a sandy beach at the far end of the tree-lined promenade.

Supermarkets Champion is 15 mins walk SE from the marina on roundabout. An Intermarché is about 700m further west on the Cayeux road. In town Rue de la Ferté is the main shopping street with a fair selection of food shops.

Market day Sunday morning and Wednesday morning in season, in the Place des Pilotes.

Banks Two banks and the Post Office in rue de la Ferté, all with holes-in-the-wall.

Restaurants Le Relais Guillaume de Normandie, quai du Romerel, ☎ 03 22 60 82 36; €14.70–36.75 in a C19 building. Hôtel du Port et des Bains, 1 quai Blavet, (by the Tourist Office), ☎ 03 22 60 80 09; €14.70–32; views across the Baie. Les Pilotes, 62 rue de la Ferté, ☎ 03 22 60 80 39; €12.60–42, and €55.65 gastro. Le relais des Quatre Saisons, 2 place de la Croix l'Abbaye, ☎ 03 22 60 51 01; €14.70–30.45. Le Moulin, facing the Champion supermarket; ☎ 03 22 60 85 86; €11.20–29.95. Le Globe, end of rue de la Ferté, ☎ 03 22 26 89 01; views across the Baie. Le Bistrot de Saint-Val, 5 place des Pilotes. Moules galore, mass eating on the pavement.

NAVIGATION

Charts AC 2451 (1:150,000) stops short of St VsS and is far too small a scale for inshore pilotage. Get SHOM 7416 (1:75,000) for general orientation, although the buoyage is so good as virtually to do away with plotting fixes – bold words, but true!

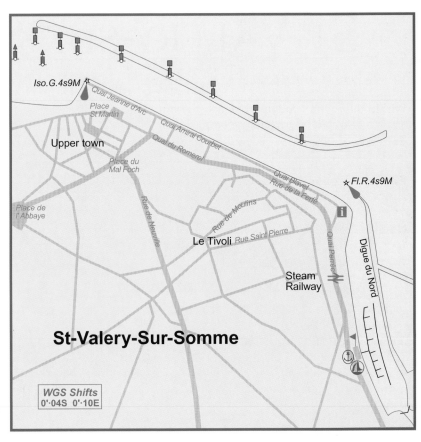

Approaches From all quadrants set course direct to ATSO buoy (see below), avoiding the various charted shoals such as the Bassure de Baas and the Vergoyer bank.

Access Tidal timing at ATSO needs to be about HW St VsS–2, which is most easily achieved from a nearby French port. Le Tréport is closest, 11M, but tidal constraints and delays in the lock may rule it out. Dieppe, 24M, and Boulogne, 31M, are much better bets. If you cannot reach St VsS until after local HW, it is best to try again another day. Weather conditions should exclude onshore winds greater than F4 and visibility less than 3M.

Landmarks The lighthouse at Cayeux is initially the key landmark. The smaller Le Hourdel lighthouse is obscured and may not be seen until it is almost abeam. The Persil-white water tower at Le Crotoy is conspic on the N shore; and the wooded slopes above St VsS mean you are getting close.

Anchorage You can anchor to seaward of ATSO buoy in about 7m on sand and shingle, purely to await the tide as it is rather exposed. Anchoring in the estuary is certainly not recommended.

Tides HW St VsS at sp and nps is 35 mins after

HW Dieppe. MHWS is 10·2m and MHWN is 8·1m. LW time and height differences are irrelevant.

Tidal streams to seaward of the ATSO buoy set roughly NE/SW at up to 2.3kn sp and 1.2kn nps. Within the estuary the flood peaks at about HW St VsS–2, ie as you start your approach and drying banks have just covered; the rise is rapid in the lower estuary.

Pilotage Waypoint is the ATSO (Atterrisage Somme) NCM light buoy 50°14´·32N 01°28´·71E. From here identify and make for the first lateral channel buoys; then follow the rest of the very well buoyed channel, with absolutely no corner-cutting, intentional or otherwise – until 6.75M later you reach the first SHM light beacon, 50°12´·30N 01°35´·95E, Fl (3) G 6s, at the head of the outer training bank. Thereafter follow the beacons to the marina 2.75M ahead. At a boat speed of 5 to 5½kn, the total time will be about 1½ to 2 hrs, ie ETA HW or a little before. Look out for seals in the channel and in the marina.

With the strong caveat that it must NOT be used for navigation because it is likely to be different when you go there, the outlined diagram of the channel (by kind permission of the HM St VsS) gives an idea of the twists and turns that it may take; some of the turns are rather sharper than the diagram suggests. Keep an open mind on the day, but for now note the following typical characteristics:

- S1/2 buoys were 1.5M SE of ATSO and during this and some other legs the tide sets strongly across the track. So perfect your tracking

No 1 Channel buoy

technique, either by watching a selected feature (the buoys or a coastal mark) to check that it does not appear to move; or by hand bearing compass or GPS. Whatever the method, the aim is to stay within what should be the best water.
- Only seven buoys are lit; the numbers are prefixed by 'L'. Your first approach should not be at night.
- The unlit WCM buoy where a channel forks left to Le Crotoy is well painted and marked BIF for Bifurcation (or Division); it was at 50°13´·20N 01°36´·00E. If bound for St VsS, you would already have seen the next pair of St VsS lateral buoys so simply shape a course to starboard and ignore BIF.
- Least depth recorded at about HW–1, coefficient 101, was 4.8m abeam No 25 buoy.

The **marina** is well sheltered by a dyke to the east and the town to the west. The flood stream ceases as you enter the marina, and the canal sluice gates upriver normally close from HW–2 to HW, so there should be no residual current. There are nine un-numbered pontoons to stbd of the fairway, and to port a long detached pontoon for locals. There are no designated ❤ berths so call Ch 09 or

Yacht club, showers and HM's office in the marina

mobile to advise your ETA (some English is spoken); their dory will then take you to a berth. If not, berth on a vacant hammerhead.

FACILITIES

Capitainerie is at the head of the access gangway. HM André Widehem; ☎ 03 22 60 24 80; 📠 03 22 60 24 82. Open 0900–1200 & 1400–1800 and at tide times in daylight hours. The Club Nautique Valéricaine (CNV) is in the same building with a friendly bar.

Tariff Daily rates (showers included) in €, in season, for LOA bands: 6–8m = 9.90; 8–10m = 13.10; 10–12m = 16.80; >12m = 18.90. Multihulls: small 16.80, large 19.20.

Showers and **launderette** To port at top of the gangway, free, accessed by code H24.

Fuel Turn left out of Capitainerie for 500m to nearest filling station at Champion supermarket on the roundabout; by cans only.

Chandlery & repairs Latitude 50, ☎ 03 22 61 21 70; 📠 03 22 26 96 10. Turn right out of the marina for 200m and it's across the road; well stocked and very obliging, closed Wednesday. Nausicaa, ☎ 03 22 26 85 85; 📠 03 22 26 73 61. Turn left out of the marina for 200m and it's by the lock

ATSO buoy leans to the tide

into the Canal d'Abbeville; smallish boatyard and chandlery, shut Wednesday. EMTCM, quai Jules Verne; ☎ 03 22 26 82 20; 📠 03 22 26 82 52. On N side of the Canal. Boatyard, engineering, CH.

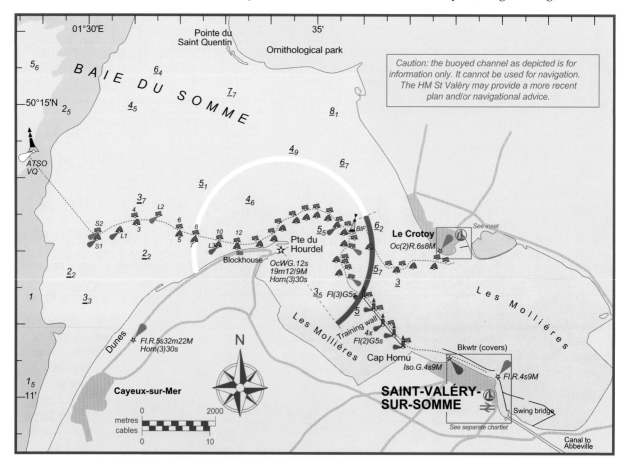

LE CROTOY

Marina – 50°13´·07N 01°37´·88E

This pleasant harbour dries completely; the HM quotes 0.8m as the maximum draught for entry. Consider visiting Crotoy by train from St VsS. If feasible for your boat, leave St VsS at HW–1½, be at BIF about HW–¾ and at Crotoy just before HW.

SHORESIDE

Tourist Office 1 rue Carnot. ☎ 03 22 27 05 25; 🖾 03 22 27 90 58. Open Jul/Aug 1000–1900 daily; other months 0900–1200 & 1400–1800, closed Tues.

What to see/do The quayside area is attractive. If staying a day or two, cycle the 10km NW to the fascinating Marquenterre bird sanctuary; keep to the back roads D4 to St Firmin and D204. Open 0930–1900; bring binoculars.

Rail Nearest stations are at Rue and Noyelles-sur-Mer, from which trains run to Boulogne/Calais or Abbeville/Amiens for Paris.

Buses none seen, but ask at the Tourist Office.

Taxi ☎ 03 22 27 90 93.

Car and bike hire Garage de l'Avenir, rue Port du Pont; ☎ 03 22 27 80 33.

Beaches Superb sandy beaches W and NW of the harbour. Near LW people walk across the channel to adjacent sandbanks, but they should be back on land by HW–3, to avoid being cut off.

All you ever wished to know about Le Crotoy

Supermarkets Shopi, rue du 8 Mai; Mon–Sat 0900–1230 & 1500–1915, Sun 0900–1230. A small Petit Casino is in rue de la Porte du Pont.

Launderette La Laverie Crotelloise, 20 ave Gen de Gaulle. Open Mon–Sat 0830–1200 & 1345–1800; Sun 0900–1200; out of season, closed Wed.

Market days One held every Friday morning in place Jeanne d'Arc, plus Tuesday mornings in season.

Banks Three banks and a Post Office in or near rue de la Port du Pont, the main street.

Restaurants Le Goëland, 8 place Jeanne d'Arc, is one of several such restaurants along the quays which cater for holidaymakers. Beyond the Tourist Office try Au P'tit Matelot, 12 rue Victor P'tit. Seafood menus €21 & 31.50. *Bon appetit!*

NAVIGATION

First read the Navigation part of St VsS. From the BIF WCM buoy to Le Crotoy Marina, read on.

Landmark A water tower close N of the marina is conspic and provides good orientation/guidance.

Tides Secondary port differences for Le Crotoy are not published, but local tide tables suggest that local HW is HW Dieppe +20 sp and +28 nps.

Pilotage About 1m less water was found near the BIF buoy than in the main channel. The Le Crotoy channel often shifts and is imprecisely buoyed.

Marina See the aerial picture for harbour layout. For a berth call Ch 09 or mobile, with ETA & draught.

FACILITIES

Capitainerie and **showers** are in the CNBS (Club Nautique de la Baie de Somme) near the head of the access gangway; bar beyond. Harbour Master Robert Jamé; ☎ 03 22 27 83 11; www.CNBS.ifrance.com Open limited hours and at tide times in daylight.

Tariff Daily rates (inc showers) in €, in season, for LOA bands: <7m = 8.40; 7–10m = 11.20; >10m = 16.

Fuel By cans, from a filling station near the Shopi.

Chandlery & repair facilities Ask the HM.

Chapter 4

LE TRÉPORT

West breakwater head – 50°03´·94N 01°22´·23E

Le Tréport is a fishing and commercial port with a locked basin for yachts and FVs.
It has long been a resort popular with Parisians (only 176km away).
But today it has lost much of its charm in a welter of glitzy stalls
and souvenir shops on the front.

SHORESIDE

Tourist Office quai Sadi-Carnot, by the marina.
☎ 02 35 86 05 69; ✉ 02 35 86 73 96. Open Jul/Aug,
0900–1300 & 1400–1900. www.ville-le-treport.fr

What to see/do Climb up from the Town Hall
to the Calvary (cross) on the west cliff top for
panoramic views of the town, harbour and English
Channel, plus a good restaurant. The Fishermen's
Quarter (Quartier des Cordiers) at the foot of the
western cliffs is worth strolling round.

   Cycle or bus 5km south to Eu on the R Bresle.
It is an ancient and pleasing town where Duc
William wed his cousin Mathilde (see Caen). The
beautiful beech forest of Eu extends over 20km
further SE.

Rail The station, ☎ 02 35 86 05 69, is on the plan.
Trains to Paris, Gare du Nord or Gare St Lazare.

Buses to Dieppe ($\frac{1}{2}$ hr) and elsewhere; bus station
is next to the railway station.

Taxi ☎ 06 07 11 47 52; 02 35 86 21 21.

Car hire Garage Moderne, 1–9 quai Sadi-Carnot.

Bike hire Place Sémard, by the rail station.

Beaches Pebbly beach and swimming pool at
Le Tréport; sandy beach at Mers-les-Bains.

Access to UK Ferry from Dieppe to Newhaven.

Supermarkets None in Le Tréport; nearest is an
Auchan in Mer-les-Bains.

Market day Tuesday & Saturday by the Casino in
summer. Mon & Thurs in Mer-les-Bains.

Banks Three on quai François I.

Restaurants These abound along quai François I.

The access channel and Avant Port from the NW

Some of the better ones, with menus from €12.60 to 31.50, plus gastronomique at €40–62, are: La Matelôte, ☎ 02 35 86 01 13; L'Aquarius, ☎ 02 35 86 59 62; Le St Louis, ☎ 02 35 86 20 70; L'Homard Bleu, ☎ 02 35 86 15 89; Comptoir de l'Océan, ☎ 02 35 86 24 92; Les Pêcheurs, ☎ 02 35 86 09 92; Marco Polo, ☎ 02 35 86 07 91.

A welcoming bar/pub, Le François I, sells no less than 80 different European beers.

Elsewhere in the town: L'Éscale, 5 rue Jules Verne (Old Quarter), ☎ 02 35 86 20 96; La Renaissance, 12 rue Brasseur (Old Quarter), ☎ 02 35 86 04 35; Le Saint-Yves Hôtel/Restaurant, place de la Gare (by the rail station), ☎ 02 35 86 34 66; Le Trianon, 44 bd du Calvaire, on the west clifftop; ☎ 02 35 86 27 01.

NAVIGATION

Charts AC 2147 (1:50,000) and 1352 (1:15,000). SHOM 7416 (1:75,000) and 7207 (1:12,500).

Approaches From the N/NE depths are fairly shallow under the influence of the Somme estuary. There are many obstructions (0.1m to 4.1m) NW of Ault lighthouse out to 2.7M. From the SW keep about 1M offshore to clear drying rocks which in places extend 4 cables to seaward. Beware many fishing floats in the near approaches. At night it is feasible to approach with the two jetty lights in transit 110°, but be wary of Les Granges rocks drying 1.1m 300m to starboard.

Lock, fishing boats and marina looking NNE

Landmarks are the church tower perched on the hillside S of the Avant Port; a 49m high silo on the N side of the Commercial basin; a Calvary (floodlit at night) high on the W cliff; and a statue of the Virgin Mary on the E cliff above Mer-les-Bains. Le Tréport is in a gap between the alabaster cliffs of Normandy which rise up at Ault, 4M to the NE.

Anchorage A rather exposed anchorage is 1.1M NW of the pierheads in 9m on sand and shingle.

Tides HW Le Tréport at sp and nps is 5 mins after HW Dieppe; LW at nps and sp is 7 mins after LW Dieppe. MHWS is 9·4m, MLWS 0·9m; MHWN is 7·5m, MLWN 2·5m.

Tidal streams set ENE/WSW at up to 3kn across the entrance. Slack water is HW$-\frac{1}{2}$.

Access In strong onshore winds a heavy swell and surf runs in the Avant Port; a strong current sets NW, max rates at HW+$1\frac{1}{2}$ to +$2\frac{1}{2}$. The access channel dries 2m and is dredged March–May. Only shoal draught boats may be able to reach the lock at HW–4 for the first lock opening.

Pilotage Waypoint in 5m is 50°04´·28N 01°21´·95E 150°/4 cables to the jetty heads. The 150° leading marks are two white discs with red borders. A bearing of 120° on a single such disc (50m W of the lock) then leads towards the lock.

Chapter 4

IPTS are at the root of the east breakwater.

VHF Call Le Tréport Ch 12, 10 to request entry to the lock which monitors Ch 09.

The Harbour In the Avant Port the channel forks to port for the Commercial dock and to starboard for the lock into the FV basin and marina. The triangular area within this fork dries substantially (4.3 to 5.5m) and should be avoided if waiting to enter the lock. Given sufficient rise of tide secure temporarily to ladders on the S quay.

The lock opens day/night HW±4 in summer (±3 other months). Obey the IPTS 100m W of the lock. Approach between 7 R/G piles. FVs have priority.

The N wall is hazardous for yachts. Most of it is corrugated steel shuttering on which fenders can snag. The top two metres of smooth concrete project into the lock by some 0.3m from the shuttering. Stanchions and guardrails can catch below this overhang as the water rises, especially

if sandwiched between the wall and a trawler. To avoid damage it is strongly advised that yachts berth on the S wall which is smooth concrete with a ladder and six vertical wires. Beware current entering the lock from the marina, especially on departure.

The marina is the eastern half of the basin beyond the FV berths; depths become increasingly shallow at the far end. There are no designated ❶ berths so take a vacant slot and negotiate a berth with the lock-keeper in the control tower. The marina is well maintained and securely fenced.

FACILITIES

The Capitainerie is effectively in the control tower where nautical data is forthcoming in English; ☎ 02 35 50 63 06. Open daily in season at tide times.

Tariff €2/m LOA, showers included.

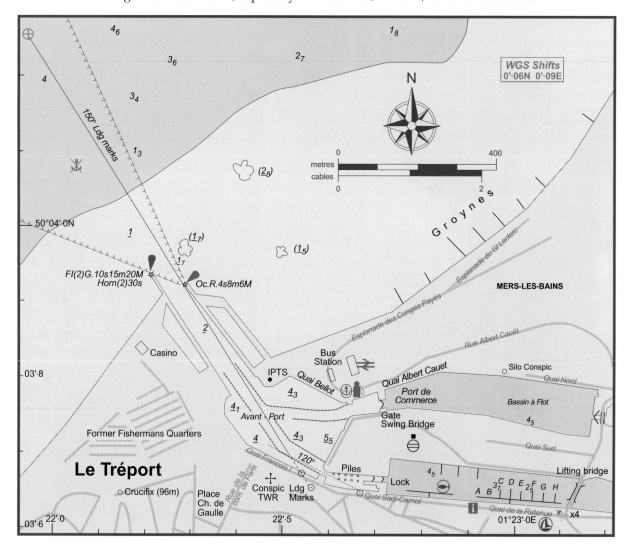

The 150° leading marks. Despite appearances they are not road traffic signs

Looking eastward into the lock. The surface of the north wall is easily seen

Chapter 4

Showers Excellent in four modern 'bathing huts' at the SE corner of the marina.

Launderette Rue Victor Hugo, one block behind the Tourist Office.

Fuel By cans from the garage behind the Tourist Office. Bulk delivery might be possible via the HM. Best to top up at Dieppe or Boulogne.

CHANDLERY & REPAIR FACILITIES

Rather limited but consult the lock-keeper. French charts are sold by the Bateau d'Ecole, quai Edouard Gelée (by the entrance to the Commercial Basin); ☎ 02 35 50 53 10.

DIEPPE

W breakwater head – 49°56´·33N 01°05´·04E

High on my list of favourites is Dieppe, one of the prettiest of ports in northern France, with its 18th century buildings facing the marina. The 1997 ferry terminal on the east side of the harbour entrance has transformed Dieppe from a not very yottie-friendly port into a hugely popular yachting centre with an excellent marina.

Dieppe's long association with Canada began 250 years ago when the Dieppoise explored that country. In WWII Canadian troops suffered heavy casualties in the disastrous raid on Dieppe 19 Aug 1942 (Operation Jubilee). Lesson learned by the Allies: don't try to take a heavily defended port. Message deduced by the enemy: The Allies can be expected to attack ports. Perhaps the successful D-Day landings may owe something to Dieppe. On 1 Sept 1944 soldiers of the Canadian 2nd Division liberated Dieppe in triumph.

SHORESIDE

Tourist Office is at the SW end of the marina, ☎ 02 32 14 40 60; 📠 02 32 14 40 61. Open Jul/Aug,

Mon–Sat 0900–1300 & 1400–2000; Sun 1000–1300 & 1500–1800. www.officetour.com

What to see/do Start the day by walking up to the chapel of Notre-Dame de Bon Secours on the cliffy plateau east of the harbour. Enjoy the views across the harbour and city; or keep walking eastward along the clifftops. Back in town visit the Cité de la Mer, rue de l'Asile Thomas, at the eastern end of the beach. This museum, in what used to be the old fishing quarter, appropriately recalls bygone fishing methods. At the far end of the beach climb up to the imposing 15th century castle. Walk round the outside for the views, then visit what is now a museum, commemorating the navy, art and ivory carving, the last named being especially unique and meticulous.

Rail The rail and bus stations are SW of Bassin Duquesne. Trains via Rouen (1 hr) to Paris (2 hrs 15 mins).

Buses to Le Tréport (30 mins), Rouen (2 hrs 30 mins) and St Valéry-en-Caux (1 hr).

Taxi Radio Taxi ☎ 02 35 84 20 05.

Car hire Europcar ☎ 02 35 04 97 10/02 35 84 40 84; Budget ☎ 02 32 14 48 48.

Bike hire ☎ 02 35 06 07 40.

Beaches A shingle beach stretches west from the harbour entrance to the Casino and castle. A swimming pool is at the W end. Kite flying on the green sward further east is popular.

Access to UK Hoverspeed to Newhaven.

Supermarkets Shopi, rue de la Barre (extension of Grande Rue), by St Remy church. Marché Plus, 22 quai Duquesne, abeam the N end of Bassin Duquesne. Auchan hypermarket is out of town on the Rouen road; Line 2 bus (5 mins) or taxi; open Mon–Sat 0830–2200.

Market day The Saturday market (best and most colourful produce market in Normandy) pulsates around the Place Nationale, the Grande Rue and St Jacques church.

Banks All in the town centre, Grande Rue.

Restaurants First slake your thirst at the vast Café des Tribuneaux in the Place du Puits Salé (Salt water well). Next to eat: Browse the quai Henri IV, where I ate well at the rather dull sounding Le Newhaven, ☎ 02 35 84 89 72, (with which Dieppe is probably twinned), by No 6 pontoon; book early. Les Écamias, ☎ 02 35 84 67 67, €12–16.80, is good value. Musardière, €11.55–26.25, earns Michelin knives & forks, ☎ 02 35 82 94 14.

The outer harbour, ferry terminal and the surrounding town

View NNE across the harbour

Le Bellevue is the first restaurant to stbd as you sail in, so should live up to its name; €11.55–24.85. Au Grand Duquesne, ☎ 02 32 14 61 10, at 15 Place St Jacques, is smallish, cosy and intimate. Eat inside or out; €11–28.70 with gastronomique at €40. Nearby at 1–3 Arcades de la Bourse, Les Arcades has menus at €15.75–30, ☎ 02 35 84 14 12. Last but not least, La Marmite Dieppoise, ☎ 02 35 84 24 26, at 8 rue St Jean features the eponymous fishy hotpot with all kinds of shellfish thrown in; menus from €15.75–40 – worth it before returning to the UK.

NAVIGATION

Charts AC 2451 (1:150,000) and 2147 (1:50,000) with a 1:15,000 inset of Dieppe. SHOM charts 6824 (1:150,000), 7417 (1:75,900) and 7317 (1:12,500).

Landmarks A nuclear power station 5M east of Dieppe is conspic, as is Pte d'Ailly lighthouse on the clifftop 5M west. Either side of Dieppe prominent cliffs give a good radar return. Closer in, the chapel & spire of Notre-Dame de Bon Secours and a Lookout station, high above the ferry terminal, dominate the outer harbour. The W breakwater is not particularly obvious at HW, but at LW its perforated concrete caissons appear very large indeed. At the W end of the beach the castle is easily identified once it is open of the cliffs.

Approach From the ENE two SPM light buoys mark a prohibited zone off the nuclear power station; see above. From the W, Roches d'Ailly NCM buoy is 1.5M offshore, marking a wreck 1.2m; it is safe to route between this and the rocks.

The western breakwater before rounding it from the NW

The DI ECM light buoy, 2.5M WNW of the harbour, marks two wrecks.

Tides Dieppe is a Standard Port; see *RNA*.

Tidal streams set ENE/WSW across the entrance at up to 1.9kn sp and 0.9kn nps.

Anchorage There is no recognised yacht anchorage. A no-anchoring area outside the hbr is on the chart, as is an underwater cable abeam the Castle.

Access At all tides, but entry can be very rough in strong onshore winds against tide.

Pilotage The waypoint 49°56´·72N 01°04´·94E is 167°/4 cables to the W breakwater head.

IPTS are shown from the W breakwater, root of, and from a repeater at the outer end of the marina wavebreak; this is visible from without/in the marina. Strict compliance with the IPTS

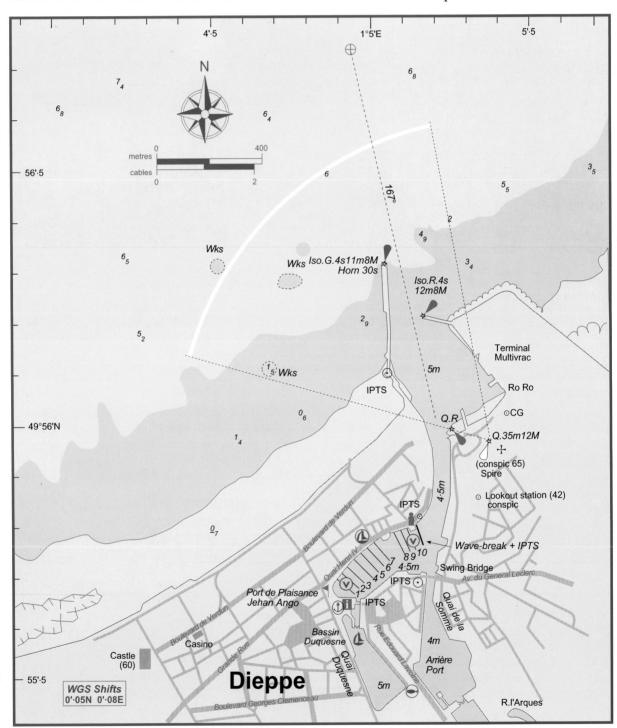

The No 1 slot closest to town

means that yachts need no longer request clearance in/out on VHF; but keep a sharp lookout for ferries and commercial vessels which have priority.

VHF Marina Ch 09. Port Ch 12.

The marina, named after Jehan Ango (a 16th century shipbuilder and privateer), has 10 pontoons in about 4m extending SSE from the quai Henri IV. These are numbered 10–1 from the entrance to the SW end. The ❶ pontoons are 10, 9 and 1. Shelter is usually good and little scend works in thanks to the very substantial wavebreak at the NE end of the marina. The marina is sometimes overflowing in high season, when it may be closed for two or three

The marina with wavebreak in the foreground, looking SW

days at a time. Long-stay yachts may arrange with the HM to berth in the Bassin Duquesne.

FACILITIES

Capitainerie is on the first floor, E end of the building next to Bassin Duquesne's entrance. **HM**, M Abadia; ☎/🖷 02 35 40 19 79; port.ango@ wanadoo.fr Open daily in season 0600–2200 & 1400–2000; off season 0900–1200 & 1400–1900.

Tariff Daily rates in €, 1 Jun–30 Sept, for LOA bands: 7–8m = 15.85; 8–9m = 19.40; 9–10m = 23.10; 10–11m = 24.30; 11–12m = 27.70; 12–13m = 32; 13–14m = 35.70; each extra metre = €3.15.

Showers (free) below the Capitainerie.

Launderette Lav-O-Clair, corner of rue Notre-Dame with Place Nationale; open 0700–2100.

Fuel Between the wavebreak and No 10 pontoon.

CHANDLERY & REPAIR FACILITIES

Latitude 45, 91 quai Henri IV, (No 8 pontoon) chandlery ☎ 02 35 84 14 69.

Thalassa–Dieppe, quai de la Marne (E side of the entry channel), chandlery/repairs, ☎ 02 35 82 16 08.

Dieppe Nautic, 9 rue de l'Ancien, chandlery, electronics, ☎ 02 35 84 13 80.

Chapter 4

St Valéry-en-Caux

Harbour entrance – 49°52´·40N 00°42´·80E

Looking up-harbour from the NNW

St Valéry-in-the-Chalk is peaceful and relaxed, full of flowers and happy people. The market place is bright and breezy, and not without charm. Try to be there on market days. My abiding memory is of the cliffs, whitish, stratified and rising sheer from the beaches, which in turn extend at low water far out to seaward.

SHORESIDE

Tourist Office is in the Maison Henri IV, a beautifully timbered Renaissance house, near the marina entry gate. ☎ 02 35 97 00 63; 📠 02 35 97 32 65. May to mid-Sep, open daily 1000–1230 & 1500–1900. www.ville-saint-valery-en-caux.fr

What to see/do Climb the east cliff where there are two monuments: One a rough-hewn granite stone memorial to the 51st Highland Division; the other a stainless steel bill-board to mark the first flight from Paris to New York in 1930. Keep walking east along the cliff tops. The silence and sense of space will take your breath away.

Pêche à pied at low water is in complete contrast and something the whole family can delight in.

Rail Trains run to Fécamp, Yvetot (31km south) and Dieppe (32km east); onward to Le Havre, Rouen and Paris. The station is S of the marina.

Buses to Fécamp and Dieppe.

Taxi ☎ 02 35 97 01 32 / Mobile 06 80 26 86 42; ☎ 02 35 97 34 32.

Car hire ☎ 02 35 97 01 88; 02 35 97 08 44; 02 35 97 00 55. BP garage by **Ⓥ** pontoon also does **bike hire** €12.60 for one day; €8 per day for five days.

Beaches Shingle beaches below the creamy-white cliffs and a swimming pool on the east seafront.

Access to UK Ferry from Dieppe to Newhaven.

Supermarkets Shopi in centre, rue des Remparts.

Leclerc is further out, on the route du Havre which leads SW from the YC.

Market day Fruit and vegetables in the market place Friday mornings and, in the summer, Sunday – a great display with much animation. Fish stalls on the east quays most mornings.

Banks Five in the market place.

Restaurants NW of the marina in the older part of town: La Barcarole is an unassuming restaurant/pizzeria facing the ❶ pontoon; €10.50 to 22. La Marine is behind the Tourist Office at 113 rue St Léger; ☎ 02 35 97 05 09. €10.50 to 29. Small, but decent food in civilised surroundings.

Near the rail station in ave Clemenceau, try the Auberge La Ferme Cauchoise, ☎ 02 35 97 00 33; €17.30–33.30.

East of the Avant Port, Le Port, ☎ 02 35 97 08 93, is arguably one of the best; €19–24 with a seafood platter for one at €28.35. Behind in rue des Remparts Le Catamaran specialises in moules €12–20. On the seafront is Les Terrasses, ☎ 02 35 97 11 22, €21 & 35. Finally at the Casino, try La Passerelle, with spectacular views to seaward, €18.90 & 24; ☎ 02 35 57 84 11.

NAVIGATION

Charts AC 2451 (1:150,000) and SHOM chart 7417 (1:75,900), both too small scale for much detail.

Approaches From Dieppe keep N of the Roches d'Ailly NCM buoy marking wrecks and rocks off Pte d'Ailly lighthouse. About 1M ENE of the port keep a safe offing from Les Ridens, an inshore bank with only 0.6m. NW of St Valéry there is a fairly exposed waiting anchorage. From Fécamp keep N of the Paluel NCM buoy.

Landmarks A TV mast is 1M east. St Valéry itself nestles down in a cleft in the cliffs. The nuclear power station at Conteville is 3M west, with Paluel NCM buoy 6 cables offshore.

Tides HW St Valéry-en-Caux at sp and nps is 5 mins before HW Dieppe; LW at nps is 15 mins and at sp 20 mins before LW Dieppe. MHWS is 8·8m, MLWS 0·7m; MHWN is 7·0m, MLWN 2·4m.

Tidal streams set ENE/WSW at up to 2.5kn sp and 1.4kn nps.

Access Strong W to NE winds cause a surf in the Avant Port. The entrance channel dries 2.5m and is therefore only accessible HW±3; hug the east side for best water.

Pilotage From the WPT 49°52´·90N 00°42´·30E the harbour entrance bears 155°/6 cables. Shingle accumulates along the W wall, so keep to the east all the way up-harbour. The spending beaches inside the entrance are marked by piles.

VHF Marina Ch 09.

Harbour and Marina Five white waiting buoys are close NNE of the Capitainerie. The marina is entered by a 9m wide gate. From 1 May to 30 Sep, it is open HW±2¼ from 0500–2359, and HW±½ from 0001 to 0500. While the gate is open, the bridge lifts at H and H+30; green or red traffic lights indicate go/no go; G + R = wait.

The ❶ pontoon is immediately to starboard

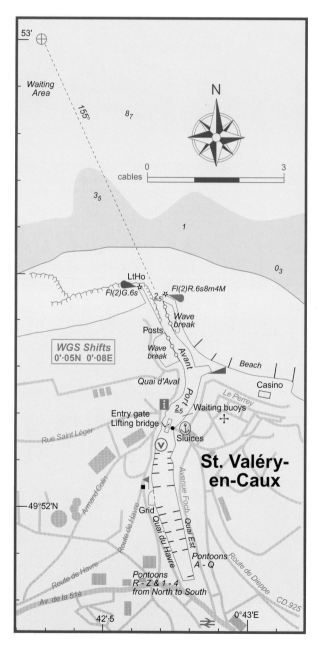

St. Valéry-en-Caux

Chapter 4

Bird's-eye view of the marina

beyond the entry gate; or berth on 'A' pontoon, to port in 3.5m. While the gate is open, currents may initially affect both pontoons. For longer stay negotiate a finger berth.

FACILITIES

Capitainerie is on the central pier between the entry gate and the sluices. HM François Gouel; ☎ 02 35 97 01 30; 📠 02 35 97 79 81. Open daily in season 0500–2359 and at tide times.

Tariff Daily rates in € for LOA bands: <8m = 12.80; 8–10m = 16; 10–12m = 21; 12–15m = 22.40; >15m = 25.60. Third night free.

Showers are excellent and free in the YC (Club Nautique Valeriquais).

Launderette on Route de Dieppe, 150m uphill from the Mairie roundabout. Open daily, 0900–1915.

Fuel From garage behind ❻ pontoon, 0700–2000 in season; 0800–1900 off season.

CHANDLERY & REPAIR FACILITIES

Nautic 76, quai du Havre, chandlery/engineering, ☎ 02 35 97 04 22; 📠 02 35 97 34 26.

U Ship on west side of marina. Sail repairs in Rouen, see HM.

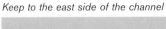

Keep to the east side of the channel

View up-harbour, Pointe Fagnet to port

FÉCAMP

Harbour entrance – 49°45′·97N 00°21′·90E

Fécamp is a welcoming place. Indeed there seems to be a mini-*entente cordiale* with British yachtsmen who flock here from Solent and Sussex harbours.
For a bird's-eye view walk to the top of Pointe Fagnet on the ancient Sentier des Matelots, the Seamen's Path;
this starts on the north side of the Arrière Port. Follow the long distance coastal path (GR 21); it is glorious in the early morning, out of the sun's heat. At the top is the ancient and partly ruined seamen's Chapel of Notre Dame de Salut, where mariners prayed for a safe voyage and gave thanks upon their return.

SHORESIDE

Tourist Office is at 113 rue Alexandre Le Grand (facing the Bénédictine Palace), ☎ 02 35 28 51 01; 🖷 02 35 27 07 77. Open Jul/Aug, Mon–Fri 1000–1800. www.fecamp.com A small office near the W corner of the marina is open Jul/Aug.

What to see Bénédictine is a spicey and subtle liqueur produced from an old recipe. In the C19 a flamboyant merchant of Fécamp, Alexander the Great, began to market it commercially. His multi-pinnacled Gothic Bénédictine Palace is an extravaganza worth visiting – if only to taste the amber liqueur; open 1000–1800 in season.

The Fishing Museum recalls the great days of cod-fishing off the Grand Banks when men were away from Feb to July; open, Jul/Aug 1000–1900.

Rail The station is beyond the east end of Bassin Bérigny. Trains to Le Havre (35 mins), with a change; and via Rouen (40 mins) to Paris (1 hr 5 mins).

Bus Le Havre (1 hr 30 mins), Rouen (2 hrs 30 mins), Dieppe (2 hrs 15 mins).

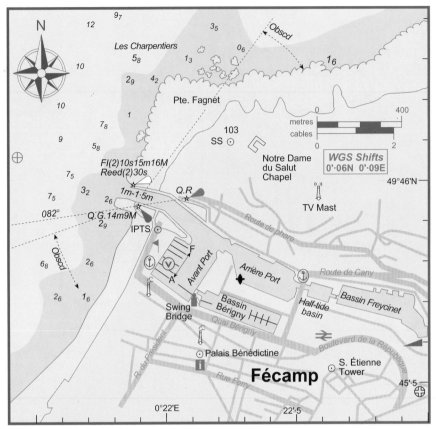

NAVIGATION

Charts AC 2451 (1:150,000) and 1352 (1:15,000). SHOM chart 7417 (1:75,900) and 7207 (1:12,500).

Approaches From the NE keep well clear of the drying Charpentier rocks extending 2 cables off Pte Fagnet. From the W be aware of a waiting anchorage for ships 1.3M west of the harbour.

Landmarks are the conspicuous Signal station and Chapel atop the 103m high, cliffy Pointe Fagnet.

Tides HW Fécamp at sp is 15 mins and at nps 10 mins before HW Dieppe; LW at nps is 30 mins and at sp 40 mins before LW Dieppe. MHWS is 8·3m, MLWS 1·2m; MHWN is 6·8m, MLWN 2·8m.

Tidal streams set NE/SW across the entrance at up to 2.4kn sp and 1.3kn nps.

Access The entrance channel is dredged between 1m and 1.5m, but silts up rapidly. The best water is on the N side. Ideally approach at HW$-\frac{1}{2}$, next best at HW±1, whilst depending on draught and sea state access is feasible HW±4. Boats drawing less than 1.2m are able to enter at all states of the tide. But even moderate onshore winds can kick up a nasty surf in the entrance. Onshore winds of F5 or more raise large seas, dangerous near LW springs. At F7 or above, divert to Le Havre or Dieppe.

Pilotage Waypoint 49°46´·07N 00°21´·42E is in about 9m, 109°/3 cables to the harbour entrance, so you can assess sea state and swell. Turn 90° stbd for the marina. The 082° transit shown on the chart is solely for pilots; the front light, QG 14m, is higher than, and may obscure, the rear, QR 10m. Beware the drying spit off the end of the S jetty.

IPTS sigs 1, 2 & 5 are shown from a grey/yellow tower near the root of the S jetty. If no main lights are shown, entry/exit is allowed. A white light on its own means that it is HW. A yellow light shown to the right of the main

Taxi ☎ 02 35 28 17 50.

Car hire ☎ 02 35 28 16 04; 02 35 27 18 67.

Bike hire Ask at the Tourist Office.

Beaches A fine sandy beach is just a few yards from your boat, across the promenade.

Access to UK Ferries from Le Havre to Portsmouth or Dieppe to Newhaven.

Supermarkets On quai Bérigny, closest to the marina, is a modestly sized Marché Plus; open Mon–Sat 0700–2100, Sun 0900–1300. Up in the town on Place Charles de Gaulle is a Monoprix.

Market day Saturday all day.

Banks Crédit Fécampois hole-in-the-wall on quai Bérigny is nearest; others in the town centre.

Restaurants The rather charming Restaurant Le Prieuré is on top of Pte Fagnet. Back at sea level, eateries line the quai Vicomté and quai Bérigny: La Marée, ☎ 02 35 29 39 15, is well recommended; a modern restaurant above a retail fishmonger; €11.25–32.80. Le Maritime, ☎ 02 35 28 21 71, at the W end of Bassin Bérigny scores well. Just up the slope, Le Vicomté is secluded; menu du jour €15. Le Progrès and La Marine on quai de la Vicomté offer menus from €12.60–28.70.

Looking east at Pointe Fagnet and the harbour entrance

lights means that the entry gates into Bassins Bérigny and Freycinet are open.

VHF Marina Ch 09. Port Ch 12, 10.

The **Marina** in the Avant Port is sheltered from all winds but can be uncomfortable when a scend works in. Visitors berth on ❶, alias 'C', pontoon (with fingers), the fourth from the entrance. Long-stay yachts can berth by arrangement in Bassin Bérigny (5m) whose entry gate opens HW–2 to +7; a waiting pontoon is close NE of the entrance.

FACILITIES

Capitainerie is at the head of 'B' pontoon with **showers** below (free) and **launderette**. **HM,** the friendly Jérôme Renier; ☎ 02 35 28 13 58; ▨ 02 35 28 60 46. Open in season 0800–1200 & 1400–2000; out of season 0900–1200 & 1400–1800.

Tariff Daily rates in €, 2 May–30 Sept, for LOA bands: 7–9m = 14.70; 9–12m = 19; 12–14m = 23.10; 14–16m = 26.25; >16m, each extra m = €2.10.

Fuel Diesel only in S corner of the Avant Port.

CHANDLERY & REPAIR FACILITIES

Alain Denis Yachting, quai de la Vicomté, chandlery, ☎ 02 35 28 30 34; ▨ 02 35 28 84 59.

Coopérative Maritime de Fécamp, quai de Verdun, ☎ 02 35 28 30 34; ▨ 02 35 28 84 59, BY.

Fécamp Marine, quai Sadi Carnot, ☎ 02 35 28 28 15.

Benedictine Palais. The tourist office is to the left of the white van

CHAPTER 5

THE BAIE DE LA SEINE AND COTENTIN
LE HAVRE TO CAP DE LA HAGUE

CONTENTS

Caen. Quartier Vaugueux for good eating

INTRODUCTION

The Baie de la Seine stretches westward for 60M from the chalk cliffs north of Le Havre to Pointe de Barfleur. It encompasses the mouth of the Seine, the Normandy beaches, the Baie du Grand Vey and the eastern side of the Cotentin peninsula. After visiting some or all of the museums which commemorate the D-Day landings, you may well feel sated by war.

But today we are free to walk those beaches on which so many men died. The sand goes on for ever to the tideline, the air is clean and fresh, the solitude and peace are absolute. Never forget.

Drying harbours From Deauville to Cherbourg almost every harbour dries in greater or lesser degree. Ouistreham is a partial exception, purely because as a ferry port its approach channel is dredged, but you must still lock into the marina.

Where access is typically limited to HW±3, this presents few problems as the harbours are mostly no more than 10–15M apart. So leave one at the earliest opportunity and enter the next before the last chance. If heading east on the Channel flood, the tidal conveyor belt can be used to reach the next harbour at, or even before, local HW.

One word of caution: In onshore winds of F4 or above some drying harbours begin to be difficult

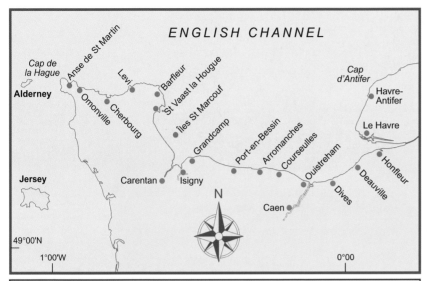

DISTANCE TABLE

Approximate distances in nautical miles are by the most direct route, while avoiding dangers

		1	2	3	4	5	6	7	8	9	10	11	12
1.	Le Havre	**1**											
2.	Honfleur	11	**2**										
3	Deauville	8	10	**3**									
4.	Dives	13	17	7	**4**								
5.	Ouistreham	19	24	14	8	**5**							
6.	Courseulles	23	28	21	17	11	**6**						
7.	Grandcamp	45	50	43	38	35	25	**7**					
8.	Carentan	56	62	56	51	46	37	13	**8**				
9.	St Vaast	53	69	53	49	46	35	16	20	**9**			
10.	Barfleur	56	62	56	53	46	39	21	26	10	**10**		
11.	Cherbourg	70	82	76	69	66	54	39	41	26	20	**11**	
12.	Cap de la Hague	88	100	94	87	84	72	57	59	42	38	18	**12**

wreck buoy and WCM buoy off the end of the Ratelets bank. Off Dives the DI SWM buoy is now larger and easier to see. Behind the town are wooded hills and the distinctive blackish Falaises des Vaches Noires.

From Deauville to Ouistreham the waters are shallow. For example, between Deauville and Dives depths are around 3m whilst off the former the 10m line is some 5M offshore. This shoaling results of course from the outflow of the River Seine which has only partly been constrained by the training walls west of Honfleur.

Ouistreham has a well marked approach channel for ferries, the inner portion lying between training walls. East of the $184\frac{1}{2}°$ leading line Merville NCM buoy warns of shoals and spoil ground to the south. West of the leading line there are three ECM wreck buoys.

Chapter 5

to enter and become dangerous if the wind exceeds F6 or thereabouts. Shallow approaches and narrow entrances compound the problem. Le Havre and Cherbourg are the only cast-iron bolt holes, so if northerlies are forecast be prudent.

PASSAGE NOTES
LE HAVRE TO OUISTREHAM

The approach channels to Le Havre and the mouth of the Seine, not to mention five Big Ship anchorages, create a very busy corner. It is described in some detail under Le Havre which yachtsmen should study in advance. The Greenwich Meridian is only 3.5M west of Le Havre, so be careful to inject the correct Longitude E/W into your GPS.

Honfleur is reached via the Chenal de Rouen, keeping to the north side of the buoyed channel until the entrance is abeam.

Deauville is easily identified by the proliferation of large white hotels and casinos. East of it the coast and the Digue du Ratier form a nautical cul-de-sac. It is best to keep west of the Semoy ECM

OUISTREHAM TO GRANDCAMP

West of Ouistreham the rocky, drying Plateau du Calvados extends 10M further west and 15M offshore; the unlit Essarts de Langrune NCM buoy marks its NE corner. It can safely be crossed near to HW, but at other times skirt round it.

Courseulles lies in amongst it with a SWM light buoy and a dog-legged approach. At its western

The Normandy flag

Juno Beach in peace at low water

end, keep clear of the ruined Mulberry harbours off Arromanches unless intending to anchor there – an emotive experience. Three wrecks NW and N of Arromanches are marked by a WCM and two ECM buoys (others are unbuoyed).

Beyond Pointe de la Percée keep to seaward of three small NCM buoys which mark various obstructions off Omaha beach (3 to 6M west of Port-en-Bessin). The beach is backed by low cliffs which were a formidable obstacle to fighting a way inland. Two miles west is the conspicuous Pointe du Hoc, scene of a daring assault by the American Rangers. Les Roches de Grandcamp is a large flat slab of drying rock extending almost 1.5M to seaward of Grandcamp itself and marked by three NCM buoys.

GRANDCAMP TO CAP LÉVI

Grandcamp is east of the Baie du Grand Vey through whose drying banks Isigny and Carentan can be reached. The former is rarely visited by British yachts; the latter is easy of access and deservedly popular.

The Îles St Marcouf lie between the Baie and St Vaast midway along a shallow bank. South of St Vaast the coast is sandy but punctuated by rocky outcrops and extensive oyster beds. From St Vaast to Barfleur keep at least 1M offshore to clear the offlying rocks which are a feature from here to Cap de la Hague and beyond.

Barfleur Race This is benign with a F4 or less and no wind against tide. In such conditions take the time-saving and straightforward inshore passage from La Grotte buoy to 49°42´·08N 01°15´·10W (off

Dives, the inside of Les Halles (see page 301)

La Jamette ECM perch) thence to Les Équets NCM buoy or vice versa. The Lat/Long is deliberately 3 cables off La Jamette so as to give some room for manoeuvre while avoiding most of the broken water. It also clears Banc St Pierre when coming from/to Les Équets, and to the south gives you a better offing on your way to La Grotte.

In heavy weather, F6 or above, the Race extends at least 3–4M to the east and north-east of Pointe de Barfleur and typical race conditions apply. If the wind is around F4, but against the tide, similar conditions will obtain. Fast tidal streams (3½kn to 4kn) sweep round this rocky, relatively shallow headland. Close off Pte de Barfleur the ESE-going stream starts at HW Cherbourg –4 and the NNW-going stream at +1. The worst conditions are likely when making for Cherbourg on a fair spring tide against a strong W or NW wind.

If your journey is really necessary, give the area a very wide berth. Rounding Pte de Barfleur in a 4M arc to the NE suggests that you keep north of 49°46′N and east of 01°10′W, but on occasions race conditions may extend up to 7M offshore.

West of Pte de Barfleur the usual route to Cap Lévi is via three cardinal buoys: Les Équets NCM 49°43′·61N 01°18′·36W; Basse du Rénier NCM 49°44′·84N 01°22′·11W and La Pierre Noire WCM buoy at 49°43′·53N 01°29′·09W. Be on the lookout for yachts buoy-hopping in the opposite direction.

It is safe to pass about 1M south of Basse du Rénier although the mileage saving is slight. Or try the inshore passage as shown on AC 1106, but the seven transits are all demanding in terms of good visibility, navigational accuracy and above all correct identification of the marks – and therefore may not be worth the candle.

CAP LÉVI TO CAP DE LA HAGUE

A race extends 2M north of Cap Lévi; expect rough patches in the vicinity especially in wind-against-tide conditions. Cherbourg presents few problems to yachts, but the Passe de l'Est demands greater attention than the West entrance because of the extensive offlying Île Pelée rocks. If west-bound from Cherbourg against a foul tide, prior to picking up the first of the SW-going stream in the Alderney Race, stay close inshore to utilise the west-going tidal eddy from HW Dover –6 to –1, contrary to the E-going Channel flood. This is shown in the large scale Tidal Stream Atlas for the Channel Islands and adjacent coasts of France, but not in the the English Channel Tidal Stream Atlas. A direct course from Cherbourg's Passe de l'Ouest to the Basse Bréfort NCM buoy is clear of dangers, but closer inshore be aware of the rocks (Raz de Bannes) marked by a NCM beacon NW of Pte de Nacqueville and those fringing the coast west of Omonville.

Anse de St Martin has two useful anchorages to await the tide; also Port Racine which is a curio inaccessible to anything larger than a dinghy.

From Basse Bréfort buoy to Cap de la Hague keep well to seaward of the offliers marked by La Plate NCM tower, the unmarked Petite and Grande Grune rocks, Gros du Raz lighthouse and La Foraine WCM beacon.

There is an inshore passage, La Haize du Raz, between Gros du Raz lighthouse and Cap de la Hague. It is a challenging way of visiting Goury or avoiding the worst of a foul tide in the Alderney Race. It is fully described in the *North France and Belgium Cruising Companion*.

Cap de la Hague lighthouse in desolate splendour

LE HAVRE

Harbour entrance, N side – 49°29´·23N 00°05´·50E

Cap de la Hève

Prohibited area

Prohibited area

The harbour entrance, marina and Cap de la Hève, looking north

Le Havre ('The Harbour') is a port of refuge with deep water, a very good marina and two ferry terminals. It is also a major commercial port with busy docks and an industrial complex extending 11M east of the harbour entrance.

After WWII the architect Auguste Perret rebuilt the city in reinforced concrete as is obvious from the public buildings and many residential blocks. The task took 20 years to finish and Perret did not live to see his dream complete.

The focal point is the Place de l'Hôtel de Ville. North of the marina looms the tower of St Joseph's church, looking for all the world like a concrete moon-rocket on its launch pad. Further east the geometric grid of streets is punctuated by the show-piece Espace Oscar Niemeyer, the sweeping curves of the Volcan building and the elegant footbridge across the Bassin de Commerce.

SHORESIDE

Tourist Office, 186 bd Clemenceau, just N of the marina. ☎ 02 32 74 04 04; 📠 02 35 42 38 39; www.lehavretourisme.com Open May–Sep, Mon–Sat 0845–1900; Sun 1000–1230 & 1430–1800.

What to see The Malraux Museum is ultra-modern and easily found next to the HM's penthouse office atop a white column at the S end of the bd Clemenceau. The museum houses a fine collection of the Impressionist painters, Boudin (see Honfleur) in particular.

The Museum of Old Havre is worth a visit to see what used to be the city's Vieux Quartier and find out about the pre-WWII city; rue Bellarmato near the SE end of the Bassin du Commerce.

Rail Mainline trains to Paris (2 hrs 15mins). The station is at the east end of the bd de Strasbourg.

Bus Bus Verts, Line 20 to Caen and Deauville; hourly Mon–Sat. Autocar Gris bus to Fécamp via Étretat. The bus and rail stations are co-located.

Taxi ☎ 02 35 25 81 81; 02 35 25 12 33.

Car hire and bike hire Ask at the Tourist Office.

Beaches A good beach runs NW from the marina.

Access to UK The P&O Portsmouth ferry terminal is at 49°29′·24N 00°06′·98E, a 25 mins walk from the marina; or a taxi if crew-changing.

Supermarkets SuperU Océane is in rue Edouard Poulet; 200m NE of the marina, through an archway by Restaurant Thalassa. Huit-à-Huit is in rue Sauvage, behind the Malraux museum. There are many small shops east of the marina.

Market The Flea market is the second Sat of the month in rue Racine, near Espace Oscar Niemeyer.

Banks All you could wish for.

Restaurants Le Thalassa, 58 rue des Sauveteurs, is near the marina; seafood €18.90–31.50; ☎ 02 35 42 63 73. The restaurant in the Société des Régates du Havre (SRH) is good, if you can find a tie. More restaurants along the sea front north of the marina; and near the Rue du Paris, south of Place de l'Hôtel de Ville.

NAVIGATION

Charts AC 2146 (1:60,000) for the eastern Baie de Seine; AC 2990 (1:15,000) for the inner approaches, port and mouth of the R Seine. AC 2994 (1:44,600) for the Seine to Honfleur and Rouen. SHOM 7418 (1:60,000) and 6683 (1:15,000) are equivalents.

Approaches The Big Ship channel leads 107° for 10M from the LHA (Le Havre landfall Lanby) to the harbour entrance. Yachts should stay outside the channel buoys to avoid impeding ships. Note: LH 1, 2 and 9 buoys do not exist.

From the N, including across-Channel, make for the waypoint, LH12 PHM buoy, about 2M from the harbour entrance; see Pilotage.

From the W & SW, cross the channel at LH11, 13 or 15 buoys, then parallel its N side to the harbour. Yachts <20m LOA do not have to cross west of LH 7/8 buoys. Never cross at the harbour entrance where visibility is restricted.

There are four additional considerations:

a. A Prohibited area (no navigation/anchoring) lies to the W, SW and ESE of the S jetty head; see chartlet. Here WWII explosives are being cleared prior to land reclamation and building work. If leaving to the S or SW, do not therefore cross the channel before LH15/16 buoys.

b. Avoid, especially at night, the five Big Ship anchorages, as shown on AC 2146.

c. Yachts coasting from/to the N or NE should cross the deep water channel to the Antifer oil terminal at, or west of, A21/22 buoys, 49°40′·50N 00°05′·00E; monitor VHF Ch 22.

d. Yachts coming from the S or SW should be alert for large vessels entering or departing the Seine via the RNA SWM and Ratier NW buoys.

Tides Le Havre is a Standard Port. MHWS is 7·9m, MLWS 1·2m; MHWN is 6·6m, MLWN 2·8m. There is a stand at HW±1½hrs; LW is sharply defined.

Tidal streams set across the approach channel at up to 1kn. In the Seine mouth the rate reaches 4kn.

Pontoon 'A' for visitors in front of the concrete moon rocket (alias St Joseph's Church)

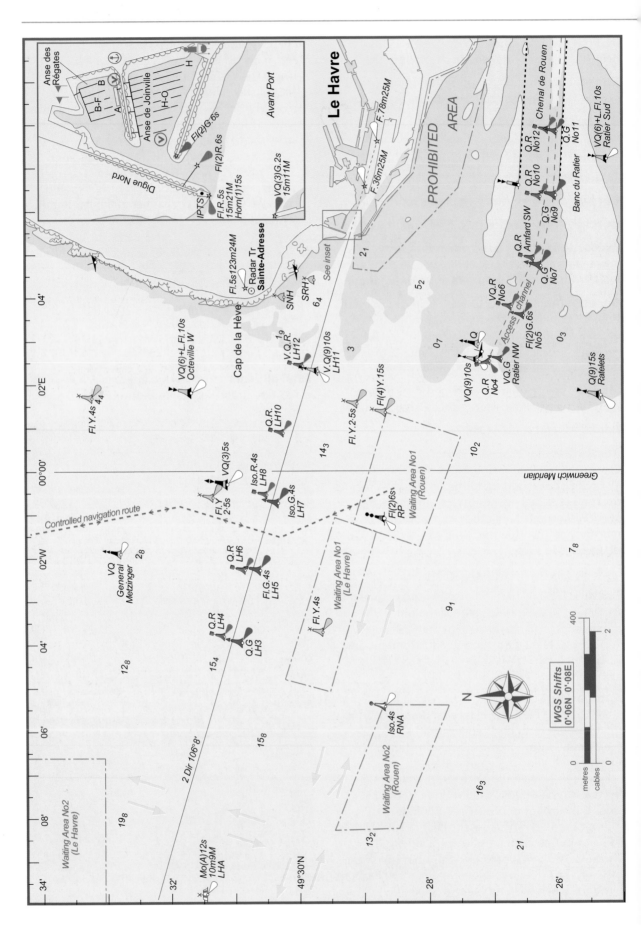

Le Havre

PROHIBITED AREA

Chenal de Rouen

VQ(6)+L.Fl.10s
Ratier Sud

Q.R No12
Q.G No11

Banc du Ratier

Q.R No10
Q.G No9

Amfard SW
Q.R No8

F.78m25M

F.36m25M

VQ.R No6
Q.R No7

Q Access channel

Fl(2)G.6s No5
VQ.G Ratier NW

VQ.R No4

VQ(9)10s
Ratier NW

2₁

5₂

0₇

0₃

Q(9)15s
Ratelets

V.Q.R. LH12
1₉

V.Q(9)10s LH11

Fl.5s123m24M
Radar Tr
Sainte-Adresse

SNH

SRH

See inset

6₄

3

Cap de la Hève

VQ(6)+L.Fl.10s
Octeville W

Fl.Y.4s
4₄

Q.R LH10

Fl(4)Y.15s

Fl.Y.2.5s

14₃

10₂

Greenwich Meridian

7₈

VQ(3)5s LH8

Iso.R.4s LH8

Iso.G.4s LH7

Fl(2)6s RP

Waiting Area No1
(Rouen)

Waiting Area No1
(Le Havre)

9₁

VQ General Metzinger
2₈

Q.R LH6

Fl.Y 2.5s

Fl.G.4s LH5

Controlled navigation route

Q.R LH4

Q.G LH3

15₄

12₈

Fl.Y.4s

15₈

Iso.4s RNA

Waiting Area No2
(Rouen)

16₃

13₂

21

2 Dir 106°8'

N

WGS Shifts
0'·06N 0'·08E

400

metres
cables

0

2

19₈

Mo(A)12s
10m9M
LHA

49°30'N

Waiting Area No2
(Le Havre)

34'   32'   28'   26'

04'   02E   00'·00   02'W   04'   06'   08'

Inset

Anse des Régates

B-F   B

A

Anse de Joinville

H-O

H

Fl(2)G.6s

Fl(2)R.6s

Digue Nord

IPTS

Fl.R.5s
15m21M
Horn(1)15s

VQ(3)G.2s
15m11M

Avant Port

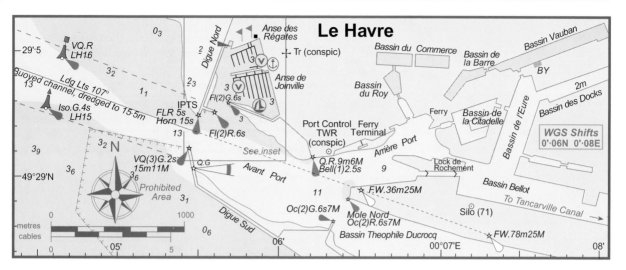

Le Havre

Landmarks are Cap de la Hève cliffs, lighthouse and radar towers, 2M NW of Le Havre; the grey tower of St Joseph's church, close E of the marina; and two, 250m high chimneys, 2.35M ESE of the hbr entrance and almost on the 107° leading line. At night the powerful ldg lts, FW 36/78m 25M, are easily seen against shore lights. The harbour entrance itself can be strangely hard to spot until quite close, especially in poor visibility.

Anchorage There is no recognised yacht anchorage either to seaward or within the port/marina. No-anchoring areas lie N and S of the channel.

Pilotage A waypoint, valid for all approaches, is the LH12 PHM buoy at 49°29′·92N 00°02′·41E. The very shallow (0.1m) tip of Banc de l'Éclat clips the N edge of the channel between LH 12 and 14.

IPTS are shown from the N jetty head. Three reds prohibit entry/exit unless a marina launch waves you through. If in doubt, stay out or in. The 250m wide entrance is narrow for a 100,000 ton vessel.

Harbour entrance looking along the 107° leading line

Access is H24, but at LW avoid shoal water off the spur, Fl (2) R 6s, at the south side of the marina.

VHF Ch 12 Port and Radar. Ch 09 Marina. Ch 67 for locks/bridges within the port.

The Marina's two basins (3m) are Anse de Joinville, where the ❶ pontoon is 'O', with fingers. Fuel and BH are in the SE corner. In Anse des Régates, the ❶ pontoon is 'A', no fingers. At the N end are the two YCs and a de-masting crane.

FACILITIES

Capitainerie HM M Robert. ☎ 02 35 21 23 95; ✉ 02 35 22 72 72. Open Mon–Fri, 0830–1230 & 1400–1830; Sat 0830–1230.

Showers and **launderette** in the Capitainerie, €2 jeton; or free in SRH.

Tariff Daily rates in €, 1 Jun–30 Sept, for LOAs up to: 8m = 80; 10m = 110; 12m = 150; 14m = 200.

Yacht Clubs Société des Régates du Havre (SRH), ☎ 02 35 42 41 21, is more formal (collar & tie) than Sport Nautique du Havre (SNH), ☎ 02 35 21 01 41.

Fuel The pumps (diesel and petrol) are activated by credit card. If your card is unable, a man from the Total filling station (100m south on the road beyond the chandlery) will do the necessary.

De-masting options are covered in *The North France and Belgium Cruising Companion*, with full guidance on the passage to/from Paris.

CHANDLERY & REPAIR FACILITIES

Accastillage Diffusion, 120 rue Augustin-Normand, ☎ 02 35 43 43 62; ✉ 02 35 21 66 07. From the Capitainerie take rue Lemaître toward St Joseph's; it's on the first corner.

ADMT, 116 rue Augustin-Normand, ☎ 02 35 43 00 41; ✉ 02 35 19 08 82. Engineering; next to the above.

Chantier Naval de la Baie de Seine, ☎ 02 35 25 30 51; ✉ 02 35 24 44 18; BY/de-mast at Bassin Vauban.

Marine Plus, BY at Bassin Vauban; ☎ 02 35 24 21 14, Fax ✉ 02 35 22 00 46. A good chandlery is near the fuel berth, on bd Clemenceau.

Delta Voiles, sailmaker, 14 rue des Sauveteurs, one block inland from the marina; ☎ 02 35 20 72 81.

The near approach, on the N edge of the access channel

IPTS

N jetty lt

LH 16 buoy

Port control - tower

Front ldg lt

HONFLEUR

Lock entrance – 49°25´·66N 00°14´·01E

Honfleur is a unique and historic fishing port, whose picturesque Vieux Bassin survives much as it was almost 400 years ago. The Bassin, shaded in the evening by the precipitous, slate-hung town-houses on the quai Ste Catherine, is blisteringly hot in the midday sun. La Lieutenance, former residence of the Governor, now houses the HM at the very top with a brilliant view over his domain.

SHORESIDE

Tourist Office, 9 rue de la Ville (SE of the Vieux Bassin), ☎ 02 31 89 23 30. Open Jul/Aug, Mon–Sat 0930–1900; Sun 1000–1300. www.ville-honfleur.fr Or www.passocean.com – for a nautical slant.

What to see The Maritime Museum in the church of St-Étienne on the SE side of the Vieux Bassin is worth a visit. Nearby are the old salt warehouses (Greniers à sel), now used for concerts, exhibitions etc. Across the Bassin, visit Ste Catherine's church, built mostly of wood in 1468 – still going strong.

Artists flock to Honfleur, art galleries abound. Eugène Boudin is the local boy and pre-Impressionist painter whose friends (Cézanne, Pisarro, Sisley *et al*) came here to capture the brilliant light. He encouraged the young Monet, some of whose works can be seen in the E. Boudin museum, 200m up the rue de l'Homme du Bois.

Down the hill in bd Charles V is the delightfully non-traditional Maison Satie. Erik Satie was a musician and composer with an original turn of mind; hear his music with English commentary. Open 1000–1900, except Tues.

Entry lock and Avant Port near low water. Notice the two fishing boats are making for the deeper water

Best water

From the sailor's chapel, Notre Dame de Grâce, enjoy the sweeping views over the Seine to west and east, taking in the elegant span of the Pont de Normandie. Visit Pont L'Evêque by No 50 bus (20 mins) to see the eponymous cheese being made. This is a gateway to the Pays d'Auge, land of fruit trees, green fields, cream, butter, cheeses, cider, Calvados and Norman gastronomy!

Rail Nearest stations are Le Havre and Deauville.

Bus Bus Verts, Line 20 to Le Havre, Deauville and Caen; Mon–Sat hourly.

Taxi ☎ 02 31 98 87 59, Mobile 06 09 34 45 77.

Car hire and **bike hire** Ask at the Tourist Office.

Beaches 15km west, by the Falaise des Fonds light, is the nearest sandy beach.

Access to UK Ferry Le Havre to Portsmouth.

Supermarkets Champion is 200m south of the Vieux Bassin in the rue de la République.

Market day Saturdays in Place Ste Catherine.

Banks CA at 26 rue du Dauphin and others SW and W of the Vieux Bassin.

Launderette Lavomatique at corner of rues Notre Dame & Bréard; open 0730–2100.

Restaurants Those around the Vieux Bassin are convenient and open-air, but invariably packed in season. Consider looking slightly further afield in two happy hunting grounds:

i. W of the Vieux Bassin, L'Assiette Gourmande, 2 quai des Passagers, ☎ 02 31 89 24 88, is one of the best in Normandy and priced accordingly. In the cobbled Place St Catherine is Auberge de la Lieutenance, ☎ 02 31 89 07 52, alfresco at €21–25.20. Thence in the rue de l'Homme du Bois, La Tortue, ☎ 02 31 89 04 93, whose narrow frontage belies the space inside. €15.75–29.40; shut Tues morning. Downhill in rue Haute is La Fleur de Sel, ☎ 02 31 89 01 92, with menus at €22 & 29.40. Au P'tit Mareyeur is strong on fishy dishes from €20, ☎ 02 31 98 84 23.

ii. East of the Vieux Bassin on the quai de la Quarantaine, in a clutch of eateries overlooking the Avant Port is L'Absinthe, ☎ 02 31 89 39 00, from €28.35. In the quiet place Arthur Boudin is Le Chat qui Pêche, ☎ 02 31 89 35 35, €11.50–24.15; and L'Escale, ☎ 02 31 89 32 22, €16.80–36.75 and shaded terrace.

NAVIGATION

Charts AC 2146 (1:60,000) and 2990 (1:15,000) for the approaches. The latter excludes Honfleur, and 2994 (1:44,600) is needed. SHOM 7418 (1:60,000), 6796 (1:45,000) and 7420 (1:10,000) are excellent; the latter has 1:10,000 blow-ups of all ports from Honfleur to Grandcamp inclusive.

Approaches a) Outer from offshore to the start of the Chenal du Rouen at No 4 PHM buoy, which is

the approach waypoint 49°27′·03N 00°02′·68E.
b) Inner from No 4 buoy to Honfleur lock.

Outer From the SW or S, make for Ratelets WCM buoy, thence to the waypoint on the North side of the Chenal du Rouen. From the W yachts

proceed direct to No 4 buoy. From the NW to N, cross the Le Havre approach channel (see page 287); when S of the channel, alter for No 4 buoy. From Le Havre Marina cross the access channel at LH 12/11 buoys; thence a dogleg to No 4 buoy.

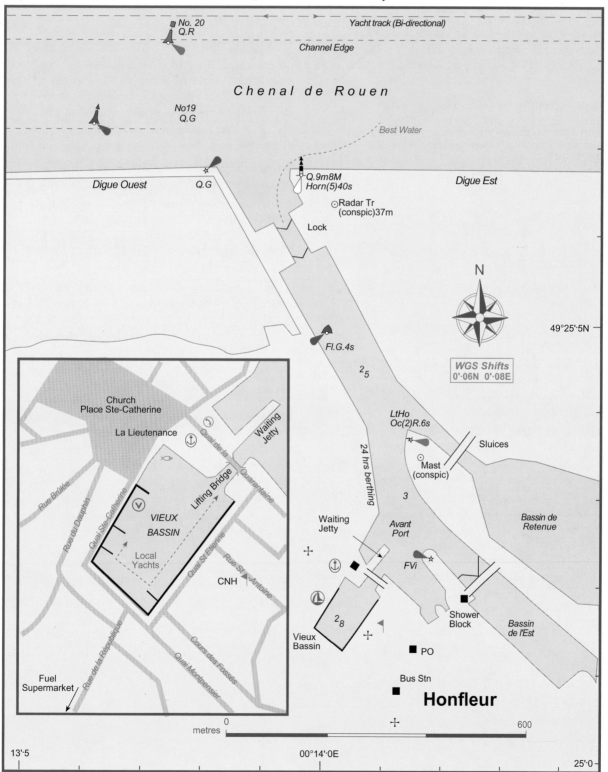

Inner Contrary to normal procedures, yachts going upstream must keep outside the PHM buoys marking the North edge of the Chenal du Rouen. In poor visibility beware a collision risk with downstream yachts also outside the north edge.

Tides HW Honfleur at sp & nps is 1 hr 35 mins before HW Le Havre; LW at nps is 15 mins and at sp 40 mins after LW Le Havre. MHWS is 8·0m, MLWS 1·5m; MHWN is 6·7m, MLWN 2·9m. In the Seine a HW stand lasts about 2¾ hrs; HW time differences are for the start of this stand.

Tidal streams in the Chenal du Rouen set E/W, often reaching 4 kn or more.

Access Pass No 4 buoy at HW Le Havre –3. With 7·5M to run, reach Honfleur just before local HW, when the lock is likely to be open for freeflow.

Landmarks are The Pont de Normandie bridge 1·7M east of Honfleur; wooded high ground SW of Honfleur; and a radar tower close E of the lock.

Pilotage Buoy-hop from Nos 4 to 20 buoys, clear of the Chenal du Rouen at all times. Buoys are approx 1M apart, so if visibility falls below 500m, consider aborting or anchoring as far north of the channel as depths permit. From No 20 buoy cross to the access channel for the lock.

VHF Radar tower Honfleur Radar and Rouen Port are Ch 73; Honfleur lock Ch 17, also ☎ 02 31 98 72 82; Port Ch 17, 73. Honfleur Radar relays messages to the lock and gives radar assistance on request.

Lock The lock operates H24, opening on the hour for arrivals and at H+30 for departures. Freeflow is usually HW±2. IPTS are shown. Four recessed floating bollards are 10m apart on each wall. Due to silting, access at LW±2 may be marginal but best water lies below the Q light on the E side, hugging the boulders. At LW+1 two days before springs, my 1.6m draught stayed afloat here and FVs routinely use this approach; see photo & chartlet.

Entry to Vieux Bassin The old lock is always open. The road bridge over the entrance lifts at:

1 May to 30 Sept: Daily 0730, 0830, 0930, 1030 and 1730, 1830, 1930 and 2030LT.
1 Oct to 30 Apr: Mon–Fri; 0830, 1130 and 1430, 1730. Sat, Sun, Hols: 0830, 0930, 1030, 1130 and 1430, 1530, 1630 and 1730.

Outbound yachts have priority and must be ready in front of the bridge at least 5 mins before the due opening. Early arrivals can wait on the jetty close to starboard of the Bassin entrance.

Waiting jetty, lifting bridge and Vieux Bassin

Visitors berths

La Lieutenance and HM

Lifting bridge

Waiting berths

NW corner of the Vieux Bassin

Vieux Bassin ⓥ berth/raft against the NW quay. If you, or your boat, are an old gaffer, you might be berthed in the N corner as camera fodder! The SW and SE quays are full of local yachts.

The Cercle Nautique d'Honfleur (CNH) oversees berthing/fees etc. The CNH office (☎ 02 31 98 87 13) and welcoming bar is in their pleasant clubhouse, 8 rue St Antoine, a side street off the SE side of the Bassin, between St Etienne church spire and the café La Voile au Vent. Office is open, supposedly, 0700–1200 & 1700–2100 in season. www.cnh.nol.fr

Floating bollard in the lock

19; 12m = 22.05; 13m = 24.15; 14m = 31.50; >14m = 35.70. Motor cruisers >12m and multihulls pay 50% more. The latter may not enter the Vieux Bassin. In the Avant Port yachts may berth for 24 hrs max against the west wall where there are four ladders. This allows locking-out when the Vieux Bassin lift bridge is not operating.

Showers (jeton FF10 from CNH) in smallish white building as on chartlet; 0730-2330 by code.

Fuel Nearest garage on the rue de la République.

FACILITIES

Capitainerie is in La Lieutenance. HM Jean-Pierre Kerangall. VHF Ch 17. ☎/📠 02 31 14 61 09. Open Mon–Fri, 0900–1200 & 1400–1700; Sat 0900–1200.

Tariff Daily rates in €, 1 Jun to 30 Sept, for LOAs up to: 8m = 11.55; 9m = 12.60; 10m = 16.60; 11m =

NAUTICAL NEEDS

Chandlery & repair facilities Honfleur Nautic, Route du Bassin Carnot, a large boatyard and chandlery. De/Re-masting can be done there with a 30 ton crane; ☎/📠 02 31 89 55 89.

Chapter 5

DEAUVILLE

Abeam the head of west training wall – 49°22´·45N 00°04´·22E

Port Deauville and Trouville, looking NE

Deauville and Trouville are often paired as though Siamese twins. But Deauville is where the yachting action is, whilst Trouville is for fishing boats. So Deauville it is – although rest assured that facilities ashore in Trouville are not omitted. Deauville is cool, elegant and sophisticated.

The charming streets and boulevards are bedecked with flowers and beautiful people. Your Cruising Companion felt instantly at ease, if a little out of pocket!

Trouville is more workaday, inhabited by real people and far cheaper than the other place. It is lively, with good entertainment for the kids.

SHORESIDE

Tourist Offices As shown on the plan. The very helpful Deauville office is open Jul/Aug, Mon–Sat 0900–1900, Sun & Hols 1000–1300 & 1500–1800. ☎ 02 31 14 40 00, www.deauville.org

Trouville office is open in season Mon–Sat 0930–1900, Sun & Public Hols 1000–1600. ☎ 02 31 14 60 70; www.trouvillesurmer.org

What to see In Deauville head for Place Morny at the hub of a 'Union Jack criss-cross' of interesting streets. Thence NW to the Casino, walk the planks (*Les Planches*) and take the ferry (*bac*) to Trouville.

East of Trouville Casino, near the white confectionery of a town-hall, turn up rue Victor Hugo into rue des Bains. Hereabouts a villagey enclave has curious shops at every turn; the quaint alleyways have changed little since the '20s and '30s.

Rail Mainline trains to Paris.

Bus Bus Verts Line 20 Caen-Deauville-Honfleur-Le Havre; Mon–Sat every hour.

Taxi ☎ 02 31 87 15 15; 02 31 88 35 33; 02 31 88 40 46.

Car hire Near Deauville railway station: Rentacar, ☎ 02 31 88 08 40. Hertz ☎ 02 31 87 36 66.

Bike hire La Deauvillaise, 11 quai de la Marine (W side of Bassin Morny), ☎ 02 31 88 56 33.

Beaches World-class sandy beaches at both places and the famous Planches – be seen rather than see. Deauville's beach huts flaunt the names of all the great movie stars.

Access to UK From Ouistreham or Le Havre.

Supermarkets In Deauville Champion is at 49 ave de la République; open Tues–Thur 0900–1300 & 1430–1945, Fri/Sat 0900–2000, Sun 0900–1300. In Trouville Monoprix faces the Casino, open Mon–Sat 0900–1230 & 1400–1930.

Market day Sunday mornings in Deauville's Place Morny. On Wed and Sun a large market stretches along the quayside at Trouville.

Banks All banks in both Deauville and Trouville.

Deauville's restaurants A tiny selection of those near the marinas: Brasserie Nautica, 2 rue Désiré-le-Hoc (behind DYC), ☎ 02 31 88 03 27; €12.60–19. Chez Marthe, 1 quai de la Marine (also behind DYC), ☎ 02 31 88 92 51, €12.60–22.05; shut Wed. Le Garage at 118 Ave de la République, opposite the Champion supermarket, ☎ 02 31 87 25 25; €15.75–26.25. Aux Trois Ormes, 22 rue Gambetta at corner of rue Mirabeau, ☎ 02 31 81 07 97; €10.50 menu, closed Wed/Thur. L'Espérance, 32 rue Victor Hugo, a favourite with race/rally organisers; ☎ 02 31 88 26 88. Warm welcome, good food at €17.85–27.30; shut Wed/Thur.

Trouville's restaurants Bd Fernand Moureaux (the quayside) is solid with

Visitors' pontoon at Port Morny

eateries of every kind/price. La Régence is recommended, ☎ 02 31 88 10 71; www.la-regence.com Le Noroit specialises in seafood. Near the Casino and the 'villagey enclave', try: La Petite Auberge, ☎ 02 31 88 11 07, 7 rue Carnot. €22.05–31.50; shut Tue/Wed. La Calèche, 87 rue des Bains, ☎ 02 31 88 74 04. €12.60–25.20.

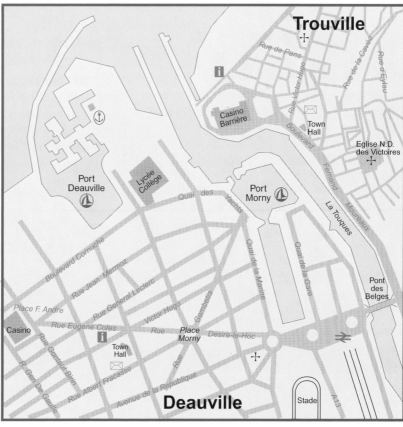

Port Deauville with Port Morny beyond

NAVIGATION

Charts AC 2146 (1:60,000) and 1349 (1:15,000). SHOM 7418 (1:60,000) and 7420 (1:10,000).

Approaches The approach is difficult or even hazardous in onshore winds of F6 or more when a diversion to Le Havre might be sensible. Study Le Havre (page 287) in advance to grasp the Big Ship anchorages and routes into Le Havre and up the Seine. From the W the approach is straightforward. Do not stray into the shoal waters to the east; ie keep west of the Ratelets WCM light buoy. NB: Deauville is just East of the Greenwich Meridian; check your GPS for Longitude East.

Anchorage The only charted anchorage is 1.4M north of the harbour in about 2m on sand/mud. Do not anchor in the drying entry channel/river.

Landmarks A large white square hotel is conspic 0.5M SW of the hbr. Trouville Casino is visible when on the 148° leading line. The light towers on the training walls are conspic when nearer.

Lights The front leading light is obscured if you deviate just 2° east of the leading line. On the ldg line, you are also in the white sectors of the lights on both training walls.

Pilotage The waypoint, 49°22′·87N 00°03′·82E, 148°/5 cables from the head of the W training wall is in about 2m. The training walls cover near HW. Note: When leaving either marina, beware FVs from/to Trouville.

VHF Ch 09 for Port Deauville and Port Morny.

Looking SE, beyond the wooden piers, at Trouville

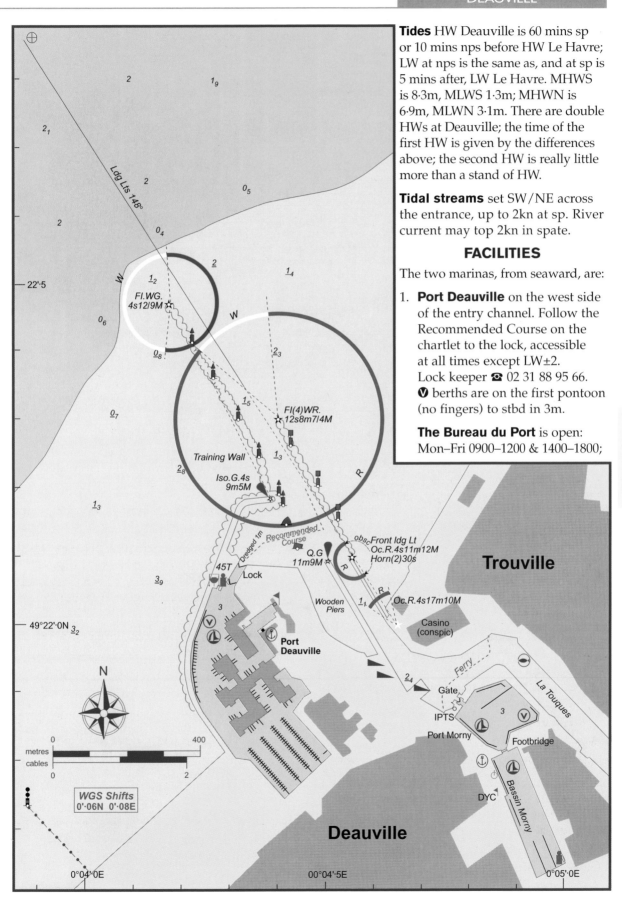

Tides HW Deauville is 60 mins sp or 10 mins nps before HW Le Havre; LW at nps is the same as, and at sp is 5 mins after, LW Le Havre. MHWS is 8·3m, MLWS 1·3m; MHWN is 6·9m, MLWN 3·1m. There are double HWs at Deauville; the time of the first HW is given by the differences above; the second HW is really little more than a stand of HW.

Tidal streams set SW/NE across the entrance, up to 2kn at sp. River current may top 2kn in spate.

FACILITIES

The two marinas, from seaward, are:

1. **Port Deauville** on the west side of the entry channel. Follow the Recommended Course on the chartlet to the lock, accessible at all times except LW±2. Lock keeper ☎ 02 31 88 95 66. Ⓥ berths are on the first pontoon (no fingers) to stbd in 3m.

   The Bureau du Port is open: Mon–Fri 0900–1200 & 1400–1800;

Chapter 5

Trouville's fishing fleet on the River Touques

closed Wed except during school hols; Sat 0900–1200 & 1500–1800; Sun 1000–1200 & 1500–1800. HM Daniel Meslay. ☎ 02 31 98 30 01; ℻ 02 31 81 98 92.

Showers (jeton €2) and **launderette**.

Fuel berth is just beyond the lock.

Tariff Daily rates in €, Jul/Aug, for LOAs up to: 8m = 10.50; 9m = 14.70; 10m = 17.85; 11m = 21; 12m = 23.10; 13m = 25.20; 15m = 28.35.

2. **Port Morny** is dead ahead at the end of the access channel. (The name avoids confusion with Port Deauville; it is also known as Deauville Yacht Harbour or Le Vieux Port). IPTS can be seen from seaward of the training walls. Enter via an entry gate, open from HW–2 to +2½ for freeflow. Gate keeper ☎ 02 31 88 57 99. Visitors berth in 3m on the SE side against a pontoon with no fingers. The inner basin, Bassin Morny, (mostly used by Deauville YC members) is entered by a gate, plus footbridge, which open when the outer gate does.

Bureau du Port (portakabin) is W of the gate into Bassin Morny; open 0830–1200 & 1330–1800. HM Serge Simonet, ☎ 02 31 98 50 40.

Showers (jeton €1.50) and **launderette** in nearby block.

Fuel Diesel only from pontoon at S end of Bassin Morny. Petrol by cans from adjacent garage.

Tariff Daily rates in €, July/Aug, for LOAs <: 8m = 12.60; 9m = 16.20; 10m = 18.40; 11m = 20.20; 12m = 23.05; 13m = 25.20; 15m = 30.90.

Deauville YC (DYC), welcomes visitors. Bar and info files on all ports from Dunkerque to St Malo.

CHANDLERY & REPAIR FACILITIES

- At Port Deauville: Localain Marine, ☎ 02 31 81 17 77. Top Marine, ☎ 02 31 81 65 55, inc Elvström Sails.
- At Port Morny: Touques Nautisme, 3 quai de la Marine, ☎ 02 31 88 45 99, behind DYC. Chantier Naval Deauvillais, quai de la Touques (SE of Port Morny), ☎ 02 31 88 05 75. Serra Marine (aka Marine Stock), 8 quai de la Gare (200m S of Ⓥ pontoon), ☎ 02 31 98 50 92. Very well stocked chandlery and specialist in stainless steel.
- At Trouville: Electronique Marine, 31 rue Biesta Monrivol, ☎ 02 31 87 87 91.

DIVES-SUR-MER

Looking ENE along the coast

Entry gate into marina – 49°17´·75N 00°05´·55W

Dives, flanked by Cabourg and Houlgate, is down-to-earth, but historic and charming in the centre. Cabourg is laid back and well-heeled, with the inevitable casino and a (very) Grand Hôtel. Houlgate is a seaside resort that, apart from its needle-sharp church steeple, does not stand out from the crowds.

Behind, pleasantly wooded hills rising to about 130m are easily seen from offshore.

William the Conqueror was here having left Barfleur en route to England. Due to a storm, he next called at St Valéry-sur-Somme, before reaching Hastings. This circuitous route was no doubt to deceive the enemy – indeed Harold was lured to York by the Vikings, when he should have been down south. The Allied planners probably noted this when they did something similar in 1944.

SHORESIDE

Tourist Office The Syndicat d'Initiative is at 9 rue Gen de Gaulle, ☎ 02 31 91 24 66.

What to see Be in Dives on a Saturday morning, to mix with locals from miles around who come to one of the best markets in Normandy. The Place de la République and adjoining streets provide a colourful setting. The perfectly preserved 14th century covered market, Les Halles, has a tiled roof supported by superb oak frames. Across the square La Lieutenance, where the Lieutenant of the Admiralty lived, retains its original striking facade. Inside the Church, above the west door, the names of 476 knights and gentlemen at arms who sailed with William to England are inscribed.

Stroll into Cabourg to visit the Casino where the streets fan out inland amid fine houses in shaded gardens. The Grand Hôtel was patronised by the writer, Marcel Proust. The restaurants, be warned, serve *gastronomique* food at *astronomique* prices.

Rail Local train to Deauville (30 mins) where change for Paris (1 hr 55 mins), via Lisieux.

Bus Local routes to Caen, Honfleur and Le Havre.

Taxi ☎ 02 31 28 94 16. At Cabourg: ☎ 02 31 24 35 85.

Car hire Caen, ☎ 02 31 84 10 10, or try Cabourg.

Bike hire Ask at Cabourg Tourist Office.

Beaches Good sandy beaches from Cabourg, past Dives to Houlgate.

Access to UK From Ouistreham or Le Havre.

Supermarkets None, but plenty of good, small food shops in the town centre, 20 mins walk. Near the marina's SW corner is a convenient gaggle of Charcuterie, Laverie, Café/Bar Le Gallia, Restaurant/Brasserie Le Pavement and, 200m further west, a well signposted Alimentation and Depôt du Pain, 0800–1230 & 1530–1930, closed Mon.

Market day The main market; see above. Fish market on the fish quay in season every morning.

Banks BNP at 2, rue Hastings; more at Cabourg.

Restaurants Enjoy a warm welcome and excellent meal, €13.65, at Le Mora, ☎ 02 31 91 25 87; across the railway line behind the fish quay. In Dives at 2 rue de Hastings Guillaume Le Conquérant is an old and picturesque coaching inn, ☎ 02 31 91 07 26. €15.75–36.75 and gastronomique at €52.50. The Auberge de la Ferme des Aulnettes near Houlgate is a good place for a meal (€14.70–42), ☎ 02 31 28 00 28.

NAVIGATION

Charts AC 2146 (1:60,000). SHOM charts are 7418 (1:60,000) and 7420 (1:10,000).

Approaches Study page 287 if coming from Le Havre. From Deauville to Ouistreham, in fresh to strong onshore winds the coast becomes a dangerous lee shore, exacerbated by the very shallow water. My boat was standing on her ends when I left at HW–1 against a NW F3–4. Otherwise there are no problems.

Landmarks Wooded hills to the east include Les Falaises des Vaches-Noires (Black Cow Cliffs), a conspic dark cliffy band. Near to, the Capitainerie and apartment buildings help to locate the marina.

Anchorage To await access and only in settled conditions, anchor on sand/mud/shingles in 5–6m to seaward of the 'DI' SWM buoy. In season there may be two waiting buoys near the DI.

Access This is a shallow water approach via a channel drying 2.6m. The entry gate opens when there is 2m over its sill which dries 2.5m, giving a window of approx HW–2½ to +3½ at neaps, and on a big spring tide –3 to +3½; for draughts >1.5m plan on ±2½. For a first visit, it is best to enter near HW. At springs beware strong currents in the marina entrance for an hour after the gate opens.

Pilotage The DI buoy at 49°19´·23N 00°05´·76W is the waypoint. The new buoy has the same light characteristics, but is taller and in slightly deeper water than its predecessor; it is easier to spot. The drying channel is well marked (see chartlet) and the buoys are moved as it shifts. In the final 90° bend towards the marina, for best water keep to the outside and 10–15m off the fish quay to port. The marina entrance opens ahead and is controlled by IPTS to stbd of the entry gate.

On a dark night the approach could be difficult. The white sector (157°–162°) of the directional Oc WRG 12s light covers the channel only as far as the Nos 3 & 4 marks. Thereafter follow the buoys and beacons closely; only three are lit. Street lights might help the final 90° bend. Moonlight and experience by day should make it achievable.

Tides HW Dives is 1 hr sp or 10 mins nps before HW Le Havre; LW at nps and sp is at LW Le Havre. MHWS is 8·2m, MLWS 1·3m;

Around the bend

Dir Lt

No 7 buoy

To marina

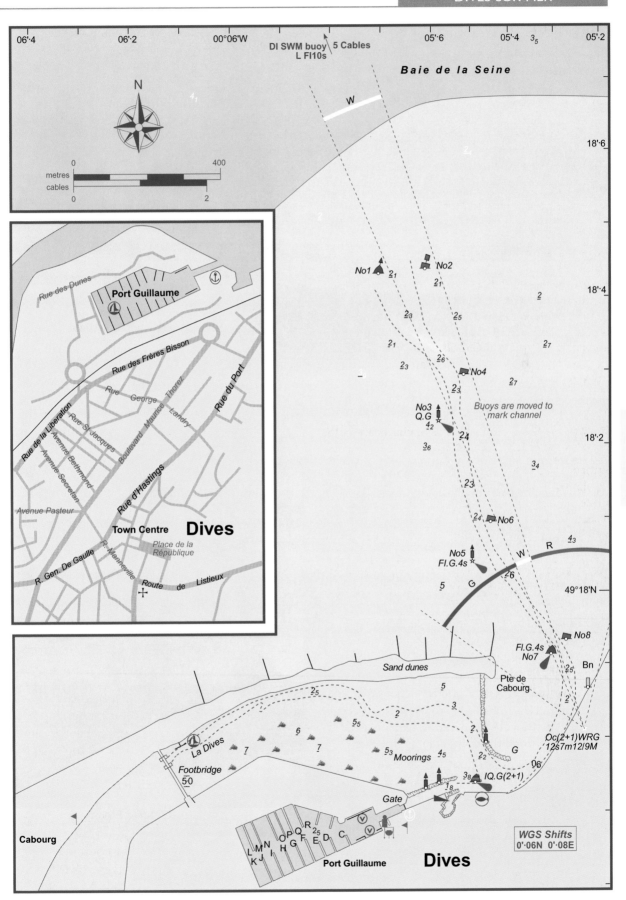

06'.4　　06'.2　　00°06'W

DI SWM buoy　5 Cables
L Fl10s

Baie de la Seine

05'.6　　05'.4　　3₅　　05'.2

N

metres
cables

0　　　　　　400

0　　　　　　2

W

18'.6

4₁

2₄

18'.4

No1　2₁　　　No2
2₁

2

2₃
2₅

2₁
2₇

2₃　　2₆　　No4
2₃　　2₇

3

No3
Q.G
4₂

*Buoys are moved to
mark channel*

18'.2

2₄
3₆

3₄

2₃

2₄　No6

No5
Fl.G.4s

W　R　4₃

2₆

49°18'N

5　　G

Fl.G.4s
No7

No8

Bn

Pte de
Cabourg

Sand dunes

Oc(2+1)WRG
12s7m12/9M

5

2₅

3

2₄

Rue des Dunes

Port Guillaume

2

5₅

2₂

G

06

Rue des Frères Bisson

6

7

5₃　*Moorings*　4₅

3₈　IQ.G(2+1)
1₈

Rue　George　Maurice　Thorez

Rue St-Jacques

Avenue Bethmond

Rue de la Liberation

Rue du Port

La Dives

7

7

Footbridge
5̲0̲

Gate

Avenue Secretan

Rue d'Hastings

Town Centre　**Dives**

Avenue Pasteur

*Place de la
République*

R. Gen. De Gaulle

R. Manneville

Route　de　Listieux

Cabourg

L　M　N
K　J

O　P　Q　R　2₅
F
H　G

E　D　C

Port Guillaume

Dives

*WGS Shifts
0'·06N 0'·08E*

Chapter 5

Marina entrance

MHWN is 6·8m, MLWN 3·0m. There is a double HW. The time of the first HW is given by the differences above; the second HW is little more than a HW stand.

Tidal streams offshore set roughly E/W at up to 1.3kn sp and 0.7kn nps. But by the fish quay they reach 4–5kn at sp, easing markedly near HW.

FACILITIES

The marina opened in 1991 as Port Guillaume and the conspicuous Capitainerie is girded with scenes from the Bayeux Tapestry. Large buildings reflecting traditional and contemporary Norman style line the N and W sides of the marina.

Capitainerie HM Christophe Loyer. VHF Ch 09. ☎ 02 31 24 48 00; 📠 02 31 24 73 02. Open in season 0900–1800; out of season 0900–1300 & 1430–1830. portguillaume@libertysurf.fr

Showers very good and only €1 by jeton; but the 'modern' toilets still feature 'a hole in the floor'. Where to berth. ❶ berths with fingers are on either side beyond the entry gate.

Tariff Daily rates in €, 1 Jun to 30 Sept, for LOA bands are: 8m = 12.60; 9m = 14.70; 10m = 16.80; 11m = 22.05; 12m = 25.20; 13m = 26.25; 14m = 27.30. A €0.50 Holiday tax is levied per night per head. Dives is cheaper than comparable places along this coast.

Fuel The fuel pontoon (diesel & petrol) is to port just before the ❶ berths; open 0700-2100 in season.

Les Halles, outside (see page 301)

CHANDLERY & REPAIR FACILITIES
Cabourg Marine ☎ 02 31 91 69 08. Mécanique Bateaux 📠 02 31 91 46 75.

OUISTREHAM

Lock entrance – 49°16´·88N 00°14´·81W

Ouistreham is really two towns: the ferry port area west of the locks; and Bella-Riva, a slightly out-moded and rather charming resort, about 8 cables NW of the marina. Ouistreham proper has little to detain you, except for four plus points:

i. It is tactically well-placed and, thanks to the waiting pontoon, is effectively accessible at all tides – though not by any means in all weathers;
ii. It has a pleasant marina and the ferry port is convenient for crew-changing;
iii. It is close enough to walk/cycle along the towpath to Pegasus Bridge;
iv It is the canalised gateway to Caen, one of the great cities of Normandy.

SHORESIDE

Tourist Office The main office (☎ 02 31 97 18 63; www.ot-ouistreham.fr) is on the seafront at Bella-Riva, near to the Casino. A Portakabin-type office is in the Place Gen de Gaulle at Ouistreham.

What to see Pegasus or Bénouville Bridge, 2M south of the marina, is the main attraction. This

important road bridge over the Caen canal was seized very early on D-Day morning by a handful of British troops who touched down by glider. Their remarkable feat of arms was only possible thanks to the glider pilots who landed in the dark on a ridiculously small field – no GPS in those days!

Today visit the impressive 'Memorial Pegasus' Museum on the east bank, open May–Sept 0930–1830 for €5.50; Oct–Apr 1000–1300 & 1400–1700. Yachts cannot berth at the bridge and the canal banks are unsuitable.

Le Grand Bunker, an observation post just W of the ferry terminal is open 1000–1200 & 1400–1800.

The Museum of No 4 Commando recalls this Anglo-French force landing on Sword beach, led by the charismatic Lord Lovat and his piper. Open daily, March–15 Oct, 1030–1800, near the Casino.

The R Orne, twinned with the Beaulieu River, joins the sea just east of the marina where the

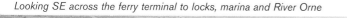

Looking SE across the ferry terminal to locks, marina and River Orne

Pegasus Bridge looking WNW

estuary is a Nature Reserve. A pleasing walk takes you 8 cables east to the Pte du Siège from where you can enjoy the peaceful scene.

Rail From Caen to Cherbourg and Paris.

Bus Bus Verts Line 1 Express bus to Caen; Mon–Sat every hour.

Taxi ☎ 02 31 97 39 41; 02 31 97 35 67; 02 31 44 45 45.

Car hire Rentacar (Caen) ☎ 02 31 84 10 10.

Bike hire ☎ 02 31 97 19 04; 02 31 96 47 47. Also via the Capitainerie.

Beaches Good sandy beaches in Riva-Bella.

Access to UK By Brittany Ferries to Portsmouth.

Supermarkets Shopi is in Riva-Bella on the ave Gen Leclerc, 500m from Place Gen de Gaulle. There is also a Champion on the Caen road south of Ouistreham. The Normandie Wine Warehouse

Airborne Museum

is at 12 quai Charcot on the W bank of the Canal almost opposite the marina. Open daily 1000–2200; ☎ 02 31 36 05 05. (See also Cherbourg, page 340).

Market day In Riva-Bella Wed-Sun in Jul/Aug at Place du Marché; May, Jun & Sep: Fri and Sun; other months, Fri only. In Ouistreham a daily fish market is at the NW corner of the West lock.

Banks Mainly in Riva-Bella on the ave de la Mer.

Restaurants Around or off the Place Général de Gaulle, ferry passengers frequent the following:
   Le Phare Hôtel; the cave-like La Broche d'Argent, €11.55–35.70; Le Goëland crêperie. Le Chalut, €14.70–57.75; Le Channel, €8.40–23.10; Le Normandie, €14.70–57.75; and at Le Roulis, €8.40–23.10, where the service was slow but the food adequate.
   In Riva-Bella, on ave Gen Leclerc or the Route de Lion, try: Le Welcome, traditional eatery; La Botte de Paille, €11.55–19; and La Maison Normande, €10.50. Nearer the Casino, check on: Le Chalet, crêperie; Hôtel de la Plage; Le Saint Georges, €16.80–49.35; and Le Belle Vue, €14.70–49.35.

NAVIGATION

Charts AC 2136 (1:60,000), 2146 (1:60,000) and 1349 (1:20,000). SHOM 7418 (1:60,000), 7421 (1:48,100) and 7420 (1:10,000).

Approaches Straightforward. From the NE, pre-study the approach channel, Big Ship anchorages and shoals off Le Havre; ditto for the Chenal de Rouen/R Seine. Merville NCM light buoy is 8 cables NE of the first channel buoys.

From the NW/N keep clear of the Plateau du Calvados, and various wreck buoys.

Anchorage The only recommended anchorage is 6 cables NW of No 1 SHM buoy in about 6m on sand and shingle. No anchoring in the buoyed channel 150m either side of the leading line.

Landmarks A large square building, Caen hospital, is visible from well offshore but closer inshore slips below the skyline. At Ouistreham the main lighthouse, next to the eastern lock, is conspic, white with a red top, Oc WR 4s 37m 17/13M. Brittany ferries are of passing interest, literally.

Pilotage The waypoint 49°19′.25N 00°14′.46W is on the 184½° leading line abeam the first channel buoys, but with 2.4M to go to the lock. An inner waypoint of 49°18′.48N 00°14′.56W is 8 cables nearer the lock in adequate water between Nos 5/6 buoys. In normal weather, by day/night this waypoint saves time. The ends of the covering training walls extend seaward to the first pair of pile beacons, Iso G4s & Oc (2) R 6s. Ensure that by then you are inside the channel. The 184½° ldg lights are synchronised Dir Oc (3+1) R 12s 10/30m 17M, shown H24, and very helpful in thick haze.

VHF Ouistreham-Caen Port is Ch 68; Lock Ch 12; Marina Ch 09; the Canal transit Ch 68; Bridges Ch 74, only if necessary; and Caen Marina Ch 09.

Tides HW Ouistreham is 45 mins sp or 10 mins nps before HW Le Havre; LW at nps is 5 mins before and at sp the same as LW Le Havre. MHWS is 7·6m, MLWS 0·9m; MHWN is 6·3m, MLWN 2·6m. There are double HWs, the time of the first given by the differences above; the second HW is little more than a stand of HW.

Tidal streams set WNW/ESE near the outer waypoint, up to 1.4kn at springs and 0.8kn neaps.

Access to the lock (and thence to the marina and Canal de Caen) is approx HW±3. The table below gives scheduled openings.

A 70m long waiting pontoon, east of the channel and north of the lock, is solely to await the next lock opening (max stay 7 hrs), not for yachts on passage to rest or wait for a fair tide. Drying

Entering the East Lock from the sea

The lock's scheduled closing times[1], relative to HW Ouistreham, are shown schematically:

Sea to canal		$-2\frac{1}{4}$	$-1\frac{1}{4}$	HW	$+\frac{1}{2}$		$+2\frac{1}{4}$	$+3\frac{1}{4}$
Canal to sea	$-3\frac{1}{4}$[4] $-2\frac{3}{4}$		$-1\frac{3}{4}$	HW[2, 3]		$+1\frac{3}{4}$	$+2\frac{3}{4}$	$+3\frac{1}{4}$[4]

(1) The above times are when the entry gates close, ie the latest time you can get into the lock.

(2) Only if the height of HW is less than 7.4m, 15 Jun–15 Sep from 0700 to 2300LT.

(3) Only if the height of HW is less than 7.2m, 16 Sep–14 Jun from 0700 to 2100LT.

(4) Additional times in red apply only at weekends and Public Holidays.

www.calvados.equipement.gouv.fr gives Ouistreham lock times and canal bridge schedules.

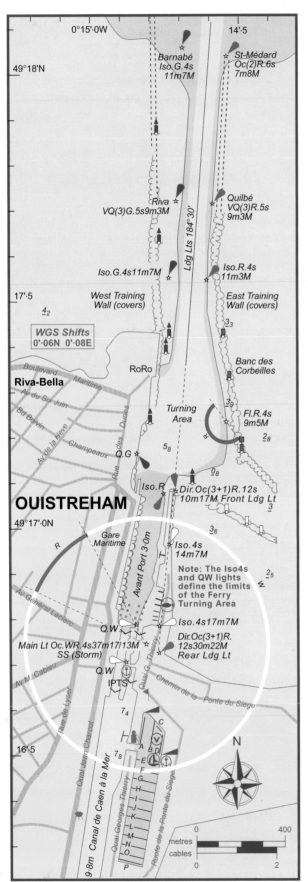

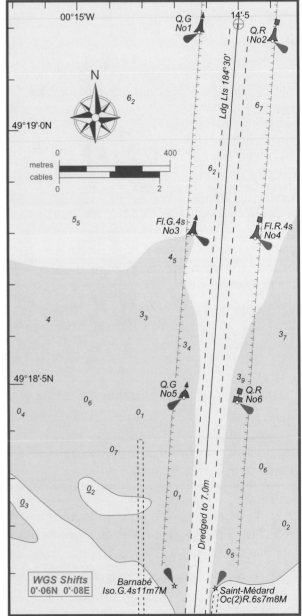

patches close N and S may prevent deeper draught (>1.6m) boats berthing near LW; at MLWS it pays to raft up (max six deep) so as to be in deeper water – usually about mid-pontoon.

Lock times for the current month are posted at the head of the waiting pontoon gangway, and at the Capitainerie. Or call the lock keeper on VHF Ch 12, 68, 74 or ☎ 02 31 36 22 00.

Lock signals IPTS, usually No 2 or 3, are shown, day/night, from atop the control tower between the locks. A fixed white light shown to east or west of the lowest of the three main lights indicates which lock is to be used by yachts/small craft, usually the east lock.

The modern Pegasus Bridge is actually a replica

Locks description The eastern lock, 181m long x 18m wide, is crossed by a yellow bridge which is normally open whilst the lock is in use. Vertical wires are rigged on the walls for warps.

FACILITIES

Capitainerie and shower block are near the S end of pontoon D. HM Alain Ezan. ☎ 02 31 96 91 37; ☎ 02 31 96 91 47; www.ouistreham-plaisance.com

Showers (jeton €2).

Launderette Washing machine €5, dryer €2.50; in the shower block.

Marina Visitors should berth/raft on pontoons 'B', 'C' and 'D'. The only fingers are on the W side of pontoon 'B' where a resident's slot may be free. For a longer stay see the HM, noting that pontoons 'F' to 'P' are all stern-to-buoy berthing.

CHANDLERY & REPAIR SERVICES

Chandlery & repairs are very good. For a major repair, take advice from the Capitainerie, SRCO or a local yachtsman as to the best company.
- On the W side of the marina are: Accastillage Diffusion ☎ 02 31 96 07 75; SNIP ☎ 02 31 97 34 47; Mécanique Marine ☎ 02 31 97 35 34; Localain Marine ☎ 02 31 97 17 41; Nauti-Plaisance ☎ 02 31 97 03 08.
- N or E of the marina on Route de la Pointe du Siège are: Chantier du Maresquier ☎ 02 31 96 30 76; JPL Marine ☎ 02 31 96 29 92.
- On the W side of the Canal (facing 'K' pontoon) is the BY, Chantier Nauti-Plaisance, ☎ 02 31 97 16 21.
- In town at 42 ave de la Redoute is the Voilerie (SM) de la Baie de l'Orne, ☎ 02 31 96 88 59.

Tariff Daily rates in €, 1 Jun–30 Sept, for LOAs up to: 8m = 15.75; 9m = 17.85; 10m = 20; 11m = 22.10; 12m = 24.15; 13m = 27.30; 14m = 28.35.

Fuel The fuel pontoon (diesel & petrol) is on the canal's E bank, close north of the marina entrance. It opens 1 hr before every outwards locking.

The **Yacht Club**, Société des Régates de Caen-Ouistreham (SRCO), is at the N end of the marina.

CAEN

Pont de la Fonderie, marina entrance – 49°11′·03N 00°21′·07W

Caen is the city of William, Duke of Normandy, King of England, and his Queen Matilda. They built, respectively, the Abbaye aux Hommes and the Abbaye aux Dames to appease the Pope who was displeased by their incestuous marriage (they were distant cousins). They lie buried next to their Abbeys which, almost nine centuries later, survived the ferocious battle for Caen in 1944. These fine buildings boast exquisite limestone stairways which look as though they are hanging in mid-air. William's Castle, at the very hub of the city, is another great Norman relic. Within its ramparts visit the Normandy Museum and the Museum of Fine Arts with its impressive art collection.

SHORESIDE

Tourist Office is in the handsome 16th century Hôtel d'Escoville; ask to see the inner courtyard. ☎ 02 31 27 14 14; tourisminfo@ville-caen.fr

www.ville-caen.fr   Hours Jul/Aug, Mon–Sat 0930–1900; Sun & Hols, 1000–1300 & 1400–1700. Other months, Mon–Sat, 0930–1300 & 1400–1800; Sun & Hols, 1000–1300.

What to see Apart from the historic buildings (see previous), a major attraction is the quite stunning MÉMORIAL museum, originally the Museum of Peace. The theme is man's eternal quest for Peace, as told through the horror of War – in particular the fearsome conflict that ravaged Normandy and the whole world. Its brilliant displays (masterly museum technology) depict the brutality of war, yet leave hope of peace on earth. Get there by No 17 bus from the city centre. Open 0900–2000 in summer. www.memorial-caen.fr

Rail The station is about 700m S of the marina. Trains to Paris (2 hrs), Cherbourg (1 hr 15 mins) and Bayeux (20 mins), but no easy route to Le Havre.

Bus Good city links and regional services; Line 20 to Le Havre (1 hr 30 mins).

Taxi ☎ 02 31 52 17 89. Car hire: Rentacar.

Access to UK See under Ouistreham.

Chapter 5

Supermarkets There is a Monoprix in rue de Bernières; head SW from NW end of the marina.

Launderette 200m NW of the marina, beyond Le Grillon restaurant; open 7/7.

Market day A traditional market is held Friday mornings in the Place St Sauveur. On Sunday mornings visit the very colourful market in the Place Courtonne near the NW end of the marina.

Banks All that you could want.

Restaurants tend to congregate in two areas:
i. The picturesque Quartier Vaugueux, a short walk towards the castle. L'Embroche, 17 rue Porte au Berger, ☎ 02 31 93 71 31, is highly recommended, from €17.85. Or try L'Insolite, ☎ 02 31 43 83 87, at 16 rue Vaugueux, €22–28.35; and others in this area.
ii. West of the castle, I enjoyed the Vietnamese Le Saigon, 13B rue du Tour de Terre, Les Quatrans, ☎ 02 31 86 13 48. Maître Courbeau at 8 rue Buquet, ☎ 02 31 93 93 00, is strong on cheese dishes; good value from about €14.70. Les Provinces, 94 rue de Geôle, ☎ 02 31 86 13 23, for traditional Norman fare.

The Town Hall and Abbaye aux Hommes

NAVIGATION

Charts AC 1349 covers Ouistreham and Caen at 1:17,500 and the Canal at 1:25,000. SHOM 7420 has 1:10,000 insets of both ports.

The Canal de Caen à la Mer is 7.6M long. The 1½ hrs passage is simple. Starting from the lock or the marina, the three bridges are: Bénouville/Pegasus (lifting), 2.3M from Ouistreham; Colombelles (swing), 2.3M from Caen Marina; and La Fonderie (swing) at the entrance to Caen Marina. Calix viaduct has 33m air clearance. The dredged depth is 9.8m, reducing to 3.6m nearing La Fonderie.

Bridge openings By sticking to scheduled start times, in both directions, you enjoy free bridge openings. Other times are by prior arrangement and bridge fees will be charged. Start times are linked to a Ouistreham lock time such that a boat entering from sea can go direct to Caen and vice versa. The south-bound start time is at Pegasus bridge, not the marina or lock. With a few exceptions, the S-bound start time is in the afternoon and the N-bound from La Fonderie in the morning. On Fridays in Jun–Aug, and possibly other months, an additional 1830 start time from La Fonderie allows Caen-based boats, and others, to get to sea for the weekend. Bridge times are posted at Ouistreham & Caen Capitaineries and on www.calvados.equipement.gouv.fr

Pilotage Max speed 7kn, no overtaking. Outbound vessels have priority at bridges. Monitor VHF Ch 68, but Ch 74 if you need to call a bridge keeper (they do their best not to delay you). Waypoints are scarcely necessary, but the Lat/Long of La Fonderie bridge is given in the Caen title. This bridge is 12m wide and leads into the marina at Bassin St Pierre in the city centre; turn 90° starboard for the pontoons.

Marina berths The pontoons, with fingers, are lettered 'F' to 'A' from the entrance. **Ⓥ** pontoon

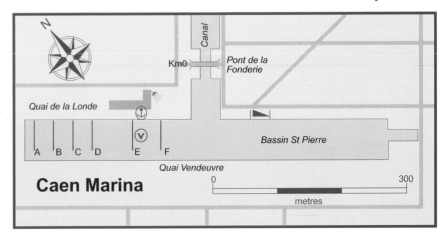

Caen Marina

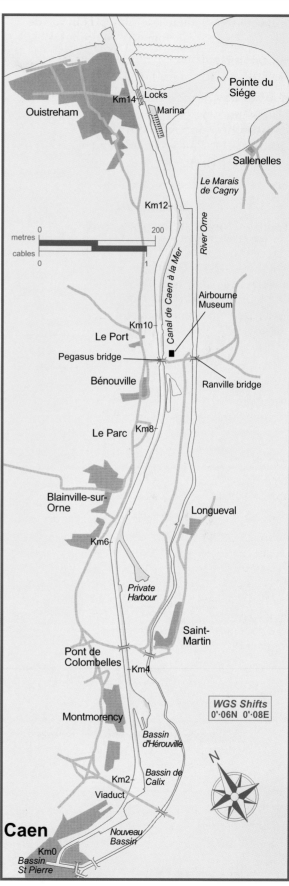

is 'E', second to stbd, unless directed elsewhere by the HM.

Bureau du Port, 2 quai de la Lande, 14000 Caen. HM Jerome Tribouillard, ☎ 02 31 95 24 47; ⟨fax⟩ 02 31 93 97 86. VHF Ch 09. Opening hours: Jul/Aug, morning during the hour prior to opening of La Fonderie (but not before 0830); afternoon during the hour after the opening of La Fonderie (but not after 1930). Mid-Apr to 30 Jun, and 1 Sep to mid-Oct: at 'convoy' times and 1100–1200 & 1700–1800. Showers €2.

Tariff Daily rates € for LOAs on pontoons: 8m = 10.50; 9m = 12.60; 10m = 13.65; 11m = 15.75; 12m = 16.80; 14m = 20; 15m = 22.05. The third consecutive night is free.

Fuel The only fuel by hose is at Ouistreham.

NAUTICAL NEEDS

Chandlery & repairs Comptoir Maritime, ☎ 02 98 92 02 98. Electrics/Electronics.

BAYEUX is easily visited from Caen, either by car (29km) or by train (20 mins). The incomparable Bayeux tapestry is the 11th century masterpiece depicting the conquest of England in 1066 and the accession of William the Conqueror to the throne of England. Designed to hang round the nave of Bayeux cathedral, it is therefore very long (70m), but only 0.5m deep. Excellent English commentary through headphones. The centre is open 0900–1900, May–Aug, €6.50. Bayeux itself is a lively mixture of thronging streets, quiet squares and a picturesque river.

COURSEULLES-SUR-MER

West training wall – 49°20´·47N 00°27´·29W

Courseulles lies at the mouth of the River Seulles which flows out across the western flank of JUNO Beach where the Canadian 3rd Division landed. Today it has a relaxed and unhurried atmosphere. The marina is central and reasonably quiet; the fish stalls are as intriguing as ever; the seafront will keep the kids happy for a while.

SHORESIDE

Tourist Office is at the corner of rue A Leduc and rue de la Mer. Open 1000–1900 daily.

What to see Apart from the inevitable aquarium and a substantial collection of seashells, there is a Duplex Drive (DD) tank which was able to 'swim' ashore from the parent Landing Craft Tank (LCT). West of the port a huge Cross of Lorraine marks the spot where Gen de Gaulle returned to France on 14 June, pre-empted by Winston Churchill who had landed two days before.

For a non-beach picnic, go no further than the SE corner of the marina where the Parc du Chant des Oiseaux has gardens, trees and play areas; a small millpond and river form an oasis of greenery.

Bassin Joinville (marina) in the foreground

Rail Nearest stations are Bayeux and Caen.

Bus Bus Verts Line 75 to Arromanches, Bayeux, Luc-sur-Mer and Ouistreham. Lines 3 and 4 both meander to Caen, via a host of little rural stops.

Taxi ☎ 02 31 37 90 37; 02 31 37 46 00.

Beaches Good beaches lie E & W of the harbour.

Access to UK See under Ouistreham (see page 306).

Supermarket Shopi on rue de la Mer opens Tues–Sat 0930–1230 & 1500–1915; Sun morning only.

Market days are Tuesday and Friday.

Banks Three, in rue de la Mer or Place du Marché.

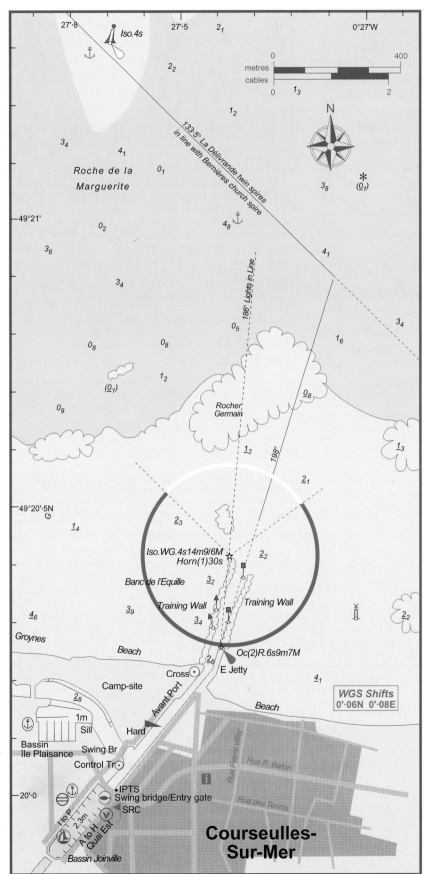

Restaurants La Belle Aurore is an old favourite, close east of the entry gate, ☎ 02 31 37 46 23; friendly bar and menus €12.60–31.50. Le Brin de Folie, 22 rue Amiral Robert (almost opposite the church) is the hot favourite for truly gastronomic delights, but is small so book early, ☎ 02 31 37 53 05. Full of character with sheltered terrace at the back and menus at €12.60 and 22.05. West of the marina, try Au Petit Mousse, €9.45–27.50; ☎ 02 31 37 46 32. Or Le Bistro du Port for grills and pizzas. More restaurants cluster round Place du 6 Juin and on the eastern seafront.

NAVIGATION

Charts AC 2136 (1:60,000) and 1349 (1:20,000). SHOM 7421 (1:48,100) and 7420 (1:10,000).

Approaches Straightforward from east or west, provided the Plateau du Calvados is given a safe offing. Strong onshore winds make conditions difficult on this lee shore; if in doubt, abort sooner rather than too late.

Pilotage A waypoint of 49°22´·00N 00°28´·70W is in 5m depth on the 133½° leading line at 9.5 cables from the SWM buoy. Depths vary from 2.5m to 5.5m. After the SWM buoy follow the dog-legged track as shown on the chartlet. Abeam Roche de la Marguerite is a least depth of 1.4m.

The front 133½° ldg mark, Bernières church spire, should not be confused with two other spires 1M and 2M further east. The rear ldg mark, Douvres-La-Délivrande's twin spires, is 5M from the SWM buoy and hard to see. Closer to, the spires sink out of sight below a wooded ridge.

The approach however is not too demanding and, near HW, is possible from anywhere within the white sector (135°–235°) of the Iso WG 4s light. At night, this light and the Oc (2) R 6s light on the east jetty form a 186° leading line. Both bouldered training walls cover, but are marked by perches. A Calvary, or Cross, is conspic at the root of the west training wall. In the entry channel keep to the east side all the way to the entry gate, for best water.

Tides HW Courseulles is 45 mins sp or 15 mins nps before HW Le Havre; LWs are 25 mins sp or 20 mins nps before LW Le Havre. MHWS is 7·4m, MLWS 1·1m; MHWN is 6·1m, MLWN 2·7m. There is a stand of some 1½ hrs at HW.

Tidal streams offshore set E/W, briefly reaching 1.8kn at springs and 1.1kn at neaps.

Access At HW±2. The entry channel dries about 2.6m. Do not try to enter in strong onshore winds.

Marina The first of two marinas, Bassin de l'Île de Plaisance, is for local shoal draught boats only. The second marina, Bassin Joinville, is accessed by an entry gate which stays open HW±2. It is 9.6m wide, and a sill 2.3m above CD retains 3m inside. The associated swing bridge opens when the eagle-eyed gate keeper (☎ 02 31 37 46 03) sees you, or call VHF Ch 09. IPTS show from the bridge, port side.

Visitors berth as directed by the diminutive and welcoming HM, Mme Angèle Bienek (with yellow baseball cap), often on a hammerhead. The fairway is narrow and there is more room to turn round at the far end. Pontoon 'X', the first to port, is only used by visitors when all vacant slots are full.

Calvary to the west, best water to the east

Anchorages are shown on AC 1349.

FACILITIES

Capitainerie on the NW side of the marina opens HW±3. VHF Ch 09. ☎ 02 31 37 51 69.

Showers (free) are to the left of the Capitainerie.

Launderette is in the Place du Marché.

Tariff Daily rates are: First 5m LOA = €7.35, each additional whole metre = €3.15; eg a 10m boat cost €23.10 + €0.50 tax per night = €23.60. This is dearer than adjacent marinas where €20, also including shower, is more the norm.

Fuel Cans from nearest garage 300m to the west.

CHANDLERY & REPAIR FACILITIES

Quai Ouest Marine, ☎ 02 31 37 42 34. Chantiers Navals de la Seulles, is also on the west quay; plus a sailmaker.

Looking up-harbour to the entry gate at low water

ARROMANCHES

SHM entry buoy – 49°21´·45N 00°37´·16W

When no conventional port was available, the innovative Mulberries (artificial harbours in kit form) allowed supplies to reach the advancing Allied armies. One was built at Arromanches by 12 June 1944. The other, on Omaha beach, was destroyed in a severe storm on 19 June.

Today many of the huge concrete caissons are clearly visible, whilst parts of the piers lie at crazy angles just off the beach. Yachts can anchor within the wide outer semi-circle, about twice the size of Dover Harbour.

SHORESIDE

What to see The major attraction is obviously the Mulberry harbour and the excellent D-Day Landings Museum. This includes a huge model of the harbour and its various components. A short film contains original footage shot by the Royal Navy in 1944. It is open 0900–1900 daily May-Sep, and shorter periods off season.

Another cinema, Arromanches 360, high up on the eastern cliff, shows similar films on a dramatic circular screen. Open Jun–Aug, 0940–1840; €4.20. Film show every H+10 and +40.

Rail The nearest station is at Bayeux (10km).

Bus Bus Verts Line 75 leaves at 0830, 1129, 1350, 1618 & 1828 for Bayeux, 30 mins; also goes to Ouistreham.

Remains of the landing jetties

Beaches Excellent at LW, in front of the town. If swimming from the boat beware the tidal stream.

Facilities Arromanches is a small town, thronging with tourists and a fair selection of eating places, bars, shops. The average yachtsman will probably go ashore solely to see the Museum and the bird's-eye view of the harbour from the east cliff.

NAVIGATION

Charts AC 2136 (1:60,000). SHOM 7056 (1:45,000), 7421 (1:48,100) and 7420 (1:10,000).

Approaches From the east keep north of Plateau du Calvados, but near HW an inshore track may be possible, depending on draught. From the west avoid wrecks, some unmarked.

Pilotage A waypoint of 49°21´·45N 00°37´·16W is the small SHM buoy at the harbour entrance; its PHM twin is some 30m away; both are hard to see until close. From the west they are obscured by the line of half-sunken caissons. The west and east entrances are unmarked and possibly

The starboard hand entry buoy

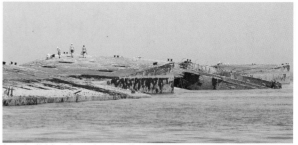

Locals fishing from the derelict caissons

unsurveyed – so not worth the risk of hitting an obstruction.

Tides HW Arromanches is 55 mins sp or 25 mins nps before HW Le Havre; LW is 35 mins sp or 27 mins nps before LW Le Havre. MHWS is 7·3m, MLWS 1·0m; MHWN is 6·0m, MLWN 2·6m.

Tidal streams set E/W at about 1·0kn.

Access At all tides, but in strong onshore winds it would be rough – as it was almost sixty years ago.

Anchorage As shown on AC 2136 anchor in about 5–6m on sand and rock about 4 cables south of the entry buoys. The caissons give little shelter, so this is very much an open-sea anchorage; even on a calm day the boat is restless. As a lunch stop, or to await a fair tide, it is adequate. Buoy the anchor, lest you hook up wartime debris.

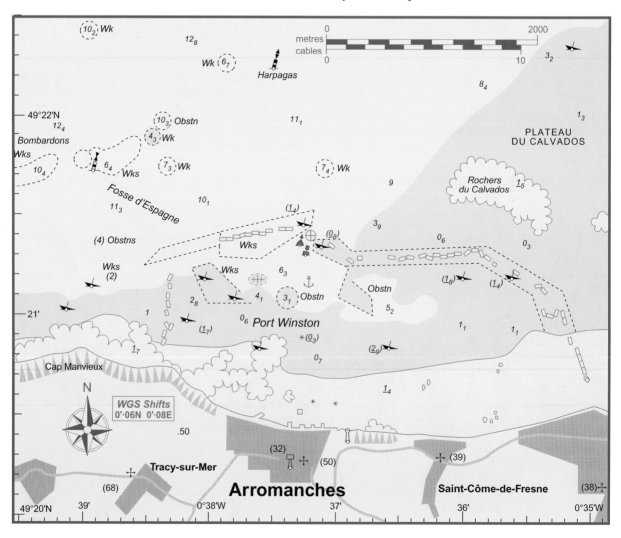

General view looking southeast

PORT-EN-BESSIN

West jetty head – 49°21´·24N 00°45´·39W

Port-en-Bessin (PeB) is home to a great fleet of large trawlers. Of course some local yachts dry out in the Avant Port, but the belief that Philippe Lefranc, the HM, shuns visiting yachts is wrong. He is friendly, efficient and reasonable, but his port is dedicated to FVs.

If you accept that, by all means visit – but berth where directed without complaint. In season do not stay more than one or two nights, due to lack of space; there are no berthing fees. It is better that you know the lie of the land.

SHORESIDE

Tourist Office, 2 rue du Croiseur Montcalm, is up the hill; ☎ 02 31 21 92 33; ▨ 02 31 22 08 40.

What to see The photogenic fleet of fishing boats – not to mention weather-beaten old tars mending their nets – is always an attraction.

The Museum of Wrecks, 1km out of PeB on the Bayeaux road, is unusual. Here WWII tanks, guns, torpedoes, bits of warships and aircraft have come to rest; open Jun–Sep, 1000–1200 & 1400–1800.

Omaha beach is 14km west by bike. Here the heaviest casualties of D-Day occurred as American troops struggled off the beaches, up the narrow paths through the bluffs to the plateau on top. The Museum of Omaha and, not far away, the American military cemetery pay tribute to these events.

Rail Bayeux is the nearest railway station.

Bus Bus Verts Line 70 from the church 0824, 1409, 1531, 1639 & 1844 to Bayeux (15 mins).

Beaches The beach east of the harbour is shingle.

Access to UK See Cherbourg and Ouistreham.

Supermarket Shopi in rue Cousteau, see chartlet.

Market day Sunday, plus daily fish market.

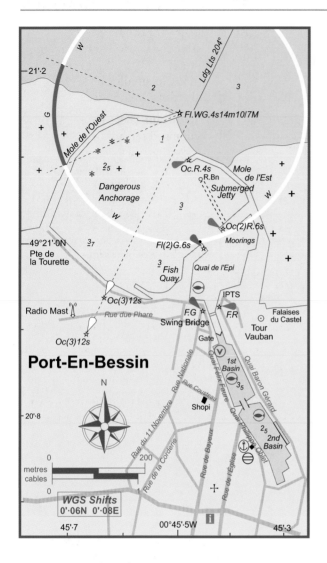

Port-En-Bessin

(chart labels)
Ldg Lts 204°
—21'·2
W
G
2
3
☆ Fl.WG.4s14m10/7M
Mole de l'Ouest
1
Oc.R.4s
R.Bn
Mole de l'Est
Submerged Jetty
*2·5
Dangerous Anchorage
3
W
Oc(2)R.6s
49°21'·0N
*3·7
Fl(2)G.6s
Moorings
Pte de la Tourette
3 Fish Quay
Quai de l'Epi
IPTS
Radio Mast
Rue due Phare
F.G ☆
Swing Bridge
F.R ☆
Falaises du Castel
Oc(3)12s
Gate
Tour Vauban
Oc(3)12s
1st Basin
*3·5
N
Quai Félix Faure
Rue Cousteau
Shopi
Quai Baron Gérard
Quai Philippe Oblet
*2·5
2nd Basin
20'·8
Rue du 11 Novembre
Rue Nationale
Rue de Bayeux
Rue de la Corderie
Rue de l'Église
0
200
metres
cables
0

WGS Shifts
0'·06N 0'·08E

45'·7
00°45'·5W
45'·3

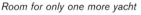

Room for only one more yacht

Banks The usual, plus cash dispenser at the PO.

Restaurants Opposite your berth, try La Marie du Port, from €11.55. Behind in rue Le Tournier is Le Bistro d'à Côte, €15.25–24.15. At No 6 rue du Nord, Le Vauban is possibly the best in PeB, €12–28.35. Or enjoy a cheap and cheerful *ouvrier* lunch at the Brasserie de la Criée by the fish-market; genuine atmosphere and good humour.

NAVIGATION

Charts AC 2136 (1:60,000). SHOM 7056 (1:45,000) and 7421 (1:48,100).

Approaches Straightforward, except in strong onshore winds when it becomes dangerous; divert to St Vaast or Le Havre. Approach direct to the harbour entrance or follow the leading line (see Pilotage). Landmarks E and W of the harbour include low cliffs; a disused Signal station, backed by a high water tower, $1\frac{3}{4}$M east; and an active Signal station 6 cables west.

Pilotage The waypoint at 49°21'·68N 00°45'·08W is on the 204° leading line, 0.5M from the harbour entrance in 10m. The leading daymarks are: Front a small white structure halfway up the scrubby hillside, and rear a white gabled chapel atop the hill. Ldg lts are synchronised, as per the chartlet.

After rounding the E jetty, steer 153° for the inner harbour. Do not stray to port where a drying jetty, marked by a small PHM perch, is a trap for the unwary. Avoid the western half of the Avant Port due to rocky shoals.

Tides HW PeB is 55 mins sp or 30 mins nps before HW Le Havre; LW is 35 mins sp or 30 mins nps before LW Le Havre. MHWS is 7·2m, MLWS 1·1m; MHWN is 5·9m, MLWN 2·6m.

Tidal streams off the harbour entrance average 1.5kn at sp and 0.9kn at neaps, setting E/W.

Access The 10.5m wide entry gate into the wet basins has a sill drying 2.0m and is open HW±2. During this period the swing bridge opens at H and H+30 for 5 mins. In practice the Gatekeeper makes every effort to open it whenever a yacht (or other vessel) is seen to be ready to enter/leave. IPTS (3 R or 3 G) are shown from the NE side of the swing bridge.

Berthing The gatekeeper will probably direct you to turn 90° starboard immediately after the entry gate, to berth NE/SW in the adjacent corner. This is marked *Plaisance* but may already be partially filled by a FV. Berth/raft up against the wall. The max LOA that will clear the fairway is about 11m. Both basins are often full of FVs and yachts might be regarded as a nuisance, at risk of inadvertent damage. The E wall of Bassin 1 cannot be berthed on due to its shallow slope.

IPTS

A man's work is never done...

The only other option is to dry out in the inner harbour against the Quai de l'Epi, subject to smaller FVs unloading their catch.

Anchorage There is no recognised anchorage. Capitainerie is at the SE end of the harbour in the large grey Fishmarket building. VHF Ch 18. ☎/🖷 02 31 21 70 49. For routine queries visit the gatekeeper or call ☎ 02 31 21 71 77.

Tariff No berthing fees for yachts.

Fuel By cans from a garage 200m away.

CHANDLERY & REPAIR FACILITIES

Cooperative Maritime, 14/18 ave Gen de Gaulle; ☎ 02 31 51 26 26.

GRANDCAMP

East breakwater head – 49°23´·60N 01°02´·90W

Grandcamp is a happy port, run by a friendly and helpful HM under whose benign influence yachts and FVs co-exist peacefully together. Stay in this small seaside resort for a couple of nights to enjoy the gentle and relaxed atmosphere. The sea front is pleasantly faded and the main street full of locals.

From the east, if not stopping at Port-en-Bessin, you can anchor off Arromanches and still comfortably make the next HW into Grandcamp. It is well placed for timing a visit to Carentan.

SHORESIDE

Tourist Office is in the main street next to the town hall. There is also a chalet-style Office on the east side of the harbour, ☎ 02 31 22 18 47.

What to see A small but interesting and well-presented museum on the seafront deals with the US Rangers (Commandos) and principally their assault on Pte du Hoc. Good film footage which you won't see elsewhere. Open Tues–Fri 1000–1300 & 1500–1800; Sat, Sun and Hols 1430–1830. You can then walk 4km east to see the real Pointe du Hoc.

The conspicuous church tower at Maisy

Looking SE into the harbour. The entry gate is shut

Rail Nearest stations are Carentan and Bayeux.

Bus Line 70 at 0736, 1320, 1550 & 1755, Mon–Sat via Port-en-Bessin to Bayeux (1 hr).

Beaches Superb, easily accessible beaches.

Access to UK See Ouistreham or Cherbourg.

Supermarket Shopi is on a roundabout about 200m south of the Capitainerie. Open Mon–Sat 0900–1300 & 1400–1930; Sun 0930–1200.

Market day Tuesday in rue Aristide Briand, the main street; Saturday at the Port. A covered, retail fish market south east of the basin is open every morning.

Banks In the main street.

Restaurants La Trinquette, ☎ 02 31 22 64 90, behind the Fish market; €14.70–25.20. Restaurant de la Mer, S of the harbour, ☎ 02 31 22 67 89; €14.70–27.30. La Marée, E side of basin, ☎ 02 31 21 41 00; €15.75–25.45, possibly the best. Le Duguesclin, 4 quai Crampon, on the sea front; ☎ 02 31 22 64 22. Traditional fare upstairs at €11.55–32. La Frégate at the E end of the main street, €9.45–13.

NAVIGATION

Charts AC 2135 (1:60,000). SHOM 7056 (1:45,000) and 7420 (1:10,000) of the port.

Approaches Straightforward. The Roches de Grandcamp, between the Baie du Grand Vey and Pointe du Hoc, extend over a mile offshore. This drying, rocky plateau is a smooth slab of almost uniform depth which can be crossed from most directions. Its northern edge is marked by Nos 1, 3 and 5 unlit NCM buoys, which are good starting points for an approach.

Pilotage The waypoint 49°25´·00N 01°04´·40W is on the 146° leading line, 1.85M from the front ldg light. Use this waypoint/leading line for a night approach or first visit to Grandcamp; otherwise the remarks under Approaches apply.

Landmarks include Maisy's 64m high, modern church tower about 6 cables SW of the harbour. A 37m high water tower is almost on the 146° ldg line – do not confuse it with two nearby water towers. Grandcamp's 47m high church spire is conspic 5 cables E of the port. Both entry beacons mark training walls which cover near HW.

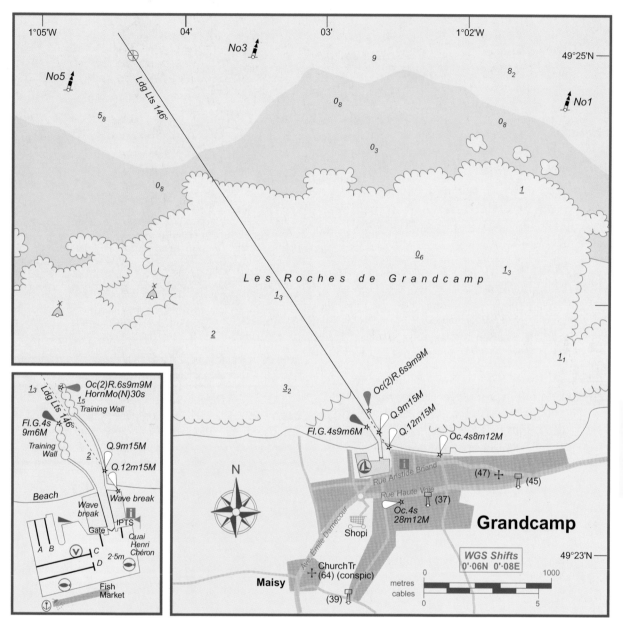

Tides Rade de la Chapelle, the roadstead at the mouth of the Baie du Grand Vey, serves as the Secondary Port for Grandcamp. HW Rade de la Chapelle is 75 mins nps or 50 mins sp after HW Cherbourg; LW is 77 mins nps or 90 mins sp after LW Cherbourg. MHWS is 7·2m, MLWS 1·2m; MHWN 5·9m, MLWN 2·6m.

Tidal streams offshore set E/W about 1kn sp.

Access At HW±2½. The approach and entrance channels dry up to 2m and are difficult in strong onshore winds. Between the jetties the best water is to the east. Yachts should give way to FVs. IPTS are shown from a small control tower east of the 14·3m wide entry gate which is open HW±2½; there is no bridge across. The sill below the gate

dries 2.3m. By coincidence the gate opens at LW Dunkerque and closes at HW Dunkerque. Gatekeeper ☎ 02 31 22 19 17.

Berthing Turn starboard and berth in about 2.3m on the near end of 'C' pontoon, with fingers. FVs berth on the E and S walls of the basin.

Anchorages There is no recognised ⚓, but in calm conditions you could ⚓ in the vicinity of Nos 1, 3 or 5 NCM buoys, clear of Les Roches de Grandcamp, to await entry.

FACILITIES

Capitainerie is in the grey Fishmarket building at the SW corner of the harbour. Open 0600–2200 in season; out of season 0800–1200 & 1400–1700. VHF Ch 09. ☎ 02 31 22 63 16. HM René Marion.

Looking east across the harbour

Very good free **showers** on the ground floor.

Tariff Daily rates € for LOAs greater than:
8m = 12.60; 9m = 14.70; 10m = 15.75; 11m = 17.85;
12m = 18.90; 13m = 21; 14–16m = 24.15.

Fuel By cans from pumps at Shopi supermarket.

ISIGNY-SUR-MER
49°19´·40N 01°06´·20W

Isigny (pronounced *'Izziny'*) is a dairy farming
centre whose butter frequently wins gold medals.
The town also boasts some rather good eating
places. But whether you elect to take your yacht
up the river and pancake into the mud is
something else. Madame in the handsome town-
hall could not remember a Brit yacht ever visiting.
I did not make it in my fin-keeler, having seen
what is on offer at LW, but with a bilge-keeler it
might have been different.

SHORESIDE

Tourist Office is next to the church at 1 rue Victor
Hugo; ☎ 02 31 21 46 00; 📠 02 31 22 90 21.

What to see The major attraction is undoubtedly
the river-bed at LW; see Berthing.

The dairy of Isigny Ste Mère, 2 rue du Dr
Boutrois (turn left at the bridge) is the co-opérative
where the famous creams, butter and cheeses are
made by traditional methods. In Jul/Aug guided
tours: Mon–Sat at 1000, 1100, 1400, 1500 & 1600;
Sept/Oct Mon–Sat at 1100 and 1500; entry €3.15.

CHANDLERY & REPAIR FACILITIES

El Gueroult Patrick, rue du Joncak;
☎/📠 02 31 21 37 79. Engineering repairs of all
kinds. Miquelot Marine, Chandlery, quai du Petit
Nice (opposite the Capitainerie).

Trains/Buses/Beaches There are none.

Access to UK See Cherbourg or Ouistreham.

Supermarkets There is a Champion in the Place
de l'Hôtel de Ville and an Intermarché on the rue
de Littry, heading out to the bypass on the SE side
of town. Smaller food shops in the town.

Market days Wednesday and Saturday.

Banks Sufficient.

Restaurants In rue Émile Démagny (the main
drag): La Flambée, ☎ 02 31 51 70 96. Hôtel de
France, Logis, fish specialities, ☎ 02 31 22 00 33.
Le Globe, 20 Place Gen de Gaulle, ☎ 02 31 51
96 70. Le Relais des marais, 21 rue Delaunay,
☎ 02 31 22 12 56.

NAVIGATION

Charts AC 2135 (1:60,000); SHOM 7056 (1:45,000).

Approaches Compared to Carentan, the channel
to Isigny is deeper, wider, at least 3M shorter and
devoid of visiting yachts. Read on...

The waypoint in about 1.5m is approximately
49°24´·05N 01°06´·30W, the 'IS' NCM buoy, a very

small, black/yellow conical buoy minus topmark. When last seen it was about 3 cables south of its charted position and was hard to spot. Be there 45 mins to 1 hr before HW Isigny, with 5M to run to the town.

Pilotage From the waypoint follow the marked channel south for about 2.5M to Pte du Grouin. Here the canalised channel runs dead-straight between training walls marked by lateral beacons. After 2M fork left into the R Aure; two fields further on you are in the town.

Tides Use differences for Rade de la Chapelle, see page 321. HW at the CI buoy is approx HW Cherbourg +1. Tidal streams are similar to Carentan.

Access Arrive at about HW; HW±2 is probably the limit of the tidal window, and then only after gaining some local knowledge of depths.

Berthing The river bed is soft mud into which keels and hulls sink; FVs fashion their own hole. The centre of the river is scoured by the current, leaving a sloping ledge or bank near the edges, in places quite steep-to and not very user-friendly.

From seaward the three possible options are:

a. To starboard abreast Miquelot's boatyard, berth bows-in, stern to buoys on a reasonably long pontoon. There are no fingers, few vacant berths and local boats are about 6m LOA or less.

b. Also to starboard, about 150m before the low arched road bridge, is a shorter pontoon on which small boats lie alongside.

c. To port is a drying inlet or slipway (thought to belong to the adjacent Atelier d'Archimède, a traditional boatyard, ☎ 02 31 22 20 12) where a shoal draught boat or small multihull might dry out, but its condition is unknown.

Anchorages There are no recognised anchorages.

FACILITIES

Capitainerie Face the fine 17th century Hôtel de Ville (town hall). Walk round to the left to a conspic door marked *Service Technique*; this serves as the Capitainerie, helpful Madame inside. ☎ 02 31 51 24 01; 🖹 02 31 51 24 09. Open Mon–Fri 0830–1200 & 1330–1715, when VHF Ch 09 might be manned. Basic free showers/heads on the quay.

Tariff The daily rate for all LOAs (5–24m) on a pontoon is €4.15.

Fuel Only by cans from garage on south quay.

CHANDLERY & REPAIR FACILITIES
Miquelot Marine, Quai Neuf, ☎ 02 31 22 10 67. Chandlery & boatyard.

Isigny near low water, looking SE

CARENTAN

Lock into marina basin – 49°19´·10N 01°13´·54W

Lock

From sea

The lock, canal, marina and town looking WSW

Carentan is delightfully different. How pleasant to see cows either side of the approach canal. And if you must go aground, how much saner to do it on the high-yielding, alluvial mud of the River Douve than on the hard rock of Ouessant. All these things, and more, are possible in Carentan and its surrounding cattle country.

Old Boney takes some of the credit. Hounded by the Royal Navy in the Chops of the Channel, he resolved to spirit his ships past the Cotentin peninsula via a canal from Portbail to the Baie de Seine. At the latter end work ceased at Carentan where fittingly the Nelson restaurant now stands.

SHORESIDE

Tourist Office Bld de Verdun, BP 204, 50500 Carentan. ☎ 02 33 71 23 50; ✉ 02 33 42 74 01. www.ot-carentan.fr Open Jun & Sep, Mon–Sat 0900–1215 & 1330–1800. Jul/Aug, Mon–Sat 0900–1230 & 1400–1830; Sun 1000–1200 & 1430–1730.

What to see Carentan is an attractive mediaeval town dominated by its 15th century Gothic church. The spire is a landmark for miles around, especially when floodlit at night. Clustered round the church are several attractive old town houses and colonnaded arcades. Carentan is a good base for travels on land, leaving your boat in total safety. Bayeux and Utah beach are easily reached.

In spring and summer visit the vast Nature Park stretching from Lessay in the west to the Bessin region in the east and from St Vaast south to St Lô. The Park reception area, 3km N of Carentan, is open 0930–1900, mid-April to mid-Sept; €3.15.

Rail Cherbourg (30 mins), Caen (45 mins), Paris (2 hrs 45 mins). The station, ☎ 02 33 42 04 00, is across town.

Bus The No 30 bus runs west to Carteret, but nothing goes east to Isigny or Grandcamp.

Taxis ☎ 02 33 42 01 95; 02 33 71 50 50; 02 33 42 21 44.

Car hire Europa, 7 Bld de Verdun; ☎ 02 33 71 50 50. Station ELF, route de Cherbourg, ☎ 02 33 42 00 93.

Bike hire Enquire at the Tourist Office.

Beaches None; no swimming in the marina basin. Open air swimming pool opposite 'G' pontoon.

Access to UK See under Cherbourg.

Supermarkets Proxi in rue Holgate (main shopping street). Shopi at rue du Dr Gaillard.

Market day Tues morning in the Place Vauban.

Banks Seven banks and one Post Office.

Restaurants On the Quai de Caligny (S end of the marina) are the Café du Port, Le Napolitain (pizzeria) and Le Nelson brasserie and restaurant; €9.60–16; good view down the marina. For more serious eating try the Auberge Normande, 11 bld de Verdun; ☎ 02 33 42 28 28. Near the station; rather nicer than its main road site suggests. €12.60–27.50.

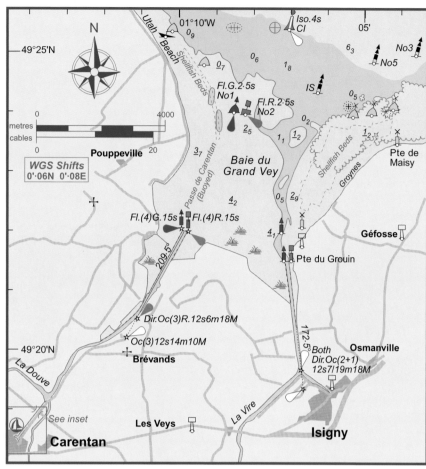

NAVIGATION

Charts AC 2135 (1:60,000). SHOM 7056 (1:45,000).

Approaches Straightforward, but do not attempt it in strong NE winds when the estuary is a bad lee shore. From the east a direct track to the waypoint will clear the Roches de Grandcamp. From the NW, keep inshore of Îles St Marcouf. The modern church tower at Maisy, by Grandcamp, is conspic from all directions and commands the bay. It is square, 64m high and shown in the photograph under Grandcamp on page 319.

Tides HW Carentan is about HW Cherbourg +1. Rade de la Chapelle, to seaward of the Baie du Grand Vey, is the Secondary Port for Carentan. HW Rade de la Chapelle is 75 mins nps or 50 mins sp after HW Cherbourg; LWs are 77 mins nps or 90 mins sp after LW Cherbourg. MHWS is 7·2m, MLWS 1·2m; MHWN is 5·9m, MLWN 2·6m.

Tidal streams in the estuary set generally N/S, max $2\frac{1}{4}$kn at springs, a seemingly high rate.

Access The graph gives access times for your draught and the tidal coefficient of the day. Note that a 2m draught yacht can enter Carentan at HW±2 on an average tide (coefficient 70–75), but only at HW when the coefficient has reduced to

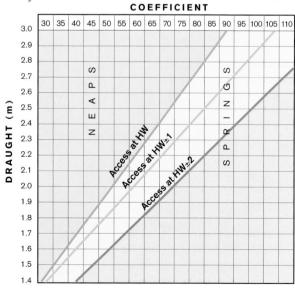

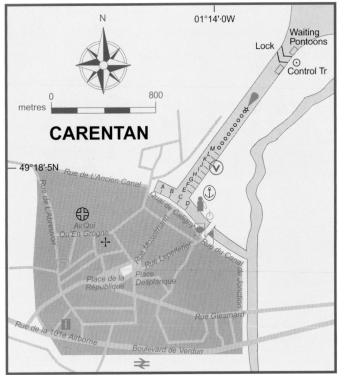

N
01°14'·0W

Lock
Waiting Pontoons
⊙ Control Tr

0   800
metres

CARENTAN

— 49°18'·5N
Rue de L'Ancien Canal

Rue de L'Abreuvoir

Av.Qui Qu'En Grogne

Place de la République

Place Desplanque

Rue de la 101e Airborne

Rue Giesmard

Boulevard de Verdun

Quai de Caligny
Rue Moselmann
Rue Lepelletier
Rue du Canal de Jonction

passed: For example from the east track direct to No 2 channel buoy at approx 49°24'·03N 01°08'·26W. Buoys are moved as the channel shifts.

The buoyed channel is wide and well marked up to the breakwater piles, but beware of shoal patches (2.3m least depth); keep well to the west side for best water. Thereafter the riverine channel is marked by perches and has adequate depths.

Night approach The CI buoy and six pairs of the 14 lateral buoys/perches are lit. The $209\frac{1}{2}°$ ldg lts are valid until the river bends to stbd, whence six street lamps on the E bank suffice to the lock.

The lock is at the junction of the Douve and Taute. In Jun–Aug it is manned HW–2 to +3; otherwise call the lock-keeper ☎ 02 33 71 10 85 or by direct line on the control tower. Small waiting pontoons are down- and up-stream. The lock can hold four to six boats depending on size and can be transited in about 10 mins. The last 1km to the marina is canalised.

50–55 (neaps). A typical draught of 1.5m is only limited at unusually small neaps (30–35).

For a first visit, aim to be at Carentan lock at local HW. To this end, leave CI buoy (7M from the lock) at about HW–$1\frac{1}{2}$, or Nos 1/2 buoys at HW–1 hr 10 mins, assuming a boat speed of 5.5 to 6kn. A slower boat should be at CI no later than HW–2.

Pilotage The CI SWM buoy is the waypoint at 49°25'·53N 01°07'·00W, but this buoy can be by-

Berths Visitors berth on 'K' which in season tends to become a crowded and sociable Little England. For a longer stay negotiate a berth nearer the town.

Anchorage There is no recognised anchorage. It is not advisable to anchor in the buoyed channel.

Leaving Carentan Lock out at HW–$1\frac{1}{2}$, bucking the last of the flood, little more than $\frac{1}{2}$kn, most of

A pastoral scene: Marina and town beyond

'E' pontoon and the Capitainerie

the way to CI. It is possible to lock out at HW–2 and enter Grandcamp before the entry gate shuts.

FACILITIES

Capitainerie HM Denis Leprevost, ☎ 02 33 42 24 44; 🖷 02 33 42 00 03. www.sctel.fr/port-carentan/ VHF Ch 09. In season 0800–1200 & 1400–1800; out of season 0800–1200 & 1330–1730. Showers free 0800–1800, Jun to mid-Sep; other hours access a single shower from outside via a coded lock.

Launderette in the shower block.

Tariff Daily rates are based on boat area (LOA x beam). May–Sep, the first 20 sq m cost €0.50 per sq m; each additional sq m costs €0.34.

Fuel Diesel & petrol pumps are on the wall at the eastern end of the T-junction; 0900-1000, Mon-Sat.

CHANDLERY & REPAIR FACILITIES

A Chandlery/Boatyard is by the SW arm of the T-junction; consult the Capitainerie.

ILES ST MARCOUF
Main anchorage – 49°29'·85N 01°08'·86W

These two uninhabited offshore islands lie almost equidistant (7M) NW of Grandcamp and SE of St Vaast; they offer interesting anchorages in calm settled weather, but even then probably only for a shortish stay. They are in the open sea, fringed by drying rocks which provide some shelter near LW. Île du Large is the NE'ly island, conspicuously fortified and lit, VQ (3) 5s. Île de Terre is a low-lying bird sanctuary where landing is prohibited.

History St Marcouf lived the life of a hermit, was patron saint of skin diseases and died 558AD – cause of death unknown. The Brits were here only from 1793 to 1802, before Napoleon moved in and built the massive fortifications as part of his plans for the invasion of England. Since WWI the islands have been inhabited only by seabirds.

Approaches The islands lie between two banks, Banc de St Marcouf to the NW and to the SE Banc du Cardonnet. In calm conditions these are not a hazard, but beware an unmarked wreck with only 0.6m over it, 2M WNW of Île du Large.

Charts AC 2135 (1:60,000) and SHOM 7056 (1:45,000) are rather smaller scale than is desirable.

Pilotage Approach on WNW or ESE aligned with with the gap between the islands. This allows you to judge your position off each island. Aim to keep well off Île de Terre whose NE tip is extended by drying rocks. Its SW tip has offlying, drying rocks marked by a WCM beacon.

Tides HW Îles St Marcouf is 78 mins nps or 52 mins sp after HW Cherbourg; LW is 70 mins nps or 85 mins sp after LW Cherbourg. MHWS is 7·0m, MLWS 1·2m; MHWN 5·7m, MLWN 2·6m.

Tidal streams The tide sets WNW–ESE between

the islands at just over 1kn, so you are unlikely to be set to one side or the other. Slack water occurs at about HW Dover −1 and +6.

Anchorages A SCM perch marks drying rocks off the W side of Île du Large. The anchorage is about 200m SE of this perch and 200m SW of the nearest point of Île du Large, in a smallish bight. Anchor in about 4–5m on rock and pebbles which may be overlaid with kelp; holding is correspondingly degraded. At LW the island provides shelter from N and E winds, but nearing HW the anchorage is increasingly exposed.

Other anchorages may be found on the SE and NE sides of Île de Terre. The former is sheltered from NW winds, the latter is rather exposed to both wind and tide.

Landing The fortified walls are interrupted on the W side by a small, but clearly visible harbour, only big enough for landing by dinghy

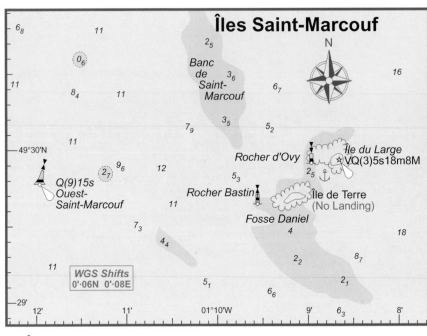

HW±2. Outside these times you will have to carry the dinghy clear, so for a longer run ashore it may be better to land on the pebbly beach, amidst discarded cannons. The fortifications are moated, so you are unlikely to be able to clamber very far. Join the seabirds for your picnic, or more probably they will join you!

Looking SW over Île du Large to Île de Terre

West cardinal beacon

South cardinal beacon

Yachts at anchor near LW

ST VAAST-LA-HOUGUE

Jetty head – 49°35′·17N 01°15′·41W

Looking north east across the town and marina to Le Run

St Vaast, abbreviated and pronounced '*SanVah*', is a long-established favourite with British yachtsmen. It is easily accessible from Cherbourg (26M) and from the south and east, well sheltered from the prevailing westerlies by the Cotentin peninsula and the marina can be entered for 5 hrs or so on every tide.

If too late to enter, the Petite Rade is a good anchorage. The only snag is that St Vaast is becoming too popular and gets over-crowded in high season – try Barfleur or Carentan.

SHORESIDE

Tourist Office 1, Place Gen de Gaulle (see plan); ☎ 02 33 23 19 32; ✉ 02 33 54 41 37; www.saint-vaast-reville.com Jul/Aug: Mon–Sat 0900–1230 & 1400 (Sun 1500)–1830. Sep–Jun 0900–1220 & 1400–1800.

What to see The working side of the harbour is invariably interesting and landing the morning catch is always a crowd-puller. Then visit the little Mariner's Chapel, a memorial to crews lost at sea.

Or indulge in *La pêche à pied* (fishing on foot) ie floundering around with the kids amongst the rocks, sand and mud of the foreshore looking for ...? An oyster tour is probably a more interesting trip for adults (or sophisticated kids). The Tourist Office does a 2 hr guided walk (turn up in your wellies) in Jul/Aug around the oyster beds and workshops; tastings included in €5.25. Île Tatihou (www.tatihou.com) can be visited by amphibious boat from the N end of the marina. Its Maritime Museum is open daily 1000–1600, Apr–Sept; €7.35. ☎ 02 33 23 19 92. There are workshops, a scientific centre, gardens, another Vauban tower and the restaurant Inter Muros; or take a picnic.

Inland, cycle round the bocage (hedgerow country) of the Val de Saire, a gentle area of green fields, woods and streams; see Michelin map 54.

Rail Valognes is the nearest (15km) station, on the Cherbourg to Paris mainline via Caen.

Bus In Jul/Aug STN Line 1 leaves at 0838, 1333 and 1657 daily to Cherbourg, 1 hr 15 mins, via Barfleur.

Taxi ☎ 02 33 54 40 29; 02 33 54 58 08.

Car hire Garage Féron, ☎ 02 33 88 57 57.

Bike hire Bar Les p'tits carreaux, 19 rue Triquet; ☎ 02 33 43 74 76.

Beaches A good beach is S of the marina, en route to the Fort de la Hougue; see chartlet.

Access to UK See Cherbourg.

Supermarkets A SuperU at Quettehou is a 2.5km bike ride west of St Vaast. Proxi, 17 rue Gautier, a mini supermarket, meets basic needs. Open Mon–Sat, 0730–1300 & 1445–2000; Sun 0730–1300 & 1630–1930; shut Wed pm Jul/Aug. L'Epicerie Gosselin 27, rue de Verrüe is a St Vaast institution, family run since 1889. It is an Aladdin's Cave of good food and fine wines.

Market Sat morning in the Place de la République.

Banks (closed Mon). Place de la République (3).

Restaurants The Restaurant des Fuschias, 20 rue Maréchal Foch is special to British and French gourmets. Eat fresh, home-grown produce in the garden or conservatory; pre-book ☎ 02 33 54 42.26.

At 5 Quai Vauban, Le Café du Port is equally popular: seafood €9.45–23.10. Nearby La Bisquine has menus €8.80–17.60. La Chasse Marée in Place Gen de Gaulle does good seafood, €13.60–23.70. Next door Le Débarcadère offers more pubby prices.

NAVIGATION

Charts AC 2135 (1:60,000) for the approach. 1349 (1:20,000) hbr plan. SHOM 7090 (1:20,000) ditto, with large scale insets of St Vaast and Barfleur.

Approaches From the E go direct to Le Gavendest SCM buoy, a convenient waypoint. The 267° ldg lts at Fort de la Hougue and Morsalines may help. From the SE and S, stay to seaward or inshore of the Banc de St Marcouf and Banc du Cardonnet. From the W and N, study the Passage Notes on page 284 before tackling the Barfleur Race. When clear, stay a mile offshore to avoid drying reefs which extend south beyond Pte de Saire to Le Gavendest.

An approach between Pte de Saire and Île de Tatihou, and through Le Run is not advised. It crosses much-prized oyster beds which dry 3.25m in places. If you run aground, the severe displeasure of the St Vaast oyster growers will be visited upon yourself, kinsmen, boat and wallet!

Pilotage From the WPT 49°34′.36N 01°13′.88W (Le Gavendest) track 315°/1.3M to the conspic white light tower on the jetty head. The harbour entrance is due west, followed by the entry gate with Capitainerie to stbd.

Landmarks Try not to confuse yourself and the rather similar towers on Île de Tatihou and Fort de la Hougue.

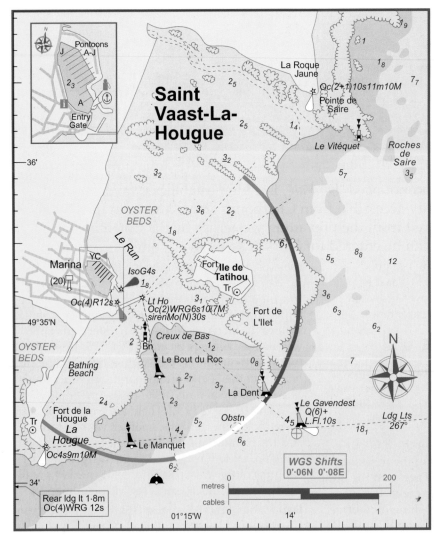

Tides HW St Vaast is 80 mins nps or 50 mins sp after HW Cherbourg; LWs are 75 mins nps or 80 mins sp after LW Cherbourg. MHWS is 6·7m, MLWS 1·0m; MHWN is 5·5m, MLWN 2·5m. The tide gauge at the gate shows the depth over the sill.

Tidal streams off St Vaast set SW/NE. Within the anchorage and in the final approach from the jetty head to the marina, be alert for tidal eddies.

Access The entry gate normally opens at HW−$2\frac{1}{4}$ and closes at HW+3, or +$3\frac{1}{2}$ on a big tide. But at nps, and if the barometer is high (>1030 mb), the gate may close at HW+$2\frac{1}{2}$. If the coefficient is <40 the gate may close at HW+$1\frac{3}{4}$ or +2. If in doubt, call the Capitainerie by ☎ or VHF Ch 09; English spoken. Go slow and give way to FVs.

Berthing Pontoon 'B' is for LOA >14m; 'C' & 'D' >11m; 'E' >10m and 'F' <10m. 'G'–'J' are for locals. On some pontoons visitors may only use the outer berths, as clearly signed. Larger boats may berth on 'B' to agree a suitable slot with the HM. Mean depth is 2.3m. Many finger pontoons are uncommonly short, narrow and springy – take care.

Anchorage Anchor in 3–5m on sand within the

Fort de la Hougue with Le Manquet east cardinal buoy in the foreground

western side, ie 330°–350°, of the jetty head light's white sector, 310°–350°. Other vessels are then free to route to/from the waypoint within the eastern part, 310°–330°. You can anchor further west in the red sector, east of a line from Le Bout du Roc to Le Manquet ECM buoys. The anchorage is open only to strong easterlies. Show an anchor light/ball.

FACILITIES

Capitainerie The HM, Mme Françoise Noël, and her staff are unfailingly helpful. VHF Ch 09. ☎ 02 33 23 61 00; ▦ 02 33 23 61 04. f.noël@saint-vaast-reville.com Open 0800–1200 & 1330–1730.

Chantier Naval Bernard and the Mariners' Chapel in the background

The harbour entrance at HW

Showers (only three for men) €2 by jeton. A night shower (when the Capitainerie is shut) is at the back of the YC, opposite 'H' pontoon.

Launderette in the Capitainerie.

Tariff Daily € rates for selected LOAs, May–Sep: <8m = 12.60; <9m = 15.20; <10m = 17.85; <11m = 21.30; <12m = 24.70; <13m = 27.80.

Fuel Diesel & petrol pumps are just before pontoon 'A'; open 0900–1200 & 1400–1800.

BARFLEUR

Harbour entrance – 49°40´·40N 01°15´·38W

Barfleur, with its archetypal Norman church standing four-square at the harbour entrance, has long been a favourite place, but change seems to be in the wind. Only a few years ago a dozen or more yachts would be drying out alongside. On my first visit in 2001 there were no yachts (other than locals);

on my second visit in August there were two. Undoubtedly fishing vessels are a valuable part of the local economy, but so too are yachts.

There may be three causes: i) A notion that the approach into Barfleur is in some way tricky. ii) A growing reluctance amongst yachtsmen to dry out against the wall, whether they be bilge or fin keelers; and iii) The seductive charms of St Vaast.

The good news is that so far nothing has come of a project to build a marina at the south end of the harbour; even with the most sensitive styling it could change the stern granite face of Barfleur.

The near approach

SHORESIDE

Tourist Office The Syndicat d'Initiative, open Apr–All Saints Day (1 Nov), is in a hut next to the church. ☎/📠 02 33 54 02 48; www.ville-barfleur.fr

What to see/do Barfleur is steeped in history. By the LB house a bronze plaque recalls the 900th anniversary of 1066 etc. Twenty eight years later Richard the Lionheart sailed in with a fleet of 100 ships en route to being crowned King of England. In 1346 Edward II sacked Barfleur, so reducing the population from 9,000 to 800; not surprisingly the area remained under English rule for the next century.

La Jamette east cardinal

Pointe de Barfleur, looking SW

In 1692 Admiral de Tourville (whose name is on today's lifeboat) won the Battle of Barfleur against a combined Anglo-Dutch fleet. Next day English fire-ships destroyed the French fleet at St Vaast.

Visit the 17th century church of St Nicholas and the mediaeval buildings at Cour St Catherine not far from the HM's shack. The present day harbour quays date from the 19th century.

The near approach, looking SW at about half tide

Chapter 5

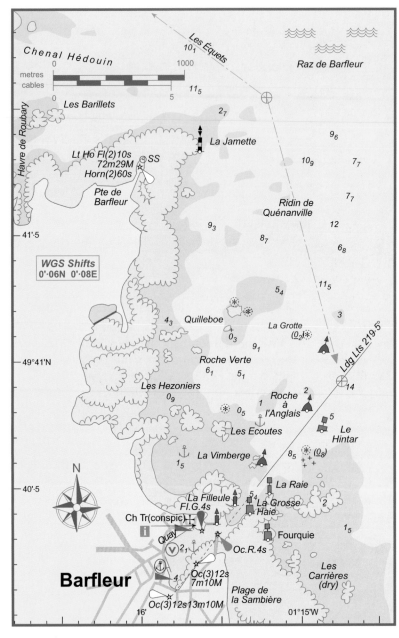

Finally walk or cycle the 3km out to the Gatteville lighthouse; climb the 365 steps for views west to Cherbourg and south to the Utah and Omaha D-day beaches and the Baie du Grand Vey. Closer to hand, study the Barfleur Race particularly in malevolent mood, and the rocks to W and S of you. Open Apr–Sep, 1000–1200 & 1400–1900; entry €2.

Rail Nearest stations are Cherbourg (27km) and Valognes (25km), thence to Paris.

Bus STN Line 1 leaves Mon–Sat 0854, 1349, 1713 to Cherbourg (45 mins); also to St Vaast.

Taxi ☎ 02 33 54 55 57.

Beaches Plage de l'Église, NW of the church, and Plage de la Sambière, E of the harbour are good.

Access to UK See Cherbourg.

Supermarkets Only a small Shopi in the main rue St Thomas Becket; Mon–Sat 0900–1300 & 1400–1930, Sun 0930–1200. See also St Vaast.

Market day Tues and Sat mornings along the quays.

Banks Crédit Agricole and the Post Office.

Restaurants Hôtel du Phare, St Thomas Becket, serves €11.55–24.15 menus in pleasant surroundings, but lacks the 'essential' sea view. Hôtel Moderne in Place Gen de Gaulle is 'a gastronomic experience best shared'; €13.65–29.40. At Le Créperie (Chez Buck) near the quayside, enjoy the fish soup for modest sums and watch the world in orbit. By the church the Café de France, an entertaining Bar / Brasserie, dispenses *moules à la Normande* at €6.30 a bowl.

NAVIGATION

Charts AC 1349 (1:20,000), plus 1106 (1:50,000) or 2135 (1:60,000) depending on your approach. SHOM 7090 (1:20,000) covers the approaches and has large scale insets of Barfleur and St Vaast.

Approaches Straightforward from the S, but keep

Gatteville Lighthouse from Barfleur

clear of the coastal reefs. From the N, after safely negotiating the Raz (page 285) – ideally by the inshore route – make for La Grotte SHM buoy, noting that La Grotte rock is 1 cable NW of the buoy; don't get set inshore. Continue to the waypoint.

Pilotage The waypoint, 49°40′·94N 01°14′·65W, is on the 219½° ldg line 7.5 cables from the harbour. Pass between Roche-a-l'Anglais and Le Hintar buoys, biased to stbd to clear the rock (0.8m). Next La Vimberge SHM buoy and La Raie, the first PHM beacon; then La Filleule, the first SHM beacon, and Grosse-Haie the second PHM beacon. Ignore totally a third PHM beacon (Fourquie) displaced well to port of the channel. Finally to starboard a beacon off the LB slip, then the W jetty head and a small SHM perch; to port is the E jetty head. Now hug the line of FVs to starboard, to berth at the far end of the quay. The squat church tower and the LB house are conspic throughout.

So good are the buoys and beacons just described that you may never have noticed the ldg lights, well inside the harbour on its SE side; not all that easy to see by day, but useful at night since all the buoys and beacons are unlit.

Tides HW Barfleur is 70 mins nps or 55 mins sp after HW Cherbourg; LWs are 52 mins nps & sp after LW Cherbourg. MHWS is 6·5m, MLWS 1·1m; MHWN is 5·3m, MLWN 2·5m.

Yachts alongside at HW

Fishing vessels alongside at LW

Tidal streams see under Barfleur Race page 284; they ease nearer the harbour.

Access HW±2½. But do not try to enter in strong onshore winds; if already in, leave asap. In strong N/NE'lies the harbour and approaches are very exposed. Drying out alongside is then likely to be at best uncomfortable and possibly dangerous.

Berthing Against the NW quay at its far SW end, beyond the FVs. The bottom dries 2.1m to firm, level sand and mud with a few small stones. The gently sloping wall is easy for fin-keelers to lean against. Ladders are suitably spaced. Ask the HM before picking up a local mooring.

Anchorages Anchor in about 6m well clear of the approach channel, La Vimberge buoy bearing 180° and Le Hintar buoy about 090°. Smaller boats can sound in further west to anchor in 2–3m, Gatteville lighthouse bearing 350° and Le Hintar buoy 083°.

FACILITIES

Capitainerie is a white hut on the quay south of the yacht berths; open Tues, Thur, Sat 1000–1200. No VHF. ☎ 02 33 54 08 29. HM is the nobly-named, but elusive Boniface Rabourt. Toilets on the quays are pretty rudimentary.

Launderette none.

Tariff Daily rates for LOAs alongside the quay: <7m = €5.25; 7–10m = €6.70; >10m = €9.45. But these modest sums are rarely collected.

Fuel None, but a local garage may deliver cans via the HM.

CHANDLERIES & REPAIR FACILITIES

There are no chandleries or boatyards.

PORT DU CAP LÉVI

Harbour entrance – 49°41´·28N 01°28´·40W

Berth in this small drying fishing harbour and enjoy the peace and a beautiful, half-mile walk through the heather to Cap Lévi lighthouse. Little or nothing changes here and therein lies part of Lévi's timeless charm. There are a few houses by the harbour, but Fermanville, 3km to the east, is the nearest community of any size. The Fort du Cap Lévi is on the headland to the NW of the harbour. It originated in Napoleonic times and has been tastefully converted into a residential venue for seminars and meetings.

NAVIGATION

Charts AC 1106 (1:50,000) will suffice, but SHOM 7092 or 5609 (both 1:20,000) would be better.

Tides HW Lévi is about HW Cherbourg +24 mins.

Access/Shelter The harbour is exposed to winds from SW to N. If moderate to fresh, the entrance will be rough and berths will be uncomfortable; it is better to wait for a light, anticyclonic easterly. Plan to arrive HW±2.

Pilotage Port Lévi is about 5M east of Cherbourg (Passe de l'Est). Start about 3.5 cables west of the harbour where a yellow SPM buoy makes a good waypoint at 49°41´·23N 01°28´·97W. From here jink slightly NE so as to approach the harbour with a rectangular whited wall on its far side

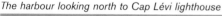

neatly aligned on about 090° between the white-painted breakwater heads. Maintain this bearing whilst avoiding numerous lobster pots and other piscatorial debris.

At night (unwise because of the risk of a line around your prop), approach in the green sector

The harbour looking north to Cap Lévi lighthouse

Keep the whited wall midway between the breakwaters

050°–109°(59°) of the directional light F RG 7m 7M which sticks up above the centre of the whited wall. Again a bearing 090° would be ideal.

Berthing A white conical buoy with mooring ring lies 100m off the head of the south breakwater; it could not be confirmed that this is a ⚓. But it could offer a convenient overnight mooring in calm conditions or at the very least allow you to row ashore and survey the scene. If you anchor outside in 3–4m a tripping line would be sensible.

Inside the breakwaters do not turn to starboard as the south part of the harbour is shoal and rocky. To the north there are four options: berth bows in to the east wall, on a sandy bottom, with stern to a buoy or anchor; or pick up a vacant buoy in the middle; or raft up on a suitable boat; or berth on the inside of the N breakwater head.

PORT DU BECQUET

Harbour entrance – 49°39′.35N 01°32′.77W

This small drying harbour lies about 1M E x S of Cherbourg's Passe Collignon and is used by small fishing boats and yachts which can dry out. It is included here as a place to potter to, if you want to explore out of Cherbourg, but a berth may be hard to find. Ashore it is backed by attractively wooded, cliffy slopes. The village has a smattering of small shops and bars. It may be worth a recce by bike or bus.

NAVIGATION

Charts AC 1106 (1:50,000) will suffice, but SHOM 7092 (1:20,000) would be better.

Access/Shelter Use Cherbourg tidal data and aim to arrive HW±2. If the wind is fresh onshore, give it a miss as quite a chop builds on the lee shore.

Approach Start about 3 cables north of the harbour close to a yellow SPM buoy which is itself just east of the 186½° leading line. The leading marks by day are two white towers, 8 and 13m high, on the shore line. At first sight, do not confuse the front tower with the large white patch on the breakwater head. At night both show Dir Oc (2+1) 12s synchronised lights, the front white 10M and the rear red 7M.

Home in on these marks, keeping well off a large red PHM beacon tower, La Tounette, which marks a rocky outcrop just east of the harbour. At this stage you have arrived! Turn starboard round the breakwater head and survey

the harbour. It is only 50m wide from the S side to the N breakwater.

Berthing There are E/W trots down the middle, but your best bet is to berth where you can, bows-in to the north breakwater with a stern buoy or kedge. The hard bottom is covered with a thin layer of mud and dries 1.4m to 3.1m. The south side, which dries about 3 to 3.4m, is unsuitable for taking the ground. Anchoring outside the harbour is feasible.

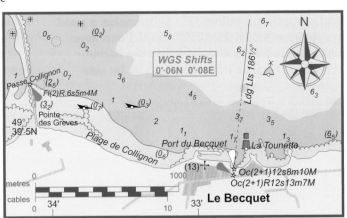

The near approach: To starboard of the leading line

CHERBOURG

Marina entrance – 49°38´·97N 01°37´·03W

Cherbourg is often a first port of call in France for thousands of British yachtsmen hellbent on going east to the Normandy beaches or west towards the Channel Islands and North Brittany. Cherbourg is a commercial port, ferry terminal, naval base, fishing harbour and yachting centre.

It is also a frontier town, geared up to the constant flow of ferry passengers scurrying south to the Med. But there is more to it than that, as a wander through the older parts of the town will reveal. In recent years new enterprises have done much to make the town a more desirable place to visit or in which to live. Cherbourg is also the gateway to many charming small towns and villages in the bocage country of the Cotentin and the high moors east of Cap de la Hague, all easily accessible by hire car.

The port enjoyed its heyday in the 1930s when the great Transatlantic liners (*Île de France*, *Queen Mary* and *Queen Elizabeth*) were regular callers. In WWII when the Allies re-captured the city, they found the port had been wrecked and sabotaged by the retreating enemy – but thanks to a swift clearance operation it was functioning again in a month. The Gare Maritime stood for years in sorry decline, but after a major face-lift this huge building opened in May 2002 as La Cité de la Mer (see overleaf).

SHORESIDE

Tourist Office is at 2 quai Alexandre III, 50100 Cherbourg – NW end of the Bassin du Commerce. Open in high season, Mon–Sat 0900–1830 and Sun 1000–1230. ☎ 02 33 93 52 02; 📠 02 33 53 66 97; ot.cherbourg-cotentin@wanadoo.fr ; www.ot.cherbourg-cotentin.fr A small kiosk

Cité de la Mer. The former transatlantic liner terminal

(Pointe Plaisance) with tourist info is at the head of 'N' pontoon, open 1000–1900 daily Jul/Aug.

What to see Undoubtedly the major attraction is La Cité de la Mer, an imaginative cultural, scientific and tourist centre concerned with all things on and under the sea. It includes a vast aquarium, the submarine *Le Redoubtable*, together with a submarine simulator, and other exhibits.

Napoleon's horse shying nervously at the Union Flag

Fort du Roule is on a rocky outcrop 112m above the town, quite a climb up the zig-zag road, but worth it for the panoramic views over Cherbourg and for the Liberation Museum which it houses. This tells the moving story of the occupation years and the liberation in 1944. Two excellent films contain much original black-and-white footage. Open 1000–1800 daily, May–Sept; €3.20, free Sun.

If seriously gale-bound, take a hire car out to Cap de la Hague to walk amidst dramatically wild scenery – especially if you haven't made it by sea.

Rail Station is S of Bassin du Commerce. TGV to Paris (3 hrs 10 mins), via Valognes (20 mins) & Caen (1 hr 15 mins).

Buses Station is close to the railway station. As well as suburban services, regional buses run to Valognes, Carteret, Diélette and Portbail (Line 3); Valognes, Ste Mère-Église, Carentan & St Lo (Line 5); Diélette (Line 7); Coutances (Line 8).

The view from Fort du Roule

Car Hire Budget ☎ 02 33 94 32 77; National/Citer ☎ 0800 20 21 21; Ada Location, 10–12 Ave de Paris, ☎ 02 33 20 65 65; Hertz ☎ 02 33 23 41 41.

Taxis ☎ 02 33 53 36 38; ☎ 02 33 53 17 04.

Bike Hire via the Tourist Office, especially the Pointe Plaisance opposite 'N' pontoon.

Ferries to UK/Eire See the Ferry Guide in Intro.

Beaches Within the harbour, none that you would swim from, but green grass near the Ⓥ pontoons is ideal for sun-bathing or a picnic.

Supermarkets Shopi in rue Gambetta is nearest, open 0830–1230 & 1430–1930, except Sun. Several general stores/alimentations near to Le Grand Gousier restaurant (see below) make food shopping infinitely more charmingly French.

The Carrefour hypermarket at the SE end of the Bassin du Commerce is well known to British regulars, not only for mega-food shopping, but also for booze – said to be the cheapest in town. Open Mon–Sat 0830–2100 (Fri to 2130). Do not fail to visit the Normandie Wine Warehouse next to the Capitainerie (also near the ferry terminal). The Wine Warehouse is run by the expansive and ever-cheerful Victoria who has lived in Cherbourg for eight years and is a mine of local and wine information. Also sells bread, croissants and

Carrefour supermarket
Bassin du Commerce
Long-stay berths
Marina
Cité de la Mer
Fort Central
Ferry terminal

Entering the marina

minor groceries. Jul/Aug 0700–1900, daily; other months: 0900–1300 & 1400–1800. Taste before you buy. Free delivery; ☎ 02 33 04 78 00; www.normandiewine.com

Market days Tues: Place de Gaulle (everything). Thur & Sat: In front of the Théatre and nearby streets (everything). Sunday: Ave de Normandie.

Banks Of every hue.

Launderette None in the marina, surprisingly; the nearest is in Rue de Blé, open 0700–2100, daily.

Restaurants Within walking distance, the following are recommended by locals or by *moi-même:* From the Place de la République (start point) head W along Rue Grande Vallée to: Le Grand Gousier, 21 rue de l'Abbaye, small and unremarkable from outside, but a gastronomic

Eastern Entrance · Île Pelée · Passe Collignon · Cap Lévi

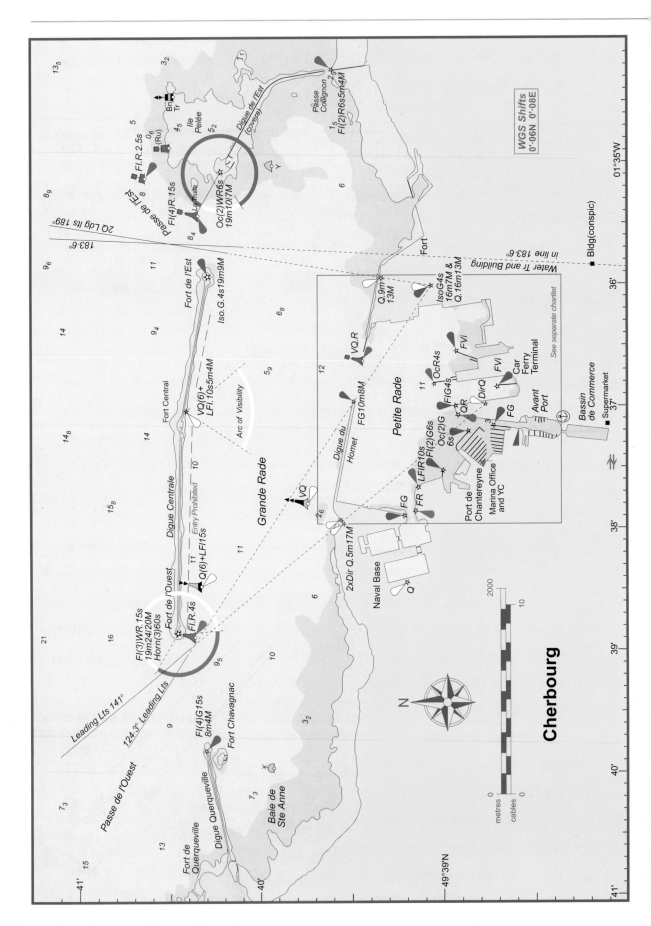

WGS Shifts
0'·06N 0'·08E

Passe Collignon
Fl(2)R.6s5m4M

Bn
Tr

(Ru)

Ile
Pelée

Digue de l'Est
(covers)

Fl.R.2.5s

Passe de l'Est

Fl(4)R.15s

La Truite

Oc(2)WR.6s
19m10/7M

2Q Ldg lts 189°

183·6°

Fort

Water Tr and Building
in line 183·6°

Bldg(conspic)

Fort de l'Est

Iso.G.4s19m9M

Q.9m
13M

IsoG.4s
16m7M &
Q.16m13M

See separate chartlet

Supermarket

VQ.R

FVi

Fort Central

FVi

OcR4s

Car
Ferry
Terminal

VQ(6)+
LFl.10s5m4M

Arc of Visibility

DirQ

FlG4s

QR

FVi

Grande Rade

FG

Avant
Port

Bassin
de Commerce

Digue Centrale

Entry Prohibited

Digue du
Homet

FG10m8M

Petite Rade

Oc(2)G
6s

Fl(2)G6s

DirQ

FG

Port de
Chantereyne

Marina Office
and YC

VQ

LFl.R10s

FR

FG

2xDir Q.5m17M

Q(6)+LFl15s

Fort de l'Ouest

Naval Base

Q

Fl(3)WR.15s
19m24/20M
Horn(3)60s

Fl.R.4s

Leading Lts 141°

124·3° Leading Lts

Fl(4)G15s
8m4M

Fort Chavagnac

Passe de l'Ouest

Fort de
Querqueville

Digue Querqueville

Baie de
Ste Anne

N

2000

metres
cables

10

Cherbourg

49°39'N

delight within; €15.75–35.70; pre-book. Back at the start point: skip the two eateries at the head of the square. Jink south on Rue Francois La Vieille to the Brasserie Le Commerce; no set menus but plenty of atmosphere, good humour and inexpensive food. Start point again, head E on Rue Tour Carrée: At Le Faitout, No 25, the food is good and affordable, the service excellent and a lot of fun was had by all (the ceiling resembles the deckhead of a ship). Next door, Au Provençal is OK, if Le Faitout is full.

Further east turn right into Rue au Blé: 50 metres up on your right is Le Laurent, an old favourite which has changed its name/ management but is still one of the best; €14.70–36.75; pre-book. Continue to the Quai de Caligny, opposite the Avant Port (FVs): Try La Régence below the Logis of that name, €15.75–30.45. Or better still Le Vauban, next to the Hôtel Ambassadeur, where the service pampers and menus €13.65–45.15 are equally good; pre-booking advised in season. Avoid the string of joints frequented by ferry passengers. *Bon appetit!*

NAVIGATION

Charts AC 1106 (1:50,000) suffices if you know the harbour well; use 2602 (1:10,000) for detail. SHOM 7120 (1:47,800), 7092 (1:20,000) and 7086 (1:7,500).

Approaches Straightforward, but please browse the section 'Cross-Channel' in the Main Introduction. The landfall buoy CH1 is 3.5M NW of the western entrance to the Grande Rade; its light, L Fl 10s, is always hard to see at night.

There are three entrances into the Grande Rade: Passe de l'Ouest is wider (5.5 cables) than Passe de l'Est, which is narrowed to 2.5 cables by the rocks off Île Pelée. Passe Collignon, SE of Île Pelée, is about 60m wide, carries 2m and is safe to use with care by day at or near HW.

Pilotage For the Passe de l'Ouest the waypoint, 49°40´·42N 01°38´·87W, is 100m clear of the PHM buoy, Fl R 4s, which guards drying rocks off Fort de l'Ouest. From here it's plain sailing across the Grande Rade to round the Digue du Homet and track 191° across the Petite Rade to the marina.

For the Passe de l'Est the waypoint, 49°41´·00N 01°35´·48W, is on the 189° leading line 7 cables to seaward of Fort de l'Est. This allows early identification of Roches du Nord-Ouest and La Truite PHM light buoys off the rocks of Île Pelée. With Fort de l'Est safely abeam, alter 216° for the PHM buoy, VQ R, at the entrance to the Petite Rade; thence 211° for the marina. Be warned, the gap between the VQ R buoy and the end of Jetée des Flamands is shallow and rocky.

Tides Cherbourg is a Standard Port. MHWS is 6·4m, MLWS 1·1m; MHWN is 5·0m, MLWN 2·5m.

Tidal streams sweep east/west across the top of the Cotentin peninsula at 3½ to 4 kn sp, and about 2 kn nps – faster around Cap de la Hague and Pte de Barfleur. Please see the 'Cross-Channel' text in the Main Introduction.

Access/Shelter Cherbourg is a port of refuge, accessible at all tides and in all weathers.

Anchorage The yacht ⚓, close

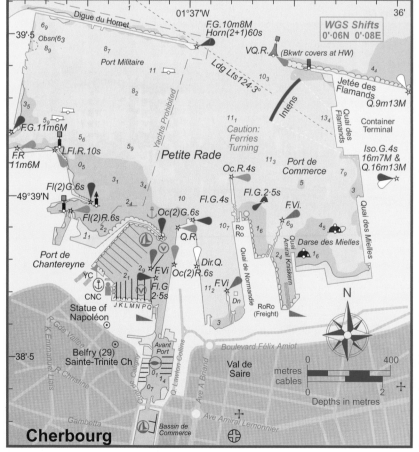

N of the marina breakwater in 2.5 to 9m, is well sheltered to S and W, but exposed to N and E.

Unlit naval mooring buoys Four near the naval base entrance pose no threat to yachts. But a single unlit white buoy, about 350m SSW of the head of Digue du Homet, is close enough to the fairway to embarrass a yacht lowering sails, for example.

Berthing Chantereyne Marina has 1,300 berths, inc 250 **Ⓥ**: Pontoons 'A' to 'I' on the NW side are for locals, as notices on the pontoons make clear. Along the S side, pontoons 'M' to 'Q' are for visitors ('O' does not exist), 'K' & 'L' are for locals; visitors may be allowed to raft up on the east side of 'J' when all else is full. Finger pontoons are standard, except on the E sides of 'J' and 'Q'; larger boats raft up alongside the latter. A detached pontoon in the middle of the marina is used by boats too large for finger berths. Caution: The pontoons are surfaced with a plastic material which, when wet, can be slippery.

In the NE corner of the Bassin du Commerce 40 pontoon berths are for long-stay/over-wintering; see the HM for details. Access from the Avant Port is by an entry gate and associated swing bridge; the gate is open from HW–45 to +45 mins, when the swing bridge opens on request VHF Ch 12. Traffic is controlled by IPTS.

Long-stay berths in Bassin du Commerce, looking NE

FACILITIES

Capitainerie ☎ 02 33 87 65 70; 🖷 02 33 53 21 12. VHF Ch 09. Hours: 0730–2300, 1 May–30 Sep; rest of the year, 0800–1900. cherbourg.marina@wanadoo.fr; www.ville-cherbourg.fr

Showers by €2 jeton, H24, plus launderette.

Tariff Daily rates €, May-Sep, for LOAs < the following: 7.5m = 11.55; 8.5m = 16.80; 9m = 16.80; 10m = 20; 11m = 23.10; 12m = 26.25; 13m = 29.40; 14m = 32.55.

Fuel Diesel & petrol next to the 30 ton boat hoist, daily 0800–1145 & 1400–1845.

CHANDLERIES & REPAIR FACILITIES

Chandlers near the marina Cherbourg Plaisance, ☎ 02 33 53 27 34; Basourdy Marine, ☎ 02 33 53 07 30; Accastillage Diffusion, ☎ 02 33 94 15 50, also a BY.

In town Comptoir Maritime, Quai de Caligny; and Le Grand Bleu on Quai Alexandre III.

Sailmakers Cousin, ☎ 02 33 93 64 81; and Voilerie (Doyle), ☎ 02 33 94 15 51.

OMONVILLE-LA-ROGUE

Visitors' buoys – 49°42'·35N 01°50'·00W

Known locally as Port Le Hâble, this includes the houses along the water's edge and close inland. Omonville proper is the small village 1km further up the hill. The setting is attractive, backed by woods and rising ground, with a good beach just south of the big stone breakwater.

Rocks abound on the S and W sides and N of the breakwater. Omonville smacks strongly of North Brittany and if that is your goal, here is the aperitif – enjoy!

SHORESIDE

Tourist Office None. The district Office is 5km south at 45 rue Jallot, BP 119, 50440 Beaumont-Hague; ☎ 02 33 52 74 94. ✉ 02 33 52 09 64. www.tourisme.lahague.org.

What to see/do The major attraction is undoubtedly to relax in quiet and pleasant surroundings. Swim and sunbathe from boat or beach; eat well at the nearby restaurant. There are scenic coastal walks on the Sentier des Douaniers (part of GR 223): 6.5km to Port Racine or 2.5km south to the Baie de Querviére – a good lunch-time anchorage.

Transport No trains/buses. Car hire: Cherbourg.

Taxi from Beaumont-Hague ☎ 02 33 08 46 46.

Access to UK See under Cherbourg.

Shopping A boulangerie, general store and a café are in Omonville, but no markets or banks.

Restaurants At the N end of the beach is the Restaurant du Port. Enter the dining room via the adjoining Café du Port (bar snacks). Good food at €20–28.35; pre-book ☎ 02 33 52 74 13 if a large crew. Brilliant view of the bay. Further S, under blue & white parasols, the Marbella Snack-Bar is just that.

NAVIGATION

Charts AC 1106 (1:50,000) barely shows the rocks either side of the fairway. SHOM 5636 (1:20,000) with a 1:7,500 inset of Omonville is far superior.

Omonville, looking SSE

Omonville Fort

Dir lt

L'Étonnard beacon

Approaches Straightforward from Cherbourg. Keep close inshore to work a W-going eddy when the main flood is setting east, but stay clear of the unlit Bannes NCM tower and its drying offliers. From the west, at Basse Bréfort NCM buoy turn SE to skirt the rocks east of Pte Jardeheu en route to the waypoint. A firing range lies close east of the harbour, but is rarely active.

Pilotage From the WPT 49°42'·46N 01°49'·12W, the Dir light Iso WRG 4s (white lattice tower, red top) on the SW side of the bay bears 257°/7 cables. Omonville's church spire in transit 255° is hard to see. Near LW especially, keep well off L'Étonnard as rocks extend SE of it and between it and the breakwater. Other marks, from S to N, include:

- A yellow SPM buoy, charted at 360m SSW of the WPT, is in fact a large, round, unlit, low-lying, rusty-white mooring buoy which is a hazard at night unless you are in the white sector.
- An old fort climbing up the hill S of the bay.
- L'Étonnard unlit SHM beacon; also spelled Le Tunard on some older charts and publications. From the W & N, the transit 195° of L'Étonnard and the old fort leads clear of drying rocks to the

east of Pte Jardeheu; but stay well E of L'Étonnard, perhaps out to the WPT before turning inbound.

Tides At nps & sp HW is 10 mins before HW Cherbourg; and LW is 15 mins before LW Cherbourg. MHWS is 6·3m, MLWS 1·1m; MHWN is 4·9m, MLWN 2·5m.

Tidal streams set across the harbour entrance, but are slight once inside.

[Chart of Omonville-La-Rogue showing depths, IsoWRG4s 13m11/8M light, Small Craft Moorings, L'Étonnard, Roche aux Moines, Le Hâble, Fort, firing range, compass rose, WGS Shifts 0'·06N 0'·08E, bearings 195°, 255°, and scale in metres/cables]

Omonville Fort

Unlit mooring buoy

L'Étonnard beacon and the breakwater

Access/shelter At all tides, the harbour is well sheltered from S and W winds. But even moderate easterlies raise quite a chop and if stronger can render the moorings untenable or dangerous. In NW to N winds a scend can work round the breakwater making the harbour uncomfortable.

Harbour Six trots of local craft fill the inner area. To seaward in 5–7m are six white conical ⚓s; raft up in season with plenty of fenders. Do not berth on the breakwater as its inner part has a drying slip and drying rocks lie seaward of its small stub pier.

Anchorage To seaward of the ⚓s, but the further out the less the shelter. Show an anchor light/ball as you will probably be close to the fairway.

Visitors' mooring buoys

FACILITIES

No mooring fees, HM, VHF, fuel, repair facilities, chandlery; only scanty toilets. PO, bank and fuel (cans) at Beaumont-Hague; an infrequent bus to Cherbourg – all part of Omonville's charm.

The near approach on 257°

Dir Lt

L'Étonnard

Chapter 5

Port Racine, looking south

ANSE DE SAINT MARTIN

Centre of the bay – 49°43'N 01°53'W

This mile-wide bay, about 3M east of Cap de la Hague, makes a pleasant anchorage, open only to winds from NW to NE. It is useful to await a fair tide through the Alderney Race – or just to walk and swim in away-from-it-all surroundings.

It also contains Port Racine, over-publicised as the smallest harbour in France. But it dries and is obstructed by small craft mooring lines, hence it is only a dinghy landing place with no facilities. Captain Racine established a naval port here in Napoleonic days.

For a run ashore, cycle or walk (preferably the latter as this is great walking country) west on the Sentier des Douaniers towards Goury, 6.5km. Half way there, book (☎ 02 33 52 75 20) your dinner at the

isolated, but well patronised Le Moulin à Vent – to cap a memorable day.

NAVIGATION

Charts AC 1106 (1:50,000) is just adequate, but

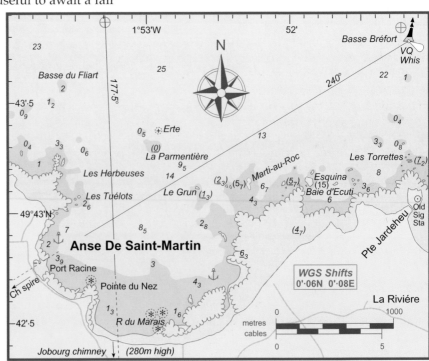

SHOM 5636 at 1:20,000 is far better, even though the current 1996 edition has rather dated black-and-white hachuring; it also contains a 1:7,500 blow-up of Omonville. Both charts have useful tidal diamonds referenced to Cherbourg.

Approaches The entrance to the bay is guarded by three sets of drying rocks: Les Herbeuses to the NW; La Parmentière awash in centre stage and Le Grun (1.9m) on the eastern flank, which is generally a mass of drying rocks. Good visibility is essential; abort if you cannot see the leading marks. A night approach is not advised even though Basse Bréfort NCM buoy is lit VQ and the Jobourg chimney has R lights; the bay itself is unlit.

Pilotage From Cherbourg, Basse Bréfort buoy is a good waypoint, 49°43'·83N 01°51'·00W, from which Port Racine bears 240°. The astern bearing 060° leads through the 3 cables wide gap between Le Grun and La Parmentière – take care at half tide when they are just covered. Port Racine is not easy to see, but two rough leading marks to the right of and above it are: Front, a long, slate-roofed house with seven dormer windows (used to be a restaurant, but is now private); and rear, the spire of Danneville church (97m high).

Le Grun   Marti-au-Roc

Port Racine at LW, looking NE

From the W or N use 49°43'·94N 01°53'·29W as a waypoint. From here the highest (280m), most substantial of several chimneys at the Jobourg nuclear waste re-processing plant bears 177·5° at 3M. Hold this bearing as accurately as possible, allowing initially for strong cross-tides, to pass through the 2.5 cables wide gap between Les Herbeuses and La Parmentière.

Tides Use differences for Omonville. Seaward of the bay and inshore of the main E-going flood which reaches 4kn @ springs, a tidal eddy sets west from HW Cherbourg –3 to +3 (HW Dover –6 to –1). Within the bay tidal streams set east <1kn.

Anchorages Outside Port Racine there are some mooring buoys for local boats up to 5m LOA; they are not man enough for a 10m yacht which may drag them in even moderate weather. In any case an adequate anchorage in 5m on pebbles/sand lies to the E or NE of the moorings, well sheltered in the lee of rising ground to the west. If the wind is easterly, anchor in 4–5m some 8 cables east of Port Racine, close SW of a rock charted as drying 6.3m. This is in the lee of the low cliffs extending SW from Pointe Jardeheu (disused signal station).

Chapter 5

CHAPTER 6

THE CHANNEL ISLANDS

Looking NE over Jethou and Crevichon to Herm

CONTENTS

INTRODUCTION

'Little bits of France dropped into the sea and gathered up by the English' was how Victor Hugo described the Channel Islands (CI), or Les Îles Anglo-Normandes as he would have called them. The islands were indeed part of Normandy until King John lost control of mainland Normandy in 1204, but retained the CI. During WWII the CI were occupied by the Germans and many concrete structures are a reminder of that unhappy time.

Today the CI enjoy considerable autonomy, with their own parliaments, known as States. Although not a part of the UK, the Sovereign is represented by a Lieutenant Governor in the two Bailiwicks of Jersey and Guernsey; the latter includes Alderney, Burhou, Herm, Jethou, Sark and Brecqhou. The two offshore reefs, Les Ecrehou and the Plateau des Minquiers (respectively NE and S of Jersey), are part of the CI.

The Islands have been portrayed as a family: Jersey is the brash Big Brother, a bit raffish but very successful. Guernsey, the next in size, is calm, prudent and tasteful. Alderney is the country bumpkin, independent but generous. Sark and Herm are just fairytale characters, too small in any event to have any worries. All are uncommonly handsome and friendly.

Alderney in French is Aurigny (hence the name of the inter-islands airline), Sark is Sercq,

Guernsey is Guernesey and Jersey is Jersey. Îles Chausey belong to France.

Weather forecasts By far the most accurate are those issued by Jersey Met Dept, ☎ 745550. After a *Securité* warning on Ch 16 & 2182kHz, they are broadcast by Jersey Radio, ☎ 01534 741121, at 0645, 0745, 0845 LT; and at 1245, 1845 and 2245 UTC on Ch 25, 82 & 1659kHz. Reception in Braye Harbour is poor/nil due to range and topography.

   Forecasts cover the CI area, defined by the French coast, 50°N and 3°W. They contain gale or strong wind warnings, a synopsis, forecast for the next 24 hrs and outlook for the following 24 hrs; plus the latest actual weather reported by Jersey, Guernsey, Alderney, Cap de la Hague, Cherbourg, Dinard, Portland and Channel light vessel. The bulletins are read at normal speed, then at dictation speed. Gale warnings are broadcast on receipt and every 6 hrs from 0307 UT.

Navigation warnings for the CI are broadcast on receipt and at 0433, 0833, 1633, 2033 UT.

Charts Admiralty charts of the CI were due to be converted to WGS 84 by end Aug 2003. So Lat/Long for the CI are here referenced to WGS 84. But SHOM charts of the adjacent French coast are only being converted to WGS 84 on a piecemeal basis, so most data remain in ED50. Check the datum.

Pilots Books which deal in more detail with tidal and pilotage matters than this volume has space for include *The N Brittany & Channel Islands Cruising Companion* (Cumberlidge /Nautical) and *The Reeds Nautical Almanac* and *The Reeds Channel Almanac*.

Tides The range, hence heights of tide, is large,

so that drying rocks can almost invariably be crossed above half tide. This puts a new perspective on navigating through rock-strewn areas, but needs an hour by hour awareness of the state of the tide.

Tidal streams are rotary anti-clockwise as the tidal stream atlas makes clear. Thus in general the tide sets NE at HW Dover–5; N at HWD–3; NW at –1; SW at +1; S at +3, and SE at +5. Streams are strongest in the N and in narrow waters.

The Casquets TSS lies from 7.5M to 25.5M NNW of the Casquets light, Racon T 25M. The lanes, orientated 075°/255°, are 20M long by 5M wide and separated by a 5M wide central zone marked by the Channel lt vessel and E Channel

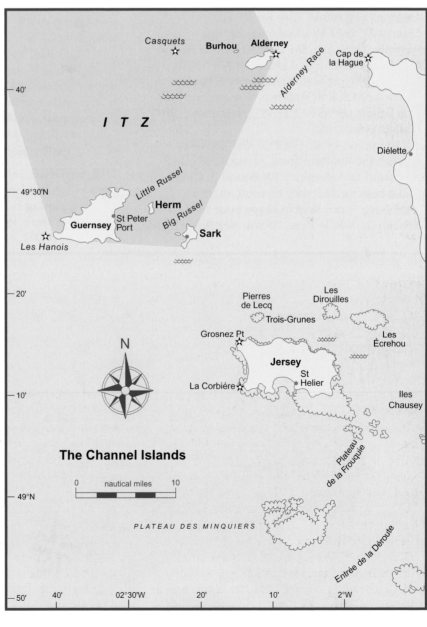

The Channel Islands

SPM buoy. The five-sided ITZ is defined by the S edge of the TSS, Alderney, Sark and Les Hanois. In general the TSS need only be crossed or avoided by yachts on passage SE from Devon towards Cherbourg or SW from Poole Bay & the Needles. *CROSS Jobourg* can provide radar surveillance and traffic info for the TSS and ITZ on request Ch 16.

PASSAGE NOTES

THE ALDERNEY RACE Tidal streams are well documented: At Alderney slack water occurs at HW Dover–1, just before the SW-going ebb starts; and at HWD+5, prior to the NE-going flood. Leave Braye for Guernsey via the Race at slack water so as to pick up the first of the SW-going stream as you round Race Rock.

Study AC 3653 to avoid areas of heavy overfalls. These are: 5M W of Cap de la Hague; Race Rocks (2M SE of Alderney's NE tip, with much white water); Alderney S Banks, approx 1.5M SSE of Alderney airport; and Banc de la Schole (49°35′N 2°13′W), perhaps too far S to affect your track.

A waypoint, 49°42′·5N 2°05′·5W, midway between the first two areas, is useful whether NE-bound to Alderney*, SW-bound to Guernsey, or just passing Alderney en route to/from Cherbourg. It can help to shape your course through the whole Race. *If you elect to go inside

Race Rocks, at least stay well clear of Brinchetais Ledge and Blanchard Rock.

If inbound to Alderney from Cherbourg, keep well north to avoid being set willy-nilly into the Race (next stop Guernsey). This means crossing 2°W at about 49°48′N, continuing W x S toward 49°47′N

Sark seen through the ruins of Grosnez Castle, Jersey

2°08′W, to pick up the leading line into Braye. All the while fix frequently so that you neither impale yourself on the NE tip of Alderney nor take the other unintentional route through The Swinge (next stop Guernsey) – but rather that you enter Braye, sweet as a nut, with a minimum of course corrections – very satisfying.

THE SWINGE, for the first time, is most safely used when heading SW out of Braye – because accurate timing is easy and you can assess conditions from atop the Breakwater. Leave spot on HWD–1, slack water in the Swinge, and you should carry a fair tide all the way to St Peter Port. From Braye hold to the south side of the channel, passing close to the 0.5m high Corbet Rock to avoid the worst of any rough stuff. The gap between Corbet Rock and Burhou is 7 cables wide.

Almost aligned with the Swinge is Pierre au Vraic (Seaweed Rock), an evil pinnacle drying 1.2m at 49°41′·61N 02°16′·93W, 2M SW of Alderney and 2.5M SSW of Burhou. It is rarely seen as yachts are usually in its vicinity near HW. Use the charted transits and/or GPS to clear it.

Keep well clear of The Casquets (lt ho, Racon T

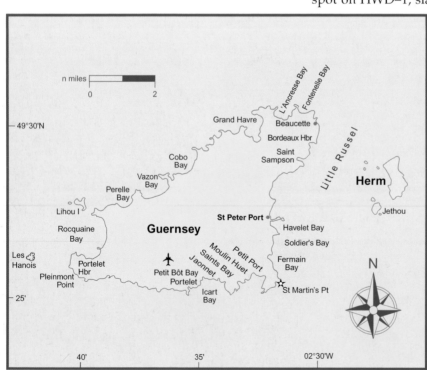

25M) and its three banks (SW, SSW and SSE), except in settled conditions; ditto the Ortac Channel and Pommier Banks.

GUERNSEY The NE entrance to the Little Russel is marked by Platte Fougère (conspic B/W lt twr, Racon P), Grande Amfroque (twin B/W & W bcns) and Tautenay (B/W bcn). Approach nearer to Platte Fougère, picking up the 198° ldg line toward Roustel, as on page 361. The Little Russel is not difficult in moderate or better visibility, but in low vis/fog the 2M wide Big Russel via Lower Heads SCM buoy is easier and safer, if rather longer.

JERSEY The near approaches are outlined on page 375. The Passage de la Déroute is a relatively shallow N/S route to the east of Jersey, running roughly parallel to the French coast from west of Carteret towards Îles Chausey and Les Minquiers.

From St Helier to St Malo there are three routes: W-about via NW and SW Minkie buoys. E-about via NE Minkie buoy; and most directly via N and SE Minkie buoys, but ensure there is sufficient rise of tide between N Minkie and Recif le Coq beacon.

INTER-ISLAND PASSAGES are generally quite straightforward, provided one works the streams to best advantage – as one does, eg leave St PP at LW for St Helier; return trip, depart St Helier at HW−2.

PASSAGES TO FRANCE, based on a 5.5kn boat speed. At St PP and St Helier it may be necessary to pre-position outside the marina to make an early start.

To Dielette, Carteret: Leave St PP at HW−4 to reach Dielette HW +1 or Carteret HW+1½: OK to enter the marinas, but timing Carteret may be tight. Leave St Helier at LW−2½ to reach Dielette HW±1. Leave at HW−5 for Carteret/Portbail HW±1.

To St Malo: leave St PP @ HW to reach St Malo HW−2, able to enter Bas Sablons or Bassin Vauban. Leave St Helier near LW, pass E of the Minkies, to reach St Malo near HW.

To Lézardrieux: Leave St PP at HW−1, passing E of Roches Douvres to reach Lézardrieux at LW +1. From St Helier similar timing applies.

Pilotage Transits are frequently used around the Channel Islands to maintain exact tracks in narrow waters or to act as clearing bearings; the marks must be correctly identified before being used. Beacons with lettered topmarks, for example 'A' for the Alligande beacon, are common especially around Herm and off SE Jersey. They are often just an iron pole or tripod structure.

Some of the bays on the NW coast of Guernsey and particularly around Little Sark require small rocks and marks to be correctly identified. For such details consult the localised pilots mentioned in this introduction.

Casquets lighthouse, looking east

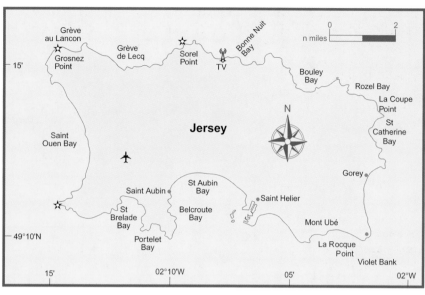

Chapter 6

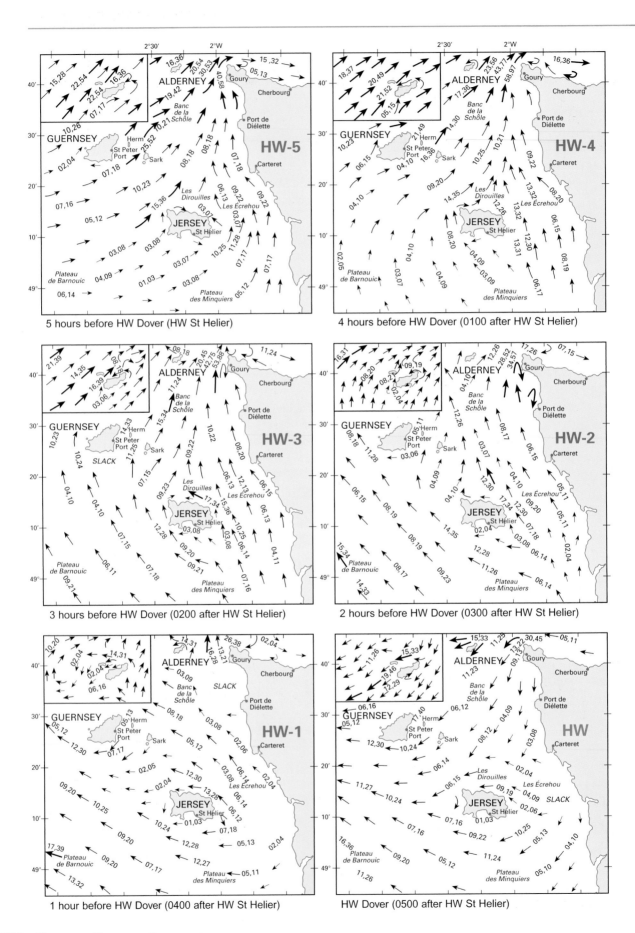

5 hours before HW Dover (HW St Helier)

4 hours before HW Dover (0100 after HW St Helier)

3 hours before HW Dover (0200 after HW St Helier)

2 hours before HW Dover (0300 after HW St Helier)

1 hour before HW Dover (0400 after HW St Helier)

HW Dover (0500 after HW St Helier)

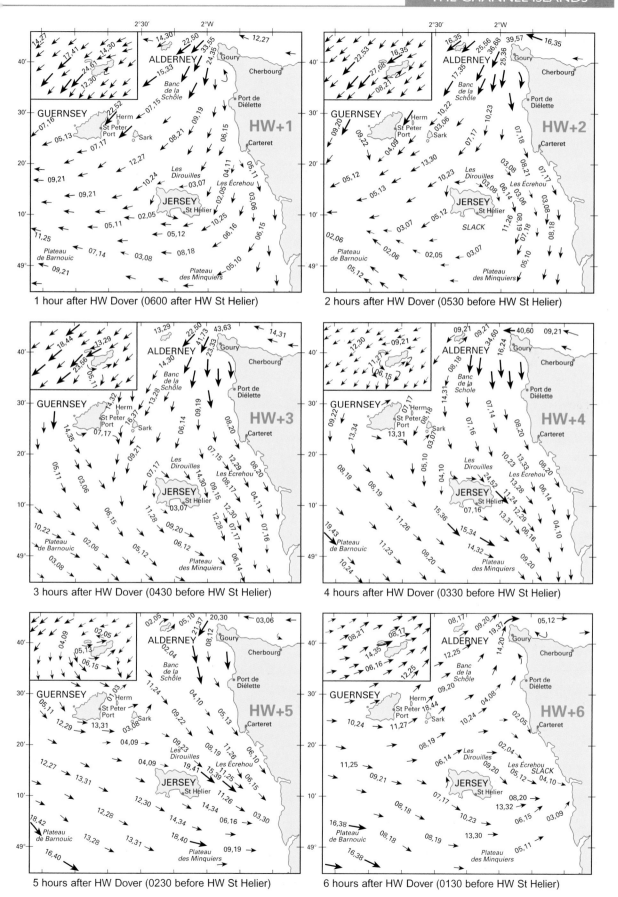

1 hour after HW Dover (0600 after HW St Helier)

2 hours after HW Dover (0530 before HW St Helier)

3 hours after HW Dover (0430 before HW St Helier)

4 hours after HW Dover (0330 before HW St Helier)

5 hours after HW Dover (0230 before HW St Helier)

6 hours after HW Dover (0130 before HW St Helier)

Chapter 6

ALDERNEY

Harbour entrance – 49°43´·74N 02°11´·54W

Looking ENE across Braye Harbour

Alderney's non-vital statistics: Population 2,200, plus approx 50,000 visitors; 12 pubs, open until 0030; four churches; 15 shops, five hotels, six guesthouses, three policemen and a partridge.... To which may be added: Several good restaurants, delightful coastal walking and peace –

but Braye Harbour may well keep you on your toes, literally.

Leave at the first hint of fresh (F5) north north easterly–easterly winds, to which the harbour is wide open. Conditions can deteriorate from soporific to tense to diabolical in a dogwatch (2 hrs for non-canines) – usually at night. Forgive the caveat, but it has to be said. In all other wind directions enjoy the change from 'marinaphilia'. And now for that run ashore ...

SHORESIDE (Telephone code 01481)

Tourist Office, Victoria St; ☎ 823737; 🕾 822436; tourism@alderney.net; www.alderney.gov.gg Open, high season, Mon–Sat 0800–1230 & 1400–1730.

What to see/do Walking or cycling is the best way to see the island; circumnavigation is approx 12M. Thirteen C19 forts on the N and E coasts include Clonque to Essex and Fort Albert overlooking the harbour. Strap-hang on an ex-London tube from the harbour to Quénard lt ho; Sat/Sun, Bank hols. The SW part of the island has high cliffs with good views to Ortac rock and the Casquets. On a rainy day visit Alderney Museum, Lower High Street, ☎ 823222; daily 1000–1200, plus 1400–1600 Mon–Fri.

Bus Riduna, ☎ 823760, runs from St Annes via the harbour to Corblets Bay, plus excursion trips.

Taxi ☎ 822992; 823760; 823181; 823823.

Car & moped hire Alderney Car Hire, ☎ 823352, by the inner harbour. Central Cars, ☎ 822971.

Bike hire Pedal Power, ☎ 822286; JB Cycle, ☎ 822294; Top Gear, ☎ 822000; Puffin Cycles, ☎ 823725.

Ferries Local boats (*Lady Maris* and *Voyager*) run scheduled trips to Cherbourg, Goury and Diélette. Condor Cats from Guernsey and Jersey to Poole, Weymouth and St Malo.

Flights Aurigny Air Services, ☎ 0871 871 0717, to Guernsey, Jersey and Southampton by Trislander. LeCocqs, ☎ 824646, to Bournemouth and Cherbourg.

Beaches Beautiful sandy beaches at Braye, thence clockwise at Saye, Arch, Corblets, Longy, Clonque (gravel) and Platte Saline Bays.

Supermarkets Iceland: Riduna Stores and Jean's Stores. Duty free prices are not all you might hope for; they are similar to a UK supermarket.

Market day Sunday in Marais Square.

Banks Natwest, Lloyds* and HSBC*; *cashpoints.

Restaurants At Braye: The First & Last, ☎ 823162/822535, is a Mecca; shut pm Sun, all Mon, except Bank Hols. Sea View Hotel, ☎ 822738, good seafood. Bumps, ☎ 823197, more good seafood.

In town: Belle Vue Hotel, ☎ 822844, top of the hill. Georgian House, ☎ 822471; good food and free wheels. Nellie Gray's, ☎ 823333, classic Indian. Out of town: The Old Barn, ☎ 822537; by Longy Bay/Essex Castle, a worthwhile 1.5M walk.

NAVIGATION

Charts AC 2669 (1:150,000), 3653 (1:50,000), 60 (1:25,000), 2845 (1:6,000), plus SC 5604.5 (1:25,000). SHOM 7158 (1:50,000), 6934 (1:25,000).

Approaches The easiest and safest approach is from the NE. If approaching via the Alderney Race or The Swinge, beware strong tidal streams which can cause dangerous overfalls. Best timing is at or near slack water; see Tidal streams on page 358. Other approaches, see page 352 for directions/tactics.

Landmarks The squat church spire at St Anne, an adjacent water tower and two radio/TV masts to the E are conspicuous from most directions. B/W vertical stripes on the Admiralty Breakwater head, L Fl 10s, may be the first thing you see from the NE in poor visibility. A Blockhouse, 350m SW of Quénard lt ho, is also conspic from the NE.

Pilotage The waypoint is 49°44´·37N 02°10´·87W,

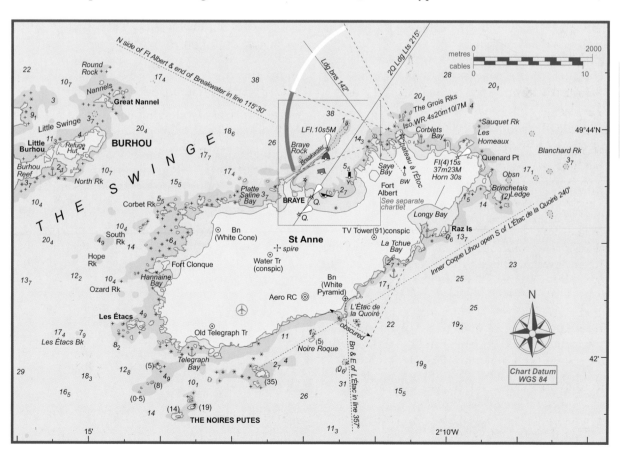

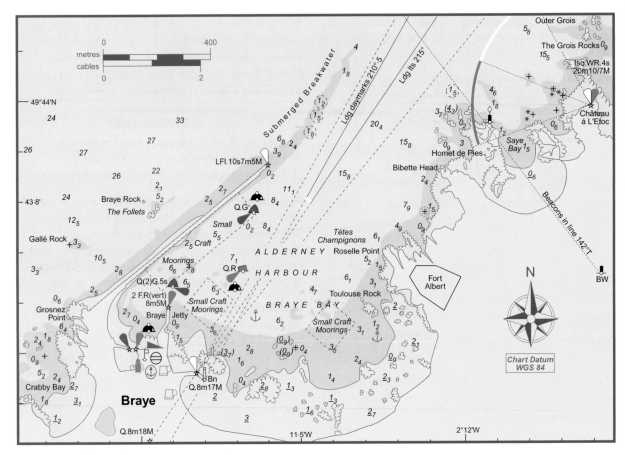

on the 215° leading line, 7·7 cables to the harbour entrance; the ldg lts are Q 8/17m 17/18M, visible 210°–220°; the rear lt is low down on the hillside. The 210.5° leading line (front daymark, white conical beacon on Douglas Quay; rear, St Anne church spire) lies just west of the 215° line. Caution: Sunken ruins, min depth 1·2m, extend 500m NE of the Admiralty Breakwater head. To clear these from the NW, track inbound 142° with a white beacon, 'hollow ○' topmark, in transit with a B/W beacon, △ topmark, E of Fort Albert. At night the 111° transit of Château à l'Étoc, Iso WR 4s, and Quénard lt ho, Fl (4) 15s, is a good clearing line. Harbour speed limit is 4kn.

Tides HW Braye at sp is 40 mins and nps 50 mins after HW St Helier. LW at sp is 25 mins and at nps 1 hr 5 mins after St Helier. MHWS is 6·2m, MLWS 0·9m; MHWN is 4·7m, MLWN 2·5m.

Tidal streams AC 60 and NP 264 (Admiralty tidal stream atlas) cover Alderney and the Casquets at large scale. Slack water is 2½ hrs after both HW and LW Braye. At HW+2½ the SW-going ebb starts to make and this is the best time to leave for Guernsey via either the Race or the Swinge. At LW+2½ the NE-going flood starts to make and this is the best time to leave for Cherbourg.

See page 352 for the Race and The Swinge.

Close inshore along the SW side of the island, a back eddy runs east when the ebb is setting SW. At mid-flood in The Swinge a back eddy sets SW past the harbour entrance and breakwater.

Access H24, at all tides, but not advised in strong NE'lies as moorings may be untenable or unsafe.

Shelter Strong NNE–E winds make Braye Hbr very uncomfortable. Persistent rolling occurs in lesser winds and with even a slight swell.

VHF *Alderney Radio* Ch 74, 16; office hours. Other times, for safety services call *St Peter Port Radio* or *CROSS Jobourg* Ch 16. Water taxi Ch M.

FACILITIES

HM's (Mr Steve Shaw) office is between Braye Jetty and Little Crabby Hbr; CG, Customs and Immigration are co-located. ☎ 822620, ▥ 823699. alderneyharbourmaster@gtonline.net Open: Apr, May, Sep daily 0800–1800; Jun–Aug daily 0800–2000; Oct–Mar, Mon–Fri 0800–1700. Crane, 25 tons max.

Moorings The 72 yellow ⚓s are mostly between the Admiralty breakwater and the fairway which is marked by two SHM buoys (the inner buoy Q

(2) G 5s was timed at 10s – Alderney time). More ⚓s are 150m east of Braye jetty and 500m further E by Toulouse Rock. Use double warps or chain. In calm weather rafting is allowed. Orange buoys are for locals only. Do not secure to Braye Jetty nor the Admiralty Breakwater. Dinghy landing at the root of Braye Jetty on a pontoon.

Anchorages Yachts can anchor in the centre of the harbour, clear of the fairway and moorings, in 5–7m. Good holding on fine sand, but avoid patches of rock and weed. In a NE'ly for best shelter tuck in S of Toulouse Rock below Fort Albert.

Other anchorages (free, no facilities; fair weather/offshore winds only) around Alderney include: Saye, Corblets, Longy, Telegraph and Hannaine Bays; also the Lug at Burhou (be advised by HM). Burhou is a bird sanctuary; no landing 15/3–21/7.

Tariff ⚓s £12 per day, anchoring £2.50; both include showers.

Water taxi *Mainbrayce Taxi* VHF Ch M; summer 0830 till late, £1 each way. State yacht's name, buoy or anchorage.

Showers free, across from the HM's Office, H24.

Launderette in the same area, H24; takes £1 coins.

Fuel Diesel & FW HW±2 from Mainbrayce in the inner harbour. Petrol by cans from Alderney Fuel Services, 823352, overlooking inner harbour.

YCs Alderney SC, next to the HM, welcomes visitors; Bar 1800–2000 daily in summer.

St Anne's church spire, the rear 210° leading mark

CHANDLERY & REPAIR FACILITIES

Mainbrayce, ☎ 822772, 🖷 823683. mainbrace@alderney.com Shop Ch 80, 0830–1800. Alderney Boating Centre, ☎ 823725, CH, opposite Sea View Hotel, Braye.

Little Crabby Harbour, looking NNE towards the moorings and Admiralty Breakwater

Chapter 6

BEAUCETTE MARINA

Harbour entrance – 49°30´·19N 02°30´·20W

Beaucette, at the northernmost tip of Guernsey, is an away-from-it-all haven of peace and quiet. If you wish to avoid the noise, over-crowding and bustle of St Peter Port's Victoria Marina, this is the place to be – for freedom, fresh air and great walking, or sailing, west toward L'Ancresse Bay and Grand Havre.

The marina was formed from a quarry by British army engineers who blasted tons of granite to carve an entrance from seaward. The rocks either side of the entrance are painted white, as per the army tradition of white-washing lumps of coal. In recent years the marina has been much upgraded by its present owners, Premier Marinas – it looks and is very good.

SHORESIDE (Telephone code 01481)

Tourist Office is in Town; see under St Peter Port. The marina office will also advise.

What to see/do Walk, cycle, take a picnic, inhale ozone, paddle amongst the rocks, enjoy all those things with your young family that you treasure from your own childhood days. These simple pleasures are richly rewarding. If you want the bright lights, St Peter Port is 20 mins away by bus.

Buses Nos 6 & 6A run to town (15 mins) from a stop about 6 mins walk from marina. Timetables in marina office.

Taxi ☎ 244444.

Car & bike hire Arrange via the marina.

Beaches The nearest sandy beach is L'Ancresse Bay, with café. Beyond is Grand Havre and a series of fine beaches stretching away to the SW.

Supermarkets A small shop in the marina office

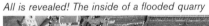
All is revealed! The inside of a flooded quarry

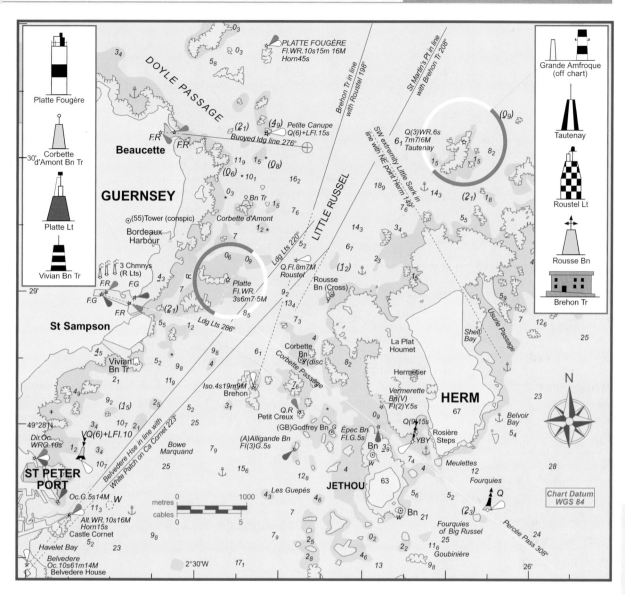

provides all basics. Opposite the bus-stop (6 mins) Dolphin Stores offers a wider range, but otherwise shop in town.

Restaurants The marina restaurant/bar, ☎ 247066, at the marina is open daily, 1200–1400 & 1900–2200. Excellent seafood and Italian cuisine. Lunch from £10, dinner from £14, plus *à la carte*.

NAVIGATION

Charts AC 2669 (1:150,000), 3654 (1:50,000), 807 (1:25,000), 808 (1:25,000) plus SC 5604.7 (1:25,000). SHOM 6966 (1:155,000), 7159 (1:50,000), 6903 (1:25,000), 6904 (1:25,000).

Approaches From the N/NE, enter the Little Russel (see page 353) on the 198° leading line (Roustel ≠ Brehon) to 49°30´·54N 02°27´·91W;

thence to the waypoint; see Pilotage.

From the NW an alternative route is the Doyle Passage: Corbette d'Amont Y bcn tower midway between Herm and Jethou on 146°. This passes close to Fort Doyle and the reefs marked by Platte Fougère light tower to intercept the ldg line into, or away from, the marina.

From the south, pass St Peter Port and navigate the Little Russel on the 220° astern ldg line until just north of Roustel bcn; thence alter for the waypoint. From the W, round Les Hanois lt ho and St Martin's Point lt ho (SW and SE corners respectively of the island), then as for the south approach.

Landmarks Platte Fougere's B/W octagonal light tower is conspicuous, 1M NE of the marina. Keep E of it, unless using the Doyle Passage. Fort Doyle is prominent; Vale Mill Tower, 8 cables SSW, is far

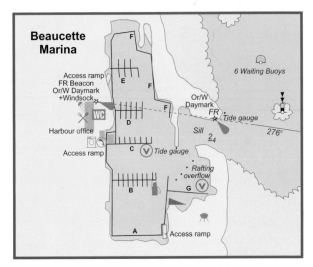

Beaucette Marina

more conspicuous, as are the three chimneys at St Sampson, 5 cables further SSW.

Pilotage The waypoint is 49°30´·09N 02°28´·69W, on the 277° ldg line, 1M to the marina entrance. This track passes about 130m S of Petite Canupé SCM beacon, Q (6) +L Fl 15s, a spindly affair which may not be seen until close. It also passes close to rocks on either hand, so counteract the cross tide with a suitable drift angle to ensure that 277° is exactly maintained.

The 277° leading marks are: Front, red vert arrow on white background; rear, white vert arrow on red background, with windsock alongside. At night both marks show a FR vertical strip light. The inner half of the channel is marked by three pairs of unlit PHM/SHM buoys. To starboard of the entrance an unlit SCM beacon marks a shoal patch. N of it are six yellow waiting buoys. The entrance is 18m wide; once through turn 90° port into the marina.

Tides Use predictions for St Peter Port, as given in the *RNA*. MHWS is 9·3m, MLWS 1·4m; MHWN is 7·0m, MLWN 3·6m.

Tidal streams The flood sets NE from HW Dover +6 to –2; the ebb runs SW from HWD –1 to +4.

Access In fresh to strong (F5/6) NE winds the approach and entrance are difficult or even dangerous. The marina is entered over a sill drying 2.37m. Access is HW±3, during which period there is at least 2m water over the sill. Depth gauges without and within the entrance show depth of water over sill. Entry is strictly controlled by the marina staff in a dory or on VHF Ch 80 in accordance with the HW±3 rule. Last minute attempts to squeak over the sill are not allowed to avoid expensive groundings.

VHF *Beaucette Marina* Ch 80.

FACILITIES

Marina Office Manager Niall Rhys-Evans. ☎ 245000; 📠 247071; Mobile 07781 102302; VHF Ch 80; beaucette@premiermarinas.com; www.premiermarinas.com

Berthing Pass details of boat etc prior to arrival so that a berth may be assigned. If none available, expect to raft up on 'G' pontoon, first to port on entry, inside five yellow buoys; depth 18m.

Tariff Daily rates on pontoons, or rafted, £1.95 per metre LOA (showers included).

Electricity £2.75 per day.

Showers (by the restaurant) are free, access code.

Launderette at the foot of the access gangway; also public telephone.

Fuel Diesel only at fuel berth on 'B' pontoon.

Chandlery & repairs Boat hoist 16 ton, crane 12 ton. Provisions, gas.The marina may assist with minor repairs. Full services at St Peter Port.

NE 6. Do not attempt entry

Looking NNW towards Fort Doyle

Castle Cornet lower left and Victoria Marina dead ahead

ST PETER PORT

Harbour entrance – 49°27´·35N 02°31´·54W

Chapter 6

St Peter Port is truly the jewel in Guernsey's crown, because like all precious stones it sparkles in a beautiful setting, relishes the sea lapping at its feet and is an international financial centre and tax haven – which is not to say that impecunious boat owners cannot squeeze into a berth there.

'Squeeze' is the operative word as those will know who have been shoe-horned into Victoria Marina in high season. But some crews are never happier than enjoying social intercourse at close quarters. Others enjoy Beaucette Marina, an oasis of calm. *Chacun à son goût ...*

Given the popularity of St Peter Port, no doubt yet more berths will be provided for the ever-growing number of visitors – who seek only to support the Guernsey economy.

SHORESIDE (Telephone code 01481)

Tourist Office is on the North Esplanade. ☎ 723552; 🖷 714951. Open Mon–Fri 0900-1700; Sat 0900–1600; Sun 0930–1230.

www.guernseytouristboard.com
enquiries@guernseytouristboard.com-

What to see/do Visit Hauteville House, where for 18 years (1851–1869) the writer Victor Hugo lived, a political exile from France's Second Empire. Now owned by the City of Paris, it is a fascinating museum – another world. Open Apr–Jun, Mon–Sat, 1000–1200 & 1400–1700; Jul/Aug 1000–1700; Sep 1000–1145 & 1400–1645; entry £4; ☎ 721911. Castle Cornet, open 1000–1600 daily, is a mighty pile with good maritime and militia museums and even an RAF squadron's exhibition 'Guernsey's Own'.

Buses Eight routes criss-cross the island. Route 7/7A circumnavigates it, but stop off on the NW

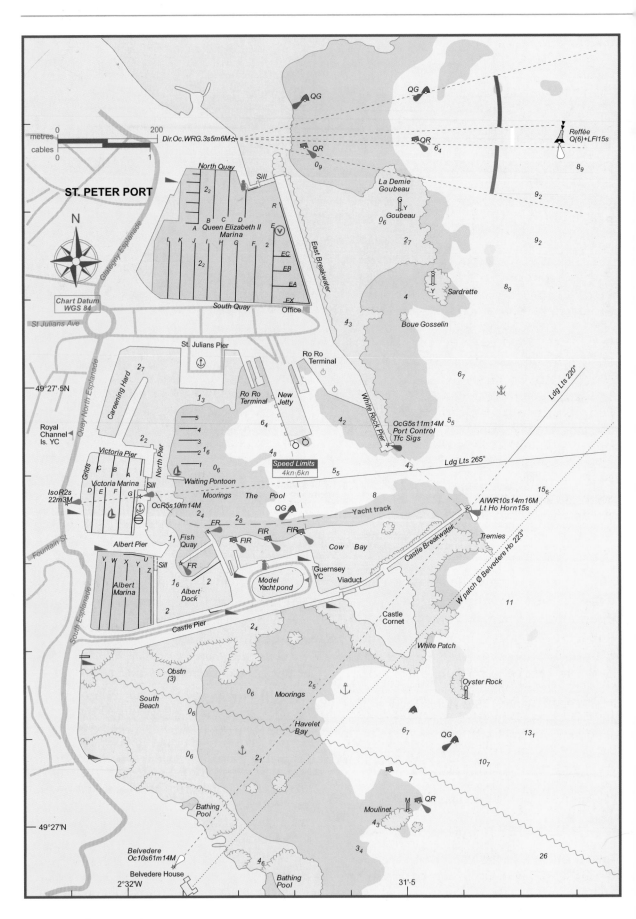

ST. PETER PORT

N

Chart Datum WGS 84

St Julians Ave

Royal Channel Is. YC

49°27'·5N

Dir.Oc.WRG.3s5m6M

metres 0 200
cables 0 1

North Quay

2_2

Sill

Queen Elizabeth II Marina

B C D

A

L K J I H G F

2_2 2_2

South Quay

R

E

EC

EB

EA

EX

Office

QG

QR

0_9

La Demie Goubeau

G Y
Goubeau

0_6

2_7

4_3

QG

QR

6_4

Reffée
Q(6)+LFl15s

8_9

9_2

9_2

8_9

4

S
Y Sardrette

Boue Gosselin

East Breakwater

St. Julians Pier

Careening Hard 2_7

2_2

Victoria Pier

C B A

Grids

D E F G

Victoria Marina

IsoR2s 22m3M

Sill

OcR5s10m14M

North Pier

1_3

5

4

3

2 1_6

1

0_6

Ro Ro Terminal

New Jetty

6_4

4_8

Ro Ro Terminal

Speed Limits
4kn 6kn

5_5

Moorings   The   Pool

QG

2_4

2_8

FR

FIR

FIR

FIR

Fish Quay

Sill

FR

1_1

Albert Pier

V W X Y U
Z

Albert Marina

2

1_6

2

Albert Dock

6_7

4_2

OcG5s11m14M
Port Control
Tfc Sigs 5_5

4_2

4_2

Ldg Lts 265°

8

Ldg Lts 220°

15_6

AIWR10s14m16M
Lt Ho Horn15s

Tremies

Castle Breakwater

W patch Ø Belvedere Ho 223°

11

White Rock Pier

Yacht track

Cow   Bay

Guernsey YC

Viaduct

Castle Cornet

White Patch

Oyster Rock

13_1

Castle Pier

2_4

Model Yacht pond

Obstn (3)

South Beach

0_6

0_6

0_6

Moorings

2_5

Havelet Bay

2_1

Bathing Pool

Belvedere
Oc10s61m14M

Belvedere House

2°32'W

4_6

Bathing Pool

0_6

6_7

7

Moulinet

M

QR

4_3

3_4

10_7

QG

26

49°27'N

31'·5

South Esplanade

Fountain St

Quay North Esplanade

Glategny Esplanade

coast for a swim or walk, then a bibulous lunch, before continuing – good fun. Timetables from the bus station or Tourist Office.

Taxi ☎ 244444. Plus taxi ranks in the town centre.

Car hire ☎ 726926, delivered to the marina. Sarnia ☎ 723933. Europcar ☎ 239696.

Bike hire Millard & Co Ltd ☎ 720777. Quay Cycle Hire, New Jetty ☎ 714146.

Ferries/flights Condor Cats to Poole, Weymouth and St Malo. Emeraude, ☎ 711414; www.emeraude.co.uk, operates direct to St Malo and via Jersey to Carteret and Granville. Flights to many UK airports.

Elizabeth College   St James Church   Victoria Tower

Victoria Marina entrance with three well-known landmarks on the skyline

Beaches Havelet Bay's sandy beach was used by Victor Hugo and is the nearest to St Peter Port. Virtually every beach around Guernsey is sandy. Along the SE and S coasts they are backed by highish cliffs which trap the sun. The NW coast is more open and and beaches are easily accessible.

Supermarkets M & S, facing Victoria Marina, has a very good food department. Safeway is about a mile out of town.

Market day The large, covered market in Market St is a hive of activity, especially in the fish hall.

Banks Mostly in the High street/Le Pollet.

Restaurants St Peter Port has a wide variety of eating places ranging from international cuisine to fish 'n chips. Here are a few within easy walking distance of Victoria Marina: Your Companion ate in considerable style and at no little expense in Le Nautique, ☎ 721714, Quay Steps, overlooking the marina and harbour. La Frégate, ☎ 724624, excellent French cuisine off St Julian's Ave/Les Cotils. Nino's, ☎723052, Lefebure St, for Italian cuisine. Nearby in Mansell St, Rosarios, ☎ 727268, for more Italian cuisine. The Chip Inn, ☎ 722108, 6 Fountain St for *pommes frites par excellence*. Hotel Jerbourg, ☎ 238826, (a taxi to St Martin's Point) for fine food and superb views.

NAVIGATION

Charts AC 2669 (1:150,000), 3654 (1:50,000), 807 (1:25,000), 808 (1:25,000), 3140 (1:6,000) plus SC 5604.6/7 (1:25,000). SHOM 6966 (1:155,000), 7159 (1:50,000), 6903 (1:25,000), 6904 (1:25,000).

Approaches The three waypoints are: From the N/NE, enter the Little Russel on the 198° leading line (Roustel ≠ Brehon) to 49°29´·46N 02°28´·66W (2 cables NNE of Roustel), to intercept the 220° ldg line (Castle bkwtr lt ho ≠ Belvedere lt) 2.8M from the harbour entrance.

From the SE or the Big Russel, make good Lower Heads SCM buoy, 49°25´·84N 02°28´·56W, thence 308°/2.4M to the harbour entrance.

From the S/W, make good 49°24´·82N 02°31´·10W (6 cables SE of St Martin's Pt lt ho), thence 355°/2.5M to the harbour entrance.

Landmarks Large cranes on the N side of the hbr and Castle Bkwtr lighthouse are conspic. From the S and E, Castle Cornet shows large white-painted patches. On the harbour skyline Victoria Tower (turreted/castellated) is conspic, ditto four spires.

Pilotage The 265° leading line into the harbour is mainly for large vessels; (the rear ldg light, Iso R 2s, is atop Woolworths). Yachts should follow the buoyed/lit channel along the S side of The Pool, noting the drying ground to port.

Speed limits 6kn in the outer harbour, E of a line south from the ferry jetty; 4kn W of that line. The 6kn limit also applies to virtually all bays around Guernsey and inshore the waters around Herm.

Traffic signals A R light is shown inwards and to seaward from White Rock pier (the N pierhead) and from New Jetty (ferry terminal) when a large vessel is under way in/near the harbour; vessels are not permitted to enter/exit.

But vessels <15m LOA may proceed under power, keeping well clear. IPTS may be fitted in the future, subject to funding.

Tides St Peter Port is a Standard Port; predictions are given in the *RNA*. MHWS is 9·3m, MLWS 1·4m; MHWN is 7·0m, MLWN is 3·6m. At sp HW is at approx 0800/2000UTC; and at nps approx 0100/1300.

Tidal streams off the hbr set N/NE at HW and S/SW at LW, max rates 5.25kn sp and 2.25kn nps. Slack water is at approx HW –3 and +3.

Shelter Very good, but the harbour is choppy/rough in fresh to strong E/NE winds, to which Victoria Marina is uncomfortably exposed. A more sheltered berth in QE II Marina may be available.

Access A waiting pontoon is close E of Victoria Marina; five more ❶ pontoons lie N of it. Beware drying ground inshore of these. There are no ⚓s.

The marina is entered over a sill drying 4.2m. A gauge at the entrance shows depth of water over the sill. Access is approx HW±2½, depending on draught; for more exact times enter the table

To find depth of water over the sill into Victoria Marina:
1. Look up predicted time and height of HW St Peter Port.
2. Enter table below on the line for height of HW.
3. Extract depth (m) of water for time before/after HW.

Ht (m) of HW St Peter Port	Depth of Water in metres over the Sill (dries 4·2 m)						
	HW	±1hr	±2hrs	±2½hrs	±3hrs	±3½hrs	±4hrs
6·20	2·00	1·85	1·55	1·33	1·10	0·88	0·65
·60	2·40	2·18	1·75	1·43	1·10	0·77	0·45
7·00	2·80	2·52	1·95	1·53	1·10	0·67	0·25
·40	3·20	2·85	2·15	1·63	1·10	0·57	0·05
·80	3·60	3·18	2·35	1·73	1·10	0·47	0·00
8·20	4·00	3·52	2·55	1·83	1·10	0·37	0·00
·60	4·40	3·85	2·75	1·93	1·10	0·28	0·00
9·00	4·80	4·18	2·95	2·03	1·10	0·18	0·00
·40	5·20	4·52	3·15	2·13	1·10	0·08	0·00
·80	5·60	4·85	3·35	2·23	1·10	0·00	0·00

below with the predicted height of HW St Peter Port. Go horizontally to the 'Depth over sill' value relevant to your draught + under-keel clearance. Extract the entry window, ie HW± ?hrs.

However entry is always controlled by the marina staff and R/G traffic lights, such that last minute attempts to cross the sill are verboten. Stranded yachts may be good spectator sport, but can also endanger or obstruct others. At peak times the patience of Job is indeed a virtue.

VHF Victoria Marina has no VHF channels. Monitor *Port Control* Ch 12 for commercial traffic (or to relay essential messages to the marina). For safety messages call *St Peter Port Radio* Ch 20.

Make link calls (remember those?) via *St Peter Port Radio* Ch 62. For D/F bearings in emergency call *St Peter Port Radio* Ch 16/67.

FACILITIES

HM's Office (Capt Robert Barton) at St Julian's Emplacement, GY1 2LW. ☎ 720229; ▨ 714177. 0900–1700. guernsey.harbour@gov.gg; www.guernseyharbours.gov.gg

Marinas Victoria Marina. Office ☎ 725987; open H24, all year. Duty Man ☎ 712422. Marina dory will direct you on arrival or berth on the waiting or ❶ pontoons outside the marina to the north. QE II & Albert Marinas are for locals, but by prior consent a few visitors may berth in QEII on 'R' pontoon.

Tariff Daily rates on pontoons (showers included) per metre for LOAs: <7m £11; <8m £12; <9m £13; <10m £14; <11m £15; <12m £16; <13m £17; <14m £18; <15m £19; <16m £20; plus £1/m thereafter.

Electricity £2 per day.

Showers are free, by access code; N side and SE corner of marina. **Launderette** same building.

Fuel Diesel & petrol at fuel berth on S side of hbr; access HW±3 (depending on draught) due to drying 1.1m. Run by Boatworks+, ☎ 726071. Fuel, inc LPG, is also available at QE II Marina which may be used if the harbour fuel berth is congested.

YCs Guernsey YC, ☎ 725342; adjacent Castle Cornet. Bar & lunches daily. Very informative website www.gyc.guernsey.net; info@gyc.guernsey.net
Royal Channel Islands YC, facing Victoria Marina; bar, ☎ 723154.

CHANDLERY & REPAIR FACILITIES

Boatworks +, ☎ 726071, ▨ 714224; boatwork@globalnet.co.uk Chandlery, BY, repairs, rigging, charts (by the fuel berth).
Marquand Bros Ltd, facing Victoria Marina; ☎ 720962, ▨ 713974. Chandlery.
Herm Seaway, Castle Embankment; ☎ 726829, ▨ 714011. Engine repairs/servicing.
Seaquest Marine, 16 Fountain St, ☎ 721773, ▨ 716738. Chandlery, electronics.
Radio & Electronic Services Ltd, Les Chênes, Rohais; 5 mins drive. ☎ 728837, ▨ 714379.

ADJACENT ANCHORAGE

Havelet Bay, S of Castle Pier, St PP. Anchor free in 2.5–5m on stone/sand/rock, well sheltered from S–W; avoid private moorings. The entrance is beaconed/buoyed/lit as per chartlet. Land at the slip W of Castle Cornet.

St Sampsons – Entrance 49°28´·91N 02°30´·72W. This is basically a commercial and fishing harbour, dries 5.2m; local boats moor in the outer harbour. All communications are via St Peter Port Control Ch 12 or ☎ 720229.

Approach from the Little Russel on the 286° leading line, front FR 3m 5M; rear FG 13m clock tower. Two chimneys are conspic N of the inner hbr. Repair facilities are good: North Quay Marine, ☎ 246561. Marine & General, ☎ 249583/ 240599. Chandlery, boatyard, engineering repairs.

St Sampsons on the 286° leading line, as seen from the fore topmast

In the W part of the harbour, work on a marina for local boats started 1 May 2003 and is due to complete Dec 2003. Access will be via a sill/retaining wall.

HERM

Harbour entrance – 49°28´·22N 02°27´·27W

This small island, only 1.3M long by 0.5M wide, is uniquely beautiful and tranquil in today's hurly-burly world, yet is only 3M east of St Peter Port. The northern part is low-lying and surrounded by pale sandy beaches which would grace any tropic isle. In the centre is farmland and in the south the land rises to 67m high and the scenery changes to craggy, gorse-covered cliffs. Even the fields rejoice in such charming names as Fairy Rings, Panto and Seagull.

In 1947 the States of Guernsey bought Herm from the Crown, so as to open it to the public. Since 1949 it has been leased to Major Peter Wood who has made many improvements whilst preserving the island's peacefulness. There are no cars.

SHORESIDE (Telephone code 01481)

Tourist Office does not exist, but the Admin Office ☎ 722377, by the harbour knows all there is to know.

What to see/do Walk, swim, sun-bathe, picnic or indulge in whatever other hedonistic delights turn you on. Walking around the island is particularly fine as the scenery is varied, the distances easily managed, sea views superb and the hills modest.

Ferries, frequent in season, go from St Peter Port's inter-island quay to Herm (20 mins): Travel Trident, ☎ 721379; Herm Seaway Express, ☎ 721342. If new to Herm, a ferry trip is a good way of seeing the beacons and marks before visiting by yacht.

Beaches Superb sandy beaches at Belvoir Bay and Shell Bay on the east coast. The latter is a magnet for conchologists seeking the exotic shells which have crossed the Atlantic on the Gulf Stream.

Supermarkets A grocery in the Mermaid Tavern provides most basics.

Banks Nearest are in St Peter Port.

Restaurants Just above the harbour, the conspic White House Hotel has two excellent restaurants: The Ship, ☎ 722159, a carvery/bar for light lunches and suppers; and the Conservatory Restaurant, ☎ 722377, for serious gourmets. A dinner menu @ £21.50 includes the ferry fare; plus

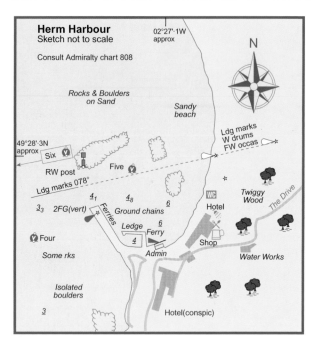

Herm Harbour
Sketch not to scale

Consult Admiralty chart 808

02°27'·1W approx

N

Rocks & Boulders on Sand

Sandy beach

Ldg marks W drums FW occas

49°28'·3N approx

Six Ⓨ

RW post

Five Ⓨ

Ldg marks 078°

4₁   4₈   6

3₃   2FG(vert)

Ground chains

Four Ⓨ

Ledge   6

Some rks

4   Ferry

Admin   Shop

WC

Hotel

Twiggy Wood

The Drive

Water Works

Isolated boulders

3

Hotel(conspic)

à la carte. The Mermaid Tavern, ☎ 710170, is pub, eatery and the social centre of the island.

NAVIGATION

Charts AC 2669 (1:150,000), 3654 (1:50,000), 807 (1:25,000), 808 (1:25,000) plus SC 5604.7 (1:25,000).

Herm Harbour from the west. The drying moorings are easily seen

SHOM 6966 (1:155,000), 7159 (1:50,000), 6903 (1:25,000), 6904 (1:25,000).

Approaches to Herm are a cat's cradle of transit lines, as shown on AC 807/8 and in some pilots. One of the three passages detailed under Pilotage should suffice for a first visit, ie Alligande Passage 074°, the most used and far easier than the chart suggests. The Corbette Passage 128° is also quite simple. The Percée Passage 308° is its reciprocal from the Big Russel. The charts list transit marks for these and other passages off Herm and Jethou.

Landmarks Brehon's squat, round tower is very conspic 1.3M W of the harbour. Close SW, Jethou's rounded bulk and Crevichon's near conical shape with a white obelisk atop are unmistakable. Most beacons have an identifying letter as topmark (see photos); of those mentioned under Pilotage, only Corbette and GB are unlit.

Pilotage Be aware of the height of tide and track accurately, laying off for the strong tidal set.
1. Alligande Passage. From the WPT 49°27'·84N 02°29'·27W, the tiny drying hbr is 074°/1.35M: Vermerette bcn, 'V' topmark, on with the white pierhead. Leave Alligande bcn 'A' and Godfrey bcn 'GB' 1 cable to starboard. When Épec bcn 'E' is abeam, alter port to bring two white drums in

Dried out E of the jetty at Herm Harbour

transit 078°; leave Vermerette to starboard.
2. *Corbette Passage.* Note: Corbette d'Amont
(Y bcn tr), 9 cables **N** of the waypoint, is **not** the
bcn used in this passage. From the waypoint
49°28´·74N 02°29´·29W identify Corbette Y bcn,
white disc; leave it 30m to port on 128°. Continue
128° with Vale Mill Twr astern twice its own
width SW of Corbette's disc (red when seen
from the E). Leave Épec bcn close to stbd; after
Percée (aka Gate Rk) WCM bcn alter slowly port
toward Rosière Steps.
3. *Percée Passage.* From the waypoint 49°27´·34N
02°26´·47W (Fourquies NCM buoy, Q) establish
on the 308° ldg line (as in 2 above). Near LW
beware Tinker & Meulettes drying rks between
Herm and Jethou. Continue to Little Russel or
as required.

Tides Use predictions for St Peter Port, as given in
the *RNA.* MHWS is 9·3m, MLWS 1·4m; MHWN is
7·0m, MLWN 3·6m.

Tidal streams In Percée Passage the stream sets
SE for 9 hrs from HW St Helier –5½ and NW for
3½ hrs from HW St Helier +3½. The NW-going
stream is weaker than the SE-going.

Access The W side of Herm is accessible HW±3,
at least until you are familiar. However from the
Big Russel you can get to the anchorages S and N
of Rosière Steps at all tides via the Percée Passage.
Belvoir and Shell Bays can be reached at all tides,
most easily from the SE with Noire Pute well to
stbd and avoiding Aiguillons and Equitelais
NW of it. The approaches are difficult or even
dangerous in fresh/strong onshore winds.

Anchorages Pleasant surroundings, well
sheltered from W'lies at: 0.6M NE of Pt
Sauzebourge anchor in about 5m between
Putrainez (9m) and Selle Roque (9m). Belvoir Bay
is best if you can get out of the tide between

Yachts afloat at LW near Rosière Steps

Caquorobert (15m) and Moulière (2m). Shell Bay
is shallow; tuck in close N of Moulière.

FACILITIES

Island admin Visiting yachts should pre-call ☎
722377 for permission to moor overnight at Herm.

Moorings/anchorages Bilge keelers and shoal
draught boats may dry out on the beach NE of
the tiny harbour, if space permits. W/SW of the
harbour are groups of 4, 5 & 6 ⚓s only intended
for short stay as they dry to sand and rock.

   Two cables south, N of Rosière Steps, are more
⚓s; further south is an anchorage where boats can
stay afloat in 3–4m. Do not berth on Rosière Steps
(except briefly for landing), as it is the LW berth
for frequent ferries.

Tariff There are no mooring charges, but a
contribution for facilities provided is much
appreciated. There is a public telephone at
the harbour.

Showers are provided free.

VHF, fuel, chandlery & repairs None.

SARK

Havre Gosselin – 49°25´·75N 02°22´·68W

There is no nautical epicentre for Sark unless it be the 'conspic' Mill, of which more anon. Hence the Lat/Long of Havre Gosselin is given above purely because it is the nearest anchorage to St Peter Port.

The island, 3M long by 1.5M wide, stands four-square with rugged 300ft high cliffs buttressing the level plateau. You will see this great chunk of granite as you head SW from Alderney or gaze north from Jersey. It cannot be mistaken for the shallow wedge-like profile of Guernsey.

Once on top you are in a time-warp: no cars, few houses, unmade lanes, hidden valleys to the sea, deserted coves, tiny fields and subsistence farming. Tourism drives the island's economy, yet it is under control and does not swamp you. A thousand people may land daily from the ferries, but they are easily absorbed and the hotels are not obtrusive. By dusk the day trippers have gone, leaving the world to darkness and to you. The night sky is like diamond-studded velvet.

SHORESIDE (Telephone code 01481)

Tourist Office is a wooden chalet, ☎ 832345, at the top of the hill from Maseline/Creux harbours. 832483; Mon–Fri 1000–1145 & 1430–1615; Sat 1000–1145. www.sark-tourism.com

NE coast of Sark with Maseline Pier and Pt Robert lt ho

Grève de la Ville

Grand Moie (25)

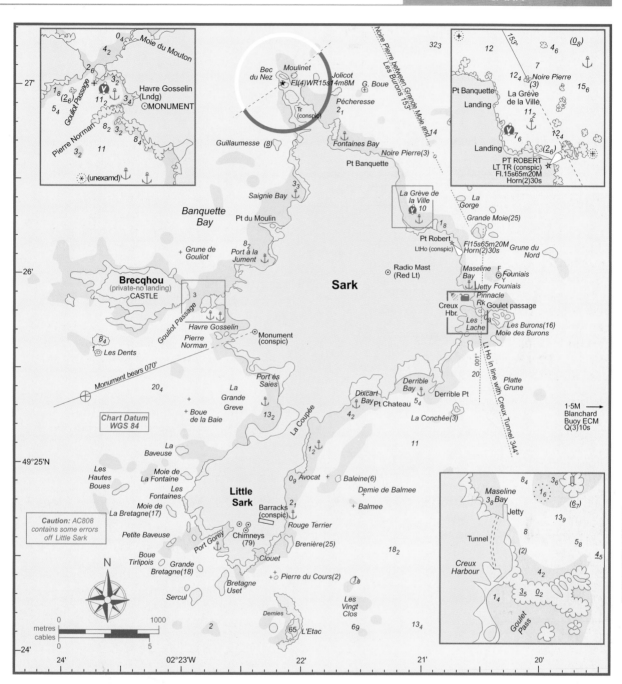

What to see/do Swim, sunbathe, walk round the island, fish, eat nobly whether ashore or afloat. Or visit the Occupation & Heritage Museum which recalls Dame Sybil Hathaway, then the Seigneur, and her spirited resistance to the German forces.

Ferries, frequent in season, to St Peter Port's inter-island quay (45 mins, £19.90 return): Isle of Sark Shipping Co, ☎ 724059. Emeraude, ☎ 01534 766566, 1 hr to Jersey.

Bike hire A to B Cycles, ☎ 832844, opposite the Mermaid. Avenue Cycle Hire, ☎ 832102, £4.50/day.

Beaches Dive in and swim ashore, but remember the steep climb to the top. Most of the anchorages have beaches, either sand, shingle or pebbles, but not Havre Gosselin.

Supermarkets None! but Island Stores, ☎ 832028, is grocer, butcher, baker, greengrocer – you name it.

Banks HSBC (opening times Mon–Fri 0930–1230 & 1330–1500) and NatWest (opening times Mon–Fri 10–1230 & 1400–1500), but neither have cashpoints.

Restaurants Six hotel/restaurants with fine food are: Stocks, ☎ 832001 (organic). Dixcart Bay, ☎ 832015, in country house style. La Sablonnerie, ☎ 832061, farmhouse comfort on Little Sark. Aval du Creux, ☎ 832036, stylish modernity by the Tourist Office. Petit Champ, ☎ 832046, overlooks Port à la Jument. La Moinerie, ☎832089, near La Seigneurie. Squires in The Avenue (the main drag) does more affordable food including an all-day breakfast; ☎ 832422. By the Tourist Office, Founiais, ☎ 832626, offers main courses at around £8. Sark Internet Café, ☎ 832580, is on The Avenue.

NAVIGATION

Charts AC 2669 (1:150,000), 3654 (1:50,000), 808 (1:25,000) plus SC 5604.6 (1:60,000) & .8 (1:25,000). SHOM 6966 (1:155,000), 7159 (1:50,000), 6904 (1:25,000).

Approaches Sark is easily approached from any direction until within 3M of it, when overfalls, as marked on the chart, and offlying rocks need to be avoided. An ECM buoy marks Blanchard Rk, 1.7M E of Creux. For inshore work heed the transits on AC 808 and the notes below about some of the more popular bays.

Landmarks SARK MILL (conspic) still appears on AC 807 & 3654, but in fact it is famously inconspic. Substantial trees totally screen the mill on its western side, whilst from the east they act as a delusive backdrop – so forget it. The Pilcher obelisk above Havre Gosselin will suffice for a general approach on 070°. The Barracks on Little Sark are also conspic, as is the isolated 65m high L'Étac, close SSE. Corbée du Nez at the N tip and Pt Robert, just N of Maseline, are the only nav lights on Sark.

Pilotage If you need a waypoint, use 49°25′·37N 02°23′·89W, 070°/1M toward the Pilcher obelisk,

as if arriving from Guernsey. The privately-owned island of Brecqhou, with its new 'mediaeval' castle and flags fluttering, lies to port; likewise by some 250m, Les Dents, an evil 1m high fang.

Some of the little bays, particularly around Little Sark, require small rocks and marks to be properly identified. For such details consult the specialised Pilots mentioned in this chapter's introduction.

Tides HW Sark (Maseline Pier) at sp is 15 mins and nps 5 mins after HW St Helier. LW at sp is 5 mins and at nps 10 mins after LW St Helier. MHWS is 8·9m, MLWS 1·1m; MHWN is 6·6m, MLWN 3·4m. HWN is approximately at midday and midnight; HWS is at mornings and evenings.

Tidal streams Offshore the main flood sets NNE from HW−3 to +3, and the ebb sets SW from LW−3 to +3. Therefore at HW−3 and +3 it is mostly slack water around Sark. Around Bec du Nez (N tip) the tide sets W from HW−1 to LW+3 (10 hrs). Around Little Sark it sets SE from LW to HW+3 (9 hrs). These simplifications help decide which way to go round the island, if for example planning the return from Creux to St Peter Port. Back eddies have considerable effect inshore, as do the fierce streams in the Goulet Pass off Creux and in the Gouliot Passage between Sark and Brecqhou.

Access Creux is accessible approx HW±2 in fair weather. Anchorages are unlit and therefore best entered by day. For a given wind direction, shelter on one side of Sark will be exposure on the other.

Anchorages Given that Sark is a mere blip (some blip!) stuck in the main Channel streams, there is often some movement in any of the following ⚓s.
• West coast, N to S (ideal in E'lies):
Saignie Bay. Tuck in N of Les Autelets (rock pillars) on sand/shingle; exposed to NW.

Percée beacon (Herm) with Brecqhou Castle and Sark beyond

L'Etac and Little Sark in the background

Creux Harbour and tunnel

Maseline Pier and Pt Robert lt ho

Port à la Jument. In 3–5m on shingle; open to NW.
Havre Gosselin. Space is limited by ⚓s (below).
Good shelter except from the SW. Land at the first
of 299 steps in SE corner. Be aware of the drying
rocks (Pierre Norman) along the S side of the bay;
and of Gouliot Passage where the stream
accelerates hard between Sark and Brecqhou.
La Grande Grève. Seemingly large bay, but avoid
two drying rocks (Boue de la Baie) in centre stage.
Anchor under La Coupée, the knife-edge Great
Wall to Little Sark or well in to Port es Saies.
• East coast, S to N (ideal in W'lies):
Dixcart and Derrible Bays. Good anchorages either
side of Pt Chateau, but can be affected by swell;
open to the S/SE. Anchor in 4–5m on sand. Land
at steps for easy access to The Avenue.
La Grève de la Ville. See below for ⚓s. Anchor close
in, on sand/mud in about 4m. Land on pebble
beach; steep path to the top. Exposed to the NE.
Les Fontaines Bay. Small bay near N tip of Sark,
well sheltered from S/SW. Tuck in close, avoiding
the drying spur to the E. Anchor in 5m on sand.

VHF *Sark Port Control* Ch 13, summer only.

FACILITIES

HM's Office at Maseline, ☎ 8323233, VHF Ch
13. Visiting yachts can anchor here, but it is
primarily for ferries and FVs. Creux harbour
is minute and dries, but smaller yachts can lie
here bows to the NE wall, stern to a kedge.
Do not berth on the pier which is used by the
supply ship and FVs. There are public telephones
at both harbours.

Moorings Havre Gosselin has four red buoys for
Sark YC and 20 yellow ⚓s laid by Sark Moorings,
☎ 832260, Mob 07781 106065 & VHF Ch 10; also
20 yellow ⚓s in La Grève de la Ville.

Tariff The ⚓s are £12 for 24 hrs. Elsewhere a
contribution for facilities is much appreciated.

Showers alongside the HM's office.

Fuel & stores The PO and Gallery Stores,
☎ 832078, sells hardware, Camping Gaz and
petrol/diesel by cans. Very limited repair
facilities; see HM.

Havre Gosselin and the Gouliot Passage

St Helier

Harbour entrance – 49°10´·49N 02°06´·42W

Inbound (probably exceeding the 5kn speed limit) on the 023° leading line

Jersey is the largest Channel Island and the best – if you ask a Jerseyman. Certainly it attracts more tourists than all the other islands put together and St Helier is jam-packed in season. But get out of town, by bike or bus, to enjoy a gentler world of pastoral beauty. By hire car you can 'do' the island in a day, but two or three would be more realistic/rewarding. The 12 parishes, all bar two named after saints, are often referred to on signposts and in addresses.

The north coast in particular is worth a visit for all its little bays, with minuscule fishing harbours; and on a clear day for views across Les Ecrehou to France or NW toward Sark and Guernsey – great coastal walking, not to mention good sailing. Try a circumnavigation (38M) or visit Les Minquiers – but first read *The Wreck of the Mary Deare* by Hammond Innes, set among these daunting reefs.

SHORESIDE (Telephone code 01534)

Tourist Office, Liberation Square, across from the marina. ☎ 500777; ▤ 500808; info@jersey.com; www.jersey.com Open May–Sep, daily, 0830–1900; Oct–Apr, Mon–Fri 0830–1730; Sat 0845–1300.

What to see/do Visit Elizabeth Castle high on its rocky outcrop, both for panoramic views and for the four small museums about the castle and its militia. Apr–Oct, daily 1000–1800; ☎ 723971; £4.70. Go by Duck amphibian or cross on foot via the causeway approx LW±2. La Mare Vineyards, ☎ 481178, 1M SW of Sorel Pt, do a light-hearted audio-visual show, plus tastings; they also make attractive wines. For a rainy day, try the Jersey museum, Maritime museum next to the marina and the CI Military museum in a bunker at the N end of St Ouen Bay.

Bus From St Helier routes 1 & 2 radiate to Gorey; 3 to Rozel Bay; 4, 5, 7 due north; 8 & 9 NW; 12 W then N; 15 to the airport. Timetables from the bus station, ☎ 721201 (Caledonia Place) or Tourist Office.

Taxi ☎ 871111; 887000; 499999; 888888; 625625.

Car hire Zebra, 9 The Esplanade, ☎ 736556.

Sovereign, ☎ 608062, 27 The Esplanade. Viceroy, 70 The Esplanade, ☎ 738698. Avis, Hertz & Europcar at the airport. 40mph/64kph max speed limit.

Bike hire Zebra, above. SGB hire shop, ☎ 873699.

Fly & ferry Flights to many UK airports. Condor Cats to Poole, Weymouth, St Malo. Emeraude to Guernsey and Sark, plus Carteret, Granville and St Malo; ☎ 766566; sales@emeraude.co.uk

Beaches Clockwise from St Helier, St Aubin Bay is one huge beach, at least at LW. St Brelade's Bay, backed by high cliffs, has considerable charm. St Ouen's Bay is 3.5M of W-facing beach, possibly exposed but rarely crowded. Along the N coast are much smaller, sandy coves: Grève au Lancon, Grève de Lecq, Bonne Nuit Bay, Bouley Bay and Rozel Bay. The E and SE coasts are more or less uninterrupted beaches from St Catherine's Bay to St Helier. Spoiled for choice?

Supermarkets Co-op on the way to the Town Hall. Stampers, at the corner of Mulcaster St and Pier Rd, is not far from the marina; Mon–Sat 0700–2100, Sun 0830–2100. A large Safeway at La Vallée de Vaux is on the N side of town; taxi advised.

Market day Saturdays an open-air market is held in Hope St. Off Halkett Place the large, covered market, noted for its ironwork, is a hive of activity.

Banks All, plus cash machines, as befits a financial centre.

Restaurants La Taverne, ☎ 725190, 6 York St, facing the Town Hall; friendly, good value Franco-Italian fare. La Capannina, ☎ 734602, 65 Halkett Place; for excellent Italian cuisine, £14.50. Nelson's Eye, ☎ 875176, Havre des Pas (close NE of power station chimney); sea view, £15.50. For details of the very wide choice the Tourist Office offer a booklet *Eating Out*; or visit www.jersey.com/eating out

NAVIGATION

Charts AC 2669 (1:150,000), 3655 (1:50,000), 1136 (1:25,000), 1137 (1:25,000), 1138 (1:25,000), 3278 (1:6,000) plus SC 5604.9 (1:60,000) & .10 (1:25,000). SHOM 6966 (1:155,000), 7160 (1:50,000), 6937 (1:25,000), 6938 (1:25,000), 6939 (1:25,000).

Approaches All approaches converge at or near a common waypoint, 49°09′·95N 02°07′·22W, close W of East Rock SHM lt buoy and on the final 023° approach into Small Road. The most used approach is from the west, rounding La Corbière lt ho about 0.5M to 1M off. Unless very knowledgeable or of unsound mind, do not cut

inside La Corbière. Continue via the NW or W Passages which meet at 49°09′·68N 02°10′·21W, betwixt Les Fours NCM buoy and Noirmont Pt. The W Passage is on the distant 082° transit of Dog's Nest Rock beacon with the Oc 5s and Oc R 5s ldg lts, 1.2–2.2M further east. Four high-rise blocks (not charted) are conspic 2 cables ESE of the front ldg lt, Oc 5s. The NW Passage parallels the coast, is undemanding and more often used.

From the S, binoculars are needed to discern all marks. Danger Rock Passage has the B/W striped head of Elizabeth Castle breakwater in transit 044° with the signal mast on Fort Regent. The Red & Green Passage enters harbour on the 023° Oc G & R 5s ldg lts. Both Passages run close to unmarked drying rocks; no problem HW±3. South Passage is the 341° transit of a B/W mark on the N shore of St Aubin Bay with Gros du Château, twin rocks.

From NE to E, use Anquette Channel via Violet SWM buoy, Canger Rk WCM buoy and Demie de Pas lt beacon, skirting Violet Bank, the extensive reefs off La Rocque Pt. From Gorey Roads and the N, route to the Violet Channel, thence as above. Tidal streams here vary by the hour and reach 4kn at springs. The inshore Boat Passage via Brett bcn and many drying rocks is not recommended.

La Mare Vineyard, N coast of Jersey

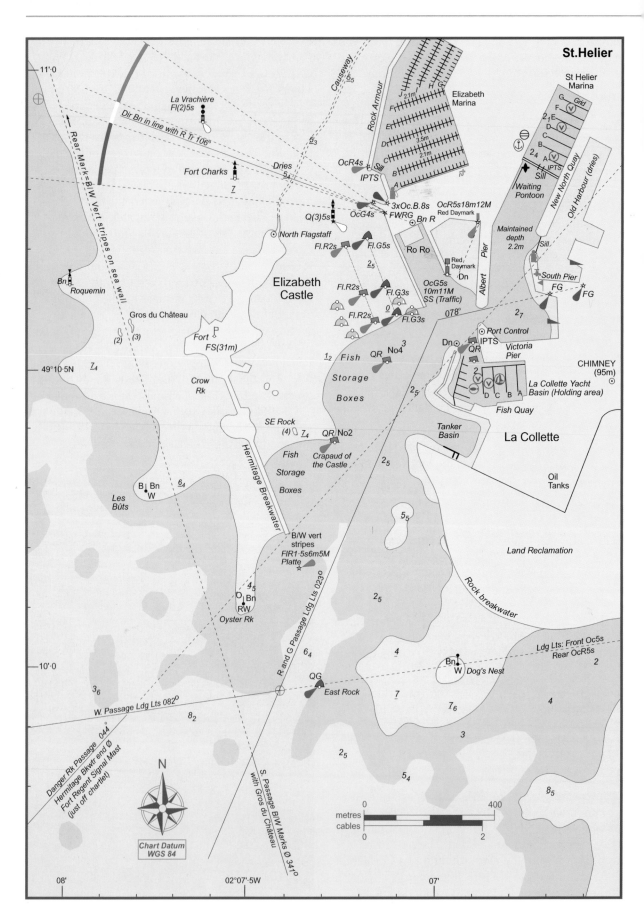

St.Helier

La Vrachière
Fl(2)5s

Dir Bn in line with R Tr 106°

Fort Charks

Dries
5·₁

7

Causeway
5·₅

5·₃

Rock Armour

Elizabeth
Marina

St Helier
Marina

J 2·1m   H G

F

Dr

C
B
A

3.5m
2·1m
2·1m

G
F
2·₁ E
D
C
B
IPTS
A

Grid

Sill
IPTS

2·₄

Waiting
Pontoon

New North Quay (dries)

Old Harbour (dries)

OcR4s
Sill
IPTS

3xOc.B.8s
OcG4s ☆FWRG
Bn R

OcR5s18m12M
Red Daymark

Maintained
depth
2.2m

Sill

Q(3)5s

North Flagstaff

Fl.R2s   Fl.G5s

Ro Ro

Red
Daymark
Dn

South Pier
FG
FG

Rear Mark = B/W Vert stripes on sea wall

Bn
Roquemin

Gros du Château

(2)   (3)

49°10·5N   7·₄

Elizabeth
Castle

Fort
FS(31m)

Crow
Rk

Fl.R2s
Fl.R2s
Fl.R2s

Fl.G3s
0
Fl.G3s

2·₅

OcG5s
10m11M
SS (Traffic)

078°

2·₇

Albert Pier

Port Control
IPTS

Dn   QR
QR

Victoria
Pier

CHIMNEY
(95m)

1·₂   Fish
Storage
Boxes

QR No4 3

No4

La Collette Yacht
Basin (Holding area)

D C B A

2·₅

2·₅

Fish Quay

La Collette

Hermitage Breakwater

SE Rock
(4) � 7·₄   QR No2

Fish
Storage
Boxes

Crapaud of
the Castle

Tanker
Basin

Oil
Tanks

B Bn
W

Les
Bûts

6·₄

2·₅

5·₅

Land Reclamation

B/W vert
stripes
FIR1·5s6m5M
Platte

O Bn
RW
Oyster Rk

4·₅

R and G Passage Ldg Lts 023°

6·₄

4

Bn
W Dog's Nest

Ldg Lts: Front Oc5s
Rear OcR5s

Rock breakwater

2

10'·0

3·₆

W. Passage Ldg Lts 082°

8·₂

QG
East Rock

7

7·₆

4

08'

Danger Rk Passage 044°
Hermitage Bkwtr end ∅
Fort Regent Signal Mast
(just off chartlet)

S. Passage B/W Marks ∅ 341°
with Gros du Château

2·₅

5·₄

3

4

8·₅

N

Chart Datum
WGS 84

metres   400
cables
0   2

02°07'·5W   07'

Elizabeth Castle from Albert Pier. Ro-Ro breakwater in right foreground

Landmarks The power station chimney (95m) is close E of the harbour, easily seen and floodlit at night. Close N the white wave-shaped roof of Fort Regent (sports centre) is fairly conspicuous, as is Elizabeth Castle on the W side of the harbour.

Pilotage From the waypoint, the entrance is easy on 023°. Check the IPTS and hold off, if needs be, in a clear area. Keep your eyes open for ferries, especially fast Cats closing from astern. Monitor VHF 14.

La Collette. The entrance is half-blind; look out for yachts leaving. Enter by turning hard starboard around a large concrete dolphin. Two PHM buoys, the first QR, must be left to port; they mark shoal ground to port, drying 0.4m.

St Helier Marina. Leave the Control Tower to stbd, ideally S of the 078° FG ldg line, as the entrance is again blind. Head N up-harbour to the marina.

Elizabeth Marina. The preferred approach is from St Aubin Bay, as this keeps yachts clear of Small Road. Keeping W of Baleine SHM buoy, make for 49°10'·94N 02°08'·08W. Here track 106°/7 cables in the white sector of a Dir F WRG lt, just S of the marina. Pass between La Vrachière IDM lt bcn and an unlit NCM bcn. This approach dries 5.3m. A secondary approach 333° from Small Road lies W of the ferry terminal, dries 2.5m and is marked by six lateral lt buoys (E1–6) and Fort Charles East ECM lt beacon.

Speed limit 5kn in Small Road, the harbour and marinas.

Tides St Helier is a Standard Port; predictions are given in the *RNA*, plus differences for Bouley Bay, St Catherine Bay, Les Ecrehou and Les Minquiers. MHWS is 11·0m, MLWS 1·4m; MHWN is 8·1m, MLWN 4·0m. HW springs is at approx 0800/2000UTC; HW neaps approx 0100/1300.

Tidal streams off the harbour and along the south coast set E/W, max rate 4kn springs. Slack water is nearly at HW and LW.

Access The harbour entrance, Small Roads, is exposed to SW winds, but all three marinas are well sheltered. Their access times are given under individual entries in FACILITIES.

IPTS, mounted halfway up the white Port Control Tower just N of La Collette, regulate commercial and ferry traffic. They are visible from within the main harbour, Small Roads, La Collette, St Helier and Elizabeth Marinas.

Long range occulting repeaters on the tower roof are shown in conjunction with IPTS: Oc R 8s with Signal 2; Oc G 8s with Signal 3; and Oc Y 4s with Signal 4. (Signal 1 and repeater are L Fl R 5s).

Signal 2 and Oc R 8s are also shown when a tanker, which at LW may be hidden by the high breakwater, leaves the Tanker Berth. It sounds a long blast if small craft are approaching.

Signals 2A and 5A exempt yachts <25m LOA from the main message. Keep to stbd and observe Rules 5 and 9 of the IRPCS meticulously.

Separate IPTS (signals 2, 3 & 4)

La Corbière lt ho at Low Water

Fort Regent on the skyline; fuel berth centre foreground

included): <8m £12; <10m £14; <12m £16; <14m £18; <16m £23; <20m £31; >20m £1.60/m.

Electricity £1 per day for <12m LOA; £2 per day >12m.

1. La Collette Yacht Basin ☎ 885529, is immediately S of the Port Control Tower and accessible H24 at all tides; least depth 1.6m in the entrance. Berth on the first two pontoons, 'D' & 'C'. FVs berth to stbd.

at the entrances to St Helier and Elizabeth Marinas (but not La Collette) control entry/exit.

Anchorage No anchoring in Small Roads (the outer hbr) due to lack of space. The nearest yacht anchorage is tucked into St Aubin's Bay

VHF Monitor *St Helier Port Control* Ch 14 for ship movements. *St Helier Pierheads* automatically gives wind direction, mean speed and gusts every 2 mins on Ch 18. There is no marina VHF but essential messages may be relayed by *Port Control* (range only about 8M) or by *Jersey Radio* Ch 16, **82**, 25. *Jersey Radio* handles safety messages etc Ch 82; link calls Ch 25; and broadcasts routine weather forecasts for the Channel Islands on 25 & 82 – see the Intro to this chapter for details. In emergency call *Jersey Radio* Ch 16/82 for D/F bearings from 49°10´·85N 02°14´·30W.

FACILITIES

HM's Office, Capt Brian Nibbs, Maritime House, La Route du Port Elizabeth, JE1 1HB. ☎ 885588, 🖳 885599. Mon–Fri, 0830–1600; jerseyharbours@jersey-harbours.com; www.jersey-harbours.com

See below for the three marinas: La Collette is an all-tide basin for yachts waiting to enter St Helier Marina (or leave early the next day); it is about 30/70% FVs/visitors. St Helier Marina is mainly for visitors. Elizabeth Marina is for local boats only, but long stay or large visiting yachts may be directed there.

Tariff The same rates apply at all marinas. 2003 daily rates on pontoons per metre LOA (showers

2. St Helier Marina Office, ☎ 885508; 🖳 879549. If you have a problem, call the office ☎ or Port Control on VHF 14. Open H24 in season.

Access Approx HW±3, depending on draught. Enter as controlled by IPTS, over a sill drying 3̲.6m with associated flapgate 1.4m high. When the flapgate first lowers, a digital gauge at the entrance shows blank; when there is 2.2m depth of water over the sill it starts to read and the IPTS are activated. A long waiting pontoon (aka No 5 berth) is located to port of the entrance in 2.2m depth.

Berthing Fingers on ❷ pontoons 'D' (N side) & 'E'; or raft on 'F' & 'G' in 2m. If draught >1.8m/LOA >12m, pre-request a berth on 'A' pontoon in 2.4m.

Showers E side of marina are free, by access code. Shut for cleaning 1200–1300 & 2359–0100.

Launderette same building. Small food shop.

3. Elizabeth Marina ☎885530; 🖳 885593. Heads pump-out, fuel, launderette and CH on site. Berth as directed.

Access Approx HW±3, depending on draught, over a sill drying 3̲.6m; the associated flapgate is 2.0m high. A digital read-out gives depth of water over sill and the rate of the tidal stream. Avoid entering in the first hour after opening, when the rate is up to 3kn at springs. Three yellow waiting buoys lie E, and 2 W, of the southern approach channel. An IPTS repeater is visible from these moorings.

Exit/entry is one-way only, alternating 10 mins in each direction, as shown by IPTS, ie for 8 mins exit, 3 FG show into the marina/ 3 FR outward. They then flash for 2 mins, before showing 3 FR in- & out-ward for a 1 min separation period. The process then reverses for inbound yachts. A siren warns when the flapgate is rising at final closure.

Fuel Diesel & petrol at S Pier (below St Helier YC). Run by S Pier Shipyard, ☎ 519700. Dries approx 3.3m; access HW±3, depending on draught. Diesel & petrol at Elizabeth Marina, S of entrance.

YCs (visitors welcome). St Helier YC, ☎ 721307, is on S Pier (at the S end of the drying Old Hbr). Open 0900–2345: Bar, restaurant, Mon–Sat for breakfast & lunch; and dinner on Fri.

Chandlery & repairs S Pier Shipyard, ☎ 519700, 🖷 519701; www.southpiershipyard.com CH, BY, fuel, repairs, rigging, electronics, charts. Iron Stores, ☎ 877755, 15/16 Commercial Buildings (E of the Old Harbour); extensive CH. Freeport Marine, ☎ 888100, New North Quay; CH, BY, ME. JE Marine Services, ☎ 626930, Elizabeth marina; CH. Bill Keating Marine Engineering Ltd, ☎ 733977; ME. DK Collins Marine Ltd, ☎ 732415, S Pier; ME. Fox Marine Services Ltd, ☎ 721312, Unit 4 La Folie Quay; ME. Island Yachts, ☎ 725048; SM. Jersey Marine Electronics, ☎ 721603, Unit 2 La Folie Quay.

CLOCKWISE AROUND THE ISLAND

St Aubin – 49°11´·27N 02°09´·94W
This charming harbour (pronounced *Oebin* as in toe) has a villagey ambience and is on the W side of the eponymous, shallow bay. It is home to the Royal Channel Islands YC (RCIYC). There are pubs, restaurants and a supermarket.

Approach via Diamond Rock PHM buoy and head to waypoint 49°11´·38N 02°09´·36W which bears 254°/4 cables to the hbr entrance. Round Grosse Rk beacon and St Aubin Fort, conspic with a Fl R 4s lt at the N end of its pier. The harbour's N pier has a Dir F WRG 254° lt and above it on the same red column a Iso R 4s lt; odd that this column is red as you will leave it to stbd. The S pier head is painted white. Tides as for St Helier.

Enter the drying harbour at HW±1, turn hard stbd and berth against the N pier on sand, drying 7m. Or anchor 7 cables SSE, off Pt de Bût (S end of Belcroute Bay) in about 2.7m; sheltered in W'lies.

RCIYC, ☎ 741023, on the S side of the hbr, is very welcoming. Bar, restaurant (shut Mon), showers. Around the hbr: Fuel (cans), FW and electricity available. Battricks BY, ☎ 743412, North Quay; most repairs. Jacksons Yacht Services, ☎ 743819, Le Boulevard; BY, CH, SM.

Bonne Nuit Bay – 49°15´·09N 02°07´·16W
This small picturesque fishing port with a steeply shelving beach and a cluster of houses is backed by low cliffs, trees and bracken. It lies 1.6M ESE of Sorel Pt lt ho and 0.5M E of a lofty (232m) TV

St Aubin's drying harbour and village from the west

mast and is well sheltered from W'lies by Fremont Pt. A beach cafe does breakfast, lunch and tea.

From the W, round a SHM buoy (marking Demie Rk) due N of Fremont Pt and steer for the waypoint, 49°15′·50N 02°06′·60W, on the 223° FG ldg lts 0.5M from the single pierhead. From the E, clear rocks extending 3 cables off Belle Hougue Pt. The front ldg lt is on the white pierhead; the rear is on a red column, low down on the hillside.

Beware Chevel Rock close SE of the leading line, marked by a pole beacon and usually visible. It is said that whoever sails round this rock on Mid-Summer Eve (23 June) will have good luck ahead; that is if he hasn't already hit the drying ledges. Dry out inside the pier if space permits, otherwise anchor where shown on AC 1136.

Bouley Bay – 49°14′·44N 02°04′·83W
This small fishing harbour protected by a short pier is similar to that at Bonne Nuit Bay, although the bay itself is much larger. Les Troupeurs is a 1.8m shoal patch 2 cables SE of the waypoint. See the *RNA* for tidal differences.

From the NW (Belle Hougue Pt) or from the SE (Tour de Rozel) go to the waypoint 49°15′·06N 02°04′·09W in mid-Bay, thence 224°/7 cables to the short, white-painted pierhead. Close-in the fairway is marked by two pairs of unlit lateral buoys. There are no lights or leading marks, but a large white building S of the harbour is the Water's Edge Hotel (and Black Dog Bar). Dry out if space permits in the harbour or anchor SE of the pier in 3–5m on sand and clear of moorings; exposed only to onshore winds.

Rozel Bay – 49°14′·23N 02°02′·65W
The village is rather larger and more picturesque than those above; the wider beach shelves steeply. Mimosa Cafe/restaurant, ☎ 864713, does lunch and dinner. Frère de Mer, ☎ 861000, is up the hill with spectacular views to France; good value food much favoured by locals. Beau Couperon Hotel, ☎ 865522, relaxed atmosphere in beautiful setting. Rozel Bay Inn, traditional pub strong on seafood.

Make for the waypoint 49°14′·44N 02°01′·96W, thence 245°/0.5M to the white-painted pierhead, tracking in the white sector (244°–246°) of a Dir F WRG light in the village. A stone building is conspic on the Nez du Gouet to the N. The fairway is marked by two pairs of unlit lateral buoys. Keep clear of the many moorings and fish boxes.

At the harbour entrance a WCM bcn, opposite the pierhead, marks a large flat rock drying about 6m. Dry out on sand if space can be found;

or anchor outside. Use tidal differences for Bouley Bay.

St Catherine Bay – 49°13′·34N 02°00′·65W
This anchorage, S of the breakwater extending 650m ESE from Verclut Pt, is used by yachts and FVs. Like Braye Hbr, Alderney, the bay was meant to shelter the British fleet, but the Navy failed to survey the centre of the bay which is full of rocks down to La Crête Pt – tut, tut.

The E side of this reef is marked by Le Fara ECM bcn. Inshore, the conspic red/white Archirondel Twr stands on the aborted S Bkwtr. Underwater power cables come ashore here. Other landmarks include: NNW, the turret on La Coupe Pt; and to the S, Mont Orgueil Castle. The bkwtr head lt is Fl 1.5s 18m 13M on a white lattice tower.

From the N, round the bkwtr head inside Pillon Rk 0.9m and anchor in 3–7m on sand/mud clear of moorings; exposed only to the SE. From the S, transit Gorey Outer Road then head N past Le Fara ECM bcn into the anchorage. See the *RNA* for tidal differences.

Do not berth on the bkwtr, but land at the slip. SC, café and a popular beach.

Rozel Bay. Local boats inside the pierhead

GOREY

Pierhead – 49°11´·80N 02°01´·34W

High Water at the drying harbour, seen from the east

Mention Gorey and everyone thinks of handsome, floodlit Mont Orgueil Castle – or they scratch their heads and wonder whether you are talking about Gorey on Little Sark or even Goury by Cap de la Hague. Worth a thought when you call Mayday and the lifeboat goes to the wrong place; they are all within 32M of each other.

So what does Gorey have going for it? Pleasant village, going on town; seasidey resort without the Blackpool trimmings; neat little harbour; benches for gazing east at France, whilst sheltered from the prevailing W'lies; golf course; decent beaches and oh... that imposing 13th century castle.

SHORESIDE (Telephone code 01534)

Tourist Office There isn't one.

What to see/do Mont Orgueil Castle, of course. It is imaginatively presented as a museum, although its history was scarcely tumultuous in the protracted wars against the French. It never made the quantum leap from bow and arrow to gunpowder and cannon. Climb to the very top for spectacular views; do the exhibits on the way down. ☎ 853292; 1000–1700; £4.70. Jersey Pottery is also rather good news, SW of the castle and back from the main road; ☎ 851119, Mon–Sat, 0900–1730.

Bus No 1 and variants to St Helier (25 mins).

Taxis, car & bike hire See St Helier.

Ferry In season Alizés run to Portbail, Carteret, Guernsey and Alderney.

Beaches Long sandy beach stretching south to La Rocque Pt. Sand and rocks to the north.

Supermarkets It's not that sort of place. Just the usual butcher, baker and chandlery (the original name for a candlestick maker).

Banks Only in St Helier.

Restaurants On the quayside below the Castle are the Dolphin Restaurant, ☎ 853370, which serves a gastronomic menu at £18.50, plus bar food. Nearly next door the Moorings Hotel, ☎ 853633, does lunch from £9.25 and *à la carte* dinner. In the village try Village Bistro, ☎ 853429; 'modern' cuisine, shut Mon.

NAVIGATION

Charts AC 2669 (1:150,000), 3655 (1:50,000), 1138 (1:25,000), plus SC 5604.8 (1:25,000) & .9 (1:60,000).

Approaches Banc du Château, least depth 0.4m, extends 1.5M SSE from a position 1M E of the Castle, and should be avoided. Inshore of it lie the Outer and Inner Roads. From the S (Violet Chan), La Coupe Turret open east of Verclut Pt leads 332° to the waypoint in Outer Road. From the NE/E, the little-used 230° transit of the Castle with Grouville Mill (1.8M beyond) leads to the N end of Banc du Château; as does the 250° transit of

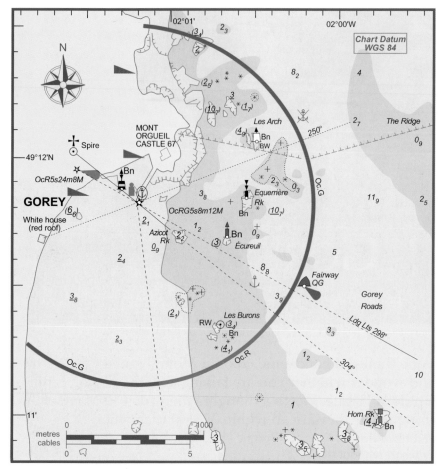

line passes very close to Azicot Rk drying 2.2m.

Équerrière Rk has a red beacon with 'fishtail' topmark = two kipper tails pointing S.

Access Approx HW±3, depending on draught. The harbour dries 4.0–7.0m and is full of local moorings. 100m WNW of the pierhead an ECM beacon marks drying rocks. Fresh to strong S'lies may make the entrance awkward.

Tides Use differences for St Catherine Bay, as given in the *RNA*. MHWS is 11·0m, MLWS 1·5m; MHWN is 8·0m, MLWN 4·0m.

Tidal streams From half flood to half ebb the stream sets strongly NE across the hbr entrance, ie onto the pierhead and toward Les Arch, B/W beacon with 'A' topmark.

Anchorage In the triangle made by the Fairway SHM buoy (QG), Les Burons R/W beacon ('B' topmark) and Écureuil Rock SHM beacon, in 2–8m on mud.

VHF *Gorey Harbour* Ch 74 at tide times.

FACILITIES

Harbour Office is on the pierhead. ☎ 853616; Mobile 07797 719336; 🖷 856927. VHF Ch 74, HW±3.

Moorings/berths Two red can-shaped ⚓s lie in deep water about 250m NW of Écureuil Rock. Twelve drying yellow ⚓s off the harbour entrance are afloat approx HW±4. There are four ♥ berths against the pier, drying to firm level sand; use a fender board.

Tariff Daily rates on moorings/alongside per metre LOA (showers included): <8m £6.20; <12m £8.30; <14m £9.30; <20m £10.40; <25m £13.50.

Showers are free.

Chandlery & repairs Virtually nil; most at St Helier. P&D HW±3, Gorey Marine Supplies ☎ 07797 742384.

the pierhead with a red-roofed house (two dormer windows) where the ruined Fort William is marked. Thence to the key Fairway SHM buoy, QG.

Landmarks Mont Orgueil Castle (67m) is conspic from all directions; the harbour is close SW of it.

Pilotage At the WPT 49°11´·07N 01°59´·22W (298°/1.6M to the pierhead) turn onto the 298° ldg line. Daymarks: Front is a white framework tower on the pierhead; rear is a white rectangle flanked by dayglow orange panels, left of and below the church spire. (Ldg lts: front, green sector of the Dir Oc RG 5s on the pierhead; rear Oc R 5s). The ldg

Mont Orgueil Castle

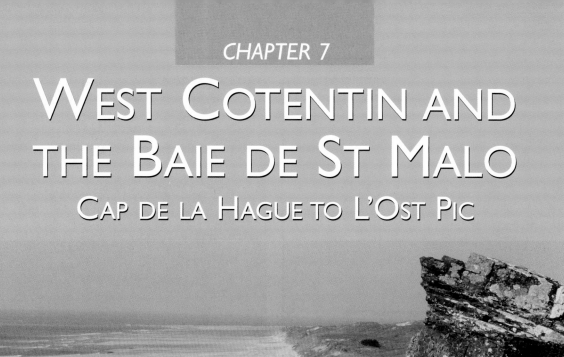

WEST COTENTIN AND THE BAIE DE ST MALO

CAP DE LA HAGUE TO L'OST PIC

CONTENTS

INTRODUCTION

From Cap de la Hague the W coast of the Cotentin peninsula runs 66M south to Mont St Michel. This is pure Normandy, as proud of its way of life and traditions as the more easterly parts of Normandy. It is also the *département* of Manche. From the high granite rocks of Jobourg to the almost mystical bay of Mont St Michel, this exposed coast is punctuated by glorious sandy coves which develop into extensive dunes further south.

There are marinas at Diélette, Carteret, Portbail (of a sort) and Granville, all of whose approaches dry. The few anchorages are only safe in offshore winds. Yachts regularly criss-cross between the Channel Islands and the Normandy ports. The French Îles Chausey lie 9M WNW of Granville,

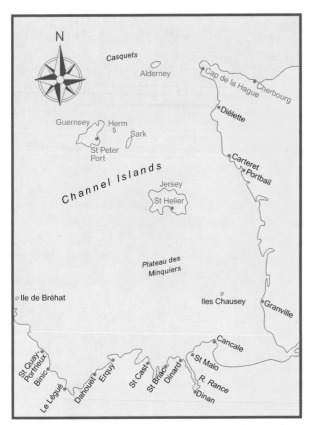

The oyster ladies of Cancale

with the English Plateau des Minquiers beyond.

Mont St Michel is an inspiring sight, but not safe to approach. It marks the boundary between Normandy and Brittany. As you skirt round the famous Cancale oyster beds and Pointe de Grouin, the rocks of Brittany are much in evidence on the way into St Malo. This historic city is hugely attractive in its own right and a perfect base for exploring inland up the River Rance to Dinan.

Between St Malo and Cap Fréhel the Emerald Coast is deeply indented by drying bays and little-visited harbours such as St Briac and St Cast. After Cap Fréhel the Baie de St Brieuc is also off the beaten track, but Erquy, Dahouet, Le Légué,

Binic and St Quay-Portrieux are all well worth visiting. The last named is truly a port of refuge and ideal as a jumping-off point for the tidally limited ports around the Bay.

PASSAGE NOTES

The tide reigns supreme around this French coast, into which the Channel Islands fit like hand in glove. Ignore tides and tidal streams at your peril; use them properly and the Kingdom of Heaven is yours, *mes amis.*

Heights of tide are amongst the largest in the world: MHWS at both Cancale and Îles Chausey reaches 13m. Compare this with Dover's 6.8m, Plymouth's 5.5m or Stornoway's 4.8m and it is obvious that your tidal thinking must undergo a sea change. The big plus is that drying rocks which look formidable on the chart can be crossed with impunity in the top half of the tide. But the downside occurs at MLWS when there may not be enough water to stay afloat. Be constantly aware, hour by hour, of the height of tide when negotiating rocks, shoals or the drying approach to many a French harbour.

Tidal range (by which the 'size' of a tide may be judged – and whether neaps or springs), is most easily

DISTANCE TABLE

Approximate distances in nautical miles are by the most direct route, whilst avoiding dangers

		1	2	3	4	5	6	7	8	9	10	11	12	13	14	15	16
1.	Omonville	1															
2.	Cap de la Hague	6	2														
3.	Braye (Alderney)	15	9	3													
4.	St Peter Port	34	28	23	4												
5.	Creux (Sark)	29	23	22	10	5											
6.	St Helier	51	45	46	29	24	6										
7.	Carteret	29	23	28	31	23	26	7									
8.	Portbail	33	27	32	35	27	25	5	8								
9.	Iles Chausey	61	55	58	48	43	25	33	30	9							
10.	Granville	67	61	66	55	50	30	38	35	9	10						
11.	Dinan	91	85	85	66	64	50	62	59	29	35	11					
12.	St Malo	79	73	73	54	52	38	50	47	17	23	12	12				
13.	Dahouet	80	74	72	54	52	41	60	59	37	45	41	29	13			
14.	Le Légué/St Brieux	86	78	76	57	56	46	69	69	41	49	45	33	8	14		
15.	Binic	84	78	75	56	55	46	70	70	43	51	45	33	10	8	15	
16.	St Quay-Portrieux	80	74	73	56	51	46	64	64	47	54	47	35	11	7	4	16

denoted by the French system of tidal coefficients. Instead of having to remember that the neap range at St Malo is 5·1m or the spring range at St Helier is 9·6m, only three figures are needed, since they apply to all ports: 40 = neaps, 70 = an average tide; and 95 = springs. These values have no units like fathoms or metres (such is the nature of coefficients). Twice-daily values appear in the *RNA* under Brest. Importantly and conveniently, the window of access to some tidally limited ports is quoted relative to coefficients: Perros-Guirec is a good example (see page 452).

Tidal streams, as skippers should be well aware, swirl anticlockwise within the huge right-angled basin formed between Paimpol, Mont St Michel and Cap de la Hague. (This rotatory effect is most noticeable around the Channel Islands which play piggy-in-the-middle).

Thus by HW St Malo the Channel flood has filled the basin, and over the next 4 hrs the water drains away, ie W-going past St Malo and N-going up the west side of the Cotentin peninsula. By HW St Malo +5 (ie LWSM) the Channel ebb is starting to run and curls S around Cap de la Hague until HW St Malo –2. At the same time it is increasingly E-going past St Malo until HW St Malo–1, thanks to a vast back eddy. So ends the 12 hour tidal cycle. If you ever doubted the need, please now study the tidal stream atlas to assess the finer points.

St Malo, Intra-Muros

THE BRETON FLAG

 Despite Brittany becoming a Dukedom in the 10th century and being incorporated into France in 1532, the Breton Flag, Gwenn ha Du (white and black), is of modern origin, created in 1925 by Morvan Marchal.

The flag, which has white and black horizontal stripes, owes much to the coat of arms of the town of Rennes, chosen as the capital of Brittany by its first Duke. The eleven ermines repeat a heraldic motif found in the flag of the Duchy 1318 and are for the Kings and Dukes who governed independent Brittany. The five black horizontal stripes represent the Gallo language regions of Brittany, Rennes, Nantes, Dol, Saint Malo and Penthlevre; the white stripes represent the four Breton-speaking regions, Léon, Trégor, Cornuailles and Vannes. These nine regions were the nine bishoprics.

It has taken fifty years for Morven Marchal's creation to be adopted generally in Brittany and for the rest of France to accept that Gwenn ha Du does not have political or separatist connotations.

Passages In relation to navigating between the CI and French ports, refer to page 353; the permutations are endless. Coasting between French ports is usually straightforward provided the streams are worked efficiently. For example, if visiting Granville, Portbail, Carteret and Diélette, it is far better to head north on the N-going flood since HW occurs later the further N you go. Heading south entails bucking a foul tide and you may not reach your destination before its tidal window closes.

Passage de la Déroute runs roughly S/N more or less parallel to the Cotentin coast and from 5M to 13M offshore. It starts between Îles Chausey and the Minkies; thence W of Chausée des Boeufs and E of Jersey and Les Écrehou. Finally it reaches open waters off Carteret, W of Les Trois-Grunes. It is shallow and narrow in places, but given fair weather and good visibility is not unduly difficult.

Westward from Granville, if not calling at St Malo and adjacent harbours, the route lies toward Grand Léjon for harbours around the Baie de St Brieuc; or direct to Paimpol. If heading for Bréhat, Lézardrieux or Tréguier make for Nord Horaine NCM buoy. Arrange your ETA to coincide with the W-going ebb, since the spring rate hereabouts is around 3–4kn. The tide rules, OK?

Diélette from WNW at half tide

DIÉLETTE

Harbour entrance – 49°33'·23N 01°51'·74W

Once upon a time Diélette was a tiny fishing port, encircled by the walls of today's innermost basin. Then the curving S jetty was built (note the older stonework) for added protection. Finally in 1996 the N jetty and substantial inner piers were added to form a marina and better facilities for FVs.

Was it worthwhile? Nothing will alter the destructive force of the sea and you would no more try to enter Diélette in onshore gales than you would Granville, Porthleven or Le Conquet. But given the right conditions you will be assured of a most friendly welcome. Berths are not all taken, and you have the convenience of a marina set amid unspoiled country (standfast Flamanville). Try it!

SHORESIDE

Tourist Office *Il n'y en a pas*! But in season there is an information desk, ☎ 02 33 93 11 86, by the Capitainerie. Or visit the Office, ☎ 02 33 52 81 60, at Les Pieux which is the nearest (6km) township.

What to see/do There are fine walks/bike rides (or charter a horse, ☎ 02 33 52 37 60), to the north along the beach or past hang-glider sites on the hillside. If energetic continue towards Vauville, Beaumont and the high moors of Nez de Jobourg. Or wander south to Le Rozel for further attractive scenery.

Rail Cherbourg (26km) or Valognes (34km) are the nearest mainline stations.

Bus No 7, Mon–Fri 0637, 0654, 0832, 1347 to Cherbourg (50 mins); return 0930, 1230, 1730, 1830.

Taxi ☎ 02 33 52 53 53 / 06 80 25 52 49; ☎ 06 08 68 08 67.

Car hire ☎ 02 33 93 10 24.

Bike hire Ask at the Capitainerie.

UK access Via Cherbourg or Channel Islands.

Ferries Alizés, ☎ 02 33 52 10 20, to Alderney, Guernsey and Jersey in season. Timetable is variable.

Beaches Extensive sandy beach N of the marina.

Supermarkets There are no shops in Diélette, but a small *épicerie* next to the Capitainerie stocks the basics. If you need more, cycle/taxi 6km to Les Pieux for a Super U; Mon–Fri 0900–1215 & 1430–1915; Sat 0900–1915; Sun (Jul/Aug) 0900–1200.

Market day Sunday 1000; also Les Pieux Fri morning; Flamanville Wed morning.

Banks Nearest banks in Les Pieux, 6km SE.

Restaurants At the marina 'Le Raz de Blanchard' (alias 'The Alderney Race'), ☎ 02 33 52 53 53, seemed in spring 2002 to have gone out of business; may it re-open asap, as it had been well patronised. For lunch in the marina, L'Escale is great on *moules* and *frites*. Left out of the marina, first right up the R Diélette valley for 500m to Le Fer d'Anse, ☎ 02 33 87 55 40; good food from €14.94. Back in Diélette two hardy perennials: Hôtel du Phare, ☎ 02 33 52 59 55, menus at €12, €16 and €22; ask for a window seat. As you head

The youngsters know no fear

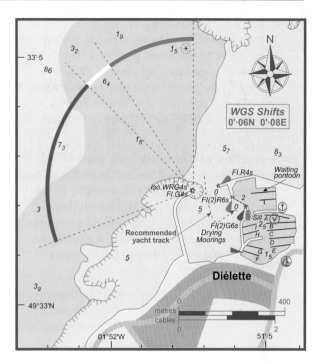

SW out of town, Hôtel de la Falaise, ☎ 02 33 04 08 40, is the large building; menus at €13.75, €21.10 and €30.50.

NAVIGATION

Charts AC 2669 (1:150,000), 3653 (1:50,000) plus SC 5604.2 (1:150,000). SHOM 6966 (1:150,000), 7158 (1:50,000) and 7133 (1:20,000).

Approaches From the NW avoid Les Huquets de Jobourg, drying rocks S of the Nez de Jobourg. From the S skirt round the WCM buoy, Q (9) 15s, marking shoals and obstructions off the nuclear power station at Flamanville.

Landmarks From all directions the chimneys and pylons of the said power station are conspicuous. From the waypoint a solitary house on the skyline is usefully aligned with the approach.

Pilotage The waypoint, 49°33'·84N 01°52'·53W, in the white sector of the Iso WRG 4s pierhead light, bears 140°/0.8M to the harbour entrance. Do not get set NE of this track by a N-going tidal stream, as drying rocks extend 700m offshore. An unlit WCM buoy about 4 cables NNW of the entrance marks a shoal.

Enter close to the outer stbd pierhead Iso WRG 4s, curve round to the inner stbd pierhead, shunning both port pierheads. The marina entrance, marked by PHM/SHM bcns, is to starboard just beyond the fuel berth.

Access The harbour is totally exposed to the

west. Entry in fresh/strong W'lies is difficult or dangerous if swell is present. A patch drying 0.5m is 70m W of the north pierhead. The entrance is dredged to 0.5m above CD, giving H24 access to the inner basin (dredged 2m) for 1.5m draught if the coeff is <75; and approx HW±4$\frac{1}{2}$ for coeff 105. The SW part of the harbour dries 5m.

Marina entrance The outer wall, marked by yellow perches, retains 2.5m inside and is crossed via a flapgate which opens when height of tide is >5m, usually HW±3$\frac{1}{4}$ to +3$\frac{3}{4}$. The sill dries 3.5m. Thus when the flapgate first drops (opens) there is 1.5m water above the sill. A gauge on the adjacent stbd pier shows depth of water above the sill.

IPTS, signals 2 or 4 indicate when the flapgate is up (closed) or down (open); shown from the SHM beacon at the flapgate. A waiting pontoon is at the NE corner of the inner basin.

Tides HW Diélette at sp is 35 mins and at nps 45 mins after HW St Malo. LW at sp is 20 mins and at nps 35 mins after LW St Malo. MHWS is 9·7m, MLWS 1·2m; MHWN is 7·4m, MLWN is 3·5m.

Tidal streams set NE across the entrance from HW St Helier –3$\frac{1}{2}$; and SW from HW StH+2$\frac{1}{4}$; max spring rate 1$\frac{3}{4}$kn in either direction. The NE-going flood may back-eddy within the harbour.

Anchorage Possible in offshore winds outside the harbour, but holding is not good.

VHF Ch 09 for the marina.

Looking east into the inner harbour

Ancient charm near the original harbour

FACILITIES

Capitainerie HM Patrick Guillard, ☎ 02 33 53 68 78, 📠 02 33 53 68 79. port-dielette@wanadoo.fr VHF Ch 09. Open Jul/Aug 0800–2000; other months, Mon–Fri 0800–1200 & 1330–1730; Sat, Sun 0800–1200.

Berthing A waiting pontoon is dead ahead in the first basin. ❶ berths on pontoons 'A', 'B' & 'C' fingers. When the retaining wall is covered boats surge fore-and-aft quite considerably; rig good springs.

Tariff Daily rates € on pontoon, 1/5–30/9, for LOA bands: <8m = 13.86; <9m = 17.75; <10m = 21.03; <11m = 23.67; <12m = 26.32; <13m = 28.81; 14m = 30.99; 15m = 33.95; >15m = 35.20.

Showers across the road from 'B' pontoon; by jeton.

Launderette In the shower block.

Fuel Diesel & petrol at fuel berth by flapgate, via HM on Ch 09.

YC ☎ 02 33 04 14 78, is part of the Raz de Blanchard building; see under restaurants.

Chandlery & repairs Diélette Nautic, ☎ 02 33 53 26 27; chandlery, repairs (below the Raz de Blanchard). BH 30 ton.

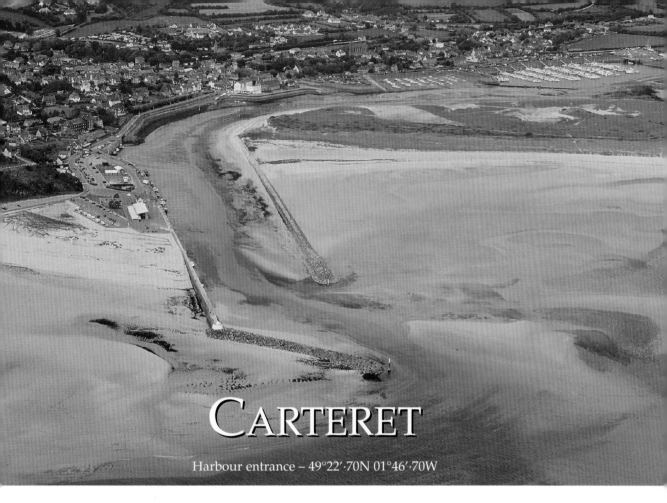

CARTERET

Harbour entrance – 49°22'·70N 01°46'·70W

Carteret is an historic port. For centuries small sailing vessels (*goëlettes*) traded from the coast of Normandy to the Channel Islands (*Les Îles Anglo-Normandes*). Today it happily combines seaside resort, fishing port, ferry terminal and marina.

The commune of Barneville-Carteret comprises Carteret, Barneville (easy bike ride NE of the marina) and Barneville-Plage on a sandy peninsula across the drying estuary of the R Gerfleur. The marina calls itself Le Port des Isles (sic) in shrewd harmony with the Channel Islands. Above the Capitainerie the flags of Jersey and Guernsey fly alongside the French tricolour and the Normandy flag. In high season the **❼** pontoon is crowded with Channel Island boats rafted *ad infinitum*, although it is believed that there are plans to improve visitor berthing.

SHORESIDE

Tourist Office in Carteret is a small kiosk open Jul/Aug daily 1000–1230 & 1500–1900. A larger Office is in Barneville, 10 rue des Écoles. Open Mon–Sat 0900–1200 & 1400–1800. ☎ 02 33 04 90 58; 📠 02 33 04 93 24; tourisme.barneville-carteret@wanadoo.fr; www.barneville-carteret.net

What to see/do There is a fine coastal walk to the lighthouse and Signal station on craggy Cap de Carteret. Deserted, sandy beaches stretch north to Cap Flamanville and beyond; see photograph on page 383. To the south sand takes over in earnest as you will discover if/when you get to Portbail. Jul/Aug a tourist train leaves Carteret at 1000 Tues & 1500 Sun for Portbail (30 mins); return at 1230 and 1630. The Americans reached Barneville 18 June 1944; see monument.

Rail Valognes (30km) is nearest mainline station for Cherbourg and Paris.

Bus No 3 dep Mon–Fri 0628, 0742, 0842* to Cherbourg (1 hr); return 1230, 1715*, 1750. * = not in school time.

Taxi ☎ 02 33 04 61 02. It takes approx 40 mins to get to Cherbourg.

Car hire Budget ☎ 02 33 52 60 73; 📠 02 33 52 65 98.

Bike hire Velosport, Le Petit Port, ☎ 02 33 93 20 73.

UK access Via Cherbourg or Channel Islands.

Ferries Emeraude, ☎ 02 33 52 61 39, sail to St Helier (1 hr) late-April to Sep. Timetable is variable.

Beaches Good sandy beach by the W Jetty and a vast one at Barneville-Plage; cycle or swim across.

Supermarkets Fruits et Legumes is a small supermarket near Hotel de la Marine for basics. Champion in Barneville (30 mins walk, 10 mins by bike).

Market day Carteret Thur, mid-Jun to mid-Sep.

Banks Crédit Agricole and PO, both with cashpoints, in Carteret. Three banks in Barneville.

Restaurants Hôtel de la Marine, ☎ 02 33 53 83 31, is the large white building port side nearing the marina; menus at €25.50 & 39. Hôtel Le Carteret, ☎ 02 33 04 95 63, turn right at the Bar du Port; menus at €15.10, 22.73*, 30.35, 39.51 and seafood platter 37.37. *Recommended, good value. L'Hermitage, 02.33.04.46.39, facing the FV berths; menus at €15, 24, 28 & 30. Hotel de la Plage et du Cap, ☎ 02 33 53 85 89, beyond L'Hermitage; menus at €12.20, 17.53, 21.34 & gastro 47.26.

NAVIGATION

Charts AC 2669 (1:150,000), 3655 (1:50,000) plus SC 5604. SHOM 6966 (1:150,000), 7157 (1:50,000) and 7133 (1:20,000).

Approaches From all directions make good the waypoint, 49°21'·70N 01°47'·41W, on the edge of the drying ledges, 010°/0.5M to the W jetty head. From N or NW avoid drying inshore rocks N of Cap de Carteret. From the W avoid Les Trois Grunes, $\underline{1}$.6m, 4.8M from the hbr entrance, marked by a WCM lt buoy. To the S,

Rounding Cap de Carteret

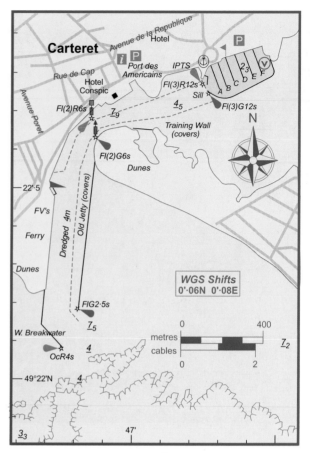

between Portbail and Les Écrehou, there are many shallow patches.

Landmarks Cap de Carteret, with lt ho, mast and signal station, is conspicuous from all directions.

Pilotage From the wpt, counter the tidal stream. The W jetty has a 100m dog-legged rock extension which covers at big springs; an Oc R 4s lt is at the head of it. Opposite this lt, on the E edge of the channel a small unlit SHM buoy marks a shifting shoal patch of no fixed address.

Initially keep mid-channel, dries $\underline{4}$.5m, but best water is on the outside of the bend towards the marina. Cross the marina entry sill squarely, ie heading NE, to clear the concrete base blocks on each side, marked by PHM/SHM lt bcns. Yellow perches mark the wall retaining 2.3m inside.

Access The approaches are rough in fresh/strong W'lies. Best timing is HW–1 to HW. The marina is entered via a flapgate which is normally open HW±2½. The flapgate sill dries $\underline{5}$m above CD. On the adjacent PHM beacon a gauge shows depth of water over the sill; when the flapgate first drops (opens) there is 1.3m above it. At small neaps, eg coeff 33, there is 2.4m over the sill at HW. Deep draught yachts should pre-calculate clearance.

Rounding the bend...

An ancient lavoir made famous in a TV advert

IPTS Nos 2 or 4 indicate when the flapgate into the marina is up (closed) or down (open); they are shown from the spur to port of the PHM beacon.

Tides HW Carteret at sp is 20 mins and at nps 30 mins after HW St Malo. LW at sp is 15 mins and at nps 30 mins after LW St Malo. MHWS is 10·6m, MLWS 1·3m; MHWN is 8·1m, MLWN 3·7m.

Tidal streams set NW across the entrance, 4kn max, when the harbour is accessible.

VHF Ch 09 for Marina and Signal station.

FACILITIES

Capitainerie HM Jean-Marc Hebert. VHF Ch 09. ☎ 02 33 04 70 84, 🖷 02 33 04 08 37. Open Jul/Aug 0800–2000; Apr–Jun & Sep 0900–1230 & 1400–1800; Oct–Mar 0930–1230 & 1400–1700.

Berthing An *accueil* (and fuel) pontoon is immediately to port on entry, but visitors should go direct to the east side of 'F'pontoon; it has no fingers, so mega-rafting is the norm.

If too late to enter the marina, dry out against the W jetty downstream of the ferry terminal on firm, flat sand/mud.

Tariff Daily rates € on pontoon, Apr–Sep, for LOA bands: <8m = 13.28; <9m = 16.56; <10m = 20.16; <11m = 23.75; <12m = 27.19; <13m = 28.75; <14m = 30.16; <15m = 31.72; <16m = 33.28.

Showers below the YC; access by code, jeton €1.

Fuel Diesel & petrol at *accueil* pontoon by credit card.

YC YC Barneville-Carteret, ☎ 02 33 52 60 73; 🖷 02 33 52 65 98. Hospitable; bar, showers.

Chandlery & repairs

Carteret Marine, ☎ 02 33 53 82 00; chandlery, crane 24 ton, BH 35 ton.
Bois Marine, ☎ 02 33 04 27 99; repairs.
Dubois Marine, ☎ 06 88 02 41 62; engineer.

Looking east from Cap de Carteret to the harbour entrance

PORTBAIL

Yacht basin – 49°19'·82N 01°42'·32W

Sand City I call this place. From seaward you can't mistake the dunes and when you reach the yacht basin (not truly a marina), all is covered in ... sand. At LW a mini-fleet of bulldozers sometimes turns up to clear the stuff, whilst the locals take to their sand yachts – until the water re-appears and real yachts get under way again. La Plage to the W has a small community on the beach, where surf and sand rule OK. Or head NE across the causeway and a famous bridge of 13 arches into Portbail. There to greet you is the church of Notre Dame, in on whose blunt spire you homed (gritty English to avoid ending a sentence with not one but two prepositions).

> The Walrus and the Carpenter
> Were walking close at hand;
> They wept like anything to see
> Such quantities of sand:
> 'If this were only cleared away'
> They said 'it *would* be grand!'
> *Lewis Carroll: Through the Looking Glass*

SHORESIDE

Tourist Office 26, rue Philippe Lebel (on the main square), ☎ 02 33 04 03 07; ⊠ 02 33 04 94 66. Open Tues–Sat 1000–1200 & 1400–1800; shut Sun, Mon & Hols. tourisme.portbail@wanadoo.fr; www.portbail.org

What to see/do Portbail is a small country town with some old buildings and a relaxed ambience. Visit the church and a Roman baptistry of the fourth century. Cycle out to the handsome Cotentin windmill at Fierville-les Mines (8km). Make sand castles. Help with dredging, sunbathe and swim. It's a hard life.

Rail Valognes (29km) is the nearest station. See Carteret for the tourist train in Jul/Aug.

Bus No 3 to Cherbourg (80 mins). Mon–Fri 0605, 0719, 0819*; back 1230, 1715*, 1750. *not in term time.

Taxi ☎ 02 33 93 01 01.

Car hire See Carteret or ask at the Tourist Office.

Bike hire Eureka, ☎ 02 33 04 81 25, Place Laquaine.

Portbail dries – and how! The training wall is clearly visible

UK access Via Cherbourg or Channel Islands.

Ferries Alizés, ☎ 02 33 52 10 01, operates to Gorey (Jersey) in season.

Beaches World class sand is everywhere.

Supermarkets Huit à Huit mini-supermarket near the main square, Place du Gouey. Écomarché, rue du Père Albert; plus butcher, baker, *épicerie* on whom the well-being of France chiefly depends.

Market days Tuesday and Sunday in season.

Banks Three banks in the little town.

Restaurants 'Le Cabestan', ☎ 02 33 04 35 30 is at the harbour, looks pleasant; menus €15 & 23. In town 'Au Rendez-vous des Pecheurs', ☎ 02 33 87 55 40, has a first floor restaurant with views out to the harbour; menus from €9.15 to 20.60.

NAVIGATION

Charts AC 2669 (1:150,000), 3655 (1:50,000) plus SC 5604. SHOM 6966 (1:150,000), 7157 (1:50,000) and 7133 (1:20,000).

Approaches From the NW approach via Écrevière SCM buoy to avoid Basses de Portbail and Banc Félés, least depths 0.2m, W of the SWM buoy.

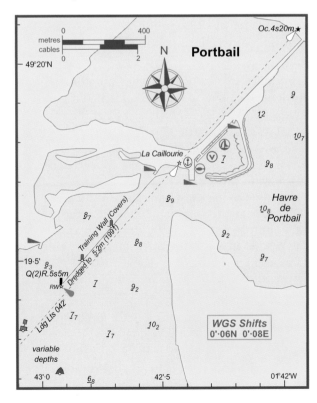

Landmarks A conspic water tower, 0.6M WNW of the harbour basin, gives general orientation.

Pilotage The waypoint 49°18'·36N 01°44'·41W is on the 042° ldg line, 300m SE of the 'PB' SWM buoy, and 1.5M from the head of the training wall. The ldg marks are front: white lattice pylon, R top, Q; rear: church spire, Oc 4s, easily seen. These lead to a pair of lateral buoys where the max drying height is $\underline{8}$.1m; the training wall is 300m ahead. Parallel the wall, marked by R perches, about 15–20m off; then ease round to stbd for the stone jetty which should be left to port. Turn port into the yacht basin which dries up to $\underline{7}$m.

Access Approx HW±2, near springs. The harbour is sheltered from most winds. The channel is dredged $\underline{5}$.2m inshore of the training wall head.

Tides HW Portbail at sp is 25 mins and at nps 30 mins after HW St Malo. LW at sp is 25 mins and at nps 30 mins after LW St Malo. MHWS is 11·4m, MLWS 1·4m; MHWN is 8·7m, MLWN is 4·0m.

Tidal streams set NW across the entrance channel on the flood.

Anchorage In settled weather, to await adequate rise of tide, anchor in 5m close N or S, but not W, of the SWM buoy. No anchoring further SE due to power cables.

VHF *Portbail Port de Plaisance* Ch 09.

FACILITIES

Capitainerie HM Jean-Marc Gaultier. VHF Ch 09. ☎ 02 33 04 83 48, 🖷 02 33 04 39 90. Open Jun–Aug 0800–2000 daily; other months at tide times.

Berthing As directed by the HM: ❶ berths on a 100m long pontoon parallel with the road; larger yachts can dry out against E side of a broad stone jetty to port of the entrance, clear of FVs; smaller yachts at the inner end; or find a vacant mooring.

Tariff Daily rates € for LOA bands: <8m = 11; <10m = 12.50; <12m = 14; 14m = 16.50.

Showers by the Capitainerie.

Electricity on the pontoon.

Fuel Only by cans from Portbail.

YC Club Nautique de Portbail, ☎ 02 33 04 86 15.

Chandlery & repairs Portbail Plaisance

GRANVILLE

Marina entrance – 48°49'·98N 01°35'·82W

Looking NNW across the marina to the Old Town. The new town is off to the right

Granville is the last port in Normandy, if wisely you discount Avranches at the head of the drying Baie de Mont St Michel. The modern part of the town is busy and lively. The adjoining marina is known as Port de Hérel to distinguish it from the commercial Avant Port and wet basin for FVs.

N of the latter the old fortified town extends SW on a craggy peninsula. Its narrow cobbled streets and 18th century granite houses are austere, even forbidding, but worth the stroll out to the lighthouse. A Carnival on Shrove Tuesday recalls the annual departure of cod fishermen to Newfoundland, if you happen to be afloat that early in the season.

SHORESIDE

Tourist Office 4 cours Jonville (main square N of the marina), ☎ 02 33 91 30 03; ⚞ 02 33 91 30 19. Mon–Sat 0900–1230 & 1400–1830; Sun 1000–1300. office-tourisme@ville-granville.fr; www.ville-granville.fr

What to see/do An unusual venture is to walk barefoot across the sands from Genêts on the N side of the bay to Mont St Michel and back, rather than joining endless busloads of grockles.

Forty mins by No 12 bus from Cours Jonville to Genêts, 23 km on the D911. Here join your guide for the 1¾ hr/4M walk, 1 hr at the Mont and 1¾ hrs back, €5. Details from Chemins de la Baie, ☎ 02 33 89 80 88, www.cheminsdelabaie.fr or the Tourist Office; it is best to pre-book.

Meanwhile back at Granville, if it rains dive into the Maison Christian Dior where the said couturier spent his childhood. In the old town hoist in the Richard Anacréon Museum of modern art with a fine collection of impressionist paintings. Or visit the local museum for the ritual dose of culture.

Rail To Paris 3 hrs 45 mins. To go N to Coutances or S to Avranches, change at Folligny, not the easiest of routes, but Granville is west of the beaten track.

Bus There is an urban network, but rural buses are slow, eg 1 hr to Avranches (26km).

Taxi Radio-taxis ☎ 02 33 50 50 06 ; 02 33 50 01 67.

Car hire Avis (rail station) ☎ 02 33 50 30 89; Picard ☎ 02 33 61 99 11; Europcar ☎ 02 33 90 64 99.

Bike hire Ask at the Tourist Office.

UK access Via Cherbourg, St Malo or CI.

Ferries Emeraude, ☎ 02 33 50 16 36, runs to Îles Chausey, Jersey, Guernsey and Sark in season.

Beaches The NW-facing Plage du Plat Gousset is up by Christian Dior's house. Plage d'Hacqueville is to the SE, beyond Pte Gautier.

Supermarkets Monoprix, 39 rue Lecampion. Marché Plus, rue Couraye.

Market days Wednesday and Saturday.

Launderette Place Godal, close NE of FV basin, 7/7 0700–2100. Lavomatic, rue St Sauveur.

Banks All banks, with cashpoints, around the town centre.

Restaurants Le Hérel (Ibis Hôtel), ☎ 02 33 90 44 52, at the marina; €12 to 21. Hôtel de la Mer, 74 rue du Port, ☎ 02 33 50 01 86; €15 to 42.60. Le Cabestan, ☎ 02 33 61 61 58, 70 rue du Port, €13 to 27. Le Phare, ☎ 02 33 50 12 94, 11 rue du Port, €15 to 39. Chez Pierrot, ☎ 02 33 50 09 29, rue Desmaisons; €15 to 23.

NAVIGATION

Charts AC 2669 (1:150,000), 3659 (1:50,000), 3672 (1:15,000) plus SC 5604. SHOM 6966 (1:150,000), 7156 (1:48,800) and 7341 (1:15,000).

Approaches From the NW, skirt at least 4 cables off the rocks around Pte du Roc. La Fourchie WCM bcn twr is not the seaward limit of drying rocks. From the W, avoid Le Videcoq WCM buoy 3.5M from Granville. From the SW, note the Banc de Tombelaine with drying patches. In the near approaches Le Loup IDM lt bcn is a key mark. Be alert for commercial vessels/FVs

entering and leaving the drying Avant Port, NE of which a wet basin for FVs is accessed via a single entry gate. Speed limits: 5kn N of a line Pte du Roc-Le Loup-Pte de Gautier; 2kn in the marina.

Landmarks Pointe du Roc is a conspic headland, 0.6M W of the marina. On it the lighthouse, signal station and spire of Notre Dame church are easily seen. The twin domes (Little & Large) of St Paul's church are visible from S of Pte du Roc.

Pilotage The WPT 48°49'.51N 01°36'.29W is 250m SSW of Le Loup. This bcn, in transit with the Fl R 4s lt on the marina's S bkwtr and the large dome of St Pauls, leads 034°/0.4M to the marina. By day approach on 055° from W of this transit, which may be used at night as there are no ldg lts. At the blind entrance leave room for outbound yachts. A covering wall to stbd shelters a windsurfing/dinghy area and is marked by five red posts, Fl Bu 4s.

Access Approx HW±3 via a flapgate above a sill drying 5.25m; when the flapgate first lowers, ie opens, there is 0.75m of water above it. At sp a 1½kn current flows in for a few minutes after first opening. On the S bkwtr a digital gauge visible from seaward shows depth of water over the sill; a reading of 29=2.9m; 00=no entry. Low-tech analogue gauges at the entrance can be seen from the ❶ pontoon. The 16m wide entrance is marked by Oc R/G 4s lts on R/G pylons, but no IPTS or traffic lights.

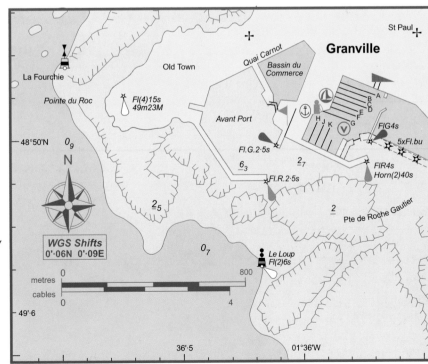

Tides HW Granville at sp and nps is 5 mins after HW St Malo. LW at sp is 20 mins and at nps 10 mins after LW St Malo. MHWS is 12·9m, MLWS 1·6m; MHWN is 9·8m, MLWN 4·5m. Note the exceptionally large spring range, 11·3m.

Tidal streams are unpredictable outside the Avant Port and marina due to eddies caused by various breakwaters; expect mean rates of 2kn at springs.

Anchorage In settled weather, to await adequate rise of tide, anchor in 2m W of Le Loup.

VHF *Port de Plaisance* Ch 09. Port Ch 12, near HW.

FACILITIES

Capitainerie HM Daniel Denis. ☎ 02 33 50 20 06, ▨ 02 33 50 17 01. VHF Ch 09. In season 0800–2200; out of season 0800–1200 & 1400–1800. dd@granville.cci.fr; www.granville.cci.fr/herel

Berthing ❂ pontoons 'G' (& 'F') are in front of the sill. 150 ❂ berths are quoted, a somewhat notional figure; berth where you can and check in at the office. Max LOA/draught is 15m/2.5m. The retaining wall maintains at least 1.7 to 2.7m inside the well sheltered marina when the flapgate is up.

Tariff Daily rates € per m² are based on the boat's area (L x B). May, Jun, Sep: 1st 20m² = €0.38, plus 0.26 for each extra m². Jul/Aug: 1st 20 m² = €0.51, plus 0.37 for each extra m². Other months: 1st 20 m² = €0.23 plus 0.18 for each extra m². Thus a 10m x 3m boat in June, for example, costs €10.20, <u>plus</u> 19.6% TVA/VAT = €12.20.

Showers behind the Capitainerie, free of charge; access code.

Fuel Diesel & petrol at the root of 'G' pontoon.

YC Granville YC, ☎ 02 33 50 04 25.

Chandlery & repairs 12 ton BH; de-masting crane, 500kg, by 'K' pontoon. SMMIG, ☎ 02 33 50 16 79, ME. Voilerie Granvillaise, ☎ 06 80 72 17 30, SM. Manche Ouest Marine, ☎ 02 33 50 74 10, CH. Méca Services, ☎ 02 33 90 19 67, ME. Granville EOLE, ☎ 02 33 51 09 56, CH. Les Régates, ☎ 02 33 50 22 53, CH. Comptoir de la Mer, ☎ 02 33 90 93 35, CH.

Future developments A major expansion of the port and marina is due to start in 2005/6 and end in 2010 (subject to the usual constraints). The present marina is unchanged. The existing W jetty will be partially demolished and a new W jetty, twice as long, will be built outside it. The NW part of the Avant Port will have 770 yacht berths. Up to 86 unusual craft/old gaffers and FVs will share the current FV basin. A large L-shaped quay area will adjoin the present marina's S breakwater, with berths for commercial vessels, ferries and FVs. All new areas will be dredged as necessary.

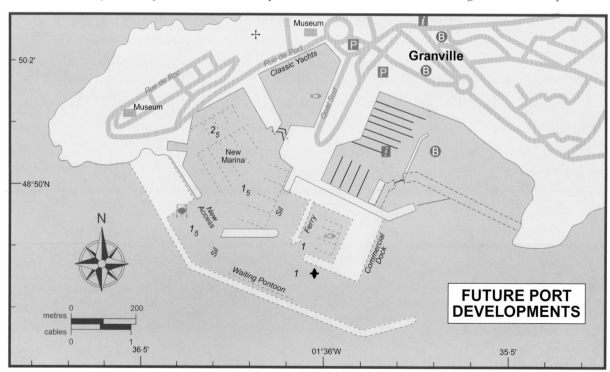

FUTURE PORT DEVELOPMENTS

ÎLES CHAUSEY

South end of the Sound – 48°52'·15N 01°49'·01W

Looking west across Grande Île. The Sound opens to the right

Isolated, yet only eight miles offshore; over-crowded in season, yet inhabited by merely seven souls plus cows in winter; a rocky archipelago, yet easy of access – that's Îles Chausey, approx 6M by 3M – a place to explore on foot and afloat. A visit is much recommended and always entrancing,

but avoid weekends when yachts from Jersey, Granville and St Malo home in like Exocets.

After the last day tripper has left by *vedette*, the silence is almost palpable. The scene at LW is in startling contrast to that at HW: A lunar landscape of rock upon rock as far as the eye can see leaves an indelible impression – hopefully only on your memory.

Îles Chausey is not a Port of Entry, ie you should have entered France at Granville, St Malo or elsewhere, before debarking in Chausey. It is actually part of the commune of Granville and the E half is a bird sanctuary – no entry 1/4 to 30/6.

SHORESIDE

Tourist Office, market day, bank, VHF, fuel, HM, chandlery and repairs *il n'y en a pas* (there are none at all).

What to see/do Enjoy the peace and solitude. Put the world to rights. Love thy neighbour. Walk the rough tracks of Grande Île to your favourite

beach; sunbathe, swim, picnic. Take the dinghy to some of the rocky islets when water re-appears.

Ferries *Vedettes* run from Granville and St Malo.

Beaches The nearest sandy beach is close NW of the lighthouse; others are there for the finding.

Supermarkets None, praise be. The general store stocks most basics.

Restaurants Choose between the Bellevue bar/restaurant, ☎ 02 33 51 80 30, and Hôtel du Fort et des Îles, ☎ 02 33 50 25 02. The latter is more up-market with menus at €16 and 24. The dining room and garden overlook the Sound.

NAVIGATION

Charts AC 2669 (1:150,000), 3656 (1:50,000), 3659 (1:50,000) plus SC 5604. SHOM 6966 (1:150,000), 7157 (1:50,000) and 7134 (1:15,000, with 1:5,000 inset of the Sound); this chart is preferred and advisable for serious rock-hopping.

Approaches The N, E and S sides of Chausey are

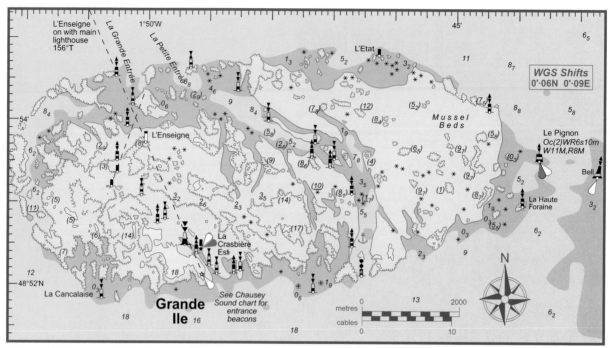

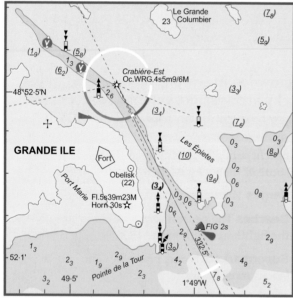

La Crabière-Est, Oc WRG 4s

adequately marked by cardinal beacons and by Le Pignon light tower; the W side is not marked. The usual and easiest approach is from the S. The waypoint 48°51'·71N 01°48'·65W is on the 332½° ldg line (L'Enseigne bcn ≠ La Crabière-Est lt bcn), 0.5M to the entrance waypoint (see title). This is in Crabière's W sector (329°–335°) and between Grande Île's lt ho and the only SHM lt buoy, Les Epiettes.

From the N, the 2M long channel is well marked by bcns which are never more than 5 cables apart. In reasonable visibility/sea state/day-only and with careful helming it presents few problems.

Landmarks The lighthouse, Fl 5s 39m 23M (grey tower with green top above the lamp), on Grande Île is conspicuous from all directions. La Crabière-Est Oc WRG 4s, is a yellow & black lattice beacon 3 cables N of the lt ho. Its white sector, 329°–335°, flanked by R and G sectors, makes a night arrival entirely feasible. The only other lights are a SHM buoy, Fl G 2s, at the entrance; and Le Pignon twr, Oc (2) WR 6s, at the E end of the reef. L'Enseigne is a W bcn twr with B top, on a 6m high islet.

Pilotage The S entry is defined by three ECM perches to port and a SHM lt buoy, plus two WCM perches to stbd (east of these ignore two SCM and a NCM bcn). La Crabière-Est is left to starboard; beyond it the channel turns approx 20° port and the moorings open up.

Grande Île lighthouse

The N entry: Having done your tidal sums (see below), make good La Grande Entrée ECM spar beacon, 48°54'·51N 01°50'·80W, on the 156° ldg line (L'Enseigne bcn twr ≠ Grande Île lt house). Hold this track until the next ECM bcn is abeam to stbd. Here pick up the 202° transit of two white bcns. Pass La Massue ECM bcn and at the front mark alter on to 139° to leave the next WCM bcn close to port. Pass between an E/W cardinal pair, then make good 126° for a SCM bcn and into the moorings.

To explore other passages and anchorages, arm yourself with SHOM 7134 and Malcolm Robson's *French Pilot*, *Vol 1*; now out of print. Have fun!

Access The approaches are rough in fresh/strong southerlies. There is sufficient water to enter from the S at all states of the tide, but from the N a drying height of 4.9m limits access to about HW±2½.

Tides HW Îles Chausey (Grande Île) at sp and at nps is 5 mins after HW St Malo. LW at sp and at nps is 15 mins after LW St Malo. MHWS is 13·0m, MLWS 1·9m; MHWN is 10·0m, MLWN is 4·8m. Note: The 11.1m sp range is amongst the largest in the Bay of St Malo. HW±2½ at neaps and springs will give at least 7.5m rise of tide, enough to cross the 4.9m high point if you elect to use the drying northern route.

Tidal streams in the Sound set NW at 2¾kn from HW St Helier −5½, and SE at 2kn from HW St H +3½. Rates are the max spring values.

Moorings Free moorings are white GRP conical buoys in profusion and mostly in enough water to stay afloat at LWS; but do your sums at the NW end of the pool or if outside the fairway. Fore and aft mooring is normal, to limit swinging; as is rafting in season, if the sea state permits.

Be wary when mooring, as some buoys have wire hawsers as risers which lack the weight of chain. When the stream is running hard, the hawser may draw more diagonally than vertically – ready to snag keel, prop or rudder – as your Companion discovered on his most recent visit; no harm done. Land at the long jetty/slipway, clear of *vedettes* in daytime; or near HW at a wooden jetty 200m SE.

Evening tranquillity in the Sound near LW. The L'Enseigne beacon tower is on the horizon to the right

CANCALE

East pierhead lt – 48°40'·16N 01°51'·03W

The problem with Cancale is OYSTERS, in their millions – little darlings! A dozen or so on your plate plus a decent dry white is all very fine, but first you have to park the *bateau* somewhere (see anchorages) – and the oysters got there first. Chart 3659 shows oyster beds both offshore (where they grow) and inshore (where they are groomed for your *assiette*). The beds are probably now more extensive than the 1985 edition of 3659 suggests, and if your keel should so much as graze a single oyster you will incur the wrath of all France. Only now are Cancale oysters recovered from a malaise which decimated them in the 1920s. Today the Cancale oyster has a distinctive tang of iodine and salt with an after-taste of hazel nuts. *Impeccable!*

If you decide not to visit Cancale by sea, may I suggest a thoroughly delightful and carefree day-trip from St Malo – by bus. Heresy, I agree, but fun albeit not of the adventurous kind.

SHORESIDE

Tourist Office At the harbour: ☎ 02 99 89 74 80; ▥ 02 99 89 77 87. Open 1400–1700, shut Wed & Sun. la_cancalaise@hotmal.com; www.la_cancalaise.fr.st In Town: ☎ 02 99 89 63 72; ▥ 02 99 89 75 08. Jul/Aug, daily 0900–2000. ot.cancale@wanadoo.fr; www.ville-cancale.fr

What to see/do You are now in Brittany, on the Côte d'Émeraude. La Houle is the lower town by the harbour. Cancale proper is the prosperous and smartish upper town, centred around a modern church. In the square is a famous bronze of ladies flushing oysters by hand. Visit La Ferme Marine, ☎ 02 99 89 69 99, 1km S of the harbour; it is both a museum and a working oyster farm; commentary in English at 1400 daily. Mont St Michel, 13.5M to the east, is usually visible but is most easily visited by train/bus from St Malo.

Rail See St Malo.

Bus 35 mins to St Malo; €4.40 return.

Taxi ☎ 06 09 39 52 52; 02 99 89 87 20.

Car hire At St Malo or ask the Tourist Office.

Bike hire Youth Hostel, Port Pican, ☎ 02 99 89 62 62.

UK access Ferry from St Malo or fly from Dinard.

Beaches There are beaches at Port Mer and Pican.

Supermarkets Marché Plus, rue de Bellevue (in main square by the church); Mon–Sat 0700–2100, Sun 0900–1200. Super-U, ave de Scissy (outskirts) H24.

Launderette near the Super-U.

Market days Sunday. Daily Oyster market at the root of the E pier. If you buy oysters you should know more elegant ways of opening them than did William Shakespeare:

> *Why then the world's my oyster*
> *Which I with sword will open.*

Banks At least three, with cashpoints, in the town centre.

Restaurants Le Querrien, 7 quai Duguay Trouin, ☎ 02 99 89 64 56; €15, 23 & 37.50. L'Armada, at NE end of seafront; menus €18.35 & 29.80. At the lower end of the scale, enjoy a bowl of soup, 6 x No 5 oysters, and glass of Muscadet for €10, at La Perle Cancalaise, ☎ 02 99 89 80 24, 21 quai Gambetta. Many and varied eateries line the harbour quays.

NAVIGATION

Charts AC 2669 (1:150,000), 3659 (1:50,000) plus SC 5604. SHOM 6966 (1:150,000), 7155 (1:48,800) and 7131 (1:20,000).

Approaches From the NE quadrant, go direct to the waypoint, keeping E of various dangers off Pte du Grouin. The majority of yachts approach from St Malo or points west, in which case Pointe du Grouin must be rounded by one of three main routes:
a) Outside La Fille NCM buoy, thence south.
b) Via Le Grand Ruet (N of Ruet WCM buoy and Herpin rock (21m) and S of Pierre d'Herpin lt ho); this route can be rough with overfalls and eddies.
c) Via Chenal de la Vieille Rivière: Passing Grande Bunouze NCM buoy, then S through the narrow, but deep cut between Pointe du Grouin and Île des Landes. Here the tide sets N for almost 9 hrs.

Landmarks Pte du Grouin with Sig Stn is easily seen. Pierre d'Herpin lighthouse, Herpin Rock, Île des Landes, like a scaly reptile, and Cancale church are all conspicuous.

Pilotage If a waypoint is needed, use 48°40'·57N 01°49'·16W, 251°/1.3M to the E pierhead. At the wpt assess the situation, especially if looking to berth in the harbour. Otherwise proceed to an anchorage as listed below.

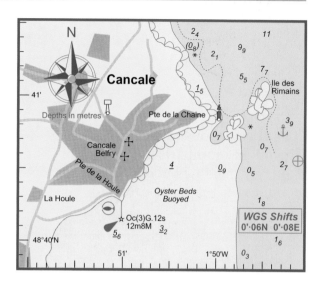

The only lights are Pierre d'Herpin lighthouse and an Oc (3) G 12s on the harbour's E pierhead.

Access to the drying harbour approx HW±2. It is of course totally exposed to E winds.

Tides HW Cancale at sp & at nps is 2 mins before HW St Malo. LW at sp & at nps is 10 mins after LW St Malo. MHWS is 13·0m, MLWS 1·6m; MHWN is 9·9m, MLWN 4·5m. Note the exceptionally large spring range, 11.4m.

Tidal streams off Pte du Grouin set NW from HW St Helier, and SE from HW St H–0555; max spring rates $4\frac{3}{4}$kn. In the anchorages off Pte de Chatry the stream sets S @ $1\frac{1}{2}$kn max from HW St H–0610, and N @ 3kn max from –0245.

Anchorages S of Pte du Grouin anchor off Port Mer or Port Picaine, close in to escape the tide, if local moorings leave space. A better anchorage is 2 cables N of the WPT (SE of Île des Rimains); good holding in about 4m, well sheltered from W'lies.

FACILITIES

Capitainerie HM via the Mairie ☎ 02 99 89 74 80; ⊠ 02 99 89 84 01.

Berthing Drying out on flat sand/mud against the E pier is possible if FVs and oyster workboats allow. Port La Houle generally is crowded with local boats, FVs and workboats. There are said to be deep water ⚓s to seaward.

Chandlery & repairs Coopérative Maritime, 23 quai Gambetta; ☎ 02 99 89 62 25, CH. Limited repairs at Cancale.

ST MALO & DINARD

Harbour entrance – 48°38'·54N 02°01'·82W

The conspicuous cathedral spire is always a welcoming sight, soaring high above the mighty ramparts of Intra Muros, the 'old walled city'. When nearer, its severely majestic buildings start to dominate the skyline. These were rebuilt with exquisite care after being flattened during WWII.

The unmistakable walled city and cathedral spire

Meanwhile you will be identifying the many rocks and marks which loom ahead ...

St Malo is a favourite city, not just because of Intra Muros, but also thanks to friendly people, warm sunshine and easy access to the inland cruising ground of the Rance. To the west some intriguing, off-the-beaten-track harbours wait to be explored.

Historically you have only to walk the ramparts to meet Jacques Cartier (who discovered Canada), Surcouf and Duguay-Trouin, (in)famous Malouine corsairs (legalised pirates). *'Ni Français, ni Breton, Malouin suis'* epitomises the independence of the people of St Malo, even to this day.

SHORESIDE

Tourist Office is at the head of the pontoons in Bassin Vauban. ☎ 02 99 56 64 48; 🖷 02 99 56 67 00. office.de.tourisme.saint-malo@wanadoo.fr; www.saint-malo-tourisme.com Jul/Aug, Mon–Sat 0830–2000; Sun 1000–1900. Apr–Jun & Sep, Mon–Sat 0900–1230, 1330–1900; Sun 1000–1230, 1430–1800.

What to see/do Walk the ramparts and dive into the cobbled streets and squares of Intra Muros; it is full of character and interest. St Servan is a well-heeled township with some up-market shops in a more mellow setting. From the marina walk round the wooded hill of La Cité and down

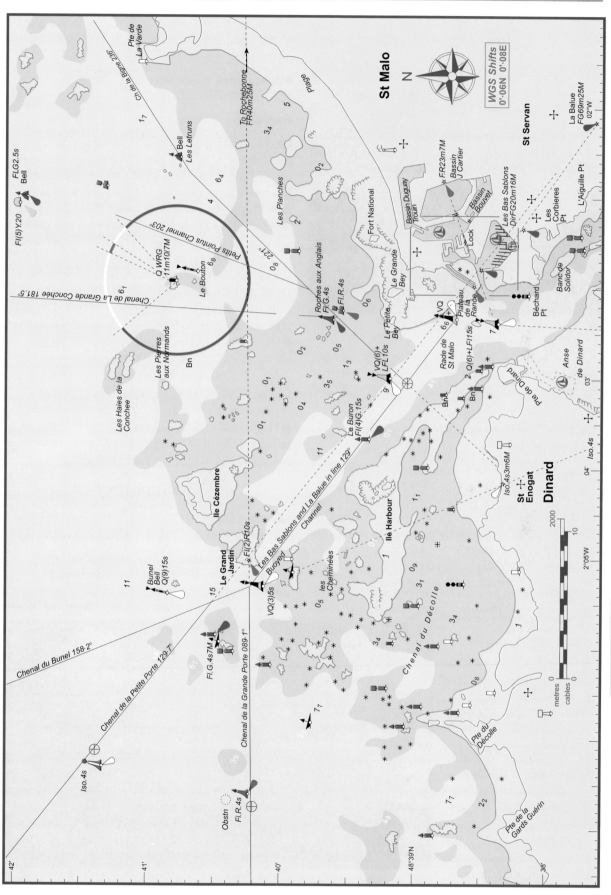

St Malo

St Servan

Pte de
La Varde

Ch de la Bigne 236°

To Rocheboone
FR40m25M

La Balue
FG69m25M
02°W

Les Letruns

FLG2.5s
Bell

Bell

FI(5)Y.20

Plage

Les Planches

Fort National

Le Grande
Bey

FR23m7M
Bassin
J Cartier

Bassin Duguay
Trouin

Les Bas Sablons
DirFG20m16M

L'Aiguille Pt

Les
Corbieres
Pt

Banc de
Solidor

Béchard
Pt

Bassin
Bouvet

Lock

Q WRG
11m107M

Le Bouton

Petits Pointus Channel 203°

227°

Chenal de La Grande Conchée 181.5°

Roches aux Anglais
FI.G.4s

FI.R.4s

Le Petite
Bey

VQ

Plateau
de la
Rance

Les Pierres
aux Normands

Bn

Les Haies de la
Conchée

VQ(6)+
LFL10s

Rade de
St Malo

2 Q(6)+LFL15s

Anse
de Dinard

Pte de Dinard

Le Buron
FI(4)G.15s

Bn

Bn

Ile Cézembre

Iso.4s

Dinard

St
Enogat

Le Bas Sablons and La Balue in line 129°

Channel

Ile Harbour

Iso.4s3m6M

Bunel
Bell
Q(9)15s

**Le Grand
Jardin**

FI(2)R10s

Les
Cheminées

2000

10

Chenal du Bunel 158.2°

FI.G.4s7M

VQ(3)5s

Buoyed

Chenal du Décolle

2°05'W

Chenal de la Petite Porte 129.7°

Chenal de la Grande Porte 089.1°

Iso.4s

Pte du
Décolle

Obstn

FI.R.4s

Pte de la
Gards Guérin

Chapter 7

The walled city, beautifully restored after WWII

into the Anse de Solidor to open up great views of Dinard and the approach to the Rance. Or go by bus to Mont St Michel; it is worth being a grockle for one day.

Rail Paris (3 hrs, 15 mins) TGV from Rennes. Dinan (1 hr).

Bus station is next to the Tourist Office (Intra Muros); also St Servan. Good local area network.

Taxi ☎ 02 99 81 30 30.

Car hire By the rail station: Hertz ☎ 02 99 56 31 61; Citer, ☎ 02 99 21 17 18; free delivery to Bas Sablons.

Bike hire Diazo Velos, 47 quai Duguay Trouin (300m from Intra Muros), ☎ 02 99 40 31 63. At Bas Sablons, contact Malocavelo, ☎ 02 99 56 22 02.

UK access Brittany ferries to Portsmouth. Condor Cats to Weymouth & Poole. Flights from Dinard.

Beaches There are good sandy beaches W, N and NE of Intra Muros; ditto at Anse de Solidor.

Supermarkets Marché Plus below La Malouine dept store, rue Ste Barbe (Intra Muros); Mon–Sat 0700–2100 & Sun morning. St Servan: Shopi, rue Ville Pépin. Wine, beer & cash, ☎ 02 99 82 3706, 24 quai Trichet; free delivery to marinas.

Market days Tues, Fri at Intra Muros & St Servan.

Banks Plenty in Intra Muros and St Servan.

Restaurants Within Intra Muros the number and variety of restaurants is enormous. A recce by day is time well spent. Marché aux Légumes is a lively spot, surrounded by cafés, bars and restaurants. La Porte St Pierre, 2 Place du Guet, ☎ 02 99 40 91 27, is a good family eatery; get a window seat looking seaward to Le Grand Jardin. La Chasse-Marée, ☎ 02 99 40 85 10, 4 rue du Grout St-Georges (150m W of the cathedral) is small, not too dear and does delicious seafood. Café de la Bourse, rue de Dinan €11-38. Coquille d'Oeuf, ☎ 02 99 40 92 62, rue de la Corne de Cerf, €11–24. Château des Bigorneaux, ☎ 02 99 56 61 93, 14 rue du Boyer, €11–20; tiny.

Near Bas Sablons, I can recommend: La Corderie, ☎ 02 99 81 62 38, a homely cottage-style place overlooking Port St Pierre; set menu €15 plus alcohol. Down the hill at Anse de Solidor, L'Atre, ☎ 02 99 81 68 39, is patronised by locals and visitors; good value food.

NAVIGATION

Charts AC 3659 (1:50,000), 2700 (1:15,000), plus SC 5604.4. SHOM 7155 (1:48,800), 7130 (1:15,000).

Approaches Rocks and shoals abound up to 3M offshore; they call for care but need not intimidate.

The seven approaches, clockwise from the W, are:

Looking NW from Intra Muros to Île de Cézémbre

a. Chenal du Décollé 133°; shallow and no longer fully charted; saves little or no time against (b).
b. Chenal de la Grande Porte 089°; see (c).
c. Chenal de la Petite Porte 130°. (b) and (c) are the two main channels; well buoyed/lit, deep and usable H24 in most weathers. They share with (d) a common inner section 129° after Grand Jardin.
d. Chenal du Bunel 158°; see (c).
e. Chenal de la Grande Conchée 181.5°.
f. Chenal des Petits Pointus 203°.
g. Chenal de la Bigne 222° and 236°. Useful from Granville, Îles Chausey or Cancale.
(e), (f) and (g) are only usable in good visibility by day due to a lack of ldg lights. After Roches-aux-Anglais SHM buoy, they share a common inner section 221° and shoal patches.

Landmarks include: The Cathedral spire; Le Grand Jardin, Bas Sablons, La Balue and Rochebonne lighthouses; Île de Cézembre (two rounded hummocks), with a 100m wide exclusion zone round it, due to explosives; Le Petit and Grand Bey islets, lt tower on Môle des Noires.

Pilotage A waypoint for (b) above is 48°40'·23N 02°07'·54W close SW of Buharats Ouest No 2 PHM buoy, on the 089° ldg line, 1.65M to the front mark Le Grand Jardin lt ho; rear is Rochebonne, FR. One cable before Le Grand Jardin, alter 40° stbd onto the 129° ldg line, Bas Sablons ≠ La Balue, both FG H24; then 2.7M to the harbour entrance (see under Title on page 402).

The **waypoint for (c)** is 48°41'·50N 02°07'·13W close NE of St Malo SWM buoy, on the 130° ldg line, 2M to the front mark Le Grand Jardin lt ho; rear is La Balue. Three cables before Le Grand Jardin jink 30° stbd for 250m to pick up the 129° ldg line, continuing as in (b) above.

Le Grand Jardin

The **waypoint for (g)** is 48°42'·65N 01°57'·30W close SE of an ECM buoy named Basse aux Chiens (but shown on AC 3659 as Basse Rochefort). Three unlit ldg lines (222°, 236° and 221° as chartlet) lead 5M to a SCM buoy near intersection with Ch de la Petite Porte. Marks are up to 6M distant

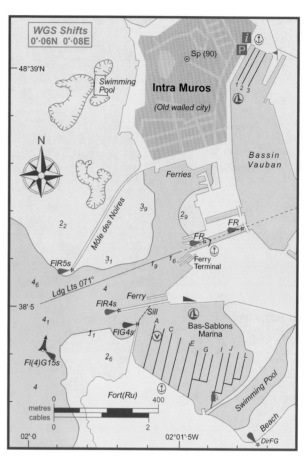

and exact tracking is needed; treat each leg separately. La Bigne is a substantial 18m high rock.

An **inner waypoint**, where all channels meet, is 48°39'·12N 02°02'·91W. From here track 129°/0.9M to the harbour entrance, as shown under the title, close to the end of Môle des Noires. Then either turn port to lock into Bassin Vauban or nip round the end of the ferry jetty into Bas Sablons Marina.

Tides St Malo is a Standard Port; predictions are given in the *RNA*. MHWS is 13·0m, MLWS 1·6m; MHWN is 9·9m, MLWN 4·5m. Note the exceptionally large spring range, 11·4m.

Tidal streams Between Le Grand Jardin and Le Buron, the streams set across the channel, ie East from HW St Helier –5, and W from HW St H+$\frac{1}{2}$; max sp rates 3$\frac{3}{4}$kn. In the Rade de St Malo the set is more nearly SSE/NNW and the rate 2$\frac{1}{4}$kn. Lay off for these powerful streams.

Access Fresh to strong W'lies can make the main approaches rough especially near Grand Jardin.

Shelter In Bas Sablons ♥ berths at the N end of 'A' and 'B' pontoons are totally exposed to NW'lies. Excellent shelter in Bassin Vauban.

Chapter 7

Looking north across Bas Sablons Marina to Intra Muros and Bassin Vauban

Anchorages An extensive 'No anchoring' area covers the NW and N approaches, the Rade de St Malo and Rade de Dinard as far SE as a line from Solidor Tower to Pte de la Vicomté – which leaves two options: ⚓ E of Dinard between the fairway and the drying moorings; or ⚓ between Pte de la Vicomté and Pte de la Jument, as charted.

VHF *St Malo Port* Ch 12. Bassin Vauban and Bas Sablons marinas Ch 09.

IPTS are shown at Écluse du Naye; see below.

FACILITIES

Marinas The two marinas are:

1. Bas Sablons Liberal access over a sill drying 2.0m. A digital gauge on the pierhead to stbd of the entrance reads the depth over the sill. On the N side of the marina another gauge is visible from all pontoons. At the SE end of the marina is a covering wall, open-air pool and a superb beach. Two white waiting buoys are close S of the entrance.

Visitors' berths 'A' pontoon, W side 43–75, E side 32–66. 'B' pontoon, W side 91–101, E side 92–102. ❶ berths have white numbers/red background. Out of season use 'B' pontoon only.

Capitainerie HM Claude Vauleon. ☎ 02 99 81 71 34; 📠 02 99 81 91 81; VHF Ch 09. Season 0700–2100; other months 0800–1200, 1400–1730. Anonymous building with dark reflective glass. port.plaisance@ville-saint-malo.fr; www.ville-saint-malo.fr

Tariff Daily rates, € for LOA bands, Jun–Aug: Rates in ( ) apply Apr, May, Sep & Oct. <8m = 13.80 (9.80); <9m = 16.70 (11.70); <10m = 19.50 (13.60); <11m = 22.70 (15.80); <12m = 25.90 (18.20); <13m = 30.80 (21.50); <14m = 35.70 (25); >14m = 48.70 (34).

Showers are free, by code. **Launderette** Au Panier à Linge, 4, rue des Bas Sablons (SE end of marina).

Fuel Diesel and petrol at fuel pontoon 'I'. Best to pre-arrange payment at Capitainerie as most UK cards will not work the pumps.

Chandlery & repairs Along the S side: Mecanique Marine, ☎ 02 99 82 62 97, BY, ME. North Sails, SM, ☎ 02 99 82 17 30. Key West, ☎ 02 99 81 46 00; CH, ME. Comptoir de la Mer, ☎ 02 99 82 25 87, quai Trichet, CH, El. Voilerie Richard, ☎ 02 99 81 63 81, SM.

2. Bassin Vauban is entered by the 'Big Ship' Écluse du Naye (no great hassle). The marina in 5.5m is at the N end, close to Intra Muros, the bus station and Tourist Office.

Lock The lock accepts inbounds at HW–2½, –1½, –½, +½ and +1½; and outbounds at HW–2, –1, HW+1 and +2. No later than HW+½, call St Malo Port Ch 12, or the lock, ☎ 02 99 81 62 86, for clearance to enter, stating your ETA (clock time and relative to HW). English is spoken; they are used to dealing with *les fou Anglais*. Enter on IPTS signal 3. Lock staff will heave you a line to take your warps. *Pas de problème*. Freeflow is unlikely due to busy road traffic over the rolling bridge. If a big ship is in transit, expect RRG and delays.

Berths Pontoons, numbered 1–3 from W–E, have no fingers and are too closely spaced for turning. Berth according to LOA: No 1, W side <8m, E side 8–9m; No 2, both sides <9–10m; No 3, W side 10–11m, E side 11–12m. No designated berths for visitors. Yachts >12m LOA may pre-arrange to berth on the quay or in the adjoining Bassin Duguay–Trouin.

Capitainerie (HM Erwann Le Calvez). VHF Ch 09. ☎ 02 99 56 51 91; ᴍ 02 99 56 57 81. Open 0700–2200.

Tariff Daily rates € on pontoon, Apr–Sep, for LOA bands: <10m = 21; <12m = 28; <14m = 36; <16m = 50. Lock fees are included.

Showers are free, access 0700–2200 by code.

Launderette In Grand Rue, dead ahead after entering Intra Muros via the Grande Porte.

Fuel Only by cans from a distant filling station.

YC E of the pontoons: Société Nautique de la Baie de St Malo (SNBSM), ☎ 02 99 40 84 42.

Chandlery & repairs Bas Sablons has much better technical support.

DINARD

Dinard is one of those fine old *fin de siècle* (the 19th) resorts with good beaches and villas slumbering amongst the trees. It still hosts the Cowes-Dinard race, at least in name, as participants now berth in St Malo's Bassin Vauban.

Dinard's Yacht Harbour near LW

Tourist Office ☎ 02 99 46 94 12, ᴍ 02 99 88 21 07. dinard.office.de.tourisme@wanadoo.fr; www.ville-dinard.fr Summer 0930–1930 daily. Other months, Mon–Sat 0900–1200, 1400–1800.

UK access St Malo ferries. Flights to Dinard from many UK airports; visit www.flightfile.com

Ferries Regular Emeraude trips from St Malo (10 mins); return €5.40.

Beaches Plage du Prieuré is at the head of the drying moorings. The oddly named Plage de l'Écluse is across the isthmus from the harbour; and Plage de St Enogat is further west. All superb.

Market days Tues, Thur, Sat in Place Crolard.

Supermarkets Marché Plus near the Tourist Office; Mon–Sat, 0700–2100, Sun morning. Intermarché, 200m from Tourist Office.

Yacht Harbour HM, Mme Crystelle Gallais. ☎ 02 99 46 65 55; ᴍ 02 99 46 64 73. 156 places in the Yacht pool; outside 476 drying moorings of which two for ♥. The pool is entered by a channel dredged 1m and marked by four pairs of R/G perches. It is marked at its NE, SE and SW corners respectively by WCM, NCM and ECM beacons. The E half of the pool is dredged 2m; the many local moorings prevent anchoring. Best to pre-arrange your visit. A proposed marina is unlikely to come to fruition due to strong environmental opposition.

Facilities P & D available near HW. The YC de Dinard, ☎ 02 99 46 67 72, has a bar and first floor restaurant with grandstand views of St Malo; menus €14 to 29. There are many restaurants in town to suit all tastes and pockets.

Chapter 7

RIVER RANCE

Barrage lock – 48°37´·12N 02°01´·63W

Dinan's port area with the old city at the top right

The Rance, between the hydro-electric barrage (*usine marémotrice*) at its mouth and Dinan some 13M south, forms an enchanting inland cruising ground. This is especially worthwhile when foul weather offshore precludes coastal cruising.

Dinan is the principal, oldest and most charming town on the lower Rance; along the banks are quiet hamlets such as St Suliac and Mordreuc, off which you can anchor/moor and stay afloat. Beyond Dinan the river shallows and becomes the Canal de l'Ille et Rance which at Rennes joins the Vilaine River. De-mast at St Malo or Dinan. Thus shoal draught <1.2m boats can reach S Brittany without the passage through the Chenal du Four and Raz de Sein – and with the bonus of a week or so in the most glorious and peaceful countryside.

SHORESIDE (Dinan)

Tourist Office at 9 rue du Château. ☎ 02 96 87 69 76; ℻ 02 96 87 69 77; infos@dinan-tourisme.com; www.dinan-tourisme.com

What to see/do This mediaeval fortress city, one of the finest in Brittany, merits some serious sight-seeing. Clamber up to the upper town by the steep cobbled rue du Petit Fort. Then walk the ramparts which encircle the city. In the centre climb the 15th century Tour d'Horloge – yes, the spire really is crooked – it's not just the local cider. Potter round the harbour in your dinghy. Go fishing. Walk the river banks and explore sleepy villages upstream.

Rail Station is 4km west of town. Change at St Brieuc and Rennes for mainline Brest/Paris.

Buses No 10 to St Malo (45 mins). No 11 to Dinard via the Rance villages. No 13 to St Cast.

Taxi ☎ 02 96 39 06 00.

Car hire ☎ 02 96 87 77 77; 02 96 85 07 51.

Bike hire See the HM or Tourist Office.

UK access Via St Malo ferries or Dinard/Pleurtuit airport, ☎ 02 96 46 18 46 (Ryanair to Stansted).

Supermarkets Monoprix at 7 rue du Marchix, first floor. Centre LeClerc is 3km west of the marina outside the ramparts.

Market day Thur in Place du Champ Clos.

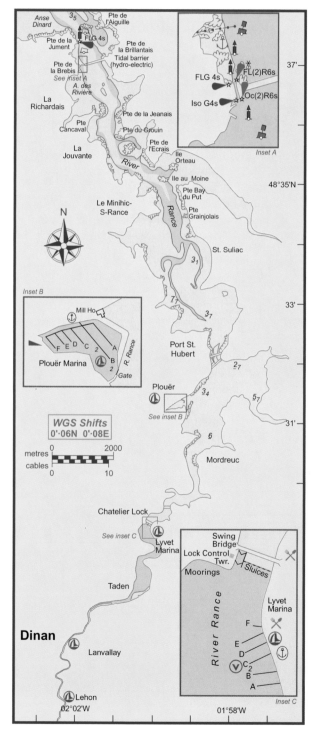

Banks Plenty in the centre of the Haute Ville.

Restaurants

Down on the quayside are two old favourites: Les Terrasses, ☎ 02 96 39 09 60; €13, 16, 27 & 39; shut Mon. And Le Relais des Corsaires, menus at €14–32. On the facing quay, L' Harlequin has a terrace

The squiffy Tour d'Horloge

which catches the last of the evening sun; €19 & 23. Up in the Haute-Ville at Place des Merciers, Chez la Mère Pourcel, ☎ 02 96 39 03 80, in a fine old timbered building does 4 star fare; menus from €17 and 27.20. Shut Sun afternoon and Mon. At 3 rue Haute Voie, L' Auberge du Pelican, ☎ 02 96 39 47 05; menus €14–42; shut Mon.

NAVIGATION

Charts AC 2700 (1:15,000) gets you to the Rance barrage. SHOM 4233, (1:15,000) fourth edition 1997, is almost essential, especially for deeper draught boats. It covers from St Malo to Châtelier lock/Lyvet marina, but should be used with caution as some charted depths stem from 1883. The IGN road map 1116 ET (1:25,000) greatly enhances your awareness of the surroundings and is useful for bike rides – one also appreciates its fine cartography.

Approaches from St Malo are simple: Round the Crapaud de la Cité SHM buoy; head S leaving La Mercière IDM bcn to port; leave the rocky Bizeux islet well to port and Pte de la Jument (G tower) 100m to stbd. Keep clear of the well-marked, no-entry zones down and up-stream of the sluices.

Landmarks The lock control tower at the extreme W end of the barrage is easily seen.

Water levels Upstream of the barrage, tides in the strictest sense have a limited effect because of the

Chapter 7

The barrage lock: Waiting to enter, northbound

way in which the turbines in the barrage operate. 'Water levels' are dictated almost exclusively by human, as opposed to sun/moon, actions.

Four metres above CD is usually maintained from 0700–2100LT, during which 8.5m is guaranteed for a stated period of 4 hrs, possibly up to 7 hrs. The significance of these two artificial, yet totally real levels is that with 4m or more you can transit the barrage lock, but due to the low water level and the ever greater drying heights upstream, you may not be able to progress much further S; unless of course the level is >8.5m. Châtelier lock needs 8.5m or more above CD before it can operate.

The times from mid-Jun to mid-Sep when water levels above CD are: (a) 4m or more; and (b) 8.5m or more are given in Electricité de France (EDF) leaflets, available from St Malo HMs; and as a recorded message (☎ 02 99 16 37 33); and in *Ouest-France*, the regional newspaper. The latter gives the times and heights of the highest and lowest levels for the next two days.

From this a simple graph can be drawn to help understand when and where you can stay afloat. Note however that the rise/fall of man-made levels can be irregular, ie not following the classic sine curve of lunar tides. St Suliac bay is used as the benchmark for these water levels.

Stories about the 'plug being pulled' and boats grounding instantly are somewhat over-stated. So long as you heed the predicted levels/times, you are unlikely to have problems.

A visit to the barrage exhibition (at the lock) to see how and when the turbines operate and water levels are adjusted is interesting and instructive.

Barrage lock Fresh to strong N'lies may make the entry from sea difficult. The lock opens day/night (on request 2030 to 0430) on the hour (H) during the period when the water level is 4m or more above CD. Arrive off the lock, ☎ 02 99 16 37 37, at H–20 mins. There are white waiting buoys.

Masted boats entering from sea must berth as far forward as possible so that the lifting road bridge can be closed astern of them; conversely, leaving to seaward they will enter after non-masted boats. Vertical wires assist berthing/warp handling.

IPTS (signals 2, 3 & 5) control entry; extra info by VHF Ch 13, loudspeaker broadcasts or an illuminated board giving access periods in French/English.

Pilotage From the barrage to St Suliac take heed of beacons (no buoys) positioned off headlands and shoals; binos needed. From St Suliac to Tour du Chêne Vert the channel is marked by R/G buoys, and by perches in the narrows leading to Châtelier lock. Keep to the outside of bends.

Châtelier lock (☎ 02 96 39 55 66; VHF Ch 14) only opens 0600–2100LT, when the level is >8.5m. Its sill dries 6.3m. Entry is controlled by two vertical R or one G (CEVNI). The swing bridge is unlit when shut; when open, a R or G controls vessels. There is room to wait on a stub jetty with vertical wires and ladder, port side of lock entrance. There are vertical ropes inside the lock.

From Châtelier to Dinan the 3M passage carries a least depth of about 1.4m, but check with the HMs at Lyvet or Dinan. It is well buoyed *à la CEVNI*, ie PHM buoys are red/brown and SHM buoys are black/white; small spar buoys.

Overhead clearances 20m for the S'ly of two

Plouër Marina, looking west

bridges at Port St Hubert (2M S of St Suliac) and Lessard rail bridge (0.5M before Châtelier). 16m for power cables 0.3M downstream of Dinan.

VHF *St Malo Port Control* Ch 12. *Barrage de la Rance* (lock) Ch 13. *Écluse du Chatelier* Ch 14. Pass your ETA at both locks to the lock-keepers.

Telephone Predicted water levels ☎ 02 99 16 37 33. Barrage lock ☎ 02 99 16 37 37. Châtelier lock ☎ 02 96 39 55 66. See also Marinas below.

FACILITIES

Marinas There are marinas at Plouër (6.3M south of the barrage), Lyvet (close upstream of Châtelier lock) and at Dinan a further 3M upstream.

1. PLOUËR (pronounced *'Plewair'*) marina is at 48°31´·54N 01°58´·95W on the west bank, well sheltered from the prevailing W/SW winds.

HM is Mlle Liliane Faustin (speaks good English) ☎ 02 96 86 83 15, ▨ 02 96 89 11 00. VHF Ch 09. plouer.portplaisance@liberty.fr Open 0900–1200 & 1400–1800.

Access There are two white waiting buoys outside. Enter over a flapgate which lowers (opens) when the water level outside reaches 8.2m, giving at that instant 1.5m over the sill. The flapgate is marked by PHM & SHM perches whose R & G lights show day/night when the flapgate is open; no lights = no entry/exit. A floodlit depth gauge on the N side of the gate indicates depth over the sill; needs binos to read. A wall, 6.5m above CD, retains at least 2m depth within; it is marked by three unlit ECM perches. Inbounds take priority over departures.

Berthing 10 ❶ finger berths on the outer end of 'B' pontoon, or as directed. Speed limit is 2kn.

Tariff Daily rates € on pontoons (showers included), in season, for LOA bands: <8m = 8.95; <9m = 11.25; <10m = 13.26; <11m = 15.88; <12m = 18.19; >12m = 20.20. No **launderette**, no **fuel**.

Electricity Free. 5 amps; 16 amps on request.

Chandlery & repairs Estuaire Marine BY, CH, ☎ 02 96 86 89 39; ▨ 02 96 86 89 41. St Samson Plaisance BY, CH, ☎ 02 96 86 95 80.

Ashore The small town of Plouër-sur-Rance is about 2km (20 mins walk) west: butcher, baker, two banks, Super-U 700m NNW of centre. Restaurant La Vieille Auberge in centre, ☎ 02 96 86 89 86; menus €14 & 19.80. Restaurant de la Cale, ☎ 02 96 86 97 24, at marina; closed Sun afternoon.

2. LYVET MARINA, 48°29´·40N 02°00´·00W. The marina is on the E bank, 250m from Châtelier lock (VHF 14). A sleepy hollow in about 2m depth.

HM is the very helpful Jean-Yves Le Gall, ☎ 02 96 83 35 57. No VHF. Open Jun–Sep, Mon–Sun 0800–1200 & 1500–1900; closed Wed.

Berthing 'D' pontoon for ❶, no specific berths.

Tariff Daily rates € on pontoons, all year, for LOAs: <8m = 8; <9m = 10.50; <10m = 12; <11m = 12.80; <12m = 14.50; <13m = 17.80; <14m = 26.50; <15m = 28.50; >15m = 30.

Showers are free. No launderette.

Electricity Daily €0.70 for 2 amp; €2.15 for 16 amp.

Chandlery & repairs None. No fuel.

Shopping Grocery in Vicomté-sur-Rance, 1.5km.

Restaurants Le Ty-Corentin on quay, inexpensive and friendly, plus bar; ☎ 02 96 83 21 10. At the bridge Le Saint-Patrick, menus €9.20 & 13.50; Guinness!

3. DINAN MARINA is situated 3M up-river from Châtelier lock.

HM, Jesse Brunelle, ☎ 02 96 39 56 44, is at 17 rue du Quai in a fine timbered house. Open Jul/Aug 0800–1900. Crane 500kg for de-masting.

Berthing Finger berths to stbd in about 1.5m.

Tariff Daily rates on fingers, in season, for LOAs: <8m = 8.54; <8.5m = 9.30; <9m = 10.06; <9.5m = 10.82; <10m = 12.50; <11m = 14.03; <12m = 18.60; >12m = 21.80.

Electricity 5 amp outlet, €2.29 per day.

Showers €1.52; Jun–Sep, Tues–Sat 0800–1830; Sun/Mon 0800–1200 & 1400–1800.

Launderette In Capitainerie. €3.05 for 4kg.

Fuel Diesel and petrol opposite Capitainerie.

Chandlery & repairs Limited, consult HM. Other facilities at Dinan: see under SHORESIDE.

Lyvet Marina on the right. Châtelier lock and swing bridge beyond, looking down river

THREE EMERALDS

West of St Malo, and still very much part of the Emerald coast, a number of deep inlets snuggle between long jutting promontories, of which Cap Fréhel is the largest. Amongst other little harbours (for which there is no space), two vivid emeralds sparkle in these inlets: St Briac and St Cast. The former is just in Ille-et-Vilaine; at the latter we are in Côtes d'Armor. Both are in a WWII mined area, but 60 years on, a Big Bang is about 0.000000001% likely – don't be off put.

West of Cap Fréhel is Erquy, the third jewel, quite different in character from the other two. But all are off the beaten track, more or less away from the crowds, sheltered by little bays and wooded headlands. Poke your bows in and swing round the hook till kingdom come, far from marinas – you'll love it.

ST BRIAC-SUR-MER

Innermost PHM perch – 48°37´·37N 02°08´·63W.

Do not confuse St Briac with St Brieuc (page 420), some 25M further W. It is one of those secluded North Brittany inlets about which British yachtsmen rhapsodise, but few visit. The moorings are in the attractive Le Béchet cove, by La Houle, NNW of the main town. Here, tucked away amongst the trees, is a smattering of shops, eateries and discreet villas. Up the hill St Briac proper has hotels and other more worrying seaside paraphernalia. The Frémur

river flows seaward under a road bridge. Pine-fringed islets and many drying rocks complete the pretty picture.

North of St Briac is St Lunaire where the eponymous saint arrived by sea in dense fog. Drawing his sword, he cut a great swathe through it and landed in brilliant sunshine – worth a thought?

SHORESIDE

Tourist Office ☎ 02 99 88 32 47; 📠 02 96 41 76 19; a kiosk at La Houle. Mon–Sat 1400–1800, Sun 1000–1230. Jul/Aug, 0900–2000 & Sun 1000–1230 & 1500–1830. contact@saint-briac.com; www.cote-emeraude.com

What to see/do Sample the nine beaches, grain by grain of clean golden sand, either by dinghy or by re-anchoring wherever the mood takes you. Good windsurfing, kayaking, sunbathing; also a good place to do nothing.

Buses No 14 crosses Frémur bridge en route via Dinard to St Malo (25 mins).

St Briac. Looking NW across the crowded moorings to Île Agot

Rail Nearest station at St Malo.

Bike hire At St Lunaire (2km), ☎ 02 99 88 92 68.

UK access Via St Malo ferry or Dinard airport.

Beaches Nine sandy beaches are advertised; the nearest, Le Béchet, faces SW to the moorings.

Market day Friday, Place du Marché. Jul/Aug, Monday at La Houle.

Banks In St Briac.

Restaurants Le Bêchet, ☎ 02 99 88 38 74, strong on moules; €12–17. Le Petit Bouchon, ☎ 02 99 88 00 38; €12, 16, 23. Dar Salam, ☎ 02 99 88 03 02; quite civilised despite the strawberry pink/cream décor.

NAVIGATION

Charts AC 2669 (1:150,000), 3659 (1:50,000), 2700 (1:15,000) plus SC 5604. SHOM 6966 (1:150,000), 7155 (1:48,800), 7129 (1:20,000) and 7130 (1:15,000).

Approaches to the WPT. From the E, via Buharats W No 2 PHM lt buoy. From the N, via Banchenou SHM lt buoy. WNW, direct from Cap Fréhel.

Landmarks Château Nessay (red brick & stucco) is visible among trees on a peninsula W of the cove. Moorings.

Pilotage The waypoint is 48°38´·32N 02°10´·68W (2.5 cables NNE of Porte des Hébihens rock) and 125°/1.66M to the innermost PHM perch. The wpt is in the 1° (124.5°–125.5°) white sector of a Dir Iso WRG 4s lt, white mast on a hut 250m N of Frémur bridge. The channel is marked by

St Briac in gale-force rain

a PHM bcn on Les Herplux and NCM bcn, La Moulière, followed by four PHM and three SHM perches. 3kn speed limit in the mooring area.

Access Difficult in strong onshore winds. Access approx HW±2½ for 1.5m draught. The channel dries progressively inshore of the first PHM perch.

Tides HW Île des Hébihens (S of the WPT) at sp & at nps is 2 mins before HW St Malo. LW at sp & at nps is 5 mins before LW St Malo. MHWS is 12·0m, MLWS 1·4m; MHWN is 9·1m, MLWN is 4·1m.

Tidal streams set NNE from HW St Helier $-5\frac{3}{4}$, and SW from -3, max spring rates $2\frac{3}{4}$kn.

Anchorage In fair weather fin keelers can anchor to seaward of the 1st PHM perch in 4–6m on sand.

FACILITIES

Bureau du Port (HM M D'Hem) is a kiosk at the E end of the cove. ☎ 02 99 88 01 75; 🖷 02 99 88 39 35. Open Mon–Fri 0830–1000 and at tide times.

Moorings There are supposedly 10 drying ⚓s and very little space to anchor except to seaward.

YC de St Briac (YCSB), ☎ 02 99 88 31 45.

Fuel Cans only from a local garage in La Houle.

Chandlery & repairs Very little; see the HM.

ST CAST

Harbour entrance – 48°38´·46N 02°14´·52W

Pleasing place, St Cast (forget Le Guildo, a handle sometimes attached to it, but in practice a quasi-commercial port 10km down the road). St Cast is quite the opposite: Acres of sand; room for yachts

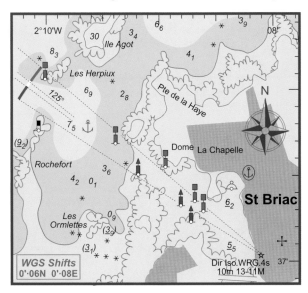

St Cast. Well organised moorings

and FVs alike; a sophisticated and chic little resort away from the drying harbour. Oh, and a very helpful and efficient HM.

On my last visit it was blowing hard and raining; the sun does not always shine. Some hard-to-please readers reckon that blue sky pics do not represent the real world.

The art of pleasing consists in being pleased.

SHORESIDE

Tourist Office ☎ 02 96 41 81 52; 🖶 02 96 41 76 19; Place Charles de Gaulle. Open Mon–Sat year round, office hours. Jul/Aug, 0900–2000 & Sun 1000–1230 & 1500–1830. saint-cast-le-guildo@wanadoo.fr; www.ot-st-cast-le-guildo.fr

What to see/do Walk S along the beach to Pte de la Garde, a fine viewpoint to N, S and E. Closer to hand and equally fine is Pointe de St Cast whence handsome Fort La Latte is visible 2M NW, with Cap Fréhel beyond. At LW walk across to Baie de la Fresnaye where mussels grow in spirals around wooden stakes; ditto in Baie de l'Arguenon. Back in town spare a look at a column commemorating a blip in 1758 (Seven Year's War) when the British lost 2,400 men in a failed attack on St Malo.

Buses No 1 to Lamballe (30 mins), for Brest/Paris train. No 13 to Dinan (55 mins). No 14 to St Malo (50 mins).

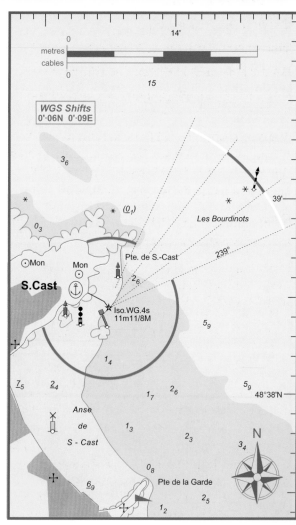

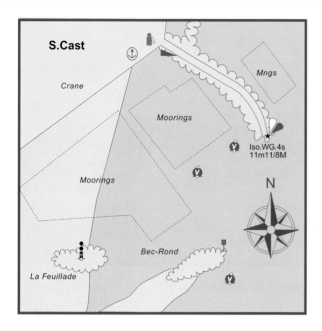

S.Cast

Crane

Mngs

Moorings

Iso.WG.4s
11m11/8M

Moorings

N

La Feuillade

Bec-Rond

Rail Lamballe (see Bus) for St Brieuc, Brest, Paris.

Taxi ☎ 02 96 41 86 16

Car hire See Tourist Office.

Bike hire M Page, rue de l'Isle; ☎ 02 96 41 87 71.

UK access Via St Malo ferry or Dinard airport.

Beaches Grande Plage stretches south forever. On the N coast: Plage de la Mare and Plage Pisotte.

Supermarkets Marché Plus, ☎ 02 96 41 86 16, in Pl C de Gaulle; Mon–Sat 0700–2100, Sun morning. Intermarché, Route Matignon, 3km SW by taxi.

Market day Fri all year. Mon 15/6–15/7.

Banks 3 in/near Pl Gén de Gaulle, with cashpoints.

Launderette Place des Mielles.

Restaurants Café Face, by the Capitainerie, does simple and inexpensive food. In town Ker Louis, ☎ 02 96 41 80 77, 15 rue Duguesclin, does regional dishes/seafood. In rue Duc d'Aiguillon choose from Le Suroit, Les Arcades and Les Halles.

NAVIGATION

Charts AC 2669 (1:150,000), 3659 (1:50,000) plus SC 5604. SHOM 6966 (1:150,000), 7155 (1:48,800) and 7129 (1:20,000).

Approaches From the E, route direct to the bkwtr head. From the NE, pass E of Les Bourdinots, rks drying 2m and marked by an unlit ECM buoy, 1M NE of the bkwtr, and in the green sector of the bkwtr head lt. From the NW, in fair weather it

is safe to pass between Les Bourdinots and drying ledges extending 2.5 cables NE of Pte de St Cast.

Landmarks Pte de St Cast and signal station. Fort La Latte 2M NW. Cap Fréhel and lt house 4M NW.

Pilotage The waypoint at 48°39´·04N 02°13´·09W, is 2 cables E of the ECM buoy, bearing 239°/1.1M to the bkwtr head. At night it is in the E'ly of two white sectors (233°–245°) of the bkwtr Iso WG 4s lt. The W'ly white sector is not advised at night.

Access Sheltered from SW to N winds. Enter the harbour between the bkwtr head and Bec Rond.

Tides HW St Cast at sp & at nps is 2 mins before HW St Malo. LW at sp & at nps is 5 mins before LW St Malo. MHWS is 12·0m, MLWS 1·4m; MHWN is 9·1m, MLWN 4·1m.

Tidal streams in the bay are mainly N-going, max spring rate 2kn.

VHF *Port de St Cast* Ch 09 (Ch 73 in winter).

Anchorages East of Bec Rond, outside moorings. Also E of Pte de la Garde in 2m; land at slip.

FACILITIES

Capitainerie (HM Dominique Delamotte) is near the breakwater root. ☎/✉ 02 96 81 04 43. VHF Ch 09. dominique.delamotte@cotesdarmor.cci.fr Season Mon–Fri 0900–1300 & 1400–2100 including tide times.

Moorings 18 fore/aft ✇s (Z1-Z18) are inside the head of the bkwtr; max LOA 13m. 20 outer ✇s (X1–X20) lie SE of Bec Rond, a large white-painted drying rock marked by a PHM perch. All ✇s are in 1.5 to 2m, sheltered from W'lies. FVs and local boats fill the rest of the harbour. At the

The outer moorings (X1–X20) at St Cast

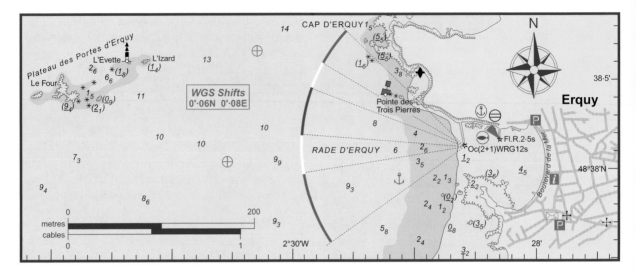

S end of the harbour, La Feuillade is another drying rock, marked by an IDM beacon.

Tariff Inner ⚓s, daily rates € (Jul, Aug) for LOA bands. Sep–Jun rates are in ( ): <8m = 11.50 (11.00); <10m = 15.50 (15.00); >10m = 20 (19). Outer ⚓s, layout as above: <8m = 10 (9.50); <10m = 14 (13); >10m = 18 (17.50).

Water taxi, *navette*, Jul/Aug 0700–2100, free of charge.

Showers in the block adjacent to the Capitainerie.

Fuel Diesel & petrol from the head of slipway at N corner, access approx HW±3.

Chandlery & repairs Coopérative Maritime at the harbour, ☎ 02 96 41 88 24; CH. Two cranes (10 & 12 ton). Rouxel Marine, ☎ 02 96 41 90 47, at the hbr; CH.

ERQUY

Outer mole head – 48°38´·12N 02°28´·60W

Say *Erquoi* and brows will furrow; *Erky* it is, short and sweet. The town is pleasant, if unremarkable. But the port area, backed by rocky cliffs and pines is far more appealing. Former fisherman's houses are converted to some extent, but without losing their charm.

If your idea of heaven is lying on a beach, then this is the place to be; prostrate next to your boat until the water re-appears and you climb aboard.

SHORESIDE

Tourist Office 29, bd de la Mer; ☎ 02 96 72 30.12; ✉ 02 96 72 02 88; tourisme.erquy@wanadoo.fr; www.erquy-tourisme.com Jul/Aug, Mon–Sat 0830–1930; Sun 0900–1230. Sep–Jun, Mon–Sat 0830–1230 & 1430–1915; Sun 0900–1230.

What to see/do If you like Coquille St Jacques (scallops) you're at the largest scallop-fishing port in Europe. Get up early for the daily fish auction or just gorge yourself in the evening. Good walks along the N coast on GR 34 will help you work up an appetite.

A day trip in the *Ste-Jeanne*, a gaff-rigged cargo sloop built in 1912, is an unusual experience; call ☎ 02 96 72 39 27, office at the port (see photo opposite).

Bus No 2 goes to St Brieuc (regional capital and rail station, 26km SW) and Lamballe; also Cap Fréhel.

Rail From St Brieuc to Brest, or Lamballe to Paris.

Taxi ☎ 02 96 72 30 37; 02 96 72 32 32; 02 96 72 49 58.

Car hire Fina, 11 rue de Corniche, ☎ 02 96 72 30 37.

Bike hire Cycles Balan, ☎ 02 96 72 10 22, rue des Hôpiteaux. Louérep, ☎ 02 96 72 02 85, 20 rue Foch.

UK access St Malo; St Brieuc or Dinard airports.

Beaches Grande Plage is a huge, crescent-shaped sandy beach stretching from the harbour to Pte de la Houssaye. It continues SW under other names. Some smaller but more interesting beaches lie E of Cap d'Erquy among rocky coves.

Supermarkets Comod, 9 rue Foch, in the town centre; 0830–2000. Super-U, 2km ESE of centre at Les Jeannettes roundabout; Mon–Sat 0900–1930.

Launderette Régina Net, ☎ 02 96 72 11 31; 8 rue des Hôpiteaux.

Market day Saturday. In Jul/Aug a free water taxi takes you and happy campers to market.

Banks Three in town centre, with cashpoints.

Restaurants Le Relais, ☎ 02 96 72 32 60, overlooks the inner hbr; €13–28. À l'Abri des Flots, a few doors away, ☎ 02 96 72 41 39, is strong on Coquilles St Jacques. In town: L'Escurial, ☎ 02 96 72 31 56, is on the seafront (bd de la Mer). La Cassolette, 6 rue de la Saline, ☎ 02 96 72 13 08, is near the Town Hall.

NAVIGATION

Charts AC 2669 (1:150,000), 3674 (1:50,000), 3672 (1:20,000) plus SC 5604. SHOM 6966 (1:150,000), 7154 (1:50,000) & 7310 (1:25,000 with inset).

Approaches From the NE, either keep N of the extensive Justières reefs to fetch Les Landas NCM lt buoy; thence to the N WPT (see Pilotage) 0.7M ENE of L'Evette NCM bcn tower. Or take the inshore Chenal d'Erquy (rocks off Cap d'Erquy ≠ 228° with Le Verdelet) a 42m high rock off Pte de Pleneuf. If this monster is hard to spot, Cap d'Erquy may be obscuring it. A good variant is to route via the two SCM lt buoys, Les Justières and Basse du Courant.

From the NW, keep N of Rohein WCM bcn twr and attendant rocks, en route to the above wpt.

From the W (eg St Quay-Portrieux), pass S of Rohein and N of Plateau des Jaunes to fetch the S WPT (see Pilotage) 7 cables SE of L'Evette.

Landmarks Le Verdelet. Craggy Cap d'Erquy. A conspic crescent of white sands SE of the harbour.

Pilotage North WPT is 48°38´·68N 02°30´·35W, 115°/1.3M to the outer mole. South WPT is 48°38´·07N 02°30´·55W, 087°/1.3M to the outer mole. Both WPTs are in the white sectors (111°–120° and 081°–094° respectively) of the Oc (2+1) WRG 12s on the outer mole; Fl R 2.5s on the inner mole.

Access Entry and mooring can be difficult or even dangerous in fresh SW'lies on a lee shore. Access is about HW±2½ for 1.5m draught.

Tides HW Erquy at sp is 5 mins and nps 10 mins before HW St Malo. LW at sp is 23 mins and at nps 17 mins before LW St Malo. MHWS is 11·6m, MLWS 1·5m; MHWN is 8·8m, MLWN 4·2m.

Tidal streams The flood sets ENE/1kn until HW St Malo –3. By HW St M–2 a back eddy sets W, reaching 2kn at HW. Caution near the inner mole.

VHF *Port d'Erquy* Ch 09.

FACILITIES

Capitainerie (HM Jean-Baptiste Besrest) is at the root of the inner mole. ☎ 02 96 72 19 32. VHF Ch 09. Open Mon–Fri 0900–1200 & 1400–1800 + tide times.

Harbour The new or outer harbour is between the outer & inner moles. Active FVs, *chalutiers*, berth on the outer mole, small leisure craft are moored at the E end. E of the inner mole, the old or inner harbour dries 4.5m and is used by various craft, some derelict. No alongside berths for yachts.

Moorings/anchorage There are four red drying ⚓s, P1–4, SW of the inner harbour on firm level sand. Or anchor in 2–4m on sand/weed patches about 2 cables SW of the outer mole in the green sector. Avoid fishing paraphernalia (buoyed) close NW of Pte de la Houssaye, and fish cages in the red sector close W of the outer mole.

Tariff Daily rates on ⚓ or at ⚓ Jul/Aug are cheap: <8m = €4.65; <10m = €5.70; <12m = €6.30.

Showers by Capitainerie/sailing school.

Fuel Fina garage, rue de la Corniche in town.

Chandlery & repairs Régina Plaisance, CH, ME, ☎ 02 96 72 13 70.

Ste-Jeanne *against a craggy backdrop*

Le Petite Muette lt ho

DAHOUET

La Petite Muette (entrance) – 48°34´·92N 02°34´·21W

Dahouet (pronounced *'Da-whette'*) is a tiny *Alice-in-Wonderland* harbour entered through a dog-legged cleft in the cliffs – like Alice you cannot see what you are letting yourself in for until you are inside. Some people say the entrance itself is hard to find, but in average

visibility La Petite Muette (LPM) can be seen from St Quay-Portrieux (10.6M); see Landmarks.

A few fishing boats dry out against the quay to port; further round to port the drying harbour opens up, full of small craft, whilst ahead is the marina sill and retaining wall. The whole lot trips over itself as if anxious to pack in yet more.

Dahouet village isn't much, but it's worth a visit for the intriguing pilotage on the way in. Le Val-André (2km) is where the action is.

SHORESIDE

Tourist Office 1 rue Winston Churchill, Val André. ☎ 02 96 72 20 55; ✉ 02 96 63 00 34; pleneuf@club-internet fr; www.val-andre.com

What to see/do Enjoy the coastal walks, taking in Val André (20 mins NE) or the low cliffs to the

SW. On a clear day take the bus (below) to Cap Fréhel for spectacular views – and that's it, apart from the Casino at Val André.

Buses No 2 connects to St Brieuc (regional capital and rail station, 26km SW) and via Erquy to Cap Fréhel to the ENE. Tourist Office has timetables.

Rail Mainline trains from St Brieuc to Paris/Brest.

Taxi ☎ 02 96 72 25 04.

Car hire Garage l'Amirauté, ☎ 02 96 72 20 20; place de l'Amirauté, Val André.

Bike hire See Val André Tourist Office.

UK access St Malo ferry or St Brieuc airport.

Beaches E of La Petite Muette is a small sandy cove. Val André sports a huge sandy beach.

Supermarkets Huit à Huit in Val André. Not much more than a boulangerie in Dahouet.

Market day Friday in season.

Banks In Val André.

Restaurants Plenty in Val André. At Dahouet on the N bank try Le Petit Navire brasserie/crêperie or Le Zef, a tiny restaurant.

NAVIGATION

Charts AC 2669 (1:150,000), 3674 (1:50,000) plus SC 5604. SHOM 6966 (1:150,000), 7154 (1:50,000) and 7310 (1:25,000).

Approaches From the E take the Chenal d'Erquy then skirt round the N and W sides of the Plateau des Jaunes off Pte de Pléneuf. From the N keep W of Rohein WCM beacon, then direct. From the NW either keep to seaward of Roches de St Quay via Les Hors and Caffa ECM buoys; or route through the Rade de St Quay via La Roselière WCM buoy.

Landmarks Le Verdelet, a prominent conical islet, 42m high, is off Pte de Pléneuf. Val André's white beach leads the eye SW to LPM, a green/white tower discernable against low cliffs. Inside, a pagoda-like shrine to Notre Dame de la Garde (Our Lady on Watch) is oddly comforting.

Pilotage The waypoint is 48°35´·21N 02°35´·35W, Dahouet NCM buoy, marking rocks to the S, and just in LPM's white sector. Traverse 6 cables east until LPM bears 160°; enter on this track midway between LPM and a PHM perch.

The channel turns ESE after a Fl (2) G 6s SHM bcn, and the shrine to port, below which two

white poles* mark a concrete ledge and slip. Hug the FV quay initially, then move mid-channel or slightly nearer to two SHM perches, until you see the marina sill between PHM & SHM beacons.

Depth over the sill is shown by two gauges, 200m before and on the sill's SHM beacon. The retaining wall is marked by five yellow SPM perches.

*These poles are not transit marks. If so used, you risk hitting rocks close W of LPM, which should always be left to stbd on entry (despite what locals may do). Ignore other white poles on the skyline.

Access Fresh/strong NW winds make entry very difficult in breaking seas. The access channel dries $\underline{4}$m initially and the marina sill $\underline{5}$·5m. For 1.5m draught access at springs is about HW±2$\frac{1}{2}$; but at neaps, for example coeff 35 HW–$\frac{1}{2}$, there is 2.3m over the sill. Think centimetres.

Tides HW Dahouet at sp & nps is 10 mins before HW St Malo. LW at sp is 25 mins and at nps 20 mins before LW St Malo. MHWS is 11·3m, MLWS 1·3m; MHWN is 8·6m, MLWN 4·0m.

Tidal streams set ESE from HW St Helier –6, and W from HW St H; about 2$\frac{1}{2}$kn at springs.

VHF Marina Ch 09.

Berths Berth/raft on the E side of the ❶ pontoon 'O', no fingers. 2.5m in the marina is quoted, but at the N end of pontoon 'O', only 1.6m was found.

FACILITIES

Capitainerie (HM Patrick Guitton) is on the E side of the marina. ☎/🖳 02 96 72 82 85. VHF Ch 09. Open Mon–Fri 0900–1200 & 1330–1700 plus tide times; Sat 0900–1200; Sun shut.

Tariff Daily rates € on pontoons, year round, for LOA bands: <8m = 12.75; <9m = 14.10; <10m = 16.60; <11m = 18.10; <12m = 20.45; <13m = 22.15; <14m = 24; <16m = 26.35; >16m = 31.55.

YC Val André (YCVA), ☎ 02 96 72 21 68, close NW of the ❶ pontoon.

Showers (very good) by jeton, in YCVA. Access by code.

Fuel None for yachts; a garage is N of the marina.

Chandlery & repairs A boatyard of sorts is up the hill S of the marina; or consult the HM.

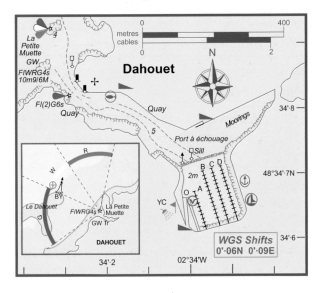

Lock

Swing bridge

Bureau du Port

LE LÉGUÉ

Outer harbour entrance – 48°32´·20N 02°42´·90W

This is no place for a gentleman's yacht – or so it used to be said. But now changes are in the wind as the inner basin is being modernised to meet the needs of today's yachtsmen. Ugly industrial sites are giving way to boatyards. Quaysides have been paved and lined with pontoons, and a Bureau du Port (Plaisance) has opened close by. A friendly welcome and helping hand are assured.

SHORESIDE

Tourist Office 7 rue St Gouéno. ☎ 02 96 33 32 50; ⊠ 02.96.61.42.16; o.t.saint-brieuc@wanadoo.fr; www.baiedestbrieuc.com

What to see/do St Brieuc is the major industrial city of the Côte d'Émeraude and self-styled 'City of Viaducts'. Climb 1.5km up the hill to the *vieux quartier*, around the stern cathedral where pretty and colourful streets are a stone's throw away from the modern shipping centre, Place du Chai.

Rail The station, ☎ 02 96 94 50 50, is 750m S of the cathedral. TGV/mainline to Brest, Rennes and Paris.

Buses See the Tourist Office for timetables.

Taxi ☎ 02 96 94 70 70.

Car hire ADA, ☎ 02 96 78 19 99; 57 rue de la Gare.

Bike hire Vélos Centre, ☎ 02 96 68 02 33, 14 rue Houvenagle.

UK access Ferry from St Malo or via the Channel Islands. Mainline trains, the N12 autoroute and a regional airport (☎ 02 96 94 95 00; 5km W of St Brieuc) give good access for crew-changing.

Beach Good sand between Iso G 4s and Pointe à l'Aigle. Further N, St Laurent is a pleasant suburb.

Supermarket Viveco on the N quay. Boulangerie.

Market days Wed, Sat at St Brieuc; Sun at Cesson.

Banks Plenty around the centre.

Restaurants In Le Légué, by N quay: La Marine, €13.50. Le Grenier à Sel, €9.15. Halfway up the hill: Aux Pesked, 59 rue du Légué, ☎ 02 96 33 34 65, up-market cuisine from €18–75, to celebrate!

In St Brieuc, rue des 3 Frères le Goff: @ No 7, La Pierre à Feu, ☎ 02 96 68 56 02. @ No 15, La Bistrot du Port, ☎ 02 96 33 83 03. Also rue de Gouët/rue Fardel.

NAVIGATION

Charts AC 2669 (1:150,000), SC 5604.2 (1:150,000), AC 3674 (1:50,000 & 1:10,000 inset). SHOM 6966 (1:155,000), 7154 (1:50,000) and 7128 (1:25,000).

Approaches From the N/NW, pass between Rohein WCM bcn tower and Caffa ECM buoy, en route to Le Légué SWM buoy, the waypoint.

From Bréhat/Paimpol, stay inshore through the Rade de St Quay-Portrieux (avoiding some shoal patches; see AC 3672), thence to the waypoint.

From the E, after Cap Fréhel either stay seaward of the extensive reefs off Cap d'Erquy and N and E of Rohein beacon; or take the inshore Chenal d'Erquy (careful pilotage), passing N of Plateau des Jaunes; thence to the waypoint.

Landmarks Pte du Roselier is a 200ft, flat-topped headland, 6 cables to stbd of the approach. High-rise blocks on the St Brieuc skyline are conspic. The ruined Tour de Cesson is on a wooded hillock about 4 cables E of the lock.

Pilotage The waypoint is 48°34´·39N 02°41´·06W, Le Légué SWM lt buoy, 206°/2.1M to the unlit No 1 buoy; thence 229°/0.4M to No 3 lt buoy at the outer harbour entrance. Pointe à l'Aigle lt is on a short pier close to stbd. Thereafter the buoyed channel trends 225°/6 cables, past Tour de Cesson, then W for the final 3 cables to the lock.

The lock, where the R Le Gouet meets the sea, is 85m x 14m; the sill dries 5.1m. Opening times, relative to the height of tide at St Malo, are:

8–10m	(MHWN 9·3m)	Local HW±1
10–11m		HW±1¼
11–11.5m		HW±1½
> 11.5m	(MHWS 12·2m)	HW–2 to +1½

There is space to jill around if the lock is not ready. Commercial ships take priority. On the N side of the entrance a depth gauge gives depth above the sill; a gauge on the S side shows depth above CD. There is a ladder at each end on either side, but no vertical ropes for reeving warps. Take heart: a lock-keeper will handle your lines.

From the lock make for the viaduct, bypassing Bassin 1 to port. Enter Bassin 2 via a low swing bridge which opens in unison with the lock.

Access In fresh/strong N–E winds the approach is difficult or even impossible. Yachts arriving to meet the lock schedule will have adequate water in the approach and inner channels.

Anchorage To await the tide, anchor between the SWM buoy and Pte du Roselier in offshore winds.

Tides HW Le Légué at sp & nps is 5 mins before HW St Malo. LW at sp is 25 mins and at nps 15 mins

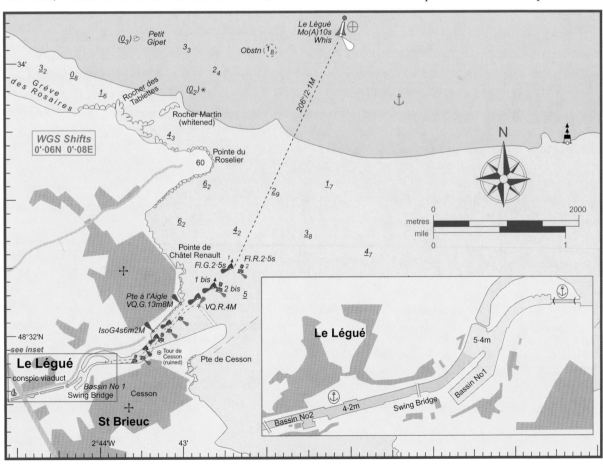

before LW St Malo. MHWS is 11·4m, MLWS 1·4m; MHWN is 8·8m, MLWN 4·0m. Persistent strong winds can alter tide heights by up to 0·7m.

Tidal streams close E of Le Légué, set S from HW St Helier –6 hrs, and N from HW St Helier.

VHF To transit the lock and bridge, call Le Légué Port Ch 12 at least 10 mins before entry/exit.

FACILITIES

Bureau du Port (HM O Perroz), Quai Nemours is N side, 350m W of the swing bridge. VHF Ch 12. ☎ 06 86 49 09 13. Opening hours as per the lock. The commercial HM, ☎ 02 96 33 35 41, ✉ 02 96 61 46 94, is N of the inner lock gate, but of no great concern. Chamber of Commerce = www.cotesdarmor.cci.fr

Berths *Accueil* berth in front of the Bureau du Port.

Berth as directed, or on the N quay in about 3m. There are some 140 berths including 20 **Ⓥ**s, but rafting on local boats is likely. At springs leave some slack on lines during sluicing, as indicated by a blue flag on the Bureau du Port.

Tariff Daily rates € (inc showers), in season, for LOA bands: <8m = 10.70; <9m = 12; <10m = 13.10; <11m = 15.50; <12m = 17.60; <13m = 19.20; <14m = 22.40; >14m = 1.59, per extra m LOA.

Electricity and **fresh water** supplies on the quayside; more being fitted.

Fuel By cans from a filling station on the quay.

YC Cercle Nautique de Légué are welcoming.

Chandlery & repairs Roger Nautique, 30 rue de la Tour, Port du Légué; ☎ 02 96 33 81 38. Engineers. J-P Vernier, 7 ave de Bretagne, 22190 Plérin; ☎ 02 96 74 45 33.

BINIC

Harbour entrance – 48°36´·12N 02°48´·85W

This bright and cheery spot is pronounced *'Bineek'*, as derived from the little River Ic which trickles through the harbour. Like all the harbours from St Malo to St Quay-Portrieux, Binic dries extensively but you can stay afloat in the marina, once used by those who fished for cod off Iceland.

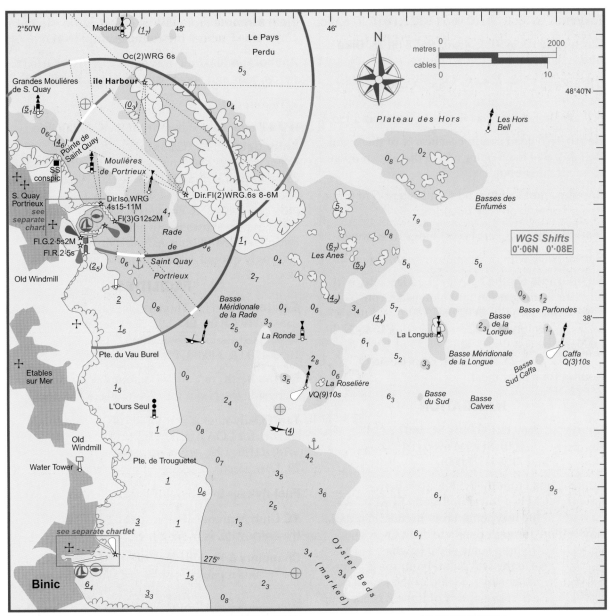

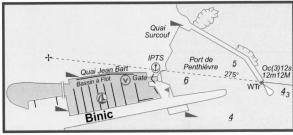

Note the access times: If you wish to be neaped, this is a better place than most and the experience will be for only two or three days.

This is the Côte du Goëlo which stretches up to Paimpol. Beyond it changes to the Trégor, another area embracing the Trieux and Jaudy rivers. Goëlo means light, but your Companion can shed few further lumens on this nebulous region.

SHORESIDE

Tourist Office, Ave Gén de Gaulle; modern block opposite a Total filling station. ☎ 02 96 73 60 12; ✉ 02 96 73 35 23. Mon–Fri, 0930 (1000)–1230 & 1400–1800 (1700); Sat, Sun, Bank hols in ( ). officedetourismedebinic@wanadoo.fr; www.ville.binic.fr

What to see/do Rather pleasant just to leap off the boat, cross Quai Jean Bart and fall into one of several goodish eateries. Or for low key culture visit the little museum by the tourist office where local traditions are recalled. There's also good cliff-top walking on GR34, to the north or south.

Rail Nearest station is St Brieuc, 14km.

Buses No 9 to St Brieuc and Paimpol.

Chapter 7

Taxi ☎ 02 96 73 31 31; 02 96 71 93 22; 06 07 57 82 46.

Car hire ☎ 02 96 94 45 45; 02 96 78 00 78. **Bike hire** Ask the HM or Tourist Office.

UK access Ferry from St Malo. A good airport (☎ 02 96 94 95 00) 5km W of St Brieuc accepts private aircraft and has flights to Jersey and Paris.

Beach Two good sandy beaches: N of the Avant Port and S of the S quay, where there is an open-air swimming pool.

Supermarket Comod, bd Gén Leclerc, S of inner basin. Super-U on NW outskirts.

Market day Thur, but Fri evenings in summer.

Banks Three with cashpoints in town; closed Mon.

Restaurants On the N Quay: La Mascotte, with an extra floating restaurant alongside, conspic blue/white awning; ☎ 02 96 73 30 77, menus €16 to 25. Le Benhuyc, ☎ 02 96 73 39 00, €15 to 27.40. Le Neptune (1st floor), ☎ 02 96 73 61 02, Pl de l'Eglise, €13 to 25. An Arvor, crêperie on Q Courcy, for a light meal.

NAVIGATION

Charts AC 2669 (1:150,000), SC 5604.2 (1:150,000), AC 3674 (1:50,000). SHOM 6966 (1:155,000), 7154 (1:50,000) and 7128 (1:25,000).

Approaches From the N/NE, pass between Rohein WCM bcn tower and Caffa ECM buoy, en route to the waypoint. From Bréhat/Paimpol, stay inshore through the Rade de St Quay-Portrieux (avoiding some shoal patches; see AC 3672), thence to the waypoint. From the E, after Cap Fréhel either stay seaward of the extensive reefs off Cap d'Erquy and N of Rohein beacon; or via the inshore Chenal d'Erquy (careful pilotage), passing N of Plateau des Jaunes, to the waypoint.

Landmarks Nothing riveting, but the pierhead lt ho and town are easily seen from the waypoint.

Pilotage The waypoint is 48°35´·92N 02°46´·60W, 278°/1·5M to the harbour entrance; the white lt ho on E pier in transit with church spire. From the pierhead the channel lies S of the moorings.

Access Enter Avant Port approx HW±3; it may be possible to wait alongside the E pier; dries 4.5m. See below for access to marina.

Tides HW Binic at sp & nps is 8 mins before HW St Malo. LW at sp is 30 mins and at nps 15 mins before LW St Malo. MHWS is 11·4m, MLWS 1·3m; MHWN is 8·6m, MLWN 4·0m.

Tidal streams From HW St Helier $-2\frac{1}{2}$ to $-1\frac{1}{2}$ an eddy runs E across the entrance at up to 1kn.

Anchorage Near the waypoint, clear of charted oyster beds and shoal patches – to await the tide.

VHF *Port de Binic* Ch 09.

IPTS 2 and 3 are shown from the Capitainerie.

Entry gate opens H24 as tide height tops 8.5m*, when there will be 3m over the sill drying 5.5m; it cannot open earlier. It closes at HW. Access at sp is about HW–2 to HW, but at nps only HW–$\frac{1}{2}$ to HW. **NB coeff <40 = No entry/exit.** A gauge (hard to read) to port shows depth above CD. A roller bridge retracts in unison. Speed limit 3kn. *Wrongly quoted as 9.5m in most guide books.

FACILITIES

Capitainerie (HM Thomas Le Gall), by the entry gate. VHF Ch 09. ☎ 02 96 73 61 86. 🖷 02 96 73 72 38. port-de-binic@wanadoo.fr Open daily, 1000–1200 & 1400–1700 and at tide times.

Berths Berth/raft on ❶ pontoon ('A') to starboard alongside the N quay, in 2–3m; max LOA 16m.

Tariff Daily rates € (inc showers), in mid/high season, for LOA bands: <8m = 14; <9m = 16; <10m = 18; <11m = 20; <12m = 21; <14m = 25; >16m = 29. Low season rates are half the above.

Fuel By cans from a filling station in town 300m.

YC Club Nautique de Binic, ☎ 02 96 73 31 67, S of the entry gate, is welcoming.

Chandlery & repairs JBM, ☎ 02 96 73 75 28, CH. For serious repairs, repair to St Quay-Portrieux.

'A' pontoon for visitors, along the N quay

St Quay-Portrieux

Harbour entrance – 48°38´·87N 02°48´·88W

Functional and friendly, but lacking charm and character

St Quay is a seaside resort NNW of neighbouring Portrieux's old drying harbour. In 1991 a large marina (Port d'Armor) was grafted onto the old harbour – to mixed reactions. But now the two communities co-exist despite differing styles; the graft has taken.

The Old Harbour has preserved its quiet charm: at the N end is a popular beach and sun-trap; local boats still moor to seaward; life goes on.

Within its huge claw-like breakwaters the marina is large, functional, well sheltered and accessible at all tides and weathers. The N part is occupied by FVs. It is an ideal base from which to work the tides and explore drying harbours like Paimpol, Binic, Le Légué, Dahouet and Erquy.

SHORESIDE

Tourist Office rue Jeanne d'Arc. ☎ 02 96 70 40 64; 🖷 02 96 70 39 99. Mon–Fri, 0900–1230 & 1330–1900 (1700); Sat, Sun 1000–1230, 1500–1800. Jul/Aug, Mon–Sat 0900–1900. saintquayportrieux @wanadoo.fr; www.saint-quay-portrieux.com

At the marina La Maison du Port is an Information Point, open 15 Jun–15 Sept; ☎ 02 96 70 50 60.

What to see/do Day sail N to nearby anchorages off Port St Marc, Port Gorey, Gwin Zégal, Pors Moguer, Plage Bonaparte and Anse de Bréhec; all on AC 3674. From this coast the French Résistance spirited away many downed aircrew in WWII.

Or walk/cycle the same stretch along the 100m high cliffs taking in Tréveneuc and Plouha. The latter is the traditional boundary between French and Breton-speaking Brittany, as will be obvious to your sensitive ear.

Rail Nearest station is St Brieuc, 21km.

Buses No 9 runs to St Brieuc (40 mins) and Paimpol (1 hr).

Taxi ☎ 02 96 70 59 46/02 96 70 46 35; 02 96 70 55 37.

Car & bike hire Via the Capitainerie.

UK access Ferry from St Malo. A good airport (☎ 02 96 94 95 00) 5km W of St Brieuc accepts private aircraft and has flights to Jersey and Paris.

Beach Good sandy beaches on NW side of the old harbour; Plages de la Comtesse (N of the marina), du Châtelet and de St Quay by the Tourist Office.

Supermarket Spar, 50 quai de la République, faces the old hbr. Intermarché, route de Paimpol on NW outskirts.

Market days Mon at the Old Hbr; Fri at St Quay.

Banks Three banks, with cashpoints, by the old harbour.

Launderette At marina; also Laverie du Port, 3 rue Clemenceau, ☎ 02 96 70 91 29.

Restaurants At the marina: Le Victoria and Le Portrieux are popular bar/brasseries. Old Hbr: Chez Fabrice, next to Spar; menus €15, 19, 26, 38.

La Bienvenue, ☎ 02 96 70 42 05, 2 place du Centre (a block behind Spar); €17.60, 23, 35.10. If feeling rich, walk N toward the Sig Stn to dine in opulent, middle Eastern splendour at the Hôtel Ker Moor.

NAVIGATION

Charts AC 2669 (1:150,000), SC 5604.2 (1:150,000), AC 3674 (1:50,000) and AC 3672 (1:25,000). SHOM 6966 (1:155,000), 7154 (1:50,000) & 7128 (1:25,000).

Approaches The harbour is guarded by Roches de St Quay, an extensive offshore reef. The inshore fairway, 6 cables wide, is well marked by buoys, beacons and directional lights.

From NW go direct to the N waypoint. From the NE, clear the reef's NW outliers (Madeux), then to the N waypoint. From the E, pass N or S of Rohein WCM beacon twr, thence via Caffa ECM and La Roselière WCM buoys, en route to the S Waypoint. From the SE, go direct to La Roselière WCM buoy and on to the S waypoint.

Landmarks On Pte de St Quay the Signal Stn is a lofty, conspic building. Île Harbour light house sprouts distinctively from a white building. At the N side of hbr the round, white iceplant is conspic.

Pilotage The **S waypoint**, 48°37´·37N 02°46´·76W, bears 318°/2·0M to the hbr entrance; by day the green lt twr on E bkwtr ≠ the Signal Stn on Pte de St Quay. At night track 318° in the W sector (316°–320·5°) of the Bkwtr elbow lt, Iso WRG 4s.

The **N waypoint**, 48°39´·88N 02°49´·24W, bears 157°/1M to abeam the E bkwtr's green lt twr, whence turn stbd into the harbour. Pass 300m NE of Moulières de Pontrieux ECM bcn twr.

At night make good 48°40´·68N 02°49´·48W,

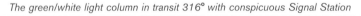
The green/white light column in transit 316° with conspicuous Signal Station

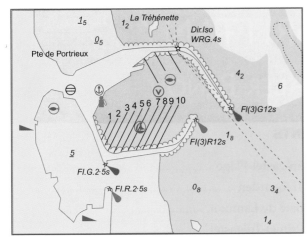

5 cables NW of Madeux WCM bcn twr. Thence utilise four Dir lt white (W) sectors in succession, as follows:

a. Track 169° in the W sector (159°–179°) of the bkwtr elbow lt, Iso WRG 4s, to the N Wpt; then

b. Track 130°in the W sector (125°–135°) of Herflux lt, Fl (2) WRG 6s, to intercept:

c. The astern W sector (358°–011°) of Île Harbour lt, Oc (2) WRG 6s, tracking 184° to intercept:

d. The W sector (316°–320.5°) of the bkwtr elbow lt, Iso WRG 4s, tracking 318° to the hbr. Note this leg can be curtailed when the entrance is seen. The sequence is more complex in the telling than in practice. It is safe and rewarding pilotage.

Access H24 at all states of the tide. The harbour is a Port of Refuge accessible in all weathers.

Tides HW St Quay at sp is 5 mins and at nps 10 mins before HW St Malo. LW at sp is 25 mins and at nps 15 mins before LW St Malo. MHWS is 11·2m, MLWS 1·4m; MHWN is 8·6m, MLWN 4·0m.

Tidal streams in the inshore fairway set SSE from HW St Helier +6 and NNW from HW St Helier –6, max rate 2kn.

Anchorage As charted at 48°38´·55N 02°48´·52W in Rade de Portrieux, 4 cables SE of hbr in 3m.

VHF *Port d'Armor* Ch 09, H24.

FACILITIES

Capitainerie (HM Olivier Guezou). VHF Ch 09. ☎ 02 96 70 81 30/06 63 67 71 77; ⌨ 02 96 70 81 31; welcome@port-armor.com; www.port-armor.com Open daily, 0700–2000 and caretaker 2000–0700. Trevor is a helpful ex-pat Brit on the marina staff.

Berths ♥ berths on pontoon 7: W side, no fingers, for LOA >11m; E side, fingers <11m.

No need to go to *accueil* berth situated in front of the Capitainerie.

Tariff Daily rates € on pontoons, 1/6–30/9, for LOA bands: <8m = 16; <9m = 18; <10m = 21; <11m = 24; <12m = 26; <13m = 28; <14m = 31; <15m = 32; >16m = 34. Rates 1/10–30/5 are half the above.

Showers by jeton €1.60 from a machine in the block which faces No 3 pontoon; there is also a **launderette**.

Fuel Diesel and petrol in front of the Capitainerie; available H24 if you have a French credit card. If not pay in cash 0800–1200 & 1400–1800.

YCs Sport Nautique de St Quay-Portrieux, ☎/⌨ 02 96 70 93 34. Cercle de la Voile du Portrieux (CVPX), ☎ 02 96 70 41 76.

CHANDLERY & REPAIR FACILITIES

U-Ship, ☎ 02 96 65 29 29, CH.
Ouest Marine Service, ☎ 02 96 70 41 93, CH, ME.
Emtec Armor, ☎ 02 96 70 90 85, electronics.
Coop Maritime, ☎ 02 96 70 42 06, CH. Alain Maintenance, ☎ 06 12 53 26 73, ME. Chantier Cras, ☎ 02 96 70 85 40, ME, hull repairs.

Future plans Various schemes are afoot ranging from expansion of the existing marina to building a retaining wall and sill across the Old Harbour. Finance and environmental opposition remain the usual stumbling blocks. Don't hold your breath.

Île Harbour lighthouse on Roches de St Quay

Chapter 7

CHAPTER 8

NORTH BRITTANY

PAIMPOL TO L'ABER BENOIT

CONTENTS

Welcome to the Côtes d'Armor, not d'Amour as one pilot book rather touchingly calls it. The real Côte d'Amour is near Le Croisic in South Brittany. Could someone please tell the Romantic Cruising Club (RCC).

Côtes d'Armor (C d'A) is a *département*, originally known as Côtes du Nord. We entered C d'A soon after leaving St Malo – flitting from the touristically labelled Côte d'Émeraude to Côte de Goëlo to Côte du Granite Rose – and will remain therein until entering Finistère at Locquirec.

C d'A is for many yachtsmen the quintessential North Brittany, to which they return year after year – with good reason. Its coastline is invariably rocky, hence navigationally challenging; ruggedly

beautiful, therefore photogenic; cleft by several rivers in which shelter is assured – and, not least graced by delightful harbours where seafood and other delights scale new gastronomic heights. If that sounds like a tourist brochure, it ain't! It's from the heart and from the stomach.

Nor does the pleasure stop at Locquirec where the *département* of Finistère begins (and continues round to Le Pouldu, just west of Lorient in South Brittany). From the Baie de Lannion to Île de Batz

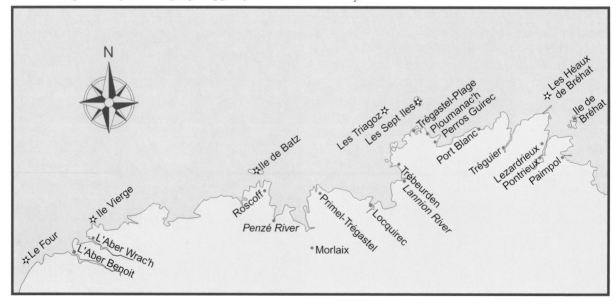

Ploumanac'h, a delightful, granite-flavoured Rosé

the principal feature is the Bay of Morlaix with its eponymous town and wide estuary to explore; plus Roscoff, handy for crew-changing.

Finistère grows wilder, more remote and more deeply Celtic the further west you go. Do not expect to find any harbour with easy access to the needs of daily life. Most British yachts making for South Brittany and beyond are at this stage intent only on carrying the tide to L'Aber Wrac'h; thence south. Moguériec and Pontusval, two very minor drying harbours, are therefore omitted.

PASSAGE NOTES

PAIMPOL TO TRÉGUIER

Tidal streams run hard around this exposed and rocky corner, especially off Île de Bréhat and in the approaches to the Trieux and Tréguier rivers. Near Plateau de la Horaine they set E at 4kn from HW Brest $-3\frac{1}{2}$; and W at $3\frac{3}{4}$kn from HWB $+2\frac{1}{2}$. Some of the more demanding minor channels, eg Chenal de la Trinité between Paimpol and Bréhat, are best not attempted for the first time at springs.

Principal landmarks include the lighthouses or bcn twrs at L'Ost Pic, Le Paon, Barnouic, Roches Douvres, Les Héaux de Bréhat and La Corne. The main outer buoys are Men-Marc'h ECM, Nord Horaine NCM and La Jument des Héaux NCM.

Correct identification of marks, some of which are distant, is crucial to safe and sound pilotage. If unsure of a mark in narrow waters it may be wise to turn back. In good weather the whole area is to be enjoyed as much for its navigational demands as for the safe havens reached by dint of your skills. Île de Bréhat, Lézardrieux, Pontrieux and Tréguier all fall into the 'must visit' category.

TRÉGUIER TO TRÉGASTEL-PLAGE

Here the coast recedes to the WSW and Les Sept Îles loom on the western horizon. From Basse Crublent PHM buoy off the mouth of the Tréguier river set course toward Basse Guazer unlit PHM buoy (NW of Port Blanc), curving north of the rhumb line to avoid Basse Laëres drying $\underline{0}$.6m and other offshore rocks.

Off Basse Crublent the stream sets west from HW Brest $+1\frac{1}{2}$; and east from $-5\frac{1}{2}$, at $3\frac{3}{4}$kn both ways. Your tidal strategy if W-bound also needs to take account of the accelerated streams in the 2.5M wide gap between Les Sept Îles and the mainland. Here the E-going stream starts at HWB $-3\frac{1}{4}$, at up to 4kn; and the W-going starts at HWB $+2\frac{3}{4}$ at up to 5kn springs. Wind over tide raises a very steep, stopping sea, so timing is crucial.

Plougrescant spire is conspic for some miles, until the lighthouse on Îles aux Moines (10M west) is in your sights.

Port Blanc, just short of Basse Guazer buoy, makes a delightfully different overnight stop in the right conditions. Otherwise consider Perros-Guirec, a traditional seaside resort with a pleasant marina. Check you are not about to be neaped.

Leave between rocky Île Tomé and the mainland, before plunging into Ploumanac'h famous for its weirdly sculpted pink granite. Around the next corner Trégastel-Plage is an equally enticing anchorage amid rocks and silver sands.

TRÉGASTEL-PLAGE TO PRIMEL-TRÉGASTEL

Next waypoint has got to be Bar-ar-Gall WCM buoy where you pass between Les Triagoz (lt ho) and the mainland's offlying reefs, en route maybe to

L'Ost Pic lighthouse

town it is interesting and well placed for a visit to the Île de Batz. But the harbour makes no concessions to yachts which must dry against a rough jetty. With the construction of a fish quay and market near Bloscon ferry terminal, a new marina is said to be planned for this area.

If passage-making to the west, squeeze through the Canal de l'Île de Batz on the first of the W-going stream at HW Brest $-4\frac{1}{2}$, so as to carry a fair tide as far as L'Aber Wrac'h, L'Aber Benoit or the Chenal du Four if everything is going for you. L'Aber Wrac'h or L'Aber Benoit are useful staging posts where you can refine your timing or await a weather improvement. From L'Aber Wrac'h it is possible to carry a fair tide, via the Chenal du Four and Raz de Sein, to Audierne – a good day's run (55M) for an average family crew.

L'ABER WRAC'H TO THE CHENAL DU FOUR

This section lies beyond the coverage of this book, but it may help those planning the next stage. The shortest practicable route (about 10M) from Libenter buoy is via Basse Paupian WCM buoy (48°35´·37N 04°46´·18W) to 48°31´·50N 4°49´·00W, 5 cables west of Le Four lt ho. From this waypoint, which can be labelled 'LF', please consult the *West France Cruising Companion* (Featherstone/Nautical Data Ltd) for the Chenal du Four proper.

The leg from Libenter to Basse Paupian passes safely about 3 cables to seaward of the outliers of Roches de Portsall (of *Amoco Cadiz* notoriety). If you feel the need for more searoom, take the slightly longer route via Grande Basse de Portsall WCM buoy (48°36´·78N 04°46´·05W), instead of Basse Paupian; thence to 'LF'.

Note that these two WCM buoys are only 1.4M apart and could be confused. Basse Paupian is however a small, unlit spar buoy; Grande Basse de Portsall is a far larger, lattice-structure light buoy with solar panels, radar reflector and whistle.

Trébeurden. The marina, with its generous tidal window, is a good base for more rock-hopping either north around Île Grande or south into the Baie de Lannion.

It is a good idea to recce Le Yaudet and the Lannion river by bike or on foot from Trébeurden (3M+), before committing yourself. Locquirec is an attractive seaside resort where you can stay afloat off the golden sands. From there it is an easy hop westward to Primel-Trégastel, passing between the offshore Plateau de la Méloine and Les Chaises de Primel – before venturing into the Baie de Morlaix.

PRIMEL-TRÉGASTEL TO L'ABER WRAC'H

At this stage, you either press on to L'Aber Wrac'h and southwards, or linger at the attractive old city of Morlaix. This is a haven away from the offshore hurly-burly, if you or your crew feel the need. The estuary requires not too demanding pilotage to lock in on the flood tide. Carantec and the Penzé river are fascinating sidelines.

Roscoff is far more than a ferryport; as a

DISTANCE TABLE
Approximate distances in nautical miles are by the most direct route, whilst avoiding dangers

		1	2	3	4	5	6	7	8	9	10	11	12	13	14	15	16
1.	St Quay-Portrieux	**1**															
2.	Paimpol	15	**2**														
3.	Bréhat (Port Clos)	15	8	**3**													
4.	Lézardrieux	21	14	6	**4**												
5.	Tréguier	46	29	22	22	**5**											
6.	Perros-Guirec	37	35	28	28	21	**6**										
7.	Ploumanac'h	40	33	27	29	25	6	**7**									
8.	Trébeurden	48	44	38	40	32	17	11	**8**								
9.	Lannion	52	48	42	44	33	21	15	6	**9**							
10.	Morlaix	67	64	58	60	46	36	30	23	24	**10**						
11.	Roscoff	59	58	52	54	41	28	22	17	19	12	**11**					
12.	L'Aberwrac'h	91	88	82	84	72	60	54	49	51	48	32	**12**				
13.	L'Aberbenoit	92	89	83	85	76	61	55	50	52	45	33	7	**13**			
14.	Lampaul	114	110	104	106	98	83	77	72	74	67	55	29	28	**14**		
15.	Le Conquet	114	110	104	106	98	83	77	72	71	68	55	29	23	17	**15**	
16.	Brest (marina)	125	119	114	114	107	92	86	83	87	79	67	42	41	31	18	**16**

PAIMPOL

Jetée de Kernoa – 48°47´·16N 03°02´·36W

Paimpol still dwells on its past, but what a past and what a nautical heritage. In the 18th century, from spring until autumn, men went to fish off Newfoundland's Grand Banks, and off Iceland in the 19th century. Kids of 12 went too, returning as young men. Conditions were harsh and 2,000 men died in one eighty year period. The catch was Cod. Today it is scallops – closer to home.

Pierre Loti, the eccentric ex-naval officer from Rochefort, championed their cause in his book *Pêcheurs d'Islande*, but by the 1930s the Icelandic trade had died. Today only a few of the shipowners' granite mansions remain; one such houses Le Repaire de Kerroc'h overlooking the harbour. The town has character as well as a welcoming ambience.

SHORESIDE

Tourist Office is SSW of the port and Place de la République. ☎ 02 96 20 83 16; ✆ 02 96 55 11 12. tourisme.paimpol@wanadoo.fr Open Mon–Sat in season 0900–1930; Sun/Hols 1000–1300.

What to see/do Musée de la Mer (rue de Labenne; 1030–1230 & 1430–1800; €4.05) recounts Paimpol's fishing history. A Museum of Costumes (Breton) is nearby. Or cycle an easy 3km SE of Paimpol to the partly ruined, 13th century Abbaye de Beauport (AC 3673). www.abbaye-beauport.com. Concerts are held there on Thur evenings; see the Tourist Office.

Buses No 9 goes 26km SW to St Brieuc and north to L'Arcouest whence vedettes run to Île de Bréhat. No 7 goes W via Lézardrieux & Tréguier to Lannion. Timetables from the Tourist Office.

Rail A local train runs scenically via Pontrieux to Guingamp (40 mins), thence TGV to Paris or Brest.

Taxi ☎ 02 96 22 05 87.

Car hire Landais, Garage Citroën, ☎ 02 96 55 33 80.

Bike hire See the Tourist Office.

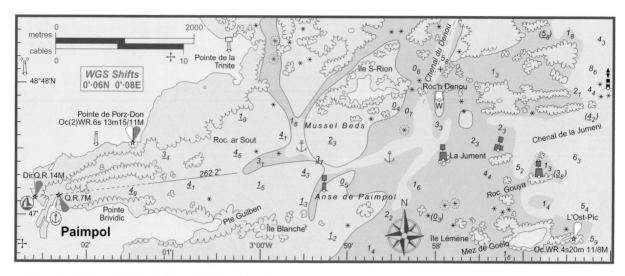

L'Ost-Pic lighthouse and islands

UK access Via St Malo ferry. Airports at Lannion and St Brieuc.

Beaches Plage de la Tossen about 600m E of the lock with LW swimming pool.

Supermarkets Marché Plus, by the Tourist Office, Mon–Sat 0700–2100 & Sun morning; also

Roc'h Denou's distinctive beacon

a small Proxi. Le Clerc hypermarket is 1km W of town on rue Becot.

Market day Tuesday mornings; fascinating fish.

Banks All the usual in town.

Launderette Lavomatique, rue de Labenne (off SE corner of Bassin 1); daily 0730–2100. Au Lavoir Paimpolais facing the rail station; daily 0800–2100.

Restaurants At the SW corner of Bassin 2 are: Le Repaire de Kerroc'h, ☎ 02 96 20 50 13; stylish, cosy dining; €13 to 29. L'Islandais, ☎ 02 96 20 93 80; next door and even more popular. Excellent €24 menu; book early for a table in the inner sanctum which replicates a timbered hull. Restaurant du Port, ☎ 02 96 20 83 18; very good seafood on the first floor overlooking the harbour. At Bassin 1's SE corner, La Cotriade, ☎ 02 96 20 81 08 catches the last of the evening sunshine; €17, 22 & 26. Le Terre-Nuevas, ☎ 02 96 55 14 14, on the corner is a traditional hotel/restaurant; €13.50, 16, 20 and 26. For a change dive into the Vieux Quartier to the Mexican El Pachuca, ☎ 02 96 20 59 22, at 26 rue des Huit Patriotes; national specialities, plus take-away.

NAVIGATION

Charts AC 2669 (1:150,000), 3670 (1:50,000), 3673 (1:20,000 including 1:10,000 inset) plus SC 5604. SHOM 6966 (1:150,000), 7152 (1:48,700), 7154 (1:50,000) and 7127 (1:20,000).

Approaches From the N, skirt E of Île de Bréhat via the charted Ch de Bréhat 167°, thence Ch du Denou 193° (wide in Breton terms and easy once Denou beacon has been identified), joining Ch de la Jument WNW of La Jument bcn twr. At HW±3 most boats will have enough water.

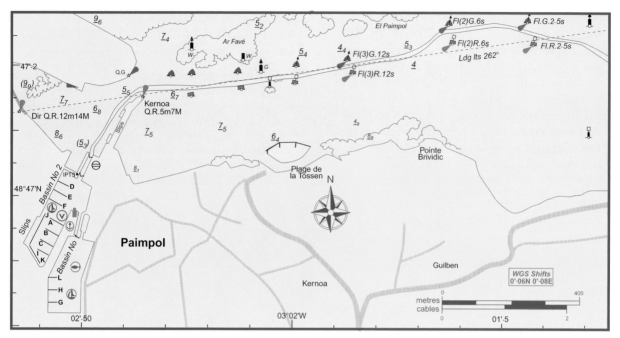

From the S, set course direct to the waypoint or cut the corner past L'Ost-Pic lt ho, Gouayan PHM bcn twr and La Gueule PHM buoy.

From the W, ie the Trieux River, pass south of Île de Bréhat heading E x N through the charted Ferlas Channel; then skirt E of Banc des Cormorandière to the outer waypoint.

Or take one of four lesser channels which short-cut south through the extensive reefs off Pointe de l'Arcouest; all require careful pilotage. From W to E they are: Chenal de la Trinité (poorly marked); Lastel (rather easier, but longer); St Rion (offshoot from Denou); or Ch du Denou 193° (see above).

Landmarks Les Charpentiers ECM bcn twr and La Jument PHM bcn twr bracket the Chenal de la Jument. Le Grand Mez de Goëlo is a substantial green island 3 cables W of L'Ost-Pic lt ho. Île St Rion is a twin-peaked island NW of La Jument. Identify all marks carefully (none is totally unique or conspicuous) – if in doubt or poor visibility, opt for Ch de la Jument.

Pilotage The outer waypoint for Ch de la Jument, the main channel, is 48°47'·84N 02°54'·93W, 260°/5M to Jetée de Kernoa. The front mark, summit of Pointe Brividic, is an ill-

The buoyed channel at LW looking E from Jetée de Kernoa

defined wooded mound easily confused with the nearer and similar Pointe de Guilbèn. The rear ldg mark is the N'ly of two spires in the town. At about 2M to run weave a way through oyster bed withies.

The inner 262° ldg lts, both QR, lead into the last 0.5M of well buoyed channel to Jetée de Kernoa (Lat/Long under Title), but are hard to see against a low evening sun. Nos 1 & 2 buoys, Fl R/G 2.5s, form an inner waypoint at 48°47′·25N 03°01′·61W.

Tides HW Paimpol at sp is 10 mins and at nps 5 mins before HW St Malo. LW at sp is 35 mins and at nps 25 mins before LW St Malo. MHWS is 10·8m, MLWS 1·4m; MHWN is 8·4m, MLWN 3·8m. Paimpol is a French Standard Port.

Tidal streams in the Anse de Paimpol set mainly S/SW on the flood and N/NE on the ebb. Rates average 2.5kn, but 3.5kn in Chenal du Denou and 5kn in Chenal de la Trinité.

Access The lock, 60m x 12m with sill drying 3.3m, is user-friendly with vertical ropes on both sides. It opens HW±2½, H24, if height of tide is >10m; if less HW±2. Freeflow may be in force near HW for as little as 10 mins to as long as 80 mins at springs. If cutting it fine, try passing your ETA to the lock-keeper, VHF Ch 09 or ☎ 02 96 20 90 02.

VHF Call Ch 09 *Écluse de Paimpol* for lock; *Maison des Plaisanciers* for marina.

IPTS (sigs 2 and 3) are shown from the W side of the lock entrance. No signals mean either that the lock is not operating or that freeflow is in force.

Anchorages Yachts can stay afloat 1 cable W of La Jument PHM bcn twr in 7m; 1 cable SW of Denou beacon in 6.6m; or 4 cables NNW of Roc'h ar Zel PHM beacon in 6m.

FACILITIES

The Bureau du Port (HM the very helpful Jean-Louis Le Bitoux) is on the E side of Bassin No 2. ☎/🖷 02 96 20 47 65. VHF Ch 09. Hours are variable as posted, plus lock times.

Berthing ⓥ berths in Bassin No 2 on pontoon 'A', with fingers, dead ahead as you exit the lock; or as directed by the HM. Yachts larger than 12m LOA may berth/raft on the pontoon along the W side of the Bassin. Bassin No 1 is for mega yachts, FVs and locals; its former lock gates are always open.

Tariff Daily rates € on pontoons, year round, for LOA bands: <8m = 14.30; <9m = 15.40; <10m = 16.65; <11m = 17.55; <12m = 18.50; <13m = 19.45; <14m = 20.35; <15m = 21.45; <16m = 22.70.

Showers by access code and jetons €1.

Fuel Diesel only at fuel pontoon, N of 'A' pontoon.

YC CNPL by the Maison des Plaisanciers.

Chandlery & repairs ENE of Bassin 2 are several largish boatyards: Dauphin Nautic, ☎ 02 96 22 01 72, CH, repairs, open daily. Le Lionnais, ☎ 02 96 20 85 18, motors (Yamaha, Volvo). Charpentiers Paimpolais, ☎ 02 96 22 09 27, traditional wood repairs. Christian Reynaud, ☎ 02 96 20 82 72, mechanical repairs. Paimpol-Voiles, ☎ 02 96 55 00 25, sailmaker. In town Cooperative Maritime, 46 ave Gen de Gaulle, CH, ☎ 02 96 20 80 22.

Maison des Plaisanciers (HM's office)

ÎLE DE BRÉHAT

Men Joliguet beacon – 48°50´·18N 03°00´·12W

Bréhat has been likened to a jewel which fell to earth and shattered into a thousand fragments. The two large fragments, linked by a tiny bridge, are those that we treasure and enjoy; the other 998 pieces we do our best to avoid.

Inevitably this heavenly spot is invaded every day in season by Gallic hordes, yet somehow they are absorbed. If you seek peace, become a creature of the night (when they have all gone home) – or at least dry out in La Corderie, since only the hardier invaders reach the northern fragment.

In the southern fragment Le Bourg (the town) is a micro-metropolis which threatens to lure Bréhat into the 21st century. You get the picture?

SHORESIDE

The Tourist Office (Syndicat d'Initiative) is in Le Bourg. ☎ 02 96 20 04 15; 📠 02 96 20 06 94. From 1 Apr, open Tues, Thur, Fri, Sat 1000–1230 & 1400–1730.

What to see/do Walk, swim or be lazy depending on your metabolism. Fish (*au pied* if needs be), paint or take photographs, according to your artistry. Eat, drink etc, as your palate demands. The 17th century mill SW of Chapelle St Michel has been restored and should be included on your walk.

Buses No 9 runs from St Brieuc via Binic, St Quay-Portrieux and Paimpol to Pte de l'Arcouest.

Ferry 10 mins crossing from l'Arcouest to Port Clos, €6.50 return; roughly on the hour from Port Clos and at the half-hour from l'Arcouest. NB: the LW ferry landing facing Près Noires SHM bcn twr is far enough away to cause you to miss the boat.

Bike hire At Port Clos for €11 per day.

Beaches Guerzido beach, SSE of Port Clos, is a pleasant cove with enough sand to call it a beach.

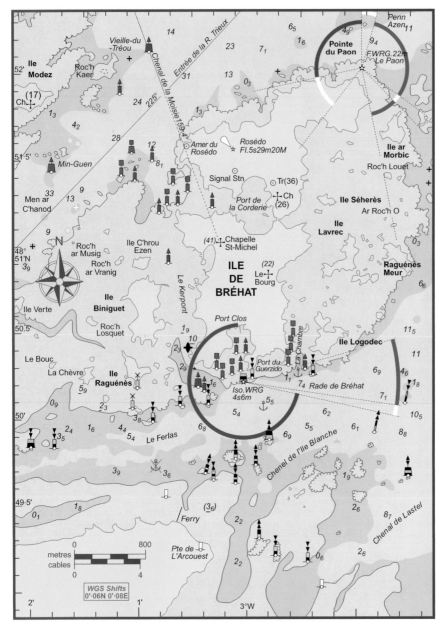

Supermarkets Huit à Huit, believe it or not, has set up shop in Le Bourg, along with butchers, bakers.

Market day Every morning in Jul/Aug.

Banks One in Le Bourg, but no cash machine.

Restaurants At Port Clos the hotel/restaurant Bellevue capitalises on its position; menus are a hefty €21 & 30.50. In Le Bourg menus are a more modest €14, 16.50 or 18 at Les Pêcheurs; but probably more at La Vieille Auberge. Far better to eat affordable moules/seafood in rather pleasant surroundings at La Potinière, a relaxed water's edge eatery by Guerzido beach.

NAVIGATION

Charts AC 2669 (1:150,000), 3670 (1:50,000), 3673 (1:20,000) plus SC 5604. SHOM 6966 (1:150,000), 7152 (1:48,700), 7154 (1:50,000) and 7127 (1:20,000).

Approaches Bréhat and its rocky archipelago are shaped like a triangle: Le Ferlas channel forms the E/W base; The Grand Chenal, ie the entry channel to the Trieux River, runs NE/SW as the hypotenuse, whilst the Chenal du Bréhat 168° is the third, eastern flank.

Le Ferlas channel leads from either end toward the anchorages off Port Clos and in La Chambre. Grand Chenal gives access to La Corderie.

Access is straightforward if on the tide and taking account of the wind of the day.

Landmarks Le Paon (the Peacock) lt ho at the NE tip is so called because of the pink/orange rocks on which it stands. SW of it Rosédo lt ho, Amer du Rosédo (a white obelisk) and the Signal Station are all conspic; as is Chapelle St Michel, with spire and red roof, high in the centre of the island.

La Corderie, looking NNW towards Chenal de la Moisie

Pilotage The two waypoints are:
a) In Le Ferlas, 48°50´·00N 03°00´·00W, 2 cables SE of the entrance to Port Clos; and
b) In Grand Chenal, 48°51´·70N 03°01´·02W, 165° 0.5M to the entrance to La Corderie. This channel is described under Lézardrieux.

Anchorages/moorings Clockwise from the S: La Chambre is a popular anchorage between Bréhat and Île Logodec; to the N it dries and there is a No Anchoring area. Pick up a ⚓ or anchor as far in as possible to escape the strong tides. Guerzido bay, close W of La Chambre, dries but anchorage or a ⚓ may be found E of Men Allan ECM bcn.

Port Clos dries completely; frequent ferries berth on HW, mid-tide and LW landings. Dry out clear of these or anchor S of Men Joliguet.

Le Kerpont leads W then N from Men Joliguet; a few moorings are laid NW of Pierres Noires SHM bcn in about 2m. Underwater cables limit anchoring space, the stream is strong but holding good. Enter La Corderie between Amer du Rosédo and Gosrod PHM bcn twr, thence lateral perches lead S and ESE. Dry out on firm, level sand; best at neaps. Shelter is good. A N/S underwater cable is just E of the last SHM perch.

Tides HW Île de Bréhat at sp is 13 mins and at nps 8 mins before HW St Malo. LW at sp is 40 mins and at nps 37 mins before LW St Malo.

MHWS is 10·4m, MLWS 1·3m; MHWN is 8·0m, MLWN 3·8m. Differences for Les Héaux de Bréhat are given in the *RNA*.

Tidal streams in Grand Chenal, abeam Rosédo, set inwards from HW Brest –4 and outward from HWB +2, max spring rates 3¾kn. In Le Ferlas the tides set E and W at the same times and rates as above.

FACILITIES

Things that do not exist at Bréhat VHF, IPTS, marinas, HMs, tariffs, showers, fuel for yachts, chandlery/repairs.

Above: Restored tidal mill SW of Chapelle St Michel
Below: Looking N into La Chambre

Chapelle St Michel, the most conspicuous daymark on Bréhat

Chapter 8

LÉZARDRIEUX

Marina, No 3 pontoon – 48°47´·39N 03°05´·81W

For many English yachtsmen Lézardrieux is the epitome of North Brittany: Accessible at all tides and in most weathers; strong tides in the outer approaches, but undemanding pilotage once in the shelter of the river. Ashore it is totally peaceful amid attractive wooded scenery.

Expect no night-clubs nor a wide choice of eating places and shops – and you will enjoy the simple pleasures of life in a small Breton village which is but a short climb up from the port.

SHORESIDE

Tourist Office is up the hill in the Place du Centre. ☎ 02 96 22 14 25. Open mid-Jun to mid-Sep, Mon–Sat 1000–1230 & 1500–1830, Sun 1000–1230.

What to see/do An attractive walk starts with a rocky scramble along the foreshore (LW only) past Perdrix, through a botanical area to Coatmer rear ldg light or Bodic; back via GR 34. A longer walk or bus/bike ride is out to the Sillon de

Talbert; this amazing sand/shingle spit projects 1.5M NE over drying rocky ledges toward Les Heaux de Bréhat lt ho and parallel with Passe de la Gaîne. Seaweed is studied and harvested here!

If you do not intend to sail up to Pontrieux, it is an enjoyable trip by bus to Paimpol, then steam train along the wooded river banks.

Bus No 7 goes E to Paimpol and W via Tréguier to Lannion; a spur branches N to L'Armor for the Sillon de Talbert. Timetables via the Tourist Office.

Rail From Paimpol (nearest station) via Pontrieux to Guingamp thence TGV to Paris/Brest.

La Croix (where else), a double-barrelled lighthouse

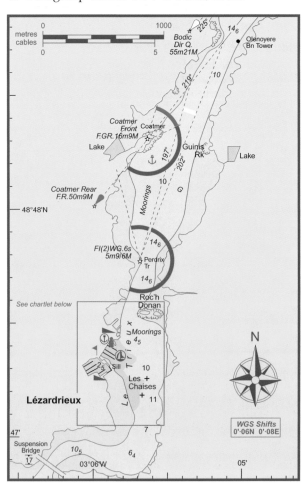

Taxi ☎ 02 96 22 65 65/06 09 82 12 12; 02 96 22 16 01.

Car & bike hire Check with the HM.

UK access Ferry from St Malo or Roscoff; or by air from Lannion or St Brieuc.

Beaches A small sandy beach is just N of the port. Plage de Traou-Treiz is close N of the bridge.

Supermarkets Casino on rue du 8 Mai, about 50m beyond the Place du Centre.

Market day Friday mornings, Place du Centre.

Banks Two in the village, both with cashpoints.

Restaurants At the port there are a few crêperies, bars, and the Restaurant du Port, ☎ 02 96 20 10 31, at the foot of the hill; €9.80 to 18. In the village, at the far end of Place du Centre turn left for 100m to L'Auberge du Trieux, ☎ 02 96 20 10 70. Strong on seafood; menus at €10 to 33. Shut Wed. The best in town – *trés, trés bon* as a local told me.

NAVIGATION

Charts AC 2669 (1:150,000), 3670 (1:50,000), 3673 (1:20,000 including 1:10,000 inset) plus SC 5604. SHOM 6966 (1:150,000), 7152 (1:48,700), 7126 (1:20,000) and 7127 (1:20,000). Note: SHOM 7126 bridges the 'gap' in the Passe de la Gaîne between AC 3672 and 3673. For walking/cycling the IGN 1:25,000 map 0814 OT covers Paimpol to Tréguier.

Approaches The Grand Chenal 225° is the main channel; see Pilotage for the waypoint. From Guernsey, the Plateau des Roches Douvres and de Barnouic (12M & 8M respectively to the waypoint) must be avoided. La Horaine lt ho (1.5M SE of the WPT) and Les Héaux de Bréhat lt ho (5.7M W of the WPT) funnel you into the Chenal de la Moisie or Grand Chenal. Lay off for the strong E-going flood across the ldg line, or the W-going ebb.

Looking south over La Croix into the Trieux River

Above: Suspension bridge upstream of the marinas. Note the coaster coming down river
Below: 159° leading marks for Chenal de la Moisie

Amer du Rosédo

Chapelle St Michel

Above: Coatmer front leading light and Lost Mor
Below: Perdrix light; marina beyond

From the E, route direct to the Ferlas Channel. From the W or NW, Chenal de la Moisie 159° joins the Grand Chenal NW of Île de Bréhat; it also links with Passe de la Gaîne, the shortest route between the Trieux and Jaudy Rivers; see Tréguier.

Landmarks Les Héaux de Bréhat is a 48m high, gaunt, grey lt ho. La Horaine is a 13m high, grey, eight-sided lt ho. On Île de Bréhat the lighthouses at Pte du Paon and Rosédo are both prominent; as are the Signal station, Rosédo's white obelisk and the distinctive Chapelle St Michel. A key feature is La Croix, a double-barrelled white/red-topped lt ho near the junction of Grand Chenal and Le Ferlas.

Pilotage Grand Chenal waypoint is 48°54′·70N 02°56′·55W, 225°/6.2M to La Croix lt ho, the front ldg mark, Oc 4s. The rear mark, Bodic, Q, appears on the skyline. About 1M before La Croix jink 10° stbd onto the inner 219° ldg line: front Coatmer, F RG; rear FR, hard to see amongst trees. The white sector (197–202.5°) of Les Perdrix then takes you the final 0.5M to the marina. By day the last 3.5M from La Croix are usually undemanding.

The Chenal de la Moisie waypoint is 48°54′·90N 03°02′·63W (also valid for the Passe de la Gaîne), on the 159° transit of Rosédo obelisk and Chapelle St Michel; least depth 1.3m. Leave La Moisie ECM twr, An Ogejou Bihan ECM bcn & Vieille du Tréou

Riverside anchorage

SHM bcn close to stbd. Watch the tidal stream.

Le Ferlas waypoint is 48°50´·38N 02°57´·09W (also valid for Chenal du Denou), 257°/3.7M to Rompa IDM bcn. Easiest to hop along the Bréhat side past seven SCM bcns to Rompa; thence enter the R Trieux 1M SW of La Croix lt ho. FVs are often moored in the stream off Loguivy. At night stay in the white sectors of Loguivy Dir lt Q WRG (257°–257.7°) and Kermouster Dir lt Fl WRG 2s (270°–272°).

Tides HW Lézardrieux at sp and nps is 10 mins before HW St Malo. LW at sp is 47 mins and at nps 37 mins before LW St Malo. MHWS is 10·5m, MLWS 1·3m; MHWN is 8·0m, MLWN 3·7m.

Tidal streams in the outer Grand Chenal reach 3¾kn at springs; the E-going stream turns S towards Bréhat and the W-going stream turns N towards Plateau des Sirlots. In the R Trieux they follow the river axis, reducing greatly as you tuck into the marina, but off the E bank and at the bridge they are strong.

Access H24 at all tides and virtually all weather. The inner marina is entered over a sill 4.9m above CD; a flapgate lowers with 6.15m rise of tide to give 1.25m or more clearance. The flapgate is marked by PHM/SHM perches with depth gauge; and the retaining wall by five SPM perches.

VHF Ch 09 Marina.

IPTS (sigs 2 and 4) are shown only at the entrance to the inner marina.

Anchorages Two outer anchorages are charted at Rade de Pommelin (4 cables NW of La Croix lt ho) in 6–9m and at La Traverse (8 cables NE of La Croix) in 11m; holding is good in both places. The river banks are mostly flanked by oyster beds, but space may still be found. There is little or no room to anchor off the marina due to mooring trots.

FACILITIES

The Bureau du Port (HM Thierry Calliot) faces pontoon 3. ☎ 02 96 20 14 22, 📠 02 96 22 18 31. VHF Ch 09. In season 0700–2200; out of season 0800–1200/1330–1730, Sun/Hols 0800–1200/ 1500–1800.

Berthing Four options: a) ♥ finger berths on N side only of No 3 pontoon, near the outer end; b) In the inner marina where up to 20 ♥ berths in 2.5m may be available, with the HM's consent; c) On a 30m long ♥ pontoon in the stream just N of Petite Chaise white beacon; and d) On ⚓s E of the marina and beween Pte de Coatmer and Perdrix beacon off the W bank.

NB: Pontoons are floodlit by shoreside arc lamps which effectively destroy your night vision; blue lights on the end of pontoons 1–3 are no more.

Tariff Daily rates € on pontoons, year round, for LOA bands: <8.5m = 14.50; <9.5m = 16.50; <10.5m = 18; <11.5m = 21; <12.5m = 25; <13.5m = 26.50; <14.5m = 28.50; <15.5m = 30.50; >15.5m = 33.50. The fee for buoys is approx two thirds of the above rates.

Shower blocks face No 3 pontoon (open H24) and the 'new' marina, access by code. Jetons €1.50.

Fuel Diesel and petrol at root of pontoon 3. Open Mon–Sat 0830–1130 & 1330–1700; Sun/ Hols 0830–1130 & 1500–1700.

YC YC de Trieux, ☎ 02 96 20 10 39; draught Guinness served.

Launderette Lavomatique in the YC de Trieux.

Chandlery & repairs Behind the inner marina are two boatyards: Trieux Marine, ☎ 02 96 20 14 71, CH, repairs; and Ateliers du Trieux, ☎ 02 96 22 16 37.

On the quay: Voiles Performance, ☎ 02 96 20 10 62, sailmaker. Technique Gréement (behind the YC), ☎ 02 96 22 10 94; rigger.

PONTRIEUX

Lock entrance – 48°42´·84N 03°08´·23W

Pontrieux is as far as yachts can navigate the Trieux River. It is also an ancient and charming town reached through the densely wooded and craggy upper reaches. Your Companion strongly recommends that you make the passage; you will not regret it and for some crew-members an inland sortie may be a welcome break from rock-dodging at sea.

The town is a haunt of artists and craft workshops and is proud of the ancient, now restored, *lavoirs* (washplaces) along the river bank. In summer the whole place is ablaze with flowers.

SHORESIDE

Tourist Office is in the Maison de la Tour Eiffel, a fine blue/white timbered house on Place Le Trocquer. ☎/📠 02 96 95 14 03. Open Jul/Aug, daily 1030–1830. tourisme.pontrieux@wanadoo.fr; www.pontrieux.com

What to see/do The sternly impressive Château de la Roche Jagu merits a visit; 4.5km from town – on your bike! Open 1000–1900 Jul/Aug; other months 1030–1230 & 1400–1800. A tourist steam train runs, mid-Jun to end Sep, along the banks of the R Trieux to Paimpol; return €20. An SNCF train continues to Guingamp, a traditional Breton town now ringed by light industry.

Rail The station is Pontrieux Gare, behind the Bureau du Port, not Portrieux Halte which is in the town. Trains to Paimpol (20 mins) and to Guingamp (25 mins) for TGV to Paris and Brest.

Buses None.

Taxi ☎ 02 96 95 67 08; 02 96 95 60 43; 02 96 95 62 89.

Car & bike hire See the HM or Tourist Office.

Supermarkets Intermarché is 300m west of the Town Hall on the rue de l'Eperonnerie.

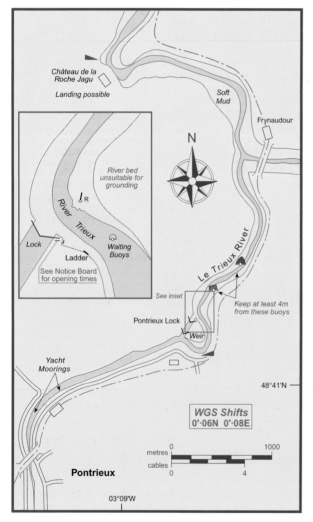

Note the sand-dredger in the lock

The port looking north

Market day Monday morning.

Launderette Le Lavoir (next to Tourist Office); 0900–1200 & 1400–1900, shut Tues.

Banks Enough in the centre.

Restaurants On the quayside are two contrasting restaurants: La Sterne, ☎ 02 96 95 19 55, with menus at €18, 26 and 36. A few doors on, Chez Jacqueline (formerly the grisly named Café de l'Abattoir) is a cheap and cheerful place for an *ouvrier* lunch. In town try: Le Pontrev, ☎ 02 96 95 60 22, at €13 & 19. Le Bilig du Trieux, crêperie, ☎ 02 96 95 33 00.

Looking up-river into the lock

NAVIGATION

Charts Admiralty and SHOM charts do not cover the R Trieux south of Lézardrieux, but Pontrieux HM has produced an excellent free plan of the river with notes. The IGN walkers' map, 0814 OT (1:25,000), gives very useful coverage (including Paimpol, Bréhat and the R Jaudy to Tréguier). It is also compatible with GPS, if you feel the need.

Timing It helps, but is not essential, to start from Lézardrieux so as to refine the timing. From there to Pontrieux lock is 6.5M. With the flood under you, allow $1\frac{1}{2}$ hrs for this passage.

The lock (see below) opens from local HW−2 to HW+$1\frac{1}{2}$ in summer; in winter HW−$1\frac{1}{2}$ to HW+$1\frac{1}{4}$. These times are straight from the *eclusier's* mouth, despite what you hear/read elsewhere!

Aim to be at the lock at local HW−1; see Tides. Not only is a rising tide always a good idea, but this time may also deconflict you from *sabliers* (sand coasters) which occasionally use the lock at HW. Therefore you should leave, or pass, Lézardrieux at $2\frac{1}{2}$ hrs before HW at the lock.

Landmarks Château de la Roche Jagu stands high above the river on a sharp bend to port, 2M from the lock; a slip and waiting buoy lie below. Beyond the lock SECMA is a large, ugly sand/gravel works to which you should turn a Nelsonian eye.

Pilotage No waypoints are given, apart from the Lat/Long of the lock (see under Title), which of course gives only a crow-fly distance to run.

Well sheltered in all winds

At Lézardrieux bridge slalom through the S-bend marked by four beacon towers; pick your way across the wide expanse opening before you to the first PHM perch; there are few marks. Thereafter stick to the outside of the high cliffy bends, shunning the shallows inside. Pause if early at Roche Jagu. 1M beyond, watch the echosounder carefully as you pass a conspic blue rail bridge where the R Leff flows in from port. Above the lock, the semi-canalised river leads about 1M to the yacht berths on the port side, with viaduct and town beyond.

Tides The river is distinctly tidal up to the lock, where the time of HW is the same as the time of HW St Malo.

Tidal streams largely follow the axis of the river.

Access The upper reaches, lock and port are all well sheltered. In a southerly gale, the calm and tranquillity were in sharp contrast to conditions downstream of Lézardrieux.

Overhead clearances Lézardrieux bridge has the least clearance at 17m above MHWS. Two sets of power cables upstream have 24m and 25m.

The lock is 65 x 12m with a sill 3.5m above CD. It is used mainly by yachts and occasional *sabliers*. With one of these in the lock (and they are well handled) there is still room for a few yachts. There are no vertical ropes on the lock sides and only a ladder at each end. The *éclusier* will therefore take your warps round minuscule metal bollards which resemble toadstools. ☎ 02 96 95 60 70, but mobile phone signal strength is poor in the valley. Two red waiting buoys lie to port of the lock as you arrive. Do not go beyond these into a drying nautical cul-de-sac for locals, with weir and salmon leap at the far end.

VHF Ch 12 for both the lock (*Écluse de Pontrieux*) and the port (*Port de Pontrieux*).

IPTS *Il n'y en a pas.* The lock-keeper is most likely to wave you into the lock or clear you in on VHF.

FACILITIES

The Bureau du Port (HM Yves Fertier) is on the quayside. ☎/🖷 02 96 95 34 87. VHF Ch 12. Open at lock times and as required.

David Fletcher, the ex-pat assistant HM, died July 2001. He did much to put Pontrieux on the map and is greatly missed.

Berths Alongside the stone quay to port or rafted; do not go beyond the blue crane (5 ton). **FW** and **electricity** available.

Tariff Daily rates €, in season, for LOA bands: <7m = 7.80; <8m = 10.70; <9m = 12; <10m = 13.10; <11m = 15.50; <12m = 17.60; <13m = 19.20; <14m = 22.40; >14m = 1.59 for each extra metre.

Showers alongside the Capitainerie, are by jeton.

Launderette Only in town.

Fuel None, but HM loans a trolley to fetch diesel and petrol from garage by the viaduct.

Chandlery & repairs None. Consult the HM.

Flower market with Tourist Office behind

TRÉGUIER

Marina, 'E' pontoon – 48°47´·29N 03°13´·17W

Tréguier, religious capital of the Trégor region, is full of appeal. Its famous cathedral steeple, perforated by geometrical shapes, only comes into view about 2M from the marina; thereafter it dominates the port and ancient market town.

Place du Martray almost encircles the cathedral and is a lively and picturesque hub, surrounded by fine timbered houses from the 15th to 17th centuries.

St Yves, patron saint of lawyers and defender of the poor (originator of Legal Aid?), is Tréguier's most famous son. Every year on the third Sunday in May a Pardon is held in his honour, attended by international lawyers. The whole town is *en fête* and traditional Breton costumes and headgear are much in evidence.

SHORESIDE

Tourist Office is on the quayside at the foot of rue Renan (next to Hotel de l'Estuaire) in a fine old house; ☎/🖷 02 96 92 22 33. Open in season, Mon–Sat 1000–1230 & 1400–1900; Sun/Hols 1100–1300 & 1500–1800. ot-pays-de-treguier@wanadoo.fr

What to see/do Wander round the cathedral and explore the back alleys. The theologian Ernest Renan lived here; his birthplace, Maison Natale,

is now a museum, open Jul/Aug daily, 1000–1300 & 1430–1830; worth a visit on a rainy day.

A 7km bike ride N on the D8 is Plougrescant, with its seriously squiffy chapel spire. Le Gouermel, crêperie/restaurant, was recommended by a local. Continue 3km N to Pte du Château to gaze at sea, rock and a photogenic little house spectacularly sandwiched between two huge rocks. Nearby the sea thunders through Le Gouffre, a rocky cleft.

Buses No 7 goes W to Lannion or E to Paimpol via Lézardrieux. Bus D does a circular route to Lannion and back via Plougrescant and Port Blanc. Timetables from the Tourist Office.

Rail Bus to Paimpol for rail to Guingamp; or bus to Lannion for rail to Plouaret: Thence mainline or TGV to Paris, or Brest via Morlaix for Roscoff.

Taxi ☎ 02 96 92 23 55; 02 96 92 49 00.

Car hire The Elf garage, ☎ 02 96 92 30 52, behind the Capitainerie.

Chapter 8

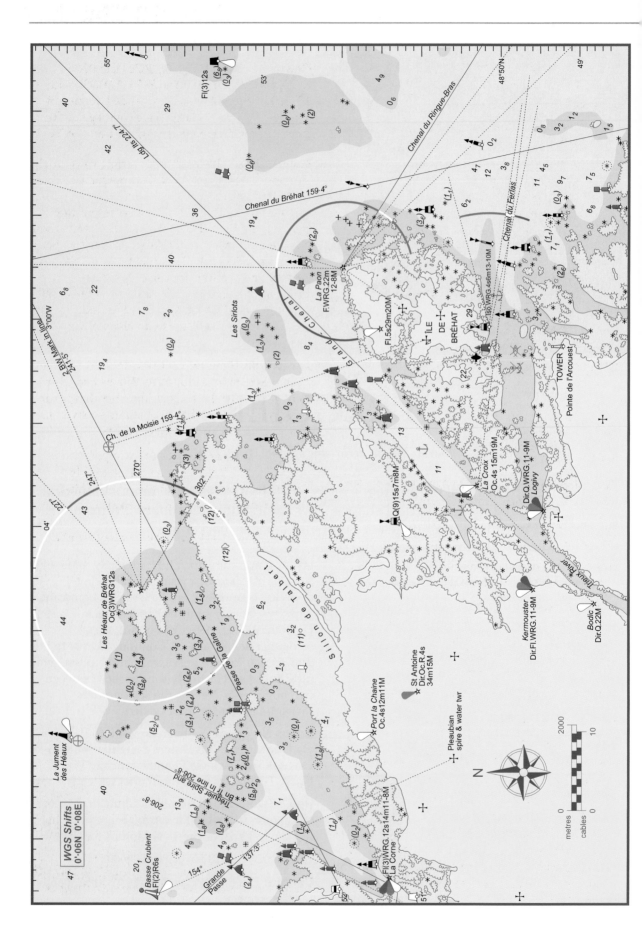

NAVIGATION

Charts AC 3670 (1:50,000), 3672 (1:15,000). SHOM 7152 (1:48,700) and 7126 (1:20,000 with 1:7,500 inset). 7126 is recommended because it bridges the 'gap' in large scale coverage of the Passe de la Gaîne between AC 3672 and 3673.

Approaches Take heed of the strong E/W tidal streams which affect the outer approaches. The three channels, from E to W, are:
a) Passe de la Gaîne 241.5°; offers interesting pilotage from the E, and is also the shortest route between Lézardrieux and Tréguier, saving about 4M against the 'outside' route. But it is relatively narrow and shallow, for use only by day.
b) Passe du Nord Est 205°/207° from the N/NE day only; distant marks are hard to find.
c) Grand Passe 137°, the main channel, by day/night.

Landmarks From the east Les Héaux de Bréhat is a 48m high, gaunt, grey lt ho. The cathedral spire may be seen whilst still offshore, but disappears behind the wooded banks when in the river. La Corne lt ho is whitish with a red base.

Pilotage a) **Passe de la Gaîne** waypoint 48°54´·90N 03°02´·63W is on the 241.5° ldg line, 3.5M from the gate at Pont de la Gaîne. (It is common to the Ch de la Moisie into Lézardrieux).

The ldg marks (front: Men Noblance white

La Corne at the mouth of the river

Bike hire Laurent Gegou, ☎ 02 96 92 31 22, ZA de Kerfolic (1.5km SW of the town).

UK access Ferry from St Malo or Roscoff; or fly from Lannion, ☎ 02 96 05 82 22.

Beaches are not much in evidence, unless you get down to the coast. Port Blanc has fine sands.

Supermarkets Huit à Huit on bd Anatole-Le-Bras, about 150m below the Mairie; open Jul/Aug, Mon–Sat 0800–2000, Sun 0900–1200; other months: Mon shut, Tues–Sat 0800–1230 & 1430–1930, Sun 0900–1200.

Market Wed all day; out of season, morning only.

Banks Several in the town with cashpoints.

Launderette Laverie 200m N of the marina on rue Marcellin Berthelot; daily 0800–2200.

Restaurants At the port Hôtel/Restaurant Aigue Marine, ☎ 02 96 92 97 00, is modern but menus from €18 to 30 are recommended. To the N next to the Tourist Office, L'Estuaire, ☎ 02 96 92 97 00, is an old favourite with first floor views across the river; €12 to 30. Up the hill in rue St Yves, L'Auberge du Trégor, ☎ 02 96 92 32 34, is cosy amongst its old stone walls; €15 to 24.50.

Les Héaux lighthouse and SHM bcn marking the N edge of Passe de la Gaîne

obelisk + black band; rear: a white wall bisected by a vert black stripe) can be hard to see due to poor visibility, low sun, distance (WPT to front mark is 6M and rear mark is 1.7M beyond). Plougrescant church spire, slightly left of the rear mark, may help.

But do not despair! From the WPT use GPS to pass close S of the first SHM perch (0.45M S of Les Héaux lt ho, as illustrated on page 447); thence to the second SHM perch and on through the gate. By then you should see the ldg marks, but ironically at this stage you scarcely need them, as you can safely head toward Le Petit Taureau SHM beacon, 300m N of La Corne.

Near LW do your tidal sums. For example, at local LW–1½ (coeff 69) least depth found at Pont de la Gaîne was 4.1m. Hug the PHM perch rather than the SHM to clear a 0.3m patch, as on SHOM 7126.

b) **Passe du Nord Est** waypoint is La Jument NCM buoy at 48°55′·42N 03°08′·03W. This Passe is little used because: It is unlit; the 205° front marks, 3M away, are hard to identify; the rear mark, Tréguier spire, is even harder, almost 9M from the WPT; and the 207° front mark, Roc'h Skeiviec, cannot easily be picked out until close. Is it worthwhile?

c) **Grand Passe** waypoint 48°54′·30N 03°11′·56W is on the 137° ldg line, 3 cables W of Basse Crublent PHM buoy. The marks (front, Port de la Chaine, Oc 4s; rear, St Antoine, Oc R 4s) are OK at night, but notoriously hard/impossible to see by day, even with binos. Instead, Pleubian spire ≠ a water tower leads 154° from Basse Crublent to Pierre à l'Anglais SHM buoy, whence Petit Pen ar Guézec SHM buoy

is only 1M on. Here turn stbd 215° for the conspic La Corne lt ho ≠ the smaller Roc'h Skeiviec white obelisk beyond. At night use La Corne's two white sectors, up and down stream. Keep E of Le Taureau, a small SHM buoy SW of La Corne.

The delightful 5M up the River Jaudy are well lit, buoyed & perched. The last 8 cables from No 12 buoy to the marina are dredged 2m and buoyed/lit, enabling a safe approach even at LW.

Tides HW Tréguier at sp is 10 mins and nps 5 mins before HW St Malo. LW at sp is 55 mins and at nps 40 mins before LW St Malo. MHWS is 9·9m, MLWS 1·3m; MHWN is 7·7m, MLWN 3·6m. Differences for Port-Béni (near La Corne lighthouse) and Les Héaux de Bréhat are given in the *RNA*.

Tidal streams set E/W at 3¾kn across the outer approaches. The E-going stream starts at HW Brest –5½ and the W-going at +1½. In the river they run true, but at a tricky angle through the marina; see Berthing.

Access Fresh to strong onshore winds, especially over tide, raise a choppy sea in the approaches.

VHF Ch 09 Marina.

Anchorages Seven anchorages are charted between Nos 1 & 10 buoys, mostly limited by

The last 3 cables to the marina are marked by small unlit buoys. Heed them well at LW

The cathedral from Pont du Canada

oyster beds, so approach carefully. Of these the last, 200m NE of No 10 buoy, is the best: clear of the fairway in a 6m pool on mud/clay, sheltered by wooded cliffs. Anchoring off the town quays is prohibited.

FACILITIES

The Bureau du Port (HM David Peron) is near pontoon 'E'. ☎/🖷 02 96 92 42 37. VHF Ch 09. In season 0700–1200 & 1330–2000; out of season 0800–1630; closed Sun, Mon, Hols.

Berthing ⓥ berths on N side fingers of 'E' pontoon (the first you reach) near outer end; or near outer ends of 'D' and 'C' pontoons; or as directed. You are strongly advised to arrive/leave at slack water which occurs at HW and LW. At these times, you won't encounter any problems.

At other times, especially mid-flood/mid-ebb, the strong tidal streams may cause difficulty. The flood sets about 190° (the ebb at 010°) through the pontoons (fingers orientated 150°/330°) – hence the tidal components are across and from astern (on the flood). OK if you are an ace on helm and throttle – if not, arrive at slack water.

One white spherical ⓥ buoy in about 1m is 450m NNW of the marina between 12 & 13 buoys.

Tariff Daily rates € (including showers) on pontoons, year round, for LOA bands: <8.5m = 13.11; <9.5m = 14.64; <10.5m = 15.40; <11.5m = 16.92; <12.5m = 19.36; <13.5m = 22.56; <14.5m = 23.93; <15.5m = 25.46; >15.5m = 26.98.

Showers below Capitainerie, access by code H24; free. **Launderette** See under SHORESIDE.

Fuel Diesel and petrol on pontoon 'E' near inner end. Open in season Mon–Sat 0800–2100 (1900 out of season); closed Sun/Hols.

YC Club Nautique du Trégor, ☎ 02 96 92 37 49.

Chandlery & repairs Co Per Marine, ☎ 02 96 92 35 72, at the E end of the Pont du Canada, is a place to travel miles for: The intoxicating smell of tarred rope, the bare creaking floorboards and above all the vast stock are reminiscent of an earlier age. Mon–Sat 0900–1200 & 1330–1900. SHOM agent.

Looking SW to the cathedral

PORT BLANC

First buoy – 48°50´.54N 03°18´.75W

Port Blanc is the very essence of a small N Brittany port. Set in spectacular rocky scenery, it happily combines a laid-back seaside resort of no great pretensions with a minor FV and yacht harbour.

If you've arrived from Lézardrieux or Tréguier, this may be your first real acquaintance with the Côte du Granite Rose. From seaward a seemingly impenetrable barrier of pink rock greets you; but from the waypoint the channel suddenly opens up – and in you go! Expect to stay longer than planned.

SHORESIDE

Tourist Office is in Place de l'Église, Penvénan, 3km south. ☎/🖷 02 96 92 81 09; www.ville-penvenan.fr Open mid-Jun to end-Aug, Mon–Sat 0930–1230 & 1400–1800; shut Sun and Hols. Other months: Thur & Sat 1000–1200.

What to see/do Walk or cycle east to Buguélès (an attractive harbour with a buoyed entry channel, recommended by the HM at Paimpol). Cross via the causeway to Île Saint-Gildas, a place of ghosts, legends and the more recent manifestation of Charles Lindbergh. Or go by dinghy to Île St-Gildas to picnic/swim off the beaches; it is an enchanted spot (old wives, fairies, elves – the lot).

Buses Line D runs infrequently to/from Tréguier and Lannion via Penvénan and Trestel.

Rail From Lannion (nearest station) to Plouaret thence TGV/mainline to Paris/Brest.

Taxi ☎ 02 96 92 64 00; 02 96 92 67 63.

Car hire ☎ 02 96 37 02 17. **Bike hire** See the HM.

UK access Ferry from Roscoff; or fly ex-Lannion airport, ☎ 02 96 05 82 22.

Beaches Good beach in front of the Grand Hotel.

Market day Saturday morning.

Supermarkets Nil, only basic alimentation.

Restaurants You can eat adequately at the Grand Hotel, ☎ 02 96 92 66 52; otherwise the usual cafés.

NAVIGATION

Charts AC 3670 (1:50,000) and 3672 (1:20,000 port plan). SHOM 7152 (1:48,700) and 7125 (1:20,000) which also has 1:10,000 insets of Perros-Guirec, Ploumanac'h and Trégastel.

Approach From the E (ie Basse Crublent PHM

Visitors' buoys, conspicuous white cottage on the left and Le Voleur lighthouse amongst the trees

buoy) stay far enough offshore to clear Basse Laëres, dries 0.6m (48°52´·93N 03°15´·80W), then make for the waypoint.

From the W approach direct, passing N of Basse Guazer PHM buoy, which marks the Plateau du Four extending 1.7M offshore. The ebb tide sets strongly west across the 150° approach toward Plateau du Four.

Landmarks Port Blanc Dir lt, an off-white tower inscribed Port Blanc, is obscured by Le Voleur (the Thief), a rocky spur in front, unless exactly on the ldg line. It is hard to spot, but with binos traverse right and up from an isolated white cottage close E to see it among trees below the skyline. The rear ldg mark, La Comtesse Mill, is 0.5M beyond on the skyline.

A white obelisk, like a Ku-Klux-Klan pointed hat, 16m amsl on an impressive rock (Île du Château Neuf) is a key mark. It is not always obvious in certain lights and tends initially to merge with the woods behind. A smaller white obelisk on Île St Gildas distracts rather than helps.

The Grand Hotel is a conspicuous white block overlooking the moorings.

Pilotage The waypoint is 48°52´·24N 03°20´·16W, on the 150° ldg line, 1.9M to the first ⚓ (see Lat/Long under Title).

From the waypoint, pass midway between the KKK hat and the only PHM perch, which define the 600m wide, deep fairway. Look out for pot floats on the way. The harbour/moorings open up in your one o'clock with the sole SHM perch beyond.

At night stay in the white sector (148°–152°) of

Ku-Klux-Klan obelisk on Île du Château Neuf

Port Blanc lt. For distance-to-go take bearings on Le Colombier light at Perros-Guirec or use GPS.

Tides Interpolate between Les Héaux de Bréhat and Perros-Guirec. MHWS is 9·0m, MHWN 6·8m.

Tidal streams set strongly across the approach; E–going from HW Brest –5, W-going from HWB+1¼. Avoid being set by the ebb onto Plateau du Four.

Access At all tides, but avoid entering in fresh to strong onshore winds, when the moorings will in any case be uncomfortable or even untenable.

VHF Ch 09 *Port Blanc*.

Moorings Five yellow ⚓s 'A'–'E', marked 'VISIT', lie close ENE of local moorings in about 5m.

Anchorages ⚓ as charted, outside the moorings in about 7m on sand/shingle. A drying ⚓ is charted S of Île St Gildas. Drying out against the jetty near the isolated white cottage or W of the Sailing School are other options.

FACILITIES

The Capitainerie (HM Thomas Le Meur) is in the Sailing School; ☎ 02 96 92 89 11. VHF Ch 09. Open 0800–1200 & 1330–1700 in season; port facilities are only available 1 Apr–31 Oct.

Tariff About €7, for all LOAs, on ⚓s.

Showers are available in the Sailing School.

Fuel, chandlery & repairs None.

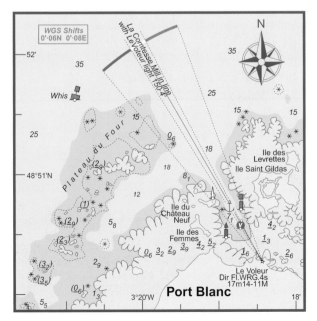

Port Blanc

Chapter 8

PERROS-GUIREC

Jetée du Linkin – 48°48´.24N 03°26´.22W

Perros, as usually abbreviated, has two souls: One the pleasant workaday harbour area, and t'other quite a classy and equally pleasant seaside resort, some 20 mins up-hill walk from the marina. Guirec, since you ask, was a 6th century saint who landed at Ploumanac'h; please read page 456 for this gripping yarn.

Perros and Ploumanac'h are overseen by the same HM in some extraordinary way, eg on my last visit in late May 2002 neither Capitainerie appeared to open at the stated times. Ploumanac'h probably only gets the full treatment in July and August.

SHORESIDE

Tourist Office is up the hill in the Place de l'Hôtel de Ville. ☎ 02 96 23 21 15, ✆ 02 96 23 04 72. Open Jul/Aug, Mon–Sat 0900–1930, Sun 1000–1230 & 1600–1900. Sep–Jun, Mon–Sat 0900–1230 & 1400–1830. infos@perros-guirec.com; www.perros-guirec.com

What to see/do Walk the coastal path (Sentier des Douaniers or GR34) from Perros to Ploumanac'h; approx 2 hrs each way with sweeping views of Les Sept Îles, Île Tomé and the pink granite sculpted by wind and weather into weird shapes which your imagination will readily identify.

See below for a brief description of Les Sept Îles.

If it's raining visit the Musée de Cire (waxworks), no match for Mme Tussaud but an interesting look at how the Revolution affected Brittany; €2.85.

Buses No 15, a round-robin route, starts/ends at Lannion taking in Perros, Trégastel, Île Grande and Trébeurden. Timetables at the Tourist Office.

Rail From Lannion (nearest station) to Plouaret (17 mins), thence TGV/mainline to Morlaix (20 mins), Brest (1 hr) or Paris (3 hrs 40 mins).

Taxi Allo Taxis ☎ 02 96 23 06 98.

Car hire ☎ Avis 02 96 91 46 23/02 96 23 20 35.

Bike hire Perros-Cycles ☎ 02 96 23 13 08, 129 rue Maréchal Joffre.

UK access Ferry via Roscoff; or fly via Lannion.

Beaches Perros boasts two immaculate N-facing beaches (Trestrignel and Trestraou) of fine sand, backed by wooded cliffs and overlooked by *fin de siècle* houses. Plage des Arcades, close N of the port, is not famous but therein lies its charm; it is uncrowded and has picnic areas – so gets my vote.

Supermarkets 200m N of the marina is Notre Marché, very small but handy, with most basics. Up in town centre a Casino is open Mon–Sat 0830–1215 & 1430–1915, Sun 0930–1230; free deliveries to boats of purchases > €85. At rue Lejeune is an Intermarché. One block away from the Tourist Office is a Marché Plus. Spoiled for choice.

Market day Friday mornings.

Launderette Laverie, close S of Capitainerie; daily.

Banks One at the port, eight in town, all of which have cashpoints.

Restaurants Facing the access pontoon Les Vieux Gréements with its bright yellow sunshades is strong on moules, very convenient and has some character. Turn left for La Marée, ☎ 02 96 23 34 13; civilised, €13 to 24.40, but closed Tues evening, all Wed & Thur evening. Le Levant, ☎ 02 96 23 23 83, is a very good first floor restaurant above Le Ponant, with marina views; €12.50 to 28.20. At the traffic lights Le Suroît, ☎ 02 96 23 23 83, is well patronised by locals; €13 to 32.

Up in town the choice is wider, especially if you include vast hotels on the cliffy tops. In the centre La Crémaillère, ☎ 02 96 23 22 08, Place de l'Eglise has menus at €14.50 to 29. Au St Yves, 11 Bd Aristide Briand, ☎ 02 96 23 21 31, is a more upmarket hotel, €12.75 to 45.75.

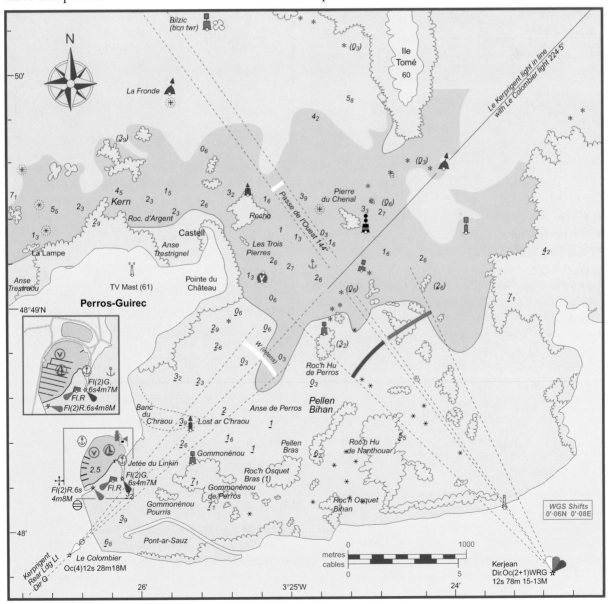

Entry gate and IPTS at High Water (top) and Low Water (above)

NAVIGATION

Charts AC 3670 (1:50,000) and 3672 (1:20,000).
SHOM 7152 (1:48,700) and 7125 (1:20,000 with
1:10,000 inset).

Approaches There are two: a) From the E, Passe
de l'Est 224.5° ldg lts lead south of Île Tomé
nearly to the marina entrance. Le Colombier, the
front mark is a white gable end below the skyline,
hard to see amid trees. Kerprigent, rear mark, is
1.5M beyond, too far away to see by day.
b) From the W/NW, Passe de l'Ouest lies

between Île Tomé and Pte du Château, in the
white sector of Kerjean 144° Dir lt on the SE shore
of Anse de Perros. It intercepts the 224.5° ldg line
400m SSW of Pierre du Chenal IDM bcn twr.

Landmarks Les Sept Îles and Île Tomé's barren
dorsal ridge are easily seen from E & W. So too is
Pte du Château with a radio mast 4 cables W of it.

Pilotage The waypoint (shared with Port Blanc)
for the 224.5° ldg line is 48°52´·24N 03°20´·16W,
5.6M from Jetée du Linkin. Respect Basse Guazer,
a small unlit PHM buoy marking Plateau du
Four. From S of Île Tomé the line is marked by a
small SHM buoy, an IDM twr (leave to stbd),
Cribineyer PHM buoy and Roc'h hu de Perros
PHM twr. After the last SHM perch, two
uncharted SHM buoys mark the channel as it
jinks S then W around local moorings.

Passe de l'Ouest waypoint, 48°51´·10N
03°26´·90W bears 144°/2.4M to the intersection
with the 224.5° ldg line. Adjacent shoals are
marked but unlit. By day Kerjean is insignificant,
and the old light, a gable end on the shoreline, is
easier to see.

Tides HW Perros-Guirec at sp is 40 mins and nps
30 mins before HW St Malo. LW at sp is 65 mins
and at nps 55 mins before LW St Malo. MHWS is
9·3m, MLWS 1·3m; MHWN is 7·4m, MLWN 3·4m.

Tidal streams in Passe de L'Est set ENE from
HW Brest –4½, and WSW from HWB +2¾; 3kn max
spring rate. In Passe de L'Ouest, at the same times,
streams set SE and NW respectively; 2¾kn max.

Access After rounding the Jetée du Linkin the
entry gate is 1 cable ahead. It is only 5.85m wide,
so care is needed. Do not emulate the more macho
French by sailing through under spinnaker.

Gate opening times, published in advance by
the HM as a function of tidal coefficients, are:

Coeff	Hours before/after HW
>70	HW±1½
60–70	HW±1
50–60	HW–1 to +½
40–50	HW–½ to HW
<40	The gate does not open.

A boat may therefore be neaped inside the marina
(or unable to enter) for one to three days; there
are many worse places to be neaped.

Entry gate opens day/night when height of tide
reaches 7.0m (the drying height of the retaining
wall). The sill below the gate dries 3.5m; so there
is 3.5m of water over the sill when the gate opens.
There is no depth gauge. Caution: For 10–15 mins

after gate opens, strong inflow/turbulence also causes a S'ly flow through the pontoons. Captain of the Gate, (Macaulay's 'brave Horatius') ☎ 02 96 23 19 03.

IPTS sigs 2 & 3, are shown from the E side of the entry gate. Outbound boats usually have priority.

VHF Marina and entry gate Ch 09.

Anchorages/moorings The nearest ⚓ is charted E of Pte du Château in about 3.5m; good holding on sand/mud. Five hard-to-see, small white waiting buoys marked VPG (Ville P–G) are closer E of Pte du Château at approx 48°49´·18N 03°25´·30W in 3m. In a S'ly gale ⚓ in complete shelter 5 cables S of La Fronde SHM buoy, off Plage de Trestrignel in 3m+. A No-Anchorage area extends 5 cables seaward of Plage de Trestraou. A good passage ⚓ is charted E of Île Tomé in 6m.

FACILITIES

The Capitainerie (HM Louis Morvan) is a former residence across the road from the access pontoon. ☎ 02 96 49 80 50; 🖷 02 96 23 37 19. VHF Ch 09. Open 0730–1200 & 1330–2000 in season and at tide times. port.perros.guirec@wanadoo.fr; www.port-perros-guirec.com

Berthing ♥ fingers are on the most N'ly pontoon (La Mutine; all pontoons are named after famous fishing boats of the past). Mean depth 2.5m.

Tariff Daily rates € on pontoons (showers inc), in season (1 Jun–30 Sep), for LOA bands: <8m = 12.50; <9m = 15.70; <10m = 17.50; <11m = 19.90; <12m = 22.50; <13m = 24.10; <14m = 25.70; <15m = 28.30; <16m = 29.90; >16m = 31.70.

Showers are free; access code to an anonymous door stbd side of Capitainerie at basement level.

Fuel Diesel and petrol at fuel pontoon N end of marina by the YC; service when the gate is open.

YC S'té des Régates Perrosienne, ☎ 02 96 91 12 65.

Chandlery & repairs Ship Marine, ☎ 02 96 91 11 88, facing the marina, is a well stocked CH. South of the town on the Lannion road are: Voilerie Erton, SM, ☎ 02 96 91 05 04. Nauti-Breiz, ☎ 02 96 91 16 07, for engineering repairs, CH, electronics. Le Locat Marine, ☎ 02 96 23 05 08, similar to the above. At the S jetty, Fl (2) R 6s, there is a slipway and concrete drying pad.

LES SEPT ÎLES

This archipelago, based on 48°52´·78N 03°29´·31W (Île aux Moines lt ho), lies 2.5M N of Mean Ruz lt ho and about 6M NNW of Perros-Guirec. The group, except for Île aux Moines and Île Bono, is a bird sanctuary, enclosed by a No Entry zone. The N side of Île Rouzic is where 18,000 pairs of gannets nest every year, whitening it with guano. Their black-tipped wings, piercing blue eyes and yellow heads are unmistakable. You may also see puffins, guillemots, cormorants, oyster catchers, auks, fulmars and grey seals.

Make good 322° from La Fronde SHM buoy toward Île aux Moines lt ho. At half tide up you will clear a 0.6m rock 300m SE of the E end of Moines. Anchor due S of the W end of Bono and E of Moines lt ho. Land at the jetty on the E tip of Moines, clear of *vedettes*.

The stream sets ENE/4kn max from HW Brest $-3\frac{1}{4}$ and WSW from HWB $+2\frac{3}{4}$. Wind against tide raises a very steep, short sea.

The same crossing can be made from Ploumanac'h on 358° with the W edge of Bono dead ahead and Men Ruz lt ho dead astern. In both cases SHOM 7125 (1:20,000) is desirable.

Île aux Moines (lt ho) and Île Bono seen from Ploumanac'h's pink granite

Château de Costaérès above and St Guirec's shrine to the right

PLOUMANAC'H

Harbour sill – 48°49´·81N 03°29´·40W

Ploumanac'h has two claims to fame: An attractive land-locked harbour and an extravaganza of pink-orange granite rocks, weirdly sculpted by wind and weather into shapes which defy belief. In season the village is gridlocked by tourists – inevitable, but a pity. The small winter population is swelled by owners of holiday homes, denizens of three large camp sites and the flood/ebb of day-trippers. But it's still worth a visit.

St Guirec came ashore at Ploumanac'h in the 6th century. Today his shrine on the beach is the object of a fanciful yarn about spinsters, desirous of marriage, sticking hairpins into his wooden nose which predictably has long since fallen off. The good Saint is now carved in granite and marriage prospects have taken a nose dive.

SHORESIDE

Tourist Office is in the village, but in early season it was never open despite a notice 'Open Mon–Sat 0900–1230 & 1400–1830' (left-over from last year?).

What to see/do Walk the coastal path (Sentier des Douaniers or GR34) from Ploumanac'h to Perros; approx 2 hrs each way with great views of Les Sept Îles and Île Tomé. Explore the omnipresent pink granite and speculate on its geological origins. Or on a more mundane level walk/cycle round the S side of the harbour to see the little tidal mill, then press on to recce your next port of call, Trégastel-Plage. Les Sept Îles can be visited by *vedette* if you don't wish to sail across.

Buses A round-robin route, Line 15, starts/ends at Lannion taking in Perros, Ploumanac'h and Trébeurden. Timetables from the Tourist Office.

Rail From Lannion (nearest station) to Plouaret (17 mins) thence TGV/mainline to Paris/Brest.

Taxi Get one from Perros.

Car hire ☎ 02 96 48 00 10.

Bike hire Check with the HM or Tourist Office.

UK access Ferry via Roscoff; or scheduled flights to Paris from Lannion airport.

Beaches The Plage de la Bastille and the Anse de St Guirec are both small sandy coves just N of the harbour entrance. The latter contains the statue of St Guirec, now in granite; see Perros-Guirec.

Supermarkets This is not a place to victual your ship, but Les Mousquetaires is NE of the port.

Banks One in the village.

Launderette In the port.

Restaurants Hôtel des Rochers, ☎ 02 96 91 44 49, overlooks the harbour; menus €15, 21 & 26. In the rather amorphous village centre, amongst various eateries jam-packed with tourists, are:

Coste Mor, ☎ 02 96 91 65 55, a Logis overlooking the Anse de St Guirec; menus €12–42. La Cotriade, ☎ 02 96 91 40 80, (Hôtel du Parc, also a Logis); menus €12.05–24.40. Plus Curraghs, Irish pub with Guinness and grub.

NAVIGATION

Charts AC 3670 (1:50,000) and 3669 (1:50,000); SHOM 7152 (1:48,700) and 7125 (1:20,000 with 1:10,000 inset). NB: AC 3670 & 3669 are too small scale to show the reefs referred to under Pilotage, the perched channel and harbour. SHOM 7125 is strongly advised, at least for a first visit.

Approaches From the E, approach between Les Sept Îles and Île Tomé, at night in the white sector of Mean Ruz lt ho. From the N (Les Sept Îles) go direct to the WPT. From the W, pass between Les Triagoz and the mainland. From E or W, if you run out of fair tide expect a rough ride if wind versus tide.

Landmarks Mean Ruz pink lt ho and the Signal Station 8 cables SSE of it are conspic. Château de Costaérès is prominent from the W, but from the E is not visible until Mean Ruz has been rounded. A cable SSW of Mean Ruz a conspic 'chapel with gargoyles' *(clocheton)* provides clearing bearings.

Pilotage The waypoint is 48°50′·47N 03°29′·12W, 2 cables NW of Mean Ruz lt ho. From here the perched channel is visible but, especially near LW, two hazards drying 1.3m must first be cleared:
   a) From the E, the reef Ar Veskleier extends 250m NW of the lt ho. To round it, track exactly 175° from the WPT until the channel opens on 216°.
   b) The rocky reef Ar Dreuzinier extends 150m NE of No 1 SHM perch; clear it by tracking as in (a).
   Keep well away from No 1 perch, aligning your track 216° with the first four PHM perches (No 2 to 8). After No 8 perch the channel trends 188° to the sill.

Tides HW Ploumanac'h at sp is 33 mins and nps 23 mins before HW St Malo. LW at sp is 1 hr 12 mins and at nps 53 mins before LW St Malo. MHWS is 9·3m, MLWS 1·4m; MHWN is 7·4m, MLWN 3·6m.

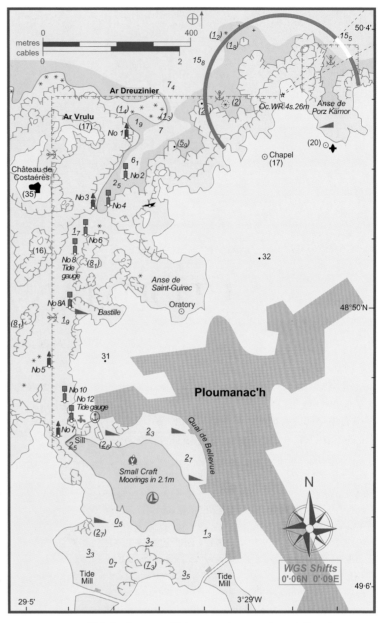

Tidal streams Take care to counteract the strong streams setting across the entrance: E-going from HW Brest –4½; W-going from HWB +1, 2¾kn max at springs but easing south of Mean Ruz.

Access In fresh to strong onshore winds the entry can be very choppy/rough; many fishing floats add to the difficulty.
   The sill which dries 2.55m is just after the last two perches, No 7 SHM and 12 PHM. Gauges on No 8 & 12 perches show depth over the sill. When the concrete base of No 5 SHM perch is covered, depth over the sill is more than 1.2m. A 1.5m draught boat with 0.5m below-keel clearance can enter approx HW±4¼ at nps and HW±3½ at springs.

The moorings seen from the east

FACILITIES

The Capitainerie (HM Guirec Galery) is above the slip. ☎ 02 96 91 44 31, 🖷 02 96 91 69 09. VHF Ch 09. Open Apr–Sep 0730–1200 & 1330–2000. Ploumanac'h is managed by Perros-Guirec; in low season the Bureaux du Port are not always open at the stated times.

Berthing Within the hbr there are 11 trots ('A'–'K') of mooring buoys orientated SW/NE. 20 **Ⓥ** berths are on the first trot 'A' in about 2m; max LOA 12m. Secure fore & aft to buoys with large dumbells as fenders; rafting is normal. The pool shallows to 1.5m and dries extensively around the edges.

Tariff Daily rates € on dumbell buoys (showers included), in season, for LOA bands: <8m = 12.50; <9m = 15.70; <10m = 17.50; <11m = 19.90; <12m = 22.50; <13m = 24.10; <13.5m = 25.70.

Showers (only two) are free; coded access.

Fuel None except by cans from nearest garage.

Chandlery & repairs Not much; consult HM or go to Perros or Trébeurden. There is a good drying grid with gauge at the root of the eastern slipway.

VHF Port Ch 09.

Anchorages/moorings Nearest anchorages are at Trégastel-Plage and off Les Sept Îles. Anchoring is prohibited everywhere within a line W from Mean Ruz lt ho thence S through Château Costaérès to the sill. Anchoring E of Mean Ruz in Anse de Porz Kamor is also prohibited (to avoid obstructing the LB). Nor is there room to anchor in the non-tidal pool. Now for the good news: Three white waiting buoys, marked VPG, are on the edge of the channel near No 6 and 8 perches in 1.5m.

A local fisherman crossing the sill. No 12 PHM perch in the foreground

TRÉGASTEL-PLAGE

Moorings – 48°50´·10N 03°31´·23W

Trégastel-Plage (TP) should not be confused with Primel-Trégastel (PT) roughly 14M WSW at the NE corner of the Baie de Morlaix. TP is about 1.5M west of Ploumanac'h, separated by acres of drying rock, Île Renote and a promontory: E of this is Ste Anne, a wholly drying, non-sailing community –

to the W yachts can anchor/moor or dry out off TP and Île Ronde. Trégastel-Bourg is 3km inland. The IGN walking map 0714 OT (1:25,000) adds to your enjoyment. End of geography lesson.

The spectacular blend of rocks with gold & silver beaches more than justifies a visit, which in settled weather may last longer than originally contemplated – such is its chemistry and charisma.

SHORESIDE

Tourist Office is in Ste Anne. ☎ 02 96 15 38 38, ▨ 02 96 23 85 97. Open Mon–Sat 0930–1230 & 1500–1830. tourisme.tregastel@free.fr; www.ville-tregastel.fr

What to see/do Walk 6km SW on the coastal path (Sentier des Douaniers/GR34) to Landrellec with great views along the rock-encumbered coastline.

For exotic fish visit the Aquarium Marin, bd du Coz-Pors, housed below huge granite boulders & a statue of the Eternal Father; daily Apr–Jun & Sep 1000–1200 & 1400–1800, Jul/Aug 1000–2000; €4.50. *Vedette* trips from Coz-Pors to Les Sept Îles.

Buses No 15 starts/ends a round-robin at Lannion taking in Perros, Trégastel-Plage and Trébeurden. Timetables from the Tourist Office.

Rail From Lannion (nearest station) to Plouaret (17 mins) thence TGV/mainline to Paris/Brest.

Taxi 27 ave de la Grève Blanche; ☎ 02 96 23 87 29.

Car & bike hire Check with the Tourist Office.

Looking SW towards the afloat anchorage

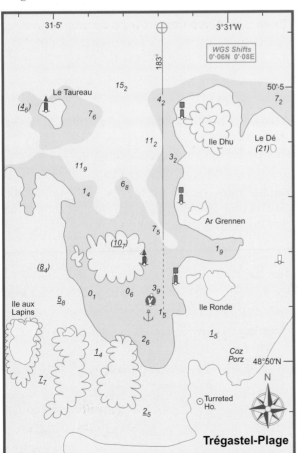

UK access Ferry via Roscoff; or scheduled flights to Paris from Lannion airport.

Beaches Silvery La Grève Blanche and golden Coz Porz are the nearest of several fine beaches.

Supermarkets Comod is near the Tourist Office. Super U, 1km SE of Ste Anne. In season Mon–Sat 0900–2000, Sun 0900–1230.

Market day Monday.

Banks Two with cashpoints in Ste Anne.

Launderette Lavomatique, rue Charles Le Goffic, Ste Anne; open daily, 0700–2200.

Restaurants Hôtel Beau Séjour, ☎ 02 96 23 88 02, has harbour views; menus €15 & 25 in its Le Roof. Armoric Hôtel, ☎ 02 96 23 88 16, is imposing but coy on menus. La Grève Blanche, ☎ 02 96 15 33 88, at the eponymous beach majors on seafood; €15 to 27.

NAVIGATION

Charts AC 3670 (1:50,000) and 3669 (1:50,000). SHOM 7152 (1:48,700) and 7125 (1:20,000 with 1:10,000 inset). Note: SHOM 7125 shows far more detail than AC 3670 & 3669 and is worth buying.

La Pierre Pendue on Île Dé

Approaches From the E stay fairly close inshore past Mean Ruz lt ho. From the W or S route via Bar-ar-Gall WCM buoy, keeping clear of the reefs E of it.

Landmarks La Pierre Pendue is conspic on Île Dé (= The Dice, an apt name for this extraordinary balancing act); its navigational significance is that the entrance is 2 cables to the west. Mean Ruz lt ho is 1.5M east of the waypoint.

Pilotage The waypoint is 48°50′·62N 03°31′·17W, 2 cables N of the first of three PHM beacons. From here it is simplest to track 183° leaving the three PHM beacons 60m to port and Le Taureau SHM bcn 400m to stbd (if knocked off its drying rock by gales, this bcn may be replaced by a SHM buoy). Pass midway between the third PHM beacon and an inner SHM beacon; this is the 'gateway' into the anchorage/moorings (Lat/Long under Title).

SHOM 7125 also shows two transits which pass quite close to Le Taureau: A chapel twr at TP ≠ 150° with a prominent water tower 2.3M inland. Or the third PHM bcn ≠ 164° with a lone turreted house *(clocheton)* on the promontory. No lights and many rocks = No entry/exit by night.

Tides Use Ploumanac'h tidal data (page 457).

Tidal streams set across the entrance, ENE-going from HW Brest −3½ and WSW-going from HWB +2½; max spring rates 3¾kn. In the approaches lay off accordingly.

Access Day only, at all states of the tide. In fresh/strong W to N winds the approach can be very choppy/rough, making it uncomfortable or even untenable inside. In calm weather, pure delight!

Anchorages Anchor 1 cable SW of the third PHM beacon in 2–3m on sand. Or dry out, if able, 100m S of Île Ronde in Coz Porz on sand/weed.

FACILITIES

The Capitainerie (HM Gilbert Leplatinec) is by the beach huts at Coz Porz. ☎ 02 96 23 49 51. Open May–Sep 1000–1200 & 1400–1800, closed Tues.

Moorings There are ⚓s 100m SSW of the third PHM beacon in 1.5m.

Tariff None is apparent and you may not be charged for a lunch stop on a buoy.

Showers at the Club Nautique (Sailing School).

Fuel By cans from nearest garage at Ste Anne.

Chandlery & repairs Nothing.

TRÉBEURDEN

Marina entrance – 48°46´·40N 03°35´·13W

Trébeurden Marina has come a long way since it opened in 1993. Legal traumas are a thing of the past, the Bureau du Port is installed in a smart new building, many more local boats are berthed there, but visitors will still find room.

The scenery has not changed at all: still a glorious mixture of sea, sand, rock, islands small and great, notably Île Milliau. Trébeurden town proper is 1.3km E of the marina – the natives are friendly.

Trébeurden is the last proper marina with generous access times between Tréguier and Camaret, not counting L'Aber Wrac'h.

SHORESIDE

Tourist Office is up the hill at Place de Crec'h Hery; ☎ 02 96 23 51 64, 🖷 02 96 15 44 87. Open Mon–Fri 0900–1230 & 1400–1800 (Sat 1700); Sun closed. tourisme.trebeurden@wanadoo.fr; www.ville.trebeurden.fr.st

What to see/do Around LW, coeff >52 (access hrs on noticeboard at S end of marina), cross the rocks/sands to explore Île Milliau; good walking and stunning views. Swim/sunbathe on brilliant beaches. At Pleurmeur-Bodou, 5km E as spaceships fly, rainy day attractions are: A Planetarium, English shows Wed at 1300 in Apr–Jun & Sep; 1300 Tues, Thur, Fri in Jul/Aug; €6.25. Nearby the Radome, an early SatCom station and space museum do English shows as above but at 1430; €7. Access by bike or tortuous No 15 bus (10 mins).

Buses A round-robin route, Line 15, starts/ends at Lannion taking in Perros, Ploumanac'h and Trébeurden. Timetables from the Tourist Office.

Rail From Lannion (nearest station) to Plouaret (17 mins) thence TGV/mainline to Paris/Brest.

Taxi ☎ 02 96 23 55 05/06 71 04 56 11; ☎ 02 96 15 48 69/06 07 36 12 66.

Car hire Car Verts ☎ 02 96 23 50 32, rue Kergonan. Lannion: Avis ☎ 02 96 48 10 98; Hertz ☎ 02 96 05 82 82.

Bike hire Le Piston Vert, ☎ 02 96 15 00 83, rue de Kergonan (close NW of Tourist Office).

UK access Ferry via Roscoff; or scheduled flights to Paris from Lannion airport.

Beaches The wide sandy Plage de Tresmeur is a hop, skip and a jump SSE of the marina. The much smaller Plage de Porz Termen is close N.

Supermarkets An *épicerie* behind the Bureau du

small but handy. Super Jodi, next to the ourist Office, is OK for most essentials. Intermarché, rue des Plages, 20 mins walk at Le Bourg; Mon–Thur 0900–1215 & 1430–1900; Fri/Sat 0900–1900; Sun shut.

Market day Tuesday.

Banks Two with cashpoints in Le Bourg, plus PO.

Restaurants By the marina: La Potinière, no set menus, ☎ 02 96 23 50 21. La Tourelle, ☎ 02 96 23 62 73, first floor; €9, 16, 24 & 34. Up the hill with fine views over the harbour, Hôtel Ker an Nod is an old favourite, justifiably, with British yachtsmen; ☎ 02 96 23 50 21; €15, 18, 25 & 28.50. Manoir de Lan Kerellec, ☎ 02 96 15 47 47, is N of the marina (near the eponymous Dir lt); worthwhile if you do not need to enquire the price. In similar vein, try Ti al Lannec, ☎ 02 96 15 01 01, country house luxury for those whose bodies yearn to be pampered.

NAVIGATION

Charts AC 3669 (1:50,000). SHOM 7151 (1:50,000) and 7124 (1:20,000 with 1:7,500 marina inset); the latter is essential for local rock-hopping.

Approaches From the E, shape a course seaward of Bar-ar-Gall and Le Crapaud WCM buoys

which mark reefs extending 2 to 3.5M offshore in an arc from Ploumanac'h to W of Trébeurden. The final approach is on an ENE track.

In offshore winds a short-cut via the 0.5M wide channel between Le Crapaud reef and the reefs N and S of Île Losket is safe, if pre-planned.

From the W route inshore of Plateau de la Méloine and S of Le Crapaud to the waypoint.

Landmarks A radome 2.5M ENE of the marina rises like a mushroom from the grass and is useful for bearings and general orientation. A conspic, flat-topped building on Île Milliau indicates that the marina is 6 cables E. On the skyline a high-rise bldg and Trébeurden church spire are prominent.

Pilotage The waypoint is 48°45′·34N 03°40′·00W, in the white sector of Lan Kerellec Dir lt (hard to see by day), bearing 066°/3M to the first PHM lt buoy, Fl (2) R 6s.

In the near approach leave Ar Gouredec SCM light buoy 1 cable to port. When 200m short of the first PHM buoy, alter ESE past a SHM and PHM buoy thence E to round the breakwater, marked by Fl G 2.5s lt and three SHM plus one PHM unlit perches.

Tides HW Trébeurden at sp is 1 hr 10 mins and nps 1 hr after HW Brest. LW at sp is 1 hr 20 mins

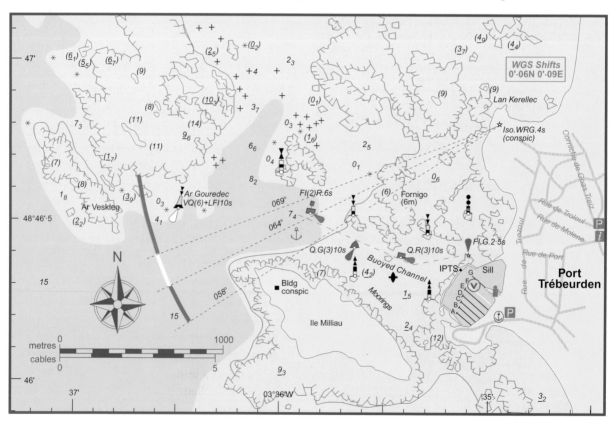

and at nps 1 hr after LW Brest. MHWS is 9·2m, MLWS 1·4m; MHWN is 7·3m, MLWN 3·5m.

Tidal streams set hard E/W in the channel between the mainland and Les Sept Îles, but ease as you come south. W of Île Losket the stream sets N from HW Brest –4 and S from +2; spring max 2kn.

Access The approach is exposed to fresh/strong W/NW winds.

The marina retaining wall is marked by four SPM perches and dries <u>3</u>.8m. Near its NW end a sill with flapgate is identified by red and green floodlit 'frames', the former with IPTS and gauge giving depth over the sill. When the flapgate first drops there is 1.7m water over the sill which dries <u>2</u>.1m.

The entry window for a 1.5m draught yacht with 0.5m under-keel clearance is approx HW±3¾ at sp and HW±5 at nps (see graph below). Wait a good 15 mins after the flapgate first drops before crossing the sill; this avoids the turbulent inrush at sp.

VHF Ch 09.

IPTS (Sigs 2 & 4) are shown to seaward from the W breakwater and internally at the sill, port side.

Moorings Yellow waiting ⚓s, marked 1–10, are S of the second PHM channel buoy, near the LB.

Anchorage 100m S of the first PHM channel buoy in about 6m on sand/weed; exposed to W/NW.

The marina is well sheltered from NW'lies

FACILITIES

Bureau du Port (HM Mme Dominique Bernabé) facing 'F' pontoon. VHF Ch 09. ☎ 02 96 23 64 00;
🖷 02 96 15 40 87. Mon–Fri 0830–1200 & 1400–1730 (Sat 1600). portrebeurden@wanadoo.fr

Berthing ♥ finger berths on 'F' pontoon, second from the entrance, in about 2.5m. Speed limit 3kn.

Tariff Daily rates € on pontoons for LOA bands in Jul/Aug; rates in ( ) are May, Jun, Sep: < 7.5m = 16 (13); < 9m = 21 (18); < 11m = 26 (21); < 13m = 30 (25); < 16m = 36 (31). Dearer than average, plus:

Showers by access code (changed weekly with no notice) and jeton €2.

Launderette Behind the Bureau du Port, open Mon–Sat 0900 (Sun 1000)–1900 from Sep–Jun; Jul/Aug Mon–Sat 0800–2100, Sun 1000–1900.

Fuel Diesel and petrol at root of 'G' pontoon.

YC YC de Trébeurden, ☎ 02 96 15 45 97.

Chandlery & repairs Cap Marine, ☎ 02 96 15 49 49, CH at the marina. ABC Marine, ☎ 02 96 23 63 55, is a BY at Chemin du Run Crec'h Du.

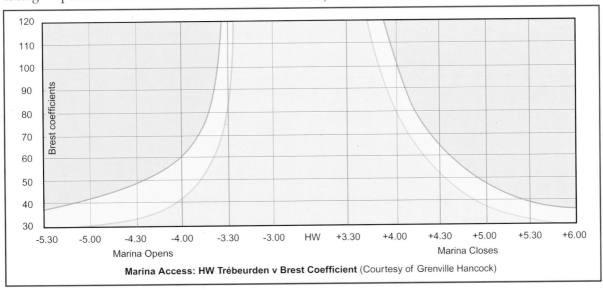

Marina Access: HW Trébeurden v Brest Coefficient (Courtesy of Grenville Hancock)

Chapter 8

BAIE DE LANNION

Le Yaudet – 48°44´·04N 03°31´·89W
Locquémeau – 48°43´·67N 03°34´·84W
Locquirec – 48°41´·46N 03°38´·68W

The title embraces three little harbours, within 4M of each other, which individually do not merit separate entries. But they do deserve your interest, especially if you wish to avoid crowded marinas.

SHORESIDE AT LE YAUDET

The Lannion (or Le Léguer) River is no longer the thriving river of bygone years when trading ships berthed at the ancient town of Lannion. Its uppermost reaches are barred by low bridges and the quays are better suited to sand dredgers. It dries extensively and the bottom may be foul.

But afloat anchorages can be found in its attractive lower reaches. Enjoy the peaceful wooded scenery and don't consider sailing up to Lannion, unless you skipper a kayak on wheels. I would not risk my fin-keeler on such a venture. It is in any case an enchanting woodland walk (6km) along the S bank to Lannion (mind the Little People), pausing at the chapel of Loguivy-lès-Lannion. Or take the more prosaic towpath along the N bank.

Le Yaudet is the place to be, standing high on a promontory with commanding views down the

estuary. Here Restaurant Ar Vro, ☎ 02 96 46 48 80, does a hikers' menu at €20. Nearby the Hôtel-Restaurant L Clairin was in refit in May 2002. No food shops to be seen. In the church there is an unusual crèche of the Virgin and infant Jesus. The beaches N and S of Beg Léguer lt ho are accessible on foot from the N bank, or by dinghy.

NAVIGATION

Charts AC 3669 (1:50,000). SHOM 7151 (1:50,000), 7152 (1:48,700) and 7124 (1:20,000, with larger scale insets of the river & Lannion); 7124 is much more preferable to AC 3669.

Approaches From the W, ie the Morlaix estuary or Île de Batz, go direct to the waypoint keeping S of Plateau de la Méloine and N of the reefs ENE of Pte de Primel.

From the N and E skirt the extensive reefs N and

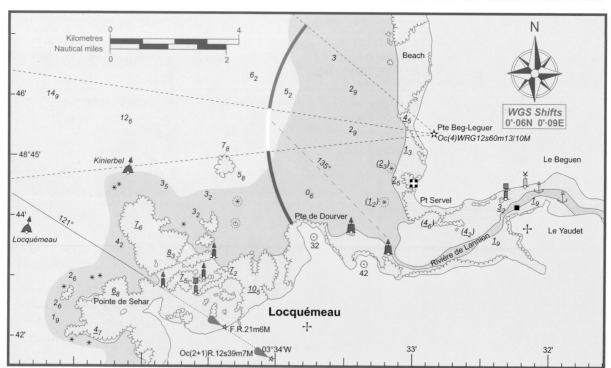

Looking west from the river mouth with Le Yaudet in the foreground

W of Ploumanac'h and Trébeurden, to make good Le Crapaud WCM buoy; thence to the WPT.

Landmarks Beg Léguer lt sits 60m above sea level, just below the skyline. The red lantern tops a squat tower grafted onto the front of a white house with red shutters.

Pilotage The waypoint is 48°44´·46N 03°36´·84W (which is also on Locquémeau's 121° ldg line). Track 092° toward Beg Léguer Dir lt (in its white sector – but a night entry is not feasible), leaving Kinierbel SHM buoy and a 0.1m reef 250m to stbd. At 03°34´·00W, or when Trébeurden spire bears 004°, alter 135° to leave two SHM bcn towers about 100m to stbd. The channel then hugs the S bank before trending gradually 057° toward a PHM perch and slip on the N bank, rounding the high rocky promontory of Le Yaudet close to stbd. As the pool opens up and Le Yaudet slipway appears to stbd, begin to sound for an anchorage in about 5m and clear of moorings.

Tides Interpolate between Trébeurden (page 461) and Locquirec.

Tidal streams set ENE/WSW 2kn near the WPT. In the river entrance the flood starts at HW Les Héaux de Bréhat –6 and the ebb at –¾; the ebb lasts 7 hrs, max spring rate 2½kn at Le Yaudet.

Access Fresh to strong W'lies make the entrance a difficult and potentially dangerous lee shore. A bar, least depth 0.3m, extends 2 cables N of Pte du Dourven. Time your approach for HW–1.

Anchorages The pool in which to anchor or moor is due N of the village and you can relish the steep climb up from the landing slip, or perish in the attempt. Anchor about 1 cable E of Le Yaudet slip in 5m on mud. If shoal draught, continue 0.4M east to a yellow perch beyond which the river dries.

Moorings There are no dedicated ⚓s; pick up a local mooring, subject to the usual constraints.

FACILITIES

Nothing other than a slip on which to land, with the satisfaction of having entered this beautiful and other-worldly spot.

LANNION is a major centre and historic town which can easily be visited from Le Yaudet, rather less easily from Locquémeau and Locquirec.

Tourist Office quai d'Aiguillon. ☎ 02 96 46 41 00, 📠 02 96 37 19 64. Jul/Aug, Mon–Sat 0900–1900; Sun 1000–1300. Sep–Jun Mon–Sat 0930–1230 & 1400–1800. infos@ot-lannion.fr; www.ot-lannion.fr

What to see/do On the NE bank wander up to

First of two SHM beacon towers

Looking up-river from Le Yaudet

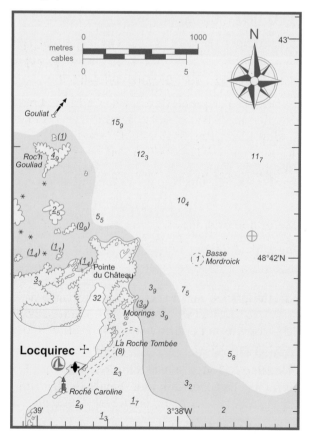

the picturesque Place du Général Leclerc and adjacent streets to see the handsome, slate roofed C15/C16 half-timbered houses; note the corbels (small stone or timber supports for a beam or cornice which give the characteristic overhang). Join the tourist trail up 143 steps to the C12 church of Brélévenez for magnificent views.

Buses No 16 from Lannion via Locquémeau (occas) and Locquirec (45 mins) to Morlaix (1 hr 15 mins). Most bus stops are near the Tourist Office.

Rail Local train to Plouaret (17 mins) to connect with the TGV/mainline to Paris/Brest. The station is on the SW bank.

Taxi ☎ 02 96 48 75 40; 06 07 06 84 27; 06 07 16 22 12.

Car hire Avis ☎ 02 96 48 10 98; Ada ☎ 02 96 48 56 70; Budget ☎ 02 96 48 05 48.

UK access Ferry via Roscoff; or scheduled flights to Paris from Lannion airport, ☎ 02 96 05 82 22.

Market day Thur in Place du Général Leclerc. Les Halles Centrales, Tues to Sat mornings.

Banks Plenty with cashpoints in the town centre.

Launderette Lavomatique, 10 rue de Kérampont.

Restaurants Roam around the Vieux Quartier and enjoy finding a suitable eatery. There is no lack of choice; in the evening it pays to eat early, by 1930, unless you have pre-booked.

LOCQUÉMEAU's little fishing harbour is at the mouth of the Léguer River. It dries completely and is the sort of place that a nautical Monro-bagger might visit; but it boasts few attractions other than two or three eateries and small food shops.

Navigation The waypoint for Lannion/Le Yaudet also serves for Locquémeau. It is on the 121° ldg line 1.5M to the front mark, a white lattice tower with red top which is easily seen; not so the rear mark, a white gable end, even with binos. With SHOM 7124 to hand, pass close to Locquémeau SHM buoy, thence to three SHM perches and one PHM, all on or near the stone jetty to stbd which projects from Pte de Séhar. A red-roofed house is conspic to stbd. Continue to the inner sanctum and local moorings. Dry out against the SE side of a second jetty.

LOCQUIREC is an attractive little resort with fine houses, a small drying harbour and a fair number of afloat moorings. It's the sort of place a French family might return to year after year and generation by generation. Even a visitor might pick up a mooring and stay rather longer than the planned lunch stop, as one does. It is the first harbour in Finistère, which extends round to Quimper.

Toull-an-Héry, 1.1M SSE across acres of drying sand, is an off-the-beaten-track anchorage if ever there was one – here the R Douron meets the sea.

Locquirec's drying harbour from the south

SHORESIDE AT LOCQUIREC

Tourist Office is on the quay. ☎ 02 98 67 40 83; 📠 02 98 79 32 50. Open Mon–Sat 0900–1200 &1430–1700. contact@locquirec.com; www.locquirec.com

Rail Morlaix and Plouaret are the nearest stations.

Buses No 16 and 51 to Morlaix and Lannion.

Taxi ☎ 02 98 67 44 06.

Car & bike hire See the Tourist Office.

UK access Via Roscoff ferry or Lannion airport.

Beaches Nine beaches at the last count. The harbour itself is a S-facing sandy beach. The whole bay at LW is a vast expanse of golden sand.

Supermarket Notre Marché, 300m up Vieille Côte, meets most needs. If not, butcher, baker...

Market day At the port Wed mornings.

Banks One on the quay with no cashpoint; CIO is just off the quay and has a cash machine.

Restaurants Hôtel du Port, ☎ 02 98 67 40 83, €18 to 28. La Presqu'Île, ☎ 02 98 79 34 27, €15 to 25. Grand Hôtel des Bains, ☎ 02 98 67 41 02, €28 and alc. Les Algues, ☎ 02 98 67 45 73, good crêperie up the hill.

NAVIGATION

Charts AC 3669 (1:50,000); SHOM 7151 (1:50,000) and 7124 (1:20,000); 7124 is preferable to AC 3669.

Approaches From the N keep W of Le Crapaud

View SSE towards Toull an Héry

WCM buoy, or inshore of Le Crapaud reef avoiding Le Four 3.5m (S of Trébeurden approach). 2M NE of Locquirec keep clear of Roc'h Parou (2.1m) and Roc'h Felusteg (1.3m).

From the WNW, pass between the Plateau de la Méloine and Les Chaises de Primel, both unlit, to the waypoint via Gouliat unlit NCM buoy, 1.1M N of the harbour.

Landmarks Kerboulic water twr, topped by a TV/radio mast, is visible 1.2M SW of the harbour.

Pilotage The waypoint is 48°42′·10N 03°37′·49W, 230°/1M to the jetty head. Close WSW of the WPT, Basse Mordroick has 1m over it.

Access Approx HW±3, but unlit so not advised at night. Good shelter from W'lies, but exposed in fresh to strong E'lies. Choppy in fresh S'lies.

Tides HW Locquirec at sp is 1 hr 8 mins and nps 58 mins after HW Brest. LW at sp is 1 hr 20 mins and nps 1 hr after LW Brest. MHWS is 9·1m, MLWS 1·3m; MHWN is 7·2m, MLWN 3·4m.

Tidal streams set NW/SE at up to 1½kn.

FACILITIES

A Capitainerie does not exist as such, but the Mairie acts the part, 200m uphill from the harbour. ☎ 02 98 67 42 20; 📠 02 98 79 32 45. Open Mon–Fri 0900–1200 &1400–1600, Sat 0900–1200. No VHF.

Berthing A fin-keeler could dry out against the jetty or on legs where space permits. The harbour dries approx 6m to firm sand/shingle. Rocks to the SW are marked by a SPM perch.

Moorings About 27 white buoys, five marked PAS (visitors), lie NE of La Roche Tombée in up to 4m.

Tariff Delightfully simple: €4.65 for a night on a buoy, regardless of LOA.

Chapter 8

PRIMEL-TRÉGASTEL

Harbour entrance – 48°42′·84N 03°49′·36W

Once again please do not confuse this place, PT for short, with Trégastel-Plage (TP; page 459) some 14M ENE near Ploumanac'h. Even without this confusion, PT has its own identity crisis, as they say.

The village of PT straggles round the NE side of the Anse de Primel with the rugged Pte de Primel jutting out northwards into La Manche. Le Diben, W of the harbour entrance, roughly relates to the fishing community. Plougasnou, about 3km SE, is the nearest place of any size – which isn't saying a lot! Morlaix is about 20km south.

But the tactical position of PT for the yachtsman is important, especially as anchorages in the Morlaix estuary are relatively few and sometimes short on shelter. PT is exposed only to W–N winds. In other winds it is useful as a passage stop or to await the tide up to Morlaix.

SHORESIDE

Tourist Office The nearest is at Morlaix, along with trains, car & bike hire, banks, serious shops, an airport and UK ferries from Roscoff.

Buses No 56 from Le Diben, and PT 10 mins later, gets you to Morlaix in 35 mins, but infrequently.

Taxi ☎ 02 98 72 35 10; 02 98 67 21 29.

Beaches The shingly Plage de Primel is the best on offer.

Restaurants Hôtel de l'Abbesse, ☎ 02 98 72 32 43, near the head of the bay, is said to be inexpensive.

NAVIGATION

Charts AC 3669 (1:50,000) and 2745 (1:20,000). SHOM 7151 (1:50,000), 7124 (1:20,000) and 7095 (1:20,000) which covers Morlaix, Roscoff and Batz.

Approaches From the E, shape a course seaward of Les Chaises de Primel and the islets/reefs NE of Pte de Primel. This can be a bumpy corner.

From the W, if you have come from Roscoff or Canal de l'Île de Batz pass S of Plateau des Duons; otherwise pass N of it.

Landmarks The craggy granite Pointe de Primel is pretty obvious. Plougasnou spire may assist.

View ENE. Visitors' moorings at one o'clock from the pierhead as seen from this angle

Pointe de Primel

152° ldg line

Pilotage The waypoint is 48°43´·63N 03°50´·00W, on the 152° ldg line 0.9M to the harbour entrance. The ldg marks/lts are plain as a pike-staff by day and night: Front, a white □ with R vert stripe, FR lt on a pylon; rear, ditto, minus the pylon. An unlit middle mark also has a white □ with R vert stripe. Stay spot on the line which leads past a large rock drying 1·7m, with green paintmark (Ar Zammeguez), then between a pair of PHM/SHM perches – to the mole, Fl G 4s.

Tides HW Anse de Primel at sp is 1 hr 10 mins and at nps 1 hr after HW Brest. LW at sp is 1 hr 20 mins and nps 1 hr after LW Brest. MHWS is 9·1m, MLWS 1·3m; MHWN is 7·1m, MLWN 3·4m.

Tidal streams set NE from HW Brest –5 and SW from HWB –2¼; spring max 2½kn. An eddy sets SW across the approach during the E-going flood.

Access by day/night at all tides. The approach and harbour are exposed to fresh/strong W–N winds which raise a choppy sea, often breaking at the narrow entrance.

VHF Ch 09 in season during office hours; out of season 0900–1200 & 1330–1730.

FACILITIES

Bureau du Port (HM Jean-Pierre Prigent). VHF Ch 09. Mobile 06 09 34 82 37. A tap & electricity on the mole.

Moorings The harbour dries to mud/weed, apart from an area (used by FVs and local yachts) S of the outer part of the mole; and a tongue of water in your 11 o'clock as you enter. Here 10 white ⚓s lie in about 1m, NE of Roc'h an Trez Braz SHM perch; five other ⚓s dry out, so do your sums.

Anchorage/berths Anchoring afloat is restricted by swinging room, but there is space to dry out further up-harbour. Berth against the mole in 2m or raft on a FV, if the HM/owner agree.

Tariff Daily rates € on ⚓s for LOA bands: < 8m = 6.10 ; < 10m = 8.30; < 12m = 11.60.

Showers may be found in Primel-Trégastel.

Fuel Only by cans from the nearest garage.

Chandlery & repairs Chantiers Navals de Primel, ☎ 02 98 72 30 06, CH, BY, ME, is at the head of the bay, accessible near HW or by road.

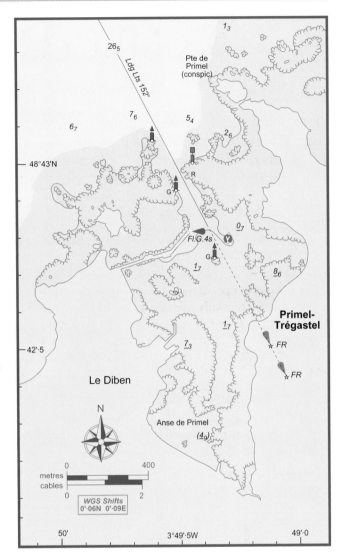

152° leading lights/marks (see Pilotage) as seen from ⚓

Chapter 8

MORLAIX
AND ITS BAY

Lock – 48°35´·35N 03°50´·20W

Morlaix, with its ancient timbered buildings, is an interesting town to wander round. The N12 road bridge just N of the lock and the high railway viaduct S of the marina emphasise the depth of the valley in which it lies – and is why it can be incredibly hot.

In 1522 British tars came up-river, plundered the town and then fell about in the wine cellars before being thrown out like football hooligans. As a result Morlaix's coat of arms sports a lion facing the English leopard and the motto *S'ils te mordent, mords-les* (If they bite you, bite them). The Château du Taureau was built to guard against further attacks. So take it easy... as one does.

SHORESIDE

Tourist Office is below the viaduct. ☎ 02 98 62 14 94, 🖷 02 98 63 84 87. Mon–Sat 1000–1200 & 1400–1800.

What to see/do The tobacco factory on the west bank has shut (a relief to the anti-smoking lobby) but is now partly a brewery: Out of the frying pan etc... Beyond the viaduct is the more interesting part of town and you should certainly call in at the house of La Reine Anne; it is a good example of a *maison à lanterne*, ie where the covered central courtyard is lit by a skylight and/or lantern.

For a spell out of town head 20km south (D785) to Plounéour-Ménez for B & B and good walking on the high moorland of Monts d'Arrée.

Rail The station is a steep climb from below the viaduct via Venelle de la Roche. TGV to Brest (30 mins), Rennes (40 mins) & Paris (4 hrs). Train to Roscoff (30 mins).

Buses Regional buses in Finistère are operated by four different companies which makes it hard to find out who goes where, when – in sharp contrast to the efficient Côtes d'Armor buses. Roscoff takes 1 hr, twice as long as the nifty little train.

Taxi ☎ 02 98 88 08 32; 02 98 88 36 42.

Car hire Europcar, ABL, Avis & Hertz are all next to the station; details via Tourist Office.

Bike hire See the Tourist Office.

UK access Roscoff-Plymouth ferry. The airport is nearby (2km), but UK flights are via Paris.

Supermarkets are all a fair walk up-town. Marché Plus in rue de Paris, near St Mathieu church. Two Intermarchés: One just W of the station; t'other at Le Queffleuth near the Théatre.

Launderette Laverie at a roundabout at the head of the marina; daily, 0800–2030.

Market day Sat, plus Wed in Jul/Aug, a large, open-air market fills most of the town centre.

Banks A 'Banditry' of banks around the centre.

Restaurants Next to the Bureau du Port is Tempo Café/Resto which is the trendy, in-place and can be noisy in the evenings; serves Coreff, the local Breton bitter. On the W bank Le Sterne is a vessel converted to bar/restaurant. La Pomme au Four is to stbd beyond the head of the marina; simple menus €10.40 to 13.60.

Just after the viaduct, turn left into Rampe St-Melaine for La Marée Bleue, ☎ 02 98 63 24 21, menus €13.50 to 36; some report poor service or food. Continue up this street and turn right along rue Ange de Guernisac which is lined with restaurants to suit all comers. The Dolce Vita is popular, so pre-book ☎ 02 98 63 37 67.

NAVIGATION

Charts AC 3669 (1:50,000) and 2745 (1:20,000 with 1:30,000 inset of the river). SHOM 7151 (1:50,000) and 7095 (1:20,000).

Approaches From the E, route south or north of Plateau de la Méloine. From the N pass between Méloine WCM buoy and Pot de Fer ECM buoy on one of the two ldg lines. From the W, either pass N of Île de Batz, thence to Pot de Fer ECM buoy. Or take the Canal de l'Île de Batz, thence eastward to Stolvezen PHM buoy on the 293.6° astern transit of Île Pigued white bcn twr and the spire of Notre Dame de Bon Secours [at night track 111° in the white sector (289.5°–293°) of Ar-Chaden].

Landmarks Île de Batz lt ho, 69m. Plougasnou spire (118m, SE of Primel-Trégastel). At St Pol-de-Léon, the twin spires of the cathedral and the even higher single spire (105m) of Kreisker chapel. The spire (77m) of Carantec church. The Château du Taureau is prominent but unlit.

Tides HW Morlaix (Château du Taureau) at sp is 1 hr 5 mins and at nps 55 mins after HW Brest. LW at sp is 1 hr 15 mins and nps 55 mins after LW Brest. MHWS is 8·9m, MLWS 1·3m; MHWN is 7·1m, MLWN 3·4m. The time of HW at Morlaix lock is virtually the same as Château du Taureau, maybe 10 mins later at springs.

Tidal streams in the two main channels reach 2½kn at springs, setting inwards from HW Brest −5 and seaward from HWB +1. The tidal diamonds on AC 2745 quote substantially lower rates.

Pilotage There are two and a half channels into the Morlaix estuary, from E to W:

1. Chenal de Tréguier Waypoint 48°43´·14N 03°51´·69W, 190°/2.1M to between Grand and Petit Aremen bcn twrs. Ldg lts 190.5°: Île Noire lt (front), La Lande lt (rear). Usable day/night, but not approx LW±2, due to unmarked rocks drying 0.9m.

2. Grand Chenal WPT 48°43´·14N 03°53´·50W, 176°/1.5M to Ricard SHM bcn twr. Ldg lts 176.4°: Île Louet lt (front), La Lande lt (rear). Usable day/night at all states of the tide, but accurate pilotage needed in the latter stages.

3. Chenal Ouest de Ricard 188.8° deviates from Grand Chenal at the WPT in (2), passing W of Île Ricard for deeper water, at which stage it is unlit.

Access All channels converge on No 1 SHM buoy, from which it is about 1 hr to Morlaix lock; best to arrange your ETA for the first opening time.

Looking south over the lock, marina and viaduct to the town centre

Chapter 8

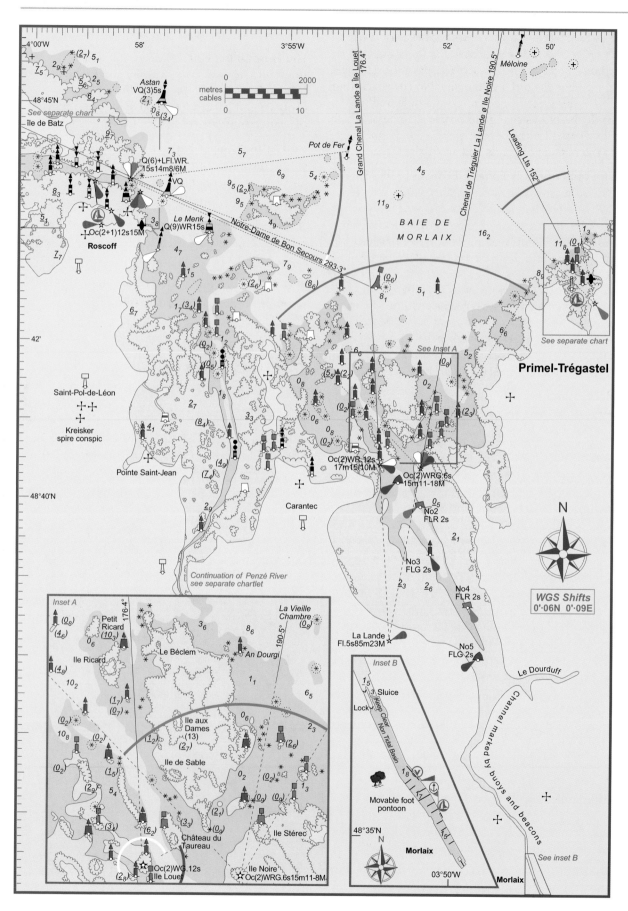

The Morlaix River From No 1 SHM buoy a track of 153°/1.8M leads past Nos 2 & 3 lt buoys to No 4 lt buoy. Here the river starts to narrow and buoy-hopping is the order of the day: No corner-cutting! Soon after passing close to Locquénolé on the W bank, the buoys change to beacons, some of which are aligned for the benefit of sand dredgers. Keep to the outside of bends and study the water.

The lock opens at HW$-1\frac{1}{2}$, HW* and HW+1, by day only, ie from sunrise to sunset. *See under Tides. In Jul/Aug there are extra openings.

Wait alongside the W bank wall where eight vertical chains are rigged (no further S); adequate depth from HW-2; raft up if needs be. E bank is shoal.

Outbound boats lock out first. There are no lights or signals; all is relaxed and unrushed. Enter when it is clear that you should. Marina staff or a lock-keeper usually help with warps. Eight vertical ropes are rigged each side. Lock-keeper ☎ 02 98 88 15 10.

VHF Lock and marina Ch 09.

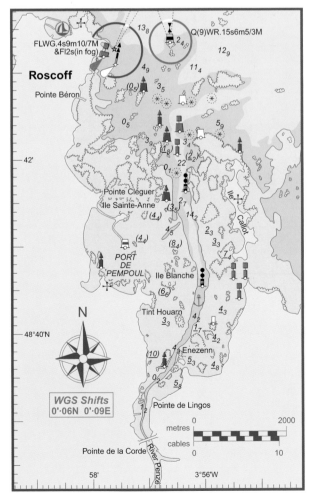

FACILITIES

The Bureau du Port (HM Fred Botcou, pronounce as *'beaucoup'*; speaks good English) is E bank by the YC. ☎/🖷 02 98 62 13 14. Daily 0830–1200 & 1400–1700 & lock hours. plaisance@morlaix.cci.fr VHF Ch 09.

Berths 16 Ⓥ finger berths are on the E bank just before the marina proper, in total shelter; or berth as directed. There are no 🛥s nor anchorage.

Tariff Daily rates per metre LOA are: On pontoons €1.40; and against the W bank quayside €1.10.

Showers are next to the Bureau du Port. Access by swipe card (€10 deposit) and jeton.

Fuel Diesel on quayside in front of the YC, a very restricted berth; more suited to filling cans.

YC YC de Morlaix, ☎ 02 98 88 27 30, next but one to the Bureau du Port.

Chandlery & repairs Loisirs Nautique, BY, CH; ☎ 02 98 88 27 30, on the W bank facing Ⓥ berths.

CRUISING THE BAIE DE MORLAIX

The Bay, entered between Pointe de Primel in the E and Roscoff to the W, is a mini-cruising ground – especially for boats able to dry out. Térénez is

Above: Château du Taureau
Below: View south in the final stretch of Chenal W of Ricard

one such anchorage, 2M SSW of Primel-Trégastel and almost in the shadow of the great tumulus on Pte de Barnénez; you may even stay afloat.

The Morlaix River, described above, is separated from the Penzé River by a peninsula at the head of which is **Carantec**, an attractive and exclusive resort town. Anchor in 0.7m N of Kergrist white ldg mark or dry out closer inshore on the sands of Plage du Kélenn. The anchorage/moorings SE of Penn al Lann are difficult for landing. Near LW you can walk across the causeway to explore Île Callot with its little chapel.

Intriguingly you can sail over this causeway near HW via the Passe aux Moutons. This short cut into the **Penzé River** is a track of about 250° between Le Goémonier PHM bcn and Le Figuier IDM bcn; numerous withies complicate the picture. Your Companion was guided by a helpful French yacht.

Otherwise enter the Penzé from the N: either W of Menke WCM bcn twr, or between Cordonnier and Les Bizeyer reef or S of that reef – in all cases continuing S between Trousken PHM and Pointe Fourche SHM beacons for 3.7M to the Pont de la Corde. Another drying anchorage is at Pempoul inside a large breakwater and a short walk, past fields of artichokes, to St Pol-de-Léon.

Upriver the marks are sparse, but almost continuous mooring trots show the way. Pick up a buoy short of the 10m high bridge and enjoy the relative solitude. There are few shore facilities. Beyond the bridge the river dries, but a dinghy trip is on the cards perhaps as far as Penzé itself (3M).

Above: The tranquil lock looking south
Below: The viaduct dominates the marina and town

ROSCOFF

Outer west jetty – 48°43´·62N 03°58´·57W

Roscoff is much more than a ferry port, although most people only know it as such. It is actually a charming old seaport once you get well away from the ferry terminal. The views NW towards Île de Batz take in a spectacular panorama of rock and sand interspersed with water.

The only problem with Roscoff is that it lacks a decent yacht harbour. Your Companion once spent several days alongside the inner jetty (for repairs); it has a very rough face and a stout fender board is essential. A retaining wall and flapgate across the entrance would be easy to build, but this is opposed by a powerful environmental lobby. Pity.

Meanwhile a modern fish quay and market has been built just south of Bloscon ferry terminal. It restricts visiting yachts wishing to anchor/moor there, especially if crew-changing. However, a new marina is said to be planned for this area.

SHORESIDE

Tourist Office 46 rue Gambetta. ☎ 02 98 61 12 13, ▨ 02 98 69 75 75. Mon–Sat 0900–1230 & 1530–1900; Sun 0930–1230. tourism.roscoff@wanadoo.fr

What to see/do At Pte Roc'h Hieveg (near the new fish quay) there is the Jardin Exotique (1000–1900 Jul/Aug) where a pleasant hour can be spent looking at botanical exotica whilst waiting for the ferry; or throw away your last euros in the garish-looking Casino. In town don't miss the indelicate-sounding Musée des Johnnies, fabled onion sellers of yesteryear who peddled their wares around the UK. Further west in the old part the inevitable Aquarium is actually the public face of the Marine Biological Institute; if you can access the latter (ask the Tourist Office) you may have a more interesting visit. If you know that you won't make it by boat, take a *vedette* to Île de Batz; every half hour (Jul/Aug) from the Vieux Port outer mole or the long boarding pier at LW. It's fun and relaxing.

Rail Train to Morlaix (30 mins), thence TGV to Brest (30 mins), Rennes (40 mins) & Paris (4 hrs). The station is close SW of the lt ho, rear ldg mark.

Buses 1 hr to Morlaix, twice as long as the train.

Taxi ☎ 02 98 29 74 53/06 72 78 20 08; 02 98 69 71 36.

Car hire Roscoff Automobiles, 69 rue Albert de Mun; ☎ 02 98 69 72 09.

Bike hire Cycles Desbordes, ☎ 02 98 69 72 44, 13 rue Brizeux; €6.10 per day.

UK access Ferries to Plymouth (Brittany Ferries ☎ 02 98 29 28 00) and Cork. Morlaix airport operates flights to Paris, thence UK.

Supermarkets Casino S/Mkt is out of town on the Morlaix road.

Launderette Laverie Ferry, rue Jules Ferry; daily, 0900–2000.

Market day Wed morning, quai d'Auxerre.

Beaches Pors ar Gored, immediately E of Vieux Port; Plage de Roc Kroum is W of town centre.

Banks Several with cashpoints in town centre.

Restaurants Le Surcouf, ☎ 02 98 69 71 89, €9.15 & 14.35, good value. Les Chardons Bleus for serious seafood at happy prices, €10 to 27; ☎ 02 98 69 72 03. Hôtel des Arcades, ☎ 02 98 69 70 45, €9.50 to 33.50, with sea views. At La Moule au Pot, ☎ 02 98 19 33 60, 13 rue Edouard Corbière (W of the church), I ate appetisingly and inexpensively.

The lighthouse is the rear 209° leading light

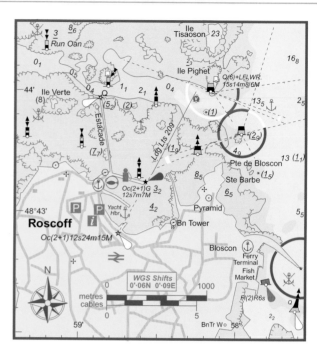

NAVIGATION

Charts AC 3669 (1:50,000) and 2745 (1:20,000 with 1:10,000 plan of the hbr). SHOM 7151 (1:50,000) and 7095 (1:20,000).

Approaches From the E, route south or north of Plateau des Duons to the entrance to Canal de l'Île de Batz. From the N route via Astan ECM buoy to round Ar-Chaden. From the W, either pass N of Île de Batz, thence as above. Or take the Canal de l'Île de Batz eastward to the waypoint (see directions under Île de Batz).

Landmarks Île de Batz lt ho, 69m, is conspic from afar. In the near approaches the churches at Île de Batz and Roscoff (W of the harbour) are obvious.

Tides HW Roscoff at sp is 1 hr 5 mins and at nps 55 mins after HW Brest. LW at sp is 1 hr 15 mins and nps 55 mins after LW Brest. MHWS is 8·8m, MLWS 1·3m; MHWN is 7·0m, MLWN 3·4m.

Tidal streams at the waypoint set E from HW Brest $-4\frac{1}{2}$ and W from HWB +1, at $3\frac{3}{4}$kn max springs. Slack water is at HWB (ie 1 hr before local HW). Between Ar-Chaden and Le Menke the stream sets S from HWB $-5\frac{1}{2}$ and N from HWB at a mere 1kn.

Pilotage The waypoint is 48°43′·95N 03°58′·29W, 1 cable WSW of Ar-Chaden bcn twr, and on the 209° ldg line, 4 cables to the head of the outer west jetty, which is the front mark Oc (2+1) G 12s; rear is the lt ho Oc (2+1) 12s.

Access to the Vieux Port S Basin, drying 5m to 6m, is approx HW±2 at springs, HW at neaps.

VHF Roscoff Vieux Port Ch 09. Bloscon Ch 12.

Roscoff church and fine old buildings

Ar Chaden marks the N side of the eastern entrance to
Canal de L'Île de Batz

FACILITIES

The Bureau du Port (HM Loïc Maron) is NW
of the S Basin. ☎ 02 98 69 76 37/06 64 46 89 43,
📠 02 98 61 11 96. VHF Ch 09. Daily 0800–1200
& 1330–1730. HM Bloscon Ferry Port ☎ 02 98 61
27 84. VHF Ch 12.

Berths/moorings In the Vieux Port S Basin yachts
dry out against the inner jetty or the road quay
(three ladders); or pick up a vacant buoy. FVs
berth in the outer N Basin. The white Ⓥs and
anchorage WNW of Ar-Chaden are exposed and
holding on sand/gravel is reported to be bad.
Do not impede ferries and FVs.

Tariff Daily rates € for LOA bands alongside: 7–9m
5.26; 9–11m 6.25; 11–12m 7.01; >12m 7.01 & 1.86 per
extra metres. Electricity €1.65. Ⓥs €7.65 per night.

Showers are near the lighthouse, where national
flags are flying. Jeton €1.60.

Fuel Diesel by cans from Coopérative Maritime or
see the HM.

YC Cercle Nautique de Roscoff, ☎ 02 98 69 72 79
Chandlery & repairs Coopérative Maritime, CH;
☎ 02 98 69 70 47, next to the lt ho.

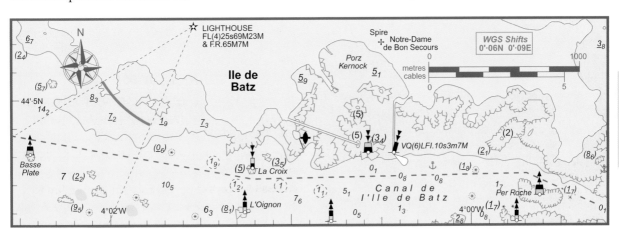

ÎLE DE BATZ

Harbour entrance – 48°44´·31N 04°00´·50W

Batz (excuse the abbreviation) is pronounced '*Ba*'. It is a fun place to be with a strong holiday feeling about it. Perhaps this is due to the sand which fills the drying harbour (Porz Kernok) – and much else on the island.

The drying harbour with Roscoff in the background

Not everybody can or wishes to dry out; consider anchoring outside and rowing ashore. Or, rather than miss the peaceful charm of Batz altogether, visit by *vedette* from Roscoff, every half hour (Jun–Aug) from the Vieux Port outer mole or the long passerelle at LW. It's fun and relaxing.

SHORESIDE

Syndicat d'Initiative (Tourist Office) at the Mairie. ☎ 02 98 61 75 70; 📠 02 98 61 75 85; mairie.iledebatz@libertysurf.fr

What to see/do Walk the island, which is only 2M long by about 0.5M wide; note the market gardening and tropical plants, but no trees. The lighthouse is open Jul–Aug daily, 1300–1730; climb 210 steps for fantastic coastal views. *Bon courage*!

Things not available on Batz Trains, buses, taxis, car hire, ferries, markets, banks, launderette.

Bike hire Vélos et Nature, ☎ 02 98 61 75 75.

Prigent, ☎ 02 98 61 76 91, next to the church.

Supermarkets Huit à Huit. Chez Thérèse. Bakery.

Beaches Pors Leyen overlooks the harbour. La Grève blanche is a superb beach near the NE tip.

Restaurants Hôtel Roch ar Mor, ☎ 02 98 61 78 28, is by the ferry landing, therefore tourist orientated. Grand Hôtel Morvan, ☎ 02 98 61 78 06, overlooks the beach. Plus four crêperies and a few bars.

NAVIGATION

Charts AC 3669 (1:50,000) and 2745 (1:20,000 with 1:10,000 plan of the hbr); SHOM 7151 (1:50,000) and 7095 (1:20,000).

Approaches From the E, route south or north of Plateau des Duons to the entrance to Canal de l'Île de Batz for which an east waypoint of 48°43´·83N 03°57´·43W will serve. From the N route via Astan ECM buoy via that waypoint to round Ar-Chaden.

From the W, make for a west waypoint 48°44´.50N 04°03´.46W, 0.7M W of Basse Plate NCM bcn twr.

Landmarks Île de Batz lt ho, 69m, is conspic from afar and dominates the island. The church and CG station are easily seen in the nearer approaches.

Pilotage through the Canal de l'Île de Batz (CIB)

This is classic pilotage through a channel which in places is narrow and shallow, but is just about adequately marked. See also Pilotage in the Introduction to the chapter on page 430.

Directions W-bound (The E-bound passage is basically a mirror image): From the east waypoint, edge closer to Ar-Chaden than to Men Guen Bras. Then make for a SCM bcn (S of Duslen white bcn twr), leaving Roc'h Zu NCM bcn to port. At the SCM bcn (which happens to be opposite the end of the long graceful pier used by *vedettes* at LW), alter stbd towards Run Oan SCM bcn. Depths of 0.5m and 0.1m will not be a problem if it is near HW with a fair ebb stream.

Now alter W x N towards the two SCM bcns at the entrance to Batz hbr; en route leave Perroch NCM bcn twr 100m to port. When Ar Polos Trez NCM bcn is abeam to port, head west to pass between La Croix SCM and L'Oignon NCM bcns. Here the channel is wider and deeper and only Basse Plate NCM bcn twr remains ahead to be left to port. All easier done than said.

Notes: You pass five SCMs and six NCMs. Tracks and distances have not been specified – a job for you! Study the tidal streams below. A least visibility of 1M is advised. Transit marks are often distant and difficult to identify positively. Ignore any beacons which are well off to either side, lest they confuse you. Consider bolt-holes in emergency, but do not contemplate a night passage.

Île de Batz from Roscoff

Tides HW Île de Batz at sp is 1 hr and at nps 45 mins after HW Brest. LW at sp is 1 hr 5 mins and nps 55 mins after LW Brest. MHWS is 8·9m, MLWS 1·4m; MHWN is 7·0m, MLWN 3·5m.

Tidal streams at the E end of CIB set E from HW Brest −4½ and W from HWB +1, at 3¾kn max springs. Slack water is at HWB (ie local HW−1). At the west waypoint, where the channel is wider, the stream is more rotatory and only briefly sets exactly E or W. For example, referenced to HW Brest, set & rates are: −5, NE 1½kn. −4 to HW, NE 2½kn. +1, ENE 1kn. +2, E 1½kn. +3, SSW 1½kn. +4, SW 3kn. +5, W 1½kn. +6, NW 1½kn.

Access to Porz Kernok, which dries 2.5m inside the entrance and 5m at the N shore, is approx:

Entrance	*N shore*
HW±3¼ @ springs	HW±2 @ springs
HW±4 @ neaps	HW @ neaps

Anchorages The nearest is 1.5 cables E of a SCM bcn at the end of the *vedettes'* LW embarkation jetty, which covers. Sound as far in as possible to escape the worst of the tide; easiest at neaps.

Porz Kernok is entered close to the said jetty to avoid rocks in the centre, ie S of Île Kernok and its white bcn. Dry out on firm sand where you can.

Between the SE tip of Batz and Roscoff's N tip, there is a No Anchoring area due to power cables.

FACILITIES

There is no Bureau du Port as such. Hence you will be left very much to your own nautical devices and may not be asked for money if only staying the odd night.

Showers are possible at Hôtel Roch ar Mor.

Fuel, chandlery & repairs None.

THE TWIN ABERS

L'Aber Wrac'h – 48°36′·00N 04°33′·55W; L'Aber Benoit – 48°34′·43N 04°35′·80W

The yacht pontoon and moorings

L'ABER WRAC'H

(The valley of the fairies) has a place in British hearts as a strategic staging post to/from the Chenal du Four and all points south. Most do not linger long, for in truth there is little to do at L'Aber Wrac'h other than wait for a fair tide and calm seas in the hope of a prosperous voyage (Goethe/Mendelssohn).

Yet it has peaceful charm, a few quite good eating places and a daunting array of lunar rocks. If you plan to linger, especially when it blows hard from the NW, move up-river to Paluden for total shelter. Future developments (below) should provide far better shelter at L'Aber Wrac'h.

The *West France Cruising Companion* (Featherstone/Nautical Data Ltd) covers L'Aber Wrac'h and the Chenal du Four southward to the Spanish border.

L'Aber Benoit (below) shares the same waypoint

and is arguably more scenic, but it has yet to entice the same number of itinerant yachtsmen as L'Aber Wrac'h, despite being better sheltered in NW'lies. The reasons may be that it is unlit and relatively unknown. Nor does it boast generous facilities, although for some this will heighten its appeal.

SHORESIDE AT L'ABER WRAC'H

Tourist Office Kiosk in season. Office in Lannilis, 4.5km SE, is open Mon–Sat 0930–1200 & 1400–1700. ☎ 02 98 04 05 43; ✉ 02 98 04 12 47. office@abers-tourisme.com; www.abers-tourisme.com

What to see/do Enjoy the coastal walk to recce L'Aber Benoit. Take a *vedette*, at someone else's risk, to rocky places not normally visited: eg Île Vierge lt ho, Fort Cézon (courtesy of Vauban), Île Stagadon. From Perros slip (on the N bank, E of Touris PHM bcn) at 1000, 1230, 1430 & 1630 Jul/Aug; €13. By contrast take a day in Brest or better still in the Armorique Nature Park (rather like Dartmoor).

Rail Brest is the nearest station: TGV/Mainline trains to Morlaix, Rennes and Paris.

Buses Line 36 runs fairly often to Brest (45 mins) and via Lannilis to Plouguerneau (15 mins) and Lilia.

Taxi ☎ 02 98 04 84 72; 02 98 04 72 76.

Car & bike hire See the HM.

UK access Ferry Roscoff–Plymouth. Flights from Brest to London (Stansted).

Beaches The problem is avoiding an oyster's bed.

Supermarkets A baker calls at the Bureau du Port 0745–0800 daily in season. The Café du Port across the road is also a bread depot. A 20 mins walk to Landéda, for a Utile supermarket (open Mon–Sat 0800–1200 & 1500–1900), plus butcher, baker etc.

Market day Thursday at Plouguerneau.

Banks Two in Landéda, one with a cashpoint. Open: 0900–1200 Tues, Wed, Fri, Sat; shut Mon & Thur.

Restaurants Hôtel La Baie des Anges has brilliant views of the river and a €15 menu, ☎ 02 98 04 82 03. L'Éscale, ☎ 02 98 04 90 11, is friendly and food good, €14 & 22; shut Wed. The bar is full of Brits yarning about their derring-do in a Force 9 – or was it a 10? La Table des Artistes, ☎ 02 98 04 85 78, imaginatively combines a restaurant and art gallery. It works! Further SE towards St Antoine: La Palue, ☎ 02 98 04 82 39, menus €16.50 & 19.00. Le Brennig, ☎ 02 98 04 81 12, €15 & 26; with first-floor views to Île Vierge lt ho.

NAVIGATION

Charts AC 3668 (1:50,000), 1432 (1:25,000 with 1:15,000 harbour plan); SHOM 7150 (1:50,000) and 7094, the same-scale, blueprint for AC 1432.

Approaches From the E, route via Lizen Ven Ouest WCM buoy, 2.2M north of Île Vierge lt ho, to keep an offing from the inshore reefs. From this buoy, and from the N, make good the **waypoint** 48°37′·56N 04°38′·37W, Libenter WCM light buoy at the entrance to the Grand (primary) Chenal.

From the W or SW, ie Chenal du Four, skirt the Roches de Portsall via the small Basse Paupian unlit WCM buoy, or the larger, lit Grande Basse Portsall WCM buoy, which is further offshore.

Landmarks Île Vierge lighthouse is a pencil-slim finger visible from afar (21M at night).

Pilotage The Grand Chenal is well marked and deep, but attentive pilotage is still needed to avoid rocks on either hand. The outer leg leads 100° 1.6M to Petit Pot de Beurre ECM bcn twr. Its ldg marks, 2.7M and 4.3M from Libenter, need binos by day but are clear by night. Plouguerneau spire is also on 100°. NB Trépied PHM looks like a little bcn twr, but is in fact an outsize unlit buoy.

The inner leg, lit by a Dir Oc (2) WRG 6s lt, leads 128°/2M to the harbour on the transit of La Palue and St Antoine towers, both white with red tops and hard to see; the river marks are adequate.

Two unlit minor channels which join the Grand Chenal at Petit Pot de Beurre, are:

i) **Chenal de la Pendante** 136° across a minefield of rocks awash. Ldg marks: front a B/W bullseye on Fort Cézon; rear a hard-to-see, orange-topped, white obelisk up the hill to Landéda.

ii) **Chenal de la Malouine** 176° requires precise pilotage through a narrow passage, but it saves 4M if coming from/going to N or E. Front mark is Petit Pot de Beurre; rear a slender white obelisk on Petite Île de la Croix. If the latter is obscured by the broad girth of PPDB, jink briefly to one side.

Tides HW L'Aber Wrac'h (Île Cézon) at sp & nps is 30 mins after HW Brest. LW at sp is 40 mins and nps 35 mins after LW Brest. MHWS is 7·7m, MLWS 1·0m; MHWN is 6·1m and MLWN 2·8m.

Tidal streams off Libenter buoy set E from HW Brest −5 and W from HWB +1, max $2\frac{1}{2}$kn springs. Off Île Cézon the stream sets SE from HWB $-5\frac{1}{4}$ and NW from HWB +1, max $1\frac{1}{2}$kn springs.

Access H24 at all tides and most weathers; fog is a possibility. The river and harbour are exposed in fresh to strong NW winds, when pontoon berths may become untenable. Complete shelter can then be found 1.8M up-river at Paluden (see below).

VHF L'Aber Wrac'h Ch 09.

Anchoring in the harbour is not permitted. A charted anchorage is just upstream of Île Cézon, clear of the fairway, in about 6m.

FACILITIES

Capitainerie (HM Jean Troadec). ☎ 02 98 04 91 62; 📠 02 98 04 85 54. VHF Ch 09. Open 0800–1200 & 1600–2130. The harbour is also known as La Palue.

Berthing Yachts <12m LOA may berth on fingers of the single pontoon; 12–14m boats only in calm conditions/fair weather. If berthing on the E side of the pontoon, take care to turn inside a WCM perch marking a 0.5m patch. Use a strong spotlight at night to avoid moored vessels; a shore floodlight

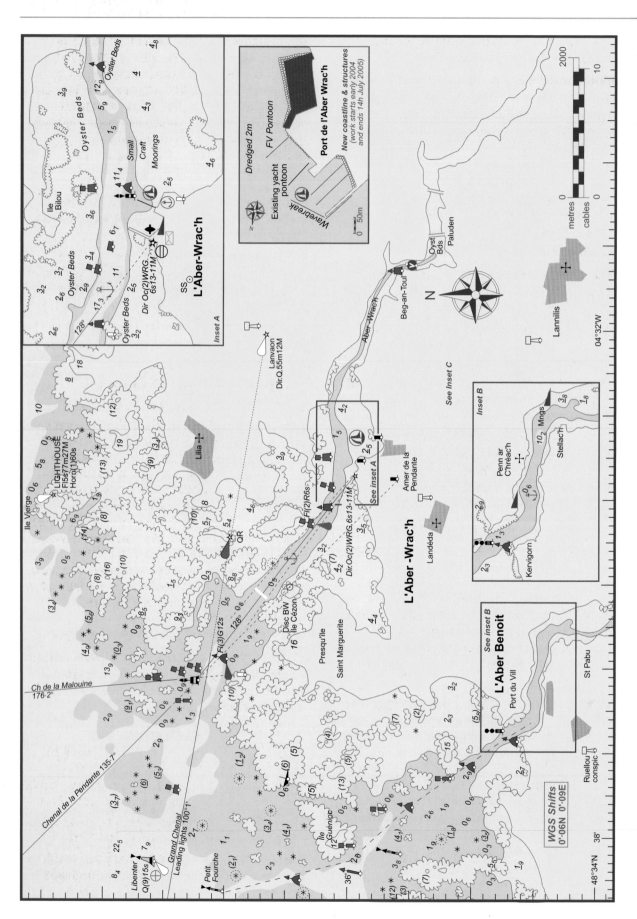

brilliantly illuminates the pontoon, but does nothing for your night vision.

Moorings 30 white ⚓s are in the pool. In season (when a free water taxi runs) rafting is normal.

Tariff Daily rates € on pontoon, ⚓s in ( ), for LOAs: <7m = 10.70 (8.70); <9m = 13.80 (11.00); <11m = 16.00 (13.10); <12m = 19.40 (15.90); <13m = 22.10 (19.90); <14m = 24.70 (20.80). Rates on ⚓s for LOAs: 14–15m = 23.20; >15m = 23.20, plus €2 for each extra metre.

Showers Behind the YC (no longer behind the bar); 0800–2100. Jeton €2 by dispenser.

Launderette Same place/hours.

YC YC des Abers, ☎ 02 98 04 92 60; friendly bar.

Fuel Diesel HW±3 (easiest at slack water) at quay by pontoon; there is a depth gauge on the wall.

Chandlery & repairs Iacomoni Bruno, BY, repairs at Ste Antoine 600m SE; ☎ 02 98 04 83 91. Shut Mon. Co-op Maritime, ☎ 02 98 04 90 16; CH. Shut Mon. At Landéda: Voilerie des Abers (SM) ☎ 02 98 37 40 26. ME, ☎ 02 98 04 93 73. At Lanilis: ME, ☎ 02 98 04 00 74.

Future developments Two new yacht pontoons are planned, sheltered by a new wavebreak and an existing breakwater. Completion date is mid-July 2005, subject to the usual hiccups. Watch this space and/or the latest *Reeds Nautical Almanac*.

PALUDEN (48°35′·50N 04°31′·23W). The channel is mostly unmarked and flanked by oyster beds. Turn S round Beg an Toul SHM bcn twr to berth/raft on dumbells or, in Jul/Aug only, on four ⚓s; fees are due. HM is Gaby Appriaual, plus mongrel dog. Land at rowing club slip on E bank for FW, showers; or at quay on W bank for FW. Access to Lannilis or Plouguerneau (2km) for all facilities. Lannilis has Casino and Leclerc supermarkets.

Paluden, 2M up-river from L'Aber Wrac'h is very well sheltered

Restaurants The Auberge du Pont, ☎ 02 98 04 16 69, is recommended; menus €18.50 to 30.50. Relais des Abers has earned mixed reports. In Lannilis (25 mins walk) Le Tournesol (sunflower) has menus at €15 to 23.70; ☎ 02 98 04 16 69. Auberge des Abers, opposite the church, ☎ 02 98 04 00 29, does a very good *ouvrier* lunch. Upstairs the expensive restaurant has a five-course *dégustation* at €48 or lobster for €89. Yes.

L'Aber Benoit. Anchor or moor along this stretch

L'ABER BENOIT This sheltered river valley sits cheek by jowl with L'Aber Wrac'h and shares some, but by no means all, similarities. For example the degree of shelter in a NW'ly is far superior at L'Aber Benoit. But it lacks even the modest facilities of L'Aber Wrac'h, both afloat and ashore. So if you seek the simple life, swinging round your anchor or someone else's buoy in perfect solitude, then L'Aber Benoit is the place for you. Come fully stored, wined, watered and fuelled. St Pabu, the nearest hamlet of any size (if that does not sound too Irish) is 3 cables SSW of the quay at Stellac'h. Houses on the N bank are well scattered.

SHORESIDE AT L'ABER BENOIT

The following do not exist: Tourist Office, trains, buses, supermarkets, car & bike hire, HM, tariff, showers, fuel, chandlery, VHF, IPTS, websites – which is why you came.

What to see/do The onus is entirely on you.

Beaches Several fine sandy beaches will have caught your eye as you came up harbour.

Market day Friday in Ploudalmézeau, 6km WSW, where the nearest Tourist Office is, ☎ 02 98 89 78 44.

Banks There may be one, or at least a Post Office with a cash dispenser – but don't bank on it.

Restaurants Your Companion did not eat ashore; it would have broken the spell, but a restaurant was glimpsed.

Taxis ☎ 02 98 89 78 21; 02 98 89 81 51.

Repairs Chantier des Abers, ☎ 02 98 89 86 55, is up-river by St Pabu.

NAVIGATION

Charts As for L'Aber Wrac'h.

Approach to the Libenter WCM buoy, but from the west a shortcut saves 1.5M (see Pilotage).

Landmarks Île Vierge lt house. Île Guénioc (12m high) and Île Garo (15m high), amid drying rocks, are two useful features, both to be left to port. A water twr is conspic, 0.7M S of the river mouth.

Pilotage From the waypoint, Libenter WCM light buoy at 48°37'·56N 04°38'·37W, make good 202°/0.5M to Petite Fourche, a WCM buoy. Then track 170°/1.2M past Ruzven Est SHM buoy to Basse du Chenal SHM buoy. Île Guénioc, and a PHM bcn off its S tip, are left 2 cables to port.

Now alter 125°/0.6M to Men Renead SHM buoy, then 157° past La Jument PHM bcn off Île Garo.

From La Jument jink port 142° to pass Ar Gazel SHM buoy, thence between Le Chien IDM bcn and Kervigorn SHM buoy. As the river opens between wooded slopes, follow the eastward bend in midstream through narrows to a broad southerly bend and pool (Lat/Long under Title on page 480).

The shortcut 100° from the W (ie Grande Basse Portsall WCM buoy) passes 2 cables N of Le Relec ECM buoy and 2 cables S of Ruzven Ouest WCM buoy to Basse du Chenal SHM buoy. Thence enter the main channel, or take a secondary channel which passes close W of Poul Orvil WCM buoy.

Tides HW L'Aber Benoit at sp is 25 mins and nps 22 mins after HW Brest. LW at sp is 35 mins

The Narrows where the streams run hard

and nps 20 mins after LW Brest. MHWS is 7·9m, MLWS 1·2m; MHWN is 6·3m, MLWN 3·0m.

Tidal streams at Petite Fourche set across track, ie ENE from HW Brest $-5\frac{1}{4}$ and W from HWB $+1$, max rate $2\frac{3}{4}$kn @ springs. From Île Guénioc to the narrows they follow the channel, reaching $2\frac{1}{2}$ to 3kn. The stream eases as the river broadens out into a pool.

Access Approach ideally between HW–3 & HW. Fresh to strong N'lies might render the approach rather too brisk for a first visit.

Anchorage A charted anchorage is 4 cables SE of Le Chien, off the S bank. This is probably full of moorings and is close to the fairway; better to continue to where the river bends S and there is more space and less tide. Not far S of Stellac'h quay the river is narrowed by oyster beds.

Moorings There are many vacant spherical mooring buoys, both white and dayglow red, but none marked for visitors. The usual rules apply.... The easiest landing place is the large quay and slip at Stellac'h.

Where the river bends S is a good area to ⚓ out of the tide

INDEX